# Unreal Game Development

# Unreal Game Development

Ashish Amresh
Alex Okita

A K Peters, Ltd.
Natick, Massachusetts

Editorial, Sales, and Customer Service Office

A K Peters, Ltd.
5 Commonwealth Road
Natick, MA 01760
www.akpeters.com



**Library of Congress Cataloging-in-Publication Data**
Amresh, Ashish.
Unreal game development / Ashish Amresh, Alex Okita.
p. cm.
ISBN 978-1-56881-459-9 (alk. paper)
1. Computer games--Programming. 2. UnrealScript (Computer program language)
I. Okita, Alex. II. Title.
QA76.76.C672.A52 2010
794.8'1526--dc22
2010010527



Printed in India
14 13 12 11 10 10 9 8 7 6 5 4 3 2 1

*I dedicate this book to my parents, Latha and Amresh, who for years have patiently withstood all my whims and fancies and to my wife, Kiran, without whose unquestioning support this book would not have been possible.*

—A. A.

*I thank my mother, Sandi Okita, for always supporting me.*

—A. O.

# Acknowledgments

When Camp Game was started seven years ago at New York University (NYU), it was by and large an experiment to see what teenagers would come up with if taught state of the art video game development skills. The magic created by the students each year eventually convinced us that that the camp curriculum needed to be shared with a larger audience. This book is an effort to help educators create similar magic by introducing the process of video game development into their schools.

First and foremost we would like to thank the students and their parents for participating in the camp game programs at NYU and Arizona State University (ASU). Secondly, we would like to thank the instructors who have lectured over the years at Camp Game, namely Dov Jacobson and Tim Fielder at NYU; Ara Shirinian, Geoff Wall, Robert Srinivasiah, Clark Morrisaint, Joseph Grossmann and Arnaud Ehgner at ASU. We would like to specifically thank Ara and Geoff for helping us with proofreading and content editing. We would like to thank the sponsors of the program over the years, especially Mark Rein, Mike Capps, and Tim Sweeney at Epic Games, Steve Singer at Nintendo, Paul Skiera at Adaptive Curriculum, Mark Buchignani at Rainbow Studios, and Maureen Higgins at Autodesk. We'd also like to thank Stan Miskiewicz, Alejandro Gil and the rest of the folks who I worked with at Black Point Studios for years of great work with the Unreal Engine, and also to wish the best for Justin Miur and Martin Murphy formerly of Midway Games. Finally we would like to thank Alice Peters and her team at A K Peters for believing in us and helping us pave the way for this fantastic curriculum to be accessible to students all over the world.

# Table of Contents

## III. Programming

# Required Tools

This book uses the Unreal Engine 3 to teach game design. We cover both the Unreal Development Kit, better known as UDK, and Unreal Tournament 3, or UT3. UT3 can be downloaded via Steam (http://store.steampowered.com/). UDK can be downloaded at http://www.udk.com/. UDK is updated monthly and many changes and advancements have been added to it. UT3 hasn't been drastically updated since its release but most of the tools found in UT3 are still in use in UDK. Both UDK and UT3 are based on Unreal Engine 3 or UE3 (licensing information available at http://www.unrealtechnology.com/).

Some of the tutorials found in this book were created using UT3: at the time of the authoring of this book, UDK was not yet available. But this book can be used with either UDK or UT3; while UT3 may have features that visually differ from UDK, much of the functionality remains unchanged. As a beginning student learning to use the Unreal Engine, you will not need to know the details of the latest releases for UDK. Many of the additions to UDK simply add new tools on top of the engine's core functionality.

When you install and play most Unreal Engine–based games, the Editor is already present: the game is also the Editor! Simply adding "editor" to the command line of the shortcut to the game will launch the game in editor mode. These sorts of topics will be covered in greater detail when we begin.

In addition to Unreal Engine 3, you'll also be required to use some 3D authoring software. Unreal Engine has very primitive modeling tools but these are not meant for building characters, vehicles, or props. For these sorts of complex models we'll be using 3D Studio Max, a leading 3D-modeling software produced by Autodesk. A 30-day free trial is available at http://autodesk.com/. Alternatively, software like Blender 3D, an open source 3D modeling application available at http://www.blender.org/, can be used.

To complete the tutorials, you'll also need 2D image-editing software. For the tutorials in this book we'll introduce you to GIMP, a popular open source 2D image-editing software available for free at http://www.gimp.org/. You may already be familiar with Adobe Photoshop (see https://www.photoshop.com/), which also works well.

To complete the programming section of this book you can use any text editor. Unreal Engine 3 uses an interpreted language called Unreal Script, or UScript for short. Unreal Script is similar to Java but has a lot of custom programming conventions specifically designed for multiplayer games. Though we don't recommend using Notepad, you don't have to have anything more than that. But we recommend text editing software capable of syntax highlighting. For this we'll be using WOTgreal, a text editor with syntax highlighting specifically designed for Unreal Script and available as freeware at http://www.wotgreal.com/. UltraEdit, available for purchase at http://www.ultraedit.com/, is another available text editor.

All content, tutorials, and resources used and created in this book are available for download at http://www.akpeters.com/unrealgamedev. The site also includes tools for instructors, including lesson plans and class presentations.

| | Preferred Tool | Alternate Tool |
|---|---|---|
| **3d Art Assets** | **Autodesk 3ds Max*, Maya**<br>www.autodesk.com | **Blender** (freeware)<br>www.blender.org |
| **2d Art Assets** | **Adobe Photoshop**<br>www.photoshop.com | **GNU Image Manipulation Program** (freeware)<br>www.gimp.org |
| **Programming** | **WOTgreal** (freeware)<br>www.wotgreal.com | **UltraEdit**<br>www.ultraedit.com |
| **Design** | **Unreal Editor of Unreal Tournament III**<br>(included) | **Unreal Development Kit**<br>www.udk.com |

* A free 30-day trial of 3ds Max is available from Autodesk's website.

# Introduction: So You Want To Make Games

## *Who This Book Is For*

I remember one of the first times I ever laid eyes on a video game. It was 1986, and I was ten years old. My mother had foolishly allowed me to loiter around a small video arcade at a Montgomery Ward department store as she went about her shopping business. It was foolish for her, of course, because it would take some considerable effort on her part to finally pry me away.

Quarter-less yet curious, I was perfectly content to gaze into the screen across some teenager's shoulder. As I stood there, everything else in the department store just faded away. The room, the arcade cabinets, the people—none of them existed any more as my complete attention was on Mario, in *Vs. Super Mario Bros.*, traversing this strange world of pipes and creatures.

I didn't fully understand what I was seeing at the time, certainly not in terms that I understand now, but the memory of that game was burned into my head so completely that I can remember the exact screens and sequence of this strange kind of emotional drama unfolding in front of me: not drama in the sense of a soap opera or of someone losing his temper—but the emotional weight of what was actually going on in the game, exaggerated by the novelty of it all. Mario stands up on a pipe, as the bad guy below wanders back and forth. How is the player going to get past this? Mesmerized, I watched him skillfully jump down from the pipe and take care of the bad guy by a few deft dodges and jumps. The action was rudimentary, but to see a video game like this for the first time was exciting! Before I could take another breath, Mario jumped up onto another pipe, and this time there were *two* bad guys below—now *this* was a serious challenge! But the pair of Goombas, as I later learned the bad guys were called, were too much for the brave player, and my introduction to Mario had come to an end.

And so began what developed into a teenage obsession with playing games, which eventually turned into a lifetime obsession with designing games. In those early years, I had no idea how I was going to do it, or even if I was smart enough to do it, but I knew for sure that I wanted to make games. While seeking my own path toward becoming a video game designer, without anyone to guide me or show direction, on that day in

Montgomery Ward began 16 years of muddling, dabbling, dreaming, and a myriad of tiny failures and successes.

If you can relate to this story—if you love playing video games, if you crave to learn how to make them but you don't know where to start, what to do, or even what is involved in making a game—then this book is for you.

## I Have No Skills (Yet), and I Must Make Games!

To get everything out of this book that we have put in, we don't expect you to have any programming ability or knowledge. You don't have to be an artist or know how to draw, and you most certainly don't have to be a game designer. This book was written for aspiring game makers who know that they want somehow to be involved in making games but aren't sure what role they want to specialize in. Even if you're uncertain whether making games is something you seriously want to pursue in the first place, this book will help you solidify your goals one way or the other.

For the most part, all you need to start out with is an interest in creating video games. However, having said that, we have made a few assumptions about your ability when it comes to using computers.

Our lessons and tutorials go over every important operation step by step, and we will spend a great amount of detail explaining how the various tools we use to create games work; but you should already be able to perform everyday tasks on any recent Windows computer without difficulty. If you check email on a regular basis and know where your files are on your computer and how to use them, you shouldn't have any issues whatsoever.

If using computers is new to you, then we recommend getting up to speed with a basic Windows user book either before or in conjunction with working on our material.

This book mirrors the curriculum we use at CampGame, a six-week summer program organized for high school students at The New York University and Arizona State University that has been running successfully for over five years. Students enter with no prior knowledge of game making whatsoever, and through the course of six intensive weeks, they finish as teams of budding game developers who have already completed fully functional games with their own designs, code, and art.

## What Can You Accomplish in Six Weeks?

Video games today are a big and serious business. Commercial projects frequently cost tens of millions of dollars and employ several dozen of development staff, including designers, programmers, artists, producers, and testers at a minimum. What's more, most game projects take at least a year of full-time effort among the staff to complete, and it's not unheard of to see this development cycle consume two or even three years of time. We've come a long way since Atari 2600 of the early 1980s. Projects in those days usually employed a staff of just one programmer. Incidentally, this programmer also happened to be the game designer, the artist, the sound designer and engineer all rolled into one.

All of this may sound quite intimidating. After all, if it took a year for a skilled jack-of-all-trades to complete a crude Atari video game, what can you hope to possibly accomplish in just six weeks, starting from scratch? For our program, the key is in the various widely-available tools we employ (more on this in the next section) and in a tight focus on the essentials of the game development process. Let's face it: No matter how smart and talented you are, it's simply not possible to make the next *Legend of Zelda* game in this span of time. However, you will have the tools and ability to create something of that scale afterward if you so desire.

Another way we make efficient use of our program, at least in the CampGame curriculum, is that we divide the course into three major tracks. In the first few weeks, we teach every student the basics of each track: Design, Programming, and Art. From that point forward, we ask each student to choose one of these specializations and spend the majority of the remainder of the program focusing their work on that track. Another essential part of the CampGame program is that we eventually divide the class into teams of four to six students, each having at least one designer, programmer, and artist. The teams spend the second half of CampGame planning and implementing their own game projects. Of course, in such a compressed space of time, our students also learn quite a bit about planning and prioritizing. The stark reality of game development is that you never have enough time to make everything that you want. The commercial nature of game making means that you have only a limited time in which to finish your projects, and so decisions about what *not to* work on are usually just as important as those about what *to* work on.

You can approach this book in one of two ways: as an individual study, or as part of a team of at least three people—a designer, a programmer, and an artist. If possible, we recommend that you gather up some of your friends who are just as interested in game making as you are and work through this book in the CampGame way: impose time limits on yourself as indicated in each chapter, pick your specializations, and use the lessons as tools for completing your own project in six weeks. Although going solo at your own leisurely pace is certainly a viable approach and will teach you a tremendous amount, working through this book with a team and time limits will also give you experience in team dynamics and prioritizing—elements that are absolutely crucial in the real world of commercial game development.

## Technologies and Tools We Use

Tools are the key to efficient game development. Over the years, game developers realized that even if they made several rather different games, they frequently had to do the same work over and over with the creation of each game. Back in the old days, there was a lot of this kind of repetition. Today, however, there are all kinds of tools (which is just another word for a computer application) available that automate the boring, repetitive stuff in game development.

If making a game is like building a house, the tools we use allow us to design the shape, looks, and composition of each room just by saying what we want and where we want each piece to go. The electrical wiring behind the walls, the plumbing, the insulation, the foundation of the house, the air conditioning system—all the required bits that nobody notices when they walk into your home—all that stuff is automatically taken care of by our tools. In this way, we can spend all our time actually making an interesting, beautiful house.

| | Preferred Tool | Alternate Tool |
|---|---|---|
| **3d Art Assets** | **Autodesk 3ds Max*, Maya** www.autodesk.com | **Blender** (freeware) www.blender.org |
| **2d Art Assets** | **Adobe Photoshop** www.photoshop.com | **GNU Image Manipulation Program** (freeware) www.gimp.org |
| **Programming** | **WOTgreal** (freeware) www.wotgreal.com | **UltraEdit** www.ultraedit.com |
| **Design** | **Unreal Editor of Unreal Tournament III** (included) | **Unreal Development Kit** www.udk.com |

* A free 30-day trial of 3ds Max is available from Autodesk's website.

Each specialty has its own tools, which are detailed in the table above. While we will focus on one particular, preferred tool for each category of work that needs to be done in our development cycle, we'll also list alternate free tools that provide the same or very similar functionality. You don't have to purchase any additional software to complete all the work in this book, but having access to the preferred tools will give you an advantage, as they are also industry standards.

Some tools are used to create (or *export*) original assets, or files, while others take those files, or *import* them, and allow you to make compositions that make up our game. The way all our tools work together is called our *work flow* or *tool chain* or *pipeline*.

In our pipeline, we use 3ds Max to create our three-dimensional (3D) models and characters and GIMP to create *textures*, or two-dimensional (2D) images that will be applied to the surfaces of those 3D models, as well as any art in your game that is 2D. We'll use WOTgreal to help us write our program code. Although you could use any text editor to accomplish this, WOTgreal has some nice features to make the whole process easier. Finally, we'll use Unreal Editor, or UnrealEd, in several important ways. With UnrealEd, you can import all the 3D and 2D assets and code we created with the other programs and place them into your game's levels. UnrealEd's main role is that of a level editor, but it's really much more than that. It's where all of the pieces come together to form your complete product, and it's even used for creating certain art elements that are not (strictly speaking) game design-related, such as particle systems, materials, and animated matinee sequences. But we're getting ahead of ourselves here.

## The Game Development Cycle

Your exposure to the game development cycle in this book will be just a hint of what usually happens in game development studios the world over. Nevertheless, it's good to have even a basic understanding of what happens when a studio tries to make a game. We'll present to you a simplified look here, as anything more is beyond the scope of this book, but if you are interested in the details of project planning and production there are all kinds of volumes out there to satisfy your curiosities.

Game development is a fascinating process. Most kinds of commercial projects or products are a bit like building a bridge—it's been done thousands of times before, so there is usually a practiced and standard way of doing things. Your bridge might have a fancy design or some fancy paint; but for the most part, all of the variables are known before you make the bridge, and so you can fairly easily say that such a bridge will take so much time to build, and you'll rarely be too far off from the reality.

The reality when it comes to making games, however, is much different. Even for experienced developers, making a game, in many cases, is a bit like trying to figure out how to make a bridge when you've never had to build a bridge before. What's more, you'll have to build your bridge while trying to figure out how to do it at the same time. But that's not all. As you're building, the pieces you're using might change shape from one day to the next. You might even have to go back and break apart bridge sections you thought were already finished. At this rate it won't be very long before you stand back and ask yourself, "What kind of crazy bridge project is this, anyway?"

There are simply too many unknowns in game making to treat it like making a bridge—at least at the start of a project. Traditionally, game projects are divided into three main phases: preproduction, production, and testing.

Essentially, preproduction is when you decide how you're going to make your game. Production is when you actually build it, and testing is when you make sure that it works the way you intended. You finish one step, and then you move onto the next. Simple, right?

The model is simple, but unfortunately it's not good for making games, because it assumes that once you're done with one phase, that part's all done, and you move on and never look back, kind of like building a bridge. If you make games in this way, you might work on your game for a long time before you realize that your original techniques are now causing you a lot of problems, and you should really have done it a different way. So now you are stuck with the dilemma of tearing down part of your game and re-doing it, or sticking with these inefficient, unwieldy techniques. It's difficult to appreciate exactly what this feels like before you've actually experienced it firsthand, but it's something that every game developer goes through.

So what now? Well, the ugly truth in game making is that pretty much all phases of the project are happing all the time during the project. You might do most of your design (as part of preproduction) in the beginning of the project, but really you will be designing all the way up until the end. You might do most of your testing at the end of a project, but really you will be testing your game all the time, even just after the first few lines of code you write.

This approach, where you are doing all parts of the process at every step over and over, is called an *iterative* process; and it very accurately captures good game-making habits. In an iterative process, you test each bit of progress you make to make sure it works. Then you stand back, look at it, and re-evaluate your plan. Maybe you decided in the beginning that your character in a game will have five lives. Now, after you have finished a couple of levels, you find that five lives won't work so well—you decide that your character needs to have a life bar instead. In this way, you stay flexible, and your current design or plan is nothing more than that: it's what you plan to do currently. You can change the plan as your product develops.

The key for you, the aspiring game maker, is not to get too stuck on one way of doing things. Be open to changing your plan, and you may find your project much better for it. However, this isn't an excuse to make sweeping changes or to do something completely different every week—you'll never finish a game that way. You'll have to decide whether your game character has lives or health bars or some other system as quickly as is practical. But with an iterative approach, you make and settle on this decision once you have something working, instead of just thinking in your head what might be good. In the end, each decision about what you want to change has a cost associated with it. If you think the change is worth the cost, go for it!

## Project Roles

Whether you are following this book as part of a team or just by yourself, eventually you will want to pick an area of specialization. More than ever, game development studios primarily look for specialists to join their teams. Although it's absolutely valuable to have knowledge in each area of expertise, complete generalists will usually have a difficult time getting hired. In this book, we distinguish between three specialties: designer, programmer, and artist.

Each of these roles can be broken down into even more precise specialties. If you want to pursue a career after learning the material in this book, it would be wise to select a specific area of expertise that best fits your talents and focus on developing that particular skill. For example, just in the category of artist, there are concept artists, modelers, texture artists, animators, particle artists, and so on. Designers can be level designers, interface designers, game designers, and mechanics or game play designers. Programmers can be AI programmers, physics programmers, graphics programmers, or game play programmers, for example.

This list may be quite daunting—it's quite all right if it is. You don't need to know which one of those roles is "you." As you try out the various tracks and lessons in this book, you'll start to get a feel for what you're naturally good at and where your preferences lie. Feel free to start any track you wish, although if you intend to ultimately make a complete game, you're either going to have to go through all of them yourself or find team partners who are willing to specialize in the other areas.

By now you probably can't wait to dig in and start making a game! In the next section, we'll jump right into Unreal Editor and show you how to build a playable level in less than a couple hours! Let's begin. . . .

# Part I: Design

# 1 Coming Up with a Plan

## What Game Do You Want to Make?

The Unreal Engine 3 was first built to create a first person shooter, but you're not limited to building an FPS. The Unreal Engine has been used to create J-RPGs (Japanese role-playing games), top-down shooters, fighting games, racing games, and even MMOs (massively multiplayer online games). Flexibility is something that the Unreal Engine affords that very few game engines do. Most game engines that have been used to make popular games today have focused so much on their particular game that modifying the engine to create any other type of game is practically impossible.

Also available on the market are more generic game engines that do afford the same flexibility but are also hindered by being very heavily dependent on a programmer to get anything at all working. Character animation in particular is a highly complex problem. Blending animations and constraints turn into a highly programmer-heavy solution. Unreal Engine has built-in artist-friendly tools that solve this problem without a line of code.

The same goes for materials, particles, level events, cinematics, and much more. The tools are what make Unreal Engine so much more advanced than any other game engine out there. Most if not all engines require a programmer, artist, and designer to work on every asset together to get anything done. Unreal Engine is one of the only engines that allow a designer to work independently of the artist, and the artist independently of the programmer, and still accomplish nearly every required task to make a game together.

## What to Expect

After the next couple of chapters, you should have a good grasp of what's involved in designing a level and building with primitive shapes to get the flow you're looking for. Then you'll learn to move on to adding scripts and events to your level to make it react to your player.

In the past, game engines depended on BSPs, or binary space partitions. BSPs were a method used to limit the number of polygons drawn to the screen. In short, if you're starting a level in one room, the game engine should not be calculating, rendering, and thinking of events happening in the last room of the level until you get closer to it. BSPs were a nice way to reduce the number of objects and events that the engine would be thinking of at once.

Modern use of BSPs has changed with different rendering techniques. In a fully-built and scripted level, the detail that is generated by BSPs can actually perform more slowly than the same scene built as a static mesh. Keep in mind that it's important to know the differences in how each is made, and the benefits of both. Starting off, we'll build an interesting scene with the BSP tools found in the Unreal Editor.

Once the scene is complete, we'll learn how easy it is to make changes with the BSP scene; we may not immediately see the performance difference between a BSP scene and a static mesh version of the same scene, but the details that can be achieved using 3ds Max's tools versus the Unreal Editor are incomparable.

Once the BSPs are finished and the level's flow is complete, we'll convert them into static mesh elements and learn how to export the various shapes with different pivot points for placement. We'll get into what a pivot point is, so don't worry about that right now.

## Reverse Engineering the Unreal Tournament Maps

### Getting Around in Unreal Editor

The Unreal editor is a fairly unique environment. The viewports are engineered to somewhat mirror 3ds Max as well as some of the basic manipulation tools. Navigation in a scene is meant to emulate the same experience as playing a level, but with a bit more control.

The editor's windows are split into two halves: the level editor and the asset editor, also known as the Generic Browser. But really, the purpose of the Generic Browser is to edit and create assets to be used in the level, so its function is more for your level's assets.

Within the editor there are dozens of other sub-editors, each one focused on a specific task. The FaceFX editor and tools, the material editor, the particle editor known as Cascade, and the physics editor known as PHaT are all available through the Generic Browser. In addition, one of the other editors that can be opened from various menus is Kismet, the level scripting and event handler; from Kismet, you can create a matinee node, which is the cinematics and level animation tool.

It's quite a remarkable set of tools! There's a reason why so many developers have chosen to go with the Unreal Editor for its artist- and designer-friendly pipeline. As a designer you'll need to focus on just a few of these editors, primarily Kismet and Matinee, the event scripting tool and the animation tool, respectively.

## UncookedPC vs. CookedPC: What's This All About?

Once you begin working on your levels, you'll be working in the MyGames directory in your MyDocuments directory. In this directory there will be another directory called Unpublished. Its name basically means that the files in this directory aren't ready for distribution to your mass of waiting fans. If objects are found in the Uncooked directory, it means that these objects have not yet been optimized and might contain extra data.

Cooking a package removes editor-only data and any objects that haven't been used in your level. Placeholder textures, materials, and various leftovers that might have been left behind from various testing will be excluded from the package once it's cooked.

PROJECT

### An Introduction to the Unreal Ed's Level Editing Tools

There are a few ways to open Unreal Tournament's editor. The first method is to create a short cut and modify it, and the other is to create a .bat file. The .bat file has a few advantages, which we'll explore later when we need to, but for now we'll go with the more simple modified shortcut.

Figure 1.1

Navigate to . . .

```
C:\Program Files\Unreal Tournament 3\Binaries
```

or to whichever directory you've installed Unreal Tournament 3; then select the UT.exe icon.

Make a new Shortcut with the UT.exe and open the Shortcuts properties [Figure 1.1]. Add editor to the end of the target line [Figure 1.2].

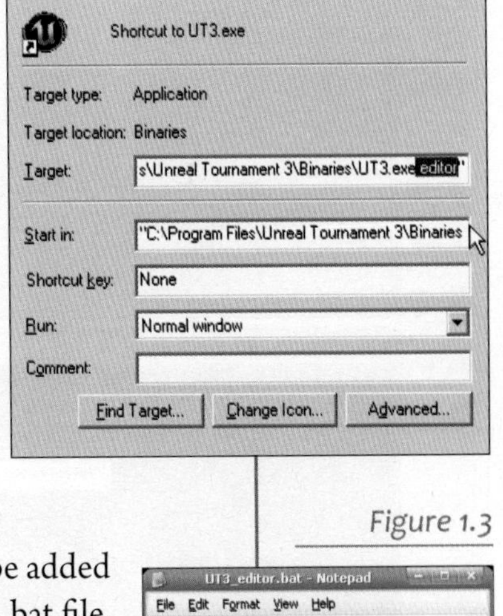


Figure 1.2

Double click on the short cut, and the editor will open rather than the game. That's it! The full line should read something like this, assuming that you installed the game onto your C: drive:

```
C:\Program Files\Unreal Tournament 3\Binaries\UT3
.exe editor
```

Alternatively, if you're a bit cleverer, you could create a new .bat file and add "Start ut.exe editor" to the first line to the .bat file [Figure 1.3]. When you're done, rename the shortcut or .bat file to UT3_Editor.bat so it'll be grouped near the exe. Other options can be added to the .bat file a bit more easily than editing the shortcut. Using the .bat file, you can add a level name and automatically jump into the level when the .bat file is run. In addition, some things, like recording game sessions as individual frames, can also be done through the .bat file.

Figure 1.3

Double click on either the .bat file or the shortcut and you should get the editor splash screen [Figure 1.4]. Awesome, now we can start making our own levels!

Figure 1.4

## Unreal Editor: A Tour

The level editor is where your level is constructed [Figure 1.5]. Game play and events are created for each level in the Kismet sequence editor. Objects placed in the level editor are usually sourced from the Generic Browser. We'll start with the most obvious file menus on the level editor part of the Unreal Editor.

Figure 1.5

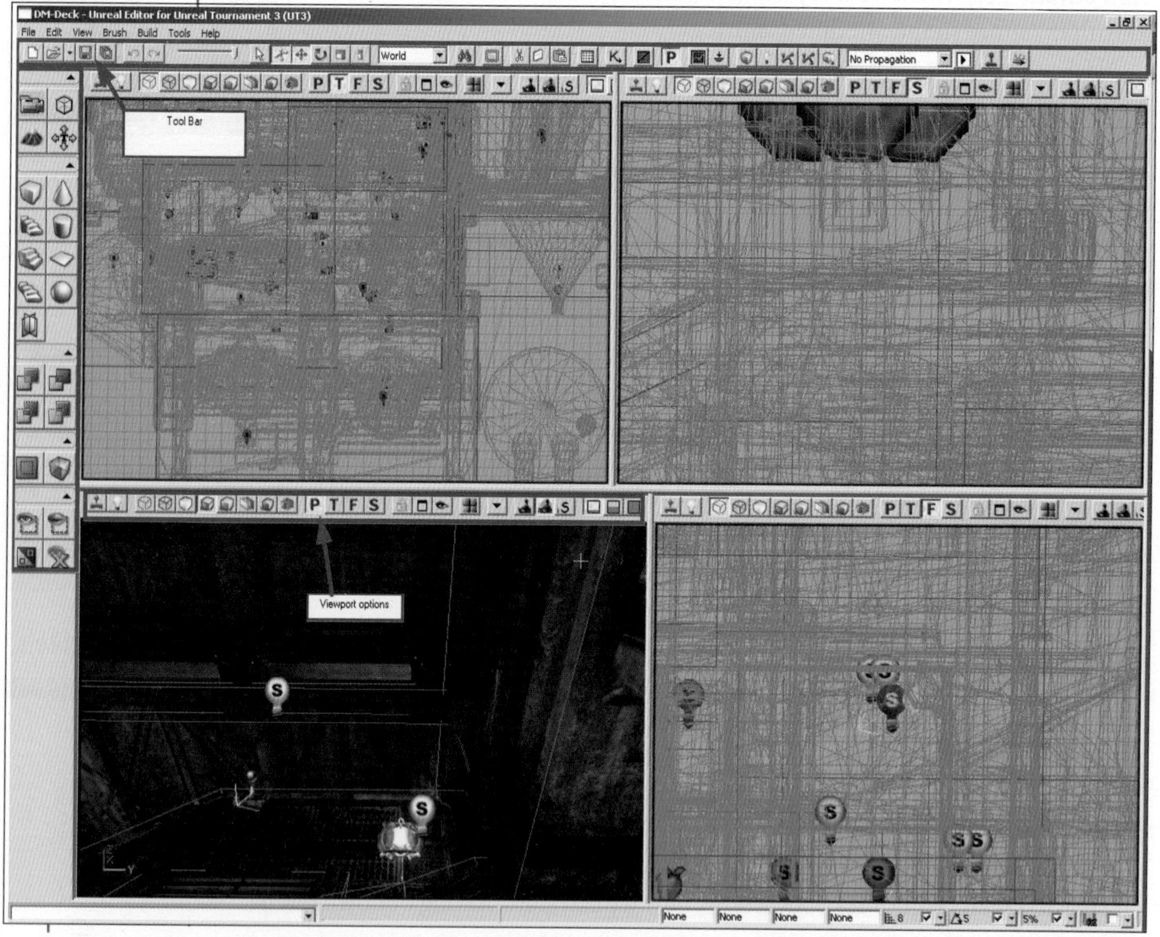

## *The Tool Bar*

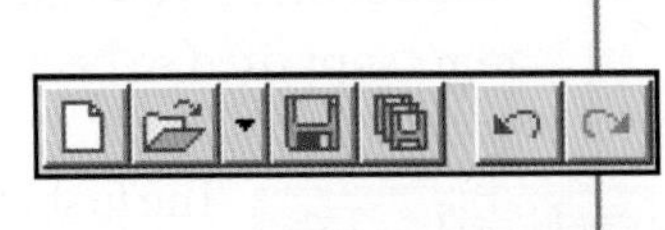

The first set of icons contains your regular new file, open file, save and save all icons. These are followed by the undo and redo buttons.

This little obscure slider is used to change what is called a far clipping plane. By default this slider is set to far; by opening a level, you can observe the effect of this slider by moving the control to the left. Switch the perspective view to wire frame and play with the slider. This will bring in the far clipping plane so you don't have to see everything placed in the level. We'll get to how to change the perspective window's viewing options in a bit.

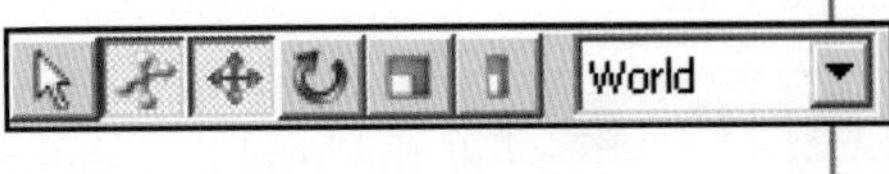


This next set of icons is related to object manipulation in the level. The first icon switches the tool to selection; the next two allow you to move objects around in the scene. The following icons are related to rotating an object and then changing the size of an object.

The popup menu is related to how the manipulation gizmo, as it's called, is oriented. By default this is set to "World"; this means that the translation gizmo is always going to point with its coordinal directions aligned to the world. Switching this to "Local" will orient the gizmo to the object that is selected. So the object's $y$-axis might be pointed in another direction different from the world once the object has been rotated and fit into a level. This is a useful option when placing objects in a specific orientation that might not be in alignment with the rectangular grid of the "World" coordinates.

Search for actors is a fairly useful button that opens a find tool, allowing you to hunt for an item somewhere in the level. With the Search for field left blank, this dialog will show you a list of all objects in the level. Selecting an object listed in this dialog and clicking the Go to button will jump the editor to the selected object in the level. Additional ease of use allows you to open the Properties dialog without even jumping to the object. This dialog makes it a bit easier to find and edit objects in your scene [Figure 1.6].

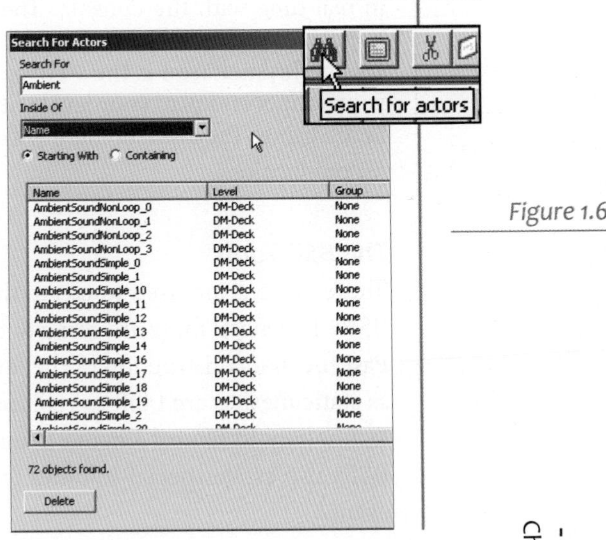


Figure 1.6

Of course if you find a bunch of objects that you don't need or can't find and know aren't supposed to be in the level, you can select them here and delete them.

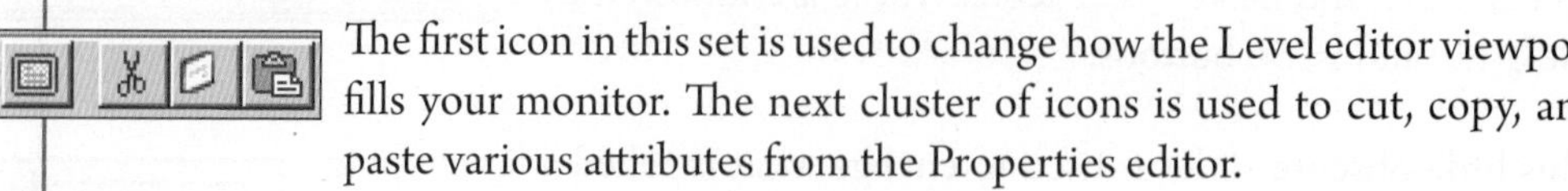

The first icon in this set is used to change how the Level editor viewport fills your monitor. The next cluster of icons is used to cut, copy, and paste various attributes from the Properties editor.

These two icons are very important. The first opens the Generic Browser, the asset manager for Unreal Editor. The Generic Browser is where many of the assets are created and edited. The next button opens the Kismet editor. Kismet is the level scripting and event manager built into Unreal Editor. It allows the game designer to create game flow and to create animations for elevators and doors.

The next set of icons contains technical items that allow you to view the level in a slightly different way. The first button turns on and off the triangles that make up all geometry in the world, in particular the BSPs that make up the level designer's level building tool kit. The second button, the *P* icon, locks prefabs together. Prefabs are useful for duplicating a collection of objects. The third button shows the graph. The last button is used to snap an object to a character socket. We'll get into what that means later on in the book.

This set of buttons is used to rebuild the level. Rebuilding geometry is not always automatic when you're working with BSPs. Lighting and AI path finding are the following three icons. The last button in the set rebuilds all of them at the same time. The following popup menu allows you to connect to an Xbox or PS3 dev kit, should you be a licensee and have a dev version of the engine. This will allow you to communicate in real time with the console. The next icon turns on the selected mode from the popup.

The Joystick icon is the `PIE`, or Play in Editor button. This is the best way to test your scripts and play your level without having to quit the editor and open the level in the game. The last icon here will cook your working packages and prep your game for publication.

### *The BSP Tools*

These buttons are used to create the various shapes used to build your level design BSPs. In general these are going to be used only to rough out the layout of your level. Past the first construction of the level design, BSPs should be deleted from the level as static meshes are built to replace them. Terrain is a bit different in that it's a new technology to Unreal Engine 3 and has been optimized to use in the game. These BSPs also create special volumes to tell the scripts to change the camera and trigger events.

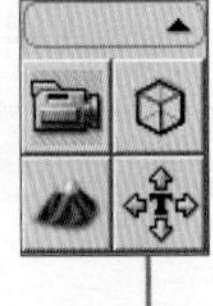

This set of buttons at the top of the tool bar contains your editing tools. Camera options are provided for moving through the level. Geometry mode is an older function left over from Unreal Engine 2; it allows you to modify BSPs on a per vertex level. Then you have a new `Terrain` button followed by another older `Texture` placement tool for use on BSPs.

This set of buttons is used to create various shapes of BSP brushes. Brushes can be thought of as a shape that you can move around your level and fill in with geometry. Each button has a different set of parameters that can be modified to change the shape of the brush before it's added to the level. Right click on the button to open the options dialog.

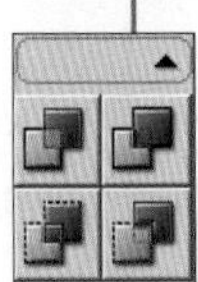

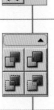

This set of icons is used to cut out, add, and divide the added BSPs. In general it's easier to stick to `Add` and `Subtract`. The other two icons are used to create more complex shapes by merging only sections where two BSPs intersect or to cut off where one of the BSPs intersects.

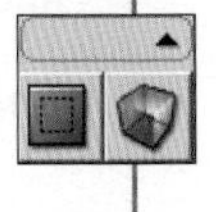

These two tools are used to add special BSPs that are used to trigger events and change certain properties of the world. Specific examples are water volumes, which tell the engine to change the properties of any character in the volume to be swimming. These volumes can also trigger events in Kismet; we'll get into more specific examples in a coming project.

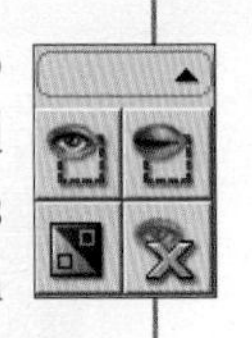

This last set of icons is used to hide and show various selections in the editor. To select multiple objects, you can move to one of the orthographic views and hold Ctrl+Alt+LMB to draw a selection box. After a selection is made, you can press the various buttons to hide your selection or hide the unselected objects. You can then unhide all or invert which objects are hidden.

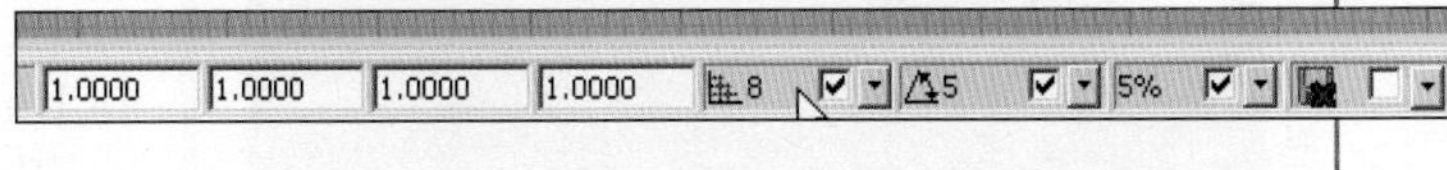


The last set of tools, found at the bottom, allows you to numerically enter various changes to a selected object. Then you're allowed to activate grid snapping and spacing. This is followed by activating rotation snapping and angle. Last, you can change the percentage of an object's scale. You have the option to have the editor automatically save, and you can change how often the level is saved.

Once you've gotten into more advanced features of the editor, you can enter commands into the command line in the level editor at the lower left.

### *Viewport Options*

Starting at the left, you have two icons that change how the level is updated as you move around. The joystick tells the viewport to update any dynamic object in real time, including objects such as particle systems or animated mesh objects. The light bulb is used to deactivate dynamic lights while moving through the level. Levels with unbaked lights can get pretty slow after a certain size.

The next set of icons is used to change the rendering style of the viewport. We'll go into more detail with these as needed. The next set of buttons, labeled `P`, `T`, `F`, and `S`, correspond to `Perspective`, `Top`, `Front`, and `Side`. The next significant icon is the box used to maximize the viewport followed by a useful but quite possibly confusing look through tool.

The black triangle button is a popup menu that changes what types of objects are shown in the viewport. The last three blue buttons are used to change the speed at which you can shuffle though the level.

A few of the functions were skipped over, but we covered the most useful tools related to the viewport. Additional information will be covered in later projects as needed.

### *The Generic Browser*

The Generic Browser is where many of the assets used to build a level are found [Figure 1.7]. The rest of the data that make up characters, items, weapons, and props can all be found in the Generic Browser. In addition, many of these assets can be edited and created here. New materials, physics assets, particle systems, and many other lumps of data are created starting in the Generic Browser. All of the data created here are saved as UPKs, or Unreal Package files.

Figure 1.7

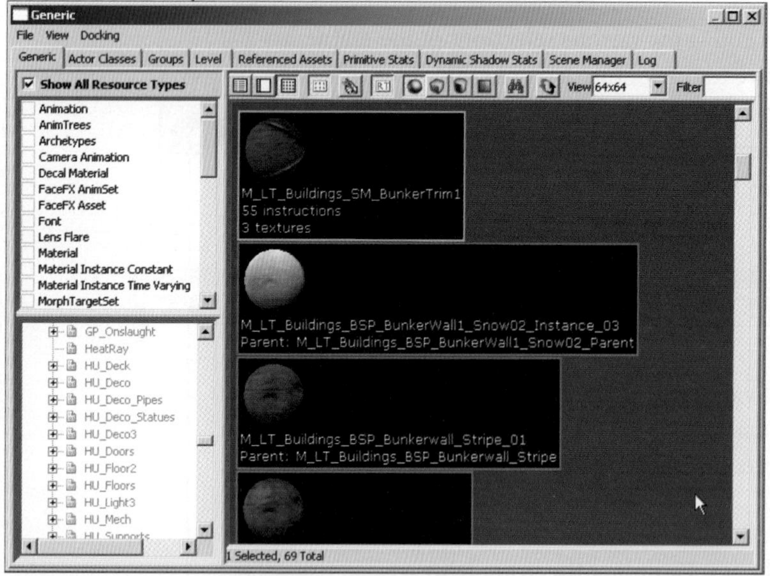


The top-left panel is defaulted to show all resource types. If you want to only show specific types of resources, you can click on options like `Material`, and the Generic Browser viewpane will only show materials. The rest of the resource types will be hidden. In addition, there are several other ways to manage how to view the resources found in the Generic Browser.

The first three icons will toggle the view from text listings, text listings with the icon of the selected item and the default; then icons only. The hand with the wrench will show only the items used in the opened level. The last `RT` icon will update the icons as changes are made to the item in view. The small icon in between the items in use and the display toggles is the `grouping` button. This button will group similar types together. Otherwise the items will be listed in alphabetical order.

The next set of icons will change the shape of material objects. Then there's another `search` icon for finding objects in the various loaded UPKs found in the Generic Browser. Next is an `update` icon followed by a popup menu that changes the size of the shown icons. The last `filter` text field will allow you to show only items in the browser pane that matches text entered into the field [Figure 1.8].

Figure 1.8

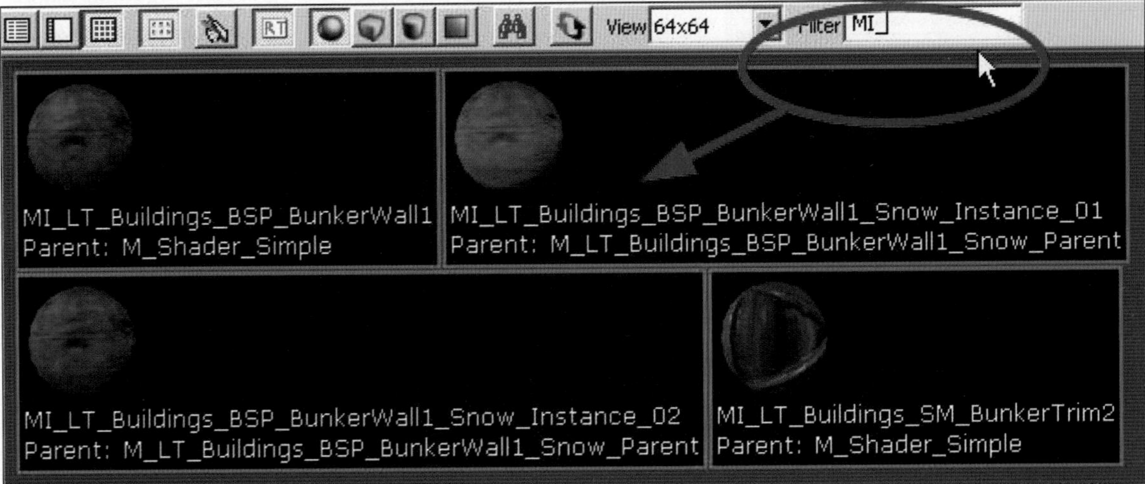


Newer builds of the Unreal Engine (like the one included with the Unreal Development Kit, which gets monthly updates) also include various other ways to store, search, and manage items in the Generic Browser. Organization is important with any game project, and the Generic Browser is going to be your main method to store and manage your game resources.

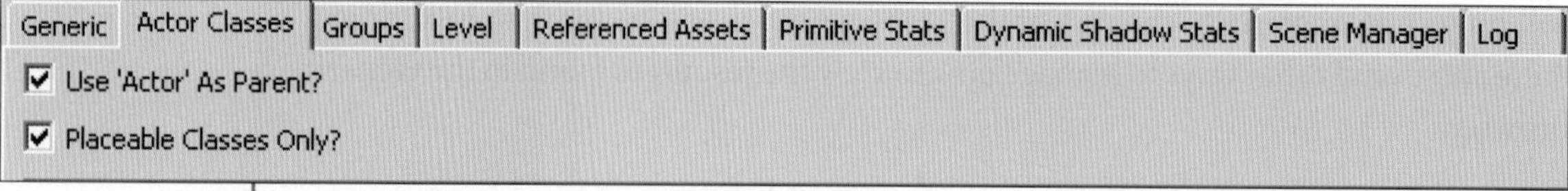


If you look at the other tabs across the top of the Generic Browser window, you'll also see a ton of other editors: Actor Classes, Groups, Level, Referenced, etc. There are a lot of different ways to see and manage your level and your resources. A major part of building a good level is keeping the level fast. A level with too many poorly placed objects and badly constructed Kismet events will be slow and clumsy. To discover the offending objects and scripts, you can use Primitive Stats, Dynamic Shadow Stats, the Scene Manager and the Log to locate them.

Figure 1.9

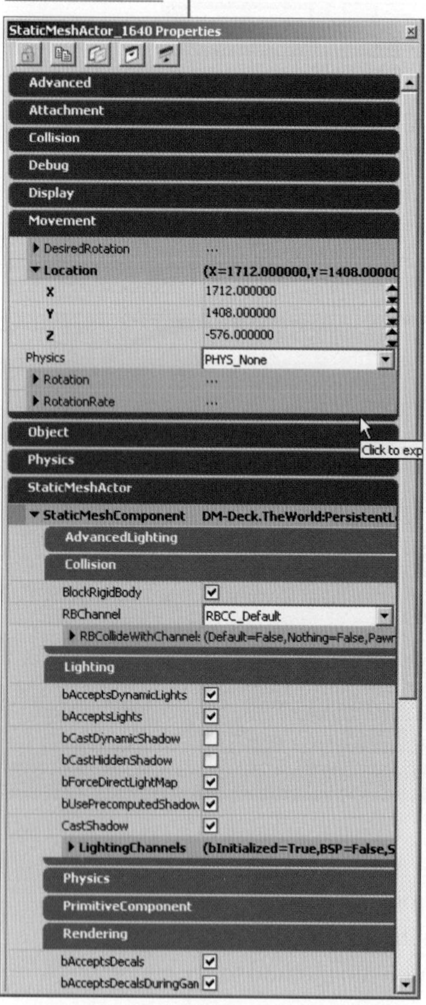


### *The Properties Editor*

Each object placed in a level has many editable properties; each property can be edited through the property editor. Many of the attributes are the same across nearly all of the placed objects. `Attachment`, `Collision`, `Display`, and `Movement` are fairly common among nearly all placed objects. Most objects that will appear in the level will also share lighting and physics parameters. Something you might notice is that all of the roll-outs found in the `Properties` dialog are arranged alphabetically. This might not be the most convenient way to organize this dialog, but once you understand how the various attributes are arranged, you might be able to locate some items a bit more easily [Figure 1.9].

The movement roll-out contains the object's placement in the scene, even though it's not actually currently moving. Almost all objects placed in the level are instances or clones of objects found in the Generic Browser's asset list. The data for the object isn't saved in the level; only the object's instance information and its placement data, as well as any specific attributes, are stored in the level.

If you need to copy attributes from one object to another, you can have more than one property editor open. To open a second dialog, turn on the `Lock` icon (located on the top left of the property editor window), and then either double click or press F4 with another object selected, and a second property editor dialog will open. This will allow you to copy and paste attributes from one dialog to another.

The levels are saved as a .ut3 map format; you can save maps using different extensions after editing your mod's .ini file settings to recognize your changes. For instance, UDK uses .umap The assets and objects that are used to construe your level are saved as a .upk file. These UPKs, or Unreal package files, contain the actual static mesh vertex data as well as textures and other sources of data that are going to be used in your level.

Here I've opened DM_Deck.ut3 and zoomed all the way out on the top view [Figure 1.10].

You can see a large sky-dome object. There are several different methods to create sky-domes, and DM_Deck has a few interesting tricks. The pair of planes to the top right of the dome are objects placed to create the sunset.

*Figure 1.10*

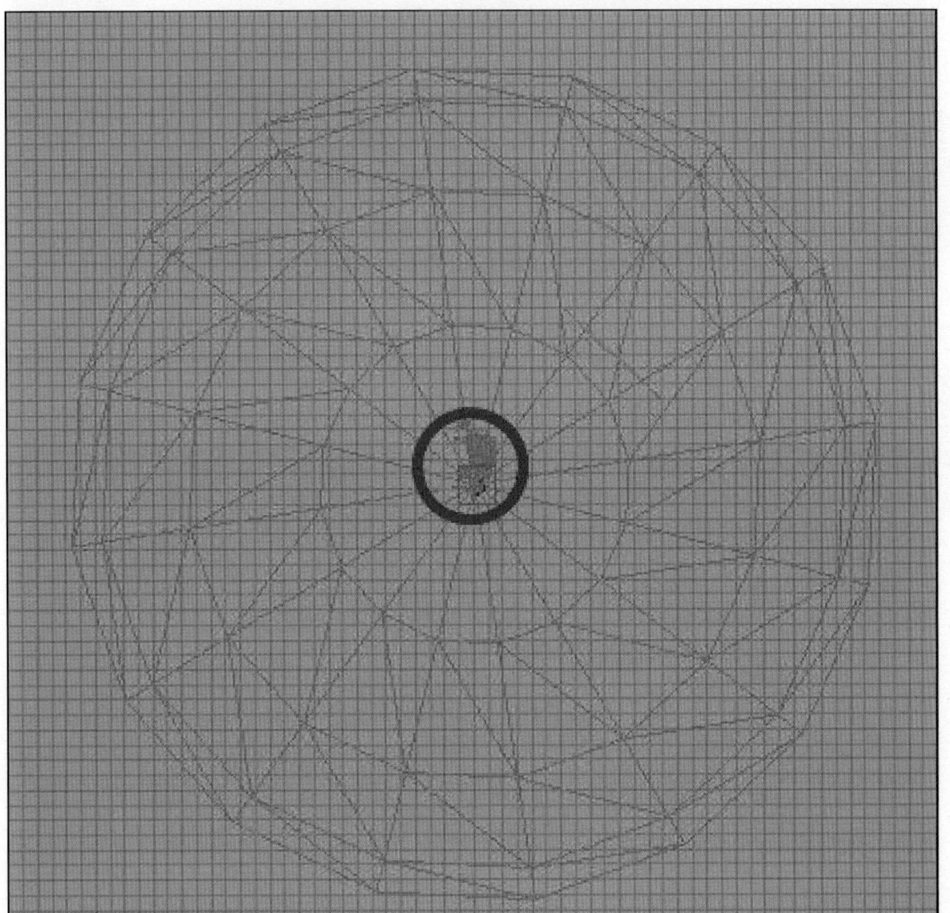

Figure 1.11

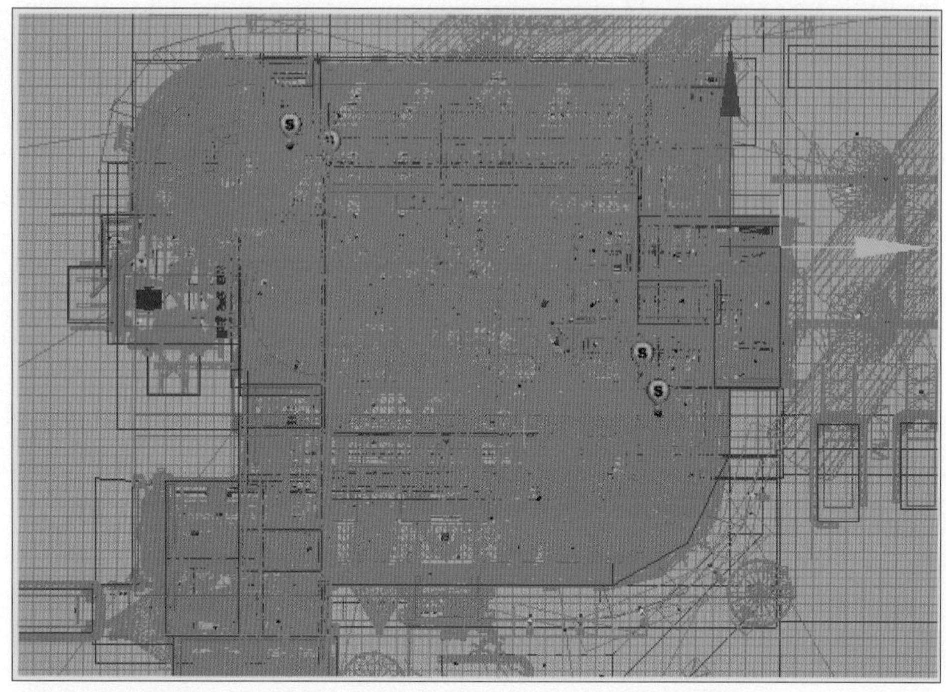

Figure 1.12

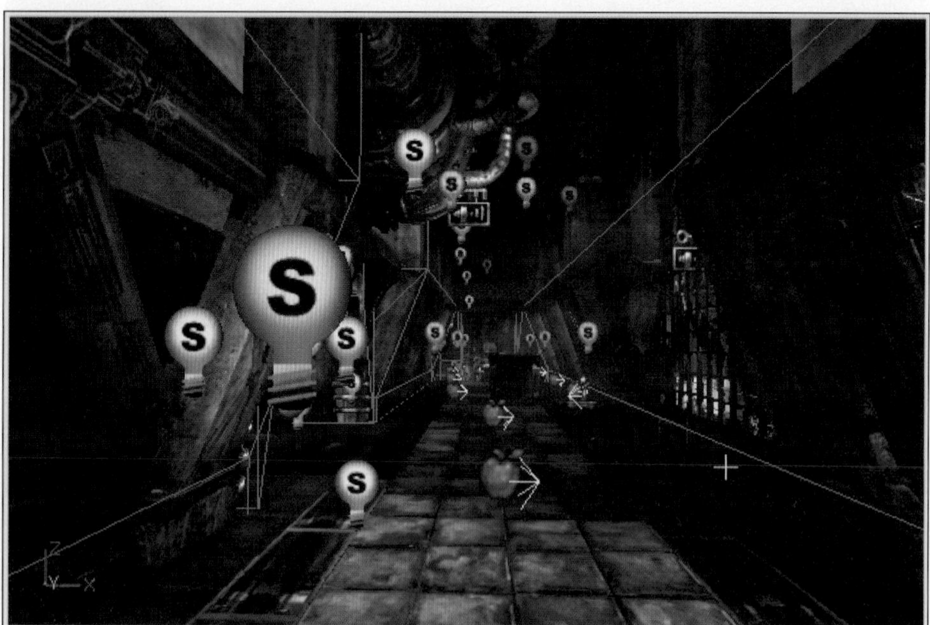

Figure 1.13

Zooming into the actual playable part of the level you can tell that there's a lot of geometry in the level [Figure 1.11]. These are almost all static mesh objects.

If you jump down into the perspective view, you can fly around and take a look at how the level is built [Figure 1.12]. One of the first things you might notice is that there are a lot of point lights scattered about the level. Many if not most of them are set to the static mesh lighting channel. That most likely makes no sense right now, but don't worry about that. We'll cover lighting channels later on when we start lighting our own levels.

Pick a light and open the properties [Figure 1.13]. Make note of the light's brightness and color. Keep some of these options in mind when you begin to set up your lights.

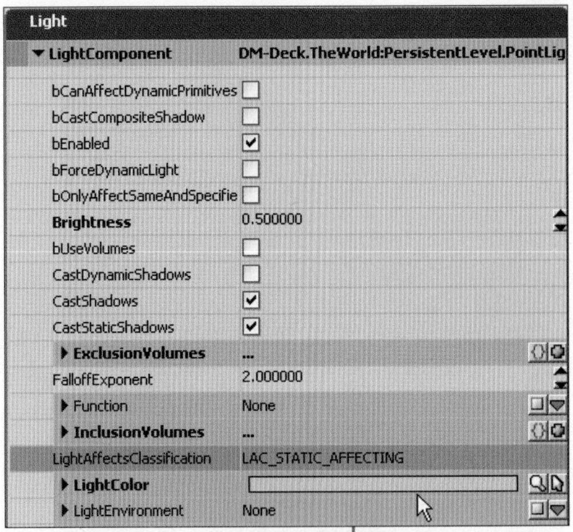

To find out how the level works, we'll open the Kismet sequence for this level. Kismet is what operates the various voices taunting you. The elevator platforms in the level are operated by the two simple sequences on the lower left of the Kismet editor. We'll take a closer look at these in a bit.

If you look at the Sequences dialog on the lower right of the Kismet editor, you can see that there's a sub-directory which contains another Kismet sequence [Figure 1.14]. This is a way to organize a lot of Kismet sequences in a level and helps keep the Kismet editor easier to view once a lot of complex sequences have been created.

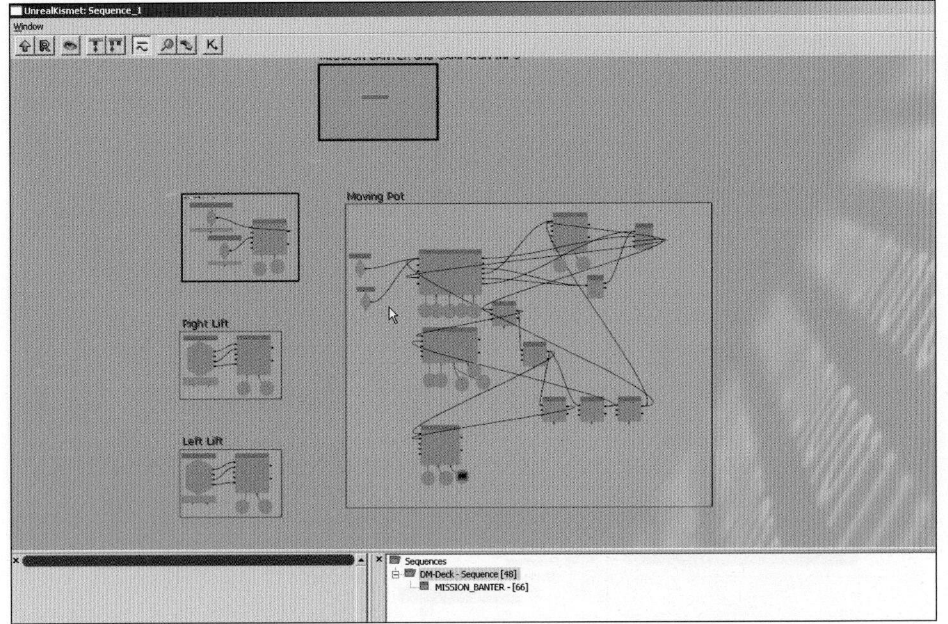


Figure 1.14

Figure 1.15

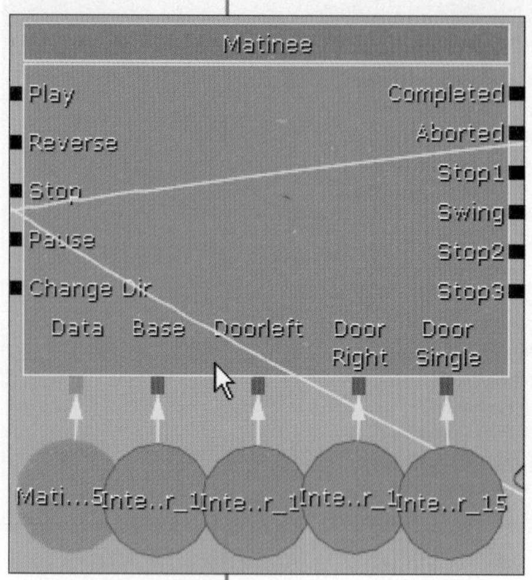


Figure 1.16

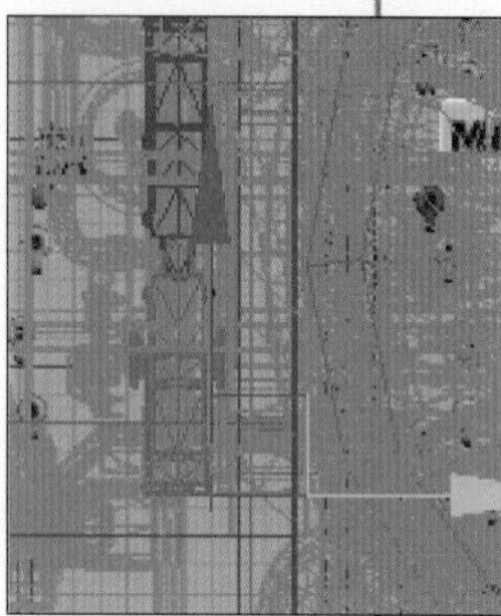

On closer inspection of a Matinee node, you can see which objects Matinee is manipulating [Figure 1.15]: Base, Doorleft, Door Right, and so forth. Double-click on one of these circular nodes, and the editor will focus on the object [Figure 1.16]. Kismet is tightly integrated with the level editor. The data that is being modified in Kismet is directly tied into the objects in the editor. Right-clicking on the object and selecting an option called "Synch to Generic Browser" will show you which UPK the object's data lives in, the generic browser or asset manager, which we are already familiar with.

Clicking on the Mission_Banter sub-sequence will open the banter sub-sequence. The number following the sequence name indicates how many nodes are found in the selected sequence. The Mission_Banter sequence contains data and events that are triggered by various events in the level. You might also notice that this is where the SCYTHE and the KRALL are unlocked when you complete the mission [Figure 1.17]. Ooh, cheats!

A completed level will have a lot of nodes. To remain in control of your project, you'll want to keep your Kismet sequences organized and neat.

Figure 1.17

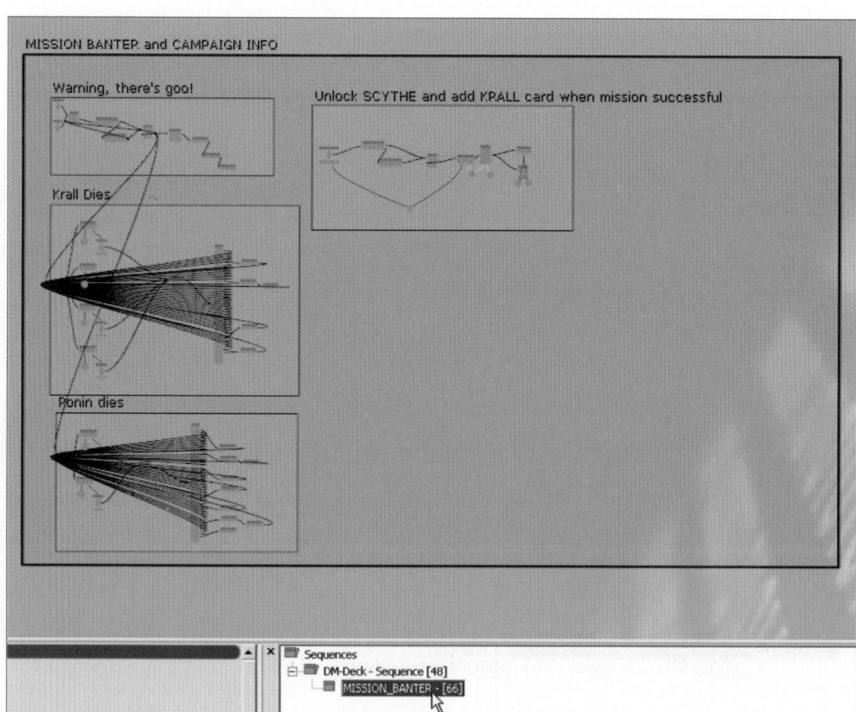

## What Have We Seen So Far?

Unreal's levels are made from a spider web of events and tons of art assets. To create such a detailed world, you need to start off simple and build up. The path taken to produce detailed worlds like these is referred to as the pipeline. The tools in the Unreal Editor are in use by many studios worldwide and for good reason. These tools provide the level designers and artists freedom to implement new ideas and see results quickly.

In the previous generation, video game development relied on programmers to accomplish many tasks. The more in depth the artist and designer tools are, the more programmers are allowed to focus on more complex problems of AI and game-specific mechanics. It's debatable if the Unreal Engine is the most efficient engine out there, but it certainly helps accomplish quite a lot out of the box.

When you're just starting out on a new game project, the Unreal Engine 3 provides a powerful set of tools to accomplish quite a lot. However, it's also quite a beast to learn. More than just a level editor, Unreal Engine 3 has animation tools, effects tools, and sound tools. This is just the beginning, and there's a ton to cover.

# 2

# Level Design

*Filling Space with Stuff to Do (Your Game Here)*

Starting off with an empty open space and filling it with a game is a daunting task. Opening a completed level and sifting through the thousands of elements that make up a level can also be overwhelming. Stepping through the process slowly will help you create a complete game level filled with all the necessary elements that create a fun gaming experience.

A good method to get the most you can out of a level is to find a specific element and find out how it's made. Select any element in the scene and open the properties editor. Take notes about what is checked on and what is checked off. For each object, find which UPK the static mesh is found in. Open the object and find out where the materials are found.

In the Generic Browser, you can open the Referenced Assets tab and discover how many ties one object has to another object. Even a simple static mesh is connected to materials, textures, lights, and physics properties. These physics properties are then tied to sounds and particle effects. One thing leads to another, and as a designer it's important to remember how these things are connected. It's all quite zen, actually.

As a level designer, you should take your experiences as a gamer and think about what you have fun doing. Then give your player the same experience. As a designer, it is not your duty to punish the player for not understanding your level design. Instead, you should work to make your level as clear as possible.

Ladders should look like ladders, dangerous areas should look dangerous, and each attribute given to objects in your scene should be readable. To help accomplish this clarity, a `Squint` button is a simple tool to help make sure your level's detail doesn't hide what's important to the player [Figure 2.1].

In this example, you can see a brighter spot in the middle of the perspective view framed by slightly brighter objects. This pattern should lead the player into another space using broad shapes and forms that add contrast and focus different from the usual dark and dirty hallway.

The `Squint` button takes the perspective camera and blurs what's in view. The concept is that small details will get blurred away and only the large obvious structures will be clear. Consider it like a myopic filter for the perspective camera. If you've made an important feature in the level too small, it will not be obvious to the player, who might not even notice it.

One of the best solutions to highlight a feature of your level is to actually highlight it. Drop some lights on the feature to brighten it up. This doesn't have to be completely obvious, but picking a specific color or pattern in an area where something important is hidden is a great way to help players find what they're looking for.

*Figure 2.1*

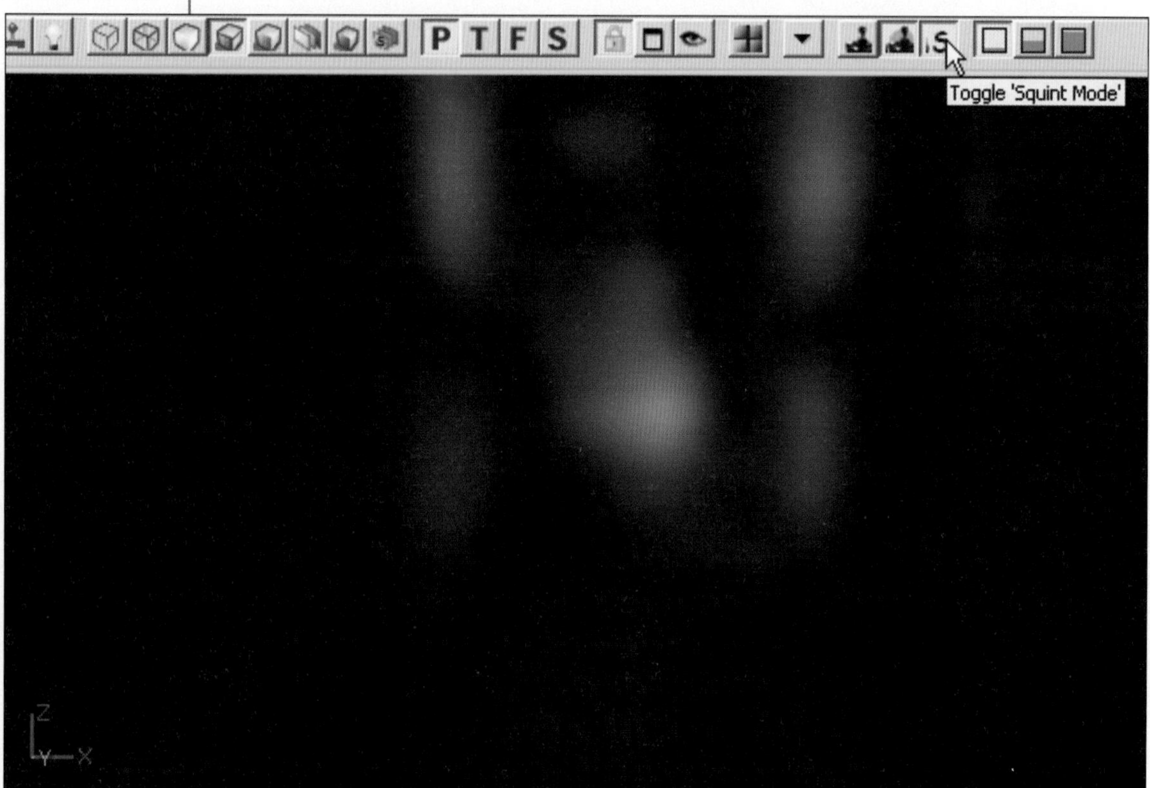


## What to Expect

Level design is a fun, challenging effort that takes a specific personality to get it right. Iterative game design allows the game designer to find and refine elements that are fun and enjoyable to play. You must want to entertain your player; that's your goal as a game designer. Something that the game designer must remember is that the level is for the player, not the designer, to enjoy. There's a difference.

Before getting too deep into building a complete level, it's best to start off with a focus, a design goal. After you've learned how to build and design levels using the

Unreal Editor 3, you should apply your efforts to very basic and simple goals at first. Then find a way to add and layer on complexity to your design when you've mastered the basics.

## Level Flow

Level flow and progression can be broken down into some very basic types. The three basic types are linear progressions, circular progressions, and radial progressions. Knowing how to understand these progressions will help you write and design how you want your level to flow. Creating a simple flow chart on paper will help communicate to your fellow team members how you want your player to interact with your game.

Linear progressions are usually story-driven events that happen in a rigid sequence. The order of the sequence cannot be changed as the players make progress, uncovering events as they come to them in the course of the game. For these types of sequences, a simple story board can be drawn to show how the level will be created and what animated sequences and objects will be needed to entertain your player or players.

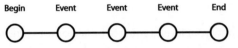

Begin Event Event Event End

An example of a linear game play setup is starting off the level without a red key, discovering a red key, and then finding a door that requires a red key to open it. The path is linear and not too exciting, and the players know pretty much what to expect when they discover a door. In some cases this can be a good way to introduce new elements to the player.

Circular progressions are either long or short linear progressions that lead back to the beginning of the sequence. Usually, when players return to the beginning of the circular progression, they have obtained something which changes how they can proceed and escape the chain of events.

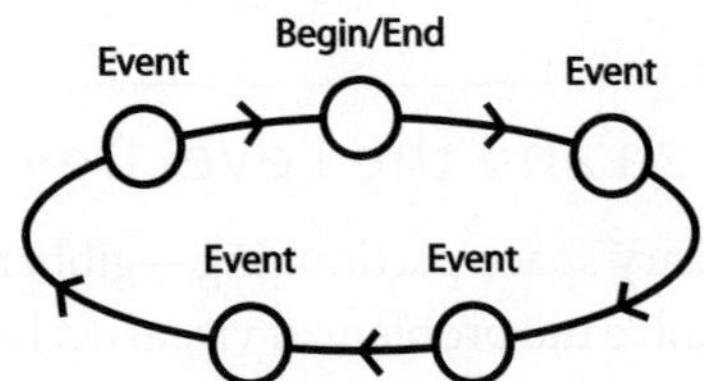


Here's an example of a circular progression: when the players begin a level, they find a door that requires a red key which they do not have; they then move to the next room and find a red key; they can then go back to the red door to open it. In this sequence there are only two events that are circularly connected, but the length of time and numbers of events that are required to find the key and then make it back to the door are up to the designer to make the game play more interesting.

Last but not least are radial sequences. These are like multiple circular events that all lead back to the same place. The difference here is that the player can jump into any one of the branches from the central point in any order and not change the outcome. These types of designs become more complex with each additional branch added from the same start point.

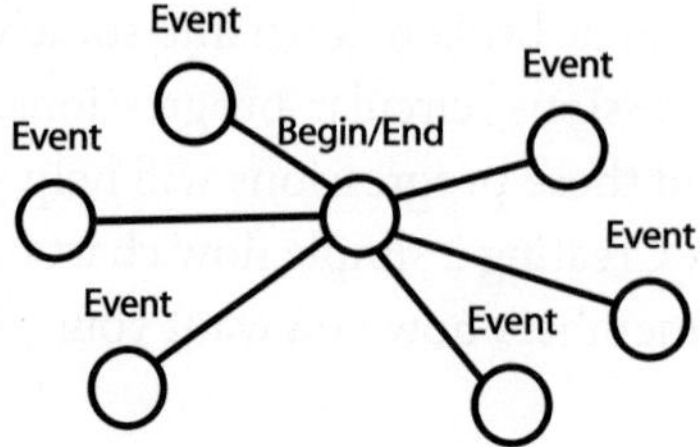


For example, the players might start off with a door that requires both a red and a blue key to open it. That means that they would have to go find both keys before returning to open the door.. The door doesn't require that the keys are found in a specific order, just that the two keys are in the players' possession.

### Building a Level

Once you've decided how your level is going to be laid out, it's time to start building. Once you start building blocks of objects and start making your level, you'll want to explore the space and see for yourself how the size of the space feels. BSPs and lighting will help you create the basic flow to your level, and the Play In Editor tool will help you get a feel for your level's flow.

If you were forced to build your level in 3ds Max, the time of iteration would be drastically increased, and the refinement of flow and timing would take longer to make it feel right. Thankfully, using the editor's tools, you can fill in space and develop the timing to make your level really feel polished. Once the level flow and timing are to a point where the game play is fun and exciting, the BSPs can be replaced with more detailed and interesting static meshes.

## Working with Design and the Level Development Pipeline

BSP is the acronym for binary space partitioning—gibberish, I know. BSPs, as they are called, were created to solve the problem of visual occlusion. In other words, BSPs were used as a very fast way to solve the problem of what players could see at any given time as they wandered through a level. These days, video cards can render highly complex scenes using tens, if not hundreds, of thousands of polygons and never skip a beat. In addition, there are many new and better ways to deal with scene complexity that do not require methods like BSPs.

The second version of the Unreal Engine made extensive use of BSPs, as did many engines of that era. The Unreal Engine's third version has moved away from BSPs and makes use of other modern visual culling methods to decide what to render to the screen. In fact, using BSPs exclusively in the Unreal Engine 3 can actually cause a loss in frame rate, as the BSP method of rendering is actually inferior to the modern rendering system!

However, BSPs still have a place in the Unreal Engine 3. As a designer, you might expect to use tools like 3ds Max, or Maya, maybe even XSI, to design your level. At some game studios that is the case, and indeed for some other game engines their use may be required. As a designer, you're not expected to build complex photorealistic structures, roads, and props, but you are expected to create the flow and layout of your level.

To use software like 3ds Max to simply create spaces, tunnels, and doors would be a somewhat slow process. Even if you were skilled with the software, the process would look something like this:

`Build objects` → `export objects` → `import objects` → `place objects` → `play level` → `repeat...`

BSPs in the Unreal Engine can help skip a few of these steps. Iteration is the key element in any good game design. Coming up with your level's timing to keep things exciting is your task as a designer. Creating contrast in space to make large rooms feel open and small rooms feel tight is important, but neither should hinder game play. These sorts of changes require playing, testing, making changes, and playing again. The BSP pipeline would look more like this:

`Build objects` → `play level` → `repeat...`

In comparison, this shorter pipeline allows for more testing of your level and much less work in exporting, importing, and placement. However, we run into the problem that BSPs are still a deprecated technology, and Unreal Engine 3 doesn't want to render the entire world as BSPs. In addition, BSPs don't allow the user to create highly detailed scenery and props. So what's a designer to do?

We'll want to replace our BSPs with static mesh elements. After you're finished or at least mostly satisfied with your level design, you're going to want to have your level artists dive into the level and start replacing the BSPs with finished art. The level artists will work on a separate level layer to allow you to continue to make tweaks and changes to the level. We'll talk more about how levels can act as layers in one of the following chapters, but for now you should feel safe in that you can work on the level design at the same time as the artists do.

What you want the artists to do with the level needs to be communicated clearly. One of the ways to clearly tell artists what goes where is to mark up the level with special materials. In a later project, you'll learn how to make some simple materials so that your artists can see what you intend to do with your level. For instance, if your plot requires your player to find the brick building, and the artist places a glass and steel building where you asked for brick, it's no one's fault for not knowing what's going on. Simple measures can be taken to avoid these situations.

You'll also want to make your levels easy to modify. Keeping in mind that you can use the same level for a death-match game, a capture-the-flag game, or any other game play option, it will be easier if you learn how to use the level manager and streaming levels. In a nutshell, a level in Unreal doesn't have to be an all-in-one set of data. A level can be made up of many small sub-level objects that all load in at the same time. One level can have your game play logic, another can have its geometry and static meshes, and yet another can contain all of the level's lighting. If you want to make changes, it's as simple as loading a different streamed level.

Excited? Sure? Now, let's get started!

PROJECT

## A Box with a Light

The three most basic elements that make up a level are something to stand on, a means of illumination, and somewhere to start. The most basic level that can be built is a hollow box with a light and a player start node. We'll start off with something like that in order to get into the groove of building with BSPs. You want to start with a new level. Making a new level will prompt you with this new level Geometry Style dialog. In general, select `Additive`. For reasons we'll go into later, `Additive` should be your default selection [Figure 2.2].

Figure 2.2

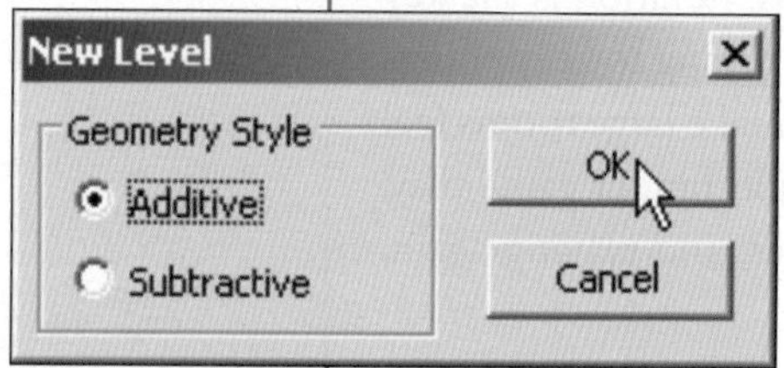


Next we'll right click on the `Box Brush builder` icon in the BSP tool bar on the left of the level editor. This will open the following dialog [Figure 2.3] and allow us to build a basic room. Fill in the following settings, remembering to check `Hollow`. This will automatically carve out a space inside of the box for us to stand around in.

Figure 2.3

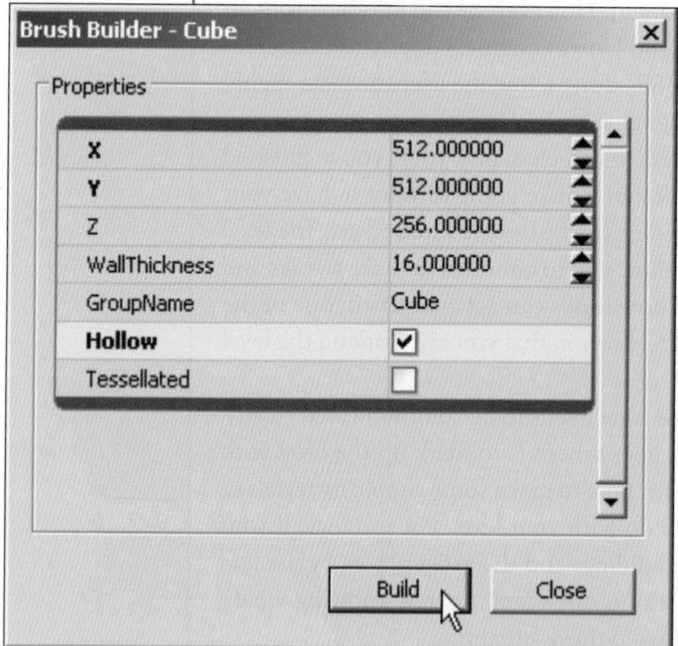


This will create what's called a builder brush. A builder brush can be described as a shape that will be filled in with geometry when the brush is applied to the world. Right now there is no actual game play geometry in the scene [Figure 2.4]. Too add this shape to the scene, we use the `Add` button from the BSP tools.

This `CSG: Add` will then fill in the builder brush with geometry that exists in the level [Figure 2.5]. A catch here is that a few of the regular hotkeys you might be used to are a bit different here. By pressing Ctrl+S, which would normally save your level, you will instead perform a

Figure 2.4

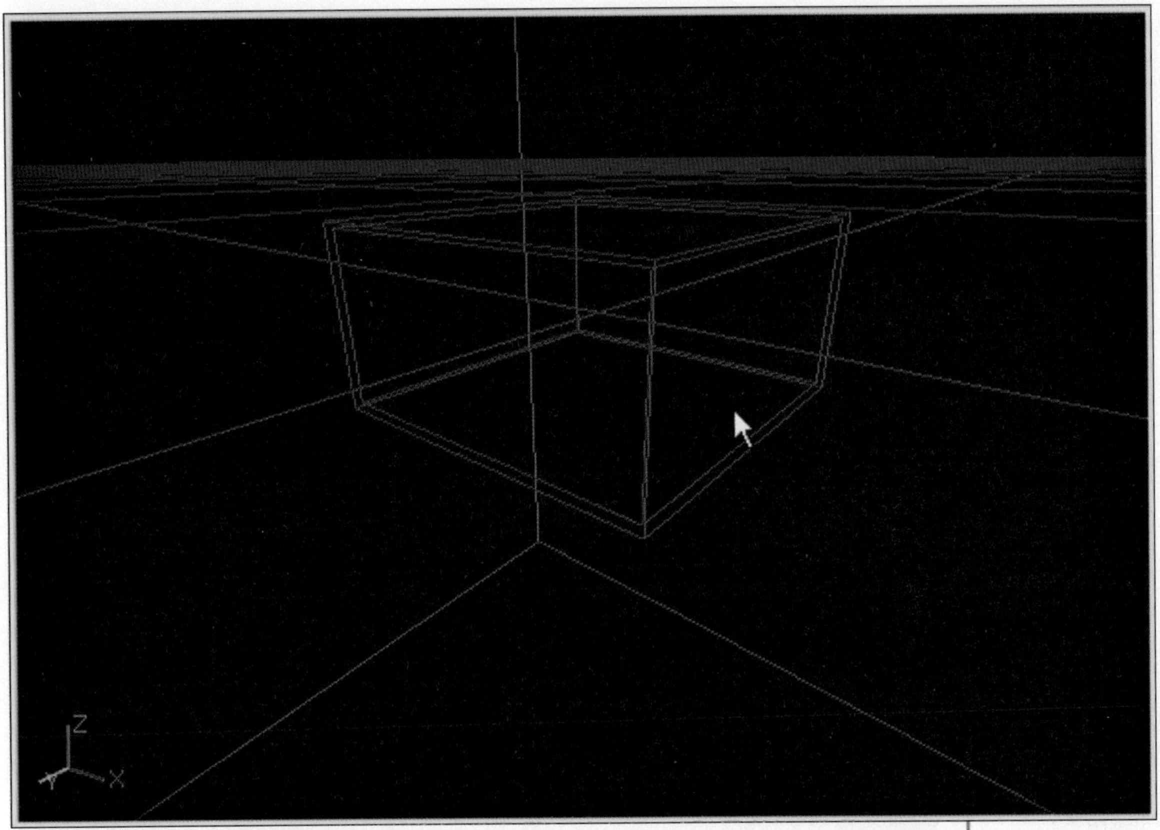

`CSG: Subtract`. If you do that now, you'll subtract the added geometry from the level, negating your efforts and adding garbage data to your level. You can delete unwanted BSPs from your scene by selecting them in the level editor view and using the delete key. By the way, CSG stands for constructive solid geometry.

Immediately after filling in the builder brush, you're not going to see much. There are no lights in the scene. To resolve this, we'll change the perspective view to `Unlit` using the icons at the top, which change how the level is viewed. Now we can see our new BSP. Move the camera to the inside of our little box-shaped room so we can add a light [Figure 2.6].

Figure 2.5

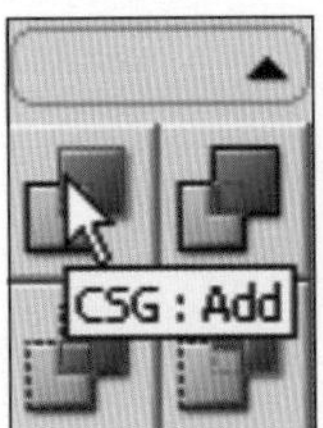

Figure 2.6

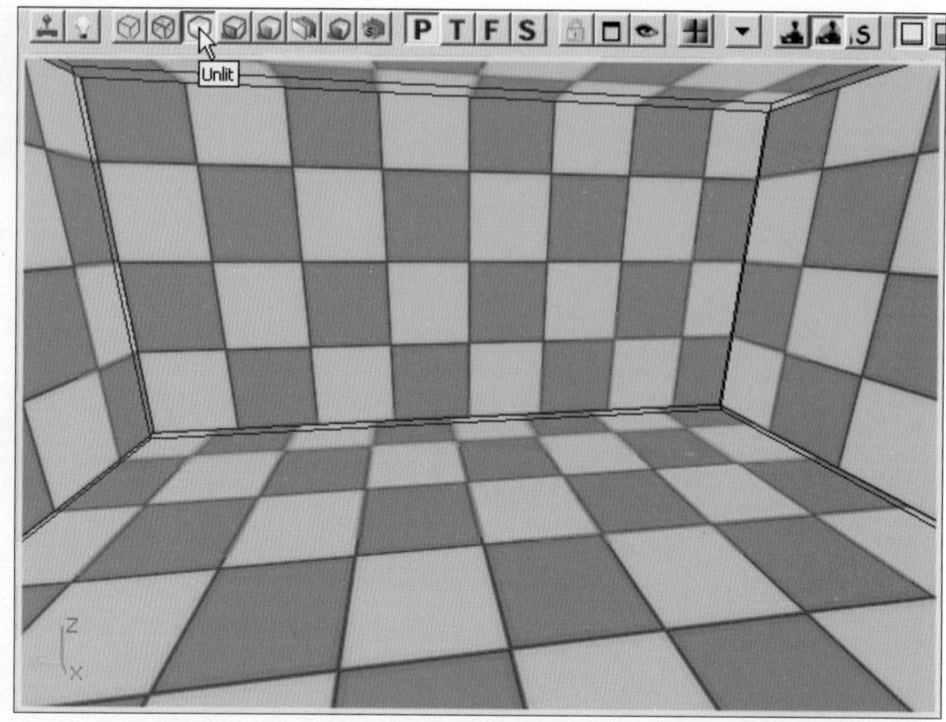


Figure 2.7

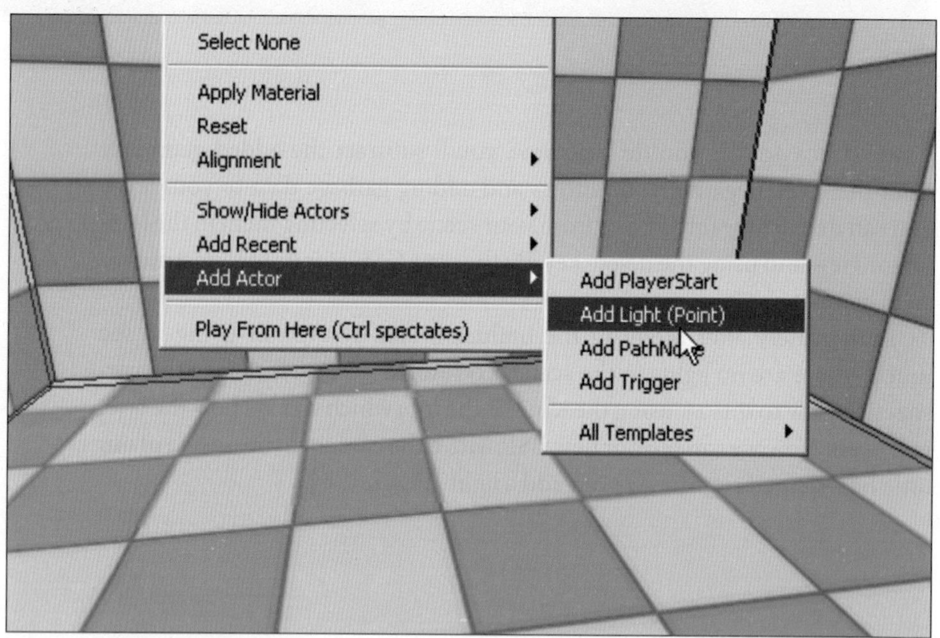

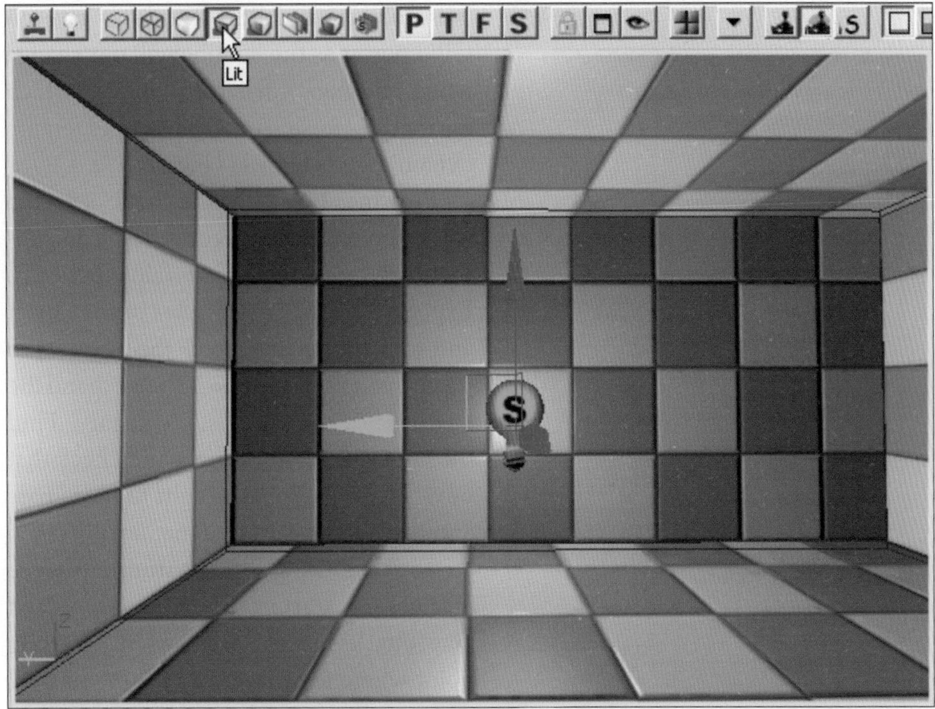


Figure 2.8

Now that we're inside our little box, we're going to want to add in a light. Right-click in the room and select `Add Actor` → `Add Light (Point)` [Figure 2.7]. This will drop a point light with default property settings into the scene. It's important to note right now that if you're going to be placing objects using the perspective viewport, you're going to want to click on something solid.

If you click in empty space in the perspective viewport and add an object, you will be placing the object somewhere in the middle of nowhere. If you do this by mistake, you can open the properties editor, expand the movement roll-out menu, and type in more reasonable coordinates, like 0,0,0. This will pop the lost object to the middle of the level editor. Otherwise, you can use the search function in the tool bar to find your lost object and enter more usable coordinates.

When your light is first created in the level, it might be placed halfway up the wall or on the floor. To move it, click and drag on one of the arrows to pull it out of the surface of the room. To see the effects of the light, change the view port coloration options to `Lit` [Figure 2.8].

Now that we have a light in the scene, we can change back to lit mode. You can still reposition the light and see the lighting effect change as you move the light around. Lights can be set to specific functions. By default, all lights added to a scene are static mesh lights. These lights will only bake their effect into the surrounding static

Figure 2.9

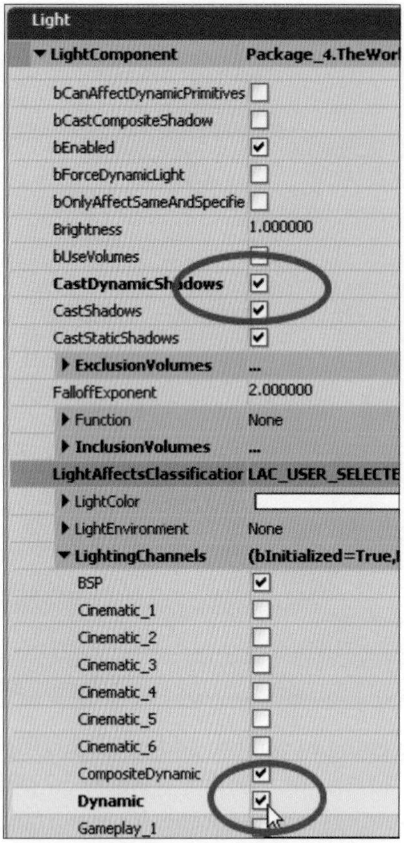

mesh objects and BSP. This is to save on GPU power as the lighting will not change while playing. Characters move, which means they are dynamic objects and require dynamic lights to be lit [Figure 2.9].

Pressing F4 with the light selected will open the light's properties. The sub-sections are organized alphabetically. Expand the `Light` attributes of the object and scroll down and check the box next to `CastDynamicShadows`. Then expand the `LightingChannels` sub-category. Find the `Dynamic` light channel and check that box. This will allow the light to illuminate and cast shadows from dynamic objects.

So far nothing too eventful, but we're just getting started. Right now we can't play our level yet as there's no starting point where the player can begin. So we'll add in a player start location by right-clicking in the scene and selecting `Add Actor` → `Add PlayerStart` to create a spawn point where we can begin [Figure 2.10].

Figure 2.10

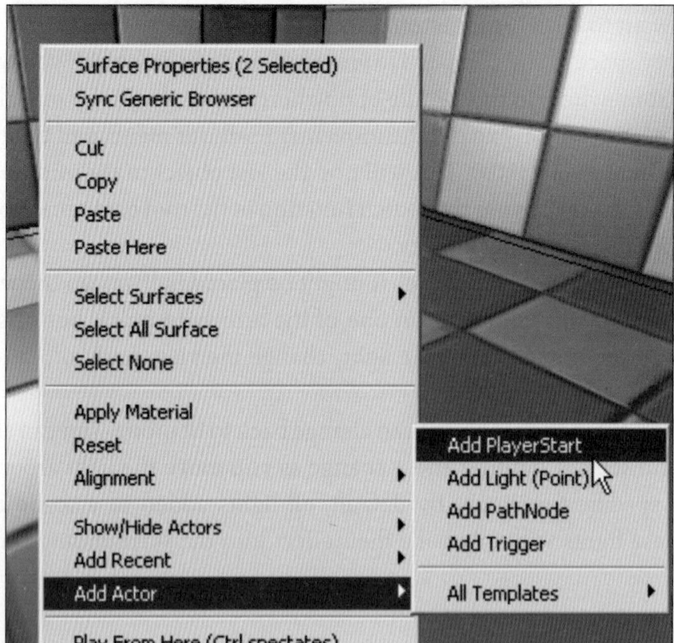

You should have two elements in this small room [Figure 2.11].

Figure 2.11

Almost there! For the level to be ready for us to play, the engine must rebuild the geometry and lighting; to do this we click the `Build All` button in the tool bar at the top of the level editor. This will cook our level so we can play it [Figure 2.12].

Building the level will also highlight a few of the errors that are associated with a new level. In a regular Unreal Tournament, you'll need at least 16 player start locations; for our simple test map, we don't have to worry about that. Likewise, we haven't added a custom material to our room, so we can also ignore our Null material reference on our BSP [Figure 2.13].

Close the map check dialog and press the `PIE` (Play In Editor) button [Figure 2.14].

Figure 2.12

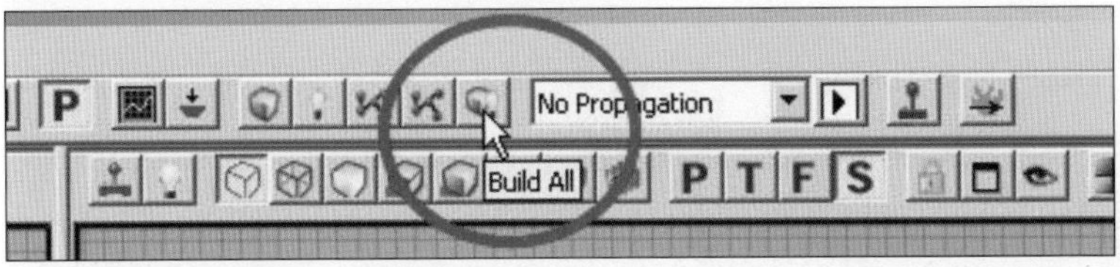

Figure 2.13

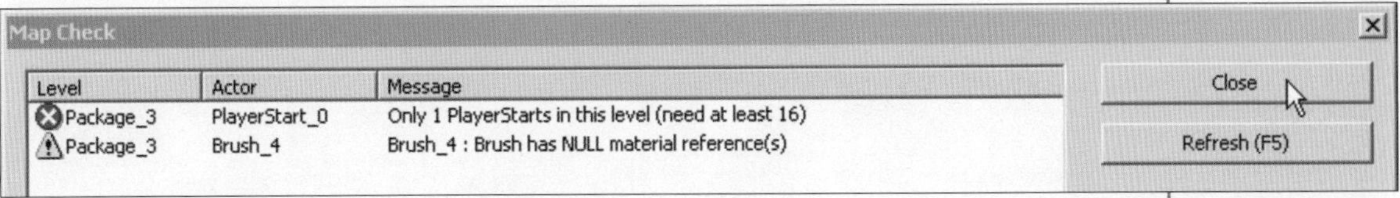


Figure 2.14

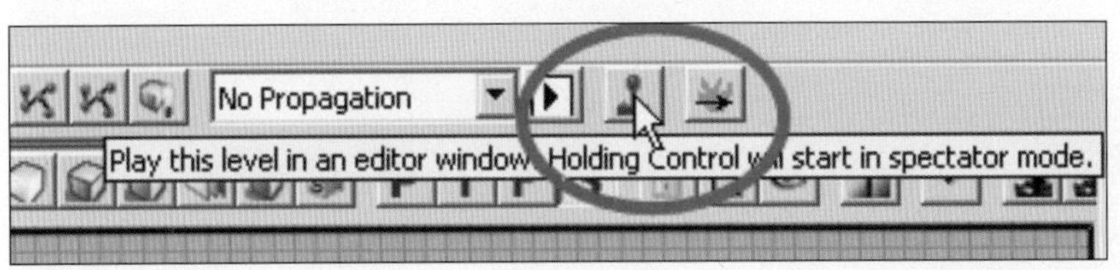

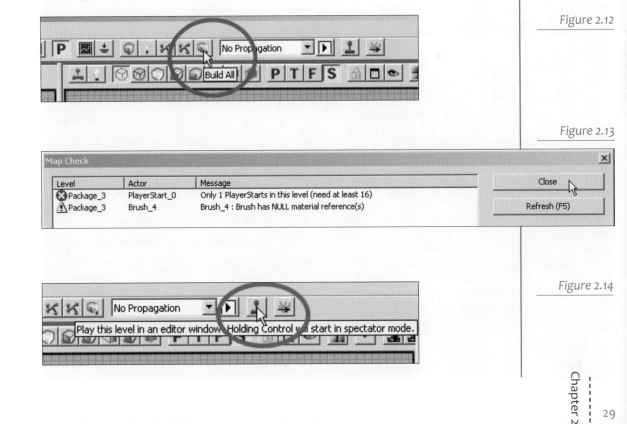

This will open a window describing what the engine is doing to prepare your level for playing. The dialog will be doing things like saving your level and creating various game play-related chunks of data. After a moment, the In Editor Game window will open. While this window is open, your mouse controls and keyboard controls will act as though you're playing the level in the game [Figure 2.15]. However, you won't have any inventory, and there will not be much of a user interface (UI), as we haven't gone through the process to make this a full death-match level.

Congrats—you've completed your first little level. We're moving in baby steps, but don't worry; you'll be building epic cathedrals and space stations in no time. To go back to the editor, simply press esc on the keyboard and the In Editor Game window will close.

Save this level in "My Documents\My Games\Unreal Tournament 3\UTGame\Unpublished\CookedPC\CustomMaps" directory as BoxRoom.ut3 because we'll be using this level a lot to test things later on.

Figure 2.15

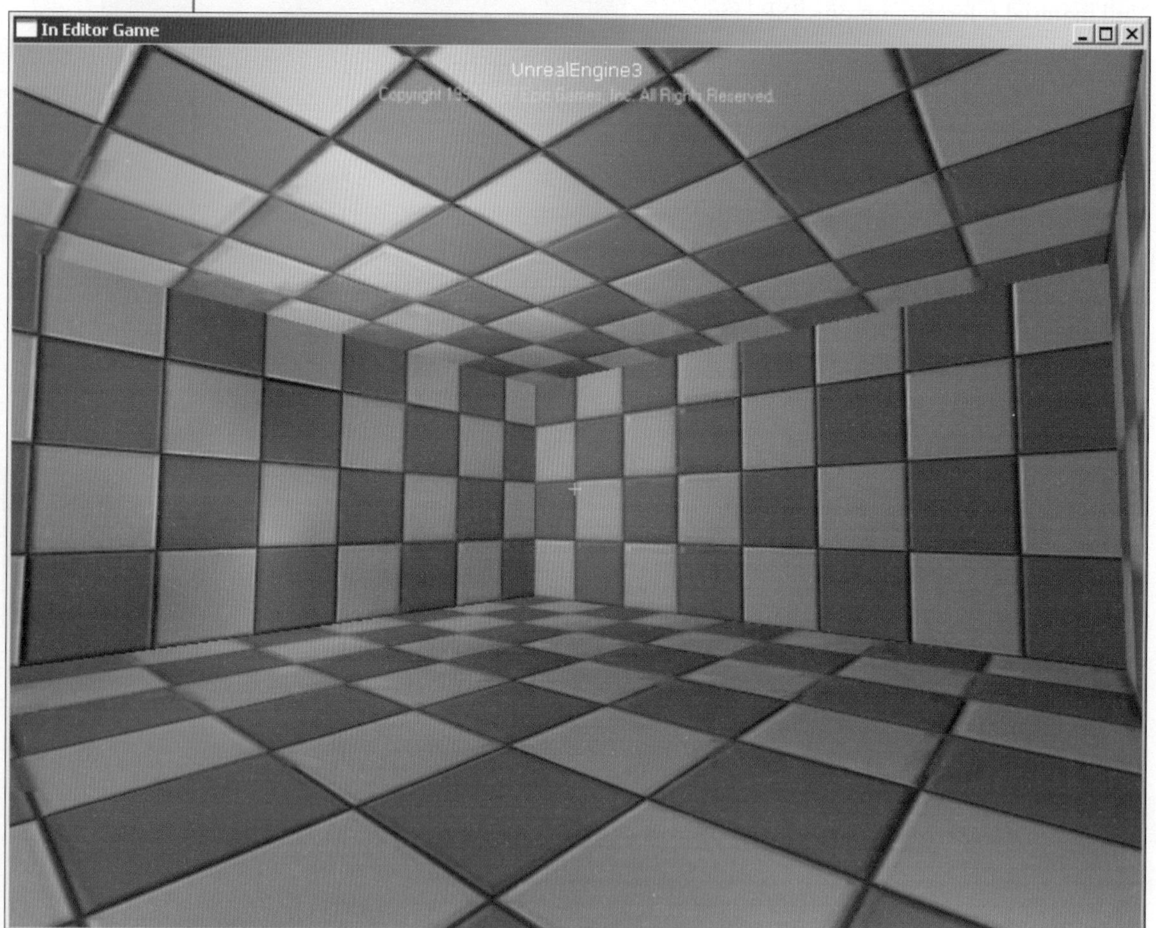

REVIEW

## What's Next?

Now that we've got a small room to start in, we're going to want to know how to move forward. The following project is basically an expanded version of the same room we just built. It might be a good idea at this point to explore the different BSP shapes on your own for a bit before moving on. You'll need to be fairly comfortable with moving around the scene, selecting and moving objects and finding objects after they've been placed in the scene.

If at all possible, you might want to build a level of your own that includes hallways, rooms, and doorways interconnected in an interesting pattern. Of course, if you want the practice, you're welcome to proceed with the following project so you can have a level that matches the projects here. However, if you want, you can also just create your own level and then open the DM_Dome.ut3 level from the disk provided and use that to follow the examples.

The projects following the DM-Dome construction also have their own isolated levels to help keep the focus of each task as simple and clear as possible. If all of the examples were focused on DM-Dome, the clutter would create spaghetti code in the Kismet, which isn't good for describing how tasks are done.

PROJECT

## Building a Basic Level DM-Dome

Additive or subtractive level building—what does that mean? In general, unless your entire game is going to happen in a subterranean environment, you're going to want to start with an additive level. Once you've started building in additive or subtractive mode, you cannot mix the two. Streaming from one level to another and switching from additive to subtractive level types will cause unpredictable results. In general, it's always best to start with an additive level.

So, for a basic death-match level, we're going to start off with your run-of-the-mill radial level design with a central arena section. Your floor plans are constrained only by a few general limitations within the Unreal Editor. That is to say, a level shouldn't be much bigger than about 200,000 units by 200,000 units by 200,000 units; past this size, the physics tends to get a bit wonky. Something called floating-point error starts to have an effect when calculations involve large numbers at such great distances from the origin.

There have been many instances of this sort of level design; it's simple and forces all of the players into the middle for a good fight. It's also difficult to get lost when all you need to do is look for a door and you'll find yourself in the middle of the arena.

So to begin, we'll start a new (additive) level. Create an additive level and save the level as DM_Dome_BSP.ut3 in your custom maps directory [Figure 2.16].

Figure 2.16

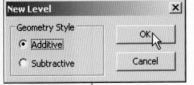

## BSP construction

We're going to position eight side rooms around a central, cathedral-like room. Then we're going to connect them together with some simple hallways (this might seem easier to do as a subtractive level), but then we're going to open up the top so we can see the sky dome. This will even allow us to shoot from one area to the next.

Figure 2.17

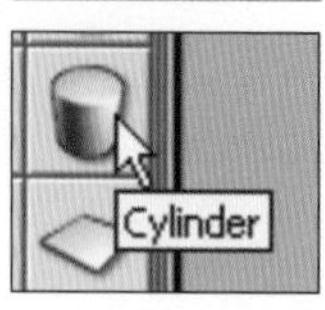


The cylinder button is located to the left of the level editor window [Figure 2.17]. Right-clicking will open the options dialog for the cylinder tool. The following dialog should open, allowing you to change the shape and size of your cylinder builder brush [Figure 2.18].

Figure 2.18

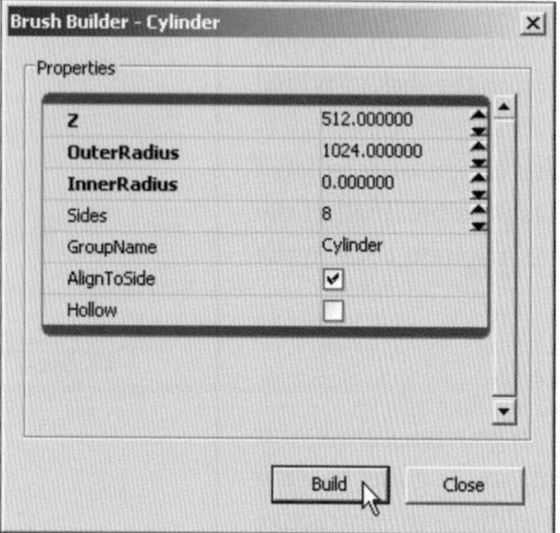


Starting with the central room we'll build a cylinder with eight sides. The height is determined by the Z value; the outer radius determines the diameter of the cylinder. If the `hollow` check box is turned on, the inner radius will carve out the center of the cylinder, turning the shape into a round wall structure. I'll leave it up to you to play with the other tools to learn how they are used, but for now let's just make our simple death-match level.

Once the cylinder is created you should see a representation of the mesh in the perspective viewport [Figure 2.19].

Figure 2.19

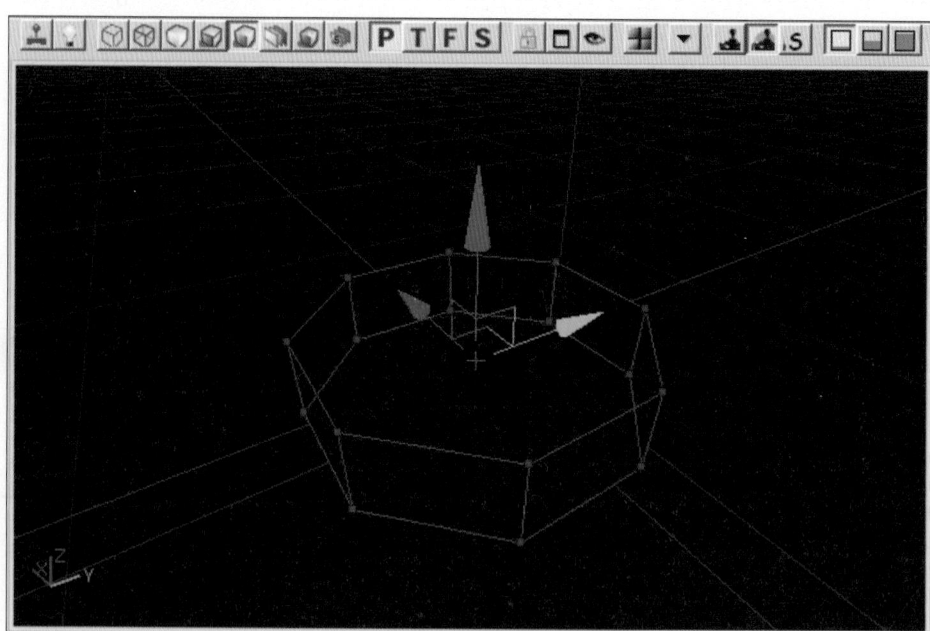

To fill in the shape with a BSP, you'll use the `Add` button located below the brush tools [Figure 2.20].

Figure 2.20

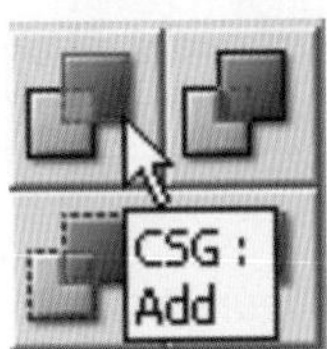


This doesn't create anything very interesting to look at since, by default, the scene has no lights and the geometry that has been created is not being lit. One quick solution is to change the lighting mode in the scene by pressing the unlit mode button at the top of the perspective view [Figure 2.21].

Figure 2.21

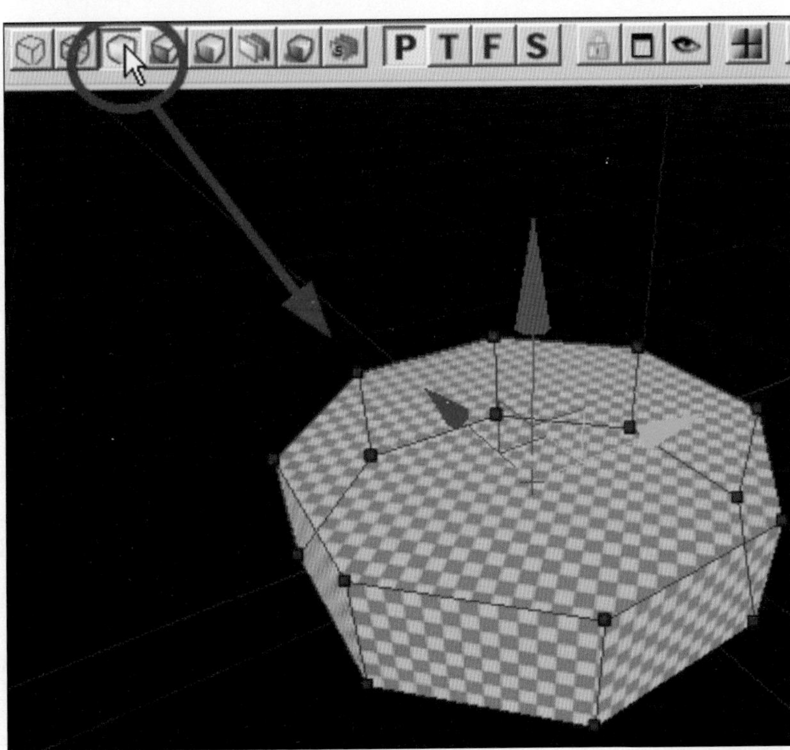


This changes how we can see the level as we build it. We'll move onto lighting the scene later on in this project, but for now we'll just work in the unlit mode. Experiment with the other buttons; some of them might not make sense at the moment, but we'll get to explaining what they all do in later chapters.

So we've built a solid octagon volume, which means there's no space in the interior of the shape. At the moment, the only place we can interact with is the top of the shape. Next we'll make a smaller cylinder shape and carve out the interior of the cylinder [Figure 2.22].

Figure 2.22

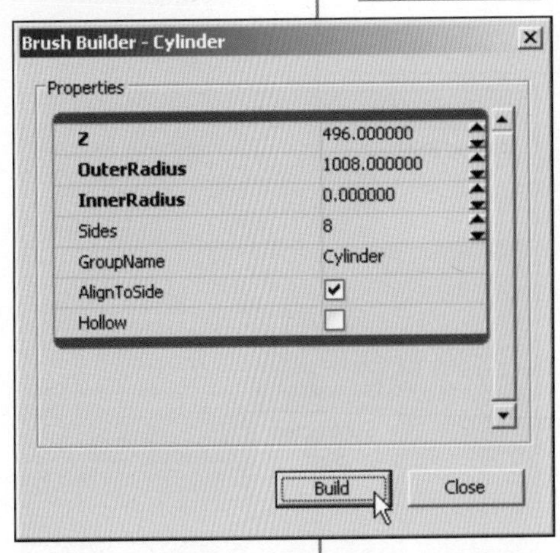

Figure 2.23

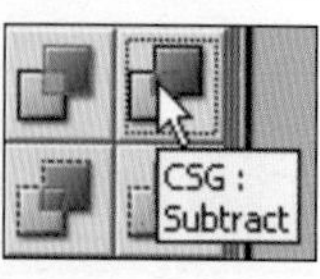


Create a new cylinder with these numbers; and this time, rather than add this brush to the scene, we'll subtract this from the scene. This will carve out the inside of the shape and create an interior space [Figure 2.23].

If you mouse to the inside of the cylinder, you should see a space something like this [Figure 2.24]. So far there's not a whole lot going on, but we'll fix that soon enough.

Figure 2.24

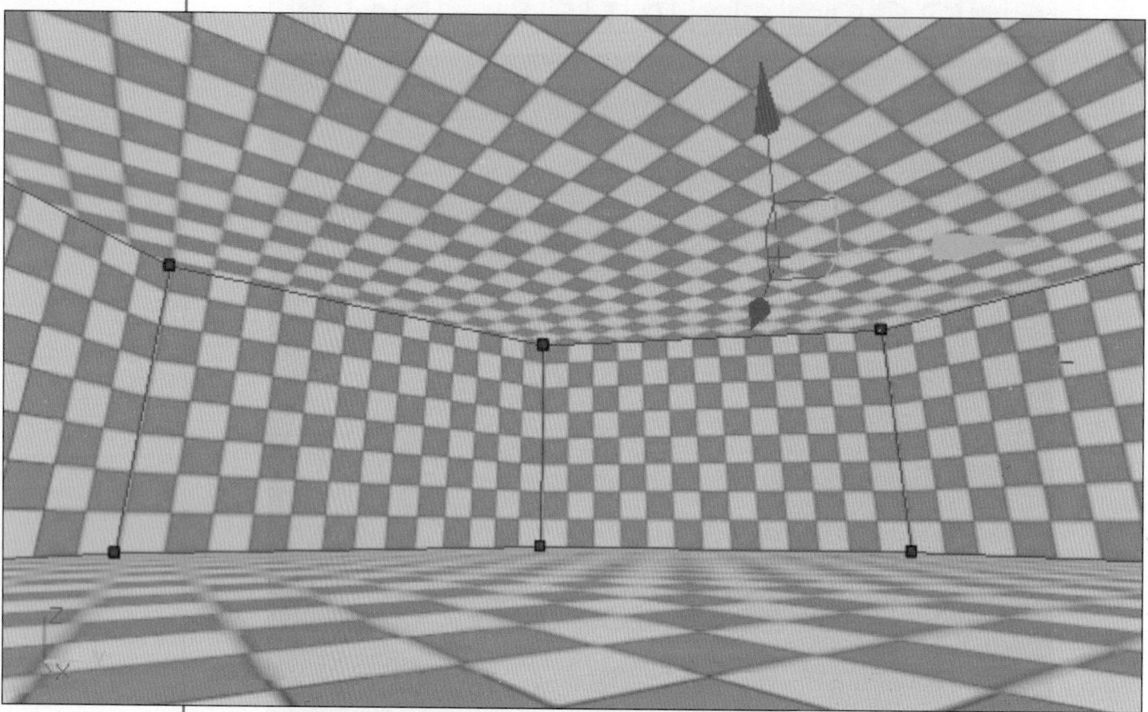

Figure 2.25

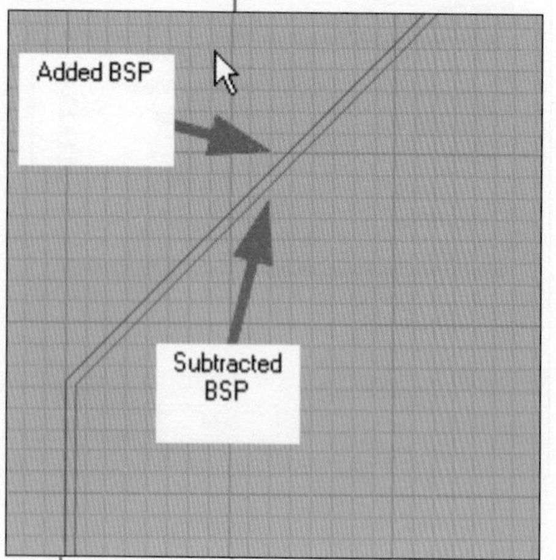


Now we have a basic central room which we'll use as the central room for our death-match level. In the future, you can use Ctrl+a to add brushes to the scene, and then you can use Ctrl+s to subtract them. One thing that might help you see what's going on when working with BSPs is a bit of the color coding that's happening in the editor while in wire frame mode. Note that added BSPs are colored in blue and subtractive BSPs are colored in brown [Figure 2.25].

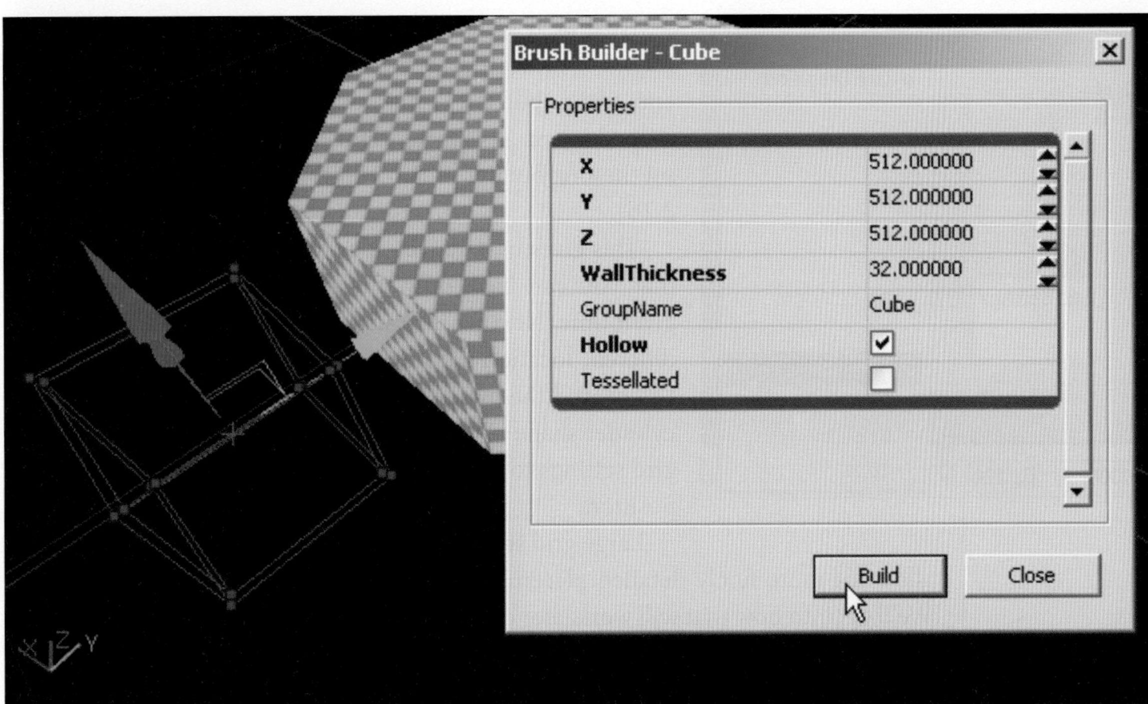


Figure 2.26

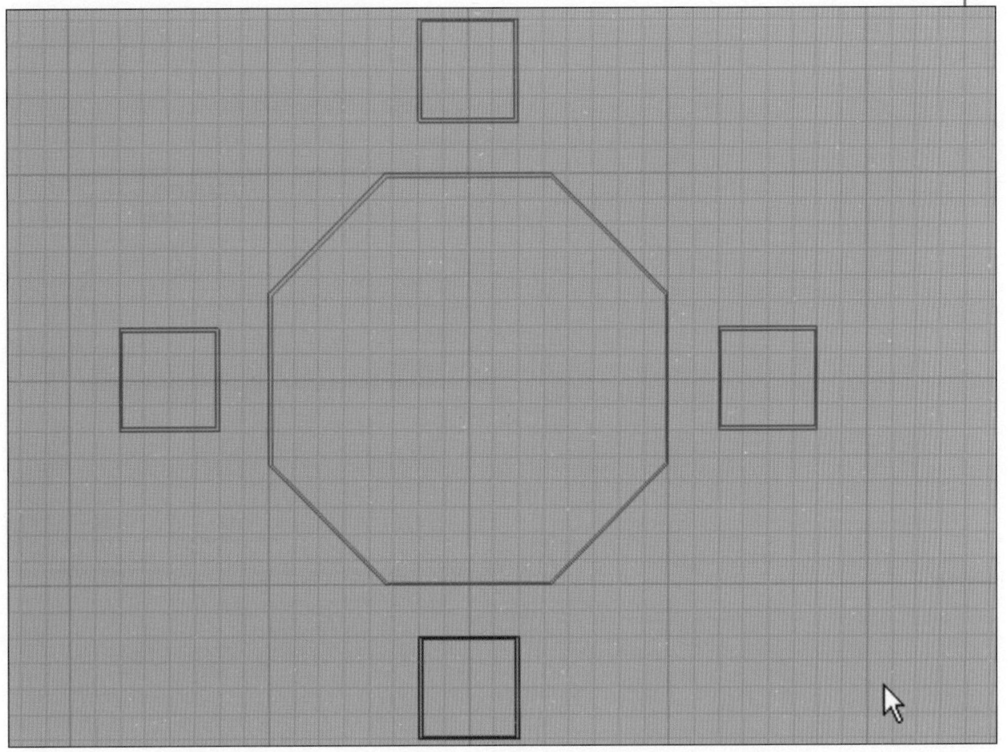

Figure 2.27

Figure 2.28

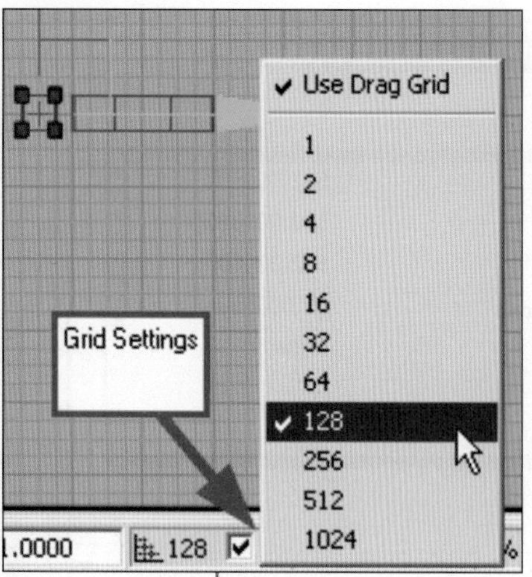


Next we'll want to create the surrounding rooms and pathways. For these we'll start with a smaller box shape, create several, and populate them around the outside of the cylinder-shaped room. This time, right-click on the `Box` button and set the Box builder brush with the following settings [Figure 2.26].

This gives us a new builder brush. It's important to know that you can have only one builder brush present at any given time. Next we're going to move our builder brush to a different location before adding the BSP to the scene. Here I've moved the builder brush to the four corners around the cylinder shape [Figure 2.27]. If you like, you can change the grid settings to snap the position of the different rooms into position.

Large grid settings make broad changes easier but will not allow for more finely detailed placement of various smaller objects [Figure 2.28]. We'll get into how that will work later on.

Next we'll change the size of the builder brush box into something slightly larger for the rooms that connect between the corners. Here I've placed them in line with the different corner sections. Now we're going to connect the different rooms with hallways [Figure 2.29].

Figure 2.29

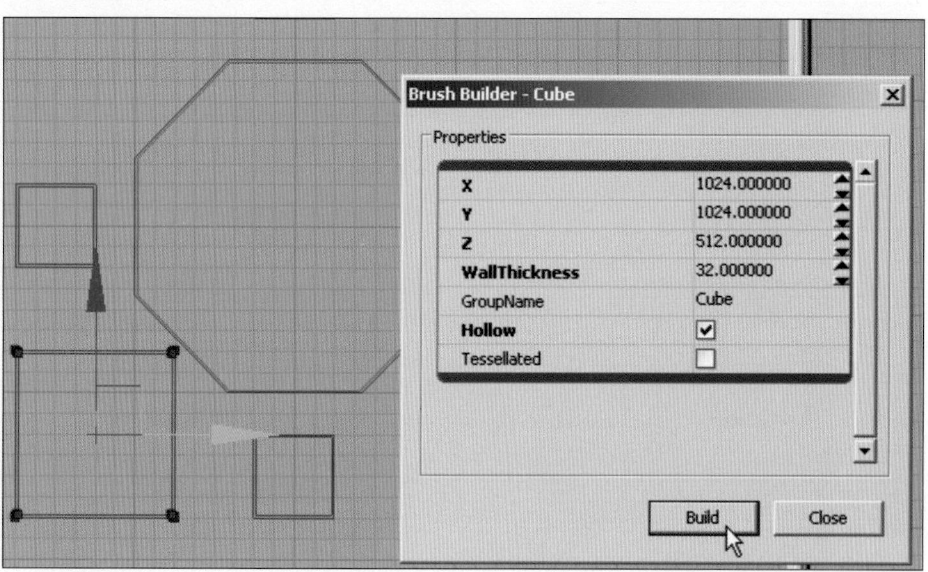

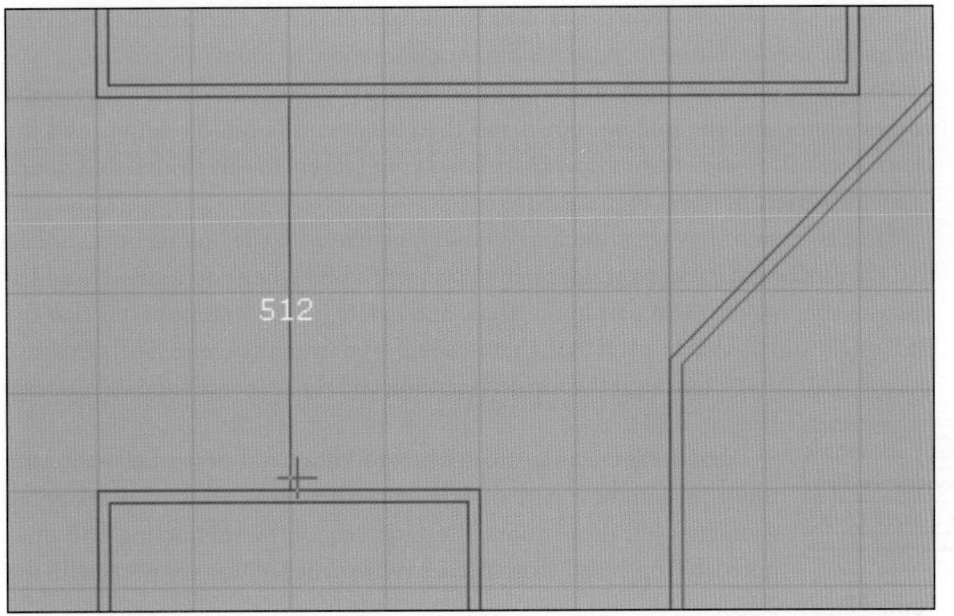

Figure 2.30

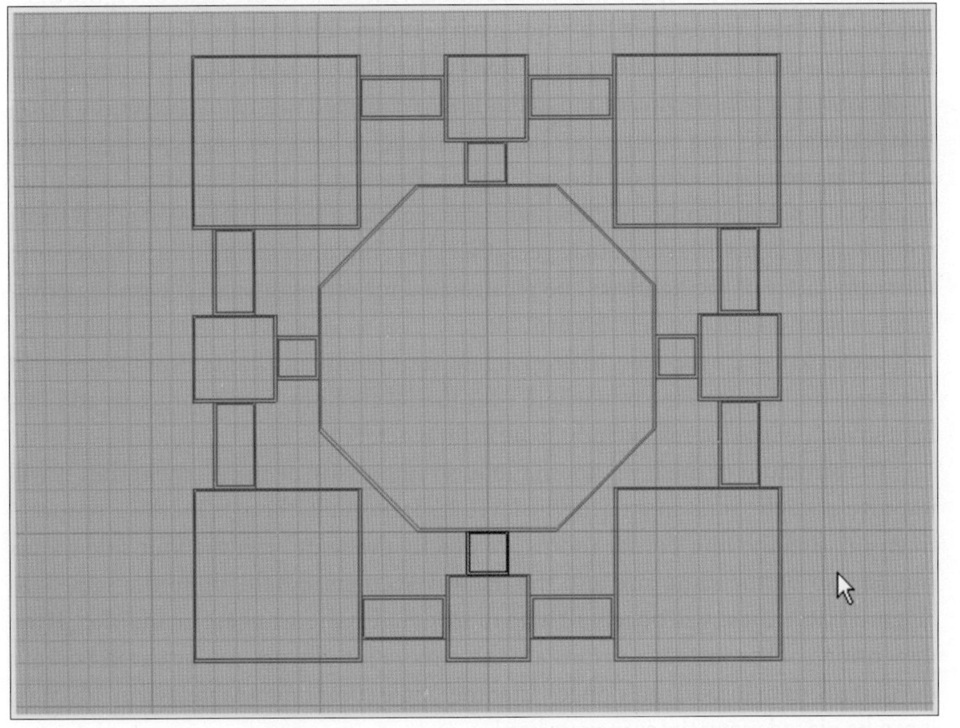
Figure 2.31

The middle mouse button can be used to measure distances. Here we click and drag the middle mouse button to judge the distance from room to room [Figure 2.30].

Following our measurements, we'll build the hallways sections to fit between the corner rooms and the middle rooms and then between the middle rooms and the central area. This will create a flow that allows your players to run around and dodge in a wide variety of ways [Figure 2.31].

Here is more or less what the map should look like with the hollow boxes added in for the hallways. If you've accidentally subtracted a BSP when you wanted to add it, you can simply select that part in the scene and delete it. The strange part is that the BSP might still be visible, even though it was removed from the scene. To fix this, use the `rebuild BSPs` button at the top of the editor, and the scene will update properly [Figure 2.32].

Figure 2.32

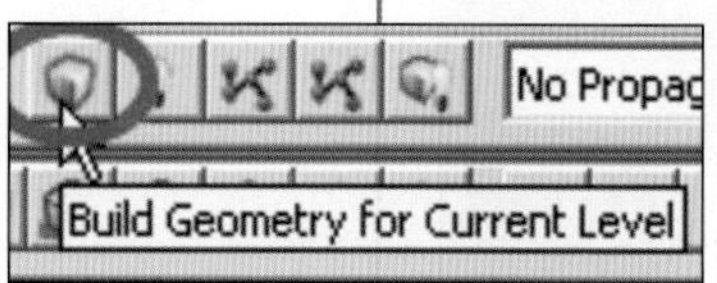


Next we'll create a smaller box to knock out doors between each room. A common part of BSP construction is a bit of overlapping geometry. For these doors, the geometry of the subtracting BSP does not match up exactly with the area where the hallway connects with the room [Figure 2.33].

Viewed from the top, the doors don't need to match the geometry exactly. These are just carving out the space that will be filled with wall. To the right of Figure 2.33, you can see that I've matched the bottom of the builder brush to the floor in the scene. Turn off the `Hollow` check box so we don't cut out any strange shapes [Figure 2.33].

Before we're able to run around in this level, we'll need to add in a player start location [Figure 2.34] and some point lights. Point lights are the most basic light to use for lighting your level. The default settings on these lights allow the designer to place hundreds if not thousands of these lights throughout a level. When you edit a scene with so many lights, the scene may get rather slow; but once the lighting is baked into the scene, none of the lights will be recalculated for each frame, so the game performance remains light and fast [Figure 2.35].

I prefer to use the top view to drop in new start points and lights. This ensures that the items are dropped in somewhere near the level's floor. Don't forget to add in a light in each of the rooms, including the central octagon.

The structure of the level doesn't look so impressive at the moment, but it will improve once the art is created for the level. It's important, though, for the art process to ensure that the four corner rooms are exactly the same size; the four side rooms should also be the same size and the hallway sections should all be the same size [Figure 2.36]. These will be rebuilt with more detail in the art phase in 3ds Max. If the dimensions of the various sections are the same, a lot of work can be saved because the part needs to be built only once. After the single component is created in 3ds Max, it can be placed many times in your level.

Figure 2.33

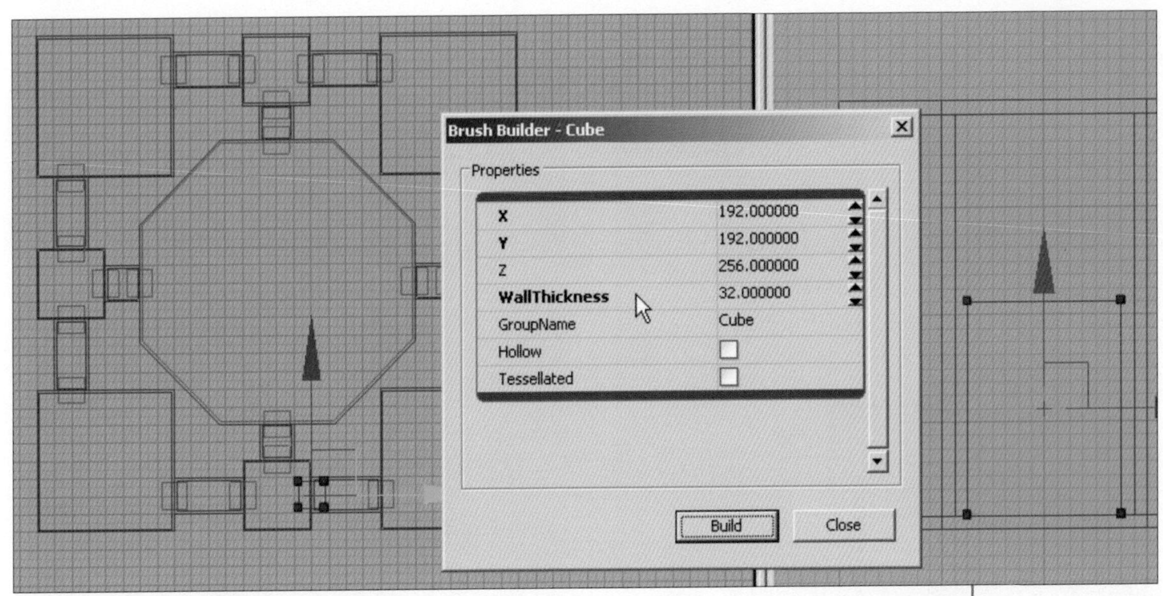


Figure 2.34

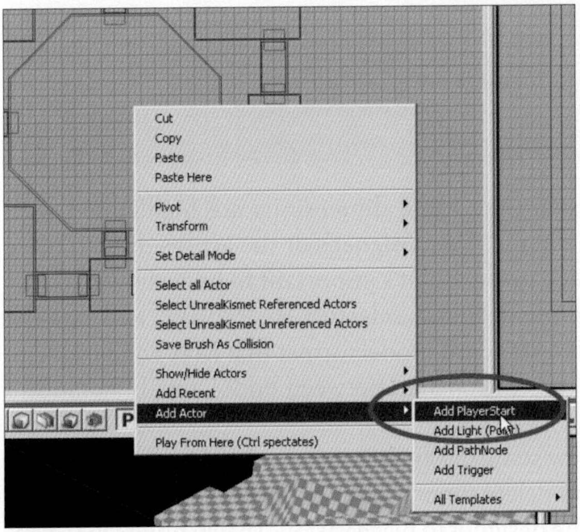

Figure 2.35

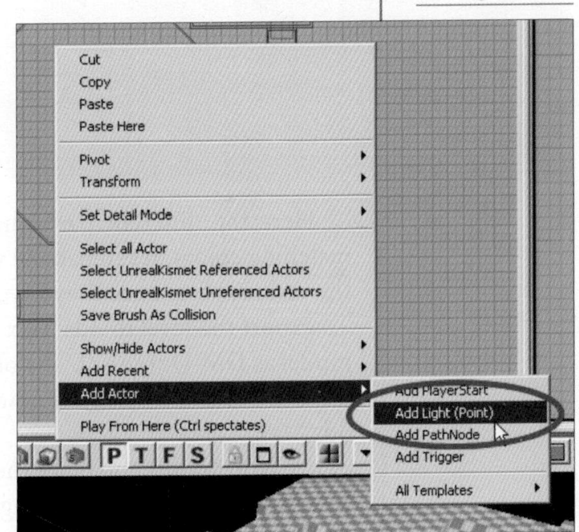

Figure 2.36

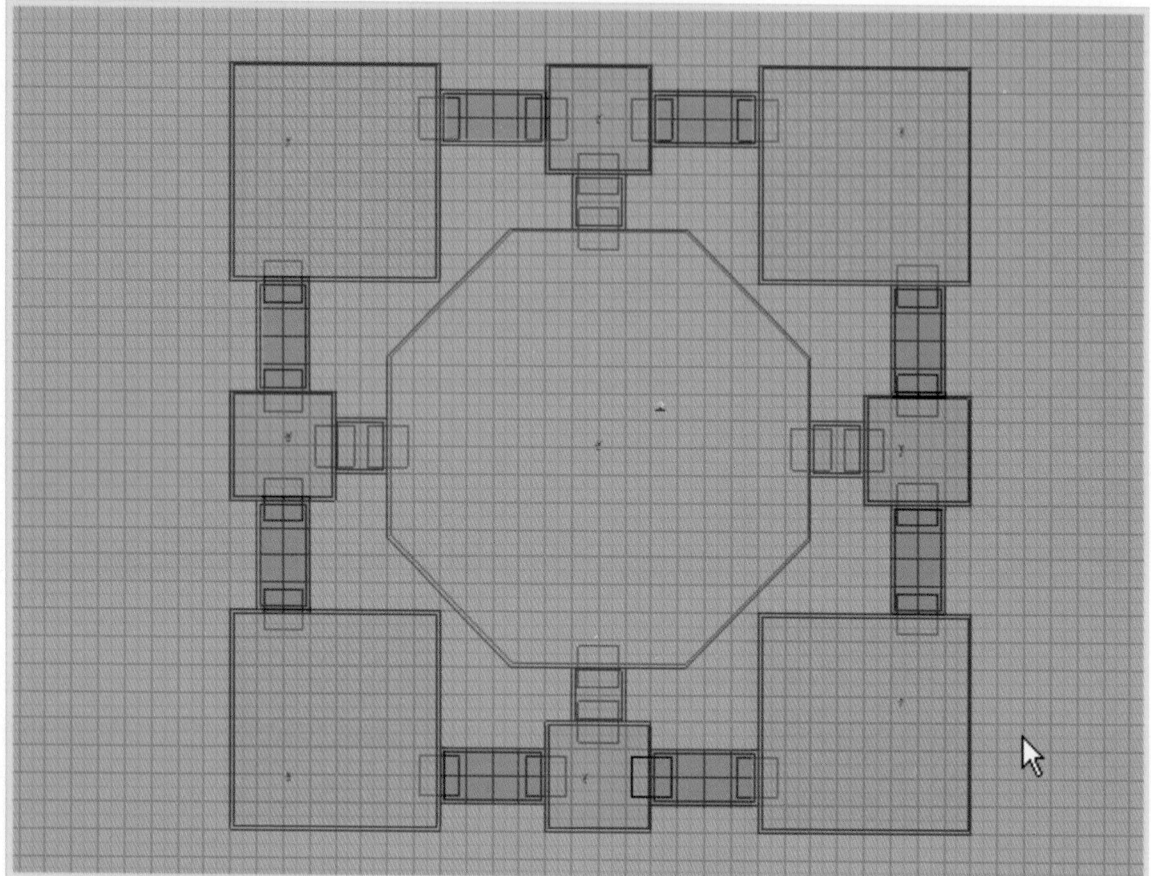

Here the different parts that share the same dimensions are highlighted with matching colors. It's debatable whether it's the designer's or the artist's duty to place the various parts once they have been made. But it's important to know how to do so. To export the level to 3ds Max for fine detailing, select `File`, `Export`, and save the model as DM-Dome.obj. The obj is a standard model format that Max will be able to import. Scale and orientation will remain constant between both Unreal Engine and 3ds Max.

As you import and place the new static mesh objects from 3ds Max, simply select the BSPs that they are replacing and delete them. Rebuild the level and test.

It will be the responsibility of the designer to place various spawn points for weapons and players once the level begins to come together. As the designer, you may also find that some parts of the level require some repositioning after they've been placed. In general, building a level is an integrated task between you as the designer and the artists who need to rebuild your level in static mesh form.

Now we've got all the geometry in place. Add a single default point light to each room to get started. We'll get deeper into lighting in the following chapters, but for now we'll just use the one light to brighten our scene; otherwise, we'll be wandering around in pitch black.

To play test our level, click on the `rebuild all` icon [Figure 2.37]. This will create all the necessary data for our level to be playable. Let the dialog digest all of the data and bake the light maps. This process shouldn't take too long with such a simple scene. In some larger productions, these light maps can take several hours to bake. Let's start off small for now [Figure 2.38].

Figure 2.37

At this point, we're going to get a dialog telling us how many BSP brushes have the NULL material assigned to them. Don't worry about that for now; we'll get around to fixing it in a later project. It is good to know, for later projects that this dialog will show up to tell you various bits of information about your level. The number of PlayerStart locations and other details like path node placements will be listed here.

Figure 2.38

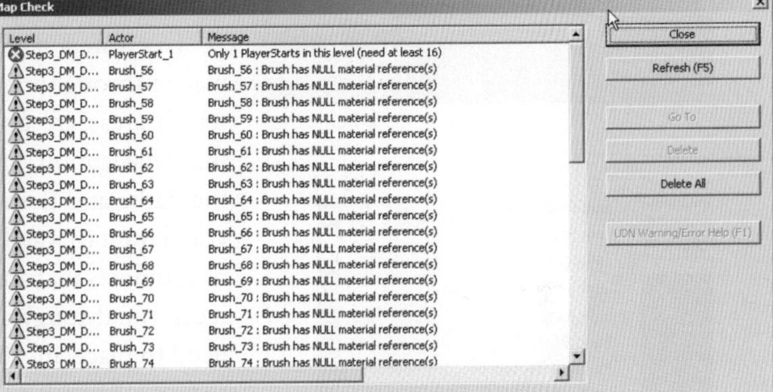


Save the BSPs and test your level. You should be able to get from room to room smoothly. Once all the necessary data has been baked into the level, click on the `PIE`, or Play In Editor, button to run around in your new level [Figure 2.39]. Congrats . . . but we're not done yet!

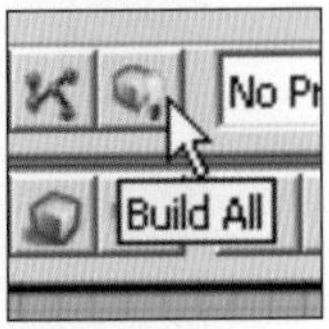

Figure 2.39

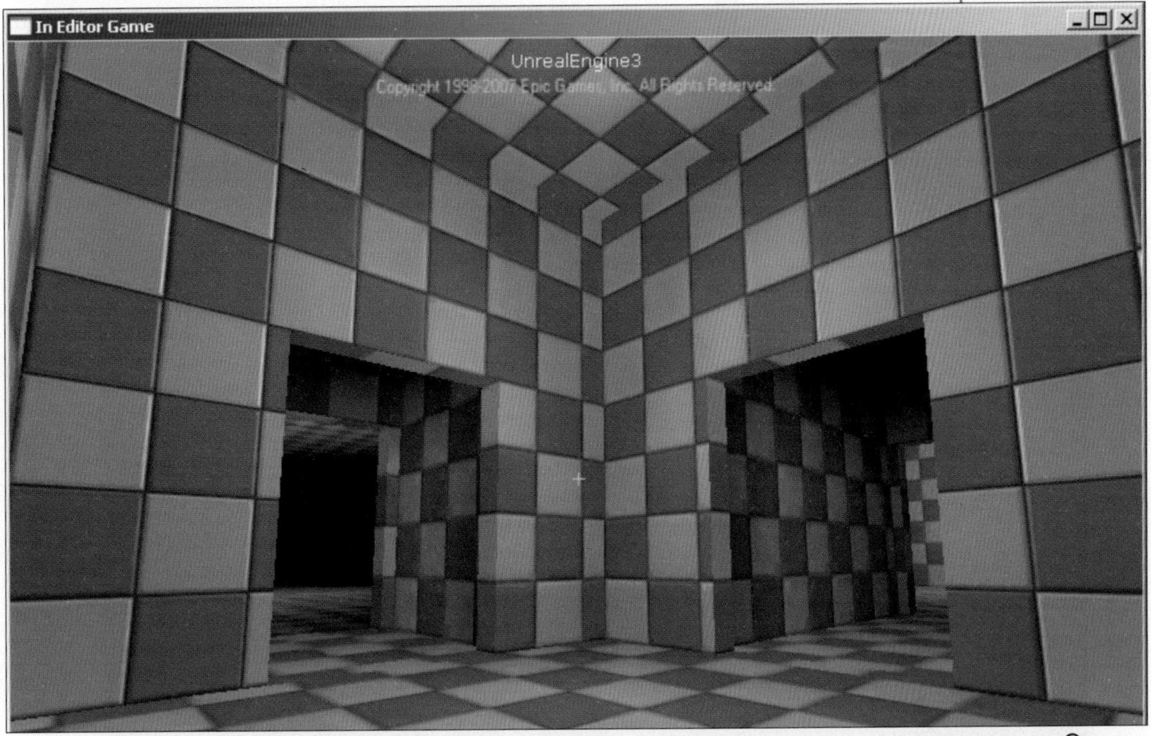

Figure 2.40

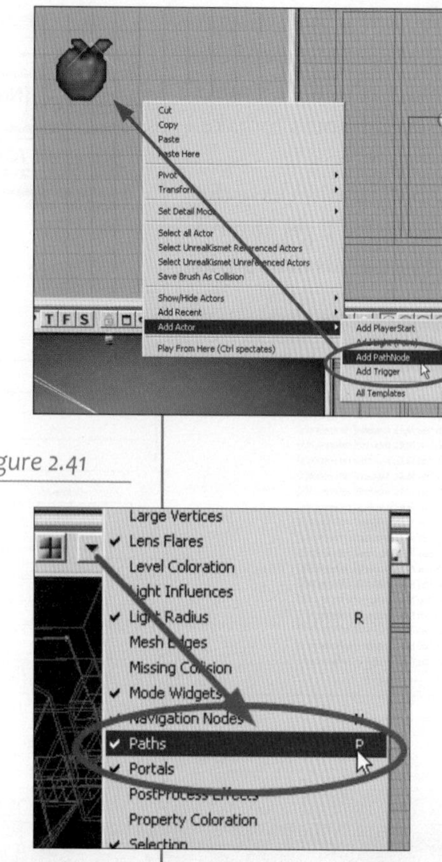


Figure 2.41

## Building Pathfinding

So now you've built a level and are able to run around in it. The Unreal Tournament AI and any new bots you program will need to know how to navigate your level. You'll want to have bots to be able to navigate the level as well. This isn't as straightforward as placing an object in the scene and spawning bots from it. Bits of data, like bread crumbs, need to be placed in the level to tell the AI where it can and it cannot go [Figure 2.40].

To create a navigation grid, the navigation points are placed throughout the level. The apple icons tell the AI which areas are open for them to run around in. Once these navigation points have been placed, it's best to build the paths and then turn on the path-finding view. What you'll want to watch out for are areas where the lines cross over objects that aren't actually passable. If the AI decides it can run through a wall, it will try. To prevent this, you'll need to place another navigation point nearby for the AI to find [Figure 2.41].

Paths can be shown using the `show flags` menu. This is the small ▾ icon located on the top of each viewport. This menu will allow you to show and hide various objects in the scene. Here I've hidden the BSPs and shown the paths after rebuilding [Figure 2.42].

Figure 2.42

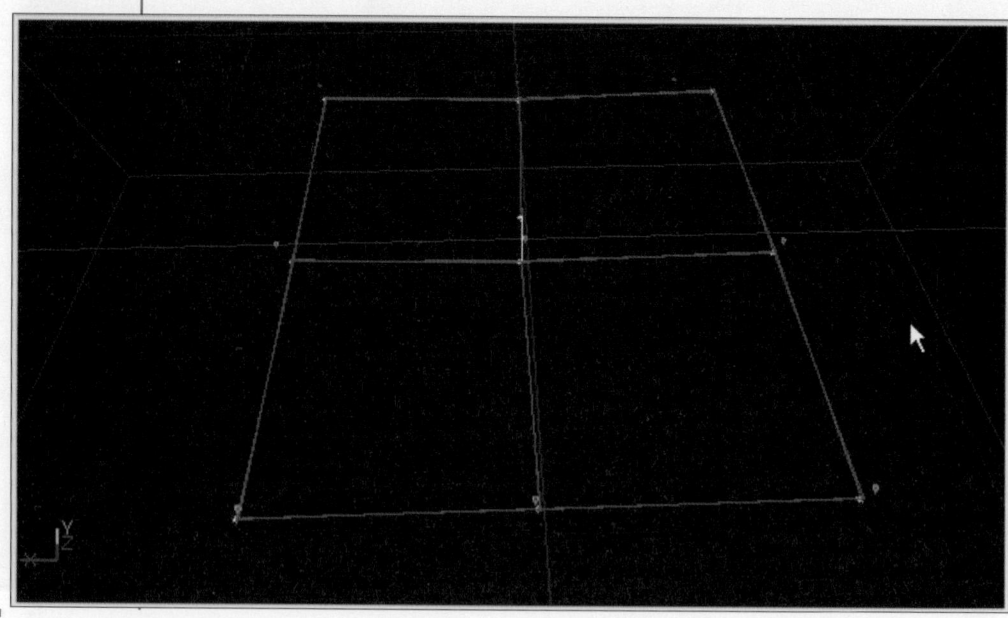

I've placed a path node in each room. The path nodes need to create a connection from one path to another so that the AI can navigate all around the map [Figure 2.43].

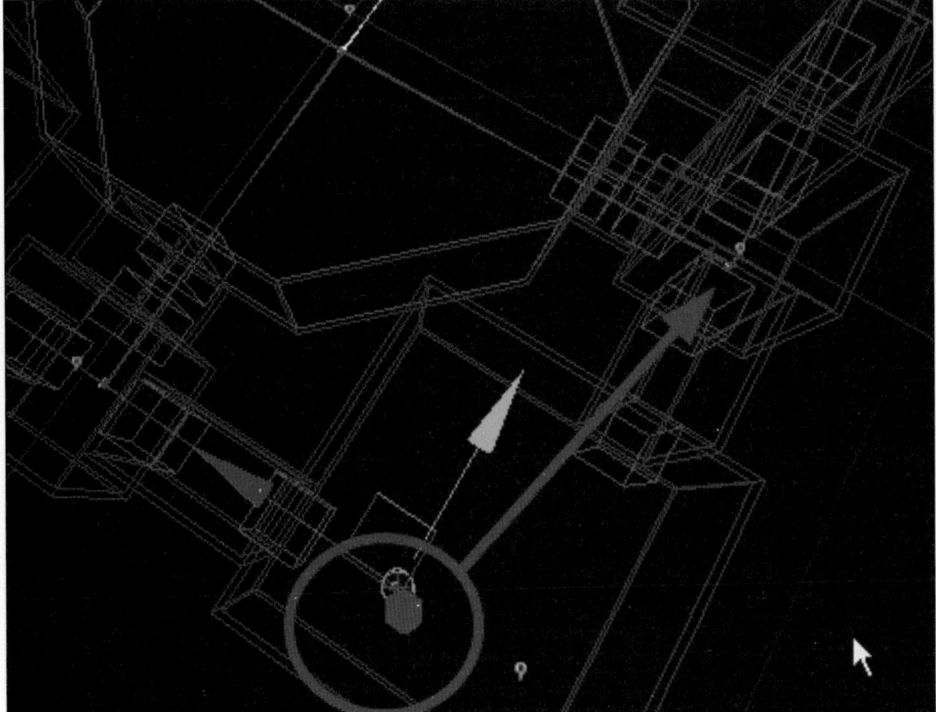

Figure 2.43

Here I've purposely moved a node away from the line of sight from a neighboring room. This will disconnect the path so that the AI will not know that the two rooms are connected. These are the sorts of things you'll need to fix to make sure that the AI can find its way around the map.

Once the AI's path-finding grid is in a reasonable shape, you'll be able to find a place for spawning the bots. Just for testing, you can spawn a bot at one of the navigation points. To do this, we'll need to open up Kismet and create a new Bot Spawner.

### Kismet: A Short Introduction

Rather than getting too deep into how Kismet works, we'll proceed by example and see firsthand how nodes are made and used. Kismet sequences usually have a trigger to start an event, then an action to do when an event is triggered. To manage the various actions, conditions and variables can be created to provide a bit of logic governing which actions are performed when an event is triggered. In a nutshell, Kismet is a bit like programming using flowchart icons.

Figure 2.44

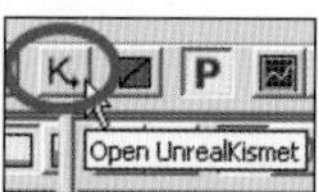


First find the Unreal Kismet button; it's the K that's in the tool bar at the top of the level editor [Figure 2.44]. In the level, select a path-finding node. In the Kismet editor, right-click and add a new pathfinder object [Figure 2.45].

This will be where our bot will spawn. Next we'll add the bot-spawning node. Right click to open the popup menu and select `New Action` → `Actor` → `Actor Factory` in Kismet [Figure 2.46]. This will create a new object in the editor that will create new bots. Round icons are variables; usually, these are filled with some sort of data. In this case, the data filling this variable is a path node.

Figure 2.45

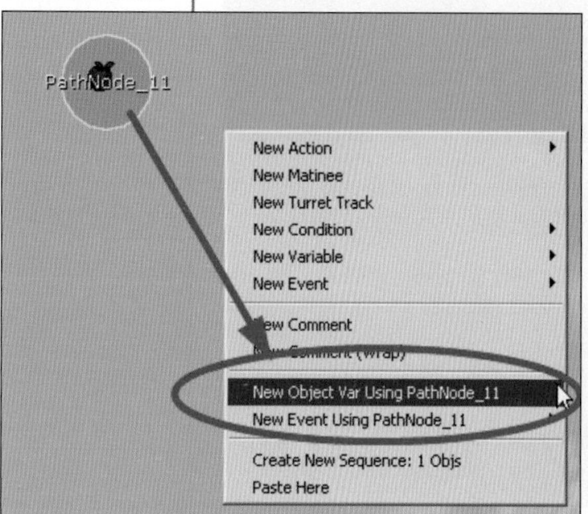


Figure 2.46

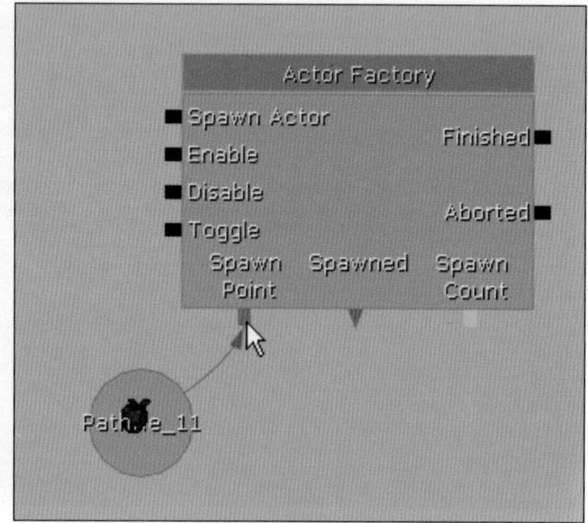


Then we'll connect the node created from the path finding and add it to the spawn point tab hanging out of the bottom of the Kismet spawn node; start dragging from the Actor Factory node's tab and connect it to the path node object [Figure 2.46]. You should notice that the colors correspond to one another. Pink tabs and lines indicate that they are both world-related objects. Various actions are connected through black lines; variables, like integers, are connected through blue lines. For now this isn't too important, but it will come into play in a later project.

Figure 2.47

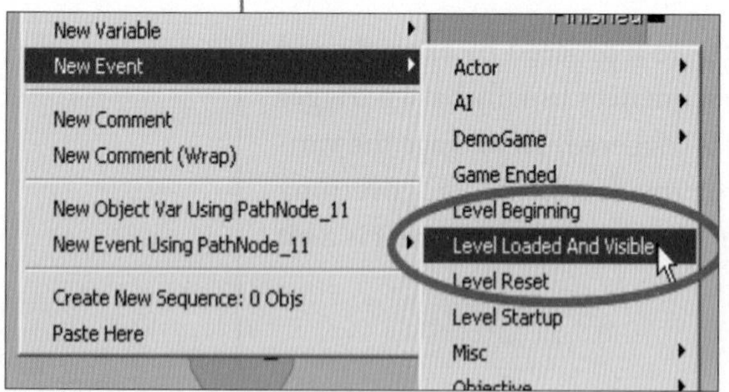


Now we'll need to add an event to tell the spawn node to actually spawn a bot. For this example, we'll simply use the `New Event` → `Level Loaded And Visible` [Figure 2.47]. We'll connect this node's output to the in tab on the spawn node. This task deserves a bit of an explanation. The event node we just placed is pretty self-explanatory. When the level is fully loaded and everything in the level is visible to the player, a signal is sent out from the

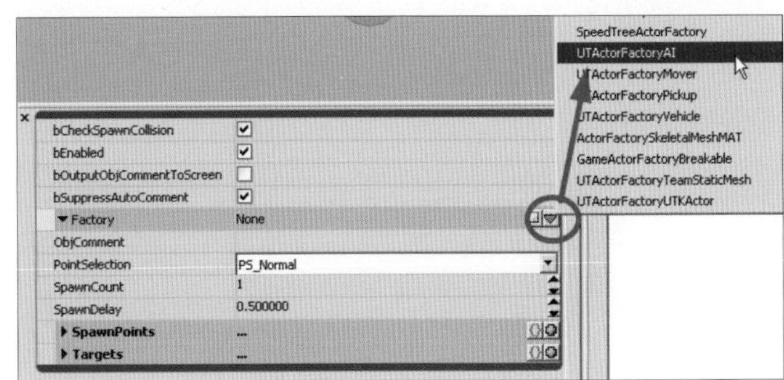

Figure 2.48

node. A black line indicates where the signal is going. In this case we've connected it to the input trigger of the spawn node. This indicates to the spawn node, when it gets an incoming signal from any node, to spawn a bot. The signal itself is not a coded message, just a trigger to tell whatever is downstream of the connection to do what it's supposed to do.

We'll need to add the parameters to the AI Factory node so it knows what sort of bot to produce. We'll select the Factory tab and click on the blue triangle to set the factory type. Select `UTActorFactoryAI`; this will set the factory's parameters [Figure 2.48].

Once the factory's parameters are opened, set the `ControllerClass` to `UTBot` and the `PawnClass` to `DemoPawn`. These two objects were created in UScript and are something that you'll be able to extend after going through the programming chapters. Last but not least, turn on `ForceDeathmatchAI` [Figure 2.49]. This will make the bot feel he has to follow you around. If he were armed, then you'd have to worry about getting shot at, but for now he's just going to stare at you angrily and follow you around if you leave the room.

| | |
|---|---|
| bCheckSpawnCollision | ☑ |
| bEnabled | ☑ |
| bOutputObjCommentToScreen | ☐ |
| bSuppressAutoComment | ☑ |
| ▾ Factory | UTActorFactoryAI'Step4_DM_Dome.TheWorld:Persist |
| **bForceDeathmatchAI** | ☑ |
| bGiveDefaultInventory | ☐ |
| bUseCompartment | ☐ |
| ControllerClass | UTBot |
| ▸ **InventoryList** | ... |
| PawnClass | DemoPawn |
| PawnName | |
| TeamIndex | 255 |

Figure 2.49

To test the new node, simply rebuild and play it in editor. Then go check whether your bot has spawned [Figure 2.50]. Once he sees you, he should follow you around. Hey, he's all dark! What's going on? We added lights to the scene, but by default lights are not connected to the dynamic lighting channel. We'll fix this in the next chapter, so don't fuss over it just yet. Save the level and play test it.

Figure 2.50

# 3 Leading the Player with Lighting

*Lighting the Way*

Telling your player important information about your level requires some visual hints. One of the best ways to provide these hints is by using creative lighting. This is something that as a game designer you can control quite well. Using light, we can tell the player where health is, where ammunition is, and where exits and pathways are found. It's important to make these hints consistent.

Colored light is a great way to tell players where they might look to find certain power-ups and necessary items in any given level. It is common to use blue or green lights to illuminate health items, red lights to make ammunition stockpiles glow, and white lights to show the player where an exit leads the player out of a dangerous room. These same hints can be subtle so as to not drag players out of their immersive experience. In order to accomplish these subtle effects, it's important to learn how to set up lights properly.

## What to Expect

We'll start off with some of the basics of lighting in Unreal. Many improvements have been made in the Unreal Tournament 3 since its initial release. Many of the features have been enhanced, and new features have been added. In these new additions, you can see many changes in how lighting might behave.

The future of real-time game engine development will focus on geometry shaders and lighting models. Good lighting can turn a bland scene into a fantastic scene. Lighting models like ray-tracing, volumetric shadow volumes, and the like will really change how we see games.

PROJECT

### Basic Level Lighting and Set-up

Lighting a scene is partially the job of the artist, but because of the direct impact on game play, the level designer should have a handle on editing lights and setting up lighting for the scene. To make our previous scene a bit more interesting, let's chop the top off the previous level. Or at the very least, if you've created your own level, cut open a bunch of windows using subtractive brushes to cut open skylights.

Now we're going to light our scene using several different light types. Unreal Tournament 3 doesn't have any global illumination built in. In reality, light reflects in many directions when it hits a surface; the bounced lighting effect can be considered an effect of global illumination. To replace this effect, we need to create many smaller point lights to fill in the shadows that natural light would normally fill.

There are a few types of lights that are accessible through the actor list in the Generic Browser window. We've already seen what we can do with a skylight; this time we'll take a look at the various other lights available in the Unreal editor.

## Light Types

Let's take a look at the different light types and see how they work. Unreal, like 3ds Max, supports various light source models. Skylights, ambient lights, spot lights, point lights, and directional lights are supplied in the Unreal Tournament Editor. Using these lights, we can create elaborate lighting set-ups for pretty much any sort of scene.

Figure 3.1

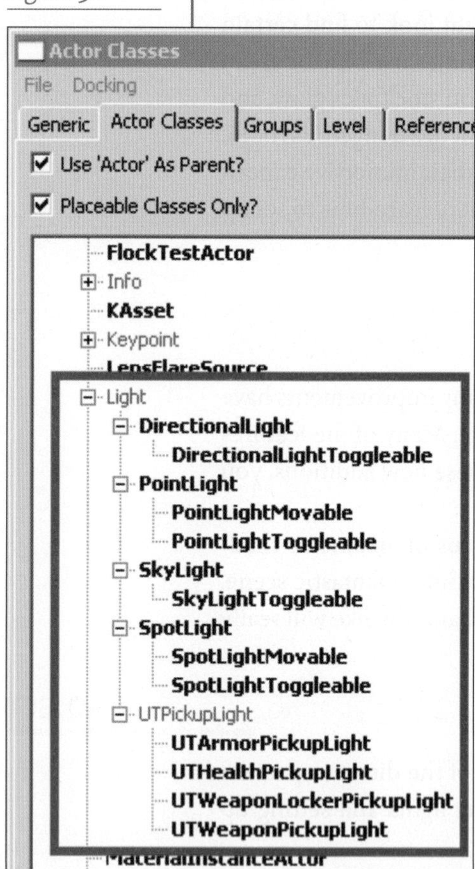


You can find these lights in the Generic Browser `Actor Classes` tab located at the top of the window [Figure 3.1]. We'll be going through the functions of the other tabs as we need them.

These lights appear in the level editor as the regular `light bulb` icon. Their effects are all quite different. Starting at the top of the list, we have `Directional lights`, `Point lights`, `Skylights`, and then `Spot lights`. These make up the basic light types that you'll use to light your level. `Pickup lights` are specifically used when placing items and other objects that require re-spawning. The important parameters for all lights are color, intensity, and size. Lights can have a value greater than 1, so if you want something to glow brightly, then set the light to around 3 or so to get the popular bloom effect seen in many games today. (*Bloom* is the glowing halo that appears around highlights on a lit surface.)

Before we're able to see the effects of each of these lights, we're going to need to chop off the top of the level we just created. To do this, let's create a large builder brush that's 4096 × 4096 × 256 [Figure 3.2]. Place the new brush so that it covers the top area of the structures; this will let light in from the top. When we place directional lights or skylights, the light will light only the exteriors of the structure. Since we're running around on the inside of the level, we'll want to expose the interior to exterior lights.

Figure 3.2

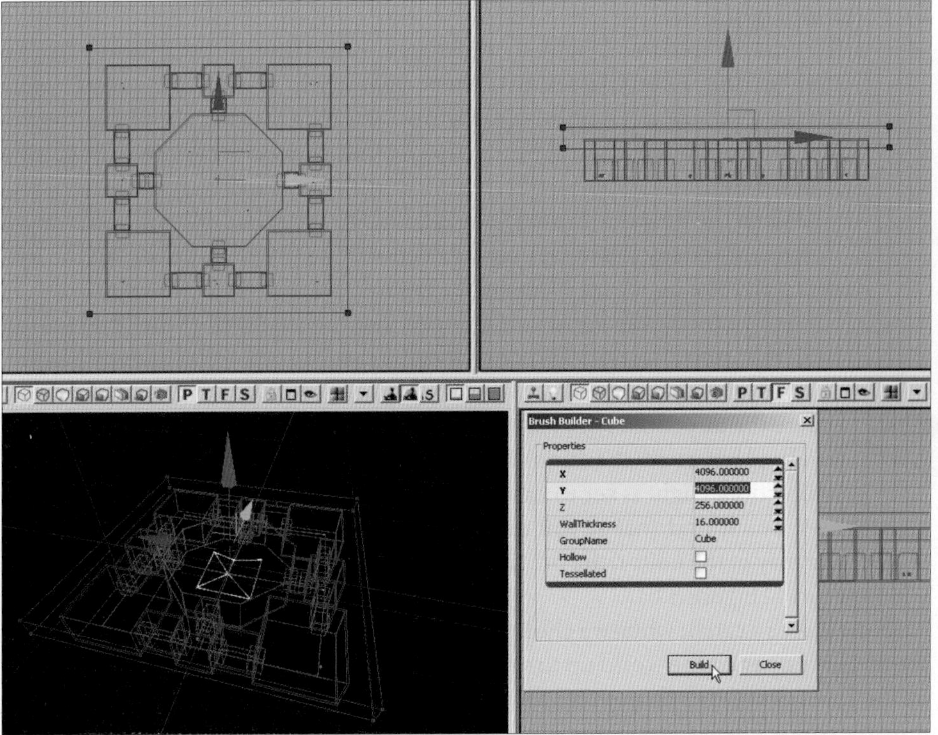


Once you subtract the builder brush from your level, you should have something that looks a bit like this [Figure 3.3]. Be careful not to chop off the level too low, or the doors will be cut off. Remember to rebuild the map geometry once you subtract the new builder brush.

Figure 3.3

Figure 3.4

Surface Properties (1 Selected)
Sync Generic Browser
Cut
Copy
Paste
Paste Here
Select Surfaces
Select All Surface
Select None
Apply Material
Reset
Alignment
Show/Hide Actors
Add DirectionalLight Here
Add Recent

## *Directional Lights*

To add a directional light to the scene, select the `DirectionalLight` item in the ActorClasses list, then right click in the scene and select `AddDirectionalLightHere`[Figure 3.4]. Don't worry about the toggle-able version for now; we'll be able to use that later on when we start getting into Kismet.

When the new directional light is added to the scene, it's pointed straight down, not usually the most useful direction. Use the `rotate` tool in the editor to give the light a bit of an angle [Figure 3.5].

As you rotate the light, you'll notice that the shadows of the level will all be in the same direction. Directional lights cast parallel light over the entire world. No matter where the directional light is placed, the entire level will be lit with the same values. By default, a directional light is set to cast dynamic shadows. You'll find that if you rebuild all in our project and play in the editor, the previously added bot will now be lit [Figure 3.6].

Figure 3.5

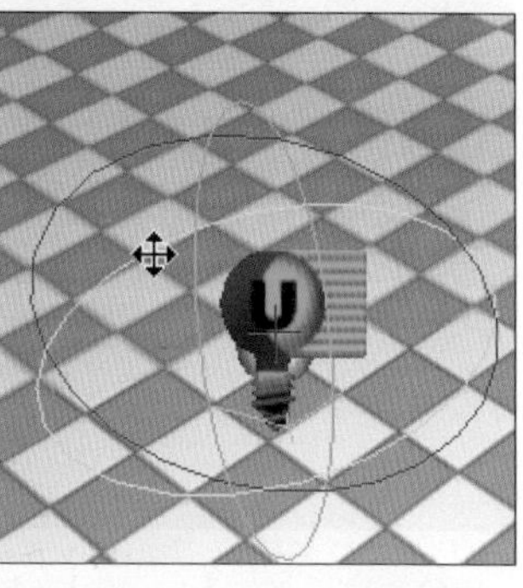

Now there's a catch: when we chopped off the top of the level, we opened the world up to seeing the outside of the level. Since there's nothing for Unreal to draw, it just leaves whatever was in the empty space last. So we'll need to add a skydome.

Figure 3.6

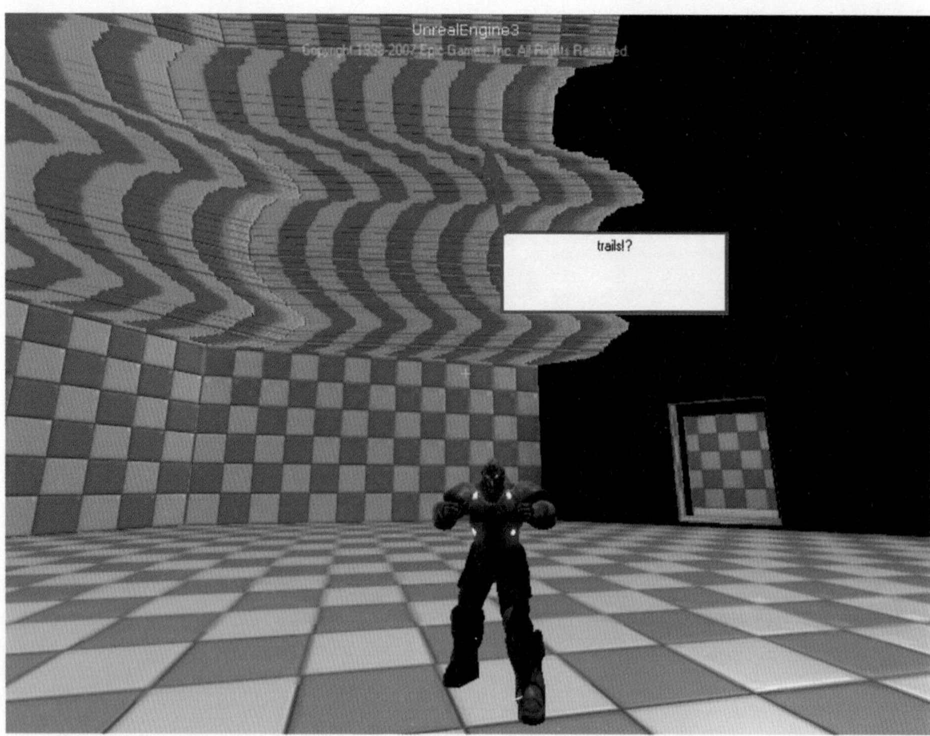

## *Skydomes*

Unreal Tournament's skydomes are simply large objects with a pretty sky texture on them. We could just add a large box around our level, but how exciting is that? Instead, we can open up a level that comes with Unreal Tournament and use its skydome. Of course, when you're going to move on to making your own content, a skydome is one of the things you'll want to add to the list of assets; but for this example we'll just *borrow* a skydome from UT3.

Save your work and open your favorite UT level. In this example, I'm opening DM-Deck. Move up and select the `skydome`. To find which package DM-Deck's skydome is hiding in, right-click and select `Sync Generic Browser` from the popup menu [Figure 3.7].

This command will highlight the model's static mesh in the Generic Browser. The package will expand to show you where the model is saved. With this command, you can select anything in any of the UT maps and find out where the asset is saved [Figure 3.8]. This is a great tool for finding where things are hidden so that you can assemble your own scenes from parts that are already in Unreal Tournament.

This skydome is saved to UN_Sky in the mesh sub-directory. If we simply add this to our level, it's going to block our directional light from lighting our scene. The skydome is still geometry and will act as a shadow-casting object.

Figure 3.7

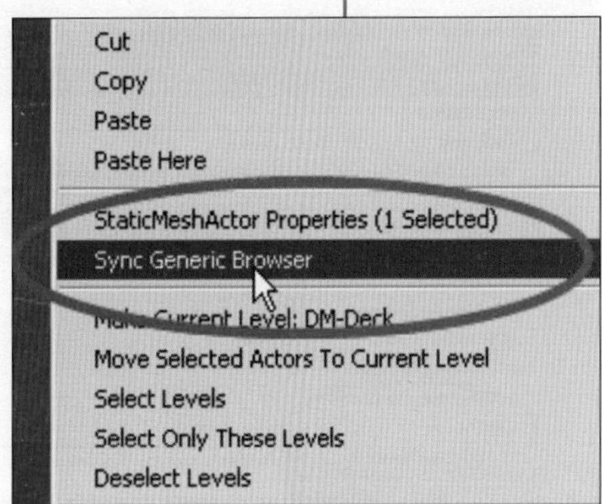


Figure 3.8

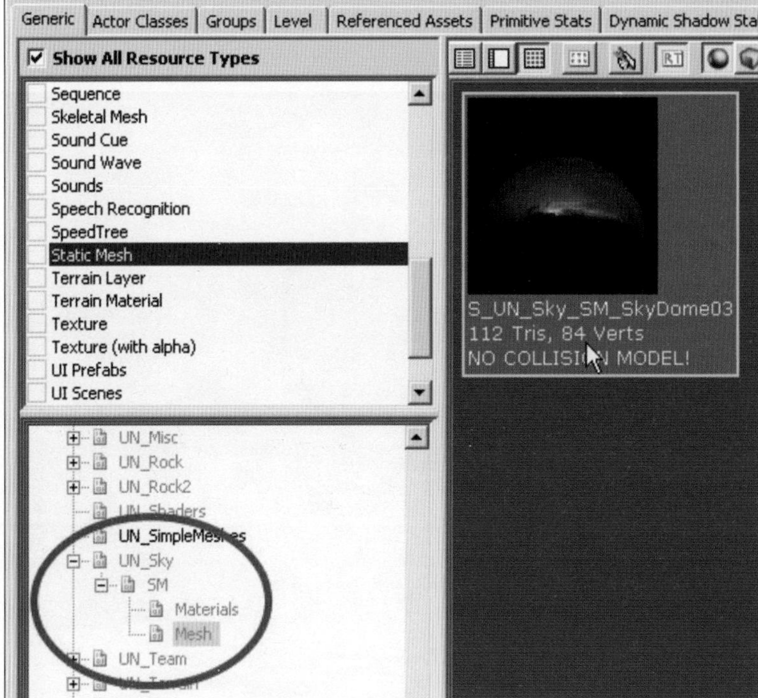

When a static mesh is placed in the level, its default lighting behavior is set to cast a shadow. We don't want this behavior in our skydome, so we can turn off the `CastShadow` check box located in the properties window [Figure 3.9]. To open the properties, double-click on the object and expand the `StaticMeshActor` roll-out; then expand the `Lighting` roll-out. This will allow you to manipulate the various lighting properties of the skydome object. You'll also want to prevent the skydome from lighting up if a rocket or something gets near it, so we'll also turn off `bAcceptsDynamicLights` and `bAcceptsLights`.

Figure 3.9

Lighting channels and lighting behaviors like these are also important for special-effect objects, light-glowing force fields, and anything that should be emitting a lot of light, like a light bulb. These objects would look out of place if they were casting a shadow rather than casting light. Make sure to keep these settings in mind as you populate your level with props.

Our level should look a bit less crazy without the trails in the sky [Figure 3.10]. Now we can get back to understanding how the rest of the lights work. We've already been introduced to the point light as one of the most basic light types. To move on, we'll jump to the Skylight type.

Figure 3.10

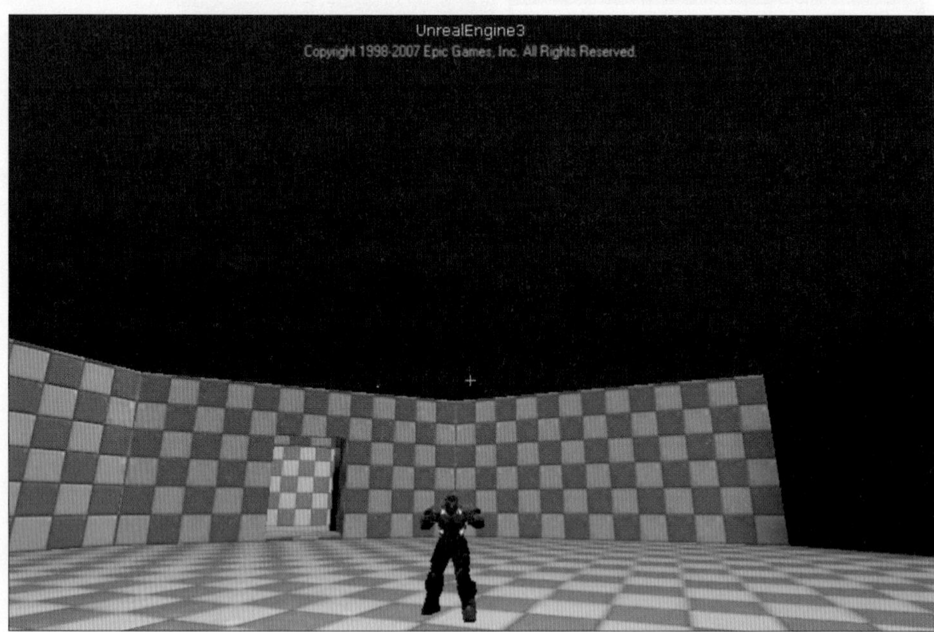

## Skylights

Skylights work a bit like the directional light. However, you may notice that with a bright scene you might get hard shadows. In the previously lit level, we added a single directional light [Figure 3.11]. This causes some of the walls to fall into complete darkness.

If we add a simple skylight to the scene, an even light will be added throughout the level. With both the skylight and the directional light brightening the scene, the light levels begin to make everything glow.

Change the skylight's Brightness to 0.2 [Figure 3.12] to bring down the overall lighting values and keep the objects in the shadows from going completely black. Of course, you'll want to adjust the brightness of all of the placed lights to suit your purposes. Dark, moody scenes can have a purple or blue tone to the shadows. This can be accomplished by adding color to the skylight [Figure 3.13].

Here a blue color has been selected for the skylight. Rather than having the walls fall into a dark grey, the shadows have a colder blue color, adding interest to the lighting in the scene. Clicking on the magnifying glass icon next to the light color parameter opens a standard color picker. Skylights are a great way to make sure your entire level has some sort of light.

Figure 3.11

Figure 3.12

| Light | |
|---|---|
| ▾ LightComponent | Step6_DM_Dome |
| bCanAffectDynamicPrimitives | ☑ |
| bCastCompositeShadow | ☑ |
| bEnabled | ☑ |
| bForceDynamicLight | ☐ |
| bOnlyAffectSameAndSpecifie | ☐ |
| **Brightness** | 0.200000 |
| **bUseVolumes** | ☑ |
| CastDynamicShadows | ☑ |
| CastShadows | ☐ |
| CastStaticShadows | ☑ |

Figure 3.13

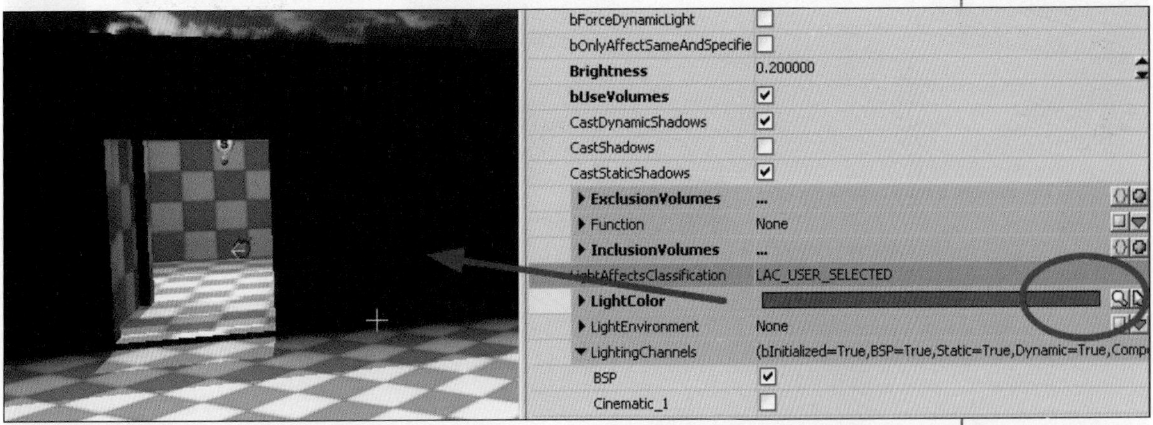


## Spotlights

A spotlight is a point light that has been cut down to lighting only a cone-shaped field. For lighting a scene using spot lights, it's a common habit to use both a spotlight and a point light in the same place. Set the spotlight to emulate the light coming out of

Figure 3.14

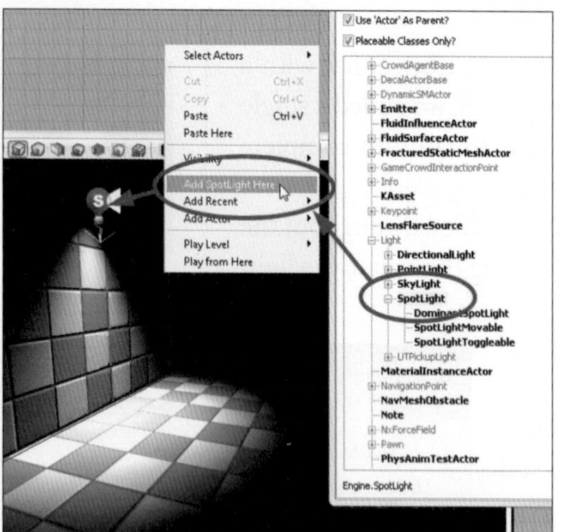


Figure 3.15

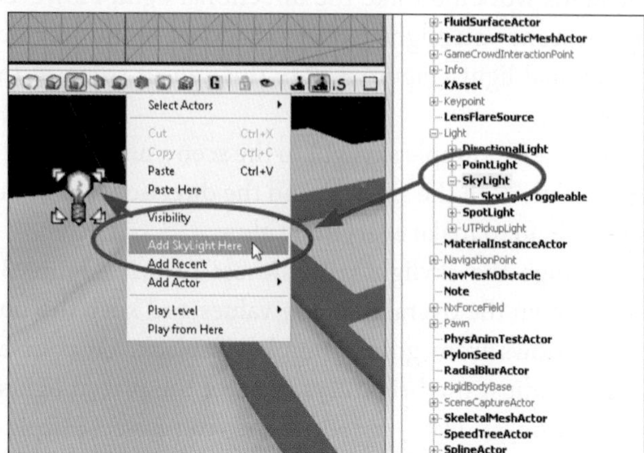


Figure 3.16

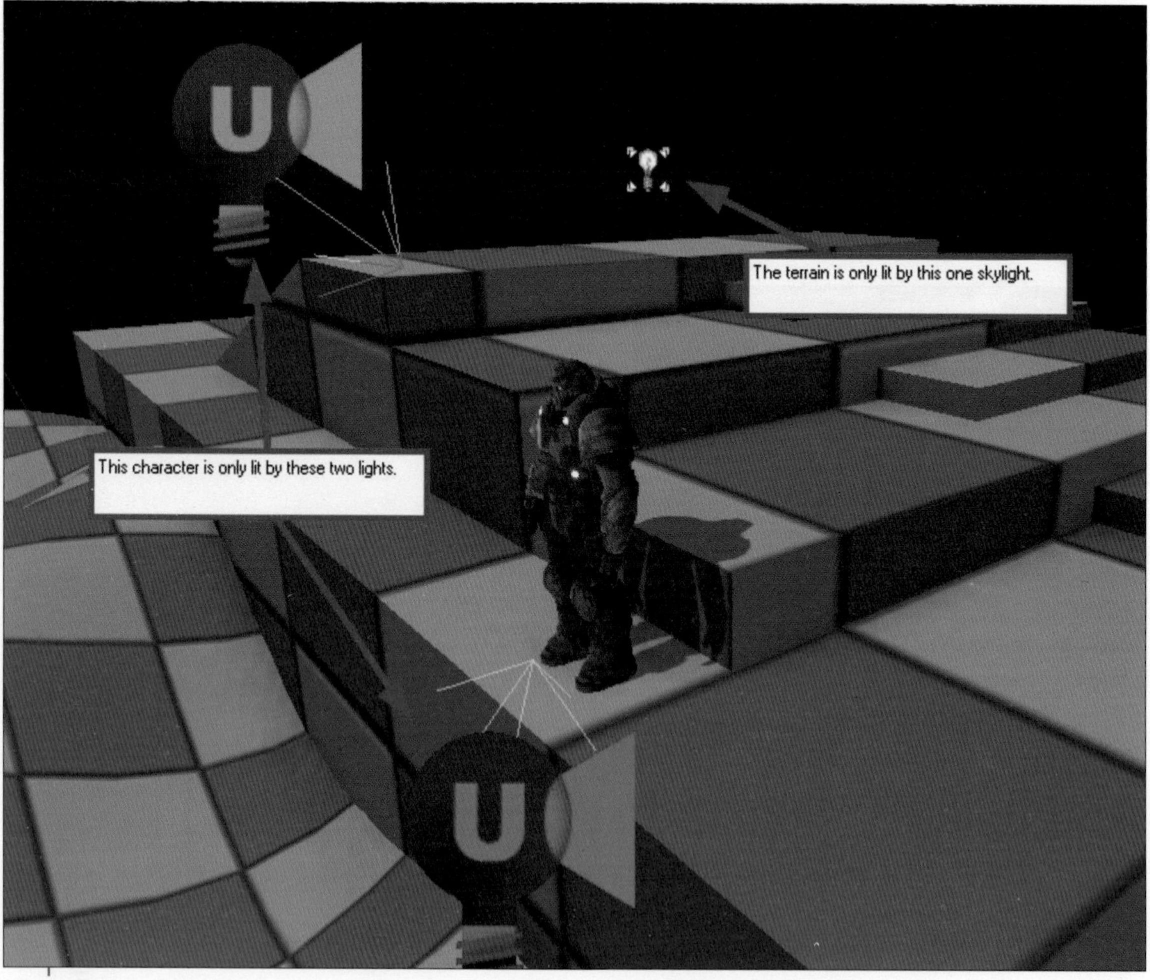

the light source and the point light to illuminate the light source itself. In most practical situations, it's easier to use several point lights in place of complicated spotlights [Figure 3.14].

Skylights are used to illuminate your entire level with a general lighting pass. This type of light is best suited for outdoor scenes where a lot of light reflects from the ground back up into the shadows created by the primary light source [Figure 3.15].

### *Shadows and Lighting Channels*

Shadows are expensive—for reasons that reach beyond the scope of this book, shadows are very demanding on the GPU. For each additional light that casts a shadow, the GPU load increases greatly. Dynamic shadows are expensive to calculate. On older video cards, more than two or three dynamic lights could destroy frame rate, even in a simple scene. The best practice here is to pick one or two lights per area that are dynamic. To control which objects cast dynamic shadows, lights can be set-up using lighting channels.

Lighting channels are a method that helps organize which lights will illuminate which objects [Figure 3.16]. By default, all static mesh objects will cast shadows and receive light from all placed light sources; but this is not true for all dynamic mesh objects like characters and other skeletal mesh objects like vehicles.

In some cases it's easier to make sure that your character is the only object that will be affected by a dynamic light source. In this case, we've created a single dynamic light for the entire scene [Figure 3.17]. This will be the only light that will affect all

Figure 3.17

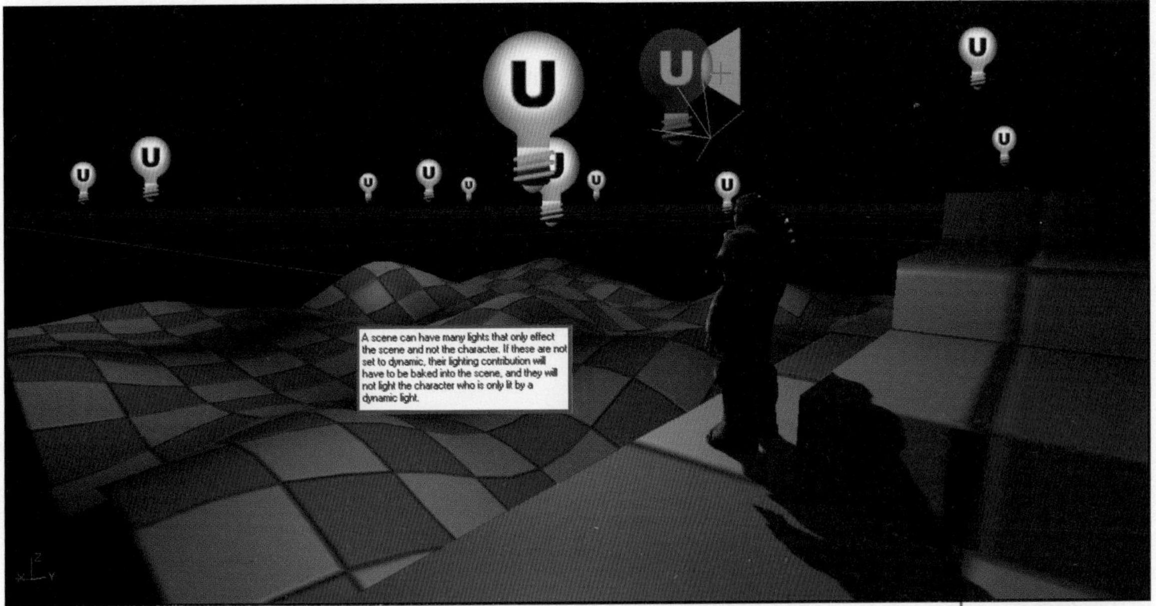
A scene can have many lights that only effect the scene and not the character. If these are not set to dynamic, their lighting contribution will have to be baked into the scene, and they will not light the character who is only lit by a dynamic light.

of the characters in the level. The rest of the lights will not have any effect on the character, so we don't need to worry about the extra cost associated with multiple dynamic lights.

PROJECT

## Highlighting Objects

Open the `lightChannels.ut3` map. This will help illustrate how light channels are used. In practice, there are instances where you'll want to guide the player using a few simple lights that illuminate only the objects in the scene that you want the player to see. In this case, you'll want to isolate the objects and the lights that will share what is called a light channel.

Figure 3.18

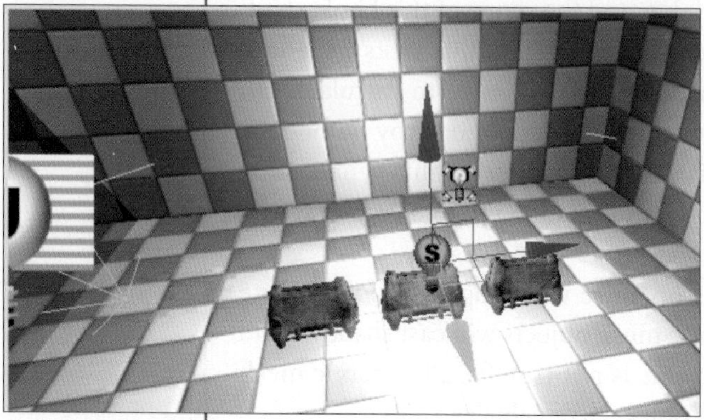

At first, this scene has a super bright light that is blowing out the surrounding area [Figure 3.18]. If we want to highlight the center barrier object, we're going to want to set up a few things to isolate it. To do so, select the light and open the property editor.

Figure 3.19



Figure 3.20



Expand the `Light properties`; then scroll down and expand the `LightingChannels` roll-out. Then turn off the `BSP` and `Static` check boxes [Figure 3.19]. You'll notice that the level will be a bit darker without the bright light blasting everything in the scene. Next we'll turn on Gameplay_1; this is the lighting channel that this light affects [Figure 3.20].

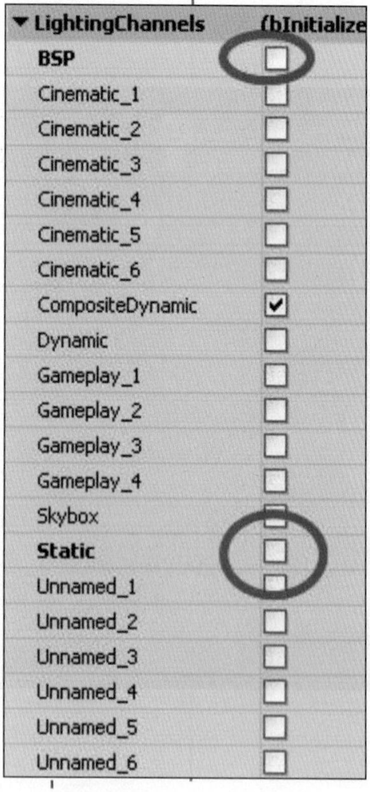

Then, we'll want the center object in the scene to also match the same lighting channel. All static mesh objects and in fact all objects that can receive light also have the same list of lighting channels. Expand the `Center Barriers` properties and open the `LightingChannels` roll-out on the barrier `Staticmesh actor`. Turn on the Gameplay_1 lighting channel [Figure 3.21].

Figure 3.21

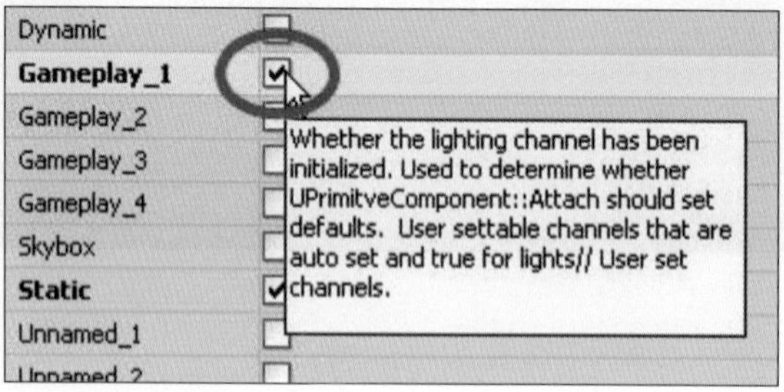

This lighting is a bit exaggerated, but it's quite clear that the center barrier is considerably brighter than the two objects that are not on the same lighting channel [Figure 3.22].

Figure 3.22

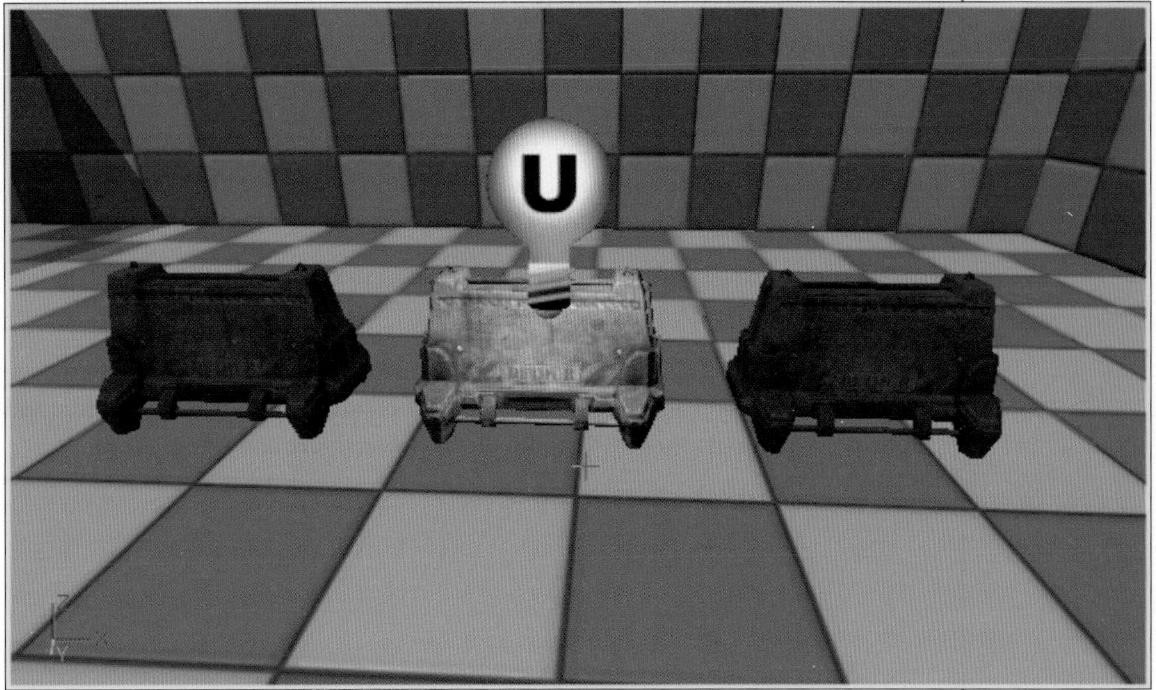

### Tips and Tricks about Light Placement

One of the best methods I've discovered while lighting large areas is turning the light into a headlight from the perspective viewport. Select the light and then select the `look` icon located on the perspective's tool bar.

This will snap the light source to the viewport's point of view. If you're using a spotlight, the light will snap into a sort of flashlight tool, allowing you to quickly and easily aim the light. Additionally, if you hold `shift` and `alt` while moving the camera, the light will be duplicated, leaving the original light behind on the last thing you were looking at. This allows you to move around a level, leaving lights behind you as you pick things to illuminate.

One thing to remember, though, is that the `lock` icon might snap randomly on other things in the camera's point of view. Static mesh objects might get snapped to your camera, so be careful when using this technique. We'll cover a few tricks later on that will help prevent this problem. Using levels as layers will help you separate the task of lighting from the task of placing static meshes in a level.

REVIEW

### BSPs Are Great, but What About Terrain?

Now that we've built some interesting shapes that represent our various buildings, we'll want to put them onto something more interesting than a flat plane. Creating a terrain is a great way to add details to a wide area, but this requires an interesting new tool.

The terrain editor can be used for small areas as well as levels, but in some cases the terrain editor is the best way for a level designer to create a space that feels natural. Our level is going to need something interesting around it. We could just ask the level artists to build us a mountain vista, but it's more fun to build one in Unreal!

This task also allows us to venture outside of the BSPs we just finished.

## On Your Own

For getting deeper into lighting, books on cinematics and photography can be a huge help. Check on line or at a library for books of this sort, and study how directors and professional photographers use light to direct viewers' gaze and create effects.

# 4 Terrain

*Shaping the Land*

The terrain tool is best suited for rolling hills and planes. Creating sheer cliffs and caves is best done using a combination of the terrain editor and static meshes. The level designer can place temporary shapes onto the terrain using BSPs to represent cliff edges and cave walls, but there are a few tricks that can be used to make this task a bit easier.

Like a regular BSP, formed level nodes must be placed for the AI to navigate the terrain. We'll have to take a look at what that means.

PROJECT

## Creating Terrain

Terrain in the Unreal Engine 3's editor is a sheet of geometry that can be modified to create hills and rolling planes. Overhanging ledges and sheer cliff structures cannot be created using the terrain editor. The terrain mesh can only be moved along the Z-axis; that is, the terrain can be shaped only by lifting and lowering the surface details. Sheer vertical or overhanging features need to be built using 3ds Max. A combination of terrain and static mesh objects can fill a terrain with lush detail.

Figure 4.1

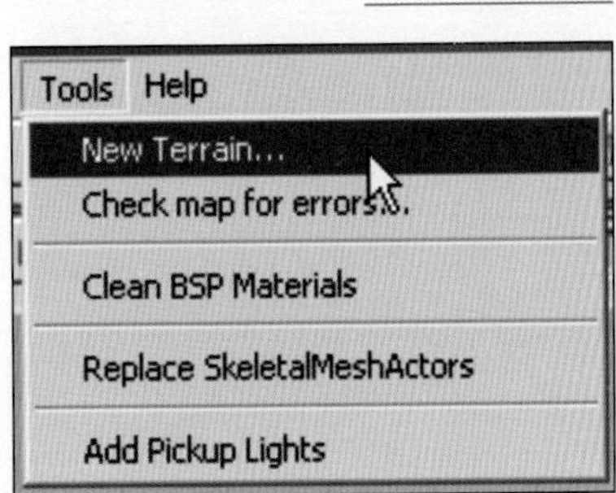


Let's start by adding a sheet of terrain to our previously modeled terrain. From the `Tools` menu in the level editor, select `New Terrain` [Figure 4.1].

This will open the new Terrain Wizard, which will prompt you for a start location and a number of patches. The number of patches is an indication of how large a space you intend to cover. By default, this is set to 16 × 16, which happens to be a 2048 × 2048 sized patch of terrain. Each patch ends up being 128 × 128 units in size.

Figure 4.2

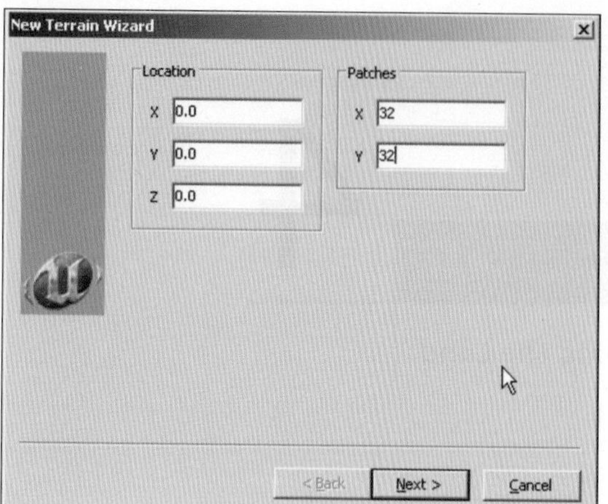


Figure 4.3

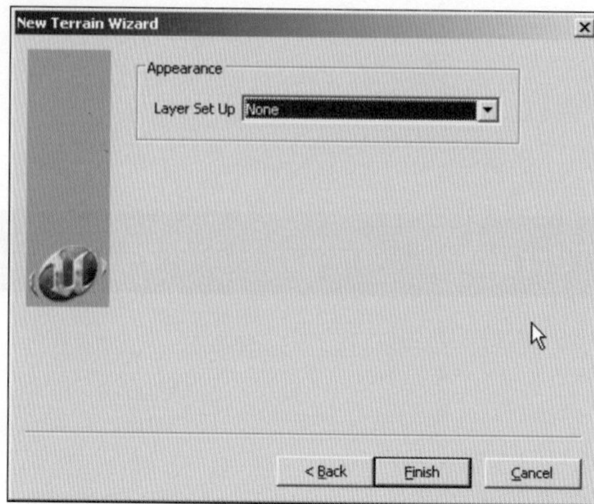


Our current level is about 4096 × 4096 units, so we'll want to make a terrain patch that's bigger so that we can build a ridge line that exists outside of our level. So we'll change the number of patches to 32 × 32 [Figure 4.2]. Since we can use grid snap, we'll leave it's start location at 0,0,0.

After that we're prompted to change the layer set-up, there are no options here as we haven't added custom set-ups through UScript [Figure 4.3].

Using snap to grid set to 256 setting, we can easily place the new terrain patch under our current level [Figure 4.4]. To make changes to the level, we'll want to open the terrain editing tool. This will allow us to lift and push the terrain into an interesting shape.

Figure 4.4

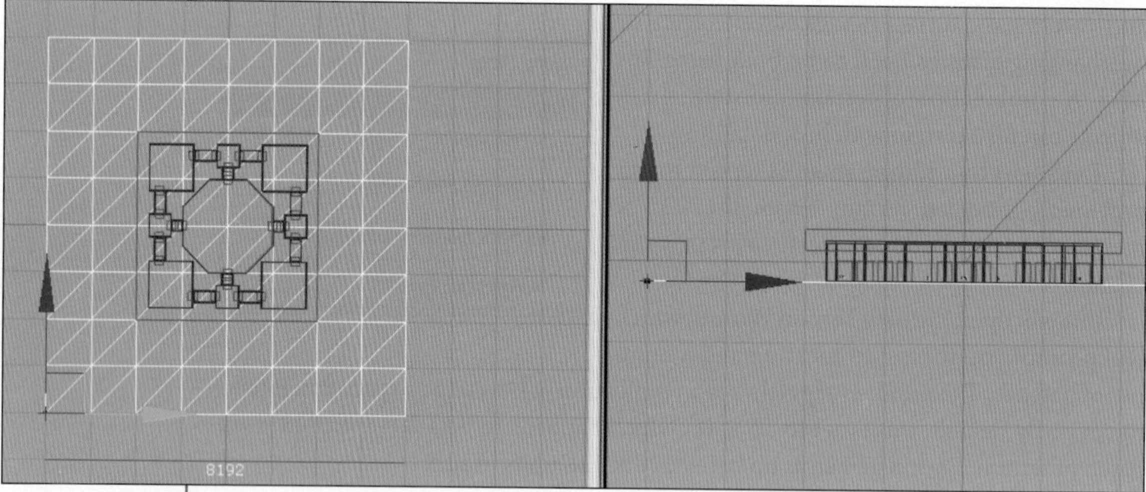

## Unreal Terrain Edit

This button from the left tool bar will open the `TerrainEdit` tool, one of the many tools built into the Unreal engine.

Figure 4.5 shows the TerrainEdit tool. The `View Settings` on the top right allow you to turn on and off the wireframe of the terrain object. The first available layer is the `HeightMap`. This is a layer of color data that translates into the shape of the terrain in the editor.

Figure 4.5

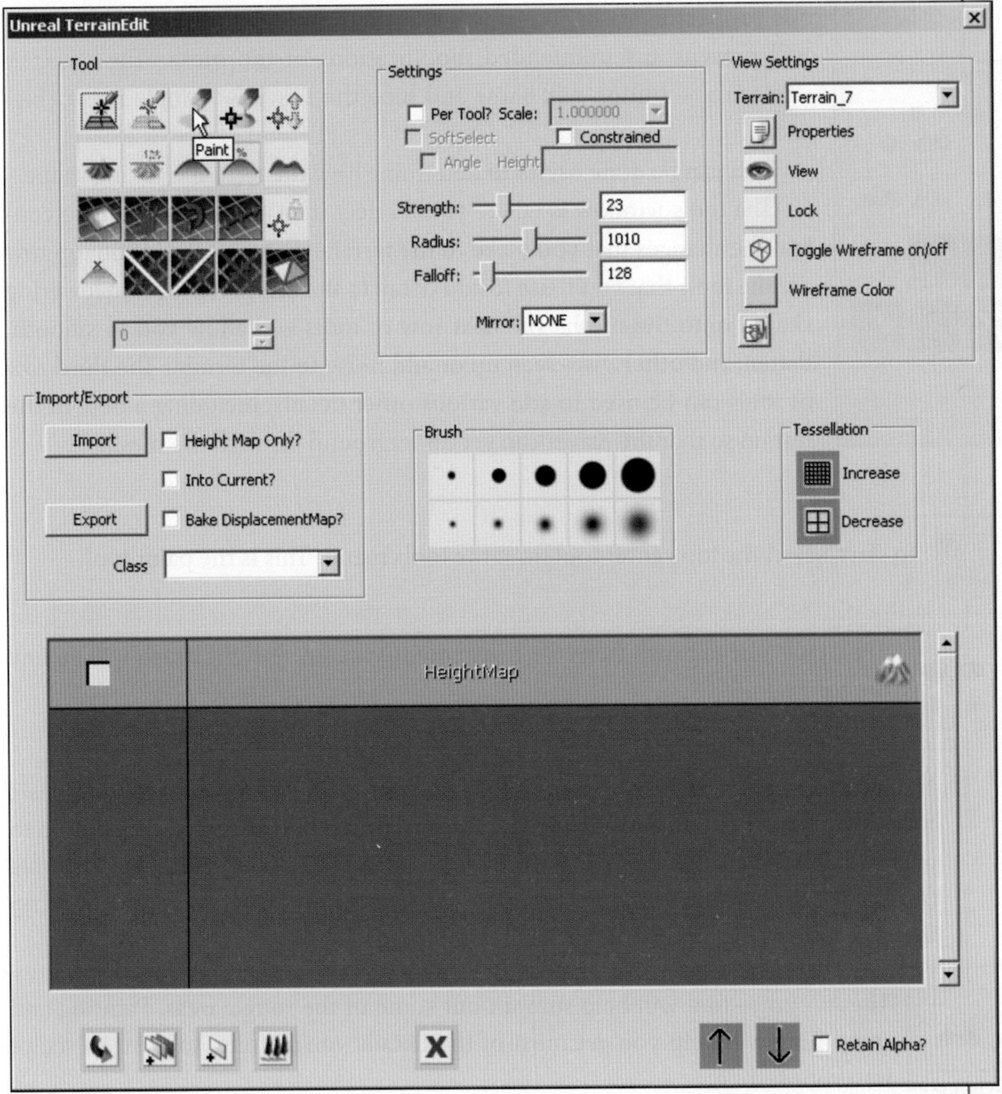

Figure 4.6

Figure 4.7

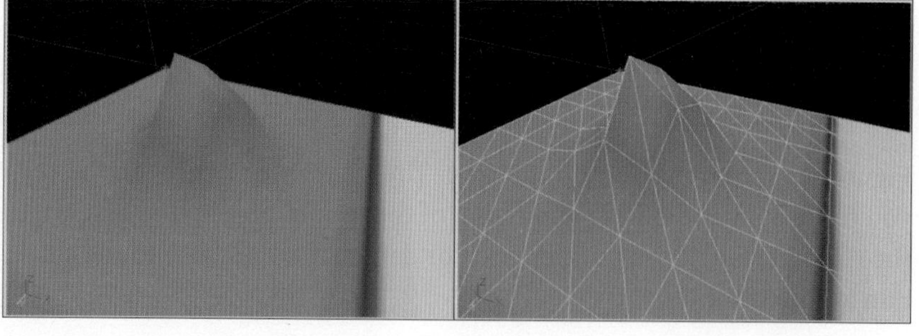

Figure 4.8

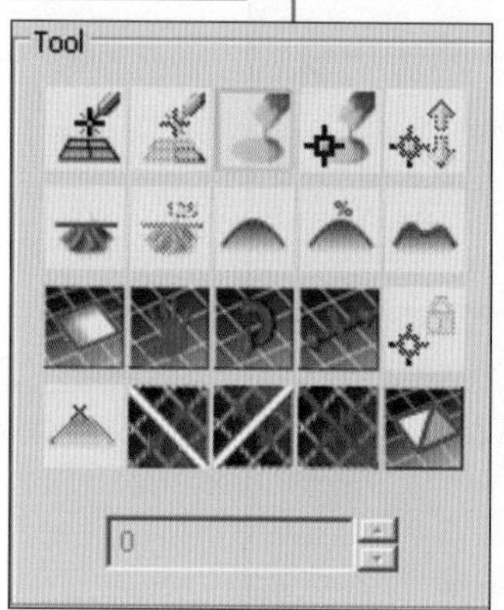


You'll want to pay particular attention to the `view, lock,` and `toggle wireframe` buttons [Figure 4.6]. These will allow you to change various properties easily. `View` will show and hide the terrain patch. `Lock` will prevent any unintended modifications of the mesh. The `toggle wireframe` button will show and hide the terrain's triangle mesh [Figure 4.7].

This can be quite useful to determine how the terrain is taking shape.

The tools window is where you'll select the various functions to control the changes that you make to the terrain [Figure 4.8]. In the top row are the tools that you'll use to add detail to the mesh, raising and lowering shapes onto the mesh. The next row of tools will allow you to smooth, flatten, and otherwise clean up or add noise to the terrain. The third row of tools can be used to add various other details, including a hole in the terrain so that the player can get underground through the mesh.

To start, select the top center tool from the tools menu. This is the paint tool.

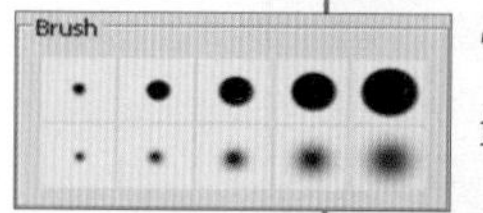


Then pick a large brush from the brush menu; the lower right brush will be fine for our example.

Navigate to a corner of the terrain. While looking more or less down over your mesh, hold down Ctrl+Left Mouse button to lift the terrain and Ctrl+Right mouse button to push it down. To change the size of the brush, you can select a different brush profile from the `Brush Menu` section, or you can change brush parameters in the `Setting` menu section in the middle of the `TerrainEdit` tool.

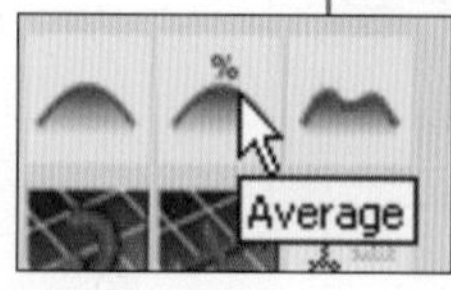


The `Average` tool will help smooth out some of the rough areas. Painting and smoothing will help you get most of the details you're going to want to sculpt into your terrain.

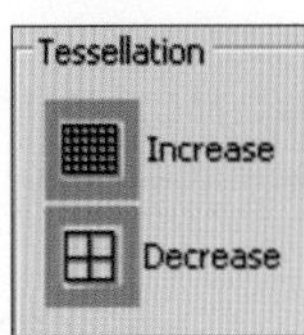


Pressing `Increase` in the `Tessellation` menu box will prompt this dialog.

Figure 4.9

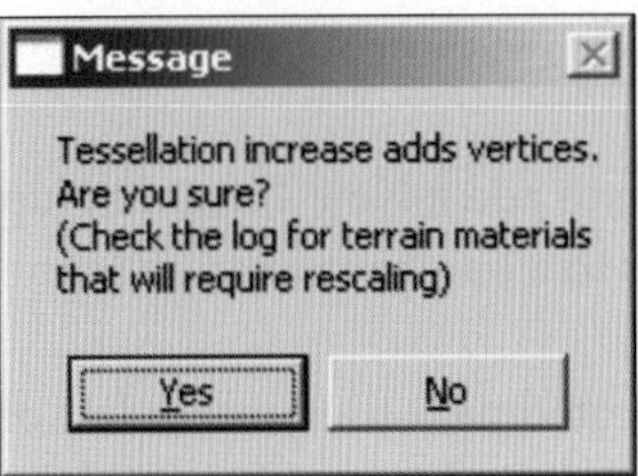


The terrain you're editing might not look too interesting; the mesh might need to be subdivided to keep the terrain from looking too blocky. To change the mesh resolution, use the `Tessellation` menu and click on the `Increase` button two or three times [Figure 4.9]. Adding too much detail will begin to kill some of the performance of your machine, while too little detail will look blocky. It's up to you to find a happy balance between detail and performance. In general, I've found that pressing `Increase` twice is high enough resolution for most uses. The previously sharp peak should look a lot much smoother now [Figure 4.10].

Figure 4.10

Depending on your graphics card and CPU power, you might want to do your terrain sculpting at a lower resolution and then up the tessellation after you're done.

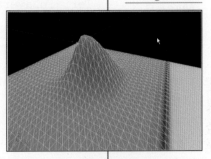

## Poking a Hole in the Terrain and Integrating the Terrain into the Level

The last few things to do with our terrain include integrating the mesh into the rest of our level. For a player to be able to go into a building underground, you'll need to clear out some faces of the terrain to allow the player to get through the mesh. The `TerrainEdit` tool has a visibility brush that allows you to punch a hole through any part of the mesh.

Using this tool you can hide and show various grid squares of the terrain. Hiding the squares will allow you to punch buildings into the terrain. As with the lifting and pushing of the terrain, you use Ctrl + Left mouse to hide and Ctrl + Right mouse to show the various grid squares of the terrain.

## Using Other Terrain Editing Tools

Unreal allows you to import and export the height map as a grayscale image. Most grayscale images are saved at 8 bits per pixel; that allows for only 255 height variations—not very smooth. To allow for more detail, Unreal supports 16 bits per pixel, which allows for over 32 thousand height variations, resulting in a smoother terrain. Various resources from the Internet can help you create more lifelike terrain maps. If you experiment with these, you'll need to import the textures from disk using this menu section in the `TerrainEditor` [Figure 4.11].

Figure 4.11

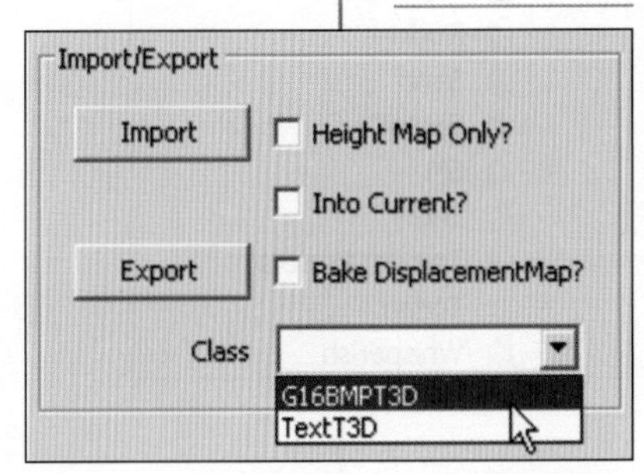

## Adding Terrain Materials

Terrain materials are handled differently from regular materials in the Unreal engine. Terrain is usually viewed from a greater distance and thus there are a number of different tricks to handle texture optimizations. A bit like GIMP or Photoshop, the Unreal engine requires the editor to use a layered masking system approach to add data onto the terrain object in the scene.

To add a texture onto our created mesh, we're going to add a New Terrain Setup Layer. A few automatic objects will be generated, thanks to a bit of automation in the Terrain editor.

Figure 4.12

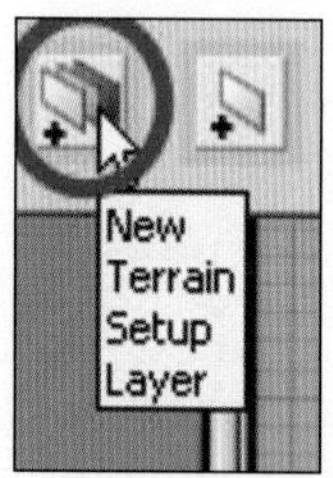


Click on the `New Terrain Setup Layer` icon located near the bottom left of the Terrain editor window [Figure 4.12]. This will open a new object dialog from the `TerrainLayerSetup` factory [Figure 4.13]. (It's interesting to note that this is one of the few things that are stored in the level package in the Generic Browser.)

Figure 4.13

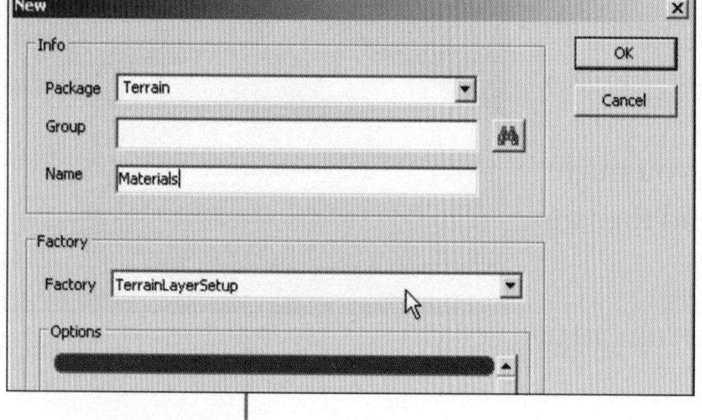


In most cases, any new object is stored in a UPK (Unreal Package) of some kind. Then, when the level is loaded, the UPKs that are used will automatically load with it. Terrain is different in that the materials and meshes created are stored inside of the level, not in a package. The level's terrain draws some shader information from the materials stored in a UPK, but the details of how they are to appear on the terrain are stored with the terrain mesh, in the level.

After you click on OK, a Terrain Setup layer will be created in the Terrain editor [Figure 4.14]. This will allow us to add various attributes to the terrain.

Figure 4.14

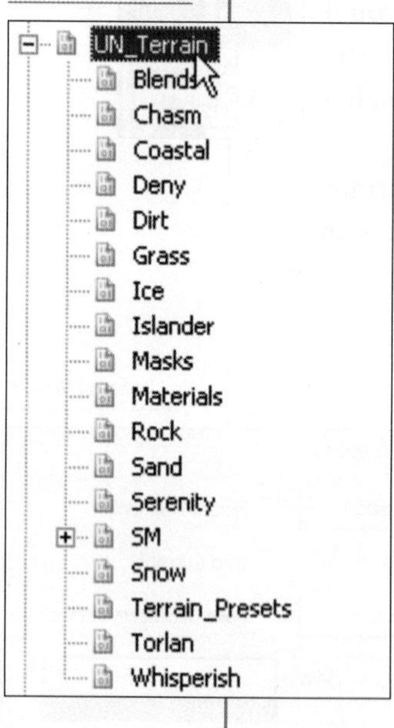


Figure 4.15

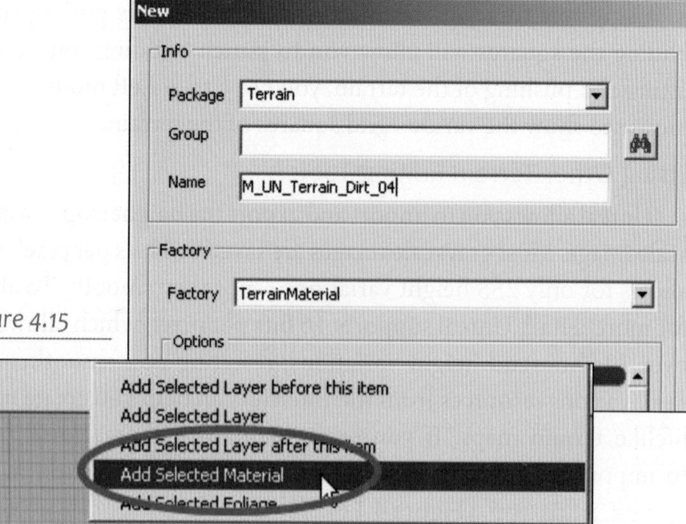

So to assign a material to our piece of terrain, I loaded up the UN_Terrain package that ships with Unreal Tournament 3. This package has a bunch of materials that tile nicely and have some interesting detail appropriate for terrain. Right-click on the UN_Terrain and select `fully load`. This will ensure that you have access to all of the stored materials in the UPK.

Highlight a material in the Generic browser. Then, back in the Terrain editor, right-click on the `Setup Layer` and select `Add Selected Material` [Figure 4.15].

Another automatic Factory will be created. This time the factory is going to be a Terrain Material. Earlier, the object that was created was a Terrain Setup Layer; this time it's a Terrain Material [Figure 4.16]. Again, these materials are a bit different from regular materials in that they are stored in the level and are not a regular UPK.

Figure 4.16

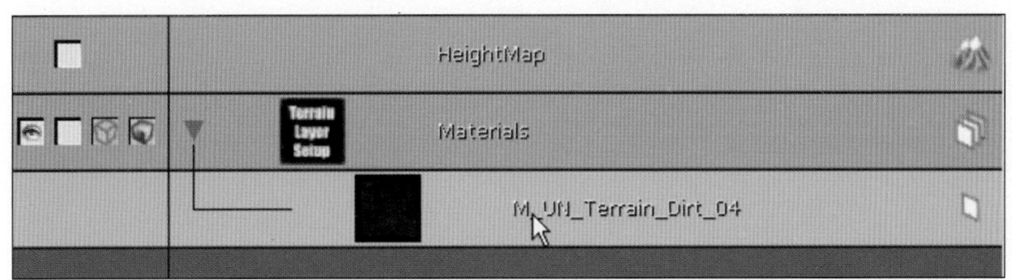


So now a new material has been added to the terrain. This should be reflected in the perspective view with the texture tiled over the terrain object in the level. For now we're going to have to settle for a single material for the terrain. Setting up multiple materials takes a bit of set-up, and there are more important things to move on to.

### Review

#### Play Testing, and Testing, and Testing . . .

It's important to make sure that your level is working out well, since you'll need to really consider how much work it will be to make changes once the level's BSPs have been converted into static mesh objects. Once the static meshes are in place, making changes requires a lot of reworking.

# 5 Managing Levels

## Managing What You've Got

Finally, we've gotten so far! We've made our own death match level and added in all the required components to make the level playable! By now we're ready to start working on the finer details that make up an Unreal level.

In a finished game, your different areas will require specific design details. A treasure room should be filled with gold and jewels, while an engine room should be filled with pipes and power systems, and so on. However, as a designer, it's difficult to tell your artists and even your programmers all your intentions for a given space.

As you build your space, using the default material will not accomplish the task of describing your level design. Setting up a few materials to tell your artists how you want the environment to be arranged is a useful method to fill your level with visual information for your artists to work from. To accomplish this, we'll need to open up GIMP to create a few basic textures; then we'll apply them as some basic materials to the walls so that your artists know what they're supposed to be looking at.

## What to Expect

You're going to need to share your work: how do you tell the artists which parts of a space are walls made of wood and which are made of concrete? How do you tell the artists the path through the terrain you're intending the player to follow?

Setting up complex materials as a designer is a distraction from your primary focus, but setting up basic materials that tell the artists what to focus on is time well spent. If it were possible to leave sign posts in a movie set telling the set builders important information like "Electric fence here" and "dinosaurs penned in this area behind the fence," that would be great. And we can do that to an extent using documentation. But it's better to draw things out exactly where you intend the objects to be.

## Setting Up Basic Marking Textures

First you'll want to think about a set of materials you want to work with. Usually, we'll want to start off with a ground, impassable walls, half-walls, etc. Once a few basic decisions have been made, then some design elements should be created. Conferring with the artists and planning on what to build before getting started is important.

Making sure that all the assets are built to the right scale takes a bit of planning. To accomplish this, we'll start in the Unreal Editor, then export some objects for the artists to get started with. From there, it's up to you, the designer, to keep the artists busy by providing approximate shapes, or *proxies,* to build from.

To help our artists understand how the level is designed, we need to create a few placeholder textures. These will tell the artist what shape things are supposed to take in the finished level. To create the textures, we will use GIMP, which is an acronym for GNU Image Manipulation Program. It is based on GNU, a set of tools that are used to make software. GIMP can be downloaded freely from http://www.gimp.org, but don't let the price tag make you think that it is inferior to its Adobe counterpart, Photoshop. It has some features different from those of Photoshop and other artist tools. After installing the latest version of GIMP, you can follow along in the next project. Of course, you can also do the same project using Photoshop or any other image editing software. To start, let's open up GIMP [Figure 5.1].

Figure 5.1

We'll make our textures small so they don't take up too much memory as we test and tweak our levels. First create a new image: we'll make the texture 256 pixels by 256 pixels. Power-of-two textures are basically numbers that the video card can handle quickly; these include 1, 2, 4, 8, 16, 32, 64, 128, 256, 512, 1024, and 2048. Textures in most, if not all, game engines are required to be a power of two in size per dimension. Non-square textures are also valid (e.g., 32 × 2048), but these are harder to use. Normally, we'd leave all of the textures up to the artist to

Figure 5.2

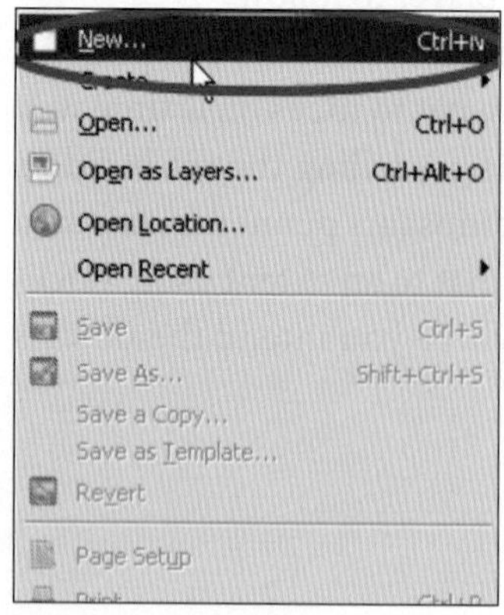


Figure 5.3

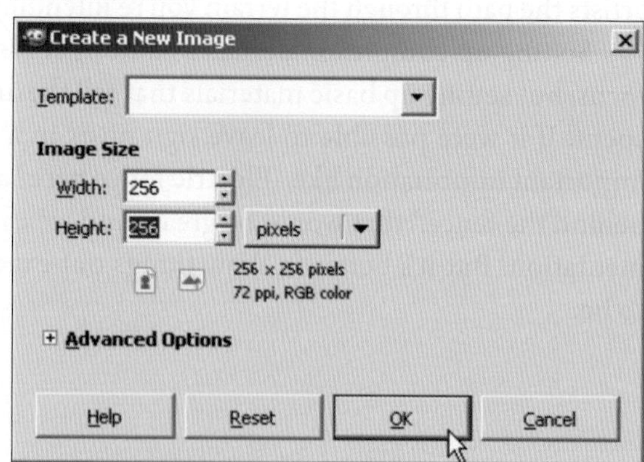

Figure 5.4

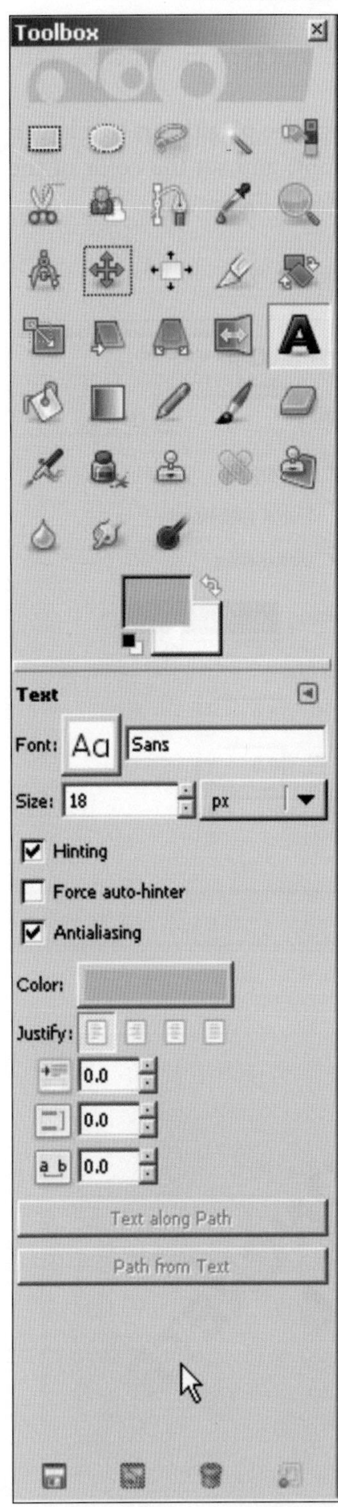


create; but we're not going to be using these textures in your final level, so you don't have to worry about making your textures too pretty.

Start a new image [Figure 5.2], and enter the following values in the dialog that follows [Figure 5.3].
Fill the first layer with a simple color. Don't pick a color that's too loud; otherwise, testing your level will turn into too much of a psychedelic experience. A faded yellow color will do to start off with. This is the tool bar in GIMP [Figure 5.4]. Depending on which tool you have selected, the lower half of the tool bar will change.

Select the `paintbucket` tool [Figure 5.5] and set the foreground color to a mustard color [Figure 5.6]. You can also experiment with the `Pattern Fill` properties, but your text might be harder to read when these are used. The purpose of these textures is to inform the artist which objects need to be replaced and what they are to be replaced with. Of course, the decision of what to fill the texture with is up to you.

Figure 5.5

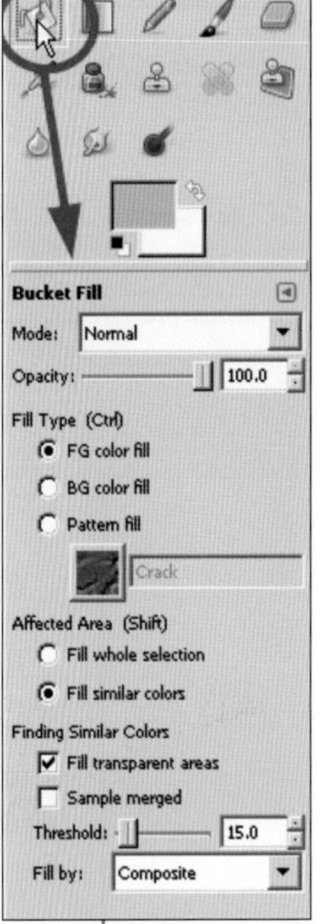


Figure 5.6

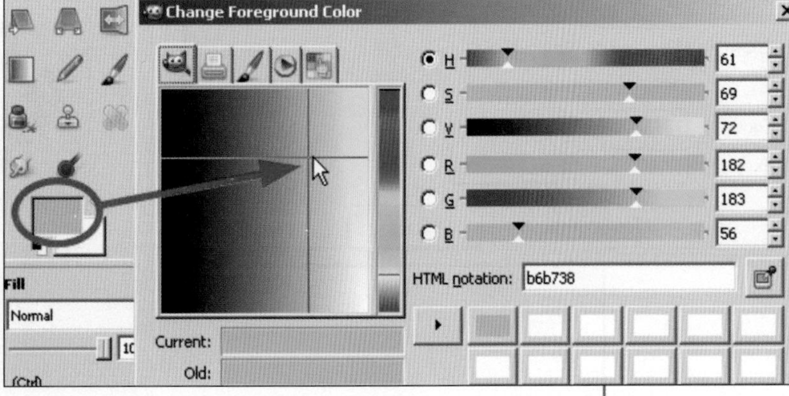

Then we'll add in a text layer with the text tool and type in "concrete wall" [Figure 5.7].

Figure 5.7

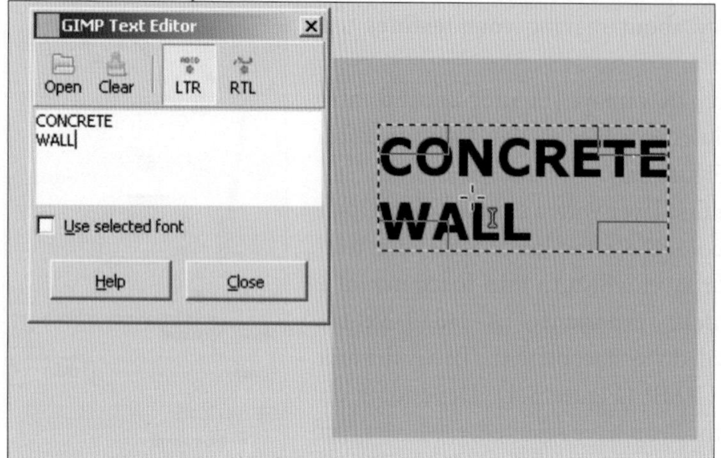


Change the parameters to a larger, bolder font; and set the color of the text to black [Figure 5.8].

Figure 5.8

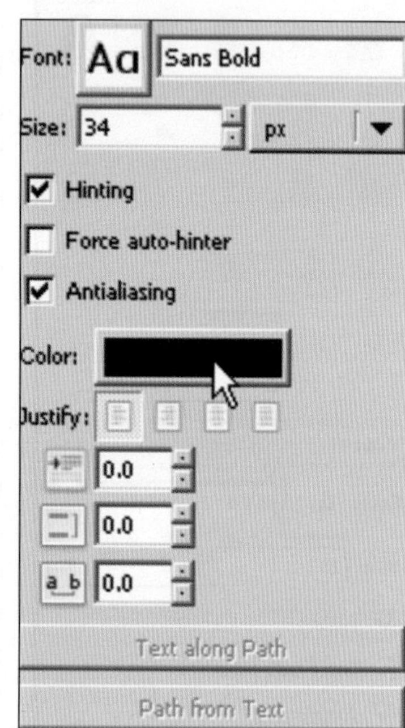


With the text layer selected, click on the Rotate tool.

The rotate center will be automatically set when you click on the text in the scene with the rotate tool [Figure 5.9].

With the move tool, recenter the text [Figure 5.10].

Figure 5.9

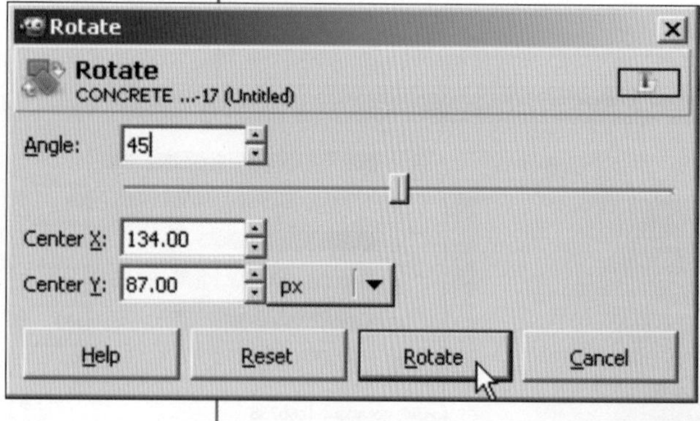


Figure 5.10

Figure 5.11

Your layers dialog should now have a filled-in layer and a concrete layer [Figure 5.11].

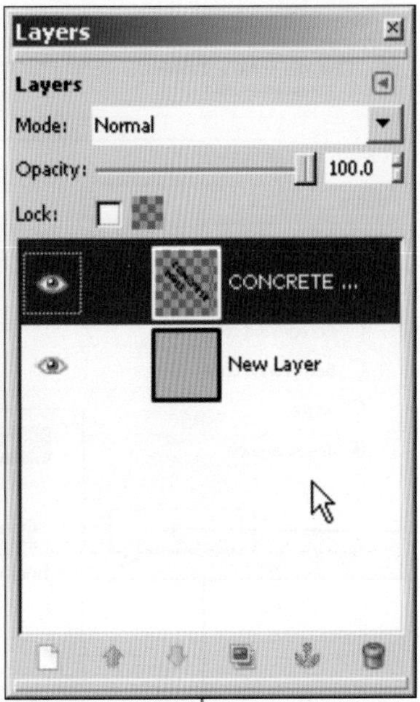

In the File menu, select `SaveAs`. Then save the file as D_ConcreteWalls.tga in your Mod's folder [Figure 5.12].

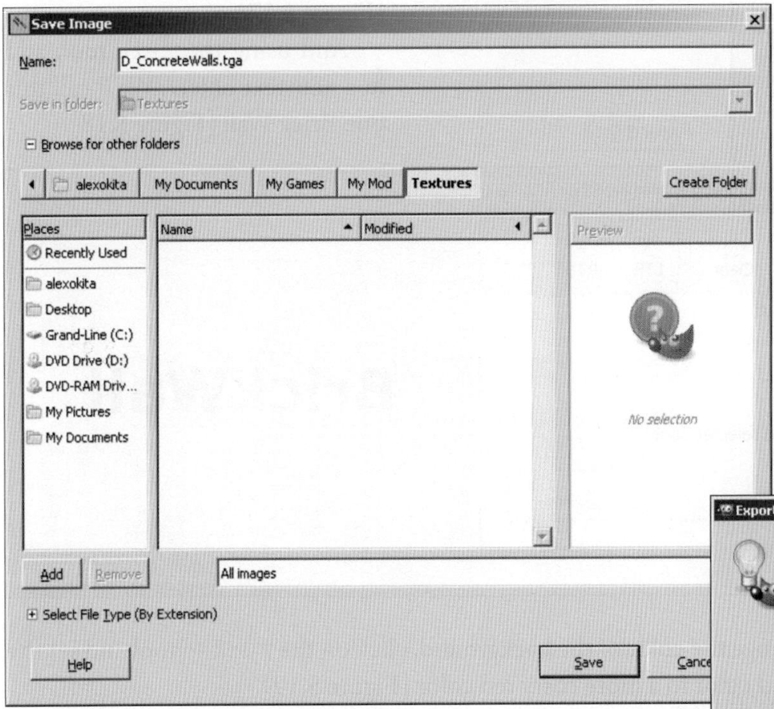

Figure 5.12

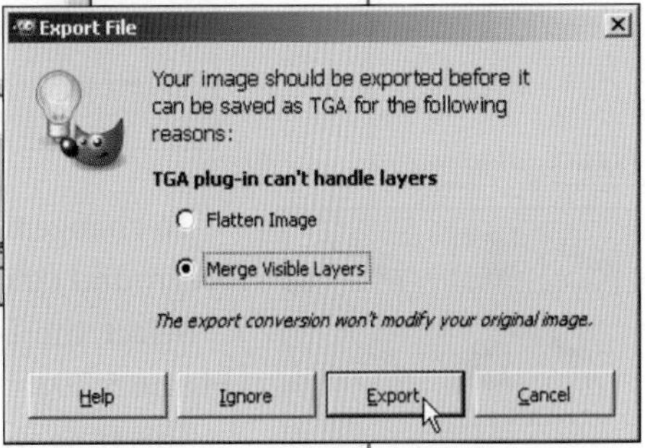

Because TGA files cannot support layers, you'll need to export the file with the `Merge Visible Layers` option and export the file with the provided name [Figure 5.13].

Disable the RLE compression and then click on `Save` [Figure 5.14]. Unreal Engine doesn't need the texture to be compressed. To create a new layer, click on the lower left of the layer's window [Figure 5.15].

This will prompt you to set the size of the new layer. Make sure

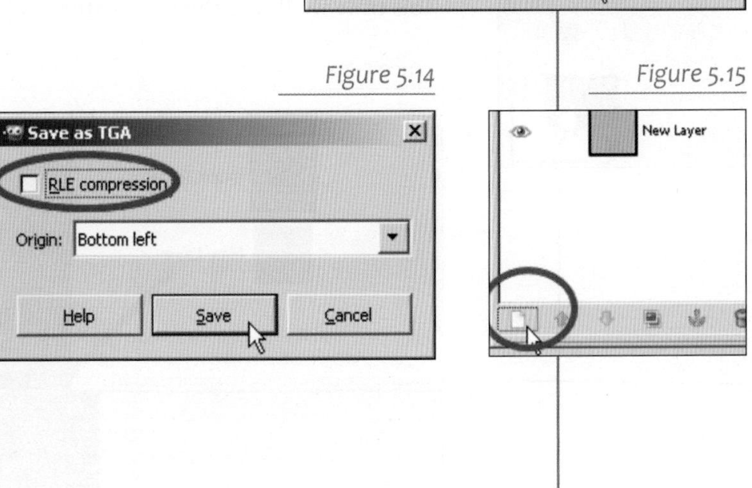


Figure 5.13

Figure 5.14

Figure 5.15

Figure 5.16

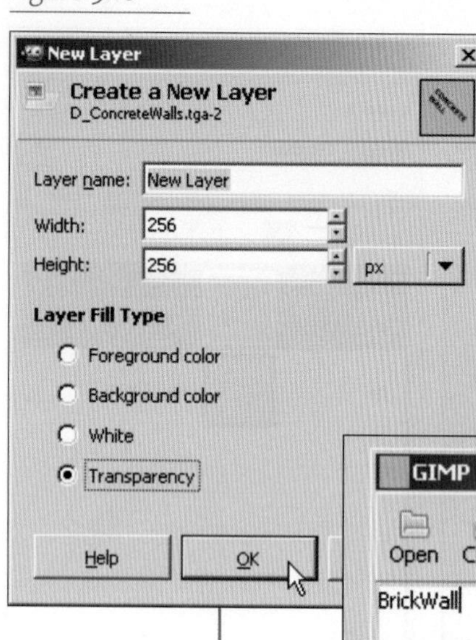


Figure 5.17

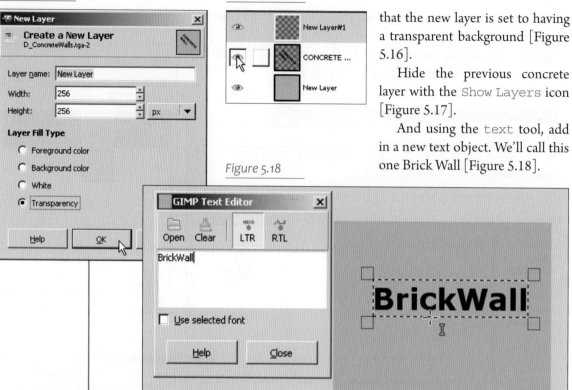

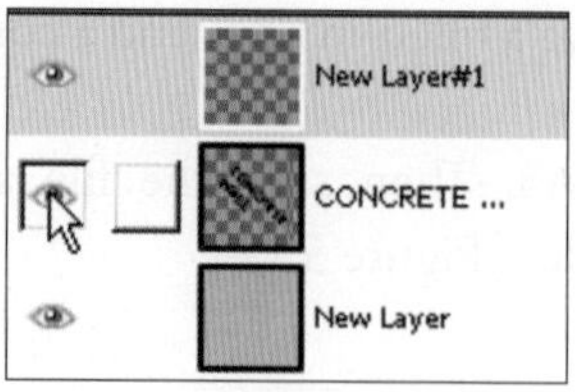

that the new layer is set to having a transparent background [Figure 5.16].

Hide the previous concrete layer with the Show Layers icon [Figure 5.17].

And using the text tool, add in a new text object. We'll call this one Brick Wall [Figure 5.18].

Figure 5.18

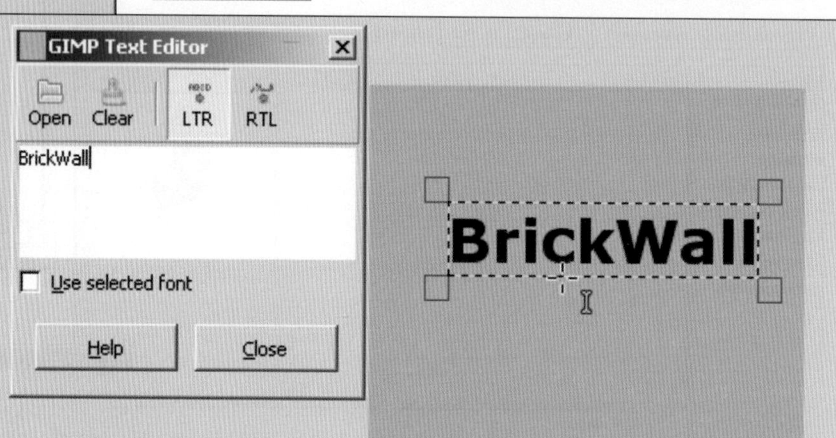


Figure 5.19

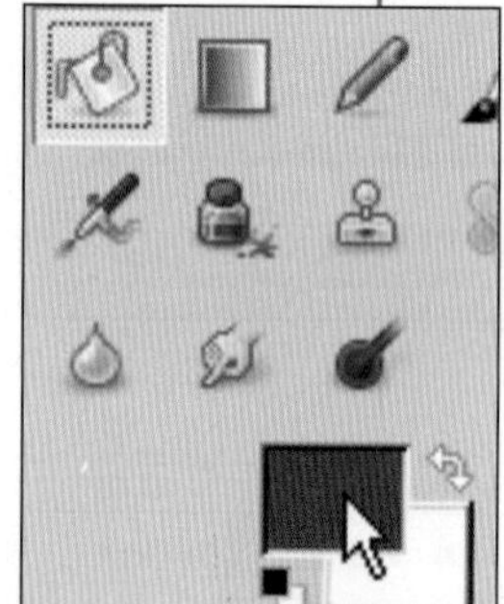

To change the color of the background, click on the Bucket tool and set the foreground color to a more rusty red color [Figure 5.19].

Select the bottommost layer and fill in the layer with the selected color [Figure 5.20].

This time we'll save the new texture as D_BrickWalls.tga [Figure 5.21].

Figure 5.20

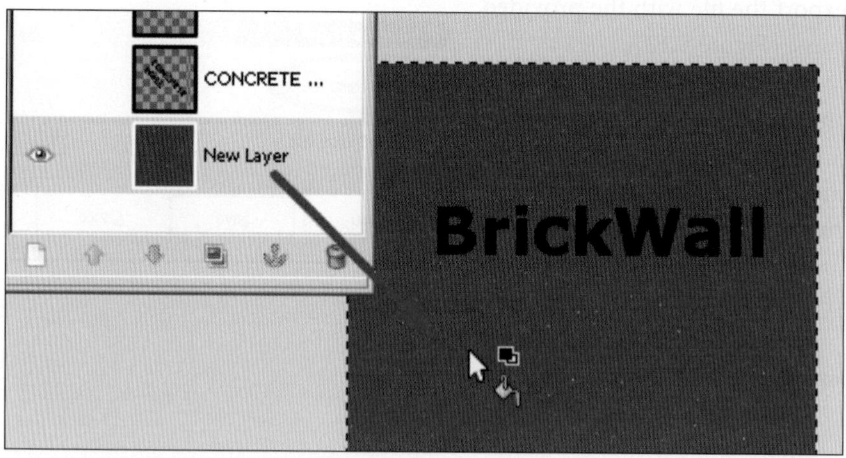

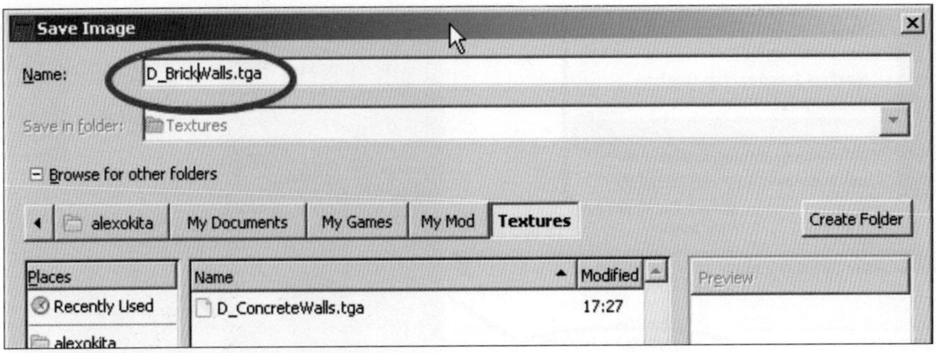

Figure 5.21

Once you're done picking the various types of materials with which you'll be populating your level, save the GIMP image as D_DesignMaterials.psd. The psd extension will make the file compatible with Photoshop, which your artists will most likely be using. Saving all of the different materials in one file will reduce the number of files you'll need to manage for your project.

This directory is where we'll be putting all of our materials specific for our BSPs. Other hint textures will also be saved into this directory. Now we can't assign the texture to a BSP without first adding it to a material. Materials are what we assign to BSP surfaces, not bitmap images.

PROJECT

## Basic Materials

We cannot assign a bitmap image to the scene. We need to build some basic materials before we can apply the textures to the BSPs in the scene. This is the first project in which we're going to be building some materials. The art chapters will go into more detail about the materials editor, but for design purposes we'll stick to the very basics of the material editor.

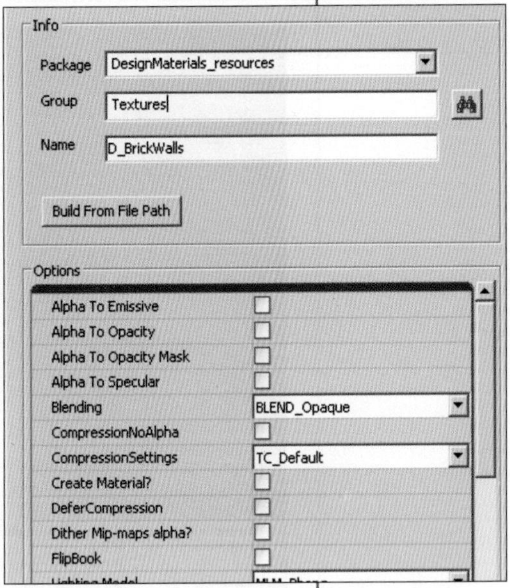

Import the texture named D_BrickWalls [Figure 5.22]. Right click in the Generic browser and select New Material to view the textures we may use for the new material [Figure 5.23]; D_BrickWalls is one of them. We'll name the new material after the texture that we're going to use [Figure 5.24]. For this, there might be a bit of overlap with some of the art chapters; but as a designer, you're going to need to know how to accomplish some of the art-related tasks as well as a few of the programmer-related tasks.

Figure 5.22

Once the new material editor is opened, highlight the texture in the Generic browser. Then select `TextureSampleParameter2D` from the menu on the

Figure 5.23

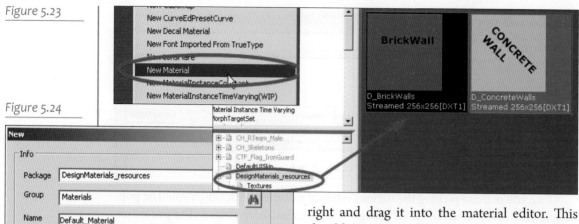

Figure 5.24

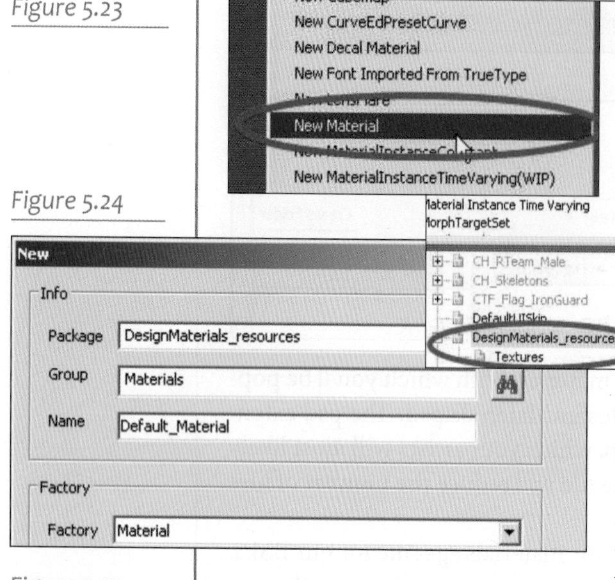


Figure 5.25

right and drag it into the material editor. This should automatically tell the new node which texture you're planning on using to attach to the node. If the node doesn't automatically fill in the texture data, select the icon in the Generic browser and click on the green arrow in the node's parameters [Figure 5.25].

Next we'll connect the node to the material's diffuse channel by clicking and dragging on the black tab on the `TextureSampleParameter2D` to the diffuse tab [Figure 5.26]. This is how the material knows where to get its color information from. Next we're going to need to tell the material what else it's made of.

Figure 5.26

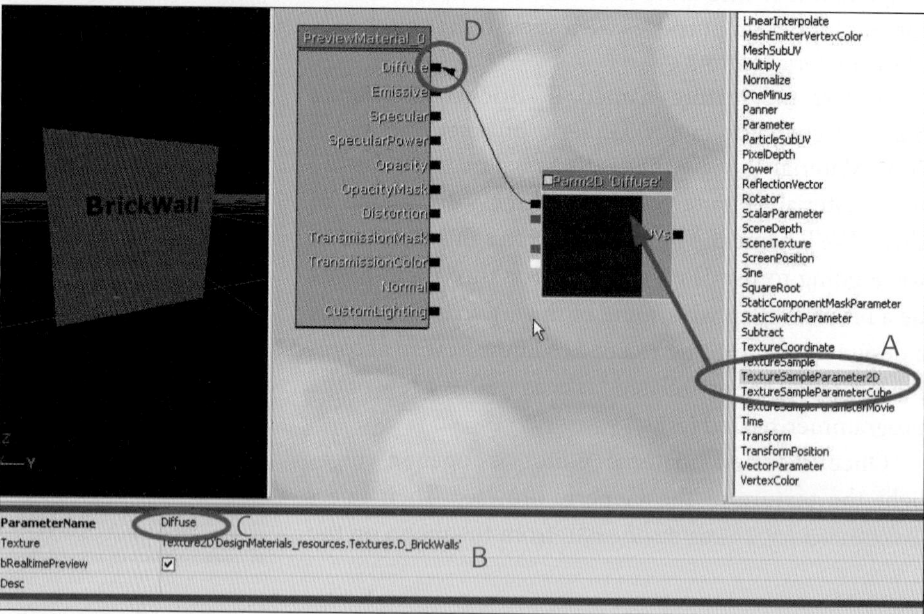

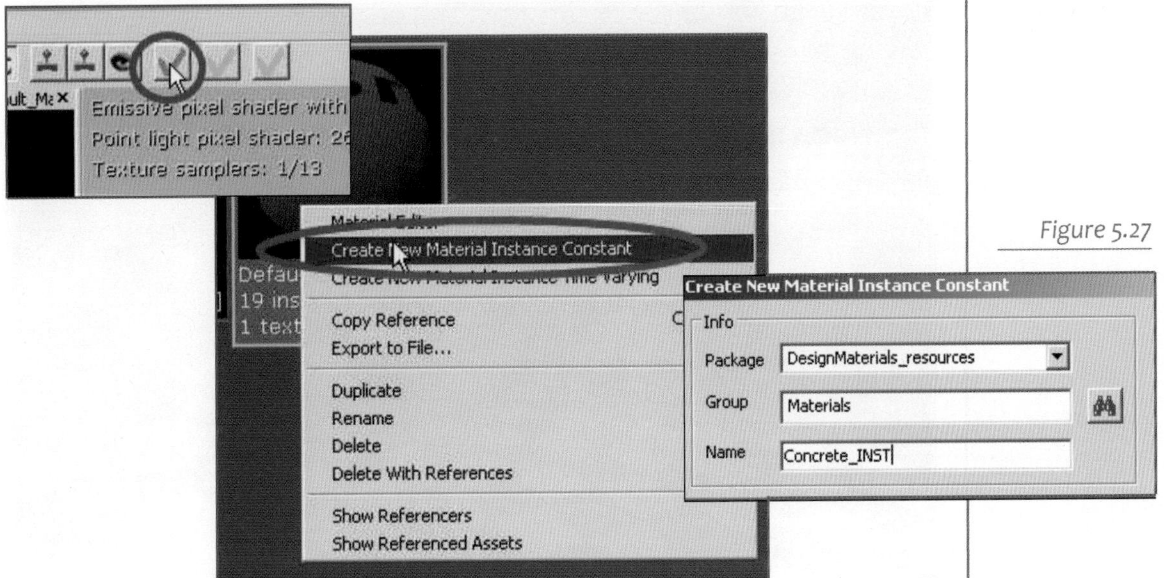


Figure 5.27

By building this material you've written a new shaders program. To reuse this work you'll create a Material Instance Constant (MIC). Right click on `Material` in the Generic browser and select `Create New Material Instance Constant`. Expand the new MIC [Figure 5.27].

The material settings tell the game what sort of effect the material is supposed to play when a bullet or rocket hits it. The sparks coming off a concrete wall will include some chunks of concrete. The hit effect on steel will include a lot of sparks. To tell the engine what sort of impact effect to play, update the settings for each material. For each material type, you're going to repeat this process of connecting a texture to the diffuse channel and setting the material type. Create new materials for the rest of the textures. Later on, in a more advanced material chapter, we could save some time by creating material instances; but for now we'll stick to this process if only to get more familiar with the process.

See the final material [Figure 5.28].

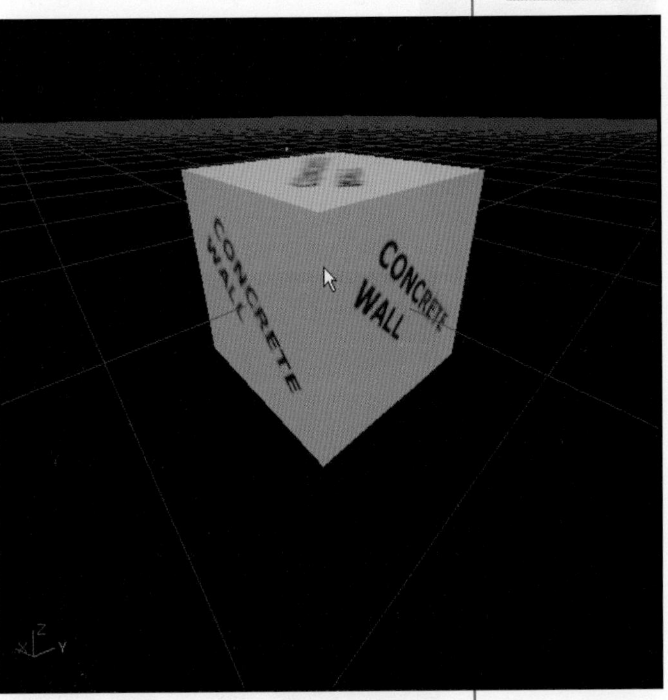


Figure 5.28

Figure 5.29

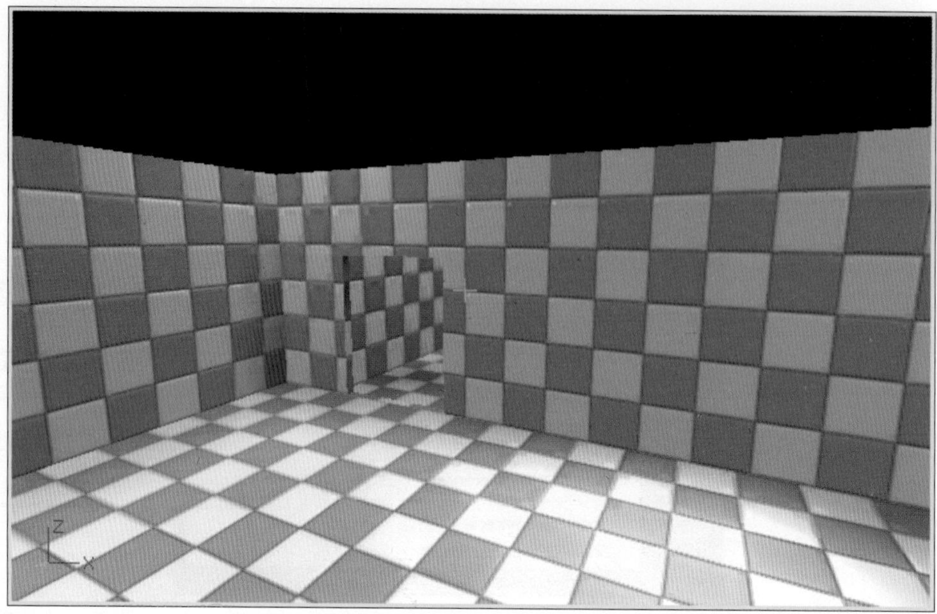

Figure 5.30

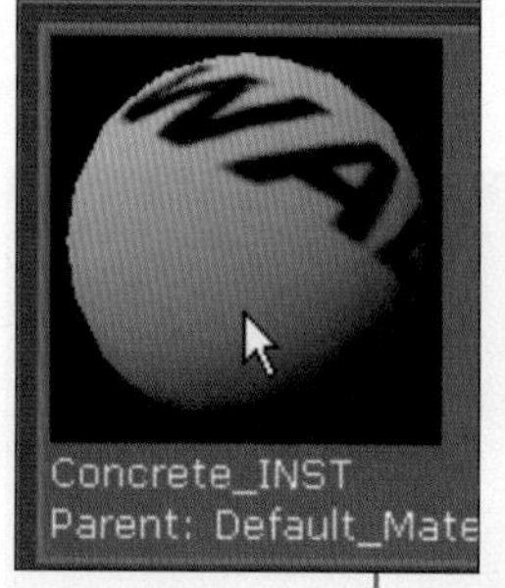


## Assigning Materials to BSPs

Now let's open the level we just made in the previous chapter [Figure 5.29]. Right now it's just a bunch of grey checkers, nothing too interesting to look at for the time being.

We'll want to mark the various walls and floors with different properties. Select the various surfaces of the BSPs highlighting them. With the surfaces highlighted, click on one of the materials in the Generic browser [Figure 5.30].

This will assign the selected texture to the highlighted BSP surfaces [Figure 5.31]. Using UDK you'll need to right click and select Assign Material from the popup menu [Figure 5.31B].

Figure 5.31

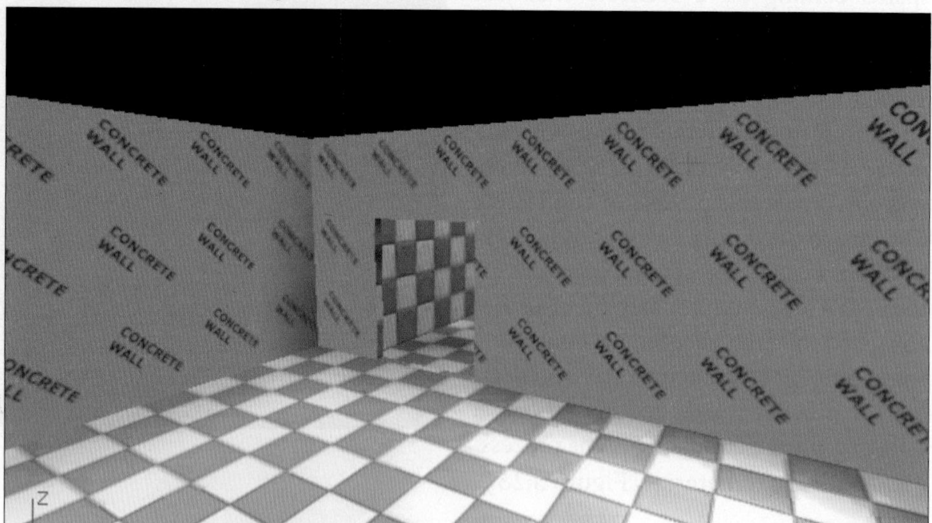

Figure 5.32

Fitting the material to the BSP isn't that important because most of the BSPs will be replaced with static meshes; but if you want to ensure that the texture is visible to the artists, then you might want to scoot the texture so that the text is in view. To do this, you'll want to open the `texture editing` tools [Figure 5.32].

Assign the different materials to the various sections of your death match level. This will go a long way toward ensuring that your design vision will be communicated to the artists properly. Objects such as cracked columns and marble walls should be indicated by marking them with a material [Figure 5.33].

Figure 5.33

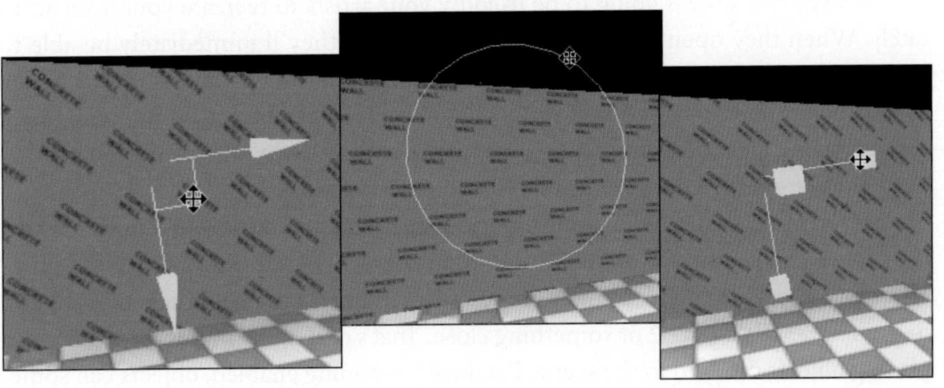

## Exporting BSPs for the Artists: What They need from You

Once all of the various objects have been tagged, you'll need to share your work with the artists. Unfortunately, the material tagging doesn't export with the objects, so your artists will need to work in both Unreal and 3D Studio Max at the same time.

Figure 5.34

Your artists should see your work in a BSP level stream while they work in their own static mesh level stream. As the artists create new assets that overlap with your BSPs, they'll need to know what to replace your BSPs with. Using this approach, it's easier for the artists to know where they need to focus their attention.

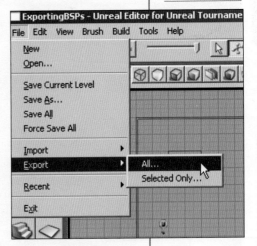

As a designer, you'll also need to talk to the artists about how the various objects you need will be used. There are two ways to build a scene. The first is to build with each object exported specifically from 3D Studio Max with the pivot point placed at the origin of the scene. These are world-space transformed objects. The more common method is to export the object with the pivot point centered on the object, or object-space transformed objects. We'll examine the differences in the following project.

First we'll open the ExportingBSPs.ut3 map in the level editor [Figure 5.34]. The first thing we'll see is a basic room with four columns at the corners. Next we'll want to fully load the ExportingBSPs _resources.upk that loaded with the level.

Figure 5.35

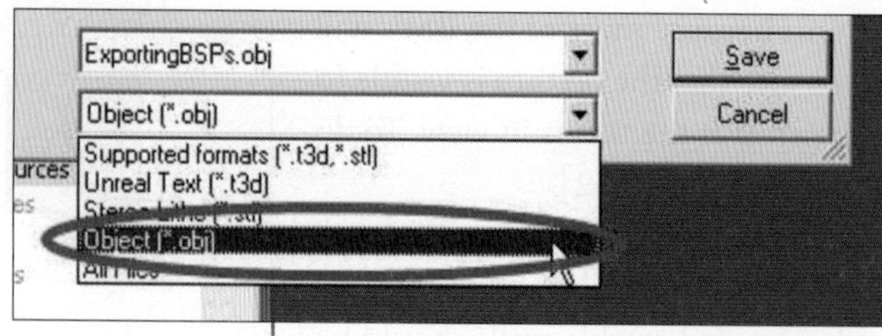


Unreal Engine has a few ways to export the geometry in the level. The OBJ file format is a tried and true format to export just about every type of geometry used by most 3D software engines, 3D Studio Max and Unreal Engine included. It's an old format, but that just means that it's simple and hasn't changed in a long time [Figure 5.35].

The exported OBJ is going to be used by your artists to recreate your level accurately. When they open the OBJ in 3D Studio Max, they'll immediately be able to build objects to the correct scale and orientation. This is important since having all of the objects built to the correct scale will make placing them into your scene much easier. Having gigantic or miniature objects and scaling them every time you need to place them from the Generic browser is an unnecessary hassle.

Select either of the red columns in the scene. The first thing you'll notice is that the pivot point is centered at the bottom of the object [Figure 5.36]. Open the properties and check on the placement of the object in the scene. You'll see 320,320,232 or possibly -320, 320, 232 or something close. That's one of the minor problems with placing objects by hand in the scene. Even with snapping enabled, objects can sometimes be very slightly off. Placing objects one at a time has a slight disadvantage of having to tweak their pivot positions one at a time as well.

Figure 5.36

Figure 5.37

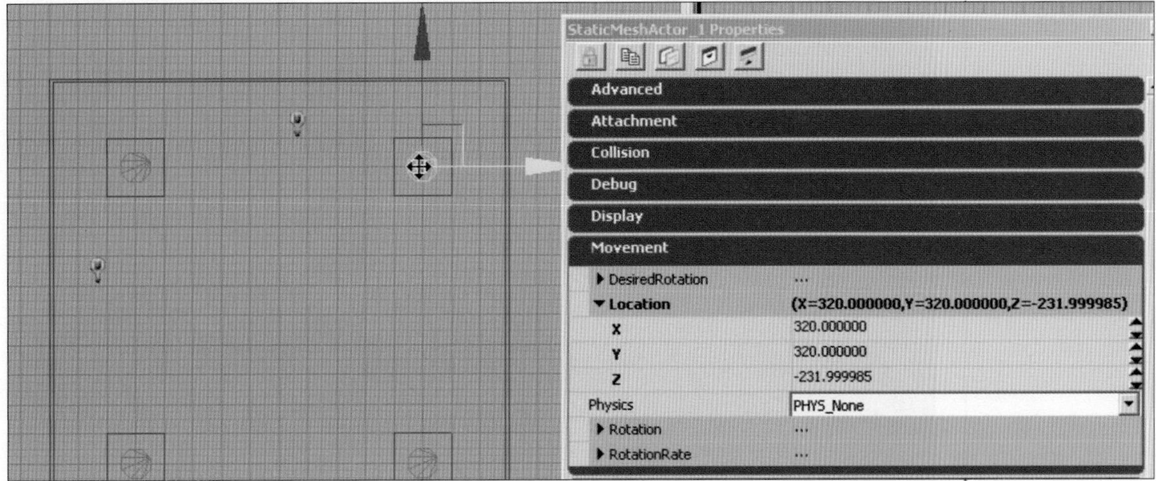


Figure 5.38

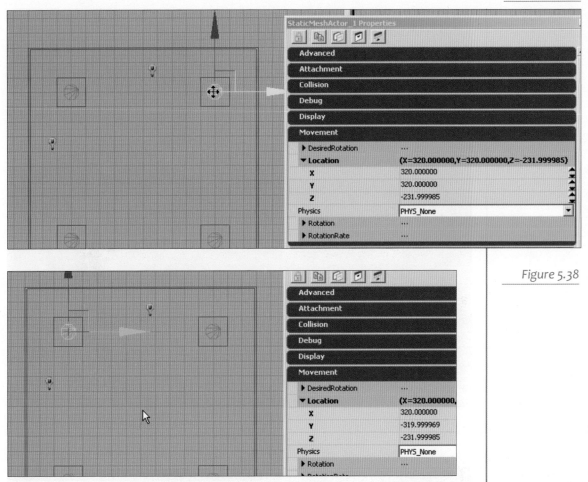

In the level editor the red column appears with the pivot point under the object [Figure 5.37]. To export objects like this, the object must be exported with the pivot point at the bottom of the object in 3D Studio Max [Figure 5.38].

The alternative is to place objects using world transformed coordinates.

From 3D Studio Max, the pivot point must be placed at the origin of the scene [Figure 5.39]. The object can be located anywhere in the scene, but when it's exported, the pivot point will not be under the object.

Figure 5.39

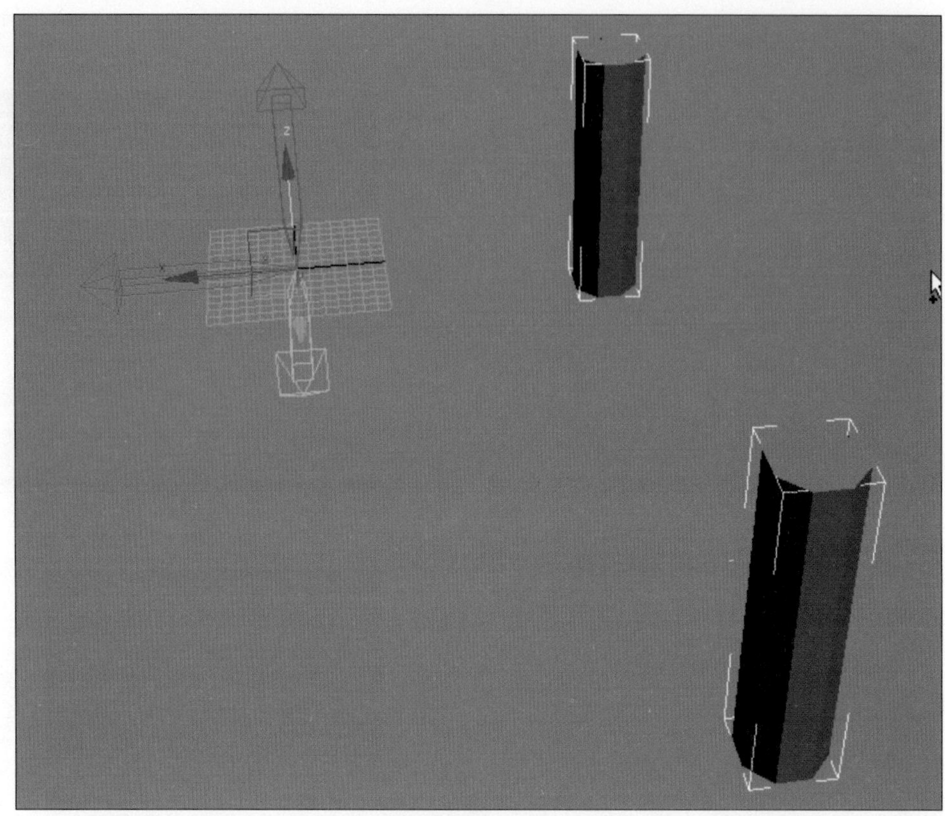

Figure 5.40

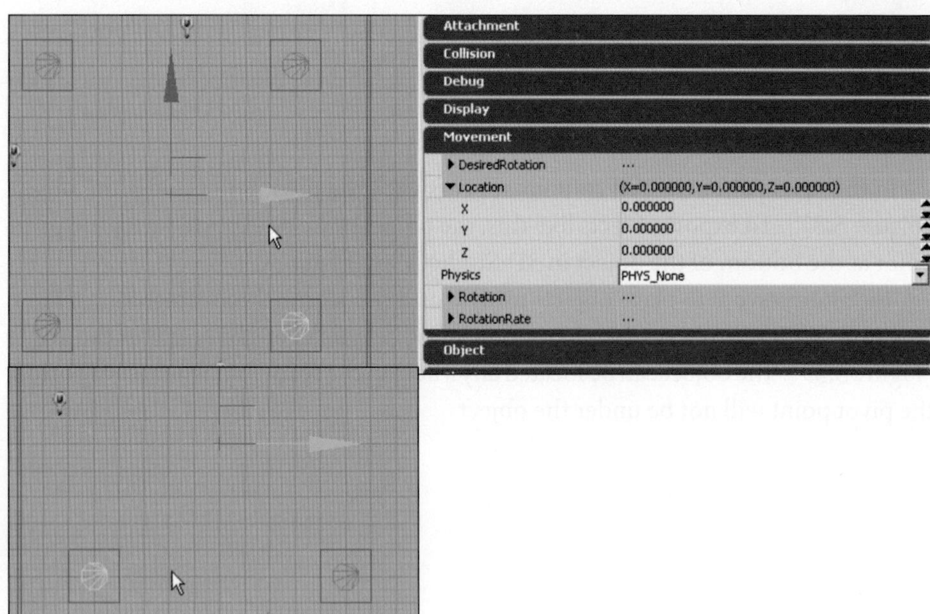

Select a green column and you'll notice that the pivot point is centered on the middle of the room (the origin of the level) [Figure 5.40]. This should reflect how it was exported from 3D Studio Max. The primary advantage of a world-space transformed object is placement accuracy. If you build a scene with many parts and the parts need to match up perfectly, it's much easier to fit them together if their placement requires only that they are moved to 0,0,0. When they are exported from 3D Studio Max, they only need to be exported as they are from the scene. However, the drawback is that the data might be redundant if the parts used to build the scene are repeated.

Of course, the advantage of an object-space transformed object is that you save memory. The time spent making sure that the object will fit into place is up to the designer, once a prop comes back from the artists. So there's a balance between when to use object-space and world-space transformed objects.

For a complex room where each chunk of geometry is unique and only used once, it might be easier to export the chunks as world-space transformed objects. For the decorations that populate the scene, like debris, or for light fixtures that are repeated in many places, it's better to use object-space transformed objects.

## Changing It Up: Overriding Materials

To take advantage of how materials in Unreal engine are managed, you can override materials in the scene after an object has been placed. In the ExportingBSPs_resources.upk, you'll find a blue material that isn't used in the scene. Open the properties of any object in the scene and expand its rendering properties [Figure 5.41].

You'll see a materials slot. Click on the green + icon and add in a new material override. Select the blue material and connect it to this slot [Figure 5.42].

The blue material is applied to a column object [Figure 5.43].

Figure 5.41

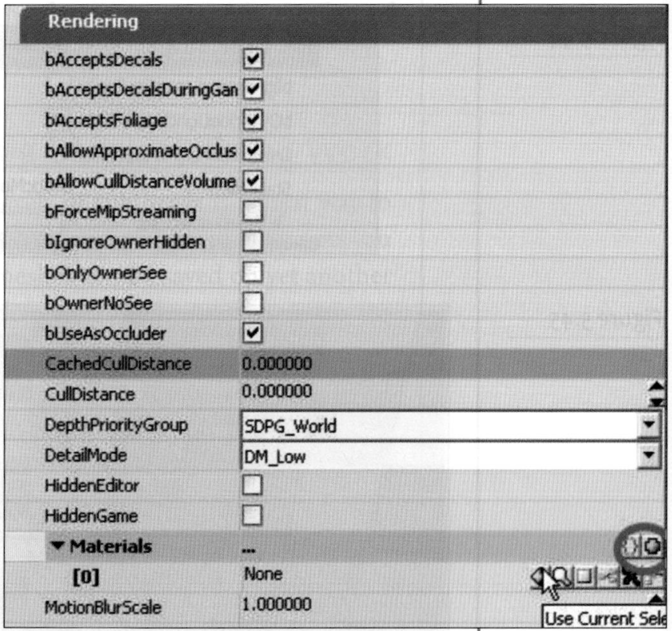

Figure 5.42

## The Level Manager

The level we've been working on is your persistent level. Any level streamed in from this level is a streamed level. This distinction is fairly important. If you load in a streamed level, none of the other associated levels will automatically load with it. Only the persistent level can load the streamed levels.

Figure 5.46

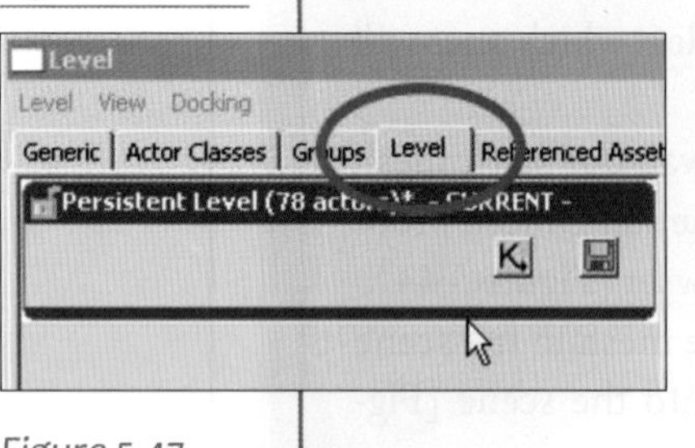


Streaming a level is a powerful tool for use with complex scenes. The sooner you begin to understand how these levels are used, the easier it will be for you to create more complex levels later on. The flexibility that streamed levels afford is akin to how layers are used in GIMP. Streaming in a level on demand allows you to mix and match behaviors, but there are a few catches you need to consider before getting too dependent on streamed levels.

Figure 5.47

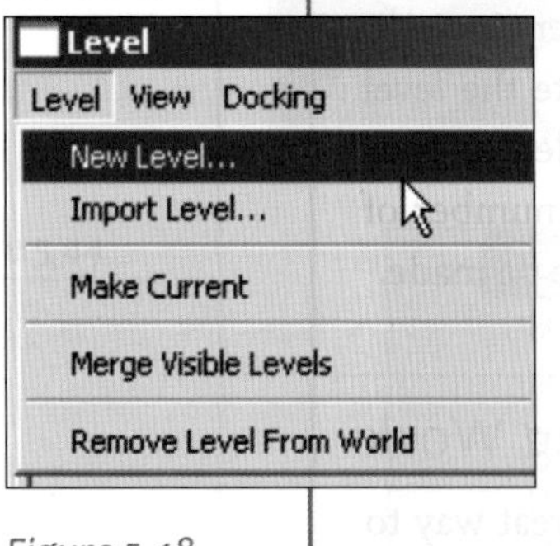


In the Generic browser, select the `Level` tab [Figure 5.46]. By default, any level you're working on will have at least one node in it. From here you can lock the level to avoid making changes. You can also open the level's Kismet sequences, and lastly, you can save changes made to that particular level with the `save` icon.

To create a new streaming level, select `Level` and then select `New Level` [Figure 5.47].

For this example, we're going to create a new level called DM_Dome_Scripts.ut3. This is the streamed level that we're going to store our persistent Kismet sequences in. To tell the base level how we plan on using the new level, the following popup needs to have the Streaming Method set to Kismet [Figure 5.48]. The alternative method is to load a level by distance. The distance method can also be useful, but it's a bit harder to control and avoids some of the more clever uses of Kismet. So for this project we'll use Kismet to load in the level [Figure 5.49].

Figure 5.48

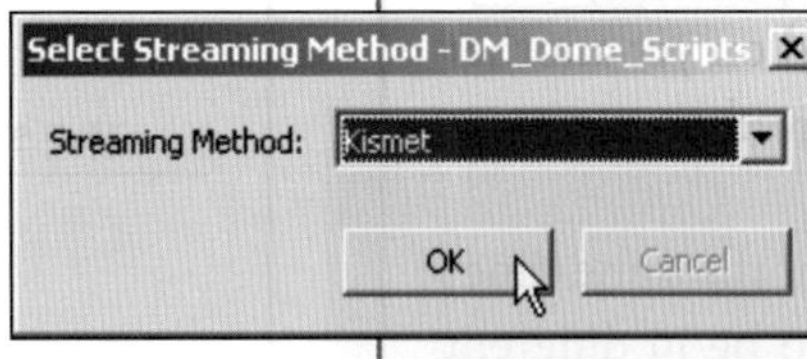


Figure 5.49

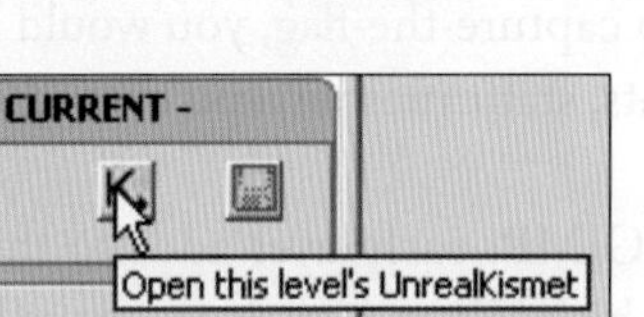


Under the `Levels` tab, you can open each level's Kismet sequence by pressing the `Kismet` icon on the level. This is one of the catches mentioned earlier. Each level has its own set of Kismet sequences. These sequences cannot communicate from one streamed level to another without special UScript written to store data in a more global sense.

In the Kismet sequence on your persistent level, you're going to want to add a new Kismet sequence that will load in your other streaming levels before playing the level. Something that should be mentioned is that just because a streamed level has been created and associated with the persistent level, the level doesn't necessarily know it's supposed to be in memory when the player begins playing.

The reason for this is simple. If you're loading a large game, and you're not going to be anywhere near the end of level until you fight your way through several other levels, the memory isn't wasted on storing parts of the game the player is nowhere near.

Figure 5.50

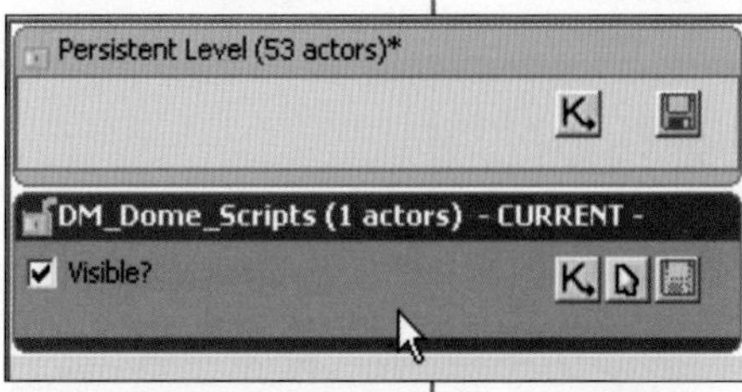


To associate a streaming level with the persistent level, you can do as we did here [Figure 5.50], or you can import a level that already exists. Either way, the same loading option will pop up to ask how you want to load in the streamed level. For this example, we're going to want to stream in the scripts level using a Kismet sequence. Kismet gives us a few more options, whereas the streaming in the level by distance is an automatic affair that can behave unreliably. There are a couple of Kismet nodes that have to be added to tell the persistent level to make the streamed levels visible. Don't worry; they're small sequences.

Figure 5.51

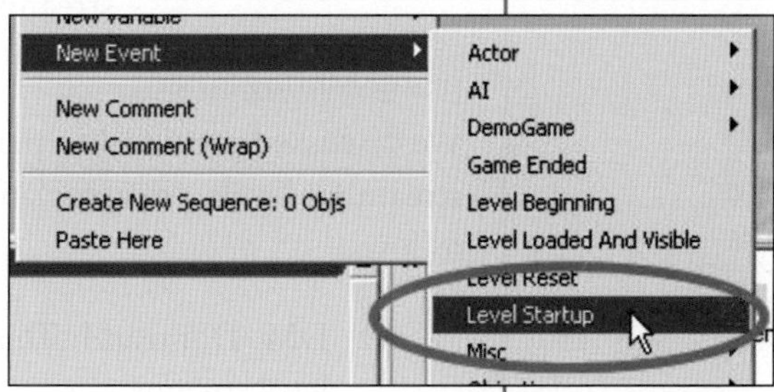


In our persistent level, create two new nodes. These will stream in the levels and make them visible when the persistent level is loaded. Streamed levels can be loaded by nearly any Kismet event. Later we can even use volume triggers to load in an oncoming level and at the same time unload a past level.

Figure 5.52

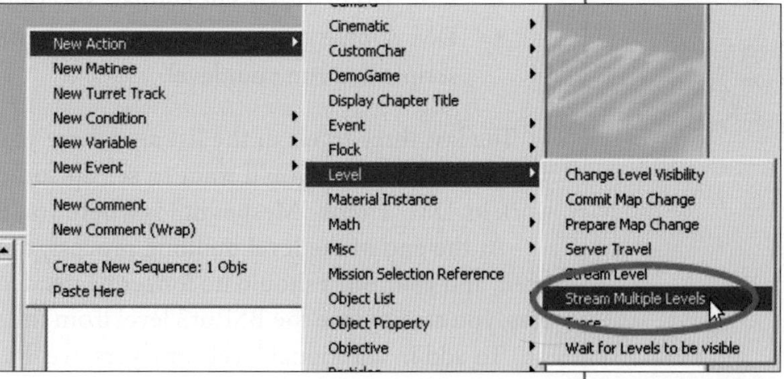


In Kismet, right-click and select the `Level Startup` node [Figure 5.51]. Add that to the Kismet sequence for the persistent level.

The next node you want to add is the `Stream Multiple Levels` node [Figure 5.52].

Connect the Level Startup node to the Load tab of the `stream multiple levels` node [Figure 5.53].

Figure 5.53

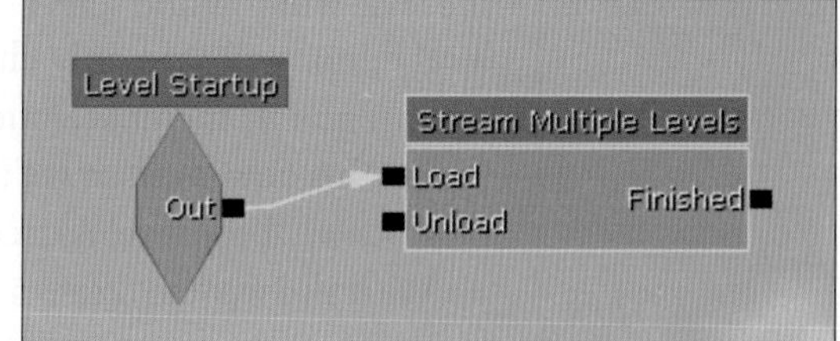


With the Stream Multiple Levels, the lower left of the Kismet editor should update with the nodes properties. Expand the Levels roll-out and add a new item with the green + icon; then type in the name of the streamed

Figure 5.54

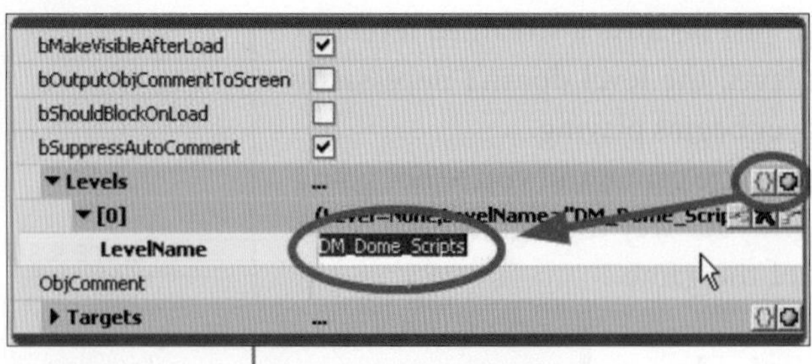


Figure 5.45

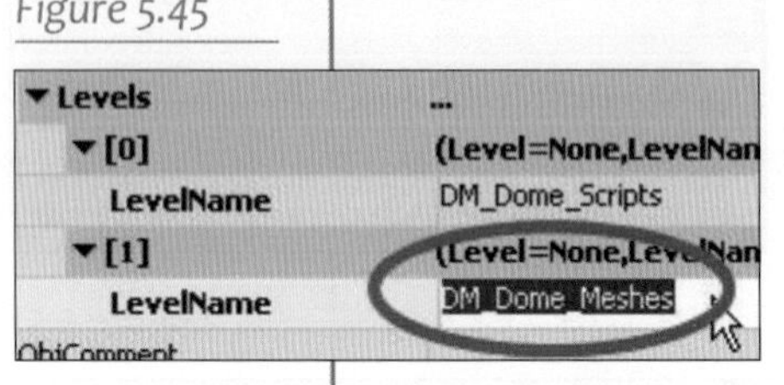


level. In this case DM_Dome_Scripts [Figure 5.54]; this will load in the scripts level when the level starts. You might also notice that bMakeVisibleAfterLoad is checked by default. This means that once the level is loaded, it will be visible. There are instances in which you will want to control when a level is visible, but in this case we want the default behavior.

You'll need to add each of the new streamed levels to this node. Adding a new level is a simple matter of clicking on the green + icon and entering the name of the level into each LevelName slot.

Here's an example of what that might look like [Figure 5.55]. Now, when your persistent level loads, the script streaming level will load with it.

## Level Management

We discussed previously a persistent level with Kismet scripts to run the level. Other streaming levels are associated with the persistent level. The usual hierarchy is as follows:

- DM_Dome.ut3: This is the persistent level that loads the remainder of the level streams.
- DM_Dome_BSP.ut3: This is the location where all of the BSPs are stored.
- DM_Dome_Lights.ut3: This level contains all of the lights for your level.
- DM_Dome_Scripts.ut3: This level contains the remainder of the Kismet scripts that run your level.

The last three levels in the list are where you as the designer will spend most of your time. However, you'll want to set up some additional levels for your artists to work in. DM_Dome_Meshes.ut3 is where you'll want your artists to be working.

At the end of the level building process, the meshes level should be fully populated, and your BSPs should no longer be needed. Once you're at this step of the process, you can remove the BSP.ut3 level from the streaming sequence of base level.

To add in additional levels or layers, we'll use the `create new level` menu as we did with the scripts level. This will create a new empty level. We can either save this new level in the level manager by clicking on the `Save` icon, or we can go to the level window and select `save` there. There's a small catch, though. The `save` in the level editor will save only changes to the active level. That's why there's a `save all open levels` menu selection and corresponding icon. We'll be creating our lighting on this new level, so we'll name the new level "DM_Dome_Lights.ut3"; this will indicate what the level is used for.

We'll also want to create new levels for scripts and another one for static meshes. This is important to remember, to be safe, we can press the save all levels icon. However if you only need to be saving changes to your scripts or your lights you can press the icon on the related level tab. The active level is indicated by the title's text in bold. We can also check out which objects are stored in which level by clicking on the `level coloration` button in the viewport.

### Level Coloration

The `level coloration` button allows you to see which objects might be placed in the wrong level. To change the level in which an object is being stored, select the object, and then select the level it's supposed to be on. Then select the menu in the Generic browser.

To pick the color of a streamed level, click on the Arrow button and choose a color from the color picker dialog [Figure 5.56]. To avoid making accidental changes to a level, click the `lock` icon on to the top left of each streamed level.

With so many people working on the same level at the same time, you might find that you need to make changes in another level. If you see a static mesh in the artist's levels, you can easily copy it and turn it into a moving object in the scripts level. Because scripts cannot communicate across levels, you'll want to move objects you need the scripts to interact with from one streamed level into your level.

Figure 5.56

StreamingLevels_LevelB (2 actors) - CURRENT -
Visible?

In this level we have a room that is streamed in, but there are some objects that are in the incorrect streaming level [Figure 5.57].

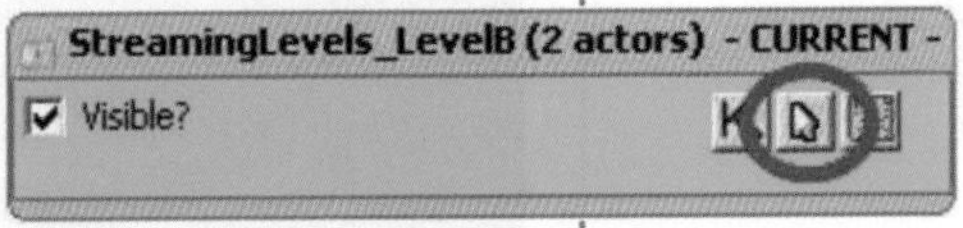

Figure 5.57

Figure 5.58

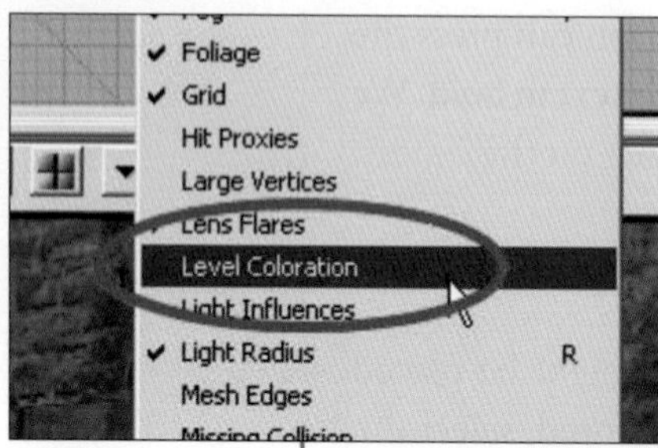


To see which objects are in the wrong stream, we can turn on `Level Coloration` in the `show flags` menu at the top of the perspective viewport [Figure 5.58].

Oops! It looks like we need to move these objects into a different stream if we want them to load in where they're supposed to be [Figure 5.59].

Figure 5.59

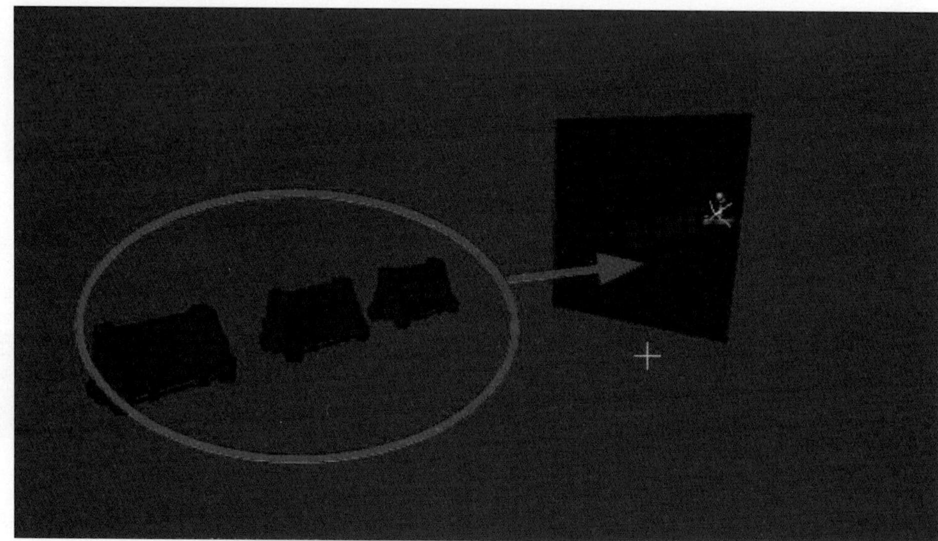

Figure 5.60

Here we can see that the levels are now colored according to the coloration in the level manager window [Figure 5.60]. In this case, we want the objects in the LevelA stream to be moved to the LevelB stream. Select the misplaced objects, change the current level, and then move the objects to the correct stream.

Right-click on the level and select `Make Current` [Figure 5.61].

Figure 5.61

Then, with the errant objects selected, right-click and then select `Move Selected Actors To Current Level`. This will move the objects into the proper level [Figure 5.62].

Figure 5.62

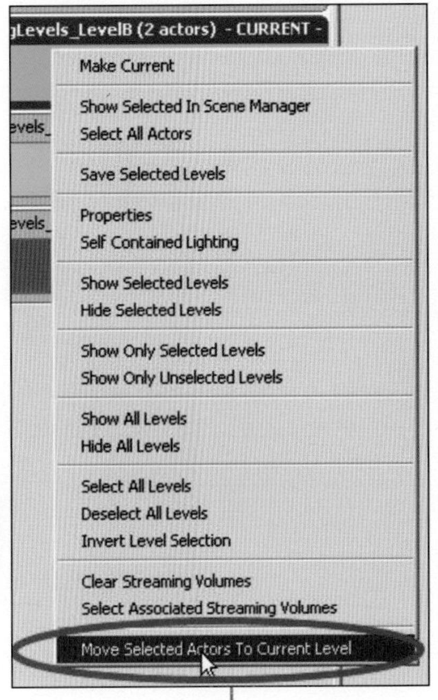


### Merging Levels

Once you've made several isolated tests and find that you need to combine them to allow the scripts to communicate, you'll have to merge the levels together.

Using this tab, you can hide some of the levels before merging them [Figure 5.63]. Doing so will prompt you with a dialog asking where you want to save the new level. This is something you'll want to do only if you want to combine the separate levels into one level. When merging levels with different Kismet sequences, only the persistent level will retain its scripts.

Figure 5.63

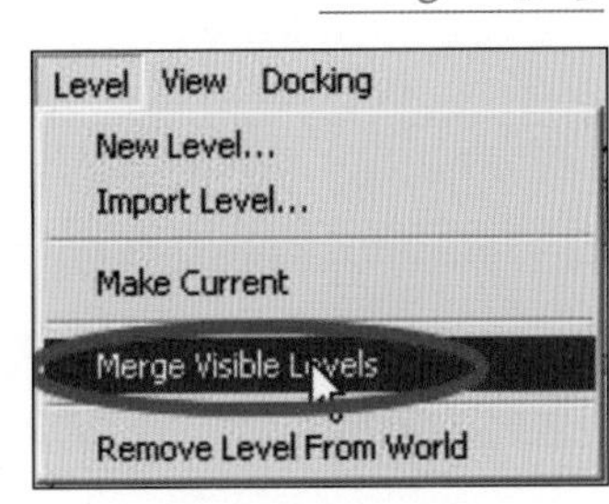


## Review

### Streaming Levels

Once you're ready to ship off your level, merge the levels and cook them. Now they're ready to be distributed!

Management of levels takes a couple of forms. First is the use of levels as layers to separate tasks. Second is the use of levels to control the use of memory. As you finish levels, you'll want to reduce the number of different levels in a given space by merging data and removing unused levels, such as the BSP levels.

A major task of the design process is to keep in mind how you're planning on dividing up your level to maintain order. As you plan your levels, it's also a good idea to write out what sort of levels will be needed for each space—meshes, scripts, static lighting, etc. These are all good things to keep separate from one another.

Planning ahead and looking forward to changing a level's use should also be kept in mind when building scripts. Knowing what parts of a level can be opened and closed off for different uses will help make updating your level faster and easier. A bit of planning ahead of time can save many hours of work later on.

# 6 Events and Triggers: What's Kismet?

*Making Movers Move*

Elevators, doors, monsters and weapons—adding the interactivity to a level is the meat and gristle of level design. Kismet is the tool that allows you to do this quickly and easily. It can be said that doing certain things using a visual tool can get complicated, but keeping the scripting environment easy to understand and organized is a part of the trick when it comes to adding a lot of interactive parts to a level.

Once a level is complete, a Kismet graph may look like a ton of spaghetti or a jumble of circles and squares connected by random lines . Understanding how to read these crazy jumbles of information will become the duty of the diligent Unreal level designer. As an Unreal level designer, your work will focus mainly in either Kismet or Matinee. Both editors allow for a lot of creative freedom, but you'll want to make your work easier by staying organized.

## What to Expect

### Kismet: Destiny—A Predetermined Course of Events

The Kismet tool in Unreal is accessed through a little button at the top of the level editor. Each level has its own Kismet sequence that can be opened in the level manager tab from the Generic browser. This is important to remember for later. The various Kismet sequences can interact with scripts only in their level. This means that a sequence cannot trigger a sequence found in another level. As a part of the practice for your level design, you're going to want to put all of the interactivity into one level.

In a previous project, we added a single Kismet event to spawn a bot—nothing too exciting just yet. Kismet allows us to add so much more than that. Kismet is commonly used to make platforms move, doors open, and monsters and weapons spawn. The various events can be triggered by objects placed in the scene either as trigger objects or trigger volumes.

The triggers can also depend on various conditions met by the player: a switch has been thrown, or a monster has been defeated. These sorts of logical conditions are set up using Kismet. Kismet has a lot of functions that allow you to control the events and manage your player.

Kismet is also easily extended by Unreal script, so when we have a solid grasp of what can be done by default in Kismet, we'll explore a bit about how we can add our own scripts on top of Unreal and create new tools for use in Kismet.

PROJECT

## An Introduction to Kismet—Making a Simple Elevator

Let's take a tour of what can be done in Kismet.

Kismet can spawn bots—we've seen that much. In the same node, we can spawn physics objects and other simple shapes in the world. Kismet is also responsible for handling making platforms move and listening to switches and levers being thrown in the level.

In addition, we can turn on and off lights, spark particles, and even cue sounds to play. The events that are triggered are all managed through Kismet—it's a powerful tool!

Figure 6.1

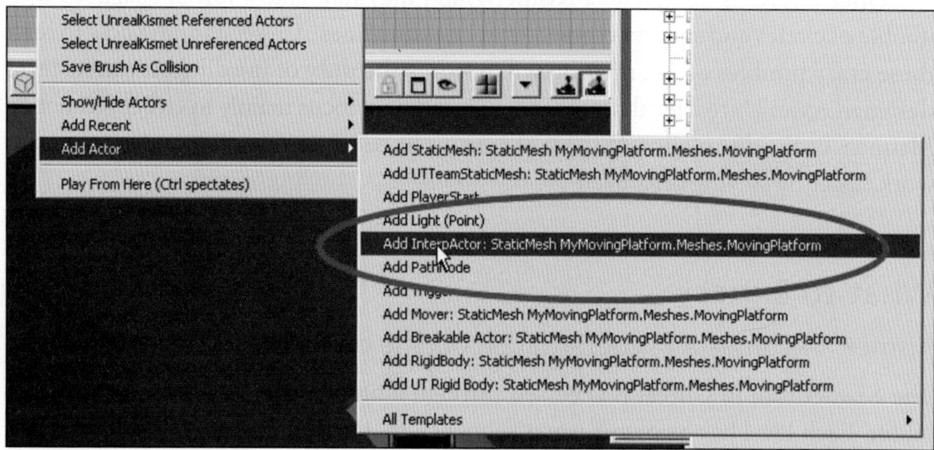


Let's start off with a simple set of BSPs. Open the Elevator project from http://www.akpeters.com/unrealgamedev. Next we'll want to place a static mesh of the elevator platform into the scene. A few things are required to set up a moving object in a scene. A static mesh is an object that remains static in the scene. In other words, a static mesh cannot move. To add a mesh that will move to a scene, you must add an interpolated mesh. Open the MyMovingPlatform.upk from the website and place the object into the scene as an interpolated mesh. Through the right-click menu on the top view, select `Add Actor` → `Add InterpActor` [Figure 6.1].

With the simple platform in place, open the properties editor and expand the `Collision` roll-out. Then set the `CollisionType` to `COLLIDE_BlockAll`

[Figure 6.2]. This setting is required for the newly added mesh to collide with the player. Without BlockRigidBody checked, the new mesh will pass through the player. You'll have to remember this for every moving object that you intend to block the player.

Place the elevator on the ground under the opening in the middle of the little level.

We can also make sure that the platform is exactly under the opening by expanding the Movement roll-out and entering 0,0,-120. It's also good to point out that this object is already set to `PHYS_Interpolating` [Figure 6.3]. This means that the object's position and orientation will be recalculated each frame for the object to remain updated. It's important to remember that for each object that's interpolated, the computer's CPU will have to check the object to make sure it's where it's supposed to be.

Next we'll want an object placed in the scene to trigger the platform's movement. Now we'll add in a trigger object [Figure 6.4]. Place the trigger in the middle of the platform. This will be used to tell the platform to rise when the player interacts with the trigger.

Make sure that the trigger is set to react when the player touches it by changing the Collision Type to `COLLIDE_TouchAll` from the `Collision` roll-out [Figure 6.5]. Now we've got the basic components needed to drive a simple Kismet sequence to lift the platform to the upper level of our level.

Open the level's Kismet sequence and select the trigger in the scene. This will allow you to add the trigger to the Kismet sequence editor.

Right click and add a `New Event Using Trigger_0` → `Touch` [Figure 6.6]. This will create a new `Trigger_0`

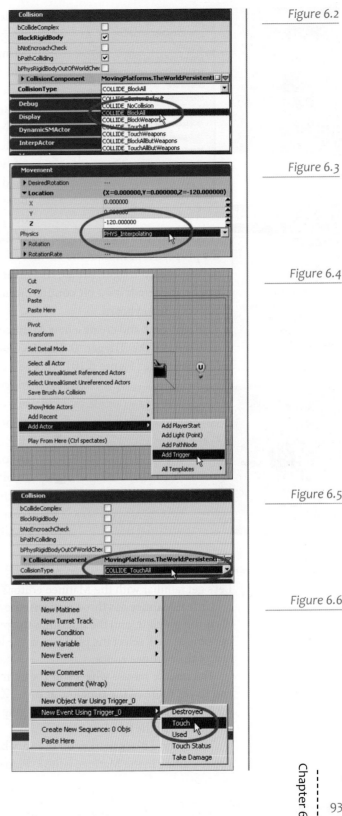

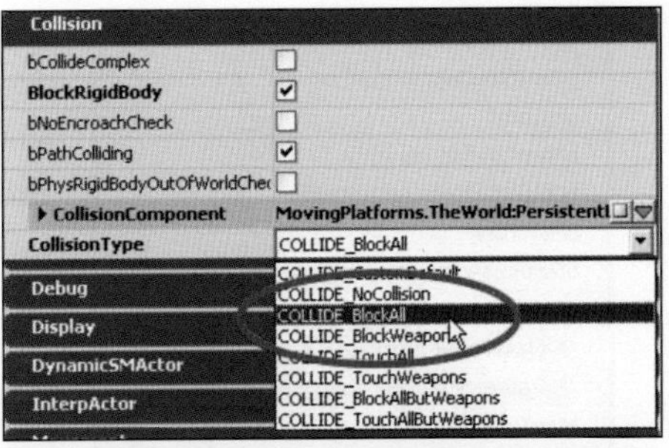


Figure 6.2

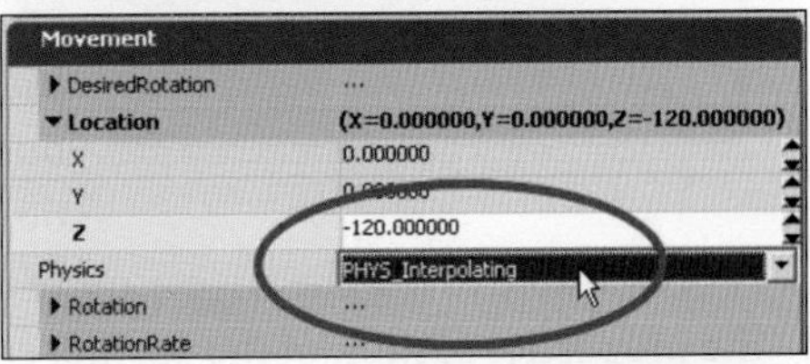


Figure 6.3

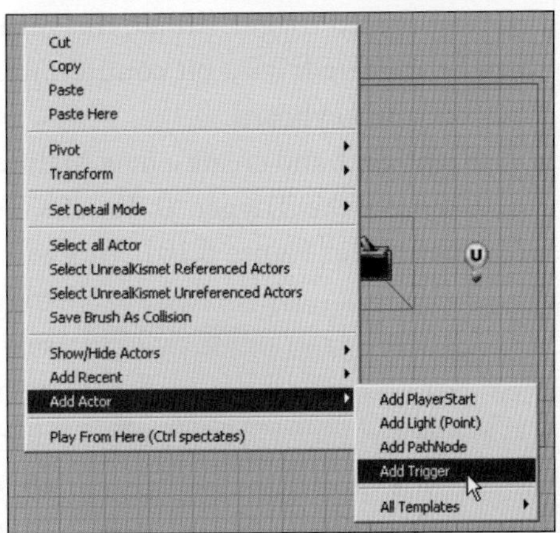


Figure 6.4

Figure 6.5

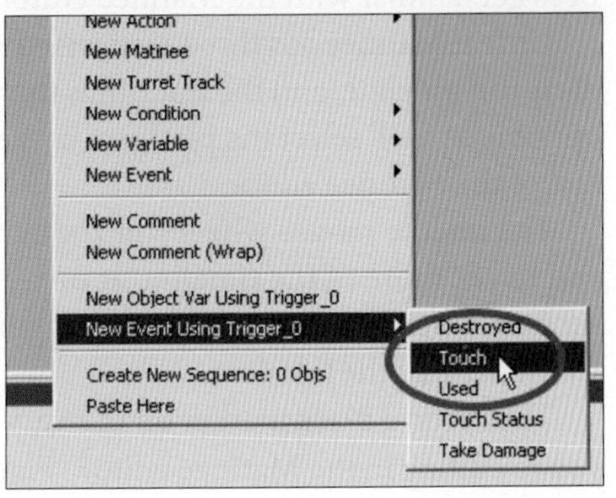


Figure 6.6

Figure 6.7

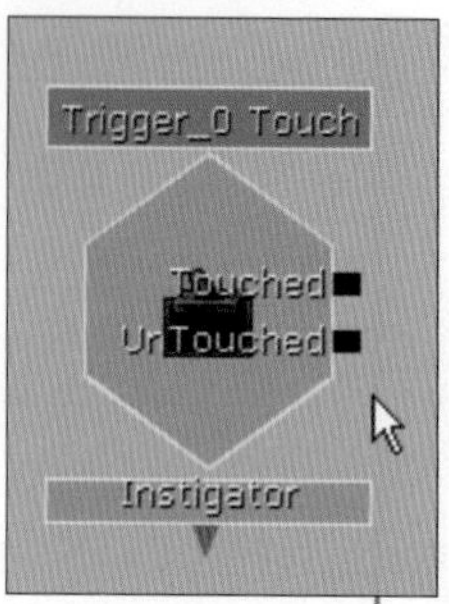


Figure 6.8

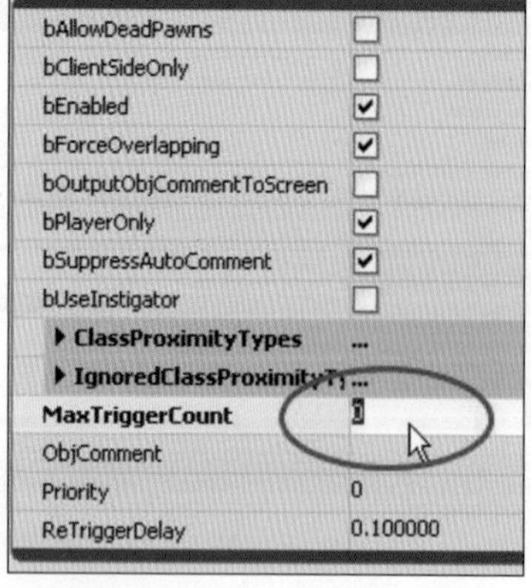


Touch node to the Kismet graph. Events using triggers allow you to begin any function in the Kismet graph. Using the outputs from `Touched` and `UnTouched` allows you to start and stop various sequences [Figure 6.7]. We'll see a simple use of this with the elevator.

Next we'll create a new Matinee node. These nodes are used to move objects around. Later on, you'll see how these Matinee nodes can be used to create elaborate cinematic sequences, but first things first. Let's just use Matinee to lift our platform.

Figure 6.9

To be able to use the trigger more than once, change its `MaxTriggerCount` in the properties section of the Kismet editor and set it to 0 [Figure 6.8]. This doesn't mean never to trigger; rather, this means never to limit how many times the node can be triggered. It's a bit counterintuitive, but it's easier than finding the infinity key on your keyboard.

Right-click and create a new Matinee node [Figure 6.9].

Connect the Trigger_0 Touch's Touched output tab to the Play Tab of the Matinee node [Figure 6.10]. This will tell the Matinee sequence to play when the trigger is touched. So far everything should be self-explanatory. Something you should notice by now is that all output events are on the right side of the nodes, and all of the inputs for a node are on the left. This remains consistent among all of the nodes. Now we have an event, but the Matinee node still has nothing in it to animate. Next we'll open the Matinee node by double-clicking on it.

Figure 6.10

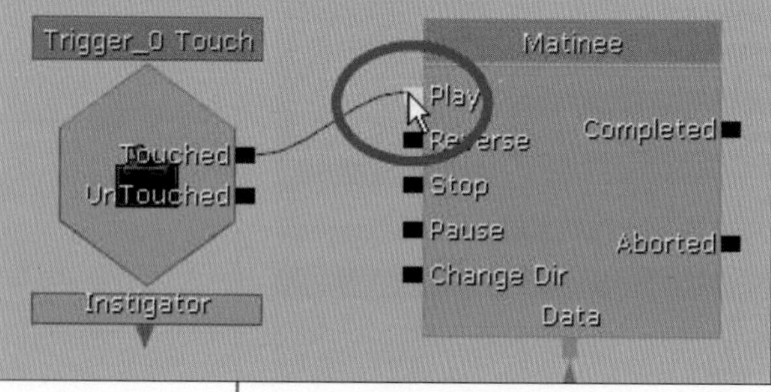


## PROJECT

### Intro to Matinee

Let's get familiar with the Matinee editor's user interface [Figure 6.11].

Unreal Matinee has three sections: the upper section is the Curve editor; the middle is the timeline, and the bottom is the properties for the selected node. To animate our object, we'll select the platform in the level editor and then right-click in the timeline of the Matinee editor.

The middle mouse wheel will zoom in and out the timeline. Zooming out allows you to see more of the timeline at once. Zooming in allows you move key frames in very small steps. Left mouse and dragging in the timeline area scrolls through to different parts of the timeline.

The vertical black marker on the very bottom of the timeline will change the time you're editing in the Matinee editor [Figure 6.12].

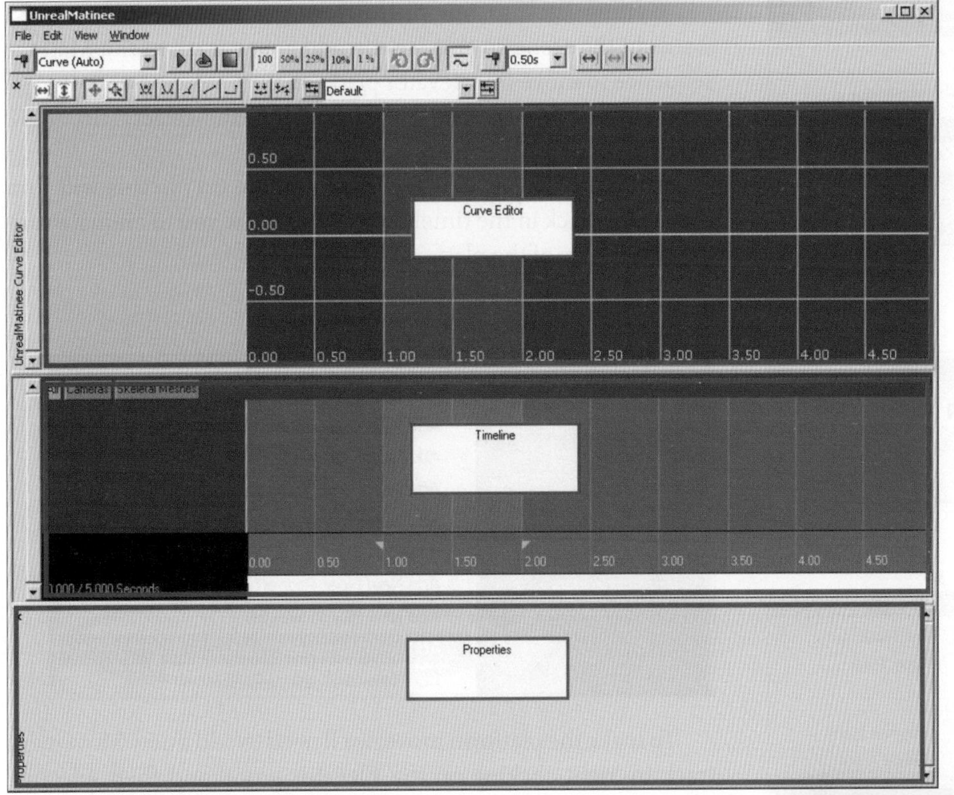


Figure 6.11

Figure 6.12

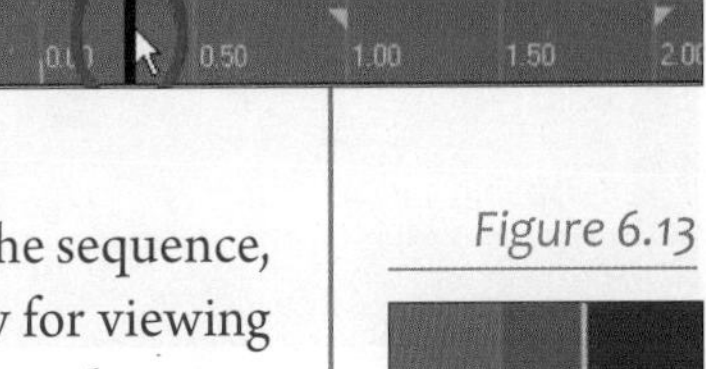

Dragging the red arrow at the far right of the timeline will change the length of the sequence [Figure 6.13].

The tool bar at the top has several sub-groups of icons. Starting at the left is the Add key frame button and a popup menu where you can select what type of interpolation will be used from the key frame [Figure 6.14].

A set of icons will allow you to play the sequence, loop a segment of the sequence, and stop the sequence [Figure 6.15]. Looping the sequence here is only for viewing in the editor. As you might have noticed, there is a green highlighted area in the timeline. The starting and ending points of the green section can be stretched using the little green triangles at the bottom of the timeline. This will change which part of the Matinee sequence is going to be looped when you press the `play loop` button, the center button in the cluster of play icons.

Figure 6.13

The next buttons, which have numbers on them, change the playback speed of the Matinee sequence. Then you have some snap, toggle, and spacing options. Then the last set of buttons, which have arrows on them, will fit the timeline to the view and change the looped area to the length of the sequence.

Figure 6.14

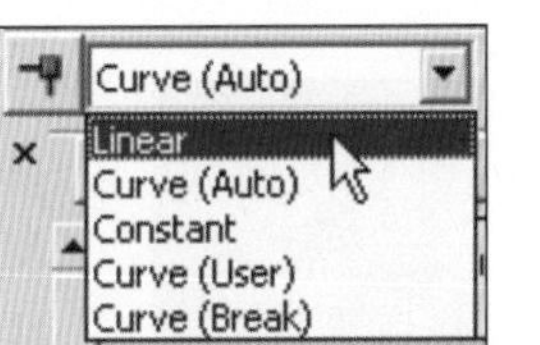


Figure 6.15

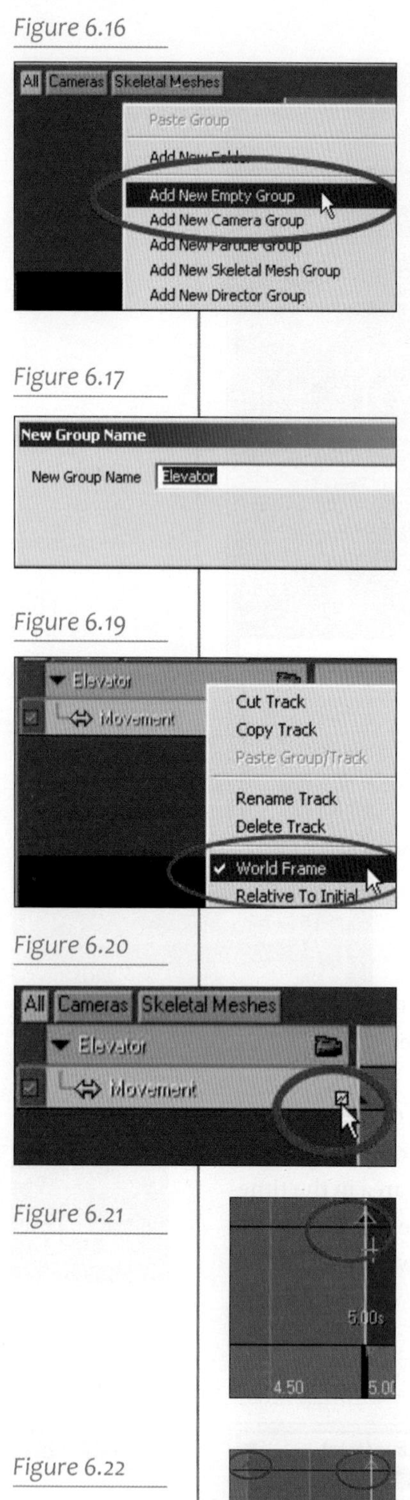
Figure 6.16
Figure 6.17
Figure 6.19
Figure 6.20
Figure 6.21
Figure 6.22

Getting back to our platform, select the `Interpolated mesh` in the scene so that we can add a new track to the Matinee sequence to move our elevator platform.

Right-click on the left darker gray area and select `Add New Empty Group` [Figure 6.16].

Name the new group "Elevator" [Figure 6.17]. This will turn into a new track in the timeline that will allow you to animate various properties of the platform object.

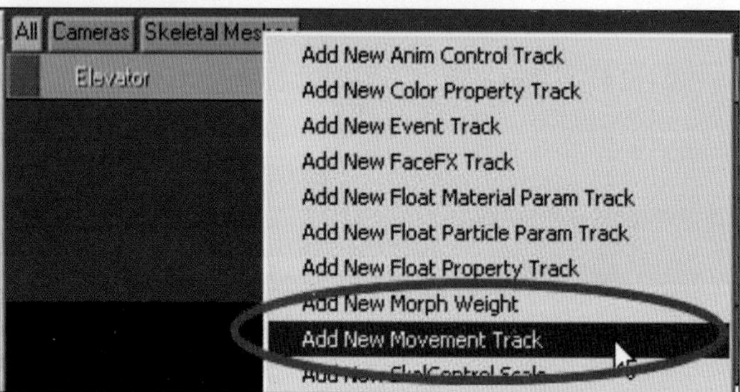

Figure 6.18

To make the platform move, we'll need to add a new Movement track by right-clicking on the Elevator group and then selecting `Add New Movement Track` [Figure 6.18]. The top Anim track is used for character animations involving skeletal meshes. We'll cover that in a later project, so don't use that one for the elevator; it's not the type of animation we can use for moving the platform.

Next, right-click on the new track and change the initial position to `World Frame` [Figure 6.19]. This is a bit hard to explain, but if the track is animating an object, this will force the object to return to where it was first placed in the level by the level designer. `Relative to Initial` will play an animation from wherever the object in question happens to be. The difference between `World Frame` and `Relative to Initial` will be explained once we get a bit deeper into how Matinee works.

To view our object's movement in the curve editor, click on the little icon on the lower right of the Movement track [Figure 6.20]. This will add the Movement track's curves to the curve editor section of the Matinee editor.

Set a key frame at the end of the timeline by dragging the play-head to the end of the time line [Figure 6.21]. Click on the Movement track and then press enter. Add two more key frames at 2 seconds and 3 seconds [Figure 6.22].

To be more precise about where the key frames are placed, you can adjust the time by right-clicking on the key frame and selecting `Set Time` [Figure 6.23].

Figure 6.23

This will allow you to change the key frame's time [Figure 6.24].

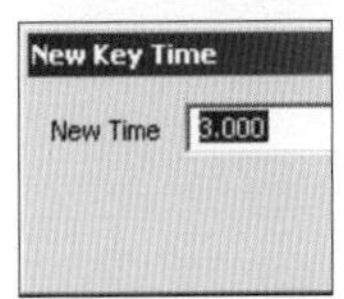


Figure 6.24

Next we'll want to change the values of each key frame. Our objective is to change the Z-height of the platform. To make the curve we're adjusting easier to see, we'll hide the X and the Y curves by clicking off the first two icons shown here [Figure 6.25].

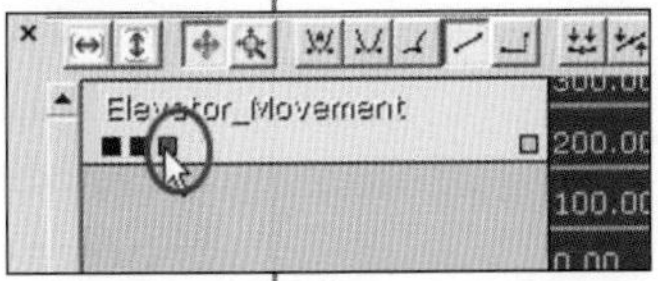

Figure 6.25

You'll be left with a single line in the curve editor.

Right-click on the middle two key frames and select `Set Value` [Figure 6.26]; set the value to 120 [Figure 6.27].

Figure 6.26

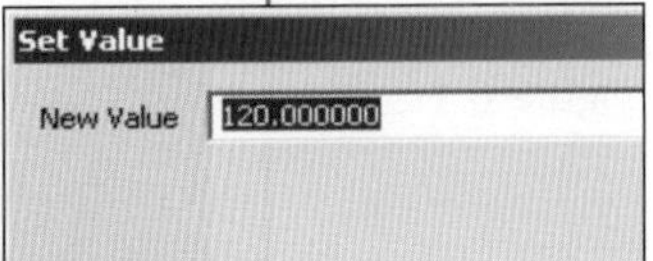


Figure 6.27

By default, your curve might look a bit like Figure 6.28. As this is, your platform will accelerate

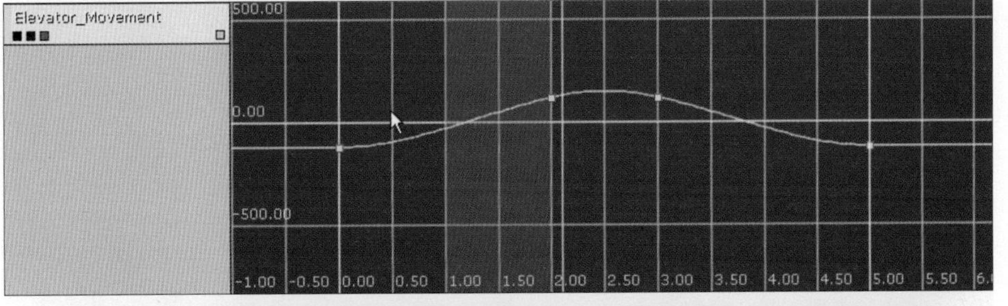


Figure 6.28

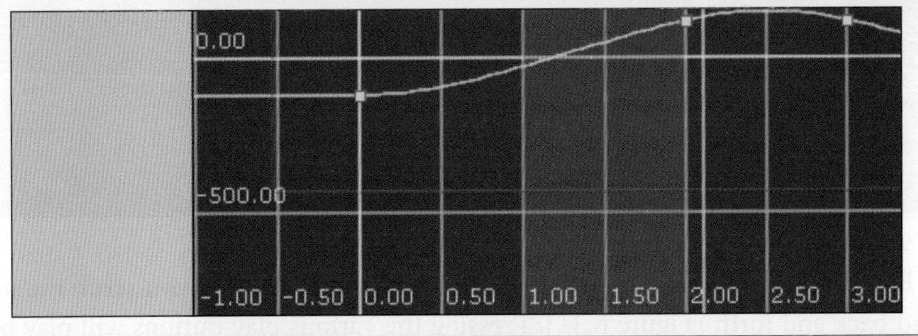


Figure 6.29

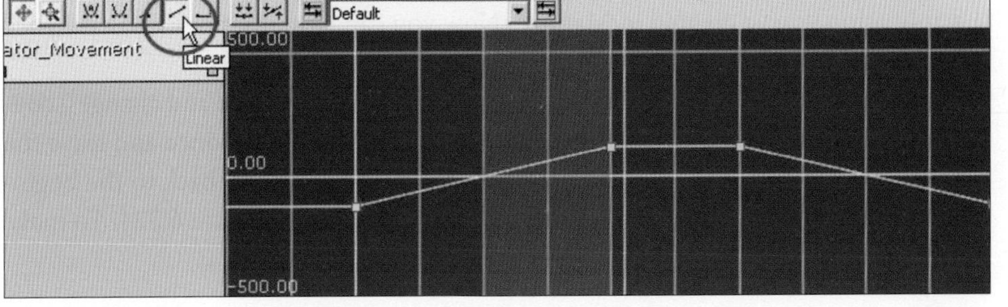


Figure 6.30

up, then actually rise up a bit from the second level, and then settle down. Then the platform will slowly descend again. The behavior we want is for the platform to stop at the top, wait, and then return down.

Hold down Ctrl+Alt and then drag a rectangle over the key frames [Figure 6.29].

This will allow you to select all the key frames at the same time. This sort of curve management is going to be useful once you've got several objects in the scene moving around at the same time.

With the four key frames selected, click on the Linear button at the top of the curve editor [Figure 6.30], and the timeline's curve will straighten out. With the line between the top two key frames flat, the platform will not be moving. To experiment, you can select an individual key frame and click on the different curve types to change the speed of the platform's ascent and descent through the air.

Figure 6.31

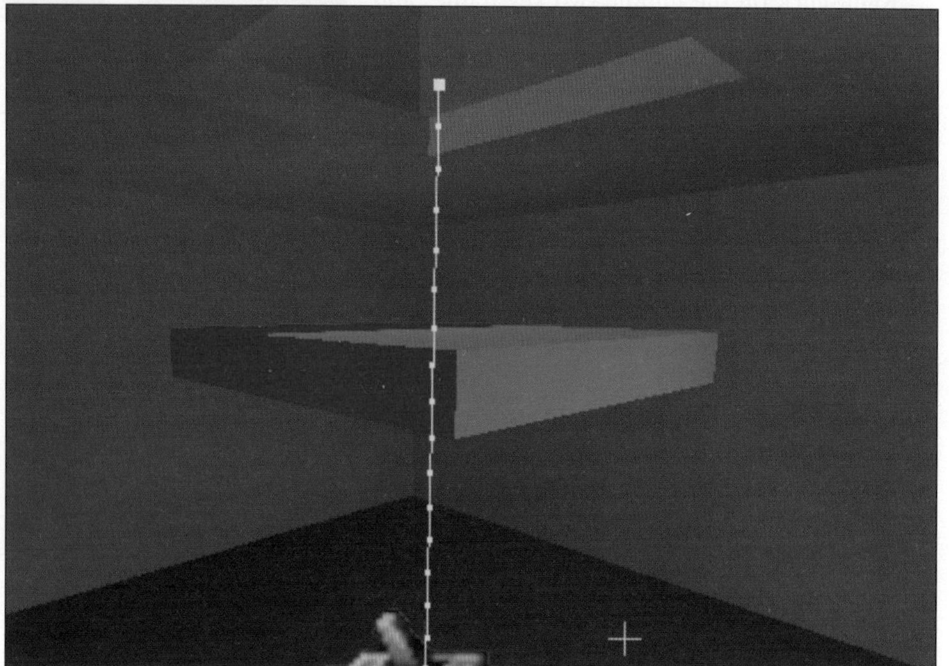

Back in the level editor, you can see the platform moving as you scrub the play-head back and forth [Figure 6.31]. Pressing the various play buttons will play back the animation you've created in Matinee. Now you can close Matinee and save your level.

Before we're done in the Kismet editor, select the Matinee node and change a couple of the parameters. By default, the Matinee sequence will play once and leave the play-head at the end of the timeline. To have the play-head jump back to the beginning of the movement sequence, turn on `bRewindOnPlay` [Figure 6.32]. To make

Figure 6.32

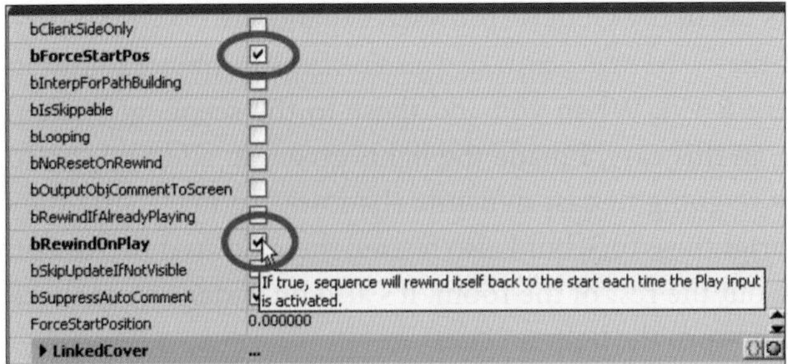


Figure 6.33

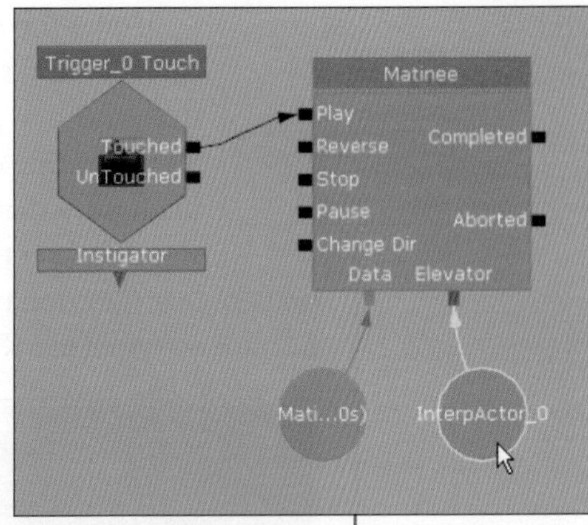


sure that the platform always starts the movement from the same position, turn on `bForceStartPos`; this will ensure that the platform will always behave the same way when the Matinee node is triggered.

Figure 6.34

One thing that's important to notice is that your Matinee node has grown a new chunk of data called Elevator [Figure 6.33]. Even more interesting is that this chunk of data happens to point to our platform. This chunk of data got its name from the name we entered when we created the track in the timeline.

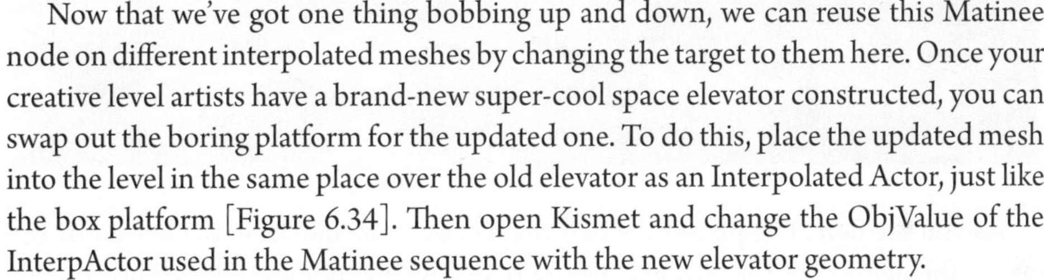

Now that we've got one thing bobbing up and down, we can reuse this Matinee node on different interpolated meshes by changing the target to them here. Once your creative level artists have a brand-new super-cool space elevator constructed, you can swap out the boring platform for the updated one. To do this, place the updated mesh into the level in the same place over the old elevator as an Interpolated Actor, just like the box platform [Figure 6.34]. Then open Kismet and change the ObjValue of the InterpActor used in the Matinee sequence with the new elevator geometry.

At this point, you should be able to click the `rebuild all` button in the level editor and hop on your elevator. There are no rails, so you might slip off the first time.

PROJECT

## Adding Some Logic to Kismet

To get started with this project, open the `SwitchesRoom.ut3` provided on the disk. This set-up involves only two rooms separated by a door. We're going to take a look at triggering multiple events with a single switch. Then we're going to open a door using two switches. We're also going to add in some new `PointLightToggleable` objects to see how those are used. Kismet has a lot of conditional nodes that will send out an event only when the condition is met.

First we'll want to set up the parts in the scene. To begin, you're going to want to add two triggers to the room. The door is already in place and is referenced from the `SwitchRoom_Resources.upk`; this is the only other object in this scene.

Figure 6.35

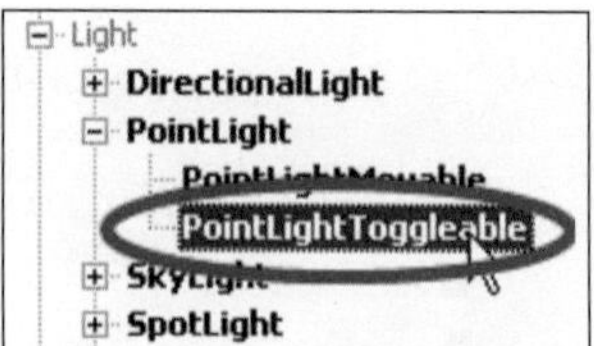


Under the Actors tab in the Generic browser, expand the PointLight category and select the PointLightToggleable sub-object found in that category [Figure 6.35]. When you add these to the scene, give them an interesting color; in this case, I made the lights green. In addition, I also made sure that they're going to cast dynamic shadows. To make sure they show up, I set their brightness to 3, but I also resized their radius down to 256 units so that they don't blow out the rest of the room. It's also important to uncheck bEnabled. We'll use Kismet to turn the light on later.

Figure 6.36

As you see here, I've placed the two triggers over the blocks in the left room and placed the lights over the triggers [Figure 6.36]. At the moment, there's no connection between the lights and the triggers. For testing, I like to show the triggers when playing the game. This makes testing our scene a bit easier. To keep the trigger showing in the game, expand the display roll-out and uncheck bHidden [Figure 6.37].

Open the level's Kismet sequence editor and right-click to add a New Event Using Trigger_0 → Touch [Figure 6.38]. Add in a New Action → Toggle → Toggle [Figure 6.39]. There are other types of toggles, but we'll start off with the most basic version for now.

Figure 6.38

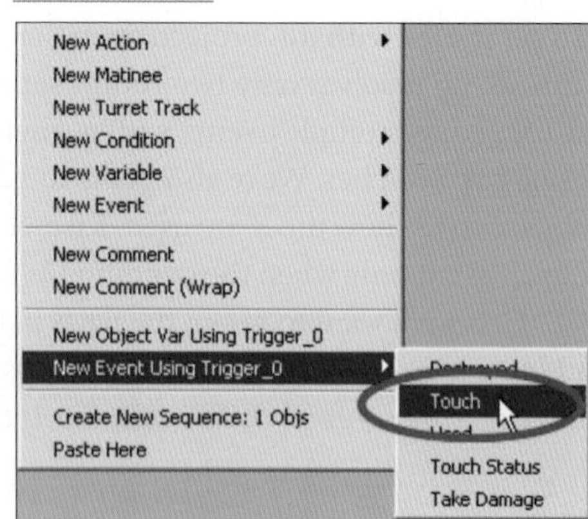


Figure 6.37

| Display | |
|---|---|
| bHidden | ☐ |
| DrawScale | 1.00000 |
| ▸ DrawScale3D | (X=1.000000,Y=1.000000,Z=1.000000) |
| ▸ PrePivot | (X=0.000000,Y=0.000000,Z=0.000000) |

We're also going to need to add in our first trigger and the light above it.

Select the `PointLightToggleable` in the level editor; then, back in Kismet, right-click and add a `New Object Var Using PointLightToggleable` to the Kismet sequence [Figure 6.40]. This is how the reference to the object in the scene gets connected in Kismet. Unless you create this object, Kismet will not know which object you're trying to communicate with.

Then we're going to add in the trigger under the light, as we did in the previous project. Once all three pieces are in the Kismet editor, attach the Touched event output from the trigger to the Turn On input tab of the Toggle node [Figure 6.41]. This will turn on an object attached to the Target tab of the toggle. In this case, we're going to attach the `PointLightToggleable` object to the target of the Toggle node.

Figure 6.39

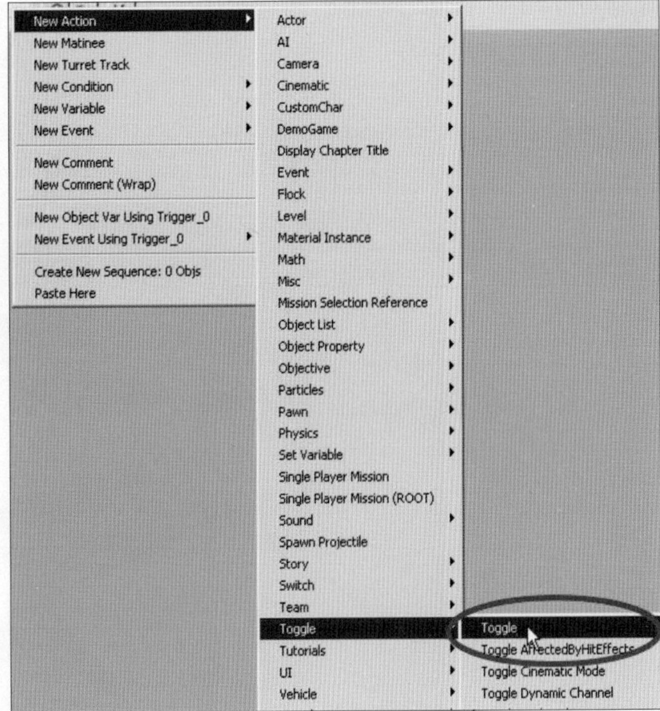


Figure 6.40

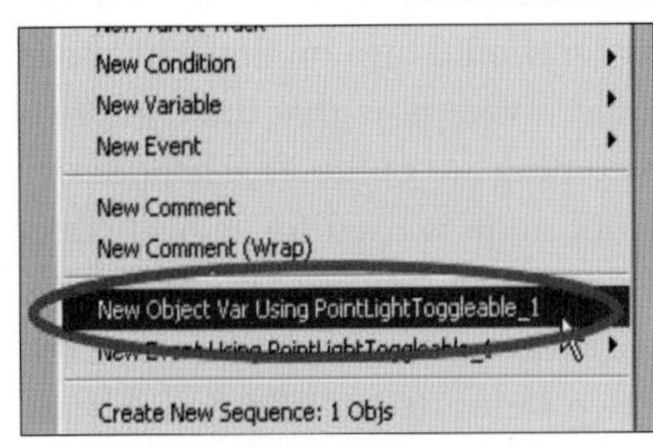


Figure 6.41

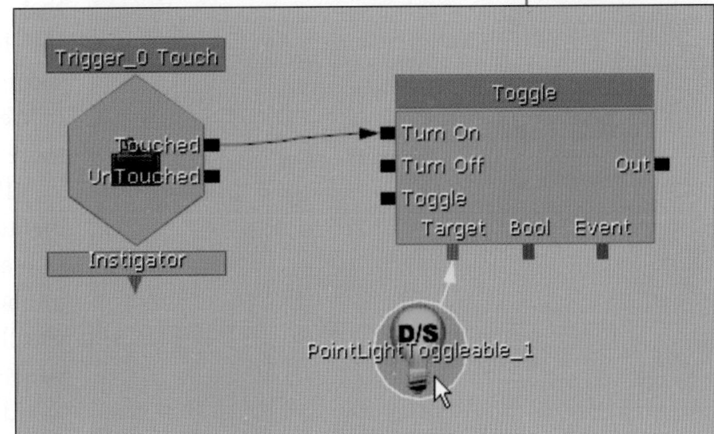


When you run the level and touch the trigger, the light will turn on—pretty straightforward, I hope [Figure 6.42]. I'll leave it up to you to hook up the other light and trigger in a similar fashion.

Figure 6.42

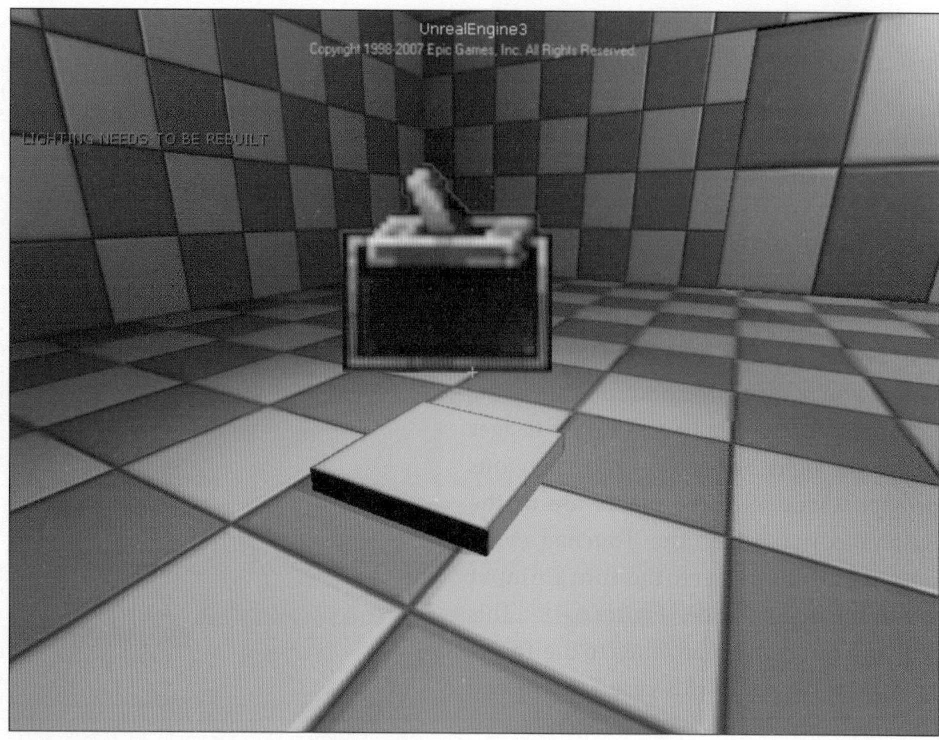


Figure 6.43

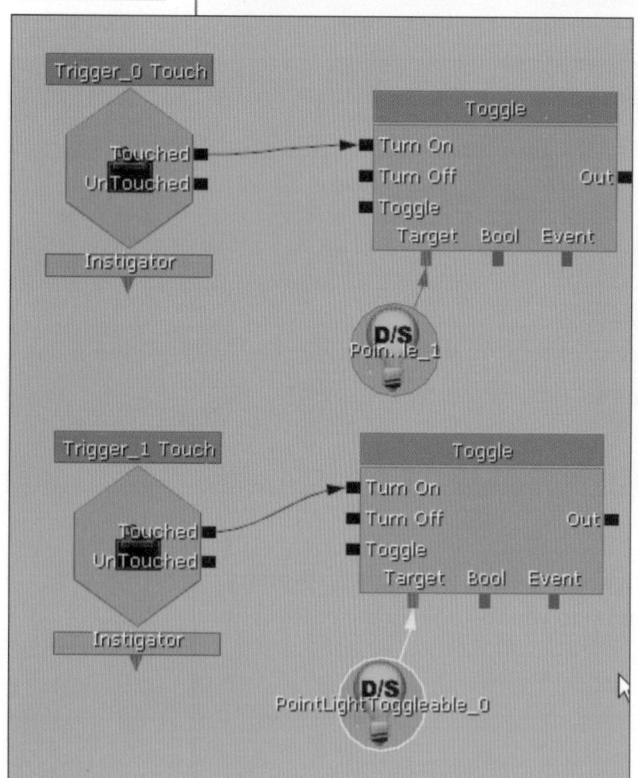


You should now have a pair of sequences that look like Figure 6.43. The first trigger should turn on the light above it, and the second trigger should turn on the light above it. We should notice now that there are two more tabs coming out of the Toggle nodes.

The Bool node is used for logical statements. Bool is shorthand for Boolean. Booleans are bits of data that can only exist in one of two states: true or false. Bools are usually a programmer tool, but as a designer, you're going to need to dive a bit into the world of programming to keep control over your game.

By default, the node tells any variable under the Bool to be false. When an event comes in to the Turn On tab, the Bool will set any variable under it to true. This sort of information isn't documented anywhere, so you'll just have to take my word that this is the case.

To make use of a Bool, we need to add one to the Kismet editor. Right-click and select `New Variable` → `Bool` from the popup menu [Figure 6.44]. To add in the logic to the Kismet sequence, add two Bool variables to the editor and connect each one to a toggle node.

Figure 6.44

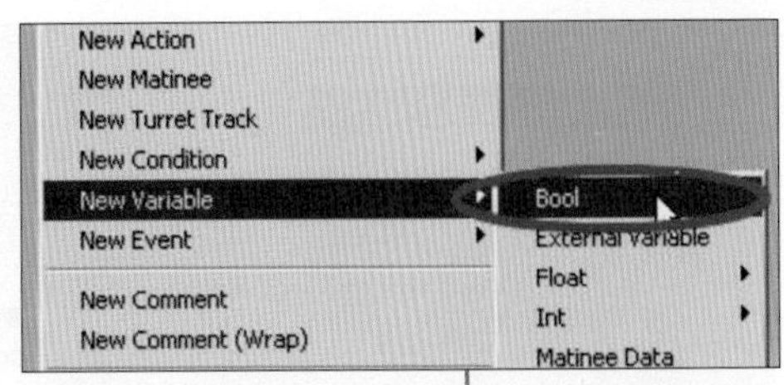


The Kismet sequence should end up like Figure 6.45. When the level starts, both lights will be off, and both variables will be set to false. Now we're going to make use of these Bools by comparing their values. Right-click and select `New Condition` → `Comparison` → `Compare Bool` from the popup menu [Figure 6.46].

Figure 6.45

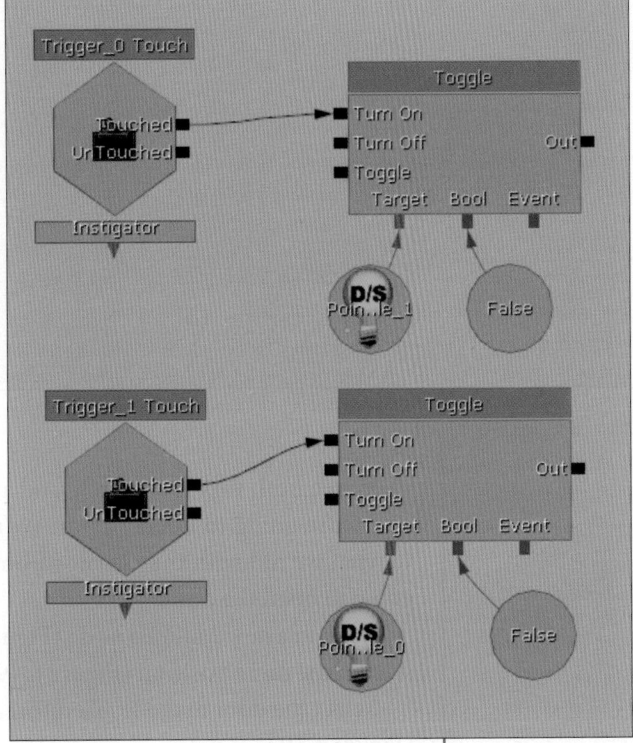


This will drop a new Compare Bool node into our Kismet sequence. Hooking this up to the logic system is simple as well: connect both Out events from the Toggles to the In tab on the Compare Bool node. Then connect both of the Bool variables to the Bool data tab on the Compare Bool node in the scene. A Compare Bool sends out an event from the True tab when all of the Bools connected to it are the same. If one of the variables doesn't match, then an event is sent from the false event output tab.

Let's step through how this works. When the level starts, both Boolean nodes are false. However, the Compare Bool node doesn't send out an event from the true output tab. Why is that? Conditions need to be told when to check up on their given task. The trigger

Figure 6.46

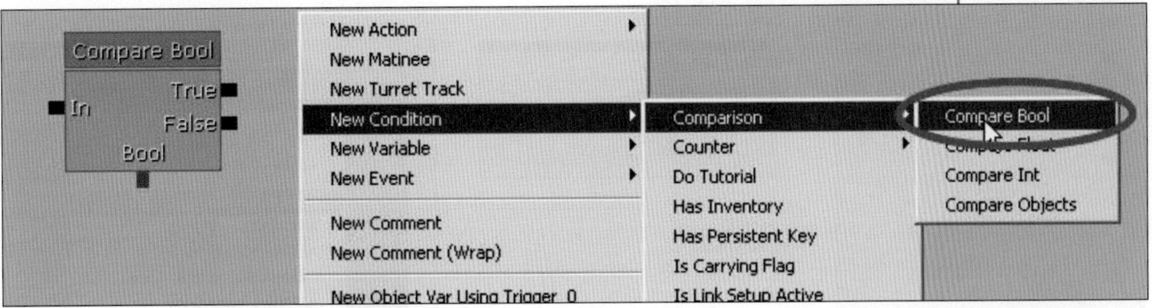

Figure 6.47

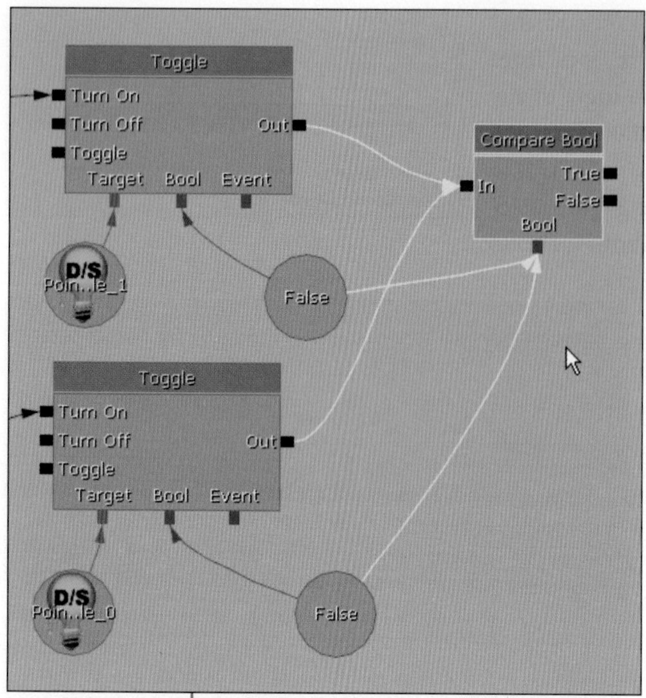


source is the Switch Touch event. The black lines that connect the nodes carry signals to each node telling the nodes to update.

If we were to add in a Level Loaded and Visible event, and connect that to the In tab on the Compare Bool node, it would then update, and then it would see that both variables are false. Then it would push out an event through the true output tab. Because the node never gets a signal until we touch a switch, it knows it doesn't need to update.

When you touch the first switch, it changes the variable to true. Then the signal from the toggle is sent out to the Compare Bool, which then updates and reads a false, because one variable is true and the other is false. It's not until both switches have been touched that both variables will match. Then, when the second switch is touched, the Compare Bool updates with true because both variables match [Figure 6.47].

When both variables match, and an event tells the Compare Bool to send a signal out, we're going to open a door. We're going to do something similar for our door to what we did with the elevator from the previous project, but this time we're only going to open the door.

Drop in a new Matinee node [Figure 6.48]; then make sure that its going to always start in the same position [Figure 6.49].

Select the door in the level editor; and back in Matinee, add in a new empty group [Figure 6.50].

Figure 6.48

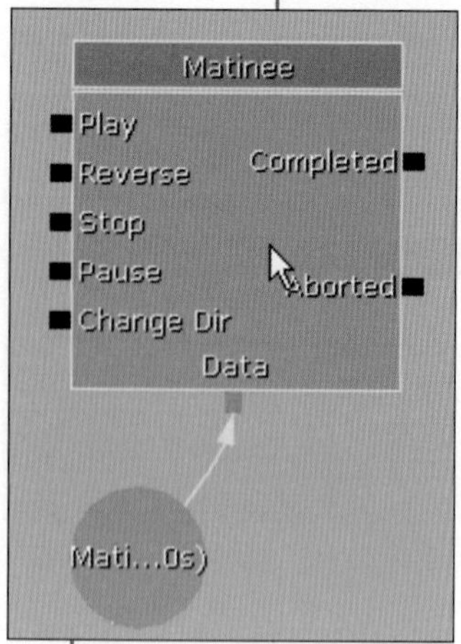


Figure 6.49

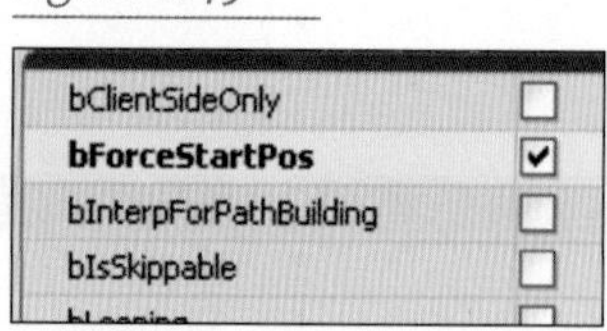


Figure 6.50

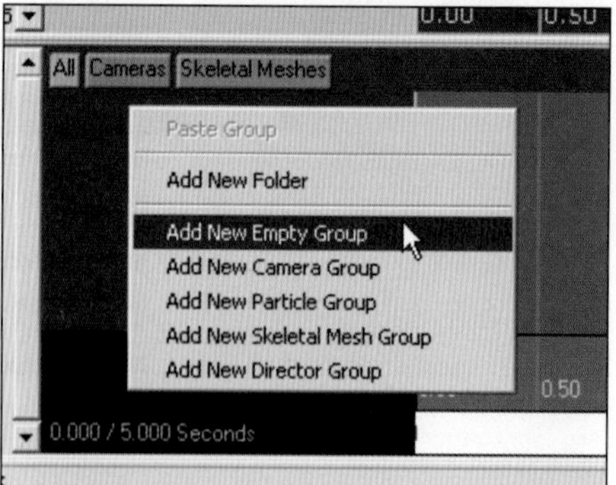

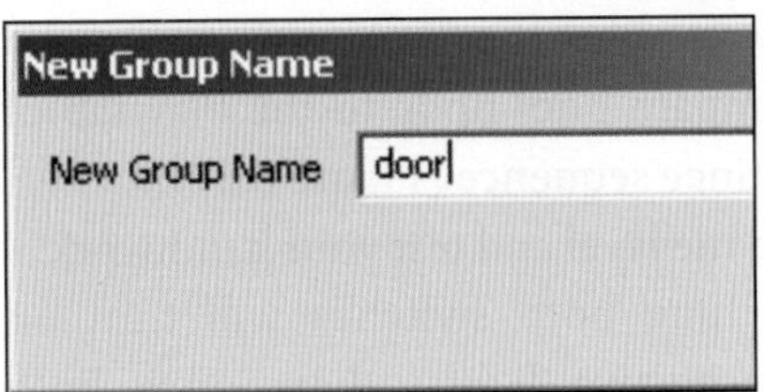


Figure 6.51

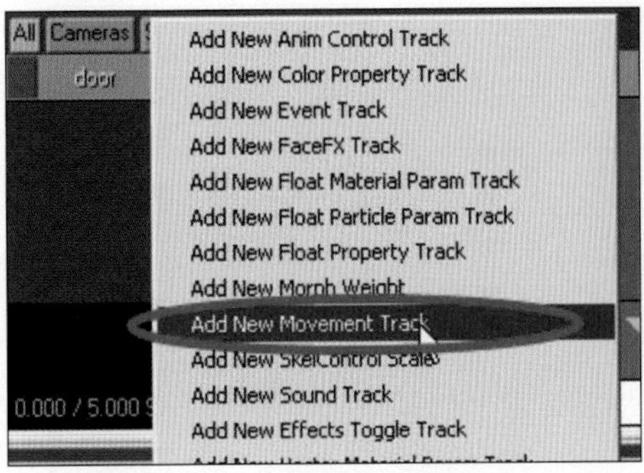


Figure 6.52

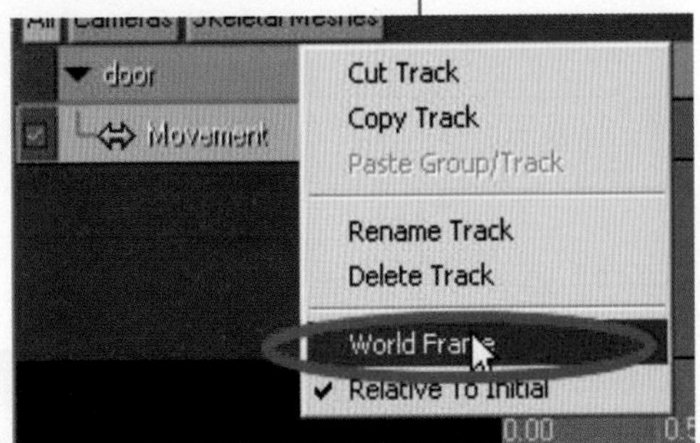


Figure 6.53

Name the new group "door" [Figure 6.51]; now we can animate the door sliding open.

Add in a new movement track under the door [Figure 6.52].

Double check that the door is set to open from the same place in the world every time the Matinee sequence is run [Figure 6.53].

Move the play-head in the Matinee editor to about 2 seconds [Figure 6.54].

Slide the door open [Figure 6.55].

Then, with the movement track highlighted, hit `enter` to add a key frame [Figure 6.56].

Figure 6.54

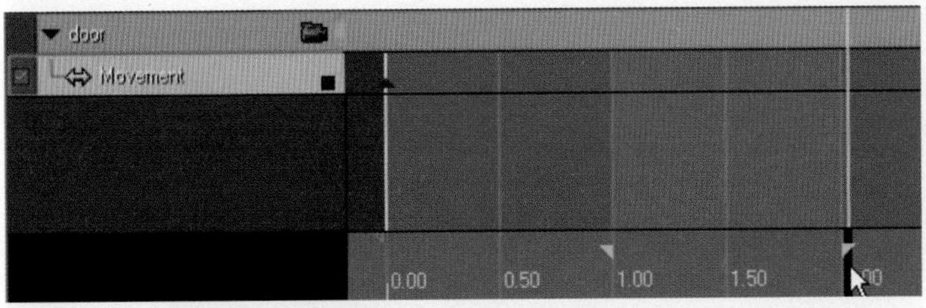

Figure 6.55

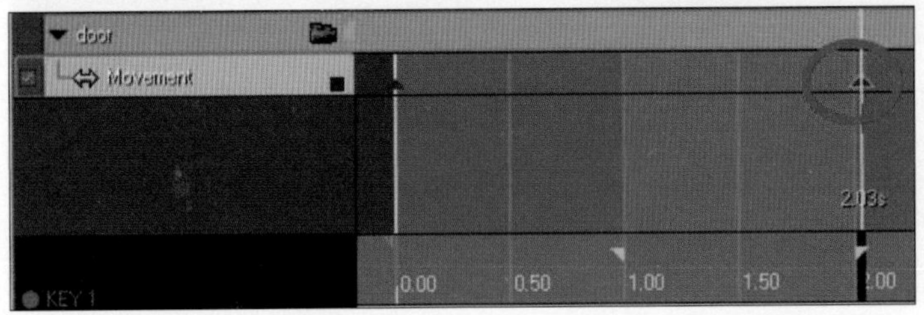


Figure 6.56

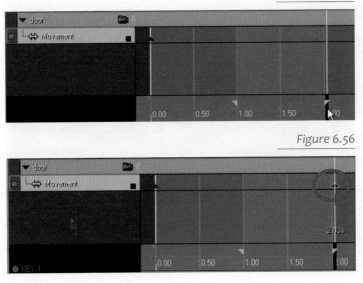

Figure 6.57

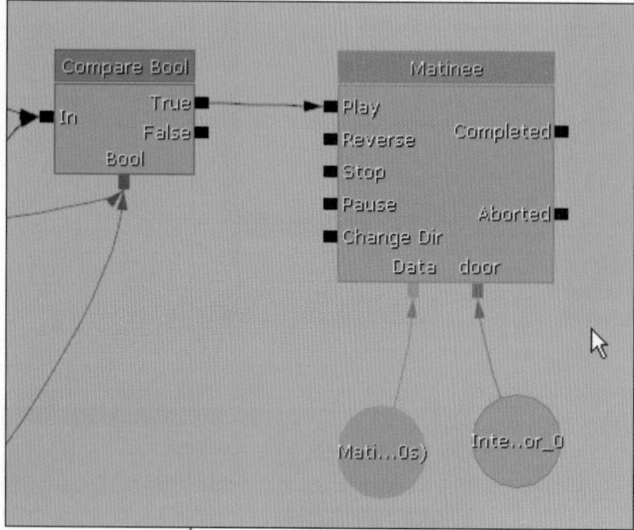


Now connect the True output tab from the Compare Bool node to the Play tab of the Matinee sequence [Figure 6.57].

Save the level and test your handiwork.

Touching both switches will turn on their respective lights; then, once both switches have been touched, the door will open [Figure 6.58]. One more thing: let's make the door close.

Add a trigger to the other side of the door [Figure 6.59].

Add in a New Event with the new trigger [Figure 6.60].

Connect our new switch to the reverse tab of the Matinee sequence [Figure 6.61].

Figure 6.58

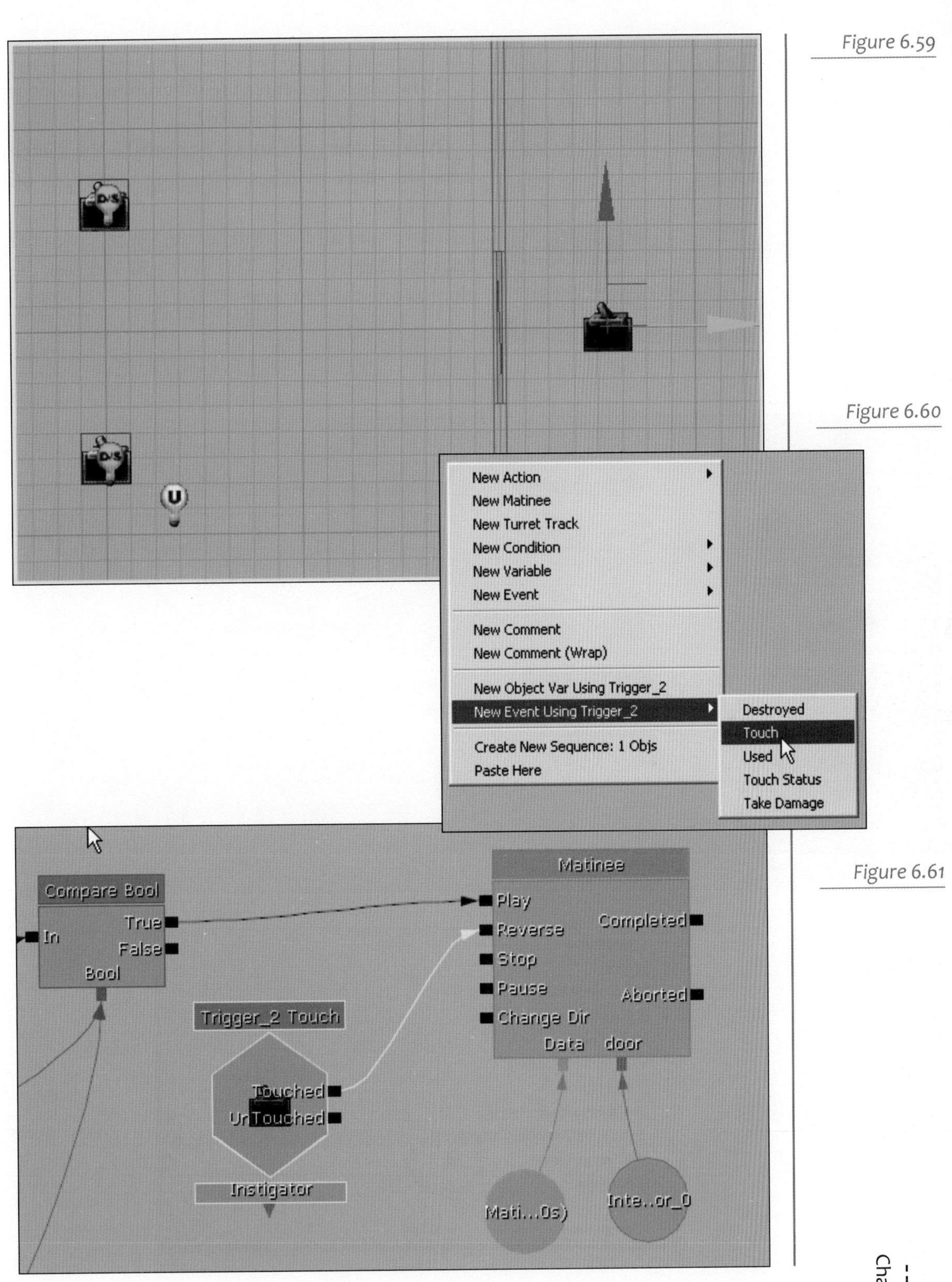
New Action
New Matinee
New Turret Track
New Condition
New Variable
New Event
New Comment
New Comment (Wrap)
New Object Var Using Trigger_2
New Event Using Trigger_2
Create New Sequence: 1 Objs
Paste Here
Destroyed
Touch
Used
Touch Status
Take Damage
Compare Bool
In
True
False
Bool
Matinee
Play
Reverse
Stop
Pause
Change Dir
Completed
Aborted
Data
door
Trigger_2 Touch
Touched
UnTouched
Instigator
Mati...0s)
Inte..or_0

*Figure 6.59*

*Figure 6.60*

*Figure 6.61*

Figure 6.62

Now when you enter the other room, the door closes behind you [Figure 6.62].

Now, if you want to, you can make the switch reset the other switches by turning them both off [Figure 6.63].

Make sure all the switches are set to unlimited triggers [Figure 6.64]. This way you can test the door as often as you want.

Figure 6.63

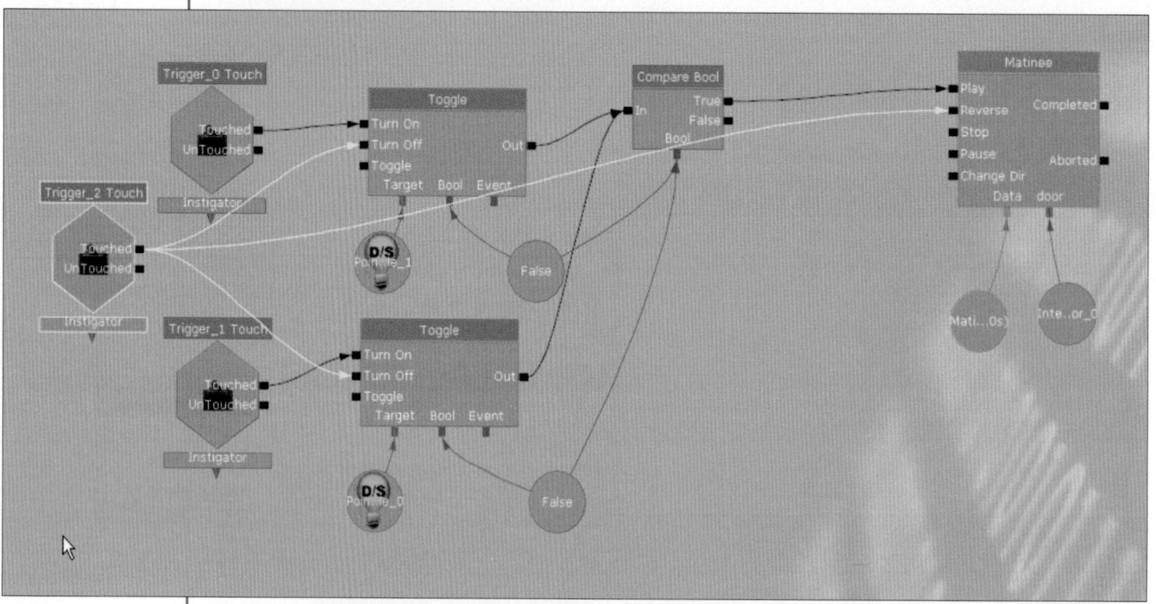


Figure 6.64

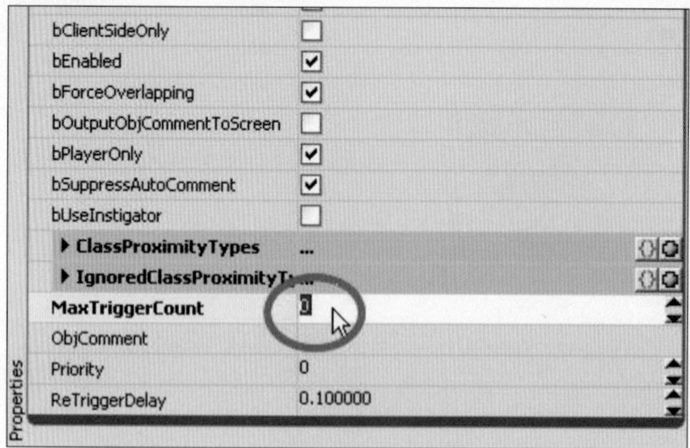

## Making Things Move

So far we've covered only the basics of what Kismet can do. We've added triggers to the scene that then activate Matinee sequences. These Matinee sequences enable interpolated objects to move around and allow us to create interesting behaviors. Using variables and conditions, we can manage what a player needs to do to open a door.

Keeping in mind that these projects have made use of just a few of the tools in Kismet, you should feel that you have enough knowledge to begin to explore the rest of the nodes in the Kismet editor. Conditions and events are labeled as to what they do. Color coding indicates what types of variables the conditions expect. In your own time, you should make an effort to explore the various uses of the different nodes available in Kismet.

# 7 User Interfaces and Menus

A user interface (UI) includes everything that exists on the screen that isn't inside of the game level itself. Objects such as menus, pop-up dialogs, icons representing weapons, for example, can all be considered parts of the user interface. It's time to start making your own dialogs and menus.

Don't get trapped into thinking that these UI objects are only for changing screen resolutions and texture quality settings. The UI is used to display health bars, weapon icons, and more. In addition, when you travel through a game, you can tell the player how and what to do by displaying various dialog screens and information boxes.

## What to Expect

So far we've been working on making the inside of the game more interesting. A big part of what completes the gaming experience is adding the front end and some additional information for the player to see. Things like popup tutorials that tell players what they need to do to play your game are essential. Menus for gathering multiplayer games and setting up various game configurations need to be built before you can distribute a mod and call it complete.

In Unreal editor, the UI is made of three parts: the widgets, the layout, and Kismet scripts to tie them together and add behavior. The widgets are what you'll want an artist to put together. These include the buttons, sliders, and health bars. You'll assemble the layout and apply the appropriate Kismet sequences to give the widgets their functionality.

While playing, you'll have what is called a HUD, or Heads Up Display, drawn on the screen. The HUD is used to tell you what items you have in your inventory and various bits of information related to the status of your character. We'll dive into how that works in a later chapter.

There have been some strides toward reduced HUD experiences in some titles. Elimination of the need for icons, text popping up, and health bars has been tried for many years, with different degrees of success. This sort of interactivity is difficult to design and even more difficult to implement. While I do suggest that you avoid a HUD-less interface for your first mod, it's important to keep in mind that too much HUD can be distracting as well.

## Getting Started

Building a GUI (Graphics User Interface) for an Unreal game can be quite simple. You can have basic buttons that lead to new screens with more buttons. The editor allows you to add tabs, columns, check boxes, radio buttons, sliders, and all sorts of lists. Of course, the more complex the GUI, the more time it will take to build it, so we'll stick to the basics for now.

The Unreal editor has a complete set of tools for editing HUDs and menus. Buttons, menus, lists, and check boxes can easily be arranged using the UI scene editor. Using the UI scene editor tool in UnrealEd, you can se tup buttons with custom graphics and functions quickly and easily. Collectively, these elements are called widgets.

When you build your UI elements, keep in mind that the game can be played at many different screen resolutions. As the dimensions and resolutions of the screen change, the placement of your buttons will change as well. The UI scene editor provides various alignment and grouping tools to allow you to manage how your buttons will flow when displayed at different screen resolutions.

If you've ever built a webpage, some of this might sound familiar. Tags that allow you to align elements to the left or right of the screen are used in a similar way inside of UnrealEd. It's also important to remember to test your GUI at various resolutions to ensure that none of the buttons fall off screen. Thankfully, the UI scene editor has a simple way to visualize how your GUI will be displayed at the different screen resolutions.

PROJECT

### A Basic Button That Closes Itself

To start, let's take a short tour of the UI scene editor. To create a new UI scene, start by right-clicking in the Generic browser to select a new UI Scene. We'll call our new UI scene "TutorialUIScene," and we'll create a package called "UIScenes." We'll put the UI scene into a new "UILayouts" group [Figure 7.1].

Figure 7.1

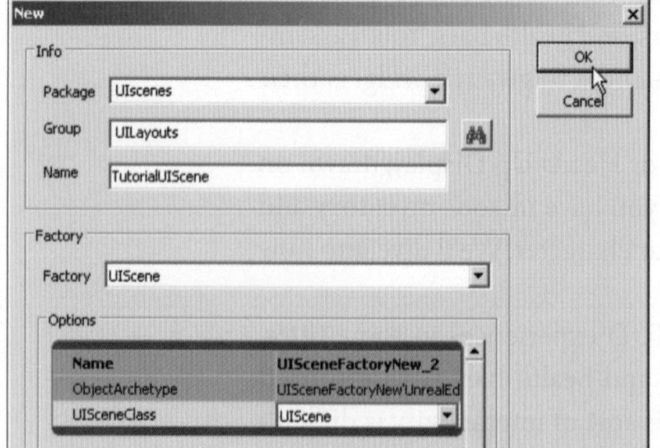


The UI scene editor will open with a blank UI scene. The open space is your UI scene; right now there's nothing in it. In this space you can arrange buttons, menus, and lists.

Let's take a quick tour of the new UI scene editor [Figure 7.2].

Along the top of the editor are tools used for aligning various elements after they have been

Figure 7.2

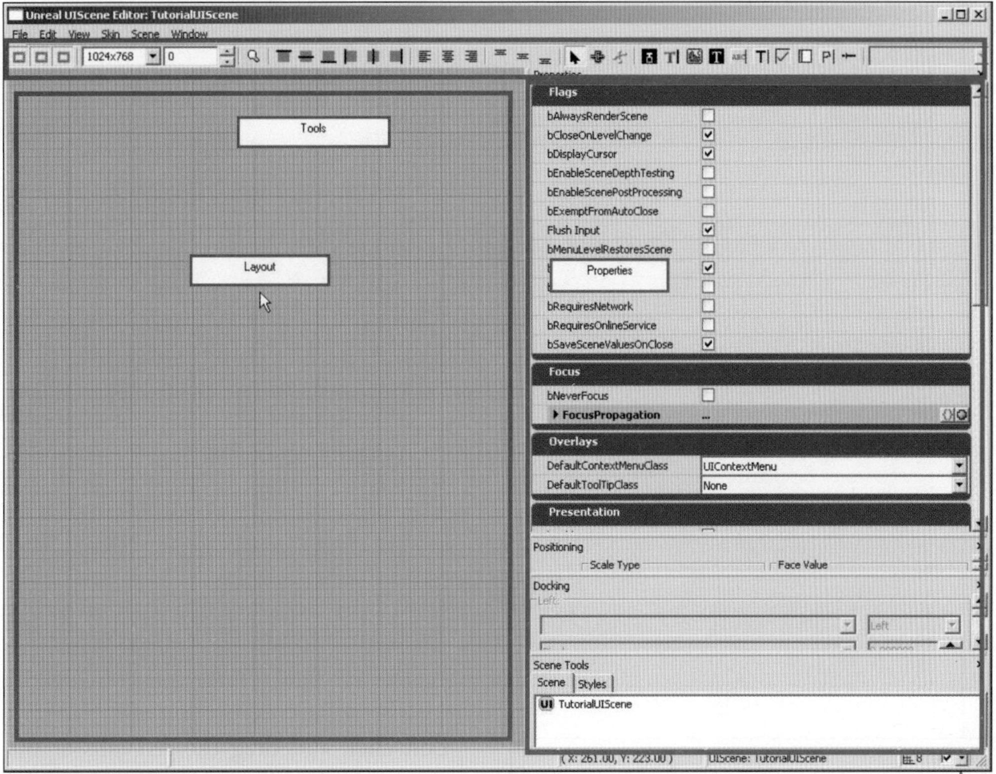


Figure 7.3

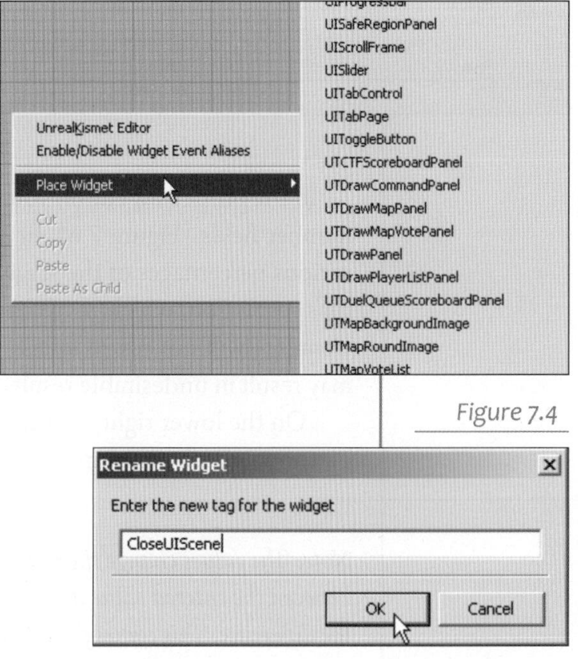


Figure 7.4

placed in the scene editor. The properties editor is located on the right of the window. Once an element is added to the UI scene, the right-click menu on the widget opens the widgets Kismet sequence. To pan through the layout editor, use Ctrl+LMB to see the rest of your scene. The mouse wheel zooms in and out of the editor.

Let's start by adding in a new button. Right-click in the scene and select `add new button`; this option appears near the top of the long list of widgets you can place in the UIScene [Figure 7.3].

Give the widget a name [Figure 7.4]. Reshape the button into a smaller widget near the center of the UIScene.

Figure 7.5

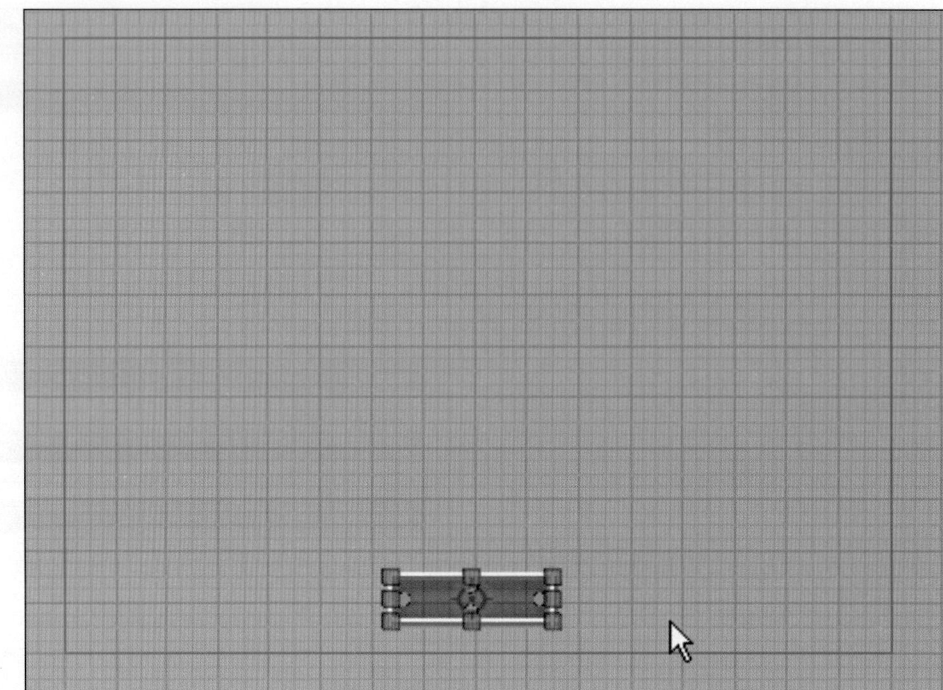

Figure 7.6

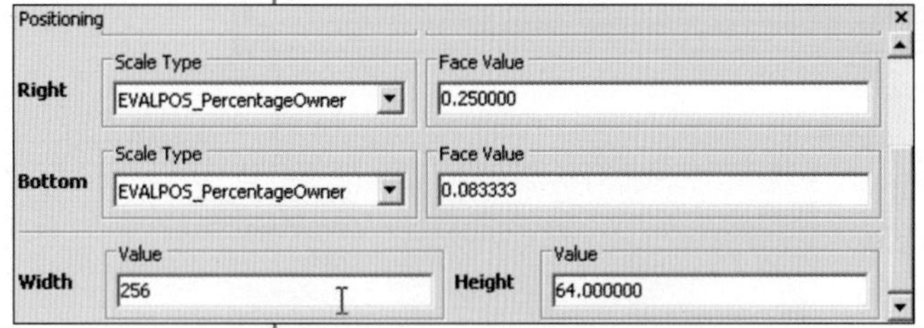

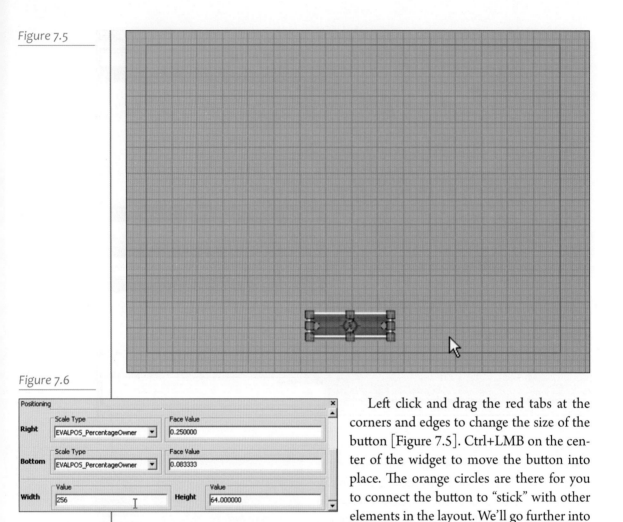

Left click and drag the red tabs at the corners and edges to change the size of the button [Figure 7.5]. Ctrl+LMB on the center of the widget to move the button into place. The orange circles are there for you to connect the button to "stick" with other elements in the layout. We'll go further into detail on this later.

In the properties editor, you can also type in specific sizes by filling in the various number fields [Figure 7.6]. In addition, the positioning of the button can be set to various percentages of the stage. This is mostly important when changing the monitor's resolution, which may change the proportions of the UI scene. The individual elements will not resize unless you specifically tell them to. Stretching the buttons may result in undesirable results.

On the lower right, you can also manually enter values to change the size of the button to match any graphics you'll be adding into the button.

*Note: The values change slightly after they're entered; don't worry about this. The difference between the entered value and the rounded value is so slight that there's no way you can see the difference. This comes from floating point error, and you'll just have to live with it.*

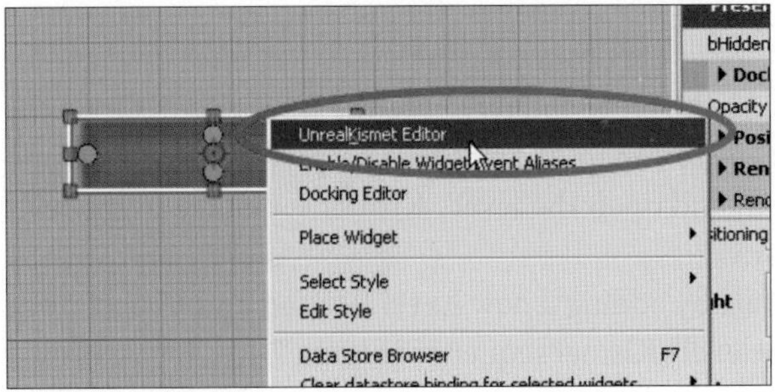


Figure 7.7

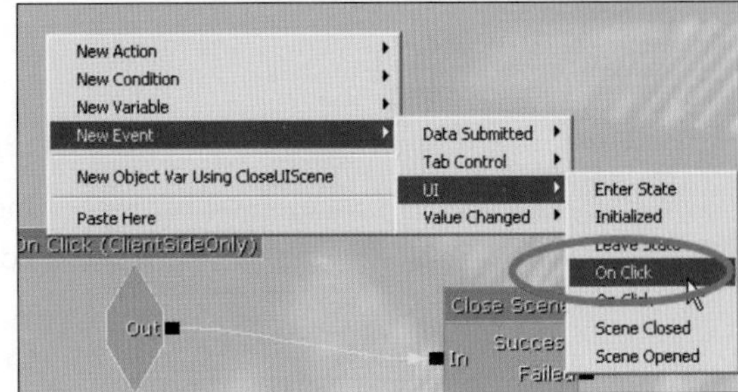


Figure 7.8

Right click on the widget and select `Unreal Kismet Editor` from the popup menu [Figure 7.7]. Each button can have its own sequence embedded in it. Try not to get too exuberant by adding clever scripts to each button; for the time being, stick to the basics so that we can get to the finish line.

With the new Kismet sequence opened for the button, add a new event called `On Click` [Figure 7.8]. This will trigger when the button is pressed. Keep in mind that each button will have its own isolated Kismet sequence. So clicking on a different button will not trigger an event in another button.

Then we'll create a new action called `Close UI scene` [Figure 7.9]. Wire the two together, save, and close Kismet and the UI scene. Your button's Kismet sequence should look a bit like Figure 7.10.

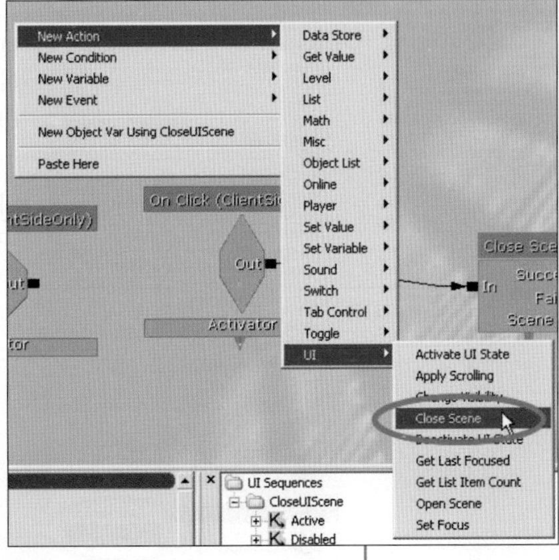


Figure 7.9

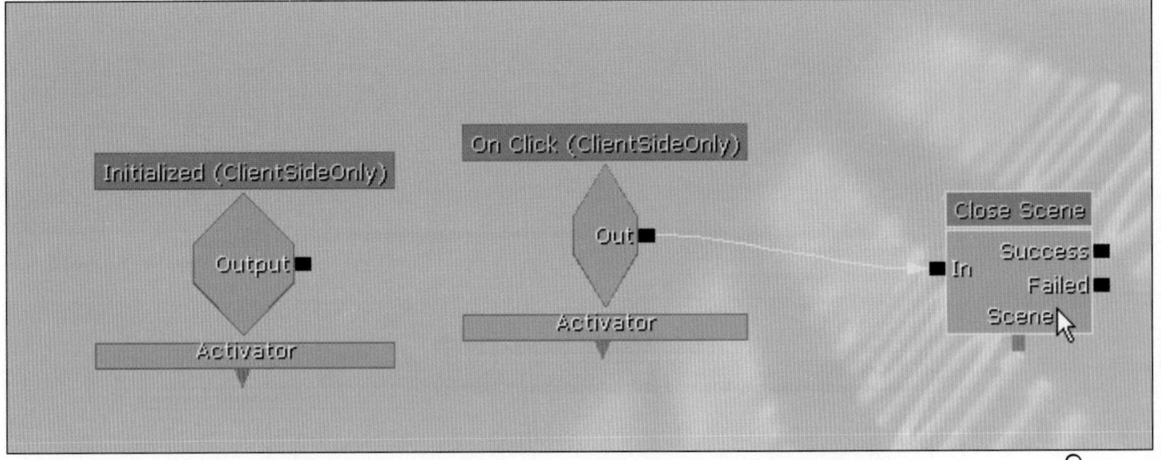


Figure 7.10

Figure 7.11

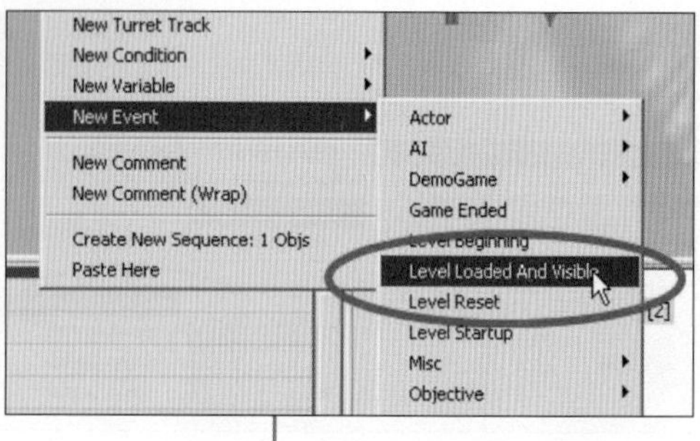


Figure 7.12

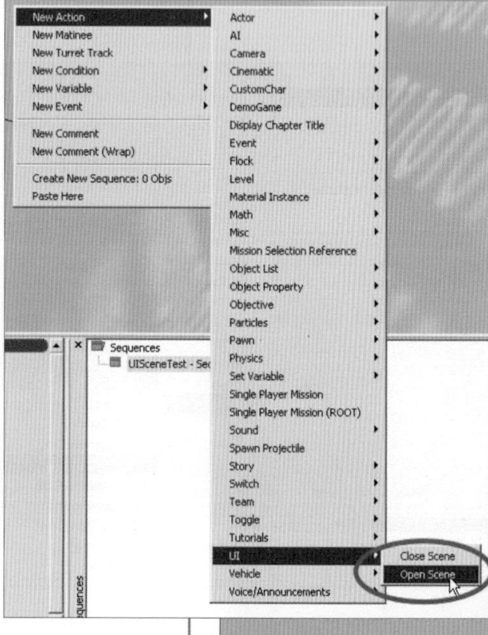


Figure 7.13

Save the UPK and return to the level editor. Open the UISceneTest.map or any other map you might be working on, and open the level's Kismet sequence in the level editor.

Start by adding a new Level Loaded and Visible node to the level's Kismet sequence [Figure 7.11]. If you already have one in the scene, then you can use that as well.

Add a new action, "Open Scene," from the UI subgroup [Figure 7.12]. This will then need to be pointed at the UIScene we just created.

With the Open Scene node selected, look at the properties editor. Highlight the `TutorialUIScene` in the Generic browser, and use the green arrow to connect the OpenUIScene node to the object [Figure 7.13]. Wire this into a new Event On Level Loaded and Visible. This will open the UI scene when the level is loaded. Run and play the level using the PIE button. Once the level is loaded, the UI scene will open [Figure 7.14].

Clicking on the button will close the UIScene. Not too bad, eh?

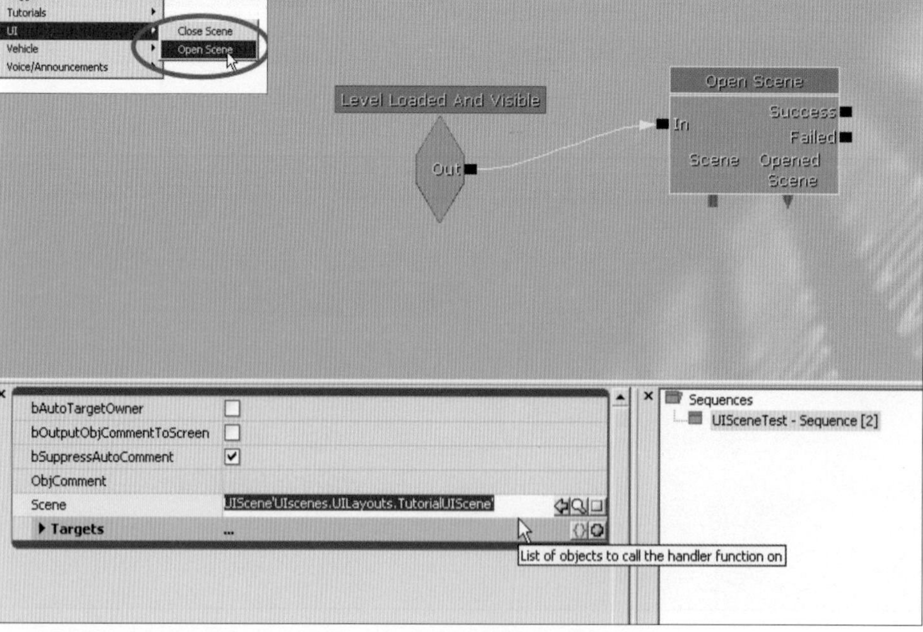

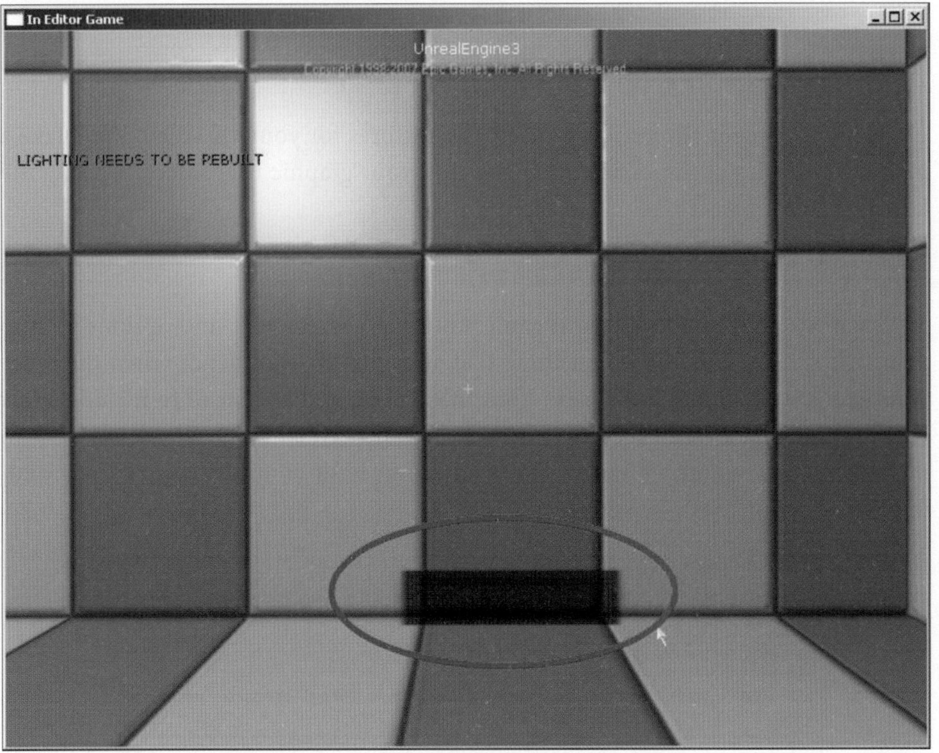


Figure 7.14

## Review

Using panels to arrange the various elements is pretty simple. Percentages allow us to keep our groups of buttons placed and still nicely arranged. It's really up to you to figure out what your layout will look like; there are plenty of tools to allow you to plan your layouts and widget placements. Once you've learned how the tools work, you're free to explore how to arrange your UI using these tools.

Once you've got a good layout for your UI, it's easy to update with new graphics as all you need to do is reimport your graphics. Changing the layouts and testing the arrangements on different monitors is also a simple task. Updating text elements for more in-game UIScenes is up to the designer, and it's a simple way to feed your player story information and plot elements.

At the moment, our UI is made of the placeholder textures. Nothing too exciting—we'll want to add our own graphics to make the UI scene more interesting. In the following exercise, we'll want to generate some images using GIMP. This sort of work is a bit like making graphics for a webpage, so we'll switch gears to a more 2D realm for the following chapter.

## On Your Own

Here's a quick, simple exercise. Create a trigger in a room. When the trigger is touched, have it open a UIScene with a bit of text to let players know they found something. Then give players a button to get back into the game.

## Adding Graphics to Your GUI

Unreal Tournament allows you to use basic textures for your UI scene. We'll take a look at the basics of importing and arranging your graphic user interface using the UIScene editor.

PROJECT

### Creating Your Title Screen

Title screens go far to define your game. Your logo, characters, and options go into your title screen. This is the first thing that your players experience when they play your game, so it should look great. Your title screen will also need to include a few basic settings dialogs, for setting screen size and player names. These are easy to include but will require a bit of footwork and some basic connections to corresponding Unreal script.

#### Basic Button Graphic

Here I'm starting with a small image that is 256 by 64 pixels [Figure 7.15].

Figure 7.15

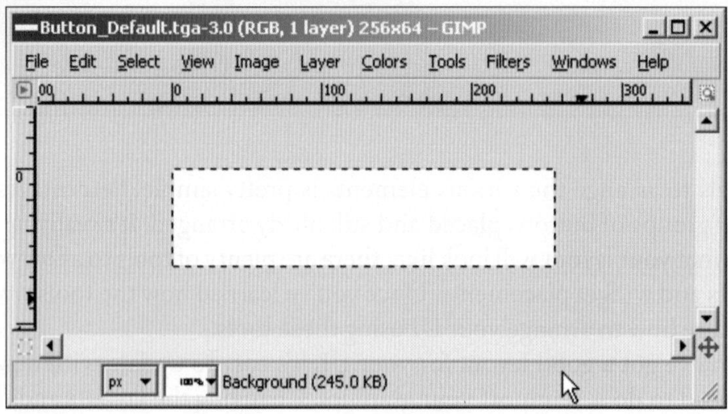


Figure 7.16

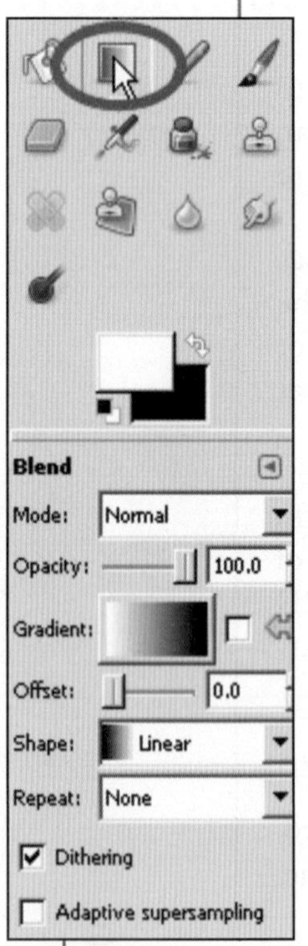


For simple demonstration purposes, we're going to avoid making this into a work of art, so we're going to make a simple gradient texture for the button. Select the `Gradient Tool` Hotkey L [Figure 7.16] and then fill in the button by dragging a vertical line. Click at the top and drag to the bottom of the canvas [Figure 7.17].

Figure 7.17

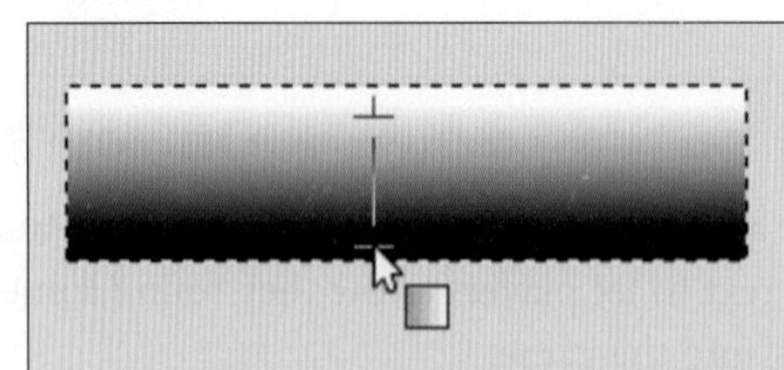

The gradient should fall nicely over the face of the button. Save this as Button_Default.tga in your game art directory. Import your graphic into the Generic browser. This will be a regular bitmap for use in the UIScene layout tool. Import the texture into a new UIScene package. Save it as Package: UIScene, Group Bitmaps, Button_Default.

Next, create a new UIScene by right-clicking in the Generic browser and selecting `New UIScene` [Figure 7.18].

Figure 7.18

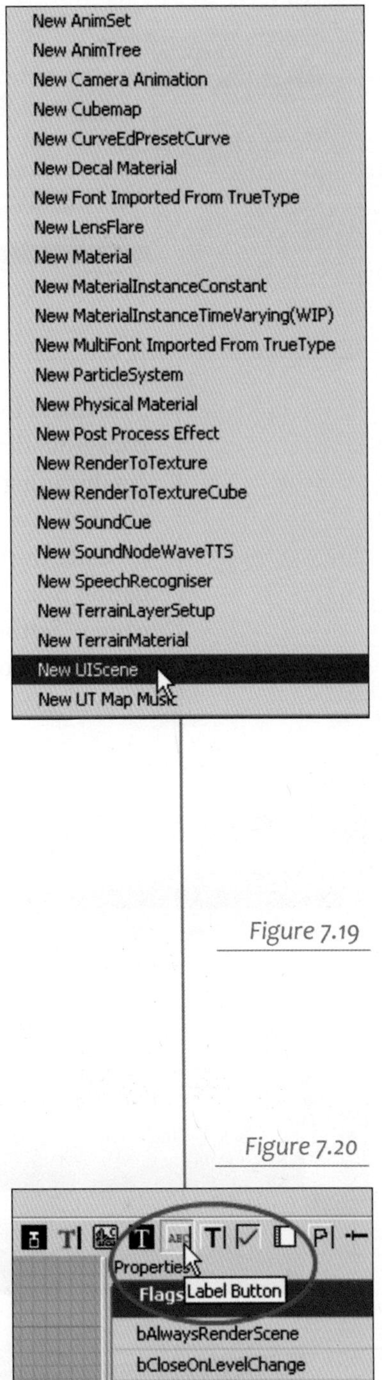


## Making Your Title Screen

Save the new UI scene as Package: UIScene, Group: Layouts, and name it SplashScreen [Figure 7.19]. The UIScene editor will open up after the new object is created.

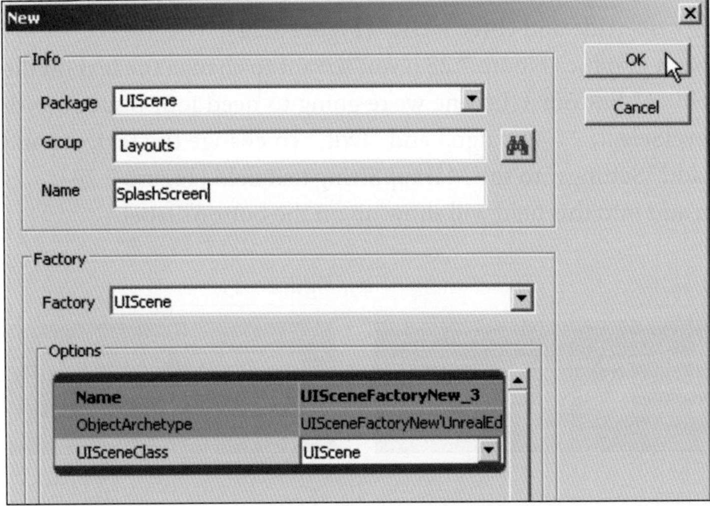


Figure 7.19

Another method to create a labeled button is to select the `Label Button` tool in the tool bar [Figure 7.20].

Figure 7.20

This will allow you to use the left mouse button to drag and create a rectangle to be your button shape in the UIScene Layout. As before, you can still adjust the size of the button to match the size of the graphic you created for the button.

You can align the tool to the center of the viewport by right-clicking on the button and selecting the `Align To Viewport` sub-menu. Then select `Center Horizontally` [Figure 7.21]. Other options are also available to align the various widgets to the layout editor. Select the bitmap in the UIScene package we just imported, and then attach the image to the button.

Figure 7.21

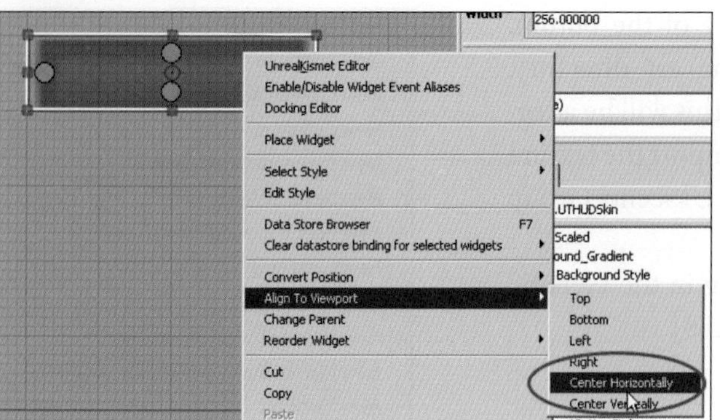


Figure 7.22

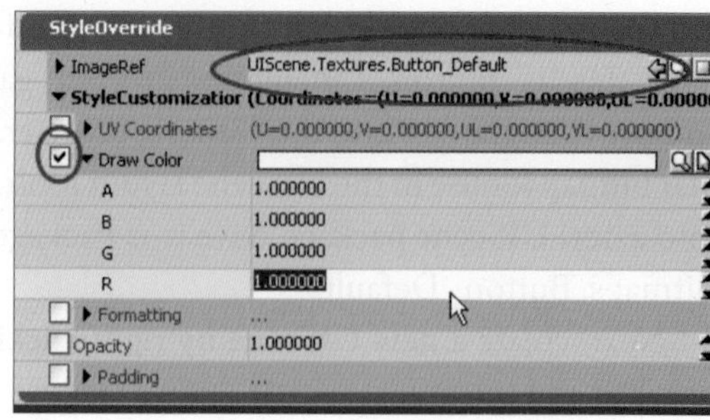


Expand the Image roll-out menu in the properties window, and then expand the BackgroundImageComponent roll-out. Target the ImageRef to the UIScene button graphic using the green arrow icon. To make sure that the graphic is properly drawn, check the `Draw Color` override and enter 1,1,1,1 [Figure 7.22].

Once the button has a graphic [Figure 7.23], you'll want to change the text on the button from "Button Text." For our UI scene we're going to need four buttons with names "Settings," "LevelSelect," "Campaign," and "Exit." To change the text, expand the data roll-out and add "Settings" to the MarkupString text field [Figure 7.24].

Whatever text you add into this field will show up on the button's label.

Figure 7.23

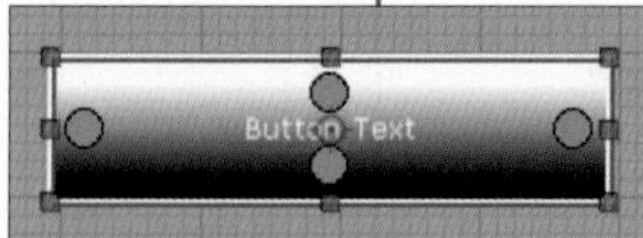


Figure 7.24

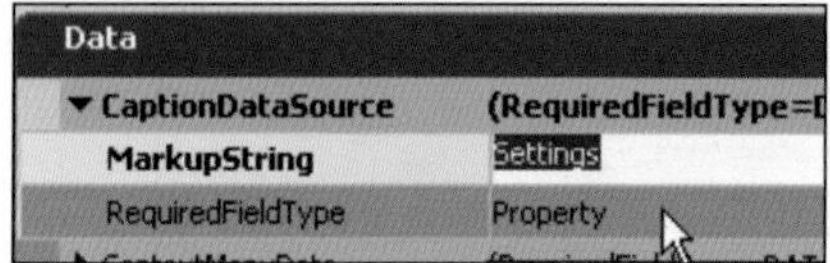


Figure 7.25

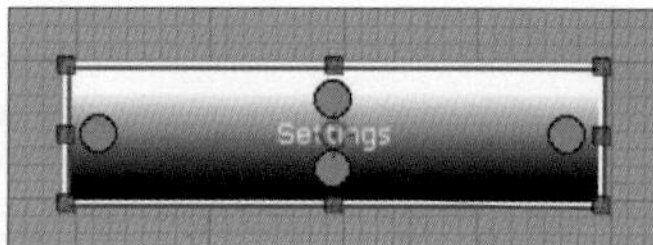

Figure 7.26

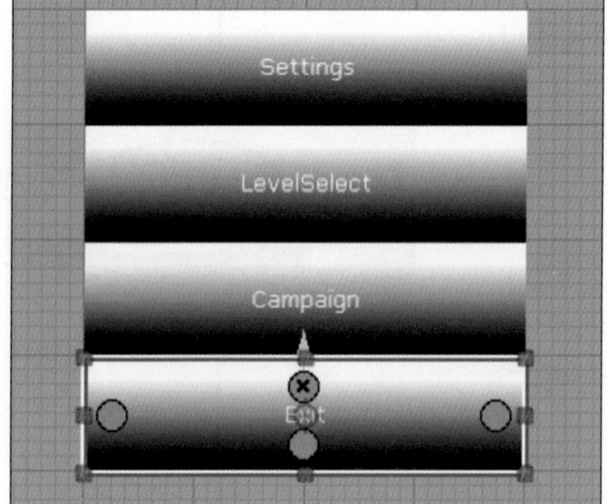


The resulting button changes should be reflected [Figure 7.25]. If they are not, then double check that you created a button with a label. There are many button types, so make sure you're using the `Label Button` tool to create your buttons.

After creating three more buttons, your scene should look a bit like Figure 7.26. Now it's up to Unreal Script to make these buttons work.

Next we'll add our title graphic.

Figure 7.27

Select the Image tool [Figure 7.27], and then drag a rectangle over our buttons. This will become our new title screen. The default sort-of-moldy-moon-cheese texture [Figure 7.28] should be replaced with your own texture.

After creating some interesting graphic in GIMP or some other image editor, you'll want to import the texture into the same sub-package along with your buttons.

Expand the Image roll-out menu; then expand the StyleOverride roll-out [Figure 7.29]. Target your ImageRef to the title you or your team created for your mod. At the moment, your title is covering over your buttons. To change the order, you can take a look at the lower right of the property editor panels.

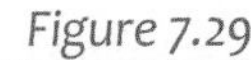

Figure 7.28

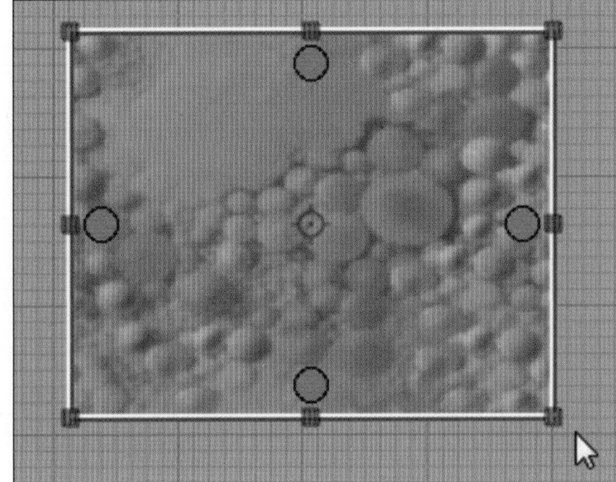

Figure 7.29

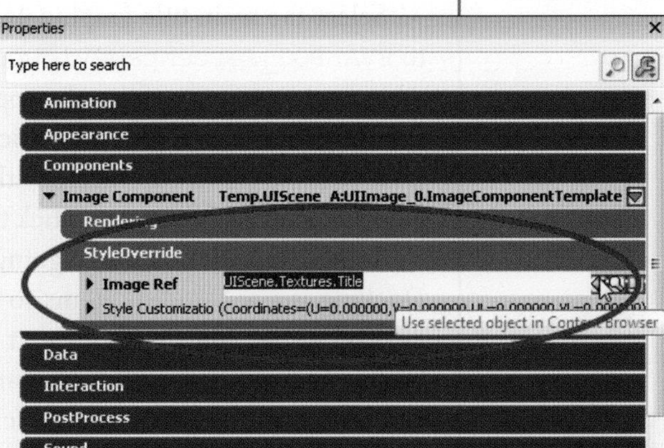


Figure 7.30

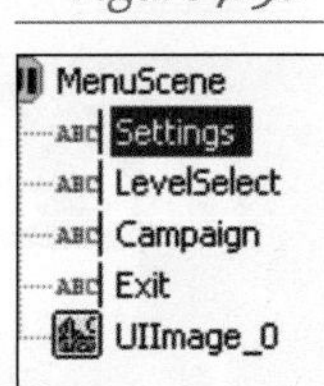


On the lower right of the UIScene editor, you'll see that your labeled buttons and the UIImage [Figure 7.30]. You can rename these to something more recognizable if you feel the need. At the moment, there aren't too many items, so it's not yet an issue; but later on, you'll want to stay organized by using readable names. We'll do a bit more than rearranging the buttons above the image; we'll create a hierarchy in which the buttons are attached to the image. Wherever the image is moved, the buttons will follow.

Figure 7.31

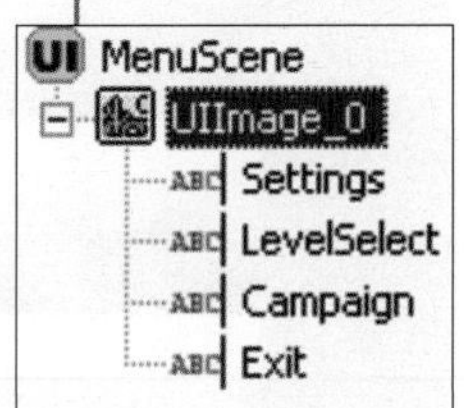


This is accomplished by dragging the button listings and dropping them onto the UIImage icon [Figure 7.31]. This will add the buttons to the image as a child object. Additionally, the order in which the objects are layered on top of one another is determined by this list view.

Now we've got a splash screen, sort of [Figure 7.32]. You'll want to work on something a bit more pleasing, but in this case, you'll at least have a good starting point and an understanding of how a UI is created.

### Arranging the Scene for Multiple Resolution Screens

We're going to want to see the rest of the logo, and we're going to want to make some changes to the buttons to make them more appealing. Graphic changes will have to come later, but we can take a look now at how to keep things in order if the layout has to be refitted to different monitor resolutions.

After some dragging and manipulation, I changed the layout to something roughly like Figure 7.33. This will be modified as we proceed because we're going to have these buttons stretch a bit when the monitor resolution changes.

Select the main title graphic. In the Positioning properties window, set the sides to `EVALPOS_PercentageViewport` [Figure 7.34]. What this will do is keep each edge a set percentage from the top left corner of the viewport. The behavior we're shooting for is that the buttons stick to the image. Also, we're going to want the buttons' sides to match up nicely with the image we're using. Just as important, we're going to want each button to stick to the topmost button.

To accomplish this, we're going to start with *docking* each button to the others. Docking is a way to link items to each other without having to enter percentages or pixel values. Start with the exit button; click to drag the top orange circle to the bottom orange circle on the campaign button [Figure 7.35]. This docks the top of the exit button to the bottom of the campaign button. Wherever the campaign button moves, the exit button's top edge will follow.

Figure 7.32

Figure 7.33

Figure 7.34

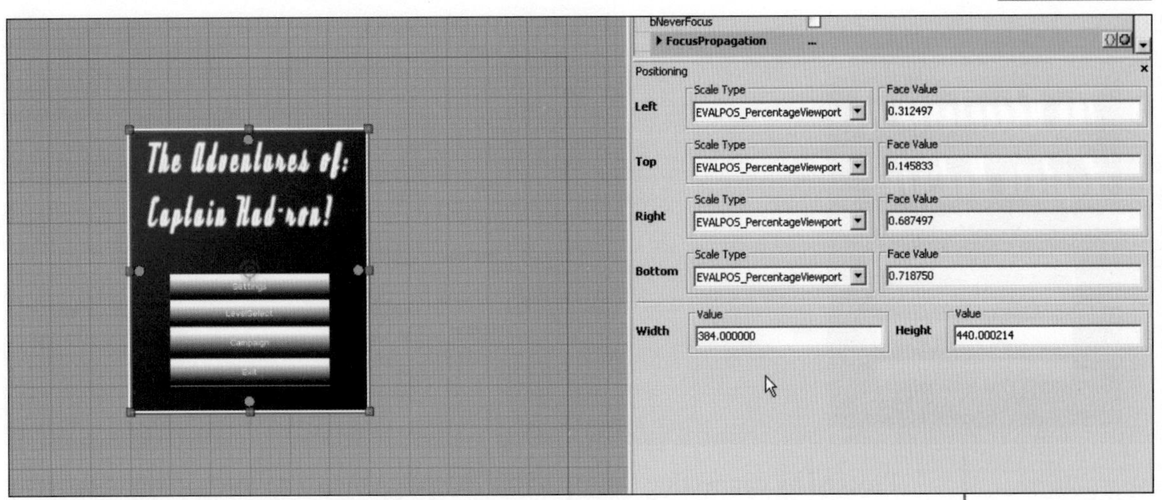


Figure 7.35

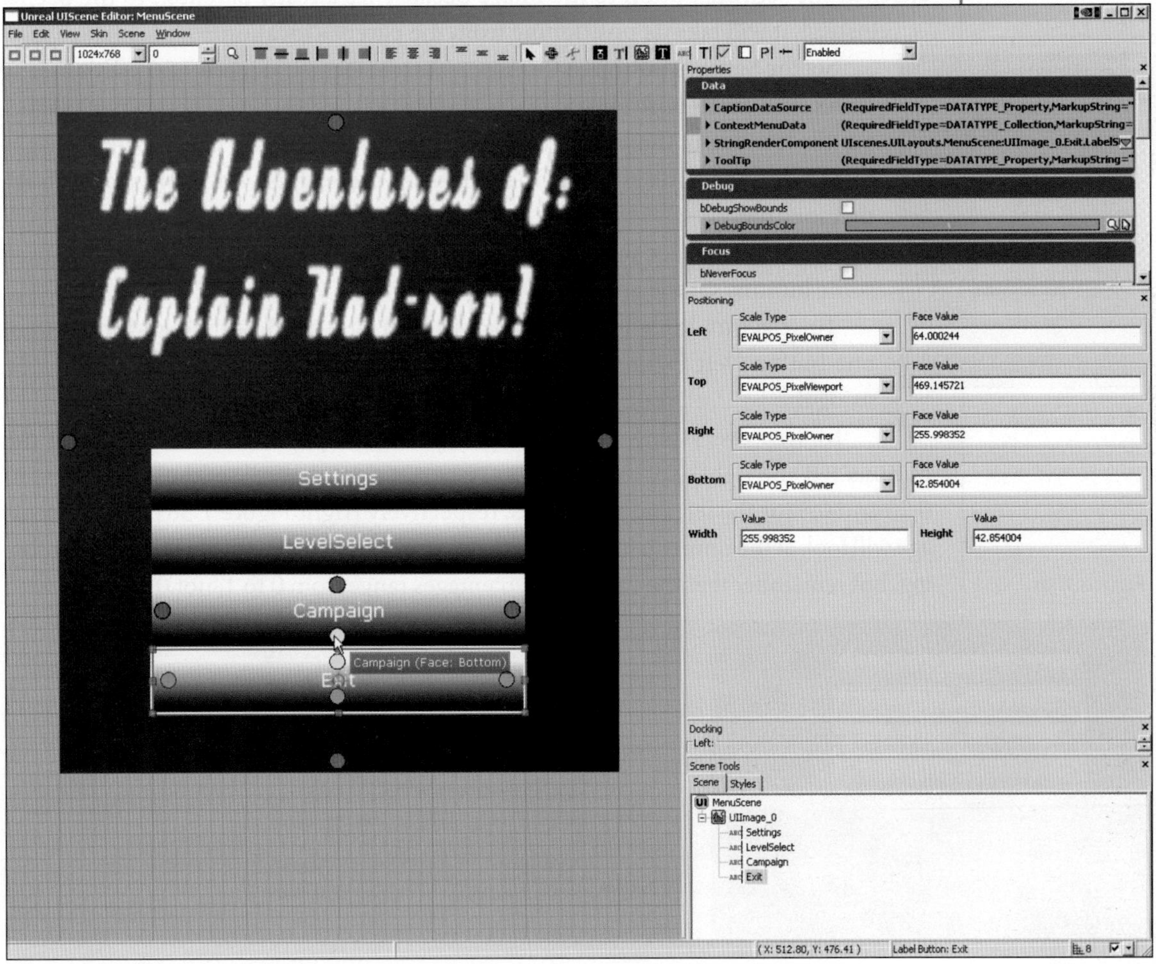

Figure 7.36

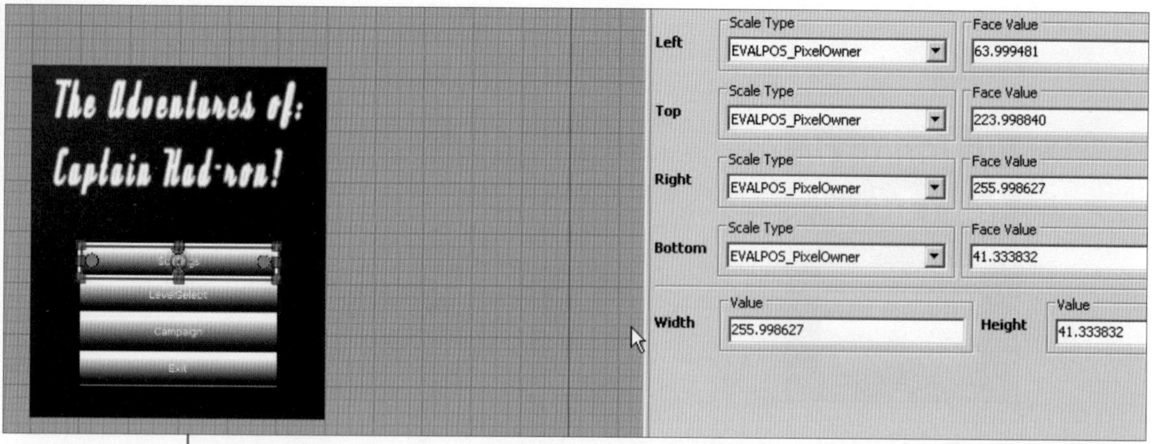

Proceed by connecting the top of the campaign button to the bottom of the level select, and the level select button's top to the bottom of the settings button. We haven't attached the settings button to the image because it's already parented to the Scene. Instead, it will take its positioning from the parent's location.

Figure 7.37

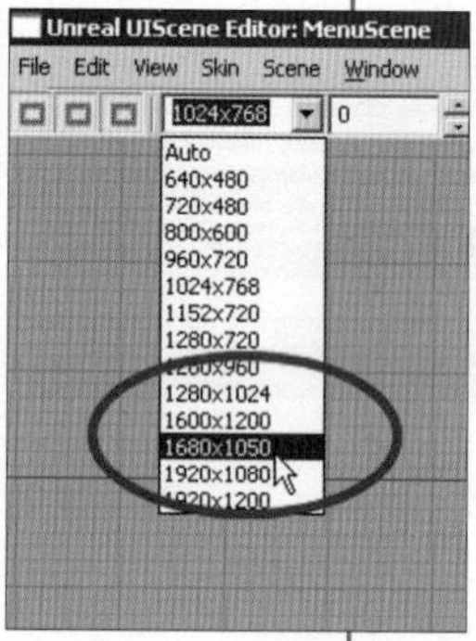

Set the Settings button to `EVALPOS_PixelOwner` [Figure 7.36]. This means it will evaluate its position relative to the pixels from its parent's or owner's shape. Set the left side of the button to 64 pixels from the left, the top to 224, the right to 256, and the bottom to 42. The numbers will readjust, but don't worry about that for now.

Now if you select another resolution at the top [Figure 7.37], you might see some buttons shuffle around!

To select multiple items, you can use CTRL+LMB to highlight more than one button [left Figure 7.38]. One thing to remember is that you need to be using the `select` tool, the black arrow in the tool bar, to do this.

To keep everything from getting all jumbled up, you can set the rest of the buttons' left and right sizes to `EVALPOS_PercentageOwner`. I set the values there to 0.25 and 0.5 for the left and right sides, respectively [right Figure 7.38]. The percentage will look at the immediate owner of the button. Some of these values can be confusing, but remember that the values of percentages range from 0 to 1, not 0 to 100.

Figure 7.38

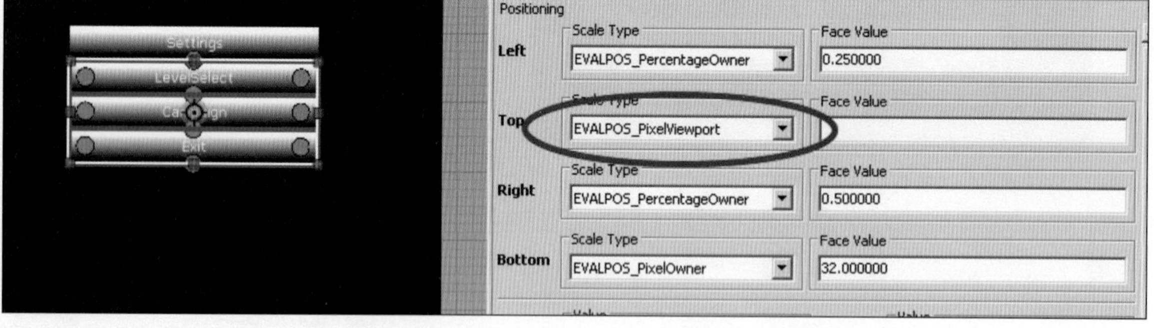

The top for each button should be set to pixel viewport [right Figure 7.38]; this should be automatically adjusted because the tops are docked to other objects. The button should be set to EVALPOS_PixelOwner, and the value should be set to 32, which happens to be the size I set for the button. See the MenuScene for the final results [Figure 7.39].

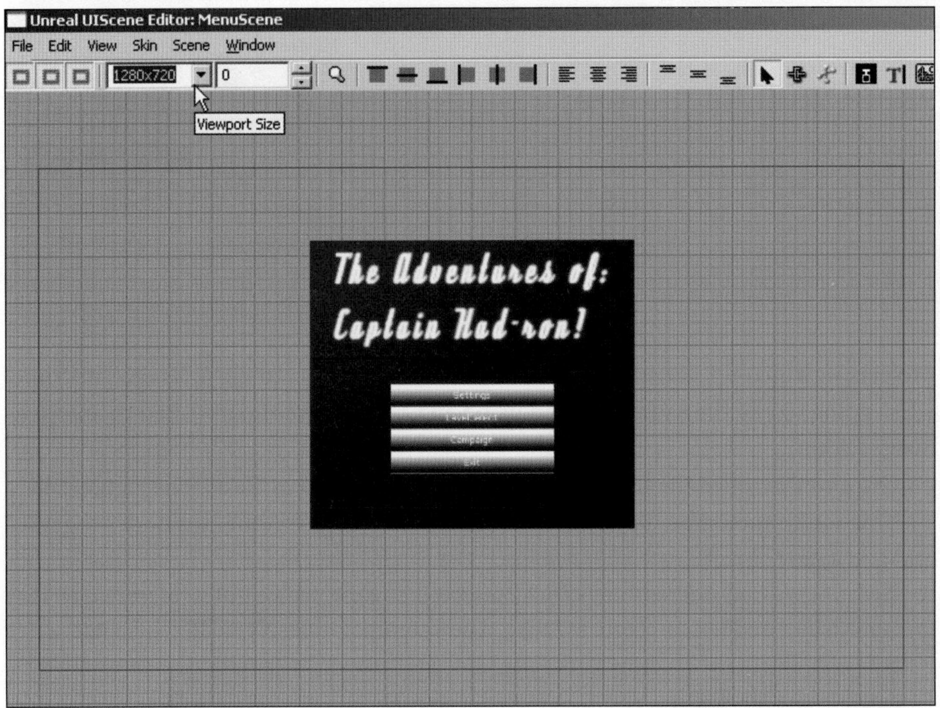


Figure 7.39

Depending on your layouts, you might have to fiddle with how the buttons are aligned, but this is something that should require a bit of experimentation in general. Punching in numbers, selecting different positioning evaluation types, and changing screen resolutions should be a part of the testing of your UI.

## Adding Functionality

Now we need to make our buttons actually work. Surprisingly, it doesn't take too much of an effort to get the basics working. There isn't much code actually necessary to make this menu do what it's supposed to.

Figure 7.40

First of all, each button has a Kismet sequence that you can assign to it [Figure 7.40]. Recall the previous

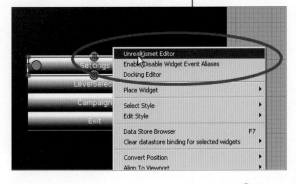

Figure 7.41

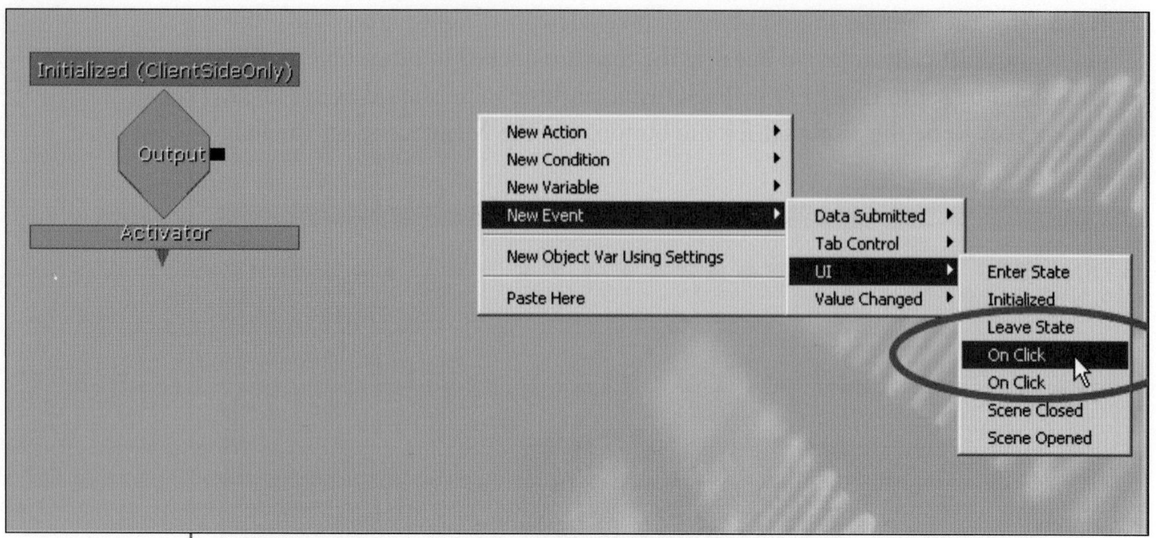


projects in which we added a simple function to a button to close itself. This time, we're going to add the same function using an OnClick event connected to an openScene action.

Once you've added the OnClick event, you'll want to add in the action [Figure 7.41].

This action should be Open Scene [Figure 7.42]. Connect the two nodes together and add a new object.

Because we had our settings object selected already, we've got a reference to that in our Kismet sequence [Figure 7.43]. The reference doesn't matter because we're

Figure 7.42

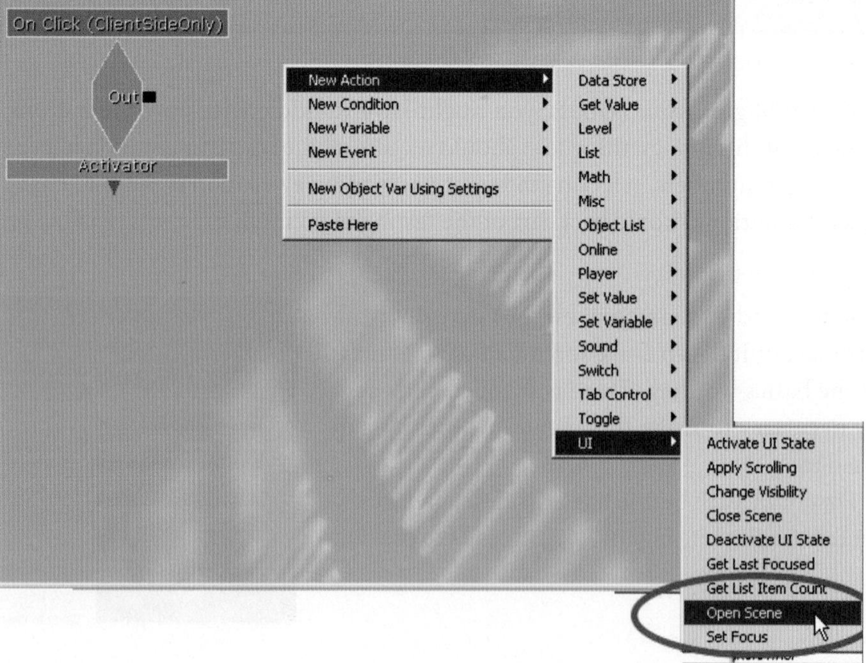

Figure 7.43

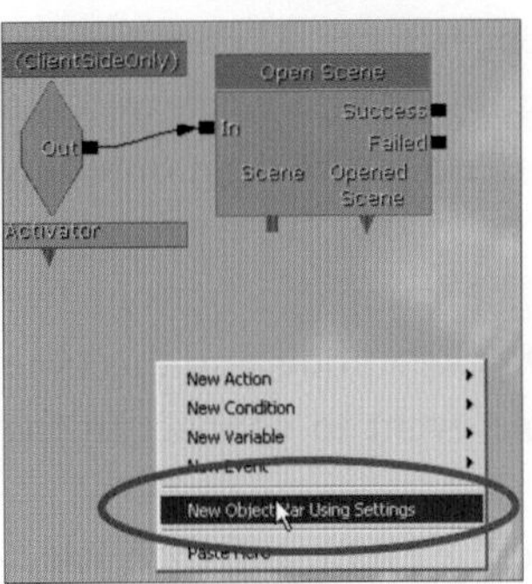


Figure 7.44

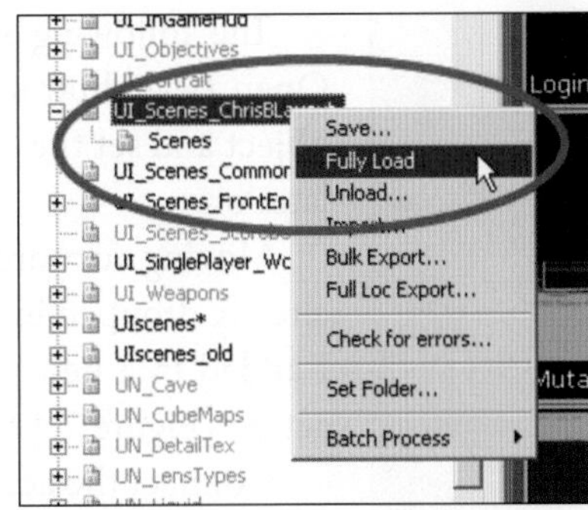


Figure 7.45

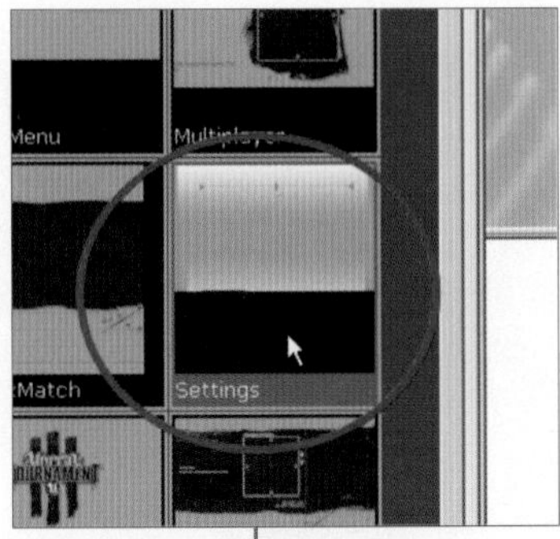


Figure 7.46

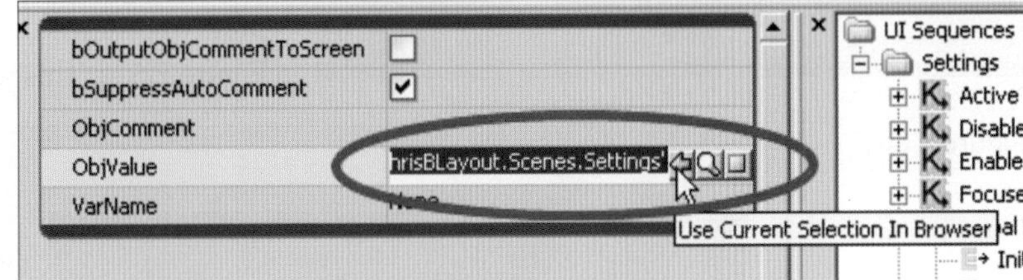


going to replace this with another object located in the Generic browser. Find the `UI_Scenes_ChrisBLayouts` package and select `Fully Load` from the right-click menu [Figure 7.44]. (If you're using UDK then you're on your own and will have to make your own UIScene.) This will expose the rest of the items that haven't been loaded and that we need to get to.

Somewhere inside of that package is the settings UI layout. Highlight this layout so that we can target the object we created in our UI's main menu.

It might also be important to note that the UI scenes are framed with a light blue color [Figure 7.45].

Enter the Settings UI scene into the ObjValue of the object in the Kismet sequence [Figure 7.46]. Finally, connect the object to the object input of the open scene node [Figure 7.47].

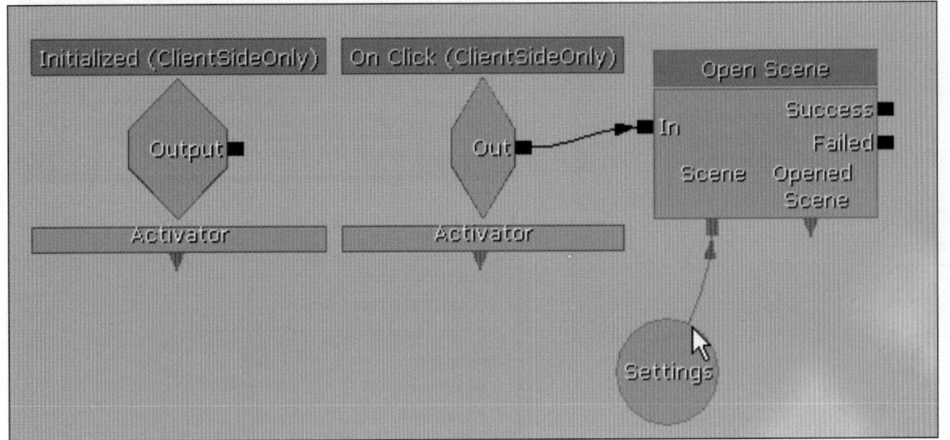


Figure 7.47

Figure 7.48

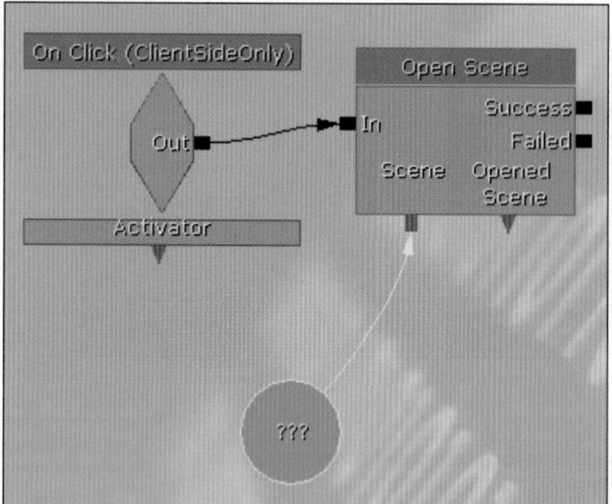


The following sequence is the Kismet for the Open Level button [Figure 7.48]. I've cleared the object and set the value to none. We'll get onto this later on.

Moving forward to the campaign button, I've already dropped in an On Click node, and this time I added in a new console event to connect to the action [Figure 7.49].

Connect the action to the event, and then select the Console Command [Figure 7.50].

In the properties of the Console Command, enter "open FM-Test_Map?game=FMod.FMGame" [Figure 7.51]. This will set the mod to your first mod,

Figure 7.49

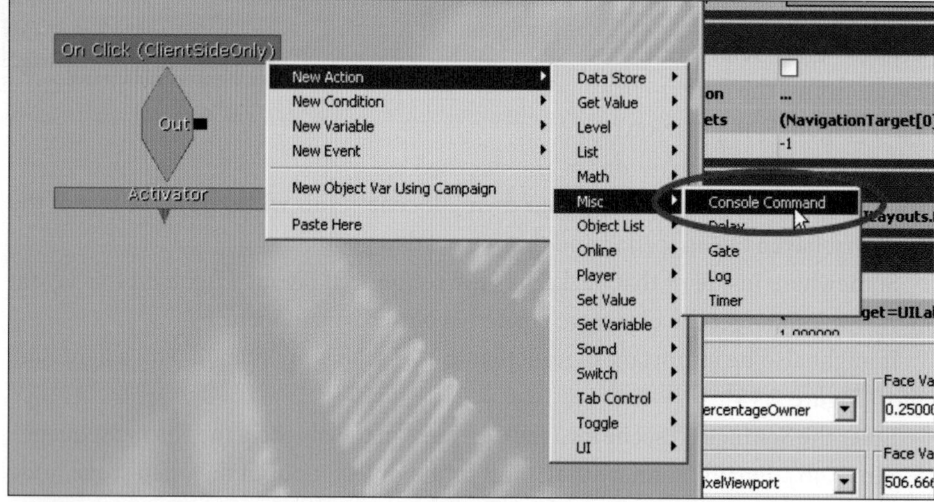


Figure 7.50

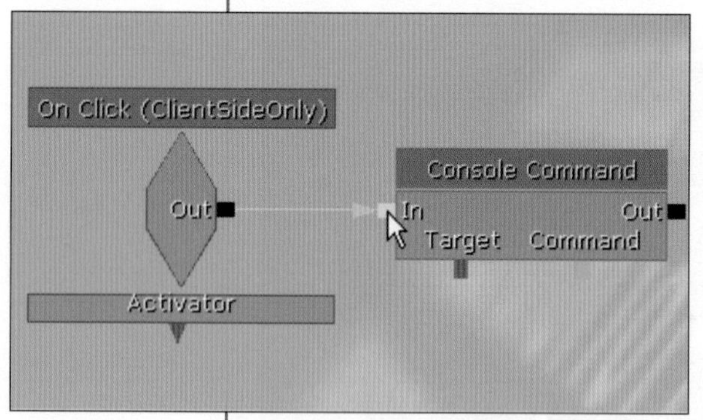


Figure 7.51

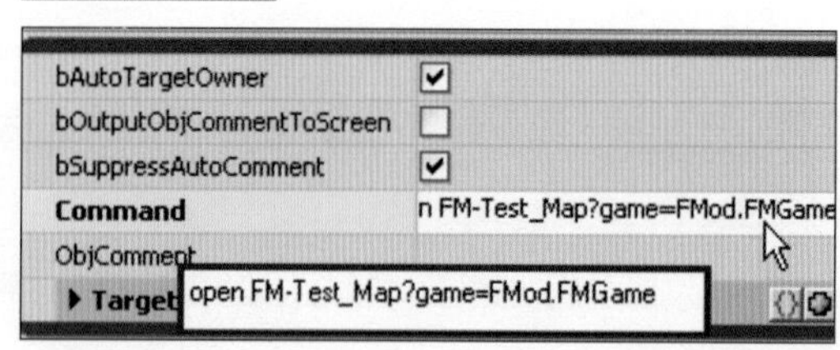


Figure 7.52

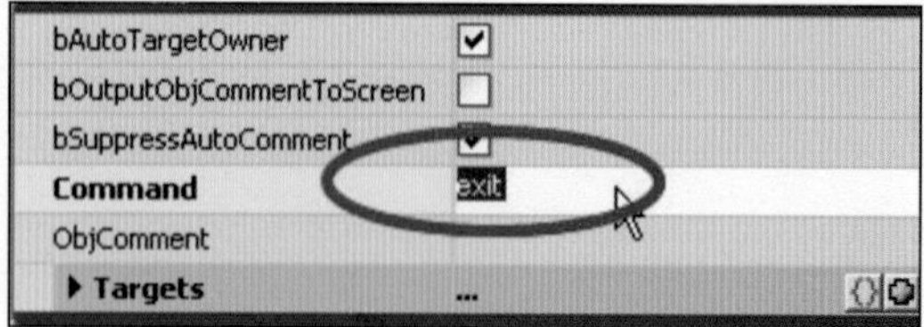

and the game type will be set to FMGame; then the FM-Test_Map will be the level that is opened. Finally, we'll move onto the exit button's Kismet sequence where the On Click action will be connected to a console command with the command being "exit" [Figure 7.52].

Close the UIScene editor and save your package. You can test the UIScene in the Play in Editor (PIE) tool. The one catch is that the PIE will not leave the level you're currently editing. So things like the console command to open the FM-Test_Map will not work. You can check the LOG panel in the Generic browser to see it execute the command, but Unreal editor will not actually launch the level.

### Attaching the Title Screen to Your Front End

To make sure that the first thing your players see when they start your mod, you're going to use BoxRoom.ut3 to load into the game first. Since there's nothing in there for the time being, it'll load quickly. We're getting quite a lot of mileage out of that level, aren't we?

Open BoxRoom.ut3 in the level editor. In the level's Kismet sequence, add the same Level Loaded and Visible node to that you added to the first UIScene project. Connect that node to a Load UIScene node that is targeted to the SplashScene in your UIScene package. Save this scene as "FirstMod_FrontEnd.ut3" in your Unpublished/CustomMaps/ directory. This will be called in the ini file, which we'll get to later on in the programming chapters. Once your mod has been set up, the player will be presented with your shiny new title screen.

*Note: To create a new font, you can export a font that comes with Unreal Tournament 3. This will give you several textures that you can then open in GIMP and modify. Each character is basically a small set of coordinates that designate the top left and lower right corners of each character. Once a new texture is created, you can import the texture into a new font. It's quite a lot of work at the moment, so if you feel adventurous, then you can take a swing at this after you've gone through the rest of these chapters.*

## Review

Creating a UI scene will take over the player controls, and an in-game mouse cursor will appear so that you know where you are clicking. Additionally, you can consider making a UI that does not take over the player controls, but that means that as you move the cursor, the in-game camera will also be trying to follow the mouse. This can feel awkward as you are controlling two different things at the same time.

Kismet is used to bind the buttons to actions. These actions include anything that Kismet can support. To add additional functionality to your UI, you or the programmer on your team need to write some Unreal script to extend your UI functions.

## On Your Own

We left the level selector empty for now. We suggest that you create a new UI scene that will open when you click on that button. The new UI scene should have any number of buttons you might need to launch console commands to open your other levels.

# 8 Refining Your Work

*Adding Details and Notes for Both the Programmers and the Artists*

Static meshes are going to fill in your space with the detail required to make a level feel rich with detail, but the behaviors and other considerations that make up a great game require a lot of planning and testing. The smaller details such as material types and how physics interacts with your objects are one of the final passes you'll have to configure when wrapping up and testing your level.

Some objects can have their attributes overridden when they've been placed in the level. This task is rather tedious but is required to add that last bit of polish to your completed level. In some cases you'll have to ask your artists to make changes to collision meshes or your programmers to add new behaviors to make the final product really shine.

Included in this chapter are methods to help highlight what's necessary to cross that final 10% of what separates a good game from a great game.

## What to Expect

From here on out, the details are going to start to get fussy. The designer's job is never done; there are going to be a lot of things you're going to need to pay attention to and problems you'll need to solve through use of various volumes and other tricks.

PROJECT

### Trigger Volumes

Now let's learn about using boxes as triggers. The usual trigger is a cylinder-shaped object that the player triggers when entering the cylinder shape. In some cases, the cylinder shape isn't so useful, and a differently shaped box would be preferable to the usual trigger. In these cases, a trigger volume is much more practical.

#### Water Volumes

A water volume is nothing more than a specially flagged BSP volume. Without a special water surface, the water volume will remain completely invisible. Create a builder brush that covers the area of the trough.

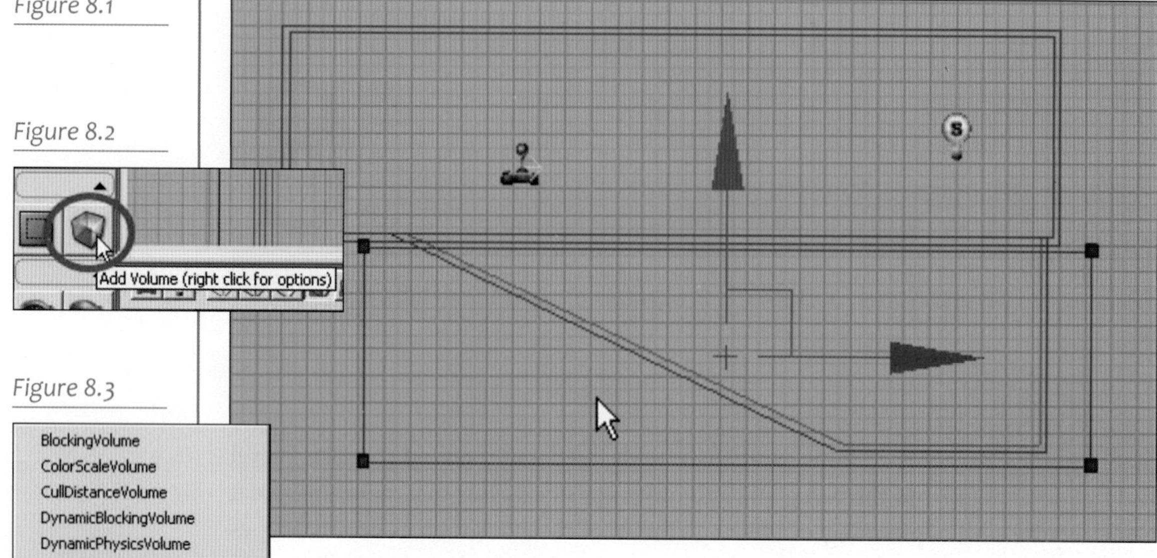


Figure 8.1

Figure 8.2

Figure 8.3

BlockingVolume
ColorScaleVolume
CullDistanceVolume
DynamicBlockingVolume
DynamicPhysicsVolume
DynamicTriggerVolume
FoliageFactory
ForcedDirVolume
GravityVolume
LadderVolume
LevelStreamingVolume
LeviathanBlockingVolume
LightVolume
PhysicsVolume
PortalVolume
PostProcessVolume
RB_ForceFieldExcludeVolume
ReverbVolume
TankBlockingVolume
TriggerVolume
UTAreaNamingVolume
UTAutoCrouchVolume
UTDynamicWaterVolume
UTKillZVolume
UTLavaVolume
UTScriptedBotVolume
UTSlimeVolume
UTSpaceVolume
UTWaterVolume

Open the WaterVolume.ut3 map. This is a basic room with a simple hole in the ground for us to fill with a volume of some sort [Figure 8.1]. To cover the basics, we'll keep this as simple as possible to avoid getting distracted. Once you've got a builder brush that will surround the trough, right-click on the `Add Volume` tool [Figure 8.2].

This will open a long list of volumes we can add to our level. For this project, select the `UTWaterVolume` from the bottom of the list [Figure 8.3].

Testing this will be rather strange. None of the usual water effects will happen other than the changes to the character's physics.

Here we've added a water volume to a simple scene [Figure 8.4]. Inside of this ramped area is water. You can't see it, but it changes the behavior of the

Figure 8.4

player character's movement. To test this, jump around outside of the brick area; then jump into the depression in the ground. Once inside, you might immediately notice that you fall more slowly and that you can even jump up out of the trough by holding down `jump`. The behavior of the controls changes to swimming, but no other feedback is provided.

Figure 8.5

To change the camera to something more water-like, keep the water volume or the builder brush selected and then, back in the `Add Volume` button, select `PostProcessVolume` [Figure 8.5]; this will allow us to change what things look like while we're inside the volume.

Post-processes are the effects that change the player camera. Bloom, motion blur, depth of field, and other effects are modified using various post-processing effects. We'll cover more about how these are used, but for now let's just make modifications to the PostProcessVolume we just created.

Figure 8.6

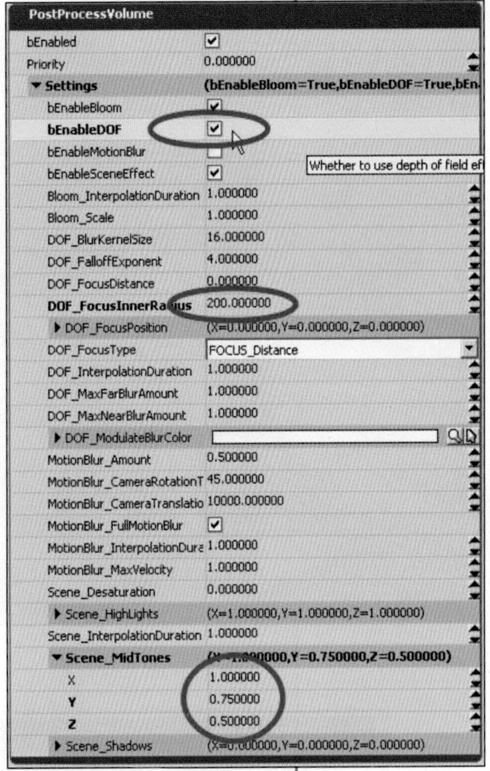


Select the volume, and in the property editor [Figure 8.6], make the following changes: `bEnableDOF` should be turned on; then the `DOF_FocusInnerRadius` should be moved in from the default setting to something much closer to the camera, so we'll change that to 200. Next we'll want to change the color to something more watery, so we'll set the `Scene_MidTones` to 1.0,0.75,0.5 for a more blue coloration. Save the level, rebuild all, and then jump in using Play in Editor.

When you jump into the volume, you should have an effect something like this [Figure 8.7]. To add to the ambience, you can add a reverb volume; then, in the properties, set the ReverbType to Underwater. All that remains is to cover the volume with a plane that looks like water. To do this, you're going to have to check out the art chapters for building some clever shaders for water, or you could simply dig through the materials available in UT3 and find a water shader to assign to a static mesh plane.

Figure 8.7

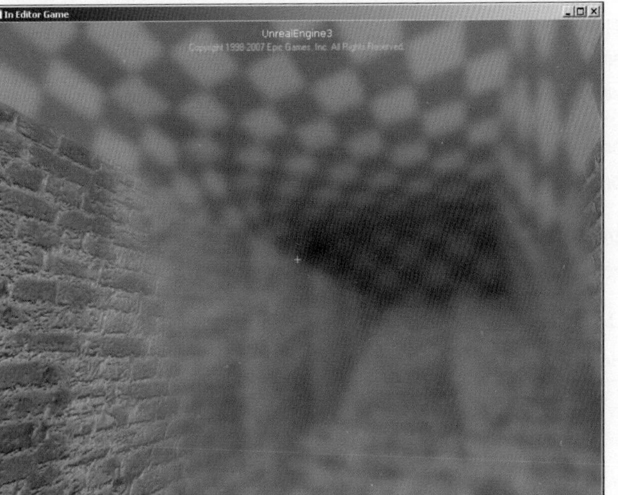

## Teleporters

Teleporters are pretty basic and simple events to set up. But the locations of some of the nodes aren't easy to find, and it's also important to know that a lot of additional sequences are required to set up a good teleport event. I've set up a new TeleportRoom.ut3; this will help speed us along through this new Kismet sequence.

Figure 8.8

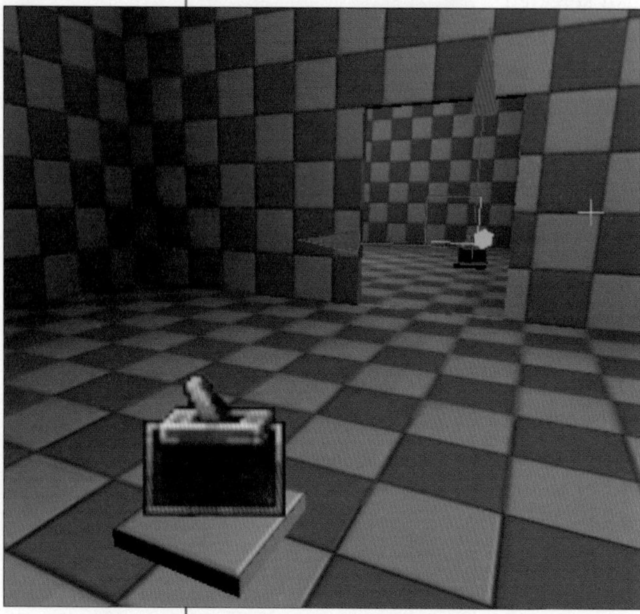

To start, I've placed a new trigger over each plate in each room [Figure 8.8].

In Kismet, add in a `New Action` → `Actor` → `Teleport` node to the editor [Figure 8.9].

Then add in a new object using a trigger [Figure 8.10]. This is an interesting use of a trigger. Triggers are mostly used as touch objects, but they have enough information to be used in different ways. In this case, we just need the location data of the trigger so that we can use it as an object.

Then, for the opposite trigger, we'll add in a regular touch event node [Figure 8.11].

Now we're going to need to know what object to teleport. In this case it's the player, so we'll add in a new object for the player. Select `New Variable` → `Object` → `Player` [Figure 8.12]. We'll use this for our teleporter.

Figure 8.9

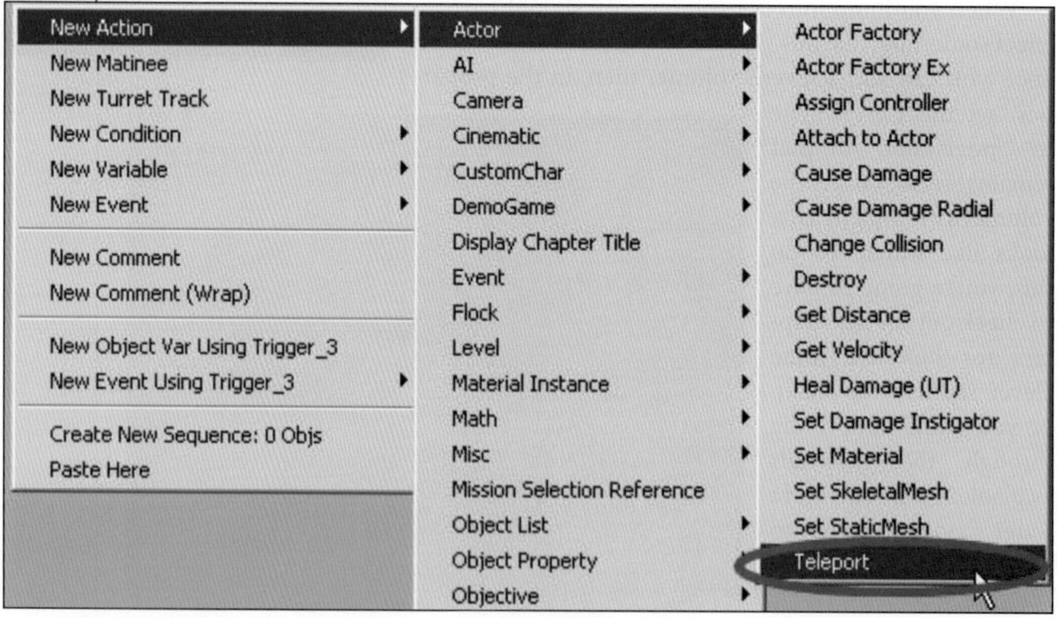

Figure 8.10

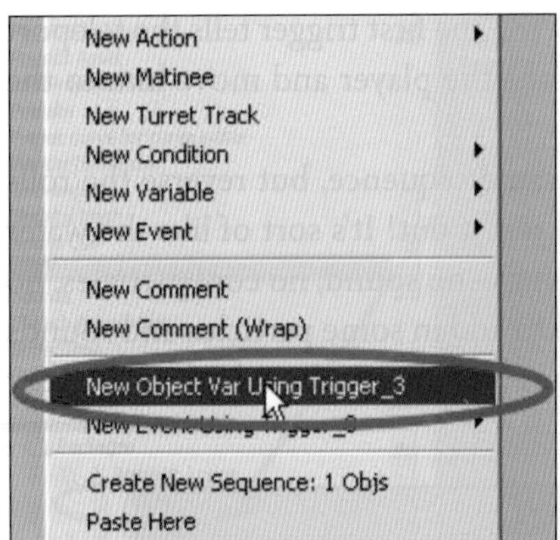

Figure 8.11

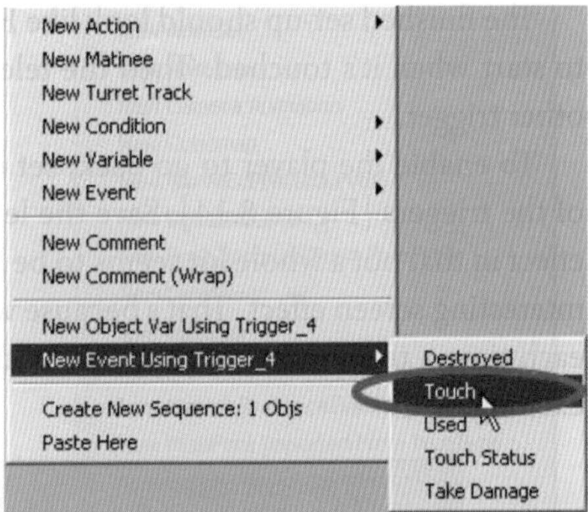


Figure 8.12

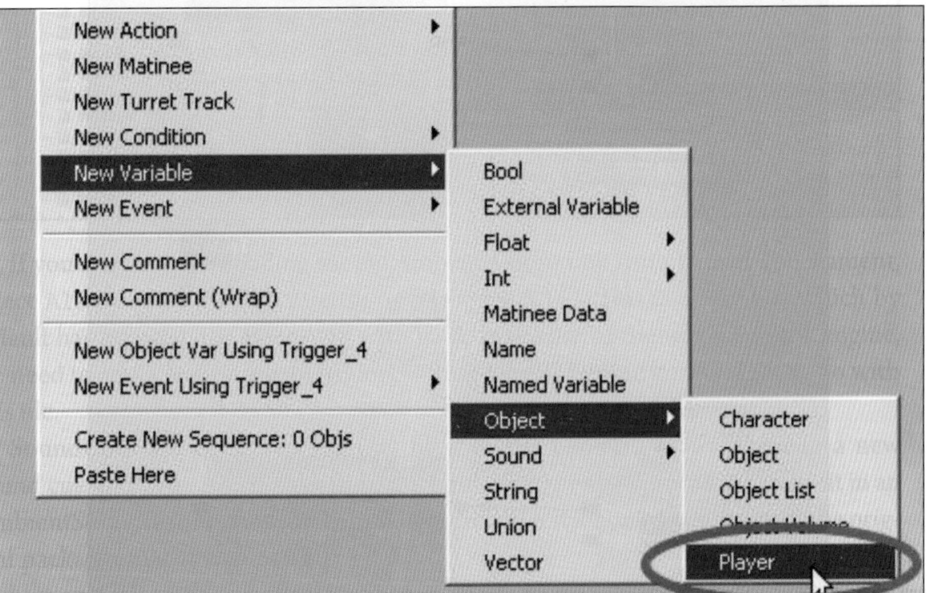


Figure 8.13

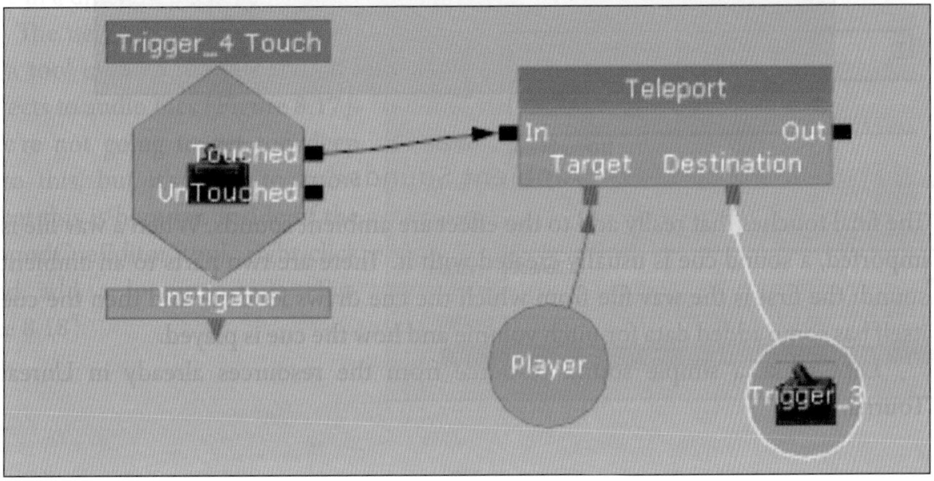

Experience shows that the more changes you can make to a scene without re-rendering and waiting on software renders, the easier the work will be. Even film studios are starting to catch on to the advantages that Machinema offers: time is money. The skill of setting up lights, cameras, and actors in a complex cinematic could translate from a game cinematic into film quite soon.

PROJECT

## Cameras and Screen Effects

So far we've used Matinee to move objects around. One of the more interesting uses of Matinee is to control cameras. Add in a camera actor into the CameraRooms.ut3 [Figure 9.1].

Figure 9.1

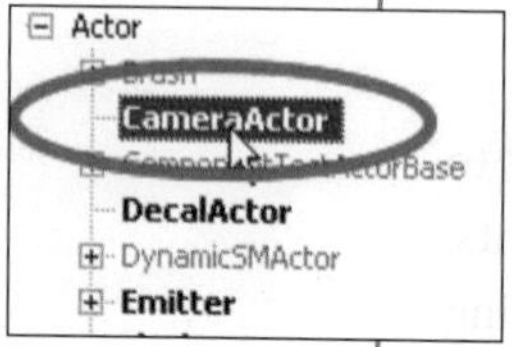

Camera actors are simple mesh objects. These are set to be hidden when you're playing, but they're easier to identify when you can see them in the editor if they look like cameras [Figure 9.2].

A great way to set up a camera point of view is to lock it to the perspective camera using the `look through object` icon. The `eye` icon at the top of the perspective view allows you to snap any selected camera to your point of view in the perspective window. When you move the selected camera, the perspective window shows you what the camera sees.

Select the camera; then click the `eye` icon to lock the selected actor to the perspective view [Figure 9.3].

Here I've moved to look at the door [Figure 9.4]. Before moving again, I need to unlock the camera from the perspective view to leave the camera aimed at the door.

Figure 9.2

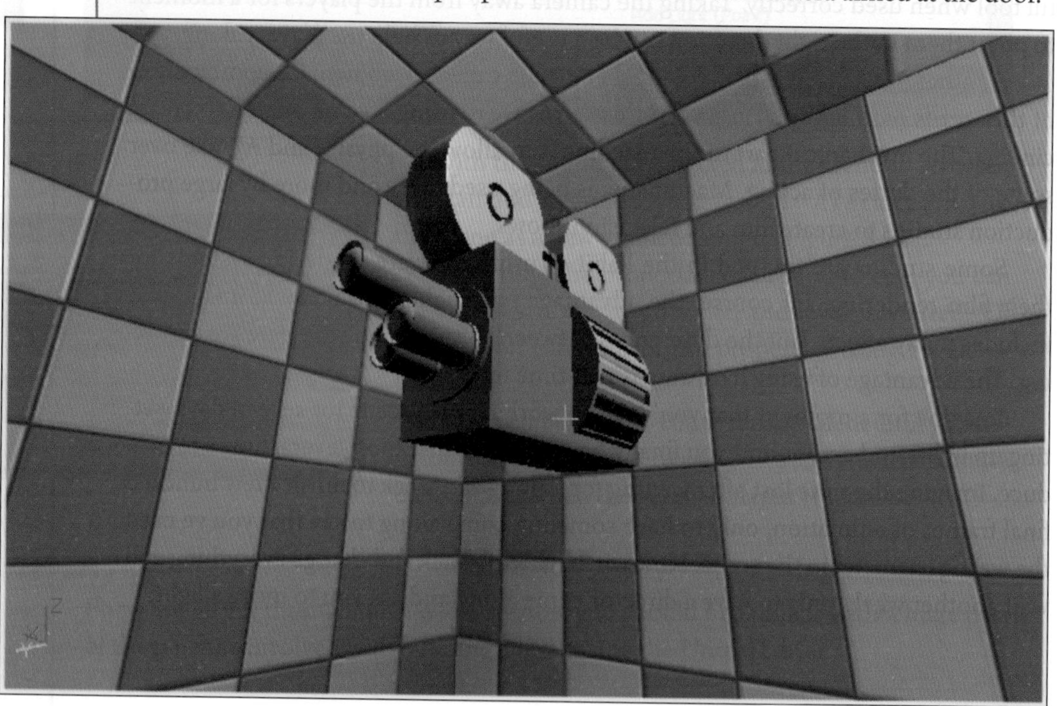

Figure 9.3

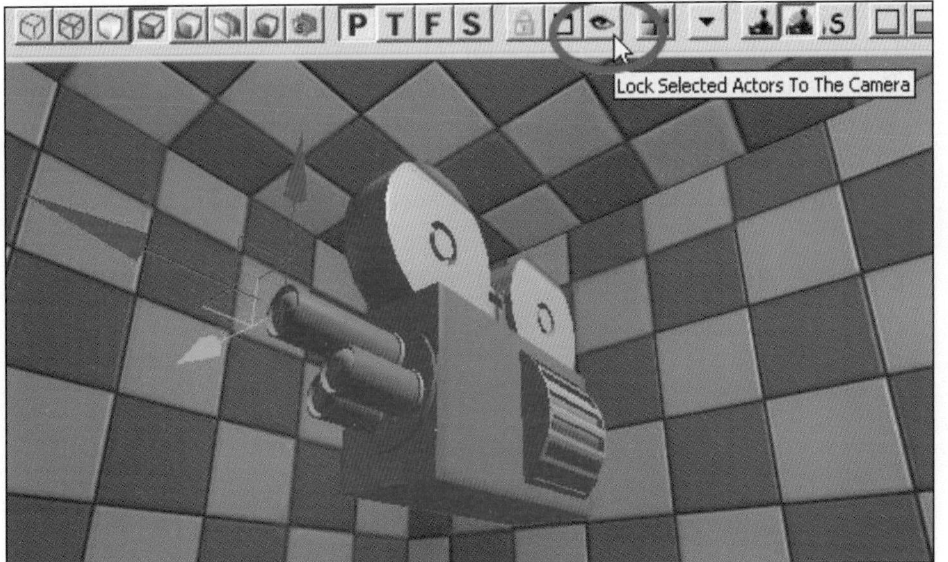


Figure 9.4

Figure 9.5

After the camera has been released from the perspective camera, I can move away and check out where I left the camera actor [Figure 9.5].

Perfect—it's looking at the door where I left it [Figure 9.6]. The lock actor to camera is a bit tricky. If I were to click on another loose actor on the scene, it would jump to the camera, and I'd be moving it around with me as I wandered about the scene. Just remember to be careful with the lock to camera tool when dealing with a complex scene.

Figure 9.6

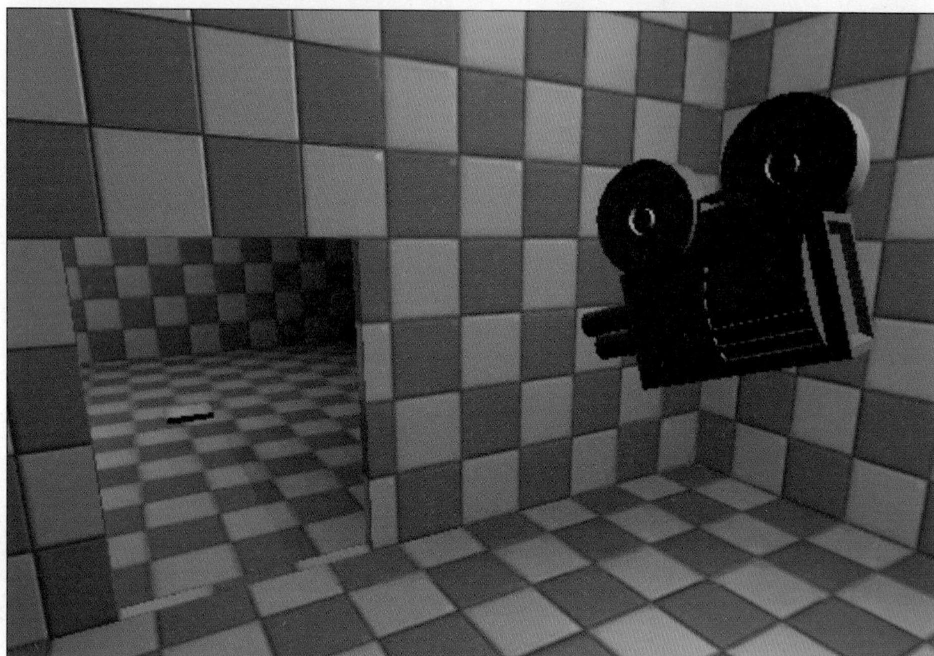

In Kismet, add in a new Matinee sequence. Next we'll add in a new camera group [Figure 9.7]. This is a special type of object that is handled a bit differently than a regular interpolated mesh actor.

We'll name the new camera track "Camera1." This makes it pretty clear what we're doing [Figure 9.8].

Next, make sure that the camera always starts in the same place when the Matinee sequence is triggered [Figure 9.9].

Figure 9.7

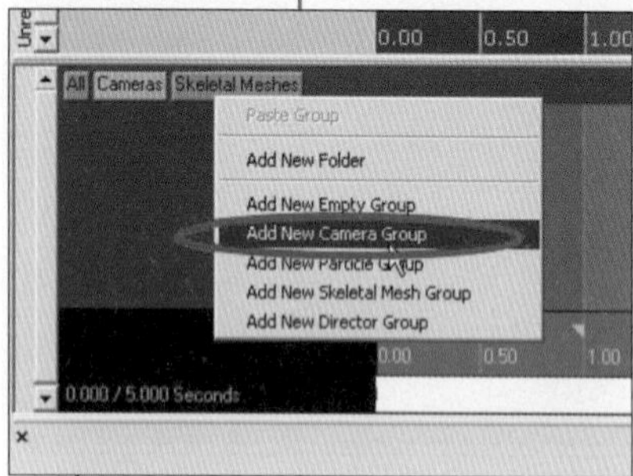


Figure 9.8

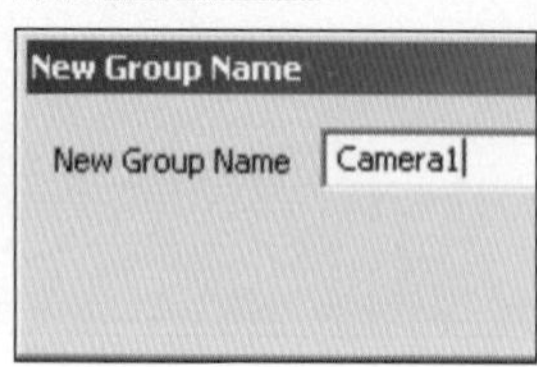


Figure 9.9

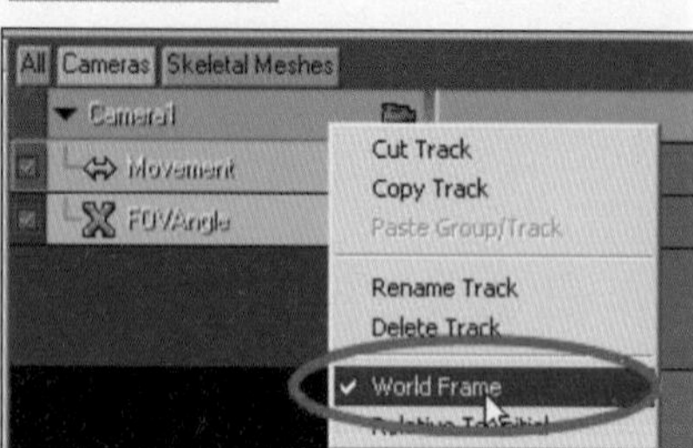

Then, to see what the camera is looking at, click on the `look through` icon [Figure 9.10].

This view should be quite familiar, but this time you might notice that the view is framed by a couple of black bars at the top and bottom of the perspective view [Figure 9.11]. That's because the camera was set to a specific aspect ratio; we can change this, but the camera is helping us know that we're looking though it.

So far, so good: we've added a simple camera to the scene. Now we're going to want to do some interesting tricks to make our camera more exciting.

Figure 9.10

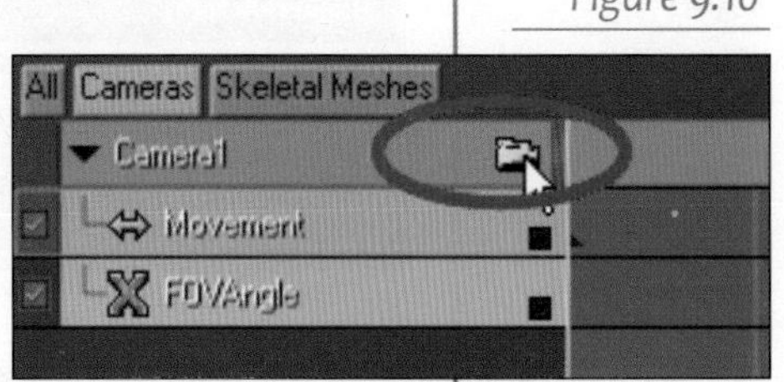


Figure 9.11

## Depth of Field

The Unreal engine uses a few tricks in 3D rendering that allow for basic image processing in real-time. One of these tricks is called post-processing. The use of the word *post* means that the effect is applied after the image is rendered. The image that is rendered to screen is stored in an off-screen chunk of memory in the video card. This chunk of memory is sometimes referred to as an off-screen buffer. While it is in this memory space, filters can be applied to the image before it's revealed to the player. Of course, this can happen many times per second.

Depth of field, or DOF, is the effect seen with many cameras: things inside of the focus range of the camera remain clear, while objects in front or behind the focus range become blurry. Unreal's camera effects include being able to manage DOF, among many other things. Adding a new camera effect is a simple way to add interest to your cinematics.

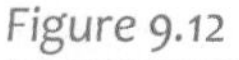

Figure 9.12

Figure 9.13

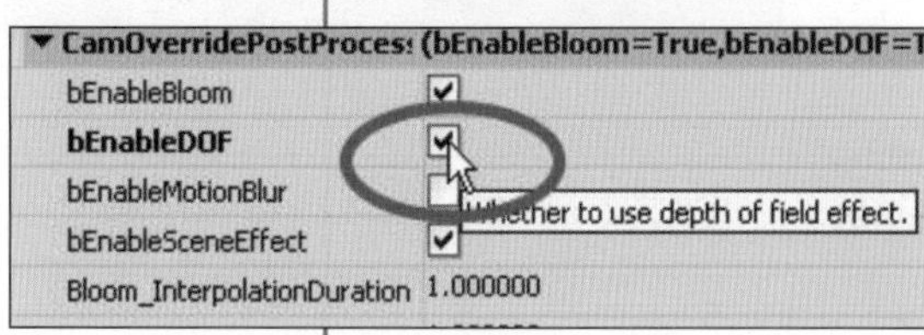


Figure 9.14

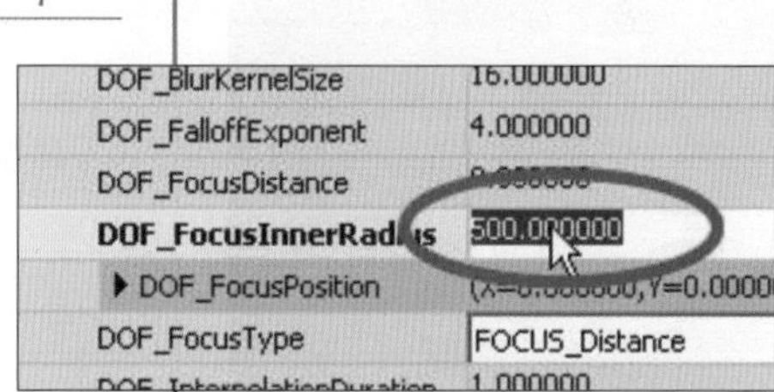

Figure 9.15

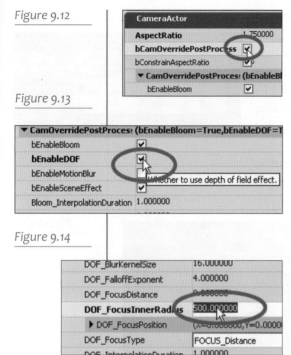

In the level editor, open the camera's properties and expand the CameraActor roll-out. To change how the camera renders the scene, turn on the `bCamOverridePostProcess` [Figure 9.12]. This will allow us to change some attributes of this particular camera to render the scene in a more interesting way.

Next we're going to turn on `bEnableDOF` [Figure 9.13]. Depth of Field was used before in the post process volume. This time we're going to make some additional adjustments to the DOF of this camera.

We're going to change the inner radius so that we can see our effect at closer distances [Figure 9.14].

With these settings active, open the Matinee editor and take a look at the scene though the camera.

The scene should be quite fuzzy [Figure 9.15], which simulates a narrow depth of field that is often seen in real world cameras with a wide aperture. Without going too much into how cameras work, an aperture is the size of the hole through which the

Figure 9.16

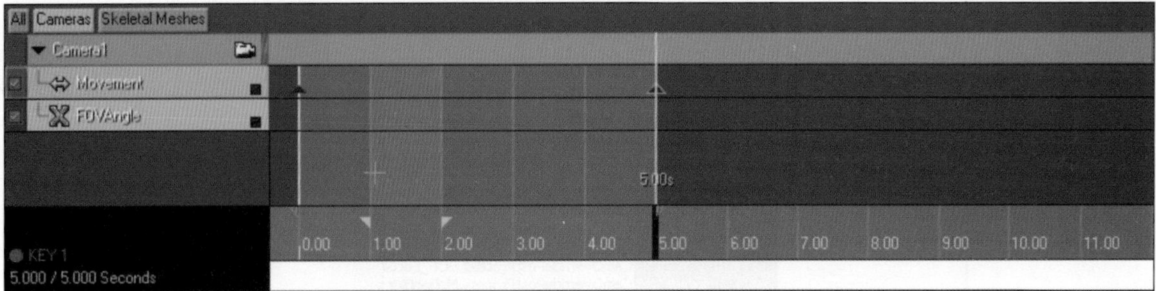


camera sees when taking a photo or video. Small apertures result in crisp images but require more light for proper exposure. Large apertures result in fuzzier images but require less light to produce an image. Of course, Unreal engine isn't going to try to simulate all of the attributes of a real-world camera, so we have to fake some of these effects using post-processing filters.

Move the play-head of the timeline to the end of the Matinee sequence, and then move the camera to look at the plate in the second room [Figure 9.16]. Set a key frame and scrub through the timeline to make sure we animated the camera flying from the first room to the second room [Figure 9.17].

To control where the DOF drops off and starts, we can add in a new property onto the camera track.

Figure 9.17

Figure 9.18

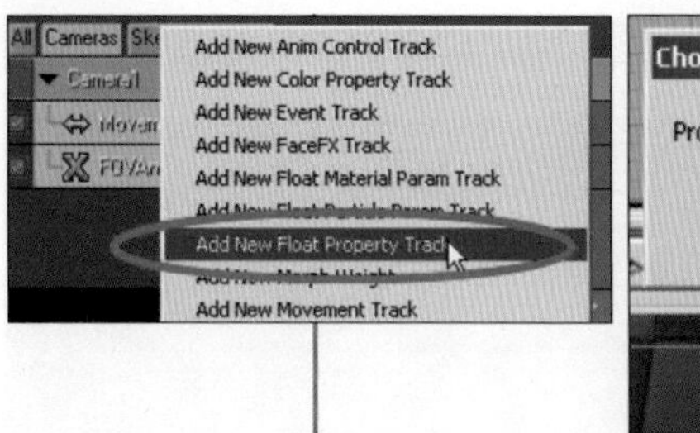


Figure 9.19

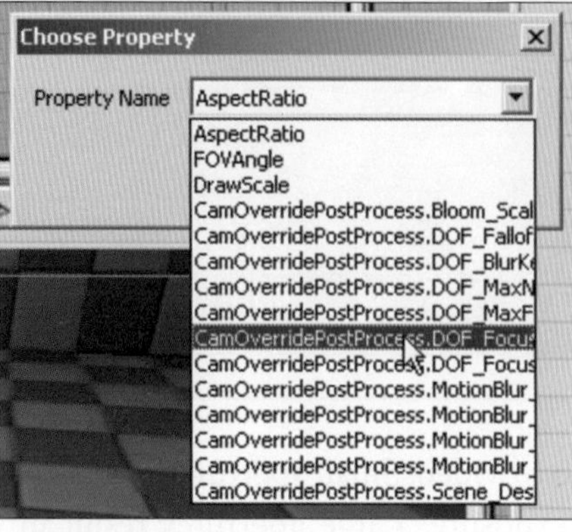


Figure 9.20

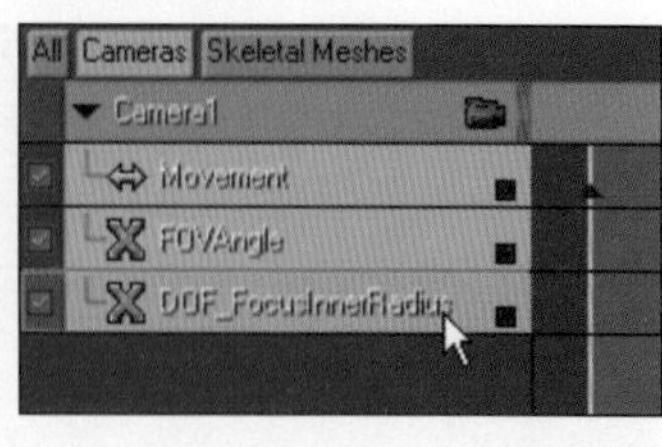


Right-click on the Camera1 track and select `Add New Float Property Track` [Figure 9.18]. This will open a dialog asking us to pick a new property to add to the track. These properties are arranged in alphabetical order. With a bit of fiddling, we can find the `DOF_FocusInnerRadius` property [Figure 9.19] and add it to the list of Camera1 properties [Figure 9.20].

It's up to you to experiment with the other settings. All of these properties can be animated in the same fashion, but we need to stay focused and pick one thing at a time.

Click on the `DOF_FocusInnerRadius` list item to see the timeline. At the beginning of the timeline, add in a key frame and then move to the end of the sequence and add in another.

Figure 9.21

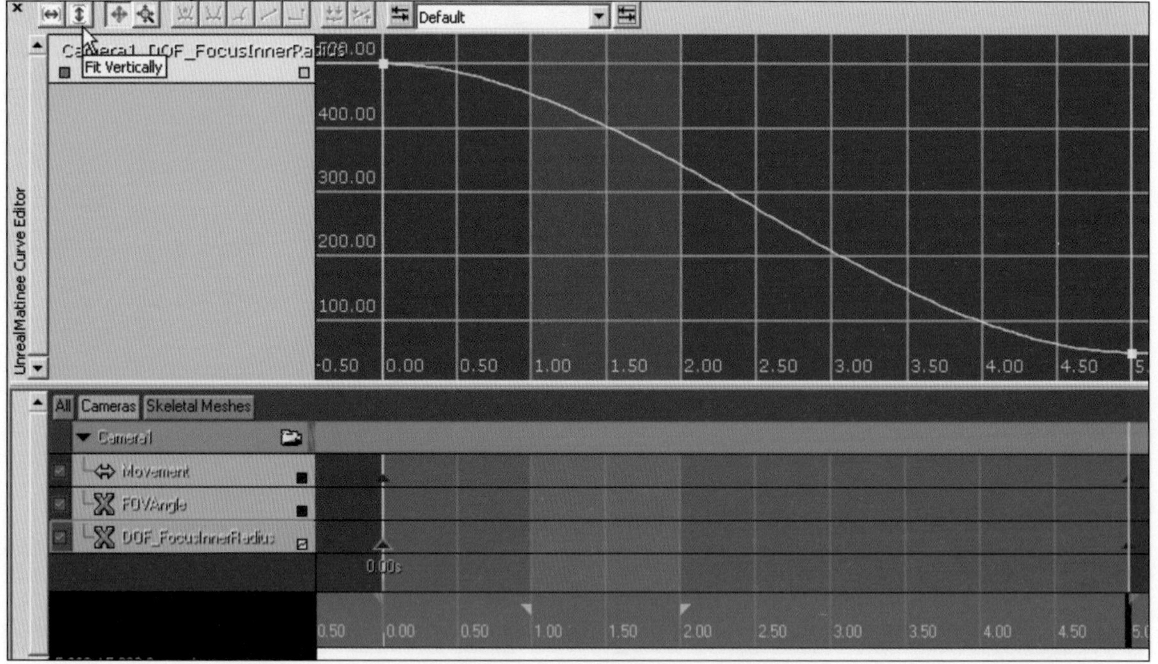

Click on the add track to the Curve editor icon so we can take a look at the property. These numbers can get pretty big, so at the top left of the Matinee editor, click on the `Fit Horizontally` and `Fit Vertically` icons so that we can see the entire curve [Figure 9.21].

From the curve, you can select a key frame and lift and lower the values to observe its effect in real time through the viewport. Unreal engine makes these sort of adjustments surprisingly fast and easy. For this example, I've adjusted the DOF to keep the plate always in focus [Figure 9.22].

Figure 9.22

These settings might be different for your scene depending on the distance from the camera you intend the focus to be. Find the proper settings for your camera before moving on [Figure 9.23]. The inner field is the distance in from the focus point where your focus starts to become fuzzy. The outer distance is the range away from the focus area where the focus becomes blurry. The focus size is a range where the focus remains clear.

In addition to depth of field, you can also change the angle of view of any camera in the scene [Figure 9.24]. Zooming in and zooming out are controlled by the `FOVAngle` track. In addition, attributes such as the scene's color, tinting, saturation and many more can all be modified and animated.

Figure 9.23

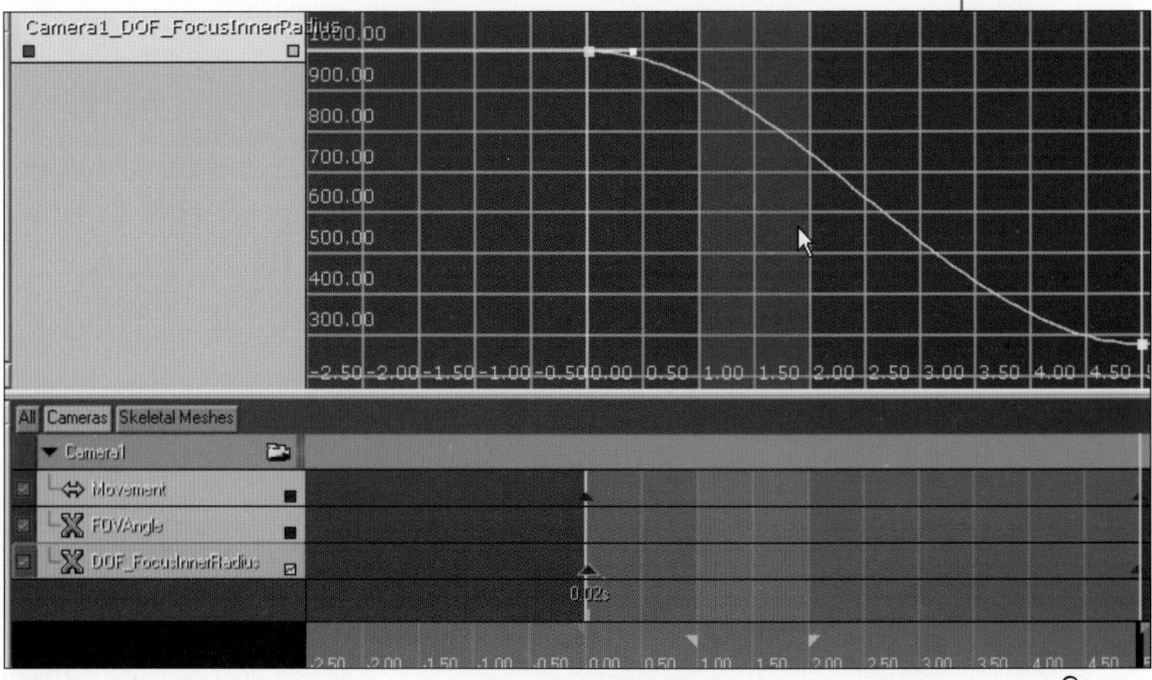

Figure 9.24

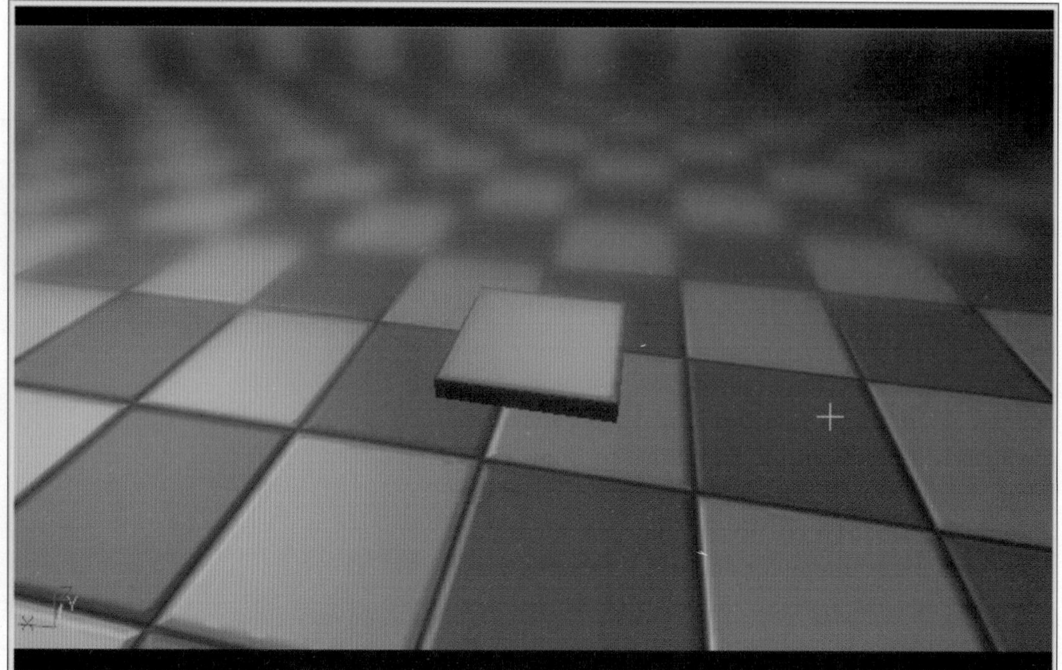

Figure 9.25

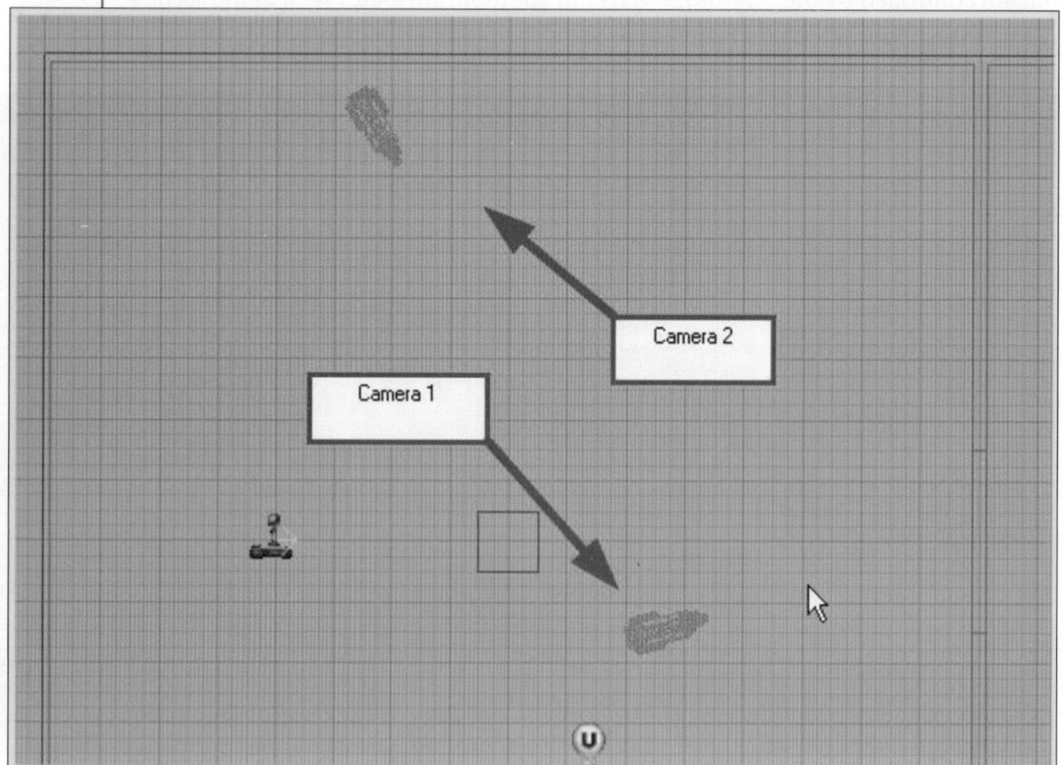

A focus field that's too small is harder to manage because things can move out of the focus range easily. A focus range that is too large negates the need for a DOF to begin with. Find some settings that appeal to your senses. This is largely an artistic decision, so explore to your own ability and find what works for you.

## Director Track: Camera 1, Camera 2

For this set-up, I've added a second camera to the previously set-up scene. Our first camera is zooming from one room to the other, focusing on the plates in the neighboring room. Our second camera will pan around the room like a surveillance camera [Figure 9.25].

To help keep Matinee from getting too cluttered, you can collapse the various animated tracks of Camera1 by clicking on the triangle on the left [Figure 9.26].

Select Camera2 and give it a key frame following the other camera out of the room.

Add in a new Director Group [Figure 9.27]. This will add another division to the lower timeline. The director track allows you to make camera edits much as you do with video editing software. This track is a method to switch from any camera in the Matinee editor to another. If the camera has not been added to Matinee, the director track cannot switch to it. As you add new cameras to the scene, they'll need to be added to the Matinee node before including them in the director track.

To make sure you can see everything in the timeline, you might have to expand the timeline. Click and drag on the horizontal bar dividing the objects in the scene from the director track [Figure 9.28].

Move the play-head to the beginning of the timeline, and in the director track, press enter. This will prompt you with a `New Cut` dialog asking which camera or object you want to cut to [Figure 9.29].

Figure 9.26

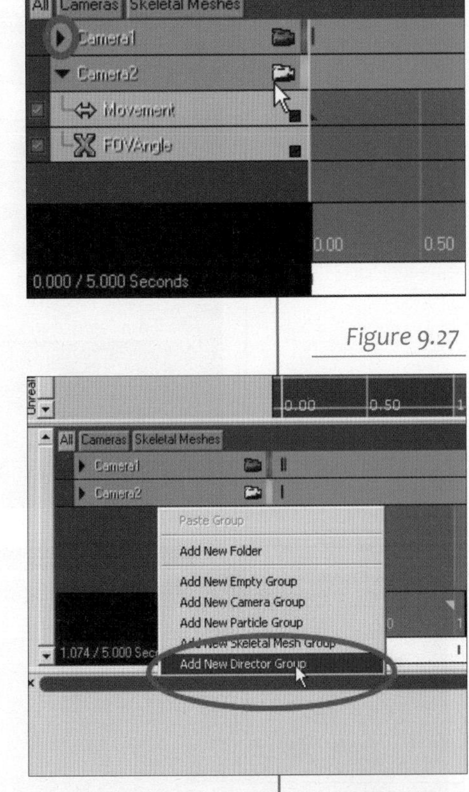


Figure 9.27

Figure 9.28

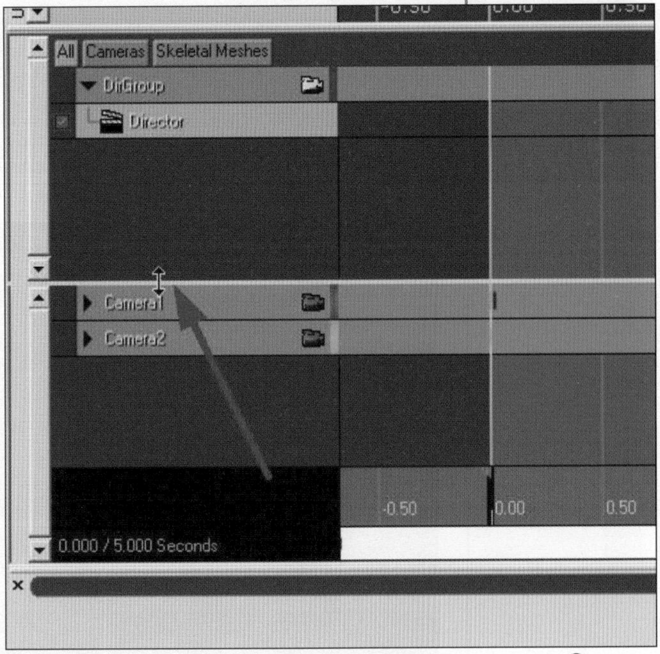

Figure 9.29

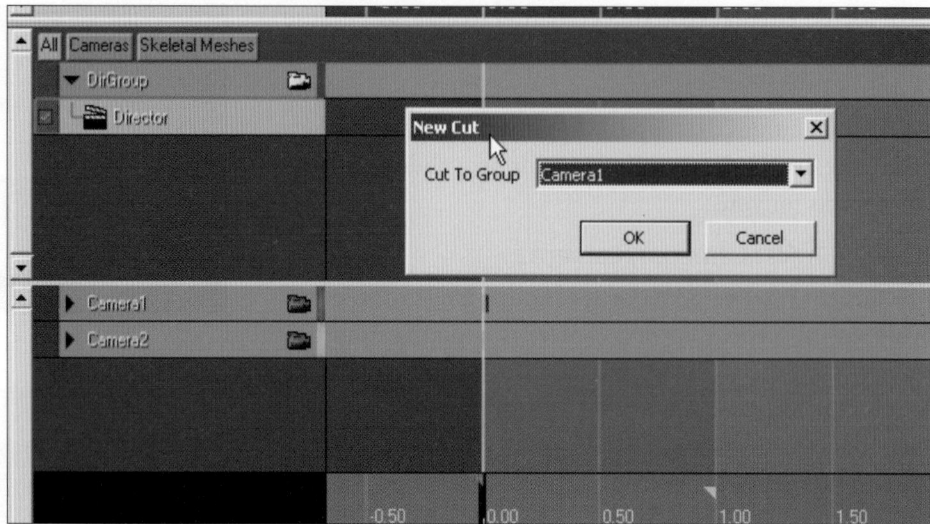


Figure 9.30

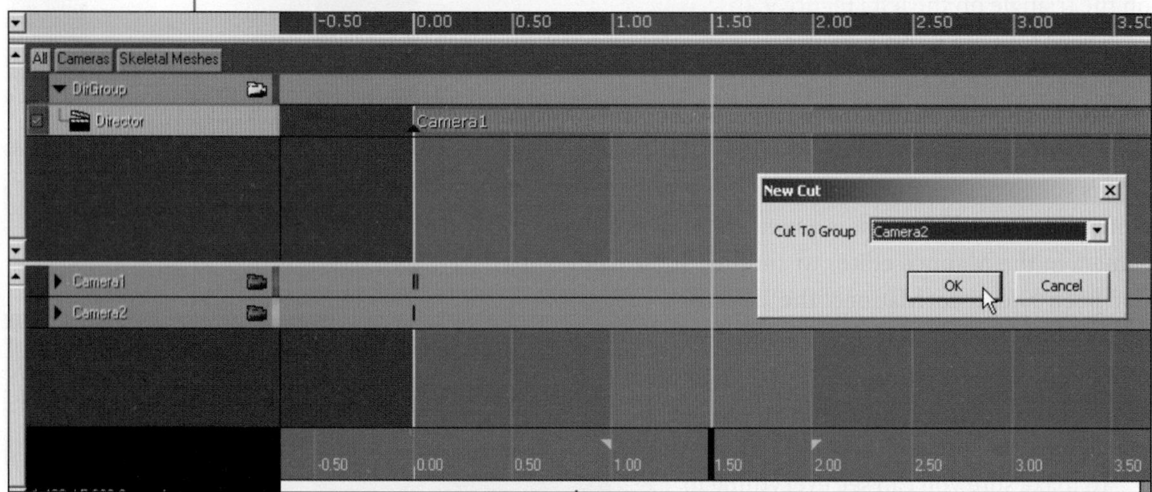


Figure 9.31

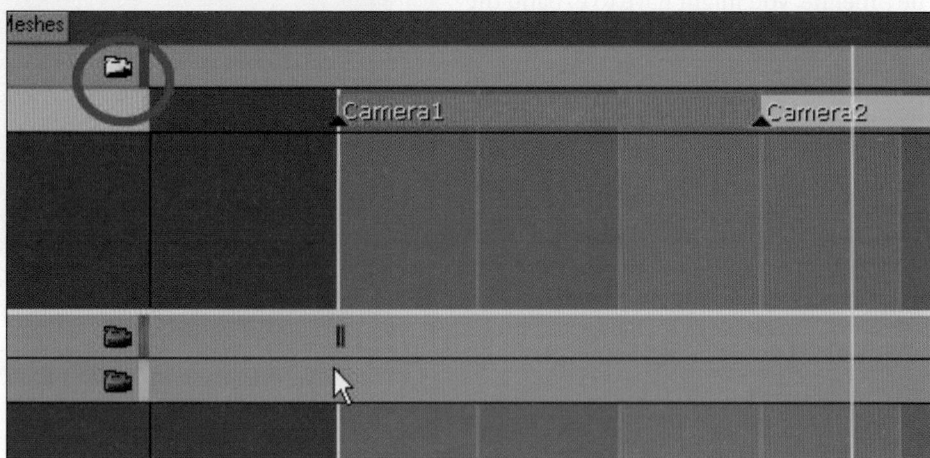

Here I've selected Camera1. The director track reflects this by adding in a new block of data labeled Camera1. Move the timeline down a bit. Then add in another key frame with the enter key and pick Camera2.

This will now add in a second edit [Figure 9.30]. You can have as many edits as needed for any effect you need. It's also important to know that you can have as many camera objects in the scene as needed to accomplish the cutscene edits you need. In theory, you could simply use two cameras and move them around between edits. While the director track is set to see through camera 1, you could move camera 2 into a new position. Once the director track switches to camera 2, camera 1 moves to another position before the director track cuts back to camera 1. In practice, this turns into quite a lot of extra work, requiring the addition of many key frames to each camera.

Figure 9.32

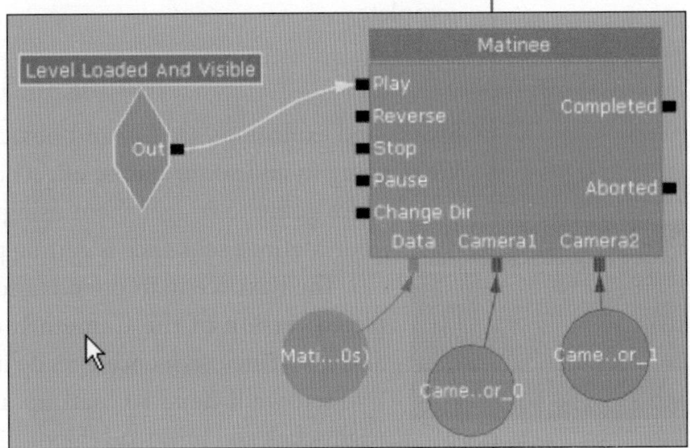


A better way to manage this is simply to add in several cameras. In a complex scene, you might end up with some two dozen cameras; but as long as they are named correctly, keeping them organized isn't so much of a problem. The added benefit of this is that it gets rid of an extra camera edit. You don't need to edit out unnecessary camera movements with it.

To see what the cinematic looks like from Matinee's point of view, click on the `Look Through` icon on the director track [Figure 9.31]. As you slide through the timeline, add key frames to the director track and select which camera you want to look through. To use this as an introduction cinematic, add in a `Level Loaded and Visible` event to play the Matinee sequence [Figure 9.32]. The director track is required to take control over the camera from the player's camera and send it to the Matinee point of view.

Figure 9.33

Now when you run the level, you'll get to watch the Matinee animation through the selected cameras!

Here's your first intro cinematic [Figure 9.33]. It's not very exciting, but we've just been going through the steps required to build up to something pretty fun!

## Particles

Particles are simple fun effects. There are two basic types of effects: single-event particles, like explosions and sparks, and others that play continuously, like smoke stacks or steam vents. You need to trigger explosions over and over if you want them to go off more than once, and the others will need an on and then an off event. After an explosion is set off, the particles remove themselves from memory when the effect is complete.

PROJECT

### Adding in Special Effects

Sparks and explosions are fun and obvious additions to any good action cinematic. We're going to add some smoke effects and explosions to our cinematic scene, and we're going to trigger them using the same Matinee sequence. At this point, your Matinee sequence is getting pretty complex.

Figure 9.34

The next scene to open is the ParticleRoom.ut3; this is basically a completed version of the CameraRoom.ut3 with a couple of moving cameras and a Matinee sequence already in place.

First we'll need to load up a few effects from Unreal Tournament 3. Right-click and fully load the `WP_FlackCannon upk`. This contains plenty of interesting particle effects for us to use in the first part of this project.

Figure 9.35

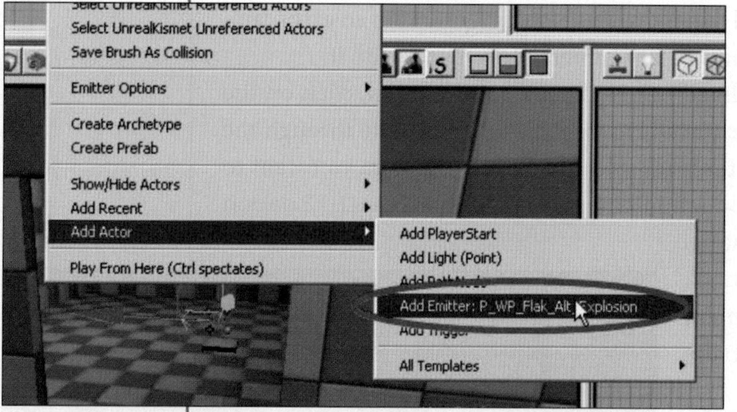


Select the particle effect in the Generic browser [Figure 9.34].

Then, back in the level editor with the ParticleRoom open, right-click and add the particle system over the second platform that the camera is moving toward. Select `Add Emitter: P_WP_Flak_Alt_Explosion` [Figure 9.35]. This will drop in a new particle emitter.

Figure 9.36

Font
Lens Flare
Material
Material Instance Constant
Material Instance Time Varying
MorphTargetSet
MorphWeights
✔ Particle System
Physical Material
Physics Asset
PostProcesss

Particle emitters don't always have to be explosions; we'll also add in a subtle smoke effect using a different particle. Load up Envy_Level_Effects and track down the P_Smoke_Stack_01 particle system. One good way to find these objects in the Generic browser is to filter what the Generic browser is showing you.

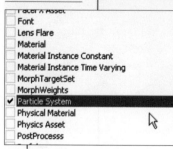

Turn on the `Particle System` check box in the Resource Type filters [Figure 9.36]. Now only the packages with particle systems in them will be listed below.

Fully load the Envy_Level_Effects [Figure 9.37] and select the smoke stack particle system. Right-click and add that to the scene right next to the flak canon explosion's particle emitter.

Once these emitters are placed in the scene, they'll automatically activate [Figure 9.38]. We want to have control over the emitters' activation, so we'll disable this by turning off the `bAutoActivate` option in the emitters' properties [Figure 9.39].

There are a couple of ways we can trigger these particle emitters. We could use a toggle, which would look something like this [Figure 9.40]. Obviously, we'd place a trigger to touch somewhere in the level, and that would turn on the particles—not all that exciting. This is just an example, but for this tutorial we're going to trigger the particle system using Matinee, not the trigger.

Going back to the Matinee, we'll have more control over the timing of these two particle systems. We'll set off the explosion a moment before the smoke starts to rise. To do this, select the smoke stack's emitter and add a new Particle Group track into Matinee [Figure 9.41].

Do the same for the explosion.

Our Matinee track should look like Figure 9.42.

Figure 9.37

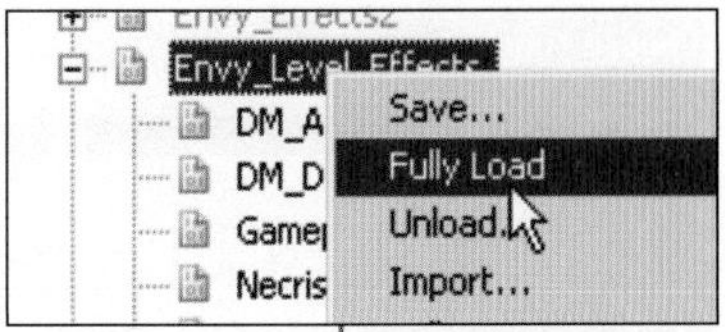

Envy_Level_Effects
DM_A
DM_D
Game
Necris
Save...
Fully Load
Unload...
Import...

Figure 9.38

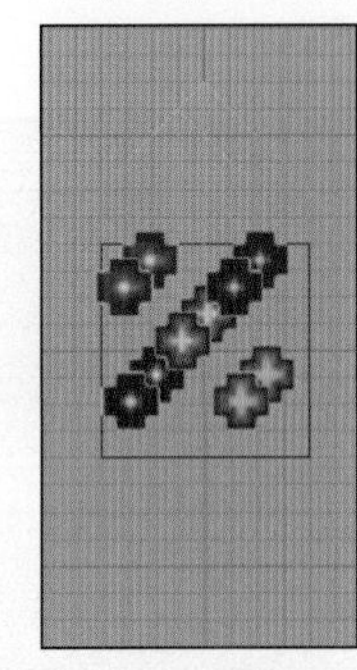

Figure 9.39

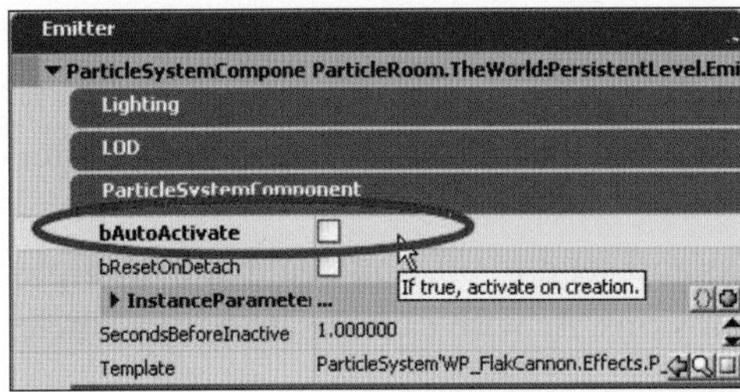


Figure 9.40

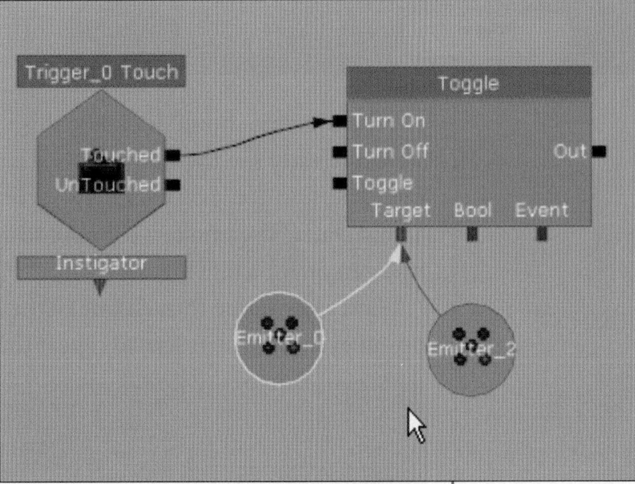


Figure 9.41

Figure 9.42

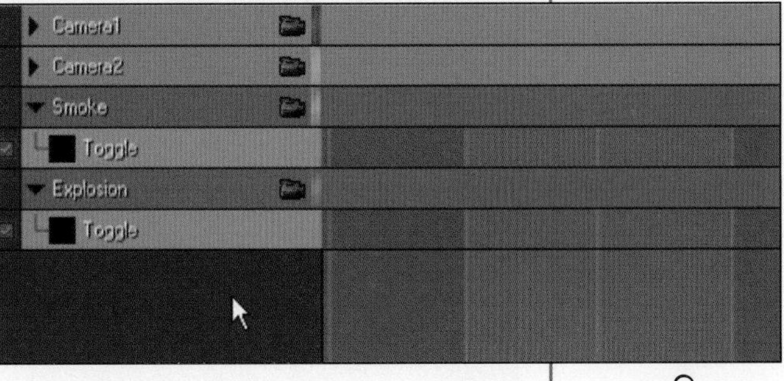

Figure 9.43

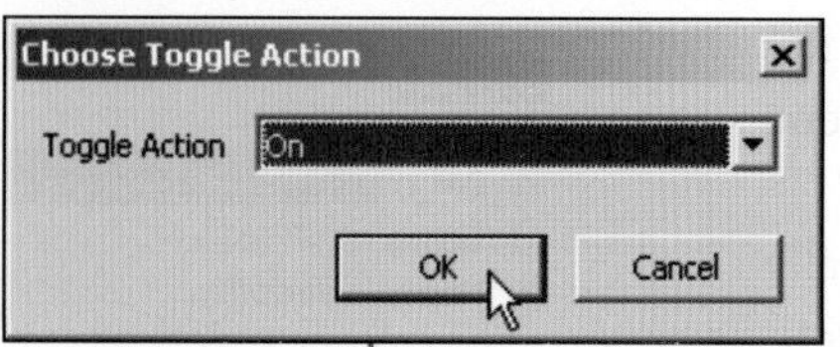


For sake of this project, I added in another cutback from Camera2 to Camera1 so that we can see our explosives at work. Then set a key frame for both the smoke and the explosion to toggle on [Figure 9.43].

This dialog should be self-explanatory. These toggles allow you to turn particle systems on and off.

Figure 9.44

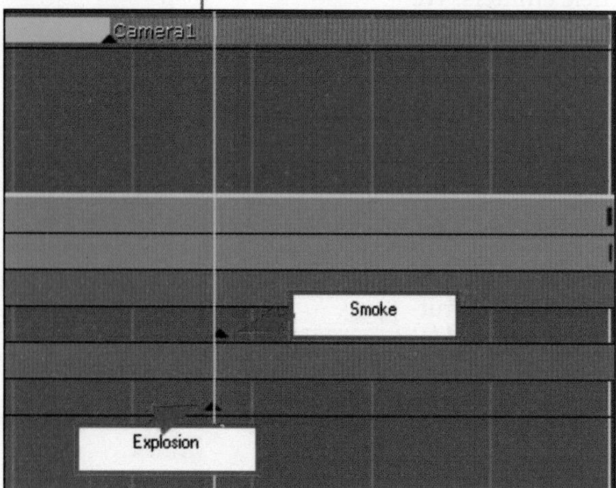


Figure 9.45

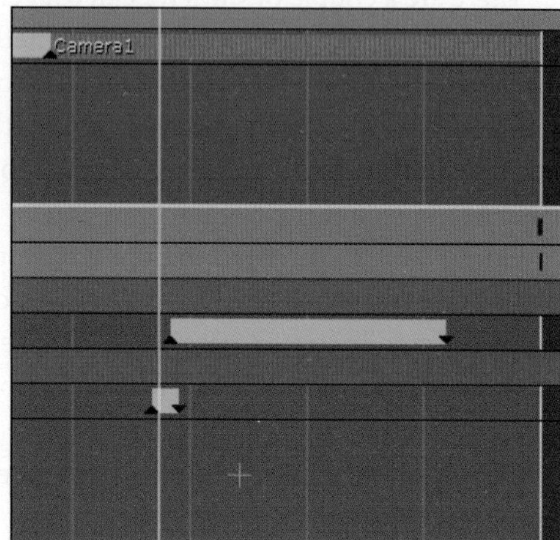


The timeline should look like this [Figure 9.44]. Our Camera1 track is set so that we can clearly see the two events start during our cinematic. So that we don't have our explosion going off every few seconds, we'll need to shut it off nearly immediately after it starts. The smoke we'll want to linger around for a bit, so we'll turn that off after it's been on for a bit [Figure 9.45].

Add a key frame to each one of the tracks and set it to off. You could add multiple on-off events to the tracks to repeat the explosions. As with cameras, to have particle

Figure 9.46

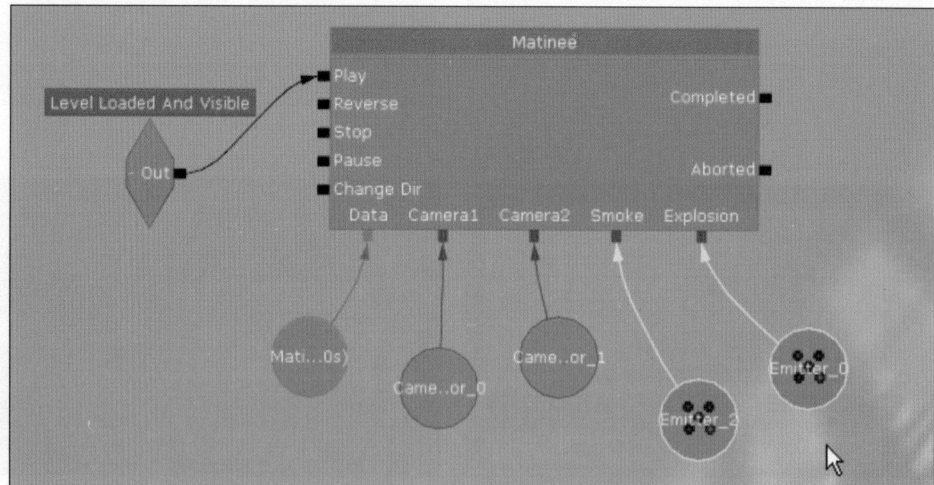

effects in more than one place in the scene, it's best to place multiple particle emitters in the scene. Once you've placed each particle emitter, you'll need to add it to the Matinee sequence to activate it [Figure 9.46].

Our Matinee sequence has grown a couple more data resources. Save your progress and test the level. One last thing: to observe the particle systems running in real time in your perspective view, you can turn on the real-time preview button on the top left of the tool bar in the viewport [Figure 9.47].

Things are starting to get a bit more interesting!

Figure 9.47

## Material Effects

Materials in Unreal editor are complex monsters—trees of nodes spanning hundreds of wires and nodes, and instances that add adjustable parameters and variables. The parameters that allow the artist to fine tune a material's various rendering properties also allow you as a designer a bit of power over the appearance of a material.

A material can be made to convert from a cold, frozen look to a molten, hot look through a single variable. This is quite useful to change the level in ways that can greatly impact the player's experience. We'll take a look at a few examples of how this can be done.

PROJECT

### Modifying Materials Using Matinee

We're going to start this project off with a very basic material system. These resources are provided in the MaterialTransitionRoom_Resources.upk on the disk. Later on,

Figure 9.48

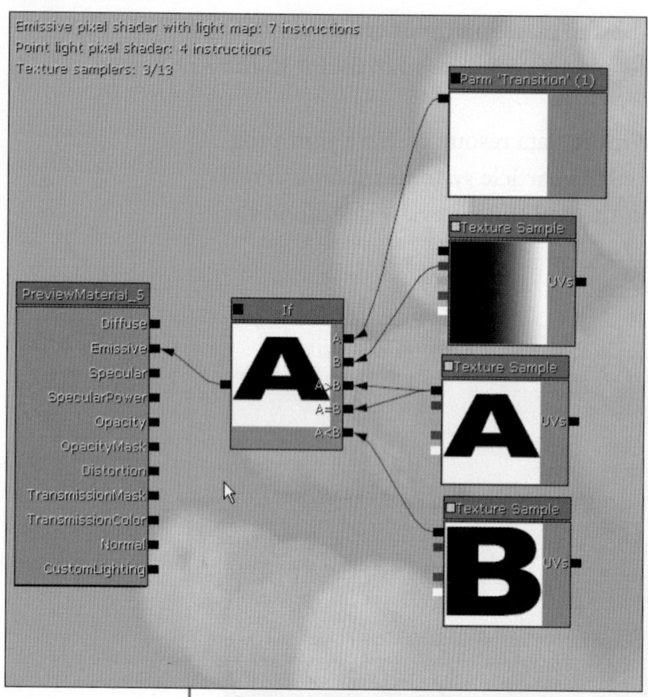


when we get to the materials chapter, we'll explain a bit more about how the material editor works; but for now we'll just discuss the couple of nodes worthy of explanation for this project.

In the middle of this material is a very interesting node called an If [Figure 9.48]. This node will allow us to clearly observe the transition of this material change from A to B and vice versa. The top data input has a Scalar Parameter node that has been named Transition; this is plugged into the A input of the If node. Under it is a simple grayscale gradient that is plugged into B. Then we have a texture sample plugged into two nodes which basically mean if the A input is greater or equal than the value from the gradient show the A texture. Then the B is plugged into the lower node where if A is less than B show the B texture.

Here is a brief explanation of how the material works. A is a value from 1 to 0. The gradient is a number of values from 1 to 0 as well, represented as a color from white to black. Each shade of gray is a value between 0 and 1. Then we have two textures plugged into the If node's evaluated inputs. The three inputs are A > B, A = B, and A < B. Translated, these mean that A is greater than B, A is equal to B, and A is less than B, respectively.

When the value going into A is compared to B, we get to see one or the other image going into the evaluated inputs of the If node. For example, if the Transition node is set to 0.5, that means that any shade of gray with a value above or equal to 0.5 will show us the A texture. Any value below 0.5 will show the B texture.

Figure 9.49

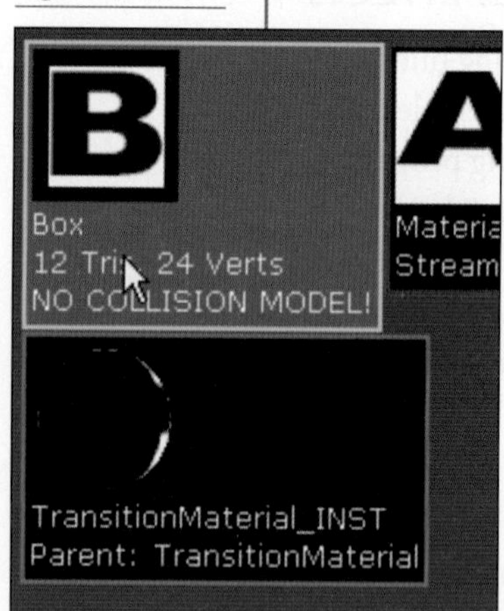


Confused? Don't worry: this will all be clear once we start to use this tool. The most important idea to get out of this is that there's a variable that has been exposed to the outside world. Any node that has "Parm" in its name means that the data can be modified in real time.

The next thing that has already been set up for you is a box that has had a material instance constant assigned to it. Place the box into the scene on the second plate that Camera1 is flying to [Figure 9.49].

Again, once we get into materials later in this book, you'll understand what a material instance constant is in more detail. Basically, a Material Instance Constant (MIC) means that the shader doesn't have to be recompiled with every modification. This allows for data

Figure 9.50

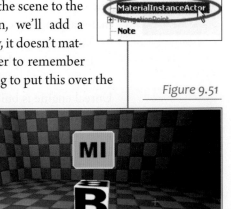

to be streamed to it in real time. For this project, we're going to stream data to the material via Matinee. To do this, we'll need a connection in the scene to the material in the Generic browser. To make this connection, we'll add a `MaterialInstanceActor` to the level [Figure 9.50]. In reality, it doesn't matter where in the level this object is placed. But to make it easier to remember what this `MaterialInstanceActor` is controlling, we're going to put this over the object in the scene we're going to be modifying.

Figure 9.51

Your scene should end up like Figure 9.51: a box with a MI over it. It's a bit odd, but don't worry. There's an interesting point to all of this—really! Select the `MaterialInstanceActor` that you just placed over the box and open the properties editor [Figure 9.52].

Figure 9.52

Expand the `MaterialInstanceActors` MatInst property, select the `TransitionMaterial_Inst` from the Generic Browser, and click on the Green Arrow to connect the actor in the scene to the material instance constant in the Generic browser. This is how the two objects will communicate with one another. Now we're going to need to control the MIC though Matinee. To do this, we'll select the `MaterialInstanceActor` in the scene and add a track for it in Matinee.

Figure 9.53

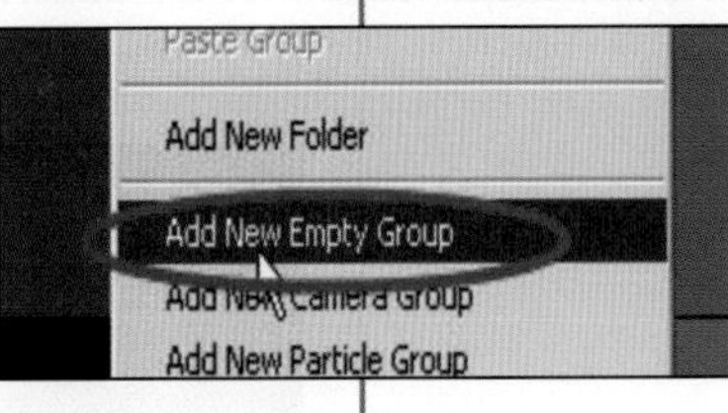


Add a new Empty Group [Figure 9.53], and name it "Material Transition."

Add in a new Float Material Param Track [Figure 9.54]. This will allow us to have control over the parameter through the Matinee timeline. In the properties window in Matinee, change the ParamName for the Float Material Param Track to "Transition" [Figure 9.55].

This is the name of the Scalar Parameter that was created in the material for the box. When we named the node in the material editor, we gave it a value to which we can now send data. Once we add key frames to the material property track, we can directly manipulate the value in the material.

Figure 9.54

Figure 9.55

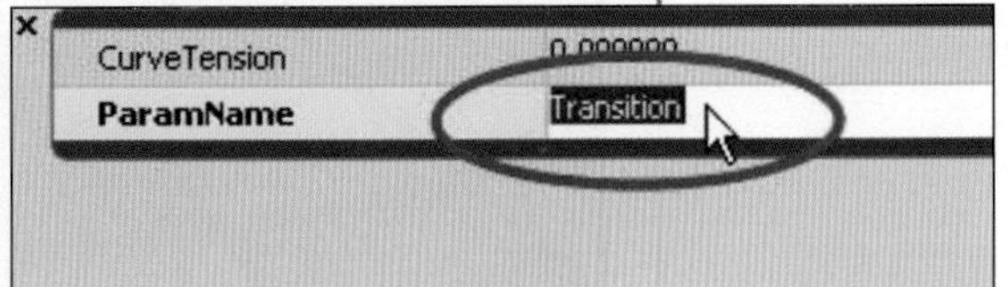

Figure 9.56

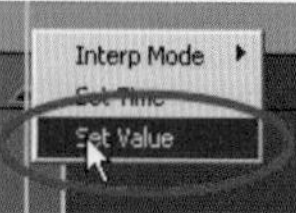


Add in three key frames [Figure 9.56]. The first two can be set to 0 and the last one should be set to 1 [Figure 9.57]. This will animate the value that is input into the material property of the material instance.

Make sure that the transition from 0 to 1 happens when camera1 can see the box.

Even without playing the level, you can scrub though the timeline and observe the material transitioning from A to B [Figure 9.58]! Materials are a huge part of what Unreal engine is built around. The materials that can be created in Unreal Engine 3 allow tricks that no other engine can afford as easily. Materials like this could help with converting characters into stone, or you could cover the ground with ice. Using some clever modifications, you could change the appearance of an entire scene from rusty iron and metal to wood, stone, and ivy.

Figure 9.57

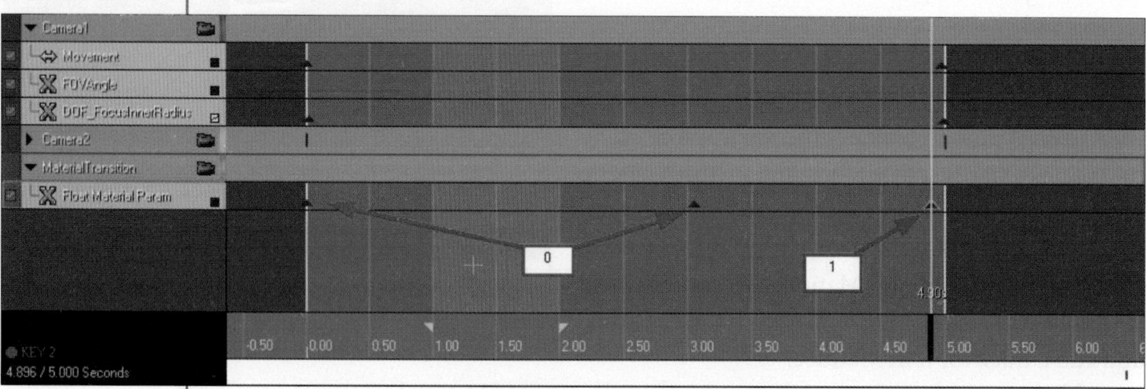


Figure 9.58

With the help of Unreal script hiding and unhiding parts of a scene to match the material changes, you could completely change the feel of any environment. In addition, characters, monsters, and particles could completely change in appearance as well.



## Camera Particles and Materials

The story so far has been something of a crash course in the Unreal engine as a whole. But take heart—we've learned a lot as well. We've made cameras fly around; we got to blow things up; and then we made a box's texture mutate. We made extensive use of Matinee, the Unreal cinematic tool. We've built some basic levels using BSP tools in the engine. We've worked with lights of all kinds. We learned how to manage level streams and learned a bit about programming logic using Kismet.

Now that we've covered the basics of how to get things done, it's up to you to take what you've seen here and extend your knowledge by experimenting with the various editors even more. Find out what the other nodes in Kismet do. There are many conditions and events we haven't even mentioned. Likewise, there are a lot of events that can be triggered and adjusted using Matinee.

# 10 Animated Characters in Cutscenes

*Machinema*

Animated characters in a cinematic automatically bring to mind long, drawn-out dialog sequences of old, tired soldiers contemplating the meaning of life. This doesn't always have to be the case. Creatures running past the player or birds flitting in the sky are both instances of animated characters that can change the overall feel of a game. Once a complex character has been set up and readied for game play, he is also ready for you to use in your cinematics.

Anim-slots are nodes in the Unreal animation tree editor that allow you to combine multiple animations. These animations layer on top of one another, blending actions like walking and talking together in an intuitive way. To avoid unnecessary complexity, you'll be spared the details of how this is done, but just accept the fact that you can animate the character's face in addition to having the character walking around in a scene just by adding a new animation track.

Once a character's anim-slot nodes are set up, they'll appear in the Matinee sequence. In general, you'll want to deal with just a few of them. You'll need a full body node of some kind. The naming is dependent on the artist or programmer who constructed the anim tree for the character. Then you'll want an upper body node of some kind, usually from the first spine node up. Finally, you'll want the character to have FaceFx added to him so he can talk. FaceFX is a complex animation tool that can do quite a number of things for the artist automatically. Without going into detail, it's quite surprising that it's a part of the Unreal Editors tool-set. It's an amazing piece of software.

## Adding in Characters, Sounds, and Dialog

PROJECT

Let's open up the Cinematic_CaptainHadron.ut3 map. This is pretty much the same sort of box room we've been using from our other projects. To get started, let's also go to the Generic browser and load in the Cinematic_CaptainHadron.upk. This contains several resources for this project. Select the Captain Hadron Skeletal mesh in the Generic browser [Figure 10.1].

Figure 10.1

Figure 10.2

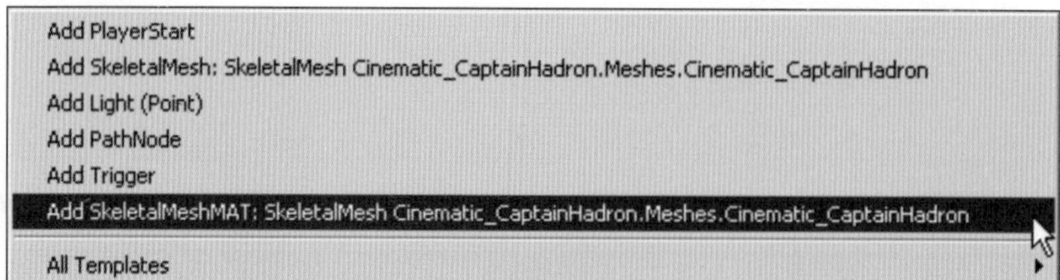


Figure 10.3

Figure 10.4

Figure 10.5

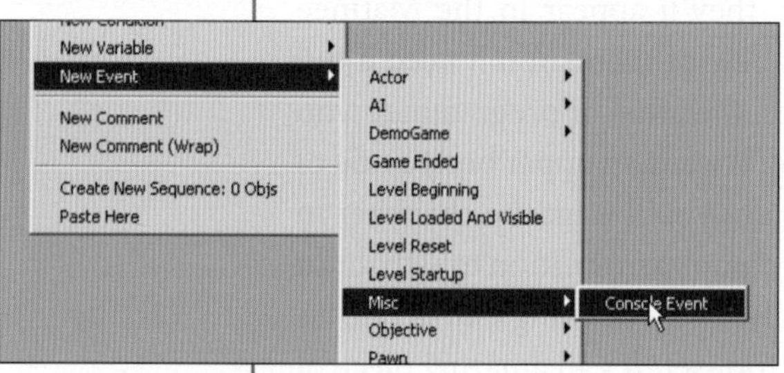


This is a regular character mesh that is also used for the character modeling projects later on. The Cinematic_CaptainHadron.upk contains the basic elements required to make a character walk and talk in the Unreal Engine 3. The addition of a FaceFX object has been included with this package. FaceFX is a powerful tool, but its use is beyond the scope of this book.

Select the captain's skeletal mesh; then go into the level editor's box and right-click to add this model to the scene as a `SkeletalMeshMAT` [Figure 10.2]. This is different from the usual skeletal mesh. The MAT at the end means that you intend to control this mesh using Matinee.

Get properties for the skeletal mesh you placed in the scene, and expand the `SkeletalMeshComponent` roll-out menu. In here you'll have access to modify many of the attributes associated with a skeletalMesh character. First, add in a new AnimSet using the green + icon in the AnimSets menu [Figure 10.3]. This will connect the skeleton in the editor to the animation assets in the Generic browser. To give the skeletalMesh some behaviors, connect the AnimTreeTemplate slot to the CaptainHadronAnimTree node in the Generic browser. AnimTrees tell the skeleton which animation to play based on various inputs from the world. Physics, actions, scripts, etc. will need to find a condition in the AnimTree to play correctly.

The AnimSets and AnimTree are found in the Cinematic_CaptainHadron.upk under the Anims subcategory.

Now we will tell the mesh it needs to update any physics conditions. Expand the movement roll-out and change the physics to `PHYS_Interpolating` [Figure 10.4]. Now we're done prepping our skeletal mesh actor for Matinee and animated cutscene goodness.

Let's hop into Kismet and add in a useful new utility called a console event [Figure 10.5].

Console events are handy little nodes in Kismet that are useful for testing levels. You can build your complex script events and connect them to difficult-to-reach triggers and puzzles. However, if you just want to test that a script is working, you could add in a simple console event node [Figure 10.6].

Figure 10.6

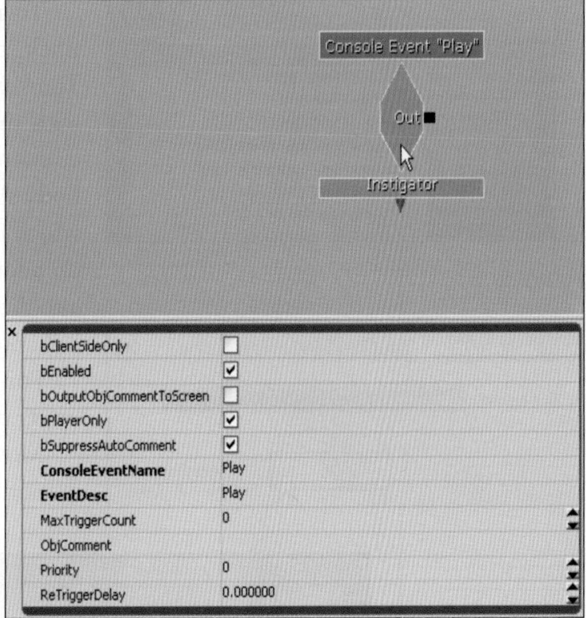


The ConsoleEventName is the command that is used in the command line to trigger the event. The EventDesc will be printed when you check for what console commands are available in the level. We'll be using this node to trigger our new Matinee object. After adding a new Matinee object, open the editor. Select the captain in the level editor; then add a skeletal mesh group to the timeline [Figure 10.7].

Figure 10.7

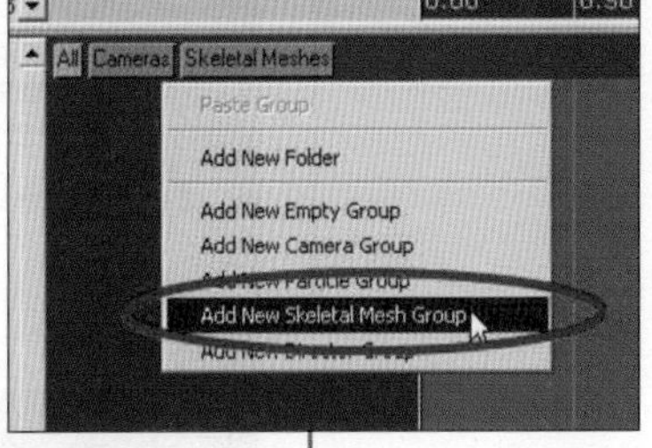


It's important to remember to always select something in the level editor before adding an object to the timeline in the Matinee editor. There isn't any other way to update the timeline's contents after it's been created. The order of operation is important and can sometimes result in confusion when you're moving an object around and adding key frames but nothing is working.

Name the new SkeletalMeshGroup "CaptainHadron" [Figure 10.8]. This will make things more identifiable if the timeline gets populated with a complex cutscene. It's not uncommon to have a Matinee object with several dozen tracks.

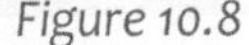
Figure 10.8

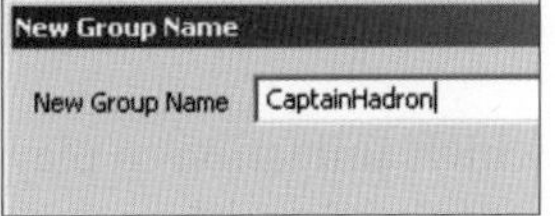


Figure 10.9

In the property editor in Matinee for the SkeletalMesh track, connect the Matinee track to the captain's animations [Figure 10.9]. This might seem redundant, but without this step, Matinee doesn't know what animations the skeletalMesh has access to. This is similar to how the skeletalMesh in the scene was connected to its animations from the Generic browser.

Now Matinee is more aware of the types of animations that can be played by the skeletalMesh actor in the scene.

Figure 10.10

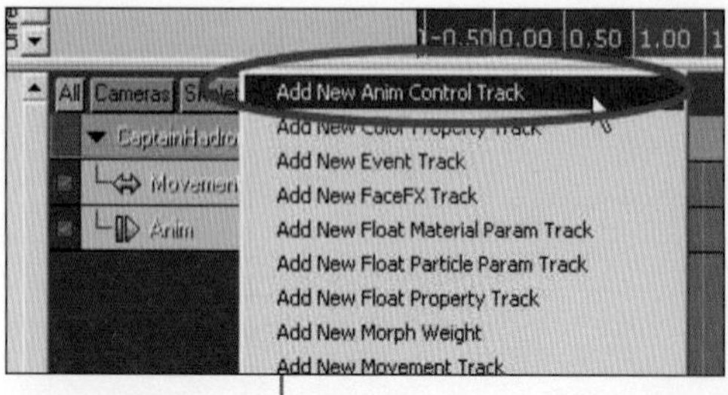


Figure 10.11

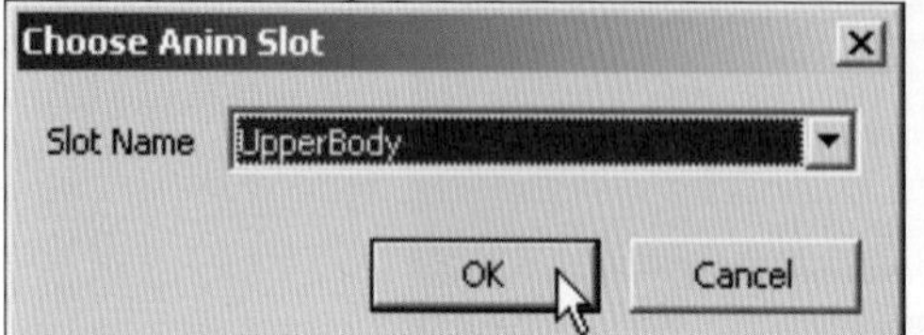


To add a new animation, we can't use the default Anim track in Matinee; we need to add a new Anim Control Track that is aware of the AnimTreeTemplate associated with the captain [Figure 10.10]. The Captain's animTree contains three animation slots: a full body slot, an upper body slot, and a lower body slot. These are used to isolate which joints an animation will play on. To remain focused on adding animation to our character, we'll avoid getting into the specifics about anim slots. These will be covered in a chapter about character animation later on.

For this animation, we'll just animate the captain's upper body [Figure 10.11].

Move the time slider to about 1 second into the animation and press the enter key to create a new key frame.

Figure 10.12

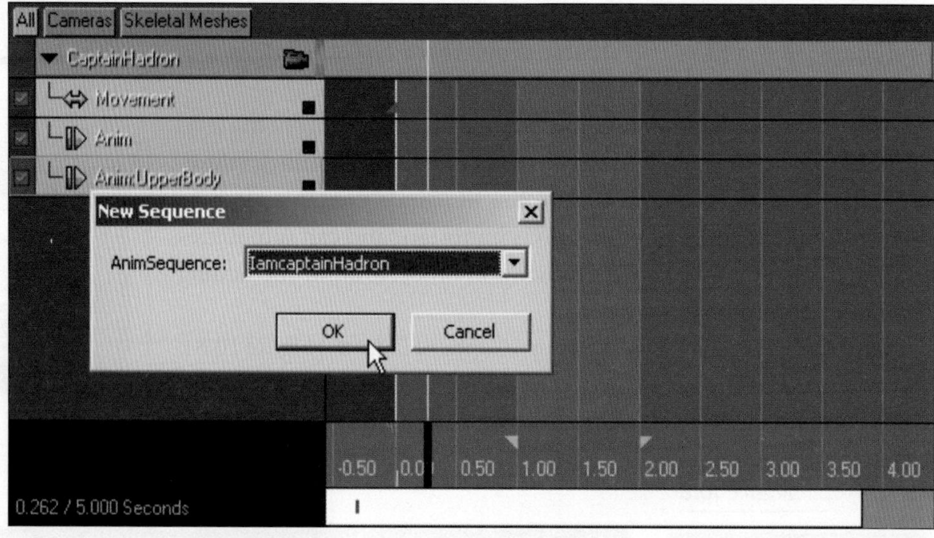


Figure 10.13

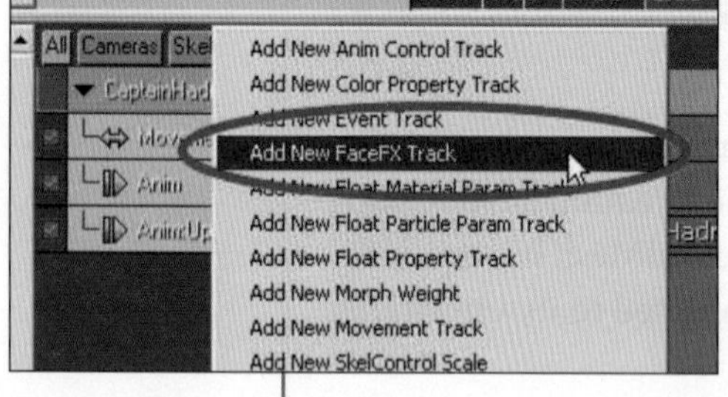


This will prompt a dialog to pick which animation to play [Figure 10.12]. Matinee is getting this list from the animSet that was added in the timeline's properties. It's important that these match with the skeletalMesh in the scene.

Next, so that our captain has something to say while acting, we'll add a new FaceFX track [Figure 10.13].

Select the IamcaptainHadron dialog in the FaceFX Animation and click on OK [Figure 10.14]. This will drop in a new track of data.

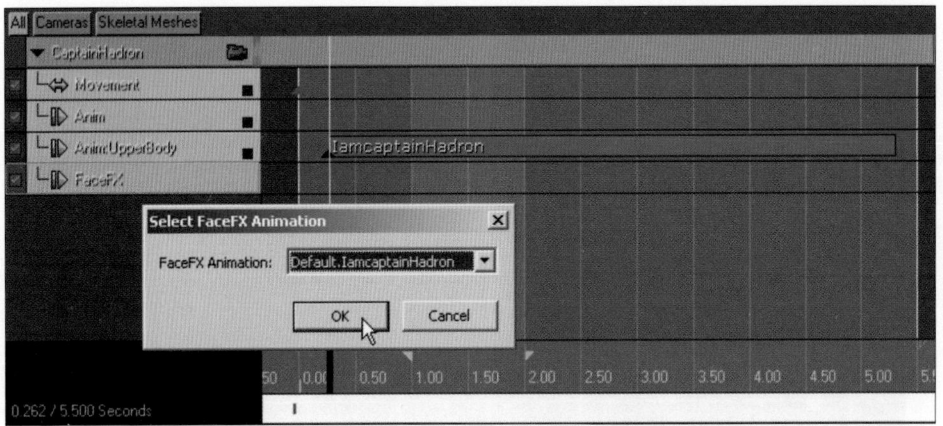

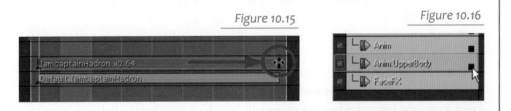

Figure 10.14

Here we have our upper body animation playing along with our FaceFX track [Figure 10.15]. But the lengths are mismatched. To solve this glitch, we can stretch out the body animation to match the length of the FaceFX animation. Hold Ctrl+LMB on the tail edge of the animation and drag it to match the length of the FaceFX track. This will slow down the animation so that it's playing the entire time that the FaceFX track is playing.

Figure 10.15

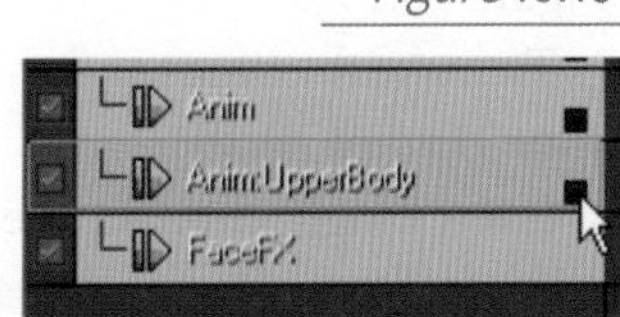

Figure 10.16

Click on the `UpperBody graph` editor button [Figure 10.16]. This will allow us to blend in the upper body animation on top of the regular animations that will be played by the AnimTreeTemplate [Figure 10.17].

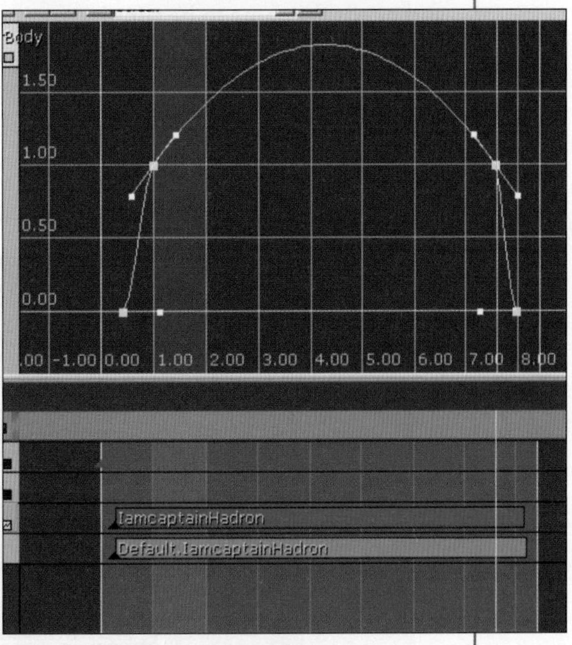


Figure 10.17

Add in a few frames: one at the beginning, one at the end, and then two just after and just before the end of the upper body animation's play length. On the graph line, you can use Ctrl+LMB to add

Figure 10.18

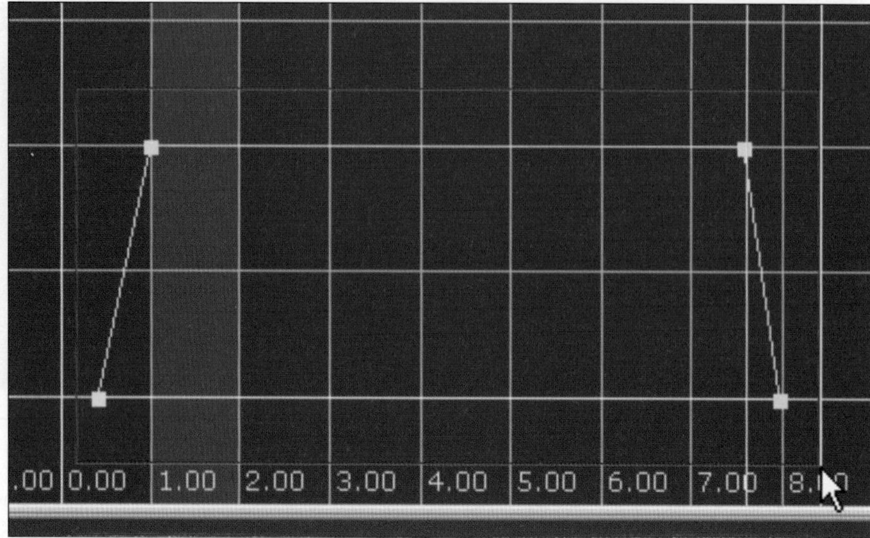


Figure 10.19

key frames. We only need values between 0 and 1, so you can use Ctrl+Alt+LMB to box select all of the key frames [Figure 10.18] and change them to linear interpolation [Figure 10.19].

To make the times and values more specific, right-click to enter values for each key frame [Figure 10.20].

Interestingly enough, the AnimTree doesn't calculate unless the game is playing. The animTree will not calculate when scrubbing through the timeline in Matinee. The FaceFX and the Upperbody animations will, but the AnimTree is a behavioral system and needs the game to be running for it to calculate which behavior to play.

When the captain is standing still, he'll simply play a basic idle animation while acting out. To see the animTree in action, move the captain around in the room and add in some key frames to make him walk [Figure 10.21].

Figure 10.20

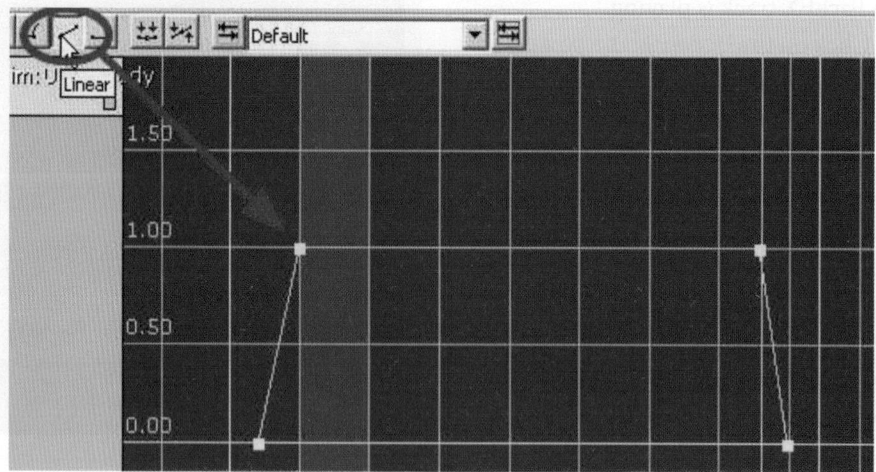

Figure 10.21

Figure 10.22

Figure 10.23

Figure 10.24

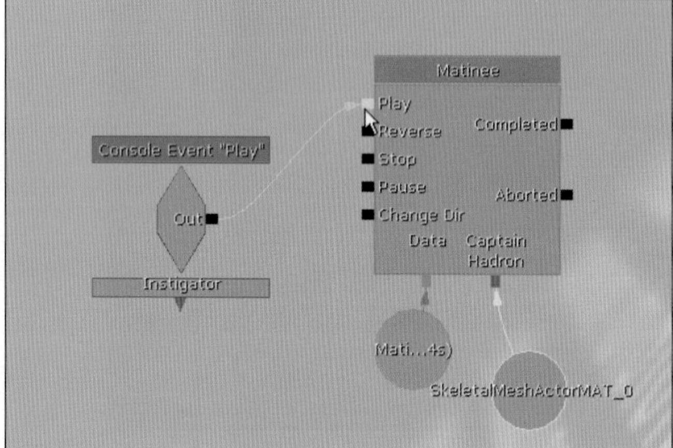


Slide him forward [Figure 10.22] and then add in a key frame in the movement track in Matinee [Figure 10.23].

Now just to double check, make sure that the console event we added earlier is connected to the play tab of our Matinee sequence [Figure 10.24].

Once we run the game, we'll see our captain idling at one end of the room [Figure 10.25]. The animTree template is allowing him to idle because he's not moving. Here's Machinema coming into play. We're allowing the software to control the animation of our character.

Figure 10.25

Figure 10.26

To run the animation, hit tab while in the in game view; this will open up a command line for us to enter commands. Type "CE Play" which means "Console Event Play" [Figure 10.25]. This will trigger the console event node we connected to the play tab of the Matinee object in Kismet.

Now we've got an acting character walking and talking [Figure 10.26]. This is a very basic cutscene animation sequence, but the building blocks are here for you to expand on. This is only the beginning; there's no difference between the cutscene we just created here and the animated events that take place in most of the gigantic games on the market today.

Just to practice, you should add in a camera and a director track to follow the character as he walks. It's just about time you started working on your own designs and building your own animated sequences. Take what you've collected here and build on these concepts and ideas. So far, we've touched a bit of everything that Unreal engine has to offer game designers. Have fun!

You're practically the Steven Spielberg of your own video game—"woot!" Cinematics don't always have to take control over the player's camera, by the way. Mini-events, or what is known as moment-to-moment events, are really what make up a modern game cinematic. As a designer, your focus should be the moment-to-moment experience your player is going to have. As players explore your level, they should constantly encounter some interesting moment that leads them to the next interesting moment.

As moments are triggered, the players should have a clue as to where they should be going next. When they arrive at the next point of interest, the next moment is triggered. This process of leading the player through your level should reveal your story in tiny parts, each one leaving bread crumbs leading the player to the next moment and the next discovery.

# Part II: Art

*The Tool Box of the Unreal Artist:*
*More Than Spanners and Wrenches*

# 11 Art, "The Unreal Way"

*Building Games the Artistic Way*

Unreal Editor 3 is a huge step beyond Unreal Editor 2. Many changes and advances have been added to the editor and the engine. Different games that use the engine have modifications and additions to the base code. You can modify the engine for building everything from fighting games to MMOs.

Unreal Editor is made of many smaller editors, each one specific to a particular task. These editors are used to build dynamic behaviors for ragdolls (PHaT) or particle systems for explosions (Cascade). Each tool has functions in it to help accelerate your work.

With some game engines, you'll have to trudge through code and add in comments into some mysterious ini file. Unreal Editor allows artists to build and complete assets using the tools they already know, with no need to edit text files so the that engine can find any particular asset.

That is not to say that you'll never edit or change any code. There are many instances where UScript needs to be edited to add your art to the game, but for testing and visualizing purposes, there's little to no need to leave Unreal Editor to see what something will look like when you're playing your game.

## What to Expect

We'll go through several of Unreal Editor's tools, but only enough for you to understand how the tool is used. Beyond the basics, you'll have to explore the depth of each tool on your own. There are a few different processes when it comes to building a level and building assets to place in a level. In addition, there are several other editors within the Unreal Engine that we'll take a look at in this section. Primarily we'll focus on the mesh editor, material editor, and animation editor. These are the three primary editors we'll need to use quite a lot throughout the rest of the projects.

We'll also see how to build assets to best fit into a level and how to use the level editor in Unreal with an external content creation tool, in this case 3D Studio Max. Alternatively, Blender is also a great tool that many artists use—and it's free!

Importing and exporting objects will be covered in later sections, but we'll see a bit of the pipeline in this chapter. Working with Max and Unreal, you'll get a better feel for how the production of your game should flow.

## What Is Provided

For this section, you'll need to set up the editor along with some of the example UPKs that Unreal uses to store data. These can be found at http://www.akpeters.com/unrealgamedev.

## More Than Just a Level Editor

Unreal Editor is much more than a level editor. Particle systems, materials, animations, and many other assets can be created and edited in the editor without any outside tools.

The AnimTree editor allows you to apply inverse kinematics for foot and hand placement. AnimTrees also give you the ability to add interesting movements to the character for real-time interaction in many complex and interesting ways.

Complex scripting behaviors can be added through Kismet, a node-based event-triggered scripting environment. Cascade is a highly advanced particle editor that gives the user the ability to create detailed, complex, and multilayered particle effects. Phat is the physics editor that allows you to add in springs, sliding joints, and other constraints to a character or dynamic object. The material editor is quite possibly one of the most immediately fun tools to begin using. Interactivity and real-time feedback make using Unreal Editor an exciting tool to learn.

We will be going into a number of the different editors in the following chapters. AnimTrees, materials, AnimSets and Phat will be a common stomping ground for the Unreal character artist. They each have a number of gotchas you'll have to learn, but once you've gotten into the pipeline, you'll be able to build characters and objects in no time at all.

# Review

Building with BSPs is a quick and easy way to rough out a level. You should spend some time exploring how they can be used for your own game design.

# 3D Design and Autodesk 3D Studio Max 12

## *3D Modeling: Creating Your World*

In a nutshell, 3D models are arrangements of points called vertices in 3D space connected by edges. Related edges form polygons. A polygon is a boundary of edges that defines a surface. A mesh is a collection of connected polygons that defines a shape. Meshes can be as simple as a box, eight vertices connected by 12 edges forming six polygons. In addition to these vertices are texture coordinates, sometimes called UV coordinates. UVs are required for any mesh in Unreal to maintain proper texture display. Of course, if you're familiar with 3D modeling, then none of this is news to you. However, one thing to remember is that the Unreal Engine 3 uses only triangles. Subdivision surfaces, nonuniform rational B-splines (NURBS), and other parametric surface types are not yet used in the Unreal Engine.

A texture is a 2D image that defines the surface's color and appearance. The texture's placement is determined by the mesh's UVs. This is somewhat like wrapping paper on a gift. In the following chapters, you'll be building a variety of objects, starting with a box and ending with a character. To get there, you'll be guided through some design processes that are used by professional 3D artists.

## What to Expect

These chapters will gloss over some of the deeper considerations when it comes to modeling complex, high-resolution shapes. There are plenty of external resources that will help you become a better 3D modeler. The most relevant things to consider for Unreal Engine are going to be our main focus. Learning any 3D tool takes time and patience, so instead of trying to teach these many skills in such a limited amount of time, we've provided many materials for you to use later. They are available at http://www.akpeters.com/unrealgamedev.

Profiles and the outlines of your meshes are the most important for quick recognition. These will define the shape of your object and make things recognizable from a distance. Once we get into building some basic props, weapons, and characters, we'll consider what makes up a distinctive profile.

When you start building, make sure that each new object you create is distinctive and not a simple copy of another basic shape. Make sure your entire world is consistent with itself. Having a few cartoony objects mixed in with photorealistic objects can make an awkward experience for the viewer.

We'll start by exporting a few simple objects. You can either build them yourself, or you can use the resources provided on the disk. Either way, the goal is to understand the process of building assets in 3D Studio Max and GIMP and then importing them into the Unreal Engine.

After we're used to how the process works, we'll apply the lessons learned to building more complex assets. By the end of these art chapters, you should be able to build and implement a complex character for your game. Your first game might not be a blockbuster triple-A title, but you should know what it might take to make such a game.

If you're already familiar with 3D modeling, or if you've spent the time it takes to learn how to better model in 3D, you'll also have the skills required build meshes and objects for Unreal. Game engines like Unreal Engine have some specific requirements that differ depending on whether you're building objects for a film or a render.

The specifics will be covered in later chapters; just keep in mind that these requirements can sometimes be quite specific. Skipping a single step or a simple detail can result in unpredictable outcomes. If something seems to be amiss, then you may want to retrace your steps and find out where things might have gone wrong.

On the book's website (http://www.akpeters.com/unrealgamedev) are materials and intermediate versions of the projects in the art chapters. If you get stuck, you should be able to use the files to help you see where you should be going. Try not to rely too much on the provided files. You should be learning how to do the work on your own. However, completed sample files are provided if you're getting stuck.

Of course, if there are some roadblocks you just can't get past or if there are sections that you're not interested in doing, you can use the completed files to move on. Learning the Unreal Engine is a gigantic undertaking. Learning from specific sections, then expanding your knowledge afterward, isn't a bad way to learn. As you grasp certain concepts, others will become more accessible. Many parts of the engine are interrelated in a way that requires an Unreal artist to be flexible and quick to learn.

In addition, there are many on-line resources and forums on which you can post specific questions: http://www.udk.com is a great resource for asking questions specific to the editor.

## Intro to 3D Studio Max

3D Studio Max is a powerful 3D modeling tool. It's used by many game and film studios worldwide for animation, special effects, and architectural visualization. We'll be using Max to learn the basics of 3D modeling. The concepts you'll learn are not specific to 3D Studio Max. You'll be able to apply your knowledge to any polygon modeling environment. Autodesk's Maya, XSI, Side Effects Houdini, and even Blender are all great tools for modeling and animation. Tools and techniques are fairly similar from program to program.

When 3D Studio Max first opens up, a dialog that has links to some movies is presented. If you're completely new to 3D Studio Max, I highly suggest that you go through them to get a better grasp of what's going to be covered in the following chapters. This book is not about learning 3D Studio Max; you should have at least a basic grasp of some general modeling techniques before getting too far into the following chapters.

To avoid being sidetracked by topics that are better covered in books focused on 3D modeling and animation, these chapters focus on Unreal Engine specifics. However, there are many specifics that will be covered that Unreal Engine requires. It's best to get what you can out of the following chapters and then, on your own time, learn the particulars of 3D modeling and animation.

Of course, if you're already familiar with 3D modeling, the projects may be redundant. However, the projects are still useful for getting to know how your models relate to what can be done in the Unreal Engine. The workflow, or pipeline, from your 3D modeling app into Unreal is the focus of the projects, so it's best to stick to the course.

There are many things that 3D Studio Max can do that Unreal Engine cannot, though you may be surprised by Unreal Engine's capabilities. Also, Unreal can surprise you with the tools and other systems available within the engine that 3D Studio Max might handle as easily.

## Getting Started

After installing 3D Studio Max, you'll want to make sure that you've also installed the Unreal Engine specific ActorX plug-ins. Navigate to the Plug-ins directory (provided at http://www.akpeters.com/unrealgamedev) and copy the ActorX plugin from the 3D Studio Max 2009 plug-ins directory to the following location [Figure 12.1].

Figure 12.1

Address C:\Program Files\Autodesk\3ds Max 2009\plugins

| Name | Size | Type |
|---|---|---|
| ActorX.dlu | 152 KB | DLU File |

Once it's copied to the plug-ins directory, the tool is accessed though the utilities panel [Figure 12.2].

Double clicking the ActorX item in the list launches the tool dialog [Figure 12.3].

In order for this to work, you must match the version of Max to the version the plug-in was made to run on.

ActorX for Unreal 2 works for Unreal 3. The output of a mesh and a skeleton haven't changed much between the two versions. The additions that make up an Unreal Engine 3 character are made in the Unreal Editor after the data has been exported from 3D Studio Max.

Figure 12.2

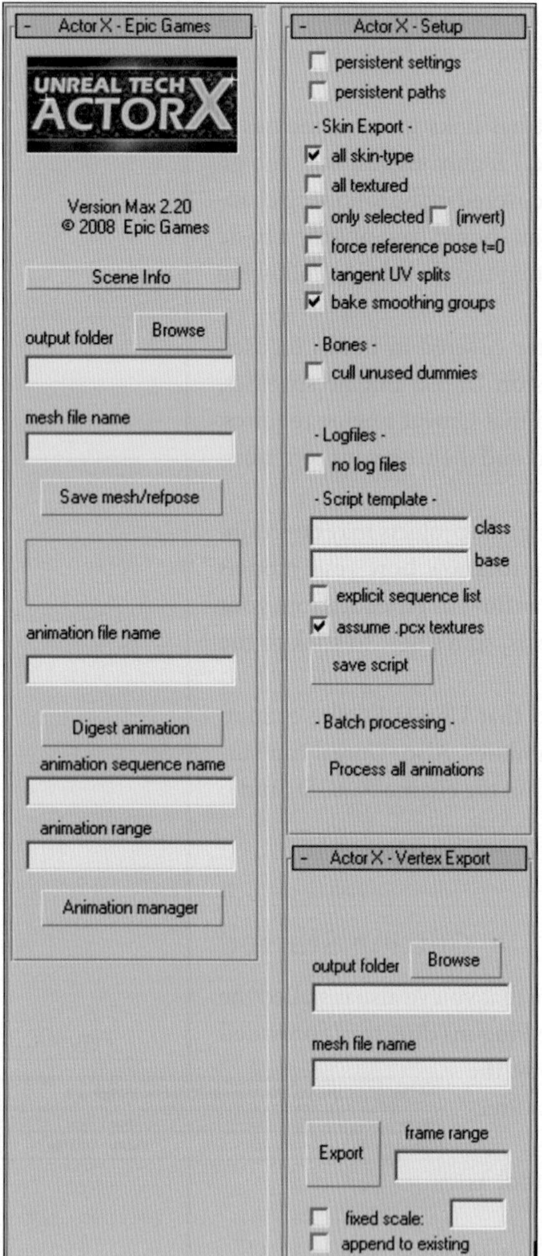


Figure 12.3

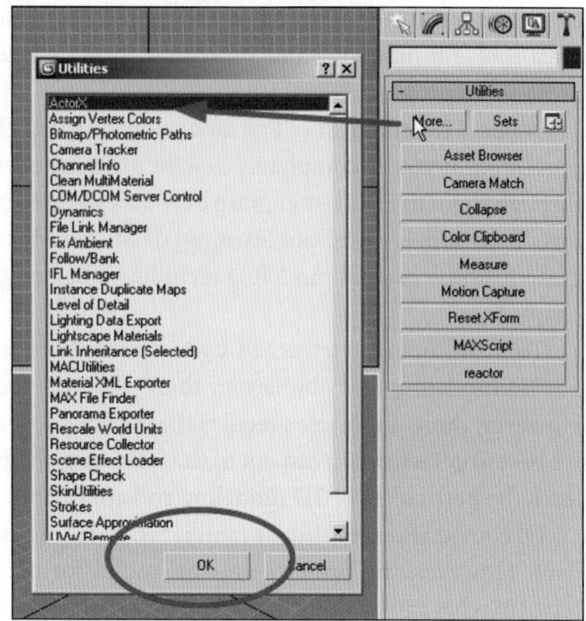


Character mesh resolutions in Unreal 2 and Unreal 3 are quite different, on the other hand. Unreal Engine 3 is quite capable of managing a character mesh with many thousands of triangles. It's not uncommon to see as many as 20k triangles on a single character. At that resolution, it's important to keep your character's mesh as clean as possible.

It's possible for a character to exceed that triangle count, but other considerations restrict how dense a mesh can be. The number of bones and materials on the mesh can start to affect overall performance. Add the character to a complex scene, multiply the character by the number of players, and then add in monsters: now you may see a performance hit, depending on your video card.

## Setting Up a Project Directory

By default, Max has no way to build a directory structure for you to work in. We're going to be building a lot of different files, so we're going to want to keep organized and put all of our work in one place. This also makes your work easier to share with the rest of your team.

Let's start with building a simple file structure for your work.

You'll be building a lot of MAX files; these are your base 3D Studio Max files that will be used to export into an ASCII scene export (ASE) format that is then imported into Unreal.

Your Max files will also be used to export character meshes as PSK files. The PSK format represents a dynamic mesh that contains skeletal hierarchy data used for characters and weapons in Unreal. In addition, a PSA file will contain animation data that is used to make a skeletal mesh move. Once we get into animating a character's face, we'll want to export an FXA file for use in Unreal to allow the character to talk.

You'll also be using GIMP to create your textures, so you'll want to save them as PSD files so that you can keep your working layers and color adjustments separated from one another, to make changes easier. Once you're done with the PSD file, you'll want to save it as a TGA file for importing into Unreal.

Finally, we'll want to keep things that come back out of Unreal organized. You'll be importing these into 3D Studio Max for reference as you build on them to make your own custom levels.

And to maintain a level of inspiration, we'll want to keep our reference images in their own directory as well.

Provided on the disk is a sample project directory. You'll want to copy this to your hard drive; it'll have plenty of references and the example projects ready to go.

It should look something like Figure 12.4.

Figure 12.4

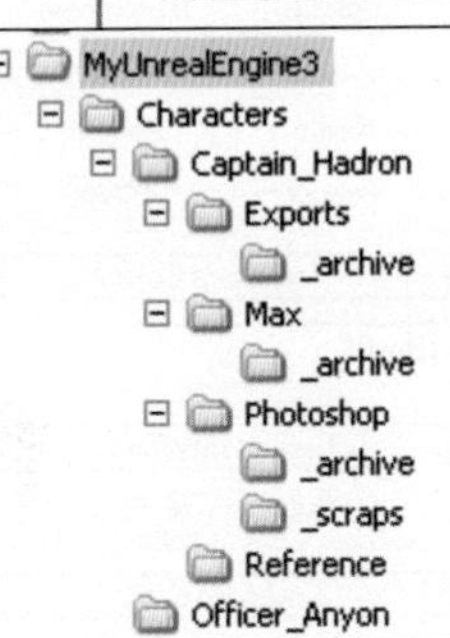


## Using 3D Studio Max

Max has a procedural modeling system that is called the modifier stack and is located in the command panel on the right. This allows you to create modifications on a model which can be re-edited after the modifier has been applied. Like a GIMP layer, these modifiers can be turned on and off to allow you to compare your model before and after modification.

Modifications include stretching, bending, and subdividing your model's surface. The order in which these modifications are applied makes a difference. If the model is tapered, then bent, it'll look different than if it were bent, then tapered. However, Unreal Engine cannot make use of the modifications created in 3D Studio Max; only the final result will be exported from Max into the Unreal Editor.

When modeling in Max, as well as any in other complex 3D environment, it's often useful to collapse a model's modification history. Leaving your model's stack too tall can slow down your computer. In general, it's just a good idea to collapse your model's stack as you work, leaving only essential modifiers in place.

Once you get to exporting dynamic mesh objects, you'll need to export the skin modifier on top of the stack. Underneath, the skin modifier doesn't matter so much as long as the overall stack is behaving properly.

## Your First Static Mesh Object

Figure 12.5

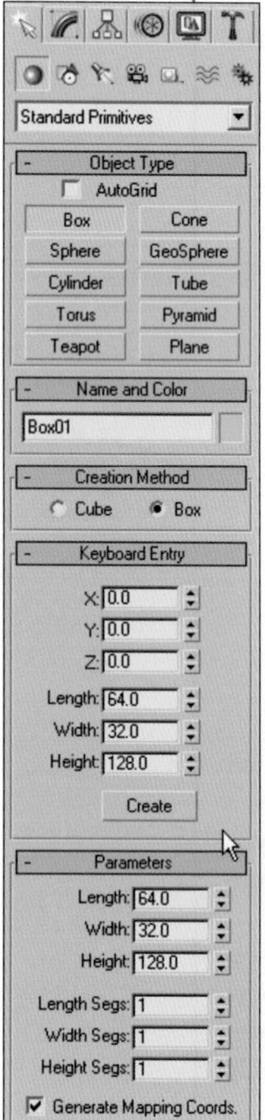


Let's start with some simple shapes and go through the steps required to get a mesh into the Unreal Engine. This project isn't going too focus much on any modeling techniques; rather, we'll focus on the steps to get any static mesh into the Unreal Engine.

For sake of simplicity, we'll start with the box primitive. Check the `Generate Mapping Coords` check box; otherwise, our mesh will not be able to support a proper texture map. Unreal units are something of a mystery. There are no real-world units with which they can immediately be associated. So that we can get a feel for how big things are once they're placed in the engine, we'll make an object with these length, width, and height parameters. Enter the Length, Width, and Height as in the figure provided [Figure 12.5].

After entering these values, click on `Create` at 0,0,0 in the Keyboard Entry roll-out menu.

We should have a simple shape like this [Figure 12.6]. Before exporting, we need to assign a material to the object.

Figure 12.6

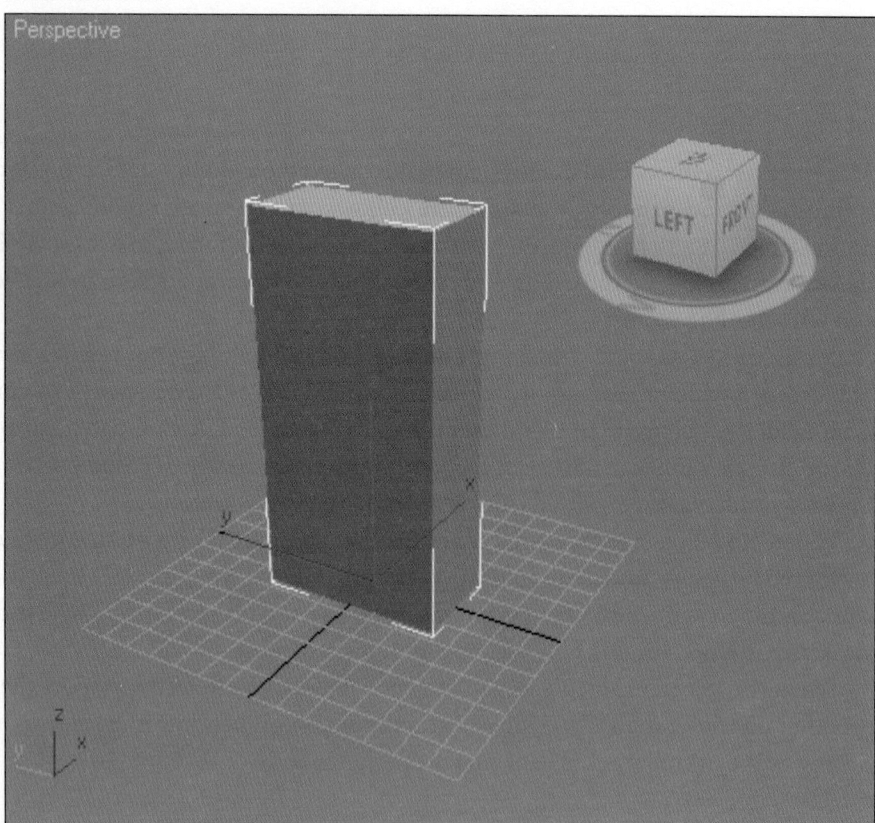

Open the material with the button on the top right of the menu bar [Figure 12.7]. Select any one of the shader balls and assign the material to the selection using the button in the following image [Figure 12.8].

Figure 12.7

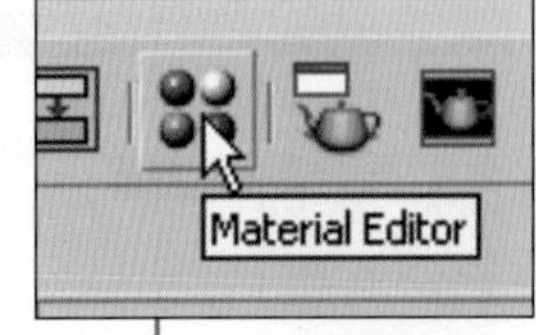


Now, with the mesh selected, go to the file menu and select `export selected`. Pick ASE from the file menu and save the mesh in our project directory in MyUnrealMod\Objects\Box\Exports as "Box.ase". You will see a dialog like Figure 12.9.

Figure 12.8

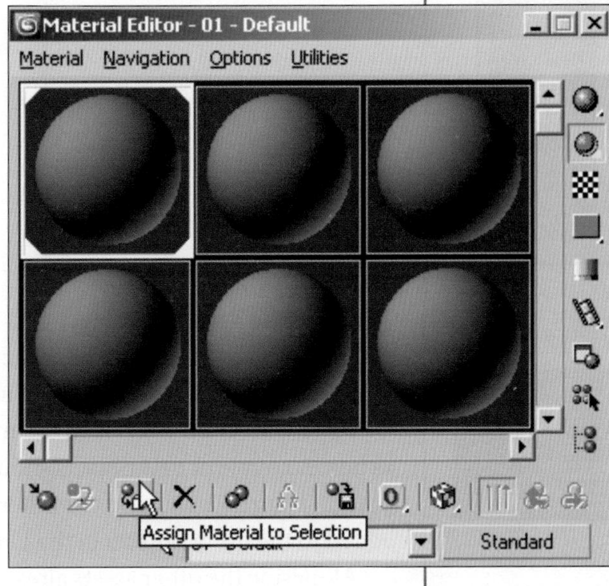


Our object is pretty simple, but we'll need to make sure that we're exporting geometric objects. If we were also exporting animation, we could export that data here; but there are better ways to do that, as we'll see in later projects. Open Unreal, navigate to the Generic browser, and select `File` → `Import`. Navigate to your Mod directory where you saved the box.ase file and select `open`.

Some of the options are legacy options for Unreal Engine 2 or other game engines that have ASE import options. Animated mesh objects will not be exported using the ASE export tool. Rather, the ActorX tool is used to export dynamic or animated mesh objects.

Back in the Unreal Editor, select Import from the `Generic Browser` → `File` → `Import` [Figure 12.10].

Figure 12.9

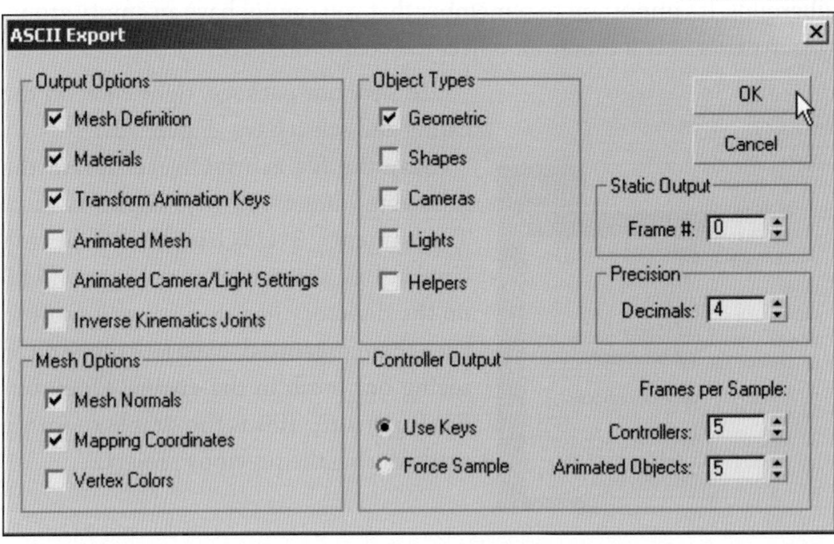


Figure 12.10

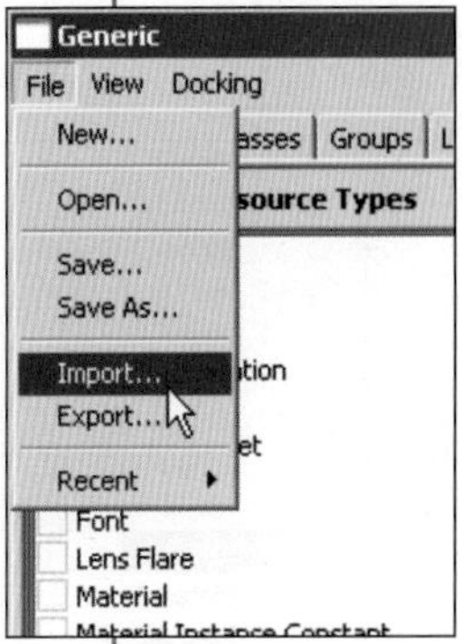

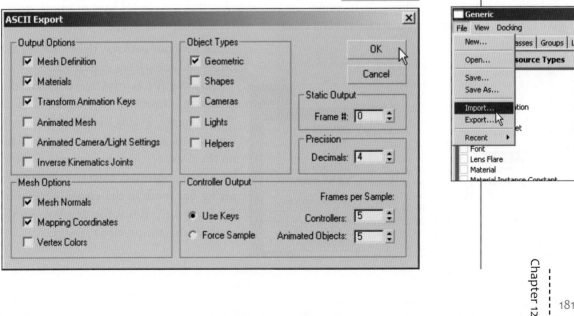

Figure 12.11

Figure 12.12

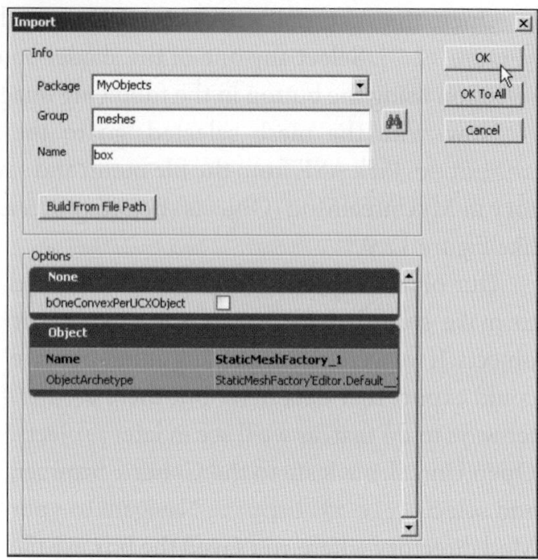


Figure 12.13

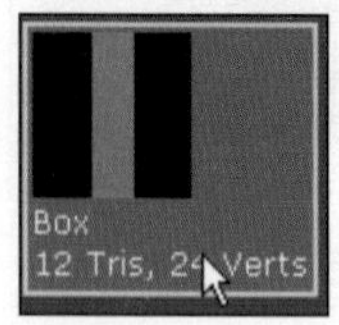


Once you select the object and import the item, an Import dialog window asks where you want to import the object to [Figure 12.11].

For this project, save the object into MyObjects [Figure 12.12]. This creates a new UPK, or Unreal Package. Add the mesh's subgroup and leave the name of the object as box. A couple of new objects should appear in the generic browser: first is your box object [Figure 12.13], and the other object is the new MyObjects.UPK that has been added to the list of objects in the Unreal Editor.

Alongside the other assets already in Unreal Tournament, a new MyObjects package should appear. In this case, I've already jumped ahead and created a few materials, but we'll get to that soon enough. One thing to note is that the subgroups all appear under the MyObjects file when expanded [Figure 12.14]. These are added as you create new subgroups. It's important to remember that you cannot have an empty group. Each subgroup exists only if there's an object to occupy the space.

Figure 12.14

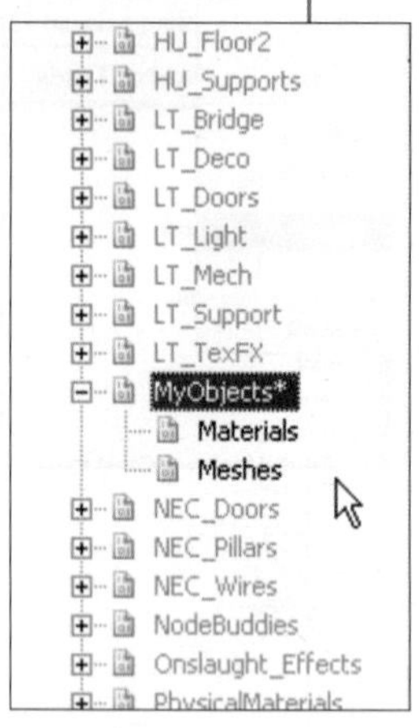


Figure 12.15

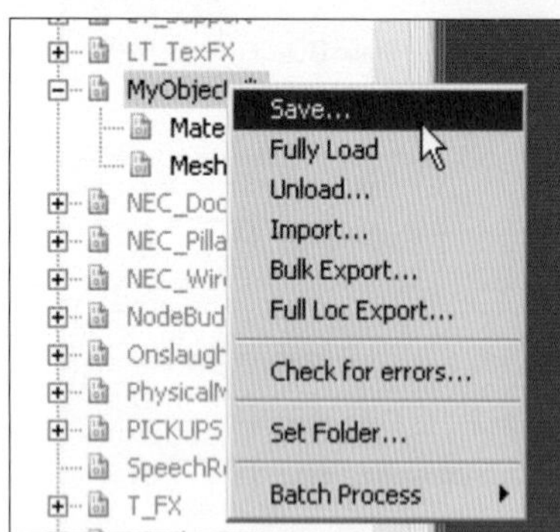


To save our package, right-click on the listing and select Save [Figure 12.15].

Save the file as MyObjects.upk in the following directory: My Games\Unreal Tournament 3\UTGame\Unpublished\CookedPC. The rest of our objects will fill up the directory like this, so we'll want to keep them organized. Next let's move on to seeing our mesh in the engine. Open our BoxRoom.ut3. This is the simple room we made during the previous project.

## A Simple Material

By default, any imported mesh will have the generic material assigned to it. We'll want to make a basic material to apply to our new object.

Start with right-clicking in the background of the Generic browser next to our box's static mesh. Select `New Material` in the following popup menu [Figure 12.16].

In the following dialog, make sure that the package is assigned as MyObjects. Add in the materials group, and name the new material "Basic_Material" [Figure 12.17].

Now our level editor viewports are looking at a simple level. In the center of the room is a player start icon.

Here's our material editor [Figure 12.18]. The left window is a preview of our material. The center is a graph of our material. On the right is a list of all the different nodes we're going to be using to build our shader graph. The top tool bar has a row of buttons for various functions to clean up and edit our material editor. The bottom panel is the parameter editor for any selected node.

Figure 12.16

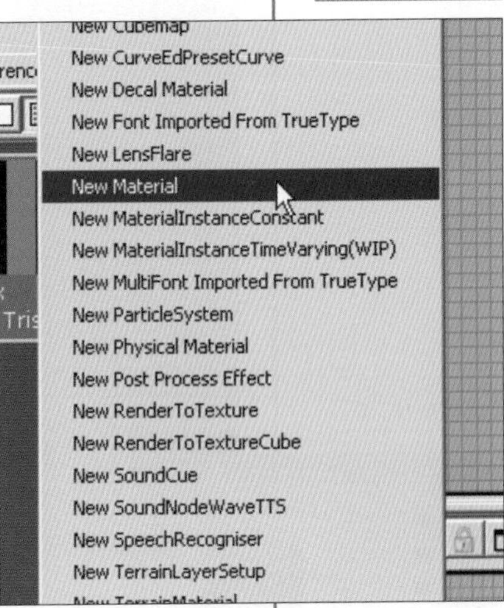


Figure 12.17

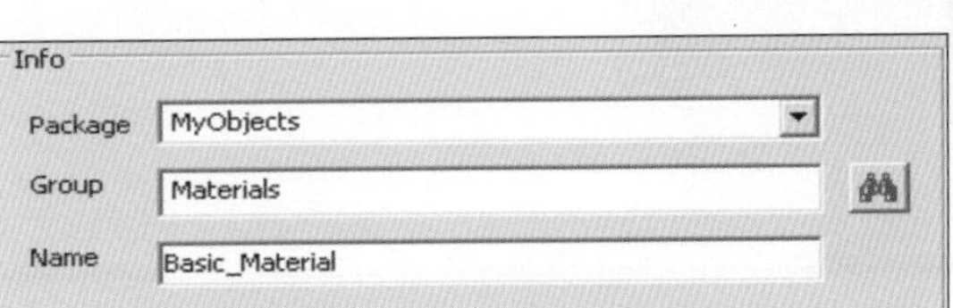


Figure 12.18

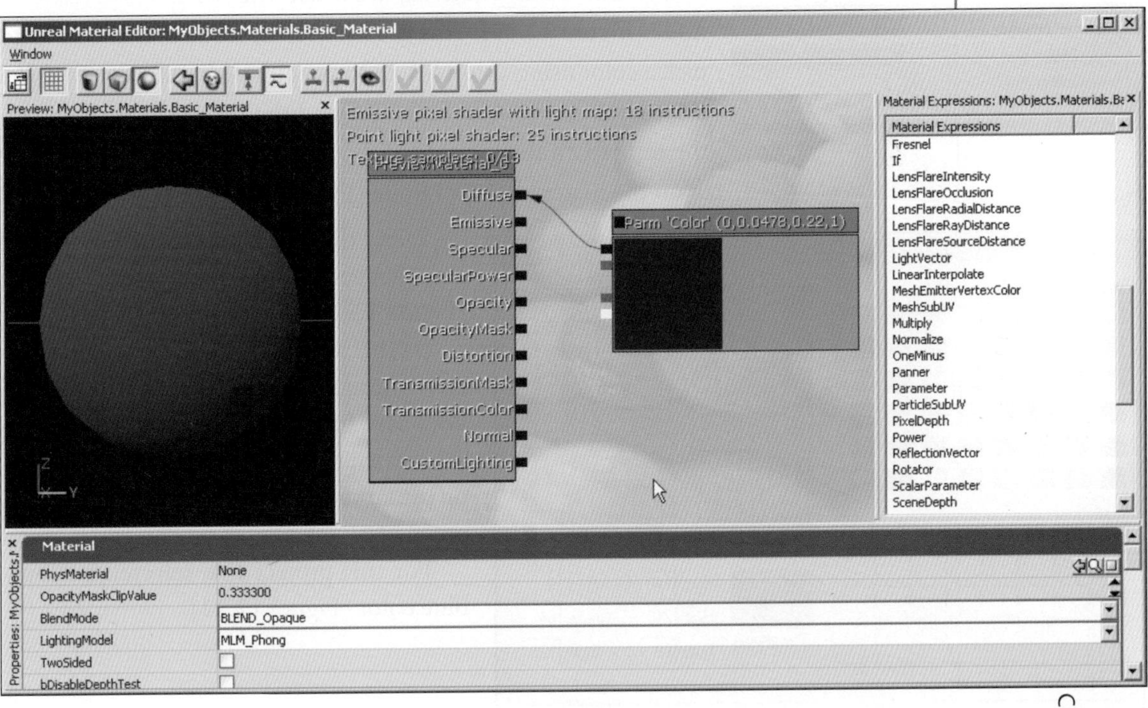

Figure 12.19

Figure 12.20

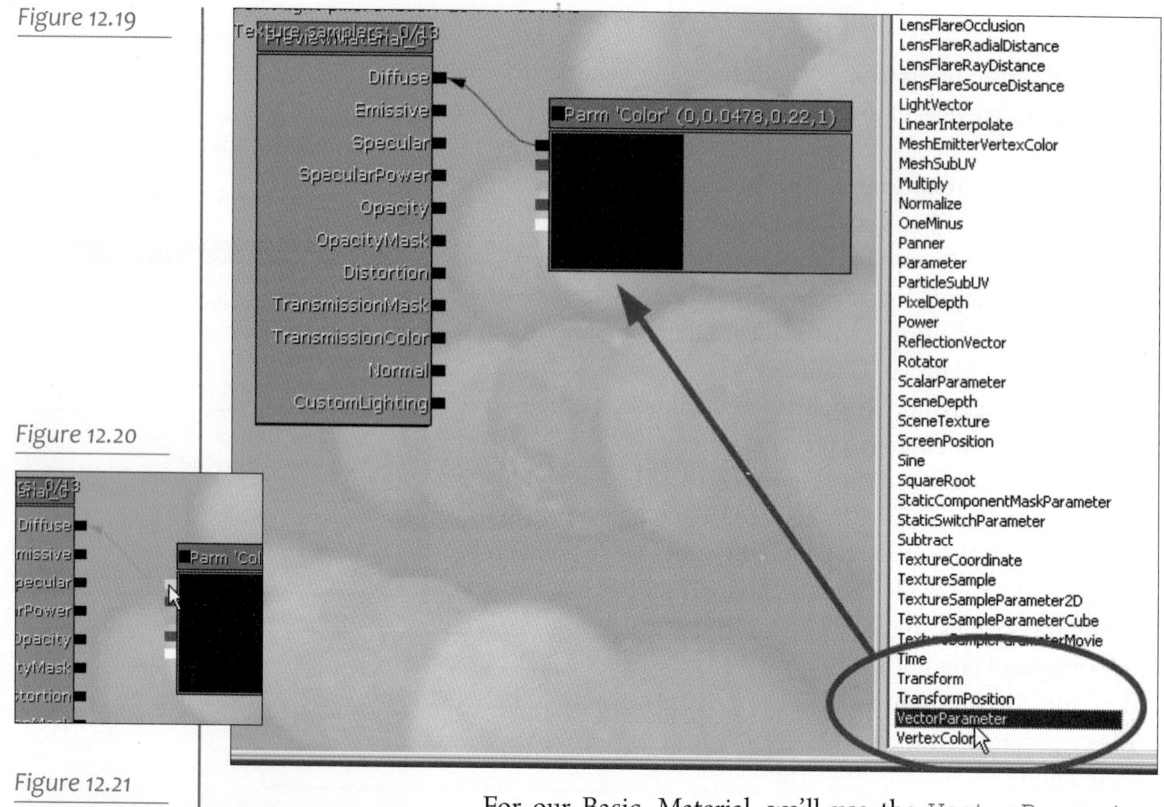


Figure 12.21

| ParameterName | Color |
|---|---|
| ▸ DefaultValue | |
| bRealtimePreview | ☐ |
| Desc | |

Figure 12.22

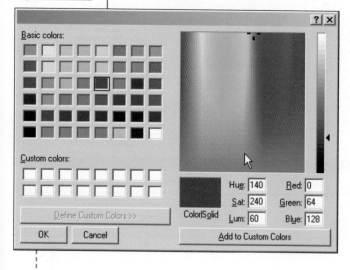

For our Basic_Material, we'll use the `VectorParameter` node [Figure 12.19]. This is a basic color node that allows us to pick a color using a simple windows color picker dialog. To make a connection between our color and the new material, click on the top tab on the left side of the node and drag it to the diffuse tab on the material output node [Figure 12.20].

Select the node, and make the following changes to the parameter's settings [Figure 12.21].

So that we can find this node's parameter settings later, we'll name it "Color." We'll also give our shader a more interesting color using the magnifying glass icon on the far right next to the `DefaultValue` parameter.

For this project I've selected a simple blue color [Figure 12.22].

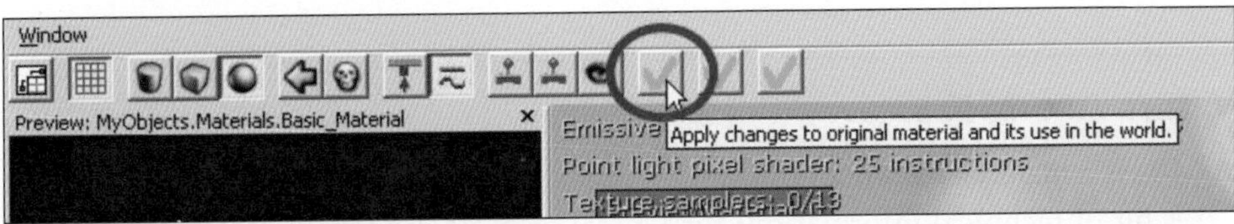


Figure 12.23

Now we're pretty much done with our first basic material. Click on the left green check icon at the top [Figure 12.23] and apply the changes to the world. This compiles our shader into a shader program that prepares it for your graphics card.

Nodes that end with "Parameter" are nodes that can be accessed through a material instance parameter. We'll get into what that means later.

Close the material editor, and save your UPK.

## The Material Editor

Here's a break-down of the different buttons along the tool bar [Figure 12.24].

Figure 12.24

Starting at the left:

- `Home`: This button will recenter the material output node back to the top left of the graph view. If you get lost navigating this view and can't find where you've wandered off to, you can use this button to jump back to the material output node.
- `Grid`: The preview window has a grid that is visible as you mouse around in that view. The grid display can be toggled with this button.
- The following group of three icons changes the primitive object showing your material.
- The green arrow can be used to show a selected model in the Generic browser in place of a cylinder, cube, or sphere.
- The skull will delete any unused nodes in the graph editor.
- The `Hide-Tab` button will hide any unused tabs, as in Figure 12.25.
- The next button toggles between curved and straight-line connections. Disable this flag for editor performance.
- The next three buttons change the various real-time views. The mesh preview output can be toggled, the graph editor can be toggled, or just one node at a time can have its real-time output previewed. We'll get into this later.
- The next three green check icons are for building the material's shader program and the fallback shader programs for legacy (old) video cards.

Figure 12.25

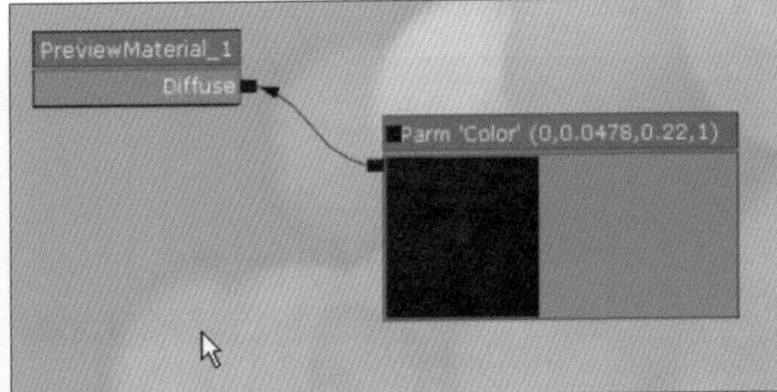

## What Are MICs?

A MIC is a material instance constant.

A bit of technical information: for Unreal or most modern games that use pixel shader programs, each unique material requires a few moments to load and unload. For each object in a game that has a different material, the graphics card needs to stop and start before rendering each material. This might not be noticeable when there are only a few different materials in the scene, but when there are a few hundred objects, performance can be lost.

To prevent this, it's best to create one material and then create instances or copies of that material with some minor changes among the instances. This is accomplished by using a material instance constant. This allows the graphics card to jump from one object to the next without loading a new material for each object since all objects share the same parent material. Thus, MICs improve performance of the application.

MICs also save a lot of development time. To make a complex material takes a bit of time. To avoid having to build complex materials over and over again, you can use a MIC. MICs also have the benefit of being interactive. Building a material requires that the material is compiled; this can take several seconds even on a fast machine. MICs are made from precompiled materials, so they don't have to be recompiled every time you make changes.

**PROJECT**

### Material Instance Constant

Of course, our basic material was pretty easy to create—it had just one node. However, if your material had several dozen nodes, having to rebuild the material for every object would immediately become a slow and tedious effort. To skip this repeated work, we can create a material instance constant [Figure 12.26].

Figure 12.26

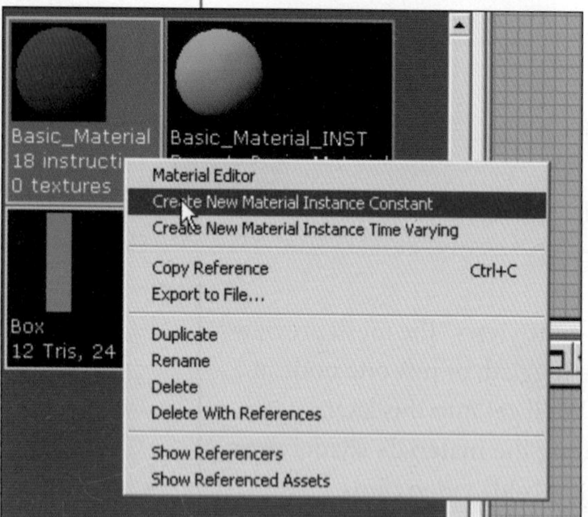


Right-click on the original material. This will become our instance's parent material object.

Name the object "Basic_Material_INST"; then click on OK [Figure 12.27].

Figure 12.27

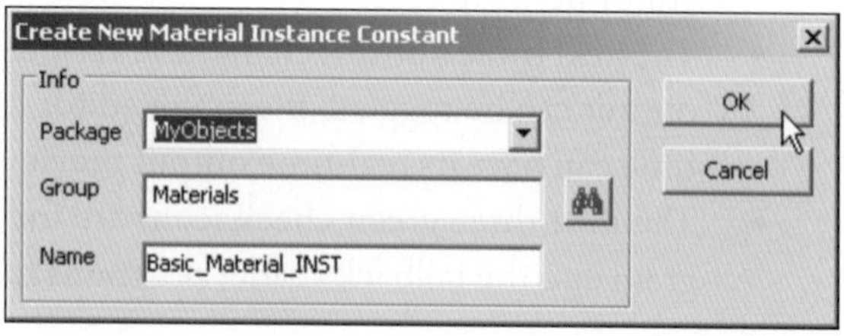

Create New Material Instance Constant
Info
Package MyObjects
Group Materials
Name Basic_Material_INST
OK
Cancel

The editor opens with some similarities to the original material editor [Figure 12.28]. This interface will allow us only to make changes to various parameters. We cannot make any changes to the material's graph.

This is where the previously named node will appear as "Color" under the `VectorParameterValues` roll-out menu. Here we can pick a different color from the parent material. Click on the check box to the left of the `Color` tab to indicate that we want to use the overriding parameters. For this project, I've selected an orange color.

We can make as many instances of the original material as we feel we need. Each one should be named uniquely before being assigned to an object.

With our new material instance created, open the static mesh editor on the box we imported in the previous project.

Here we have our static mesh object [Figure 12.29]. By default, this object will have a grey checker pattern applied. To change this, we'll want to add in our new

Figure 12.28

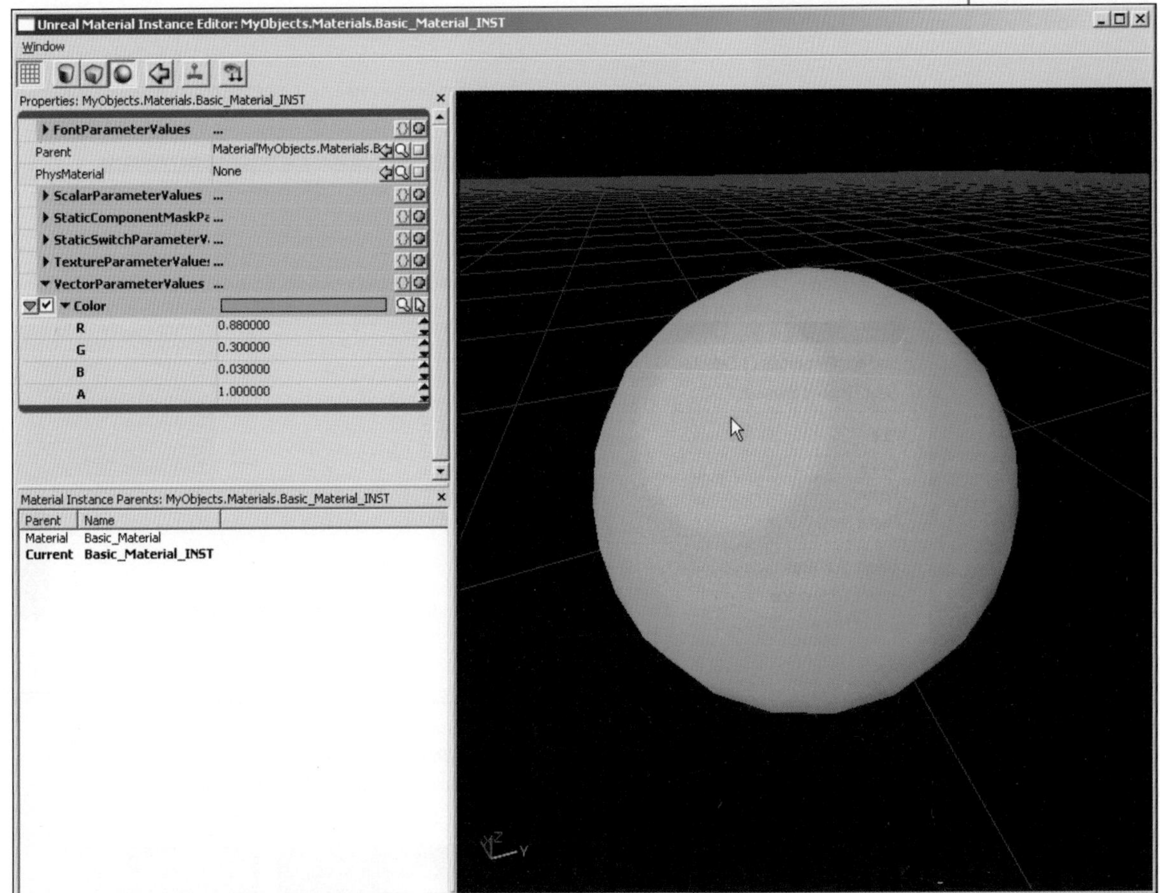

Figure 12.29

Figure 12.30

Figure 12.31

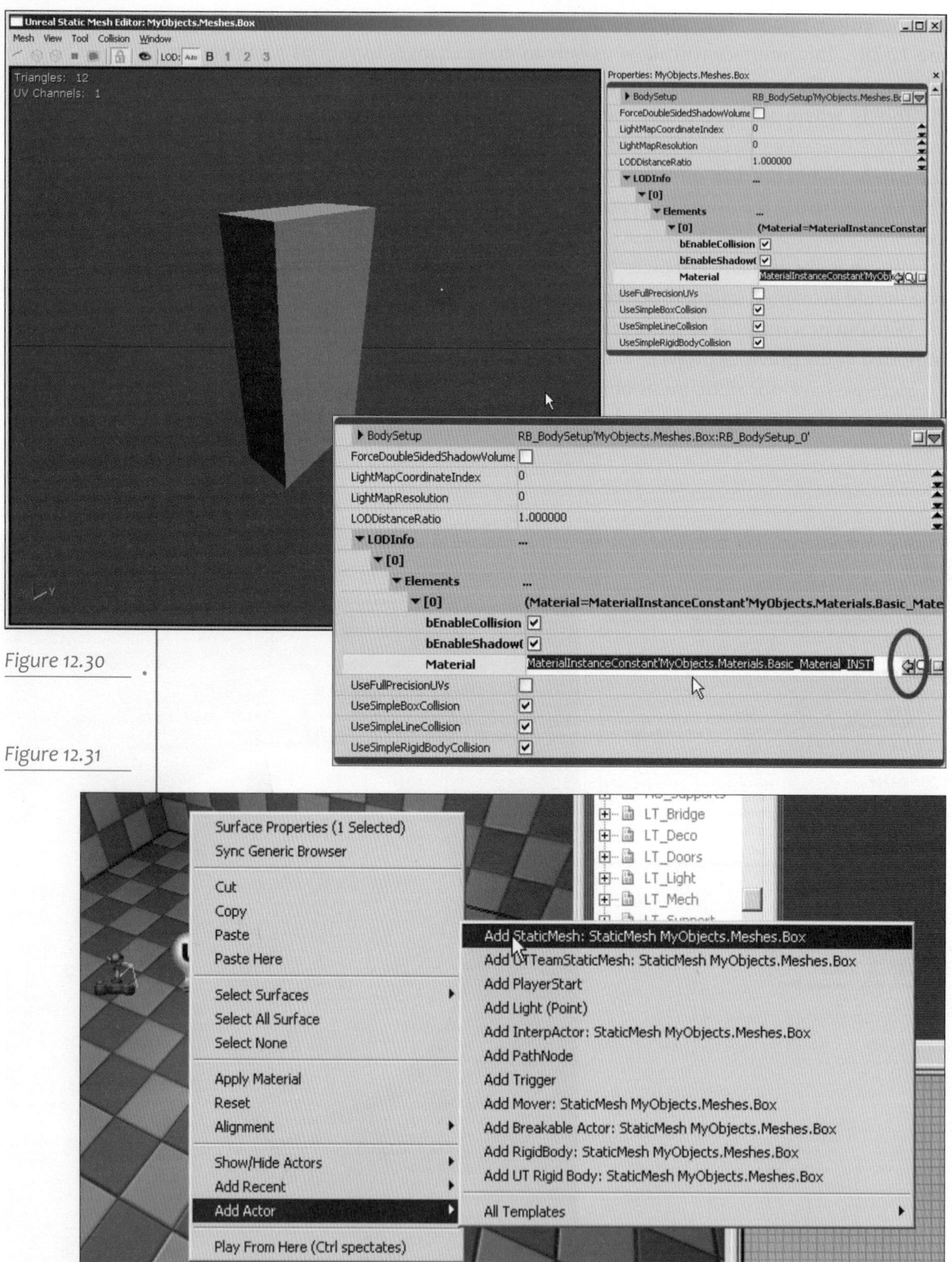

material instance, not the material parent. Of course, we can assign the material parent, but we'd be losing some of the ability to change the objects color using the material instance constant.

Select the material instance we created and add it to our static mesh's LOD[0] Material parameter [Figure 12.30]. The LODInfo roll-out only has one group for now, as well as only one element. Later, when we build more complex static mesh objects, we'll need to fill in the various material slots with different materials. Close the StaticMeshEditor and save your UPK.

Figure 12.32

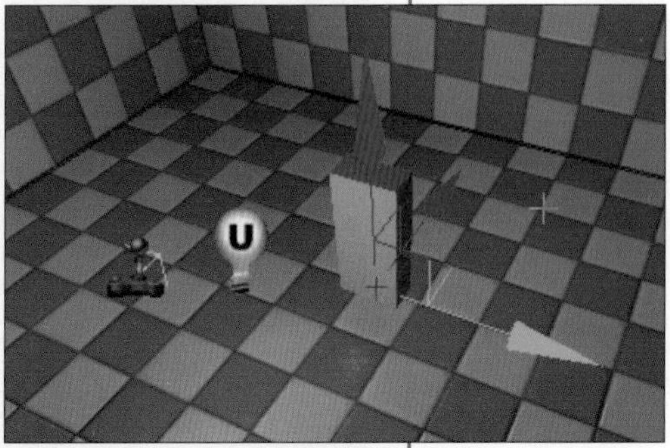

*Note: These LODs are how you could create multiple levels of detail for a single object. When seen up close, an object can have more geometric and texture data than when seen from farther away. If an object is far away, then there's no need for the video card to render several hundred polygons that cover just a few pixels on the screen.*

Going back to the level editor . . .

Highlight our mesh object in the Generic browser. This indicates to the level editor that this is the object we'll want to add to our scene. Then right-click on the floor of the scene and select `Add Actor` → `Add StaticMesh` [Figure 12.31].

You should now have an orange box in your scene [Figure 12.32].

Figure 12.33

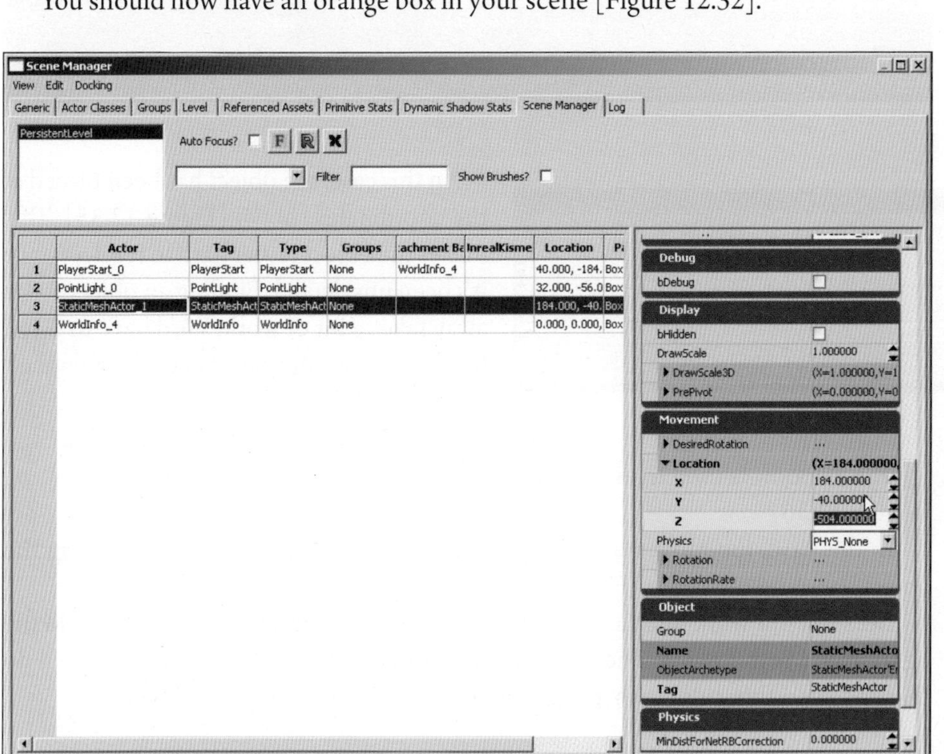

One of the useful editors in the Generic browser is the scene manager [Figure 12.33]. The scene manager tab allows us to select any object in the scene and change its location. In some cases, you might accidentally place the object in a distant place in your level.

If you placed the object while outside of our room, the object will be sent to a distant corner of the level [Figure 12.34].

Figure 12.34

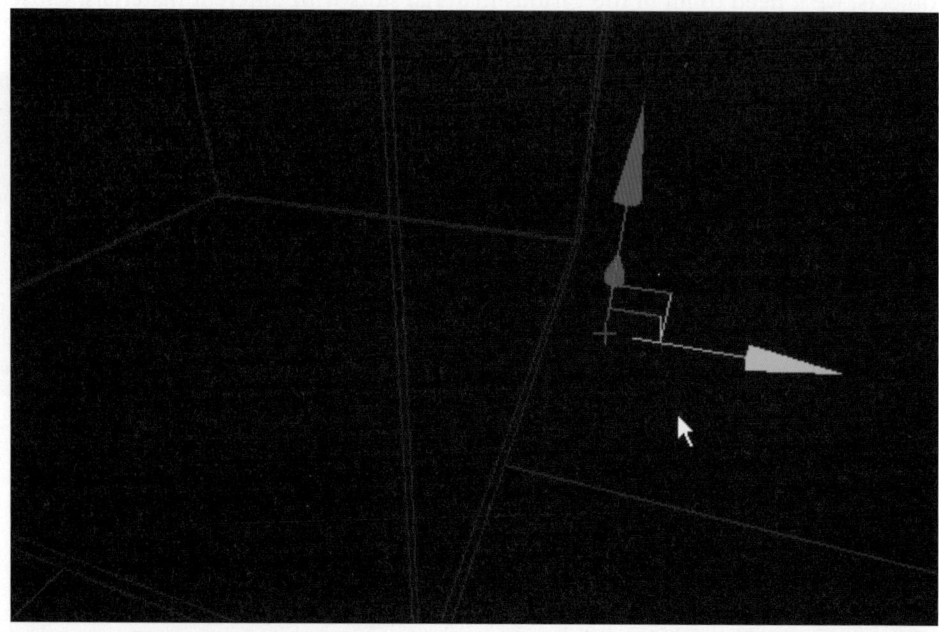

Figure 12.35

| Movement | |
|---|---|
| ▸ DesiredRotation | ... |
| ▾ Location | (X=226376.000000,Y=1144.000000,Z=-130984.000000) |
| X | 226376.000000 |
| Y | 1144.000000 |
| Z | -130984.000000 |
| Physics | PHYS_None |
| ▸ Rotation | ... |
| ▸ RotationRate | ... |

In this case, the object has been placed at the coordinates shown [Figure 12.35]. This makes the object rather hard to reselect once it's been unselected. Finding an object so far away takes a bit of work. We'd have to scroll for several minutes just to get close enough to see the object.

`F4` will open the object's properties.

This window is used to assign various changes to the selected object in the scene [Figure 12.36]

In this case, the movement's location parameters were set to 0,0,0 to bring the object back into our room [Figure 12.37].

Let's test our work thus far. Before we can play in our level, we'll need to build the lighting and path finding. There aren't many paths in such a small place, but we'll do that and everything else with a single button: `build all` [Figure 12.38].

Figure 12.36

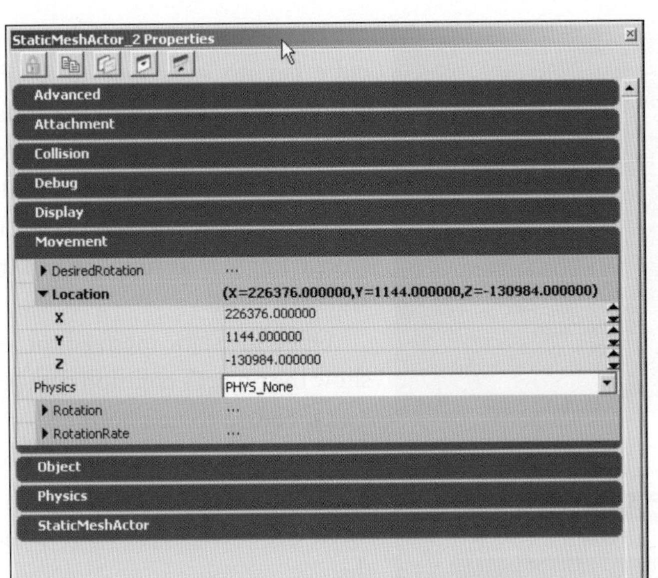


Figure 12.37

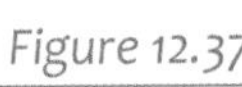

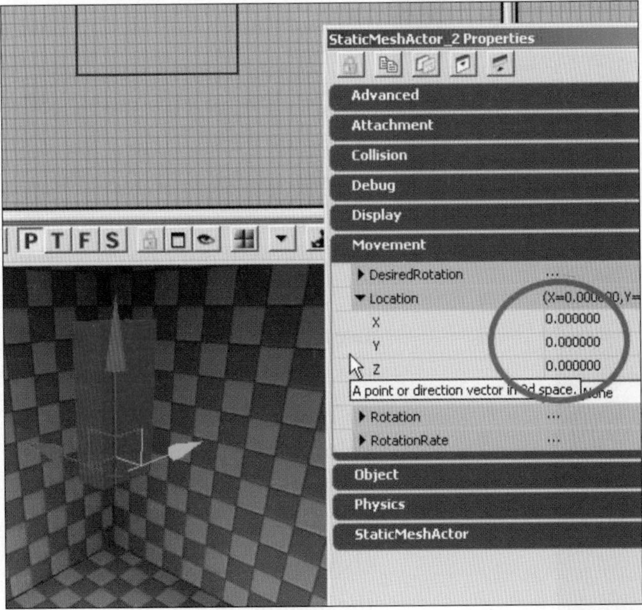


Figure 12.38

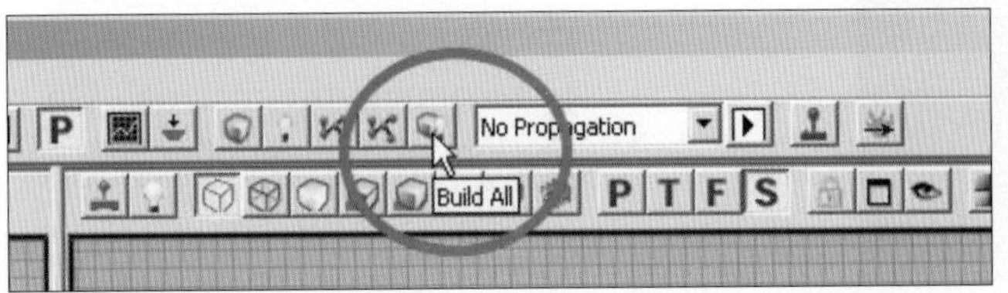

Figure 12.39

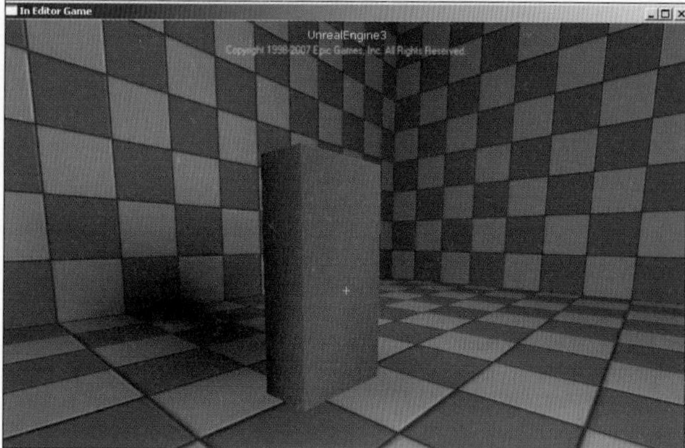


The first thing we might notice is that our cube has no substance to it [Figure 12.39]. We can walk right through it as if it weren't there. We need to add collision capabilities to our mesh and tell the editor that the object is meant to collide with the player. To do this, the Unreal Engine has supplied us with some quick and easy tools.

Open the static mesh editor for the box and show the object's collision data [Figure 12.40].

Of course there's nothing to see; we didn't create a collision object in Max to export with our object. We need not worry, as the static mesh editor has some built-in tools to do just that.

Select the Collision menu, and then select 6DOP simplified Collision [Figure 12.41]. This will automatically fit a box collision object to the same shape as our box.

Our box now has usable collision applied to it [Figure 12.42]. Close the static mesh editor, save the package, and test the scene again using the `Play in Editor` button. Now we can't walk through our object! Save the scene.

Going back to the editor, lets us see why we used a MIC instead of a regular material parent. Open the material instance parameters, and expand the vector parameter values for the color setting [Figure 12.43].

To the right of a color channel is a spinner that allows us to adjust the number's value by clicking and dragging up and down. Click on the middle of the spinner and drag up. The color should change in real time, both in the shader preview and in the editor! To see these changes using a regular material, you'd have to recompile the material. On more complex shaders, the recompile time can take several minutes to complete.

Figure 12.40

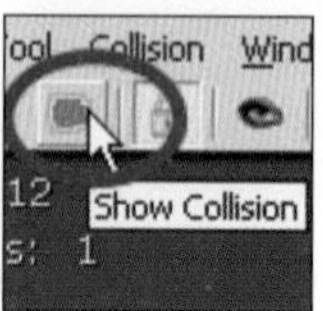


Figure 12.41

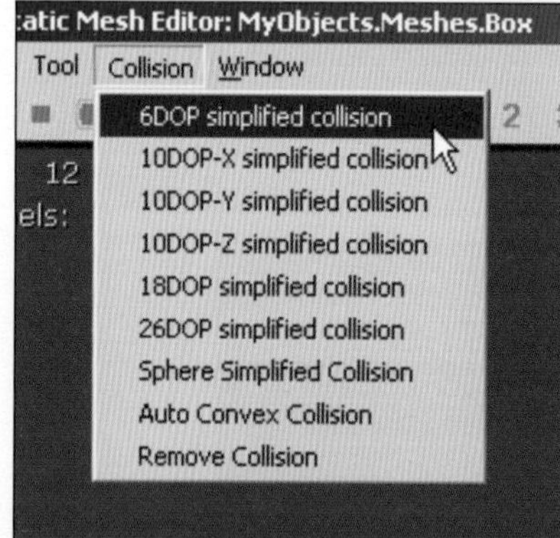


Figure 12.42

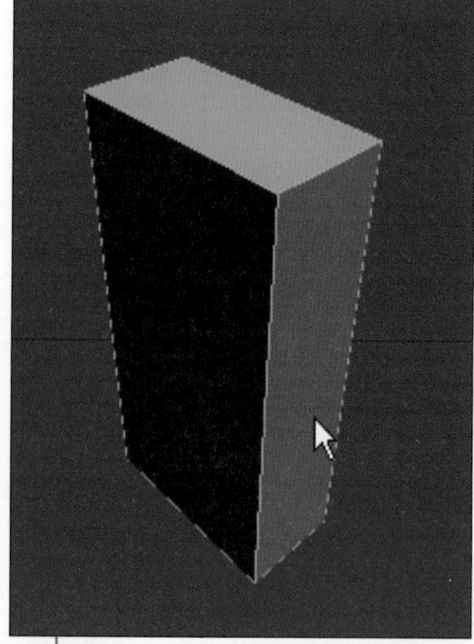

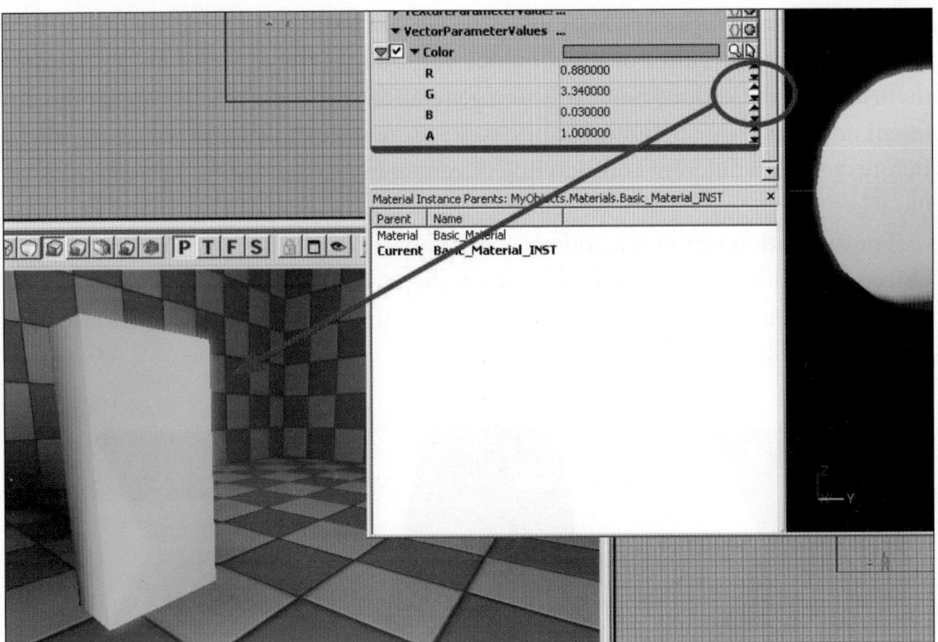


Figure 12.43

## Review

Now you should be able to export a static mesh from 3D Studio Max and then import it into Unreal. Once the mesh has been exported from Max ,the object is saved in a UPK. Once in the engine, a simple collision object can be made to fit your mesh. After the static mesh has been prepared, you should be able to place the object into your scene and set the attributes for player collision.

You should notice that your object's polygons are converted into triangles when they're imported into Unreal. Sure, all you've built is a simple box shape, but that was a lot more work than just making a cube, wasn't it? Next, we'll want to give our cube a texture that's something other than the gray tile pattern that Unreal defaults to for any object without a material.

Additionally, you should remember the units that you were using when creating this shape. 256 units tall is pretty high, but it doesn't correlate to any real-world units, inches, centimeters, or otherwise. It's somewhat useful to remember that a person is roughly 128 units tall, and a hallway is about 256 units wide. You can create your own standard for what the numbers mean. if you decide that a unit is a centimeter then you should make tall characters 200 units tall and go from there.

## On Your Own

It would be a good idea to create different shapes and then see what sort of automatic collision objects will fit them the best. It should be apparent that Unreal will not always make the best-fitting shapes for more complex meshes. We'll go into how to make a customized collision object in the following chapter.

For now, build some of the other shapes in 3D Studio Max, and try out various shapes that are not cubes or boxes. Once you build a few different shapes, import them and test the various other collision generation methods. You'll find that the different methods create different shapes, some more suited to your model than others. Before creating a different collision object, remember to remove the current collision model.

For calculation simplicity, and because of how the software was written, collision objects are made of what is called a convex shape. Convex shapes have the property that for any pair of points in the shape, the line segment connecting them is also contained by the shape.

Figure 12.44

In Figure 12.44, the shape on the left is a concave object. The shape in the middle is convex. Collision shapes should be convex, if possible. If your object requires a concave collision shape, it's better to make it out of compound convex shapes, as illustrated by the shape on the right in Figure 12.44. Just make sure there's a tiny gap between the two shapes; otherwise, when the physics is applied to the shape, the two shapes will try to push off one another.

# 13

# 2D Images and GIMP

## *2D Images: Adding Texture*

A texture is a color bitmap that wraps around a 3D model using the model's UV layout. Remember that each vertex has at least one associated UV coordinate. Your texture defines your mesh's surface appearance. Marble or limestone, gold or iron, ice or stone—these properties are best defined by painting a texture onto your model's surface. Color and texture creation is just as important as modeling, if not more so.

A texture doesn't merely have to define the material; it does much more. Details can be painted in that are too difficult to model, so a good texture can add greatly to the complexity on any 3D mesh. With a good texture, a good model can look great.

## What to Expect

Creating a texture for a 3D model is different from painting a regular 2D image. GIMP is only a part of how you'll be creating textures for your 3D model. You'll need both 3D Studio Max and GIMP open to build your textures. This also helps you find and fix your meshes' UVs before you go too far. Making fixes early helps save time later in the development process.

You'll find you'll need to paint a few different types of textures for a single mesh object. The most simple is the diffuse texture, sometimes referred to as an albedo map or color map. Using the diffuse texture as a source, you'll modify it to create a specular map. Additional maps might include a normal map, an emissive map, a specular power map, and several others.

There are also specific textures that help animate and modify a material in unexpected ways. We'll get into what all of that means when we start the material projects; just keep in mind that building a complex texture can sometimes take as much time as building a complex mesh.

## What Is Provided

On the book's website (http://www.akpeters.com/unrealgamedev) are some of the example files you should be able to recreate. You should be able to use these as reference for making your own textures.

Also on the site are some free photo images to work from. You'll want to use these to add some realistic detail to your own work in GIMP.

## Basic Considerations

Before we get started, keep in mind that drawing skills are not required for these examples. Many of the tools in GIMP simply require logic and patience. Only when it comes to creating something from scratch does the task become more difficult and complex.

Of course, more photorealistic textures require some painting skills. Painting specific details does require technique and practice. There are some simple tricks to get this sort of detail into GIMP; we'll cover these when we get to them.

GIMP will not turn you into Da Vinci. There are plenty of print and on-line resources to help you become a better computer artist. In the following chapters, we'll cover what's directly necessary for making textures and materials for Unreal.

GIMP's native file format is XCF, but we can also save files in Photoshop's native file format, PSD. It's not important that you know what all these are just yet, but it's important to remember that GIMP has lots of image data that it can preserve but that cannot be imported into Unreal Engine.

Unreal will most reliably read a Targa Truevision file, or a TGA. There are a few other import file formats, but the TGA is pretty simple and has very few export options, which are easily explained.

Targas have three or four channels of color. The first three are Red, Green, and Blue. The fourth channel is called an alpha channel. Unreal can use an alpha channel, or any channel for that matter, in a variety of ways. We'll observe how these work when we get into the project later in this section. Just for your reference, a 24-bit texture is for a Targa without an alpha channel, and a 32-bit Targa is for files with an alpha channel.

TGA is also a lossless image format. JPEGs are compressed and smaller, but in making the file size reduction, you lose detail. BMP does not allow for a fourth alpha channel, so we'll avoid using that format as well. Unreal does have support for several other file formats, but these are used for their specific reasons. For sake of brevity, we'll avoid going into what the other image formats are used for.

Working PSD files should be saved at a higher resolution than your Unreal-ready images. This is a common practice at most if not all game studios. When it comes to cooking your game, you'll have the option of resizing the textures based on how they are used in the game. This is to adjust your memory footprint depending on what your target memory size is. It's easiest to start big and reduce size. There is no practical way to reclaim lost detail once it's been cut down, so start big and reduce as needed.

*Note: For future reference, be aware that texture resizing in engine is a great practice. Unreal Tournament on the PC is allowed to use larger texture resolution than on a game console. Game consoles have a fixed memory footprint, whereas PC video cards are being made with more and more video texture memory. In most cases the same assets are used for both platforms; then, Unreal is targeted to build a version for each platform.*

### Naming Conventions and Organization

Something that you'll need to do is sort out with the rest of your team what you're going to be naming all of your files. One thing to remember is to keep the convention short and simple. So we'll be using something like "Objectname_D.tga" for your object's diffuse color. For a specular map, you'll want to use "Objectname_S.tga" for the end of the file name; and for the object's normal map we'll use "_N.tga"—a single letter—it doesn't get much shorter or simpler than that.

In the Unreal Editor there are methods to rearrange and rename files once they've been imported, but it's better that your work file names match up with the names you're using within the editor. When you're working with a team of people, you'll all want to agree to a file-naming convention before getting too far into your project.

## Intro to GIMP

Most of the game and film industry depends on 2D graphics paint and photo editing tools like Photoshop. However, it's not necessary to use Photoshop when just getting started with game development. Other paint and texturing applications are out there, but at some point either Photoshop or GIMP is involved. Basic understanding of GIMP is essential for Unreal or any other game engine, for that matter. In the following chapters, we'll learn enough to build useful textures for both 3D Studio Max and Unreal. We'll focus on learning techniques specific for Unreal. Beyond the basics, I'll leave it up to you to do your own exploration.

Because of GIMP's popularity, there are thousands of free learning resources both on-line and in the book store. Rather than getting into the specifics of GIMP, I'll leave it up to you to explore and learn the tool in more depth beyond what will be covered in the following chapters.

### UI Elements and Map

Launch GIMP. You will see the toolbox with icons that allow you to paint, erase, and fill your image with color, and to pick the brush, eraser, various selection tools, and so on [Figure 13.1].

Figure 13.1

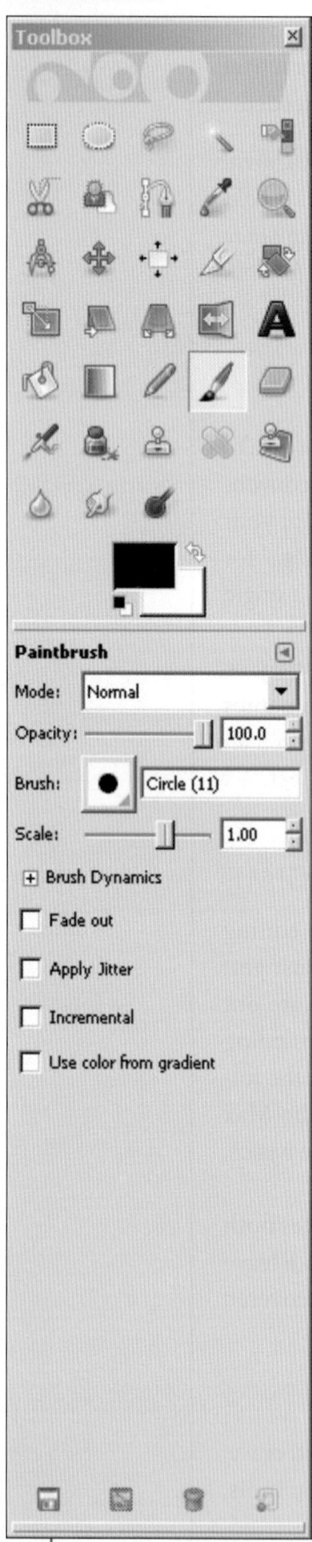


You'll want to learn the hot-keys associated with these tools, but the icons are there in case you don't remember the hot-key. Hover over each tool icon to reveal its pop-up help. The associated hot-key is highlighted as bold-face text at the end of the tool description. The brush options are different from the selection tools options. You will also see menus for saving, editing, and selecting filters.

Figure 13.2

The other panel that appears is for layer, channels, paths, and undo operations [Figure 13.2].

This is panel allows you to manage how your image is constructed. Regarding the creation of normal maps, the red and green channels are especially important for how the map is used, and the blue channel is primarily used to add depth to the lighting detail. Textures may also be created and used to manipulate another image's UV coordinates. The red and green channels can be used to push and distort the colors of that image. We will discuss such specialized textures in a later chapter.

## Tools and Filters

The top menu has your usual file menu as well as a way to access all of the regular filters and functions that GIMP is known for. Filters are used to process images to create basic effects such as blurring or adding contrast to edges. You can also manipulate the colors of an image to create some basic effects such as converting a color photograph into a gray-scale image.

## Setting Up GIMP

There's one useful plug-in for GIMP, downloadable from http://nifelheim.dyndns.org/~cocidius/normalmap/. This tool is used to create normal maps. Launch the plug-in's installer, located at http://www.akpeters.com/unrealgamedev. You must have this plug-in installed before continuing reading this chapter because we describe how to use the tool.

Normal maps are colored images that are used to add surface detail to a material. The maps can be used to add fine detail, such as bolts and panels or wrinkles and buttons, to a texture. Of course, this doesn't add geometry to a model, so the shape is not changed; rather, the lighting of the surface is modified to make it appear as if there is additional detail on the material.

## Intro to Unreal Materials

A material defines how an object's surface behaves when lit. When an object is imported, the Unreal Editor automatically assigns it a simple grey checker pattern.

By default, any imported object must have a material assigned to it to have any sort of appearance. Materials define how light interacts with the object's surface. Color, glossiness, glow, etc., are defined by the material you assign to the object. To give the surface detail, you need to assign a color texture map created in GIMP to the material.

To prepare a mesh in Max for Unreal, you need to assign materials to the various surfaces of your object. Applying a single material to the entire object tells Unreal that you intend to use only one material for the entire object. This is fine for something like a boulder, which is rock-like all around.

The faces a material is assigned to can't be changed after the mesh has been imported. For an object like a computer monitor, you'd want to apply a different material to the screen than to the case. To accomplish this, you will want to apply a multi-submaterial in 3D Studio Max or Blender to the object.

Objects with various surface properties require different materials applied to them. Assign materials by material type, not by part. Don't assign a different material to each button and switch, as that's just a bad way to work.

Material parameters created in 3D Studio Max are not imported into the Unreal Editor. Your material assignments in 3D Studio tell Unreal which polygons use different materials. These turn into empty material slots in the various editors within Unreal.

PROJECT

## A Slightly More Interesting Material

Let's start by creating a new document in GIMP. Create a new document and set the size to 256 × 256 pixels. Name the new texture "DefaultMaterial" and click OK [Figure 13.3].

Figure 13.3

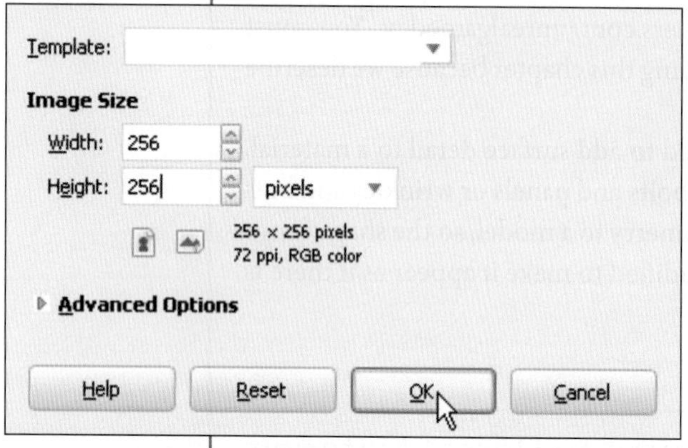


Figure 13.4

Figure 13.5

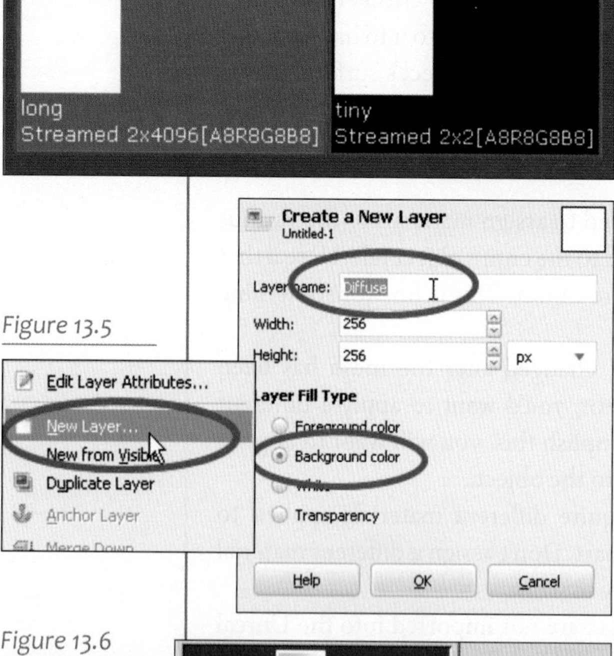


Figure 13.6

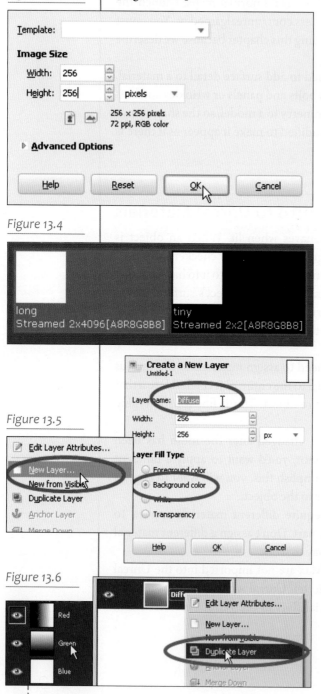

Make sure you select pixels and not inches. Dots per inch don't really matter since Unreal doesn't even know what an inch is. Unreal, like many game engines, prefers textures sized in powers of two. Each dimension can be as small as 2 pixels or as large as 4096 pixels [Figure 13.4].

The use of either of these two textures might get a bit flaky, so I'd try to stick to something more reasonable. So try to keep your materials to no more than a 4:1 ratio (height-to-width or width-to-height). If things begin to look strange in the engine, it's most likely a driver problem with the video card. Some older systems might clamp a texture at 8:1.

Right click in the `Layer Tool` window and select `New Layer`. Name the new layer "Diffuse" [Figure 13.5]. Repeat the process and make layers for a specular and a normal map. We're going to make a material for general purpose and for a few interesting experiments with the Unreal material editor.

In the red channel, make a gradient from left to right. Make a similar gradient from top to bottom in the green channel.

For now we'll leave the blue channel unchanged [Figure 13.6]. Duplicate the diffuse layer and rename it to "Specular." We're going to be making an interesting material in Unreal Editor using the color channels as data input rather than just color information. This will also be used to create a simple material for general purpose use for the following projects.

Figure 13.7

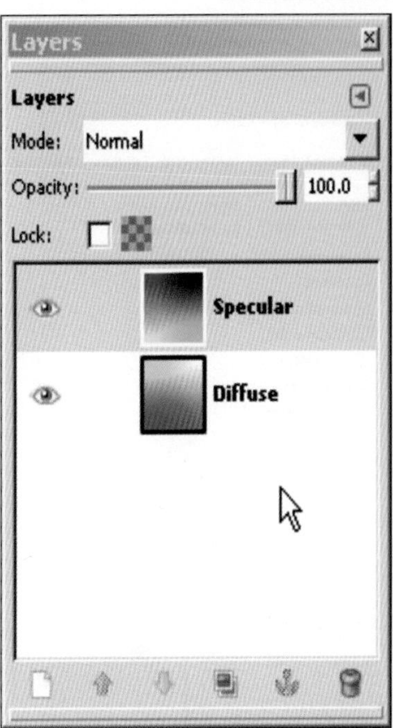


Once in the specular group, invert the color so the layers look like this [Figure 13.7]. The specular has a green and red gradient with yellow on the lower left and black to the top right. The diffuse has a white top right corner with a dark blue lower left corner, with teal and magenta in the adjacent corners. So far, we've done nothing too exciting. Next is the normal group.

On the white background of the normal layer, add a noise pattern using `Filter` → `Noise` → `HSVNoise` [Figure 13.8]. Change the settings to: Holdness 1, Hue 0, and Value 255. This will create an image with a simple black-and-white noise pattern.

To turn the noise pattern into a normal map, select `Filters` → `Map` → `NormalMap`. This will open the normal map generation tool [Figure 13.9]. This tool takes a regular image and uses the color information as a normal map. The size of the detail is determined by the sample size. The filter "4 sample" results in a finely detailed normal map, something similar to sand paper. The 9 × 9 setting results in a softer, more rounded result. Normal maps are information about the contours of a material's surface. The height of the bump is determined by the brightness of the colors used in the calculation. Bright colors are tall bumps; dark colors are pits in the surface.

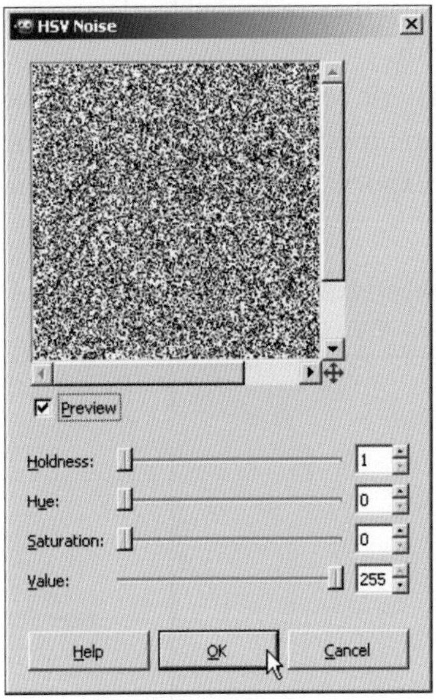

Figure 13.8

Figure 13.9

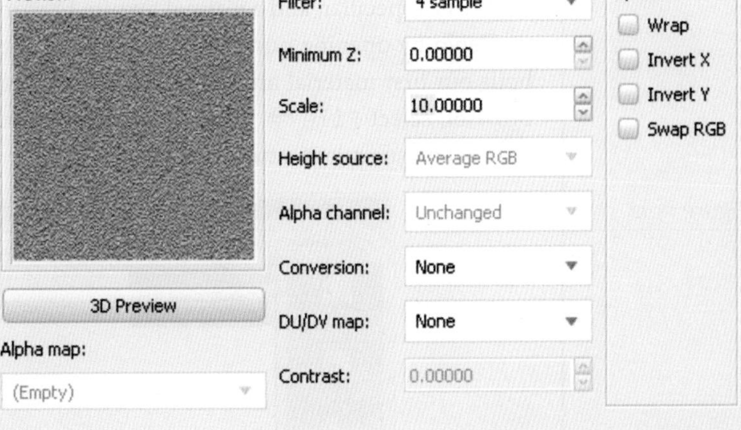

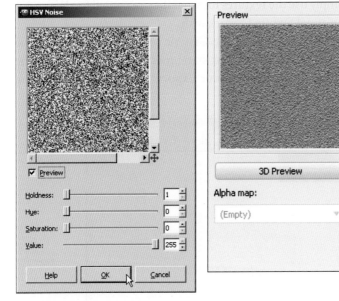

Figure 13.10

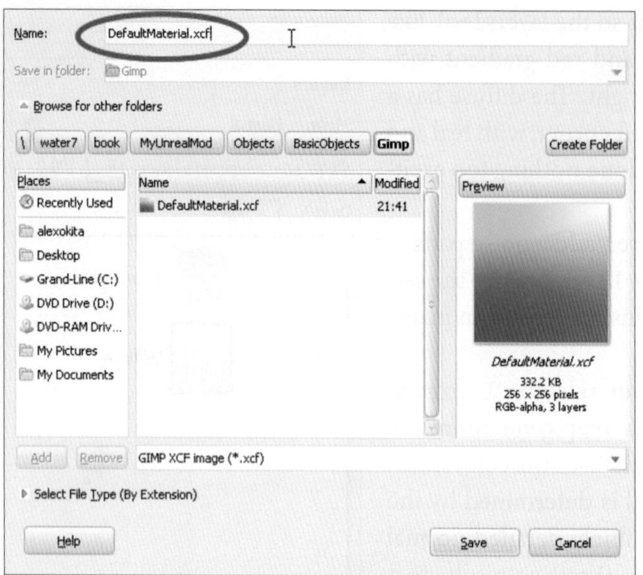


Figure 13.11

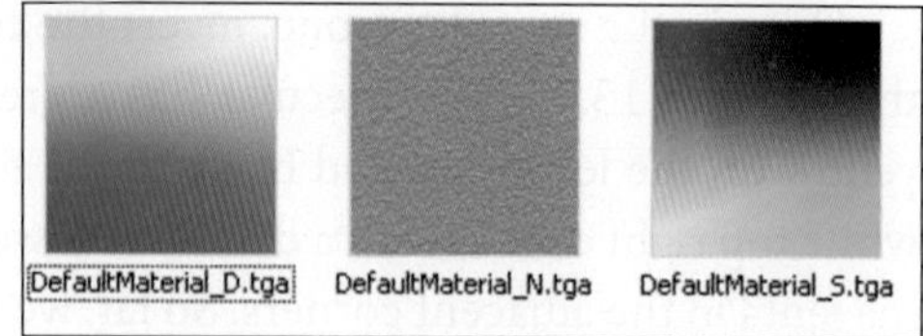


The normal map can obtain its contours from numerous sources. In this case, I've selected "Average (R,G,B)" for height information. The scale is set to 10 to make the contrast high enough to notice from any angle. Save your GIMP file in the BasicObjects/GIMP directory as DefaultMaterial.xcf [Figure 13.10]. Then set the visibility to isolate the individual layers [Figure 13.11] and save them as TGAs. That's enough for GIMP; now let's get back to the Unreal Editor.

## Project

### Building Useful Shaders

In our previous material project, we built one of the simplest practical materials I can think of. Now that we have a few bitmap images to work with, we'll get a bit further into the materials editor. We've got three basic color textures to work with. For the immediate project, we'll simply use the textures for what they're named for. We've got a diffuse, a specular, and a normal texture to work with.

Begin by opening our MyObjects.upk in the Generic browser. This is where we built our first material and applied it to our box static mesh object. In the Generic browser, select `File` → `Import`. Navigate to our Exports directory and select the diffuse and specular textures [Figure 13.12].

Figure 13.12

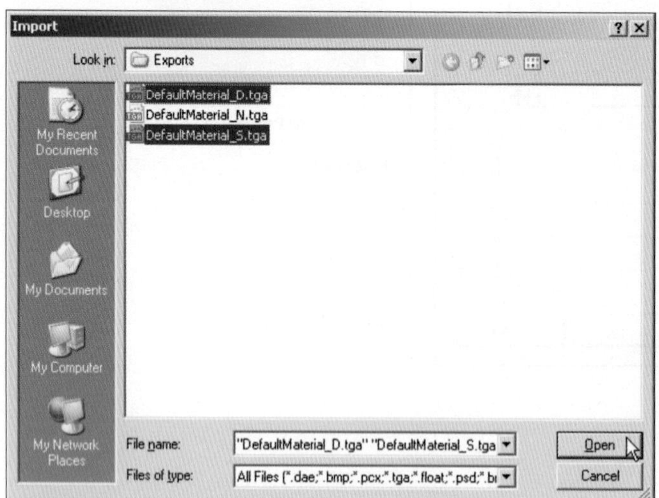

Figure 13.13

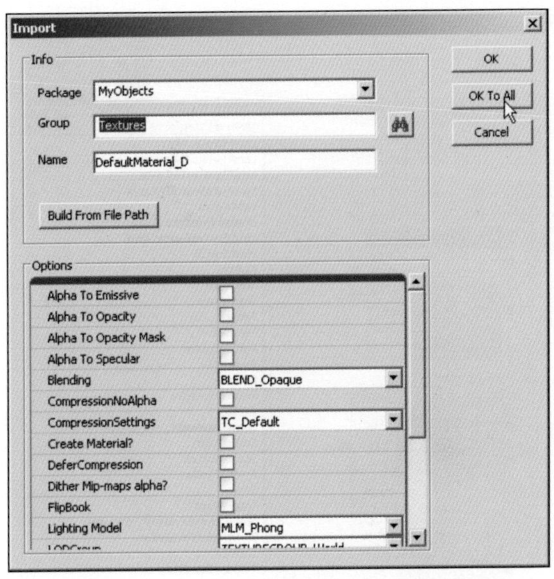


Figure 13.14

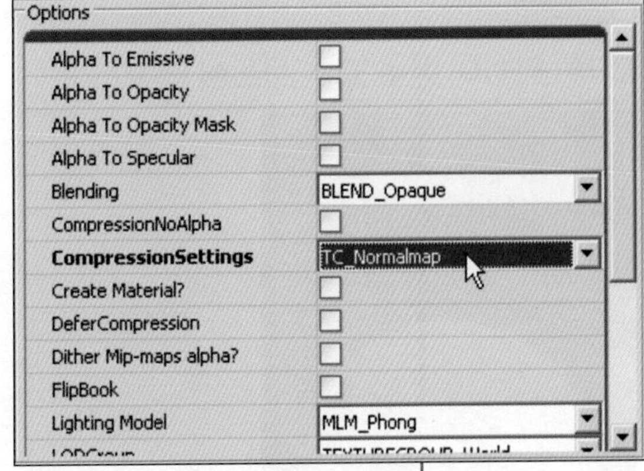


Create a new Textures group and click on `OK To All` [Figure 13.13].

It's important to note that a normal map is imported differently from a regular color texture. The main difference is the color ranges for the red and green channels. Import the normal texture separately from the diffuse and specular textures as there are a few changes to the color settings once imported [Figure 13.14].

When you import the normal map, change the Compression Settings to TC_ Normalmap and click on OK.

The normal map has SRGB unchecked and the UnpackMin values are set to -1 [Figure 13.15]. A regular texture is imported with the following settings [Figure 13.16]. Additionally. the CompressionSetting is set to TC_Default.

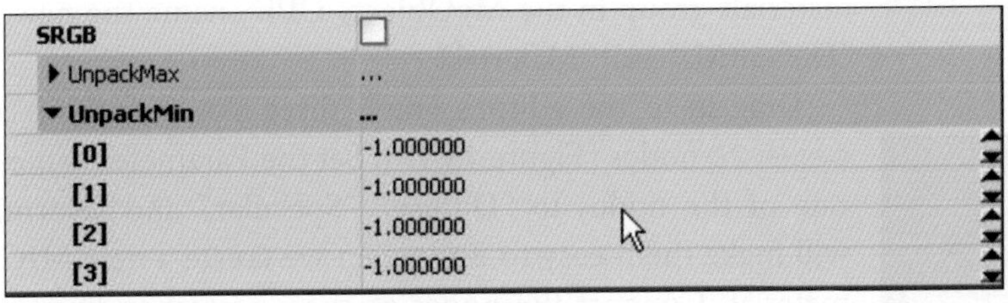

Figure 13.15

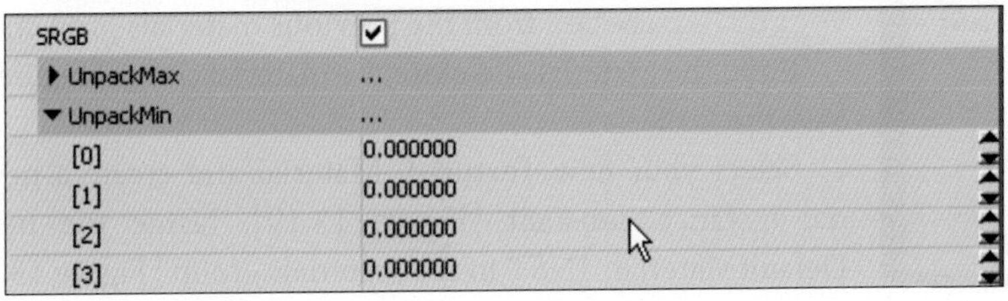

| **SRGB** | ☐ |
|---|---|
| ▶ UnpackMax | ... |
| ▼ **UnpackMin** | ... |
| **[0]** | -1.000000 |
| **[1]** | -1.000000 |
| **[2]** | -1.000000 |
| **[3]** | -1.000000 |

Figure 13.16

| SRGB | ☑ |
|---|---|
| ▶ UnpackMax | ... |
| ▼ UnpackMin | ... |
| [0] | 0.000000 |
| [1] | 0.000000 |
| [2] | 0.000000 |
| [3] | 0.000000 |

Figure 13.17

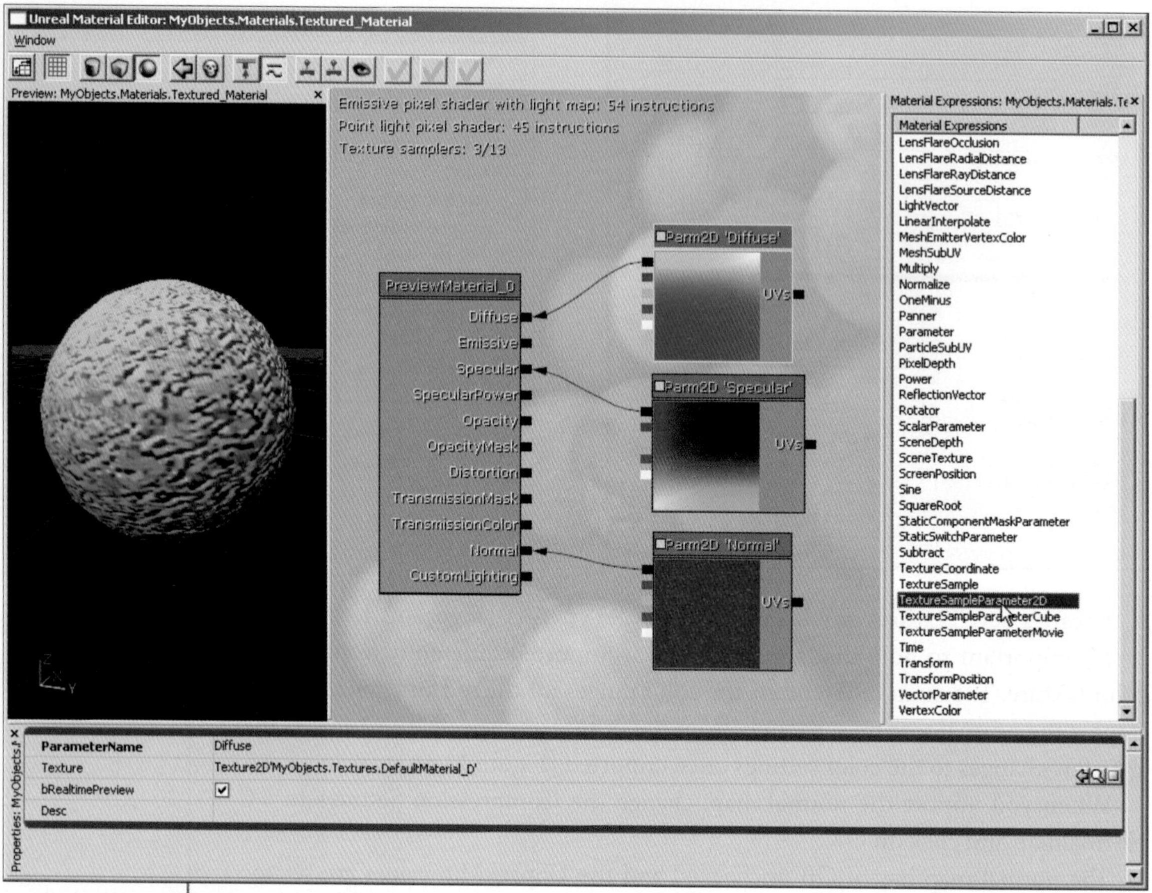

Figure 13.18

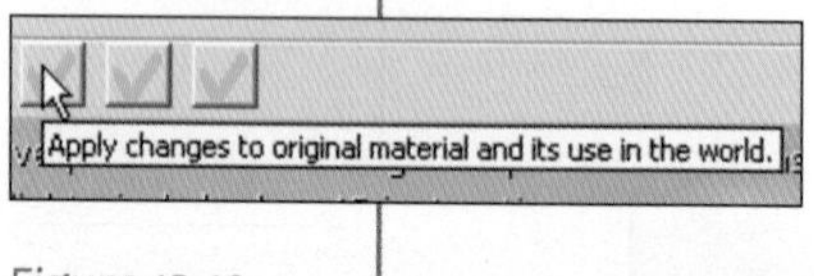


Figure 13.19

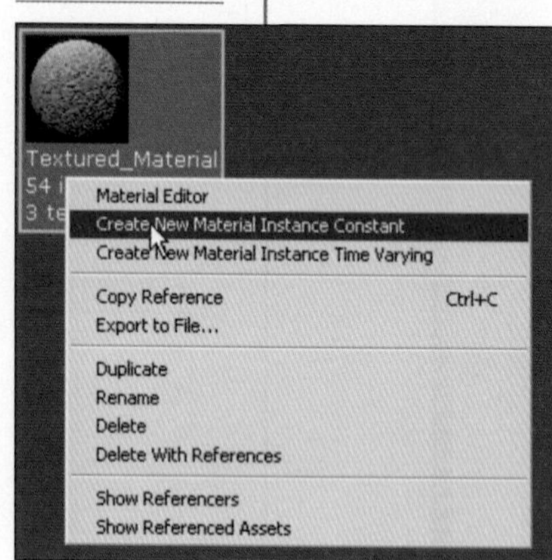


If you're having problems with a normal map not showing up correctly or displaying with seams, this might be a good place to start debugging. Create a new material and add it into the materials group in the MyObjects UPK; name the new material "DefaultMaterial_Material."

Drag in to the editor's graph three `TextureSampleParameter2D` nodes [Figure 13.17]. Set the ParameterName for each one of the nodes to "Diffuse," "Specular," and "Normal." This will make them easy to find when we create a new MIC for this material. Connect the nodes to their corresponding input tabs on the main material node. This is similar to how we dragged a `VectorParameter` from the previous materials project.

Build the material and close the material editor [Figure 13.18]. Save the UPK.

Select your new Textured_Material and create a new material instance constant [Figure 13.19]. Name the new MIC DefaultMaterial_INST in the materials group [Figure 13.20].

Figure 13.20

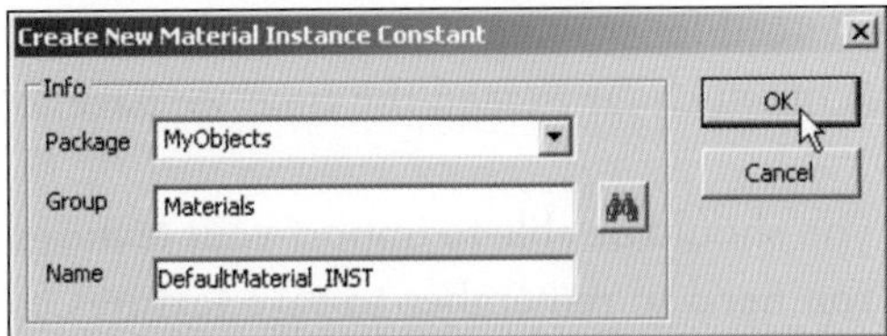


Figure 13.21

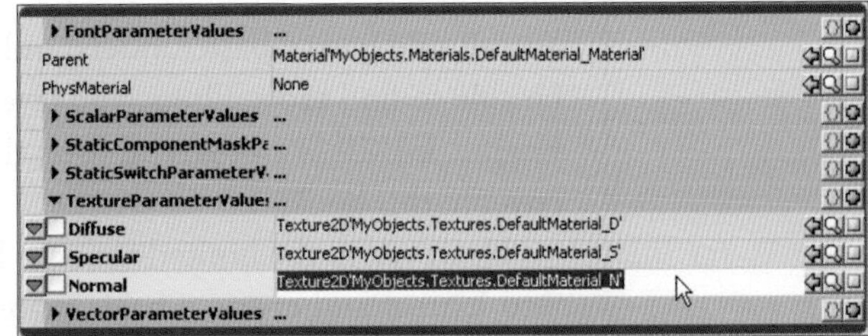


Figure 13.22

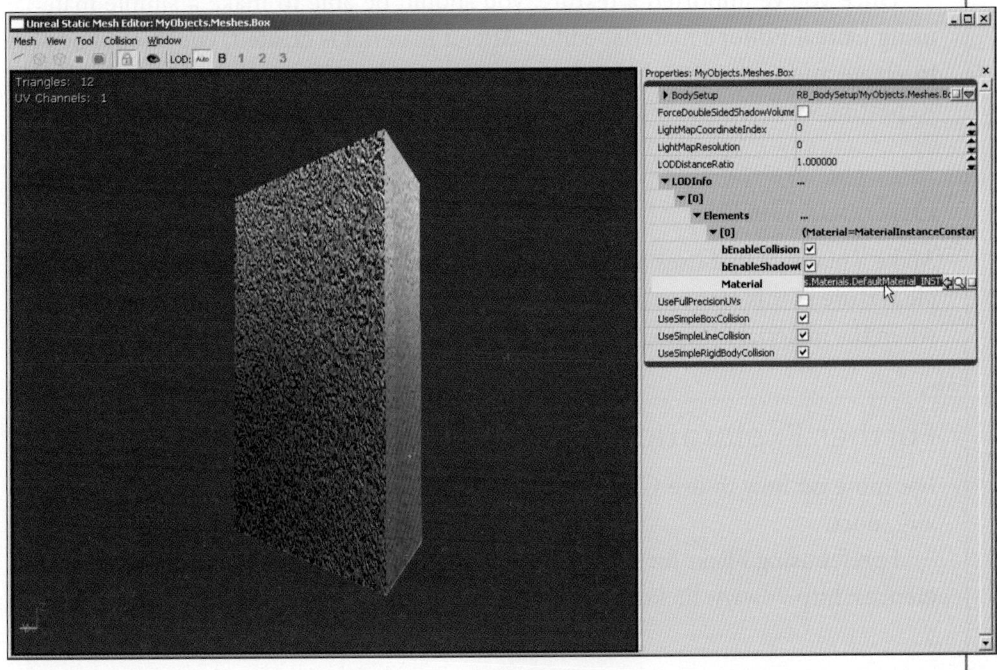


Figure 13.23

The new MIC now has three TextureParameterValues to override with textures for your new objects [Figure 13.21].

Assign the new MIC to the box object and save the UPK [Figure 13.22].

The box in the boxRoom is updated to reflect the changes from the static mesh editor [Figure 13.23]. It's time to start making some more textures!

You should have a basic understanding of the GIMP user interface; and you should be able to find tools, filters, and layers we'll need for making textures for the Unreal Engine. GIMP is a powerful tool, the uses of which far exceed the time we have to cover in this book.

However, in the limited time we have, you should be able to import your textures into Unreal and create a basic material. You need to remember to save textures as either 24- or 32-bit Targa files. You must also remember that you should save a texture with power-of-two dimensions.

Once you've imported a texture, you should be able to make a simple material using Unreal Editor's material editor. After a material is created, you should be able to create and use material instance constants and understand the value of a MIC. Repeating work is a waste of time, and we've only got six weeks!

## On Your Own

Make a material that uses a texture for both diffuse and specular colors. Using a single texture in this manner for multiple lighting channels saves texture memory space when the material is in use.

## Further Exploration

For more on how to use GIMP, read the GIMP Documentation: http://www.gimp.org/docs.

I prefer using Flickr for sifting through photos to find good texture and shape references: http://www.flickr.com/creativecommons.

# 14 Using Max with GIMP

*Making the Most of Your Model*

So far you've made a few simple things in 3D Studio Max and some simple placeholder textures in GIMP. Now let's use 3D Studio Max to create more complex textures. Using the 3D software to generate some data for use in GIMP saves a lot of time and adds basic detail that can greatly enhance your texture work.

High-resolution modeling in combination with the low-resolution in-game model allows for a few tricks that help make texturing easier. One of the most common misconceptions is that the high-resolution mesh must be built like the low-resolution mesh.

## What to Expect

Ambient occlusion is a shading method that takes into account the attenuation of light due to occlusion by objects in the scene. It is one great way to get some interesting detail on a 3D model. This detail, as well as other surface details, can be transferred to your texture. Let's see how we can use 3D Studio Max to create such detailed textures.

## Baking Textures in 3D Studio Max

With 3D Studio Max, you can model some basic details into an object. High-resolution modeling is becoming more and more essential to building detail and texture for even the most basic of props. This section provides an example of a high-resolution model suitable for baking some nice ambient occlusion maps and a normal map.

The presentation here should give you an idea about how to create your own high-resolution details. Learning how to model with so much detail is out of the scope of this book, so we'll avoid getting too deep into what is required. However, it is important to know how high-resolution models are used and what they can give you.

Once your ambient occlusion detail has been extracted from the high-resolution model and transferred to your game-ready model, additional detail can be added in

GIMP. Of course, rendering detail using 3D Studio Max isn't the last step in any texture-creation pipeline. The finishing touches and fine-grained details are added using GIMP.

Figure 14.1

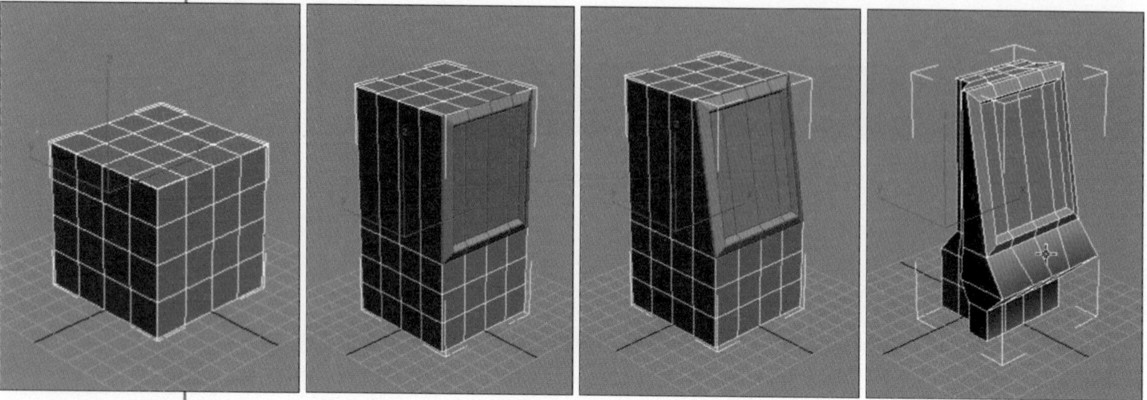

## PROJECT

### Baking Diffuse Textures from High-Resolution Sources

Let's start making a fairly basic computer console as a static mesh object [Figure 14.1]. For this we'll also make some really simple textures using the high-resolution mesh as a base.

Figure 14.2

Figure 14.3

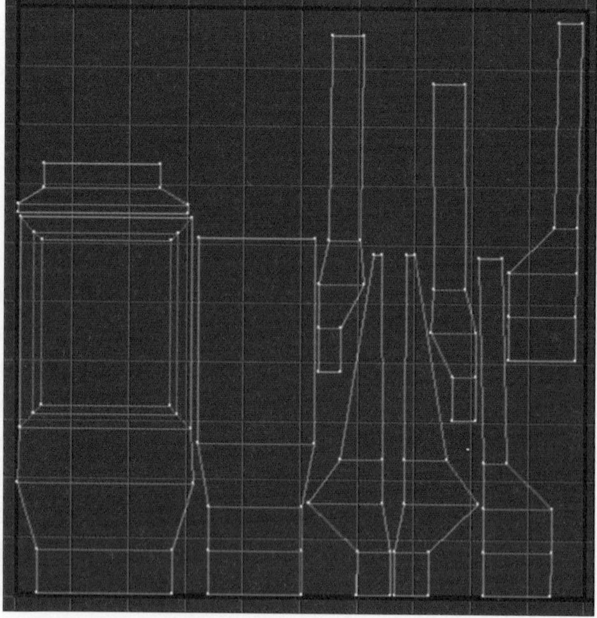

Figure 14.4

After building the basic shape, extra edges were removed as they were not needed [Figure 14.2]. The texture coordinates of the model were then unwrapped so that none of the faces were lying over the others [Figure 14.3].

The unwrapping is mostly important for when we start transferring data from the high-resolution mesh to the texture.

A more detailed version of the mesh was created by adding some chamfers, and additional objects were added to the mesh [Figure 14.4]. It's important to note that none of the new parts had to be welded into the mesh; they were simply placed on the

Figure 14.5

main mesh. After the mesh was combined into a single object, the different areas were assigned colors using a multi-submaterial. This helps speed up the texture creation for our low-resolution mesh.

On the left we have a fairly basic high-resolution mesh [Figure 14.5]. It's nothing amazing, but it's enough to demonstrate how you can use a more detailed object to create textures for a lower-resolution mesh.

As long as the low-resolution mesh and the high-resolution mesh match up, the transfer of detail should be reliable [Figure 14.6].

Figure 14.6

Figure 14.7

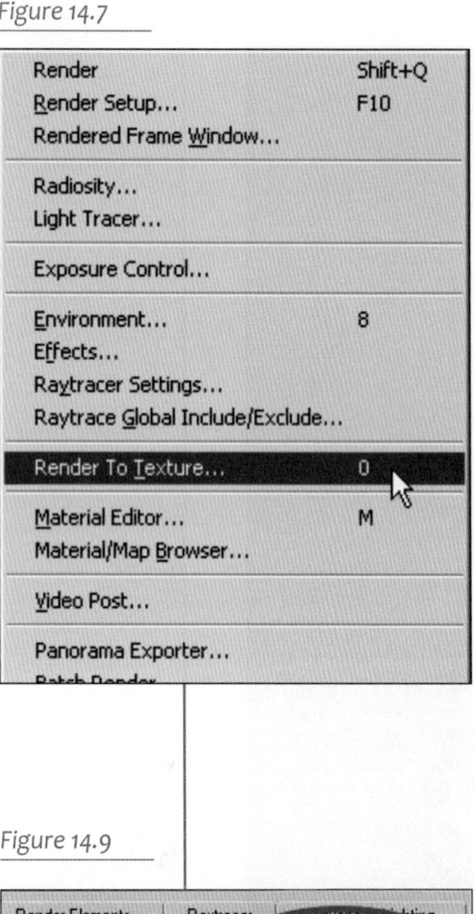


Figure 14.9

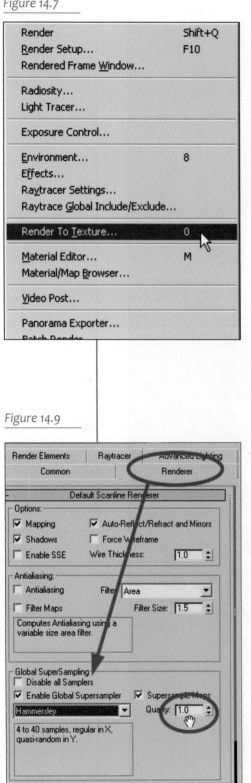

Figure 14.8

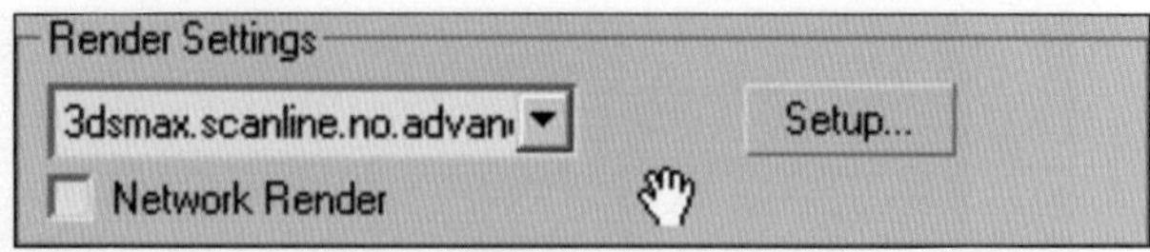


Select the low-resolution mesh. This is our "target" for all of the following rendering operations. Under the Rendering menu, select `Render To Texture` [Figure 14.7]. This will create a texture based on the low-resolution mesh's UVs.

Select one of the 3D Studio Max scanline Render settings; then click on the `Setup` button [Figure 14.8].

Pick the Renderer tab, enable `Global Supersampler`, and switch the selection to `Hammersley`. Set the Quality to 1, and then close the window [Figure 14.9].

In the Render to Texture window, enable the projection mapping and then click on the `Pick` button [Figure 14.10]. This will allow you to pick your high-resolution source object. The steps taken here add a new Projection modifier to the low-resolution mesh. The cage of the mesh is the nonrenderable geometry that the Projection modifier uses as the surface for ray-tracing the mesh in order to compute normal vectors. The automatic settings will need adjustment, so we'll take a look at how to make sure that the cage will catch all of the high-resolution data.

Let's push out the cage a bit from its original placement [Figure 14.11]; this will ensure that the buttons on the high-resolution mesh are captured by the low-resolution approximation to the mesh [Figure 14.12]. In the figure, the original cage is shown as a white wireframe that tightly encloses the high-resolution mesh. The expanded cage is shown as a purple wireframe.

Figure 14.10

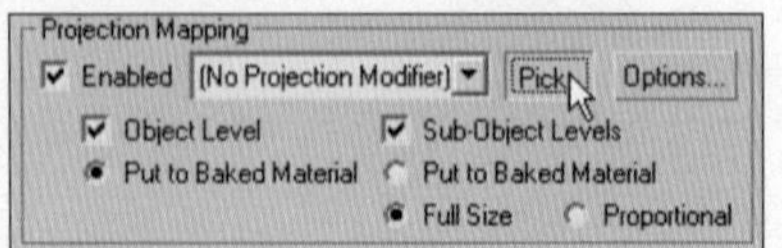


Figure 14.11

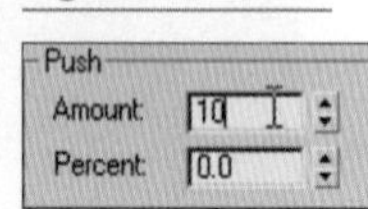

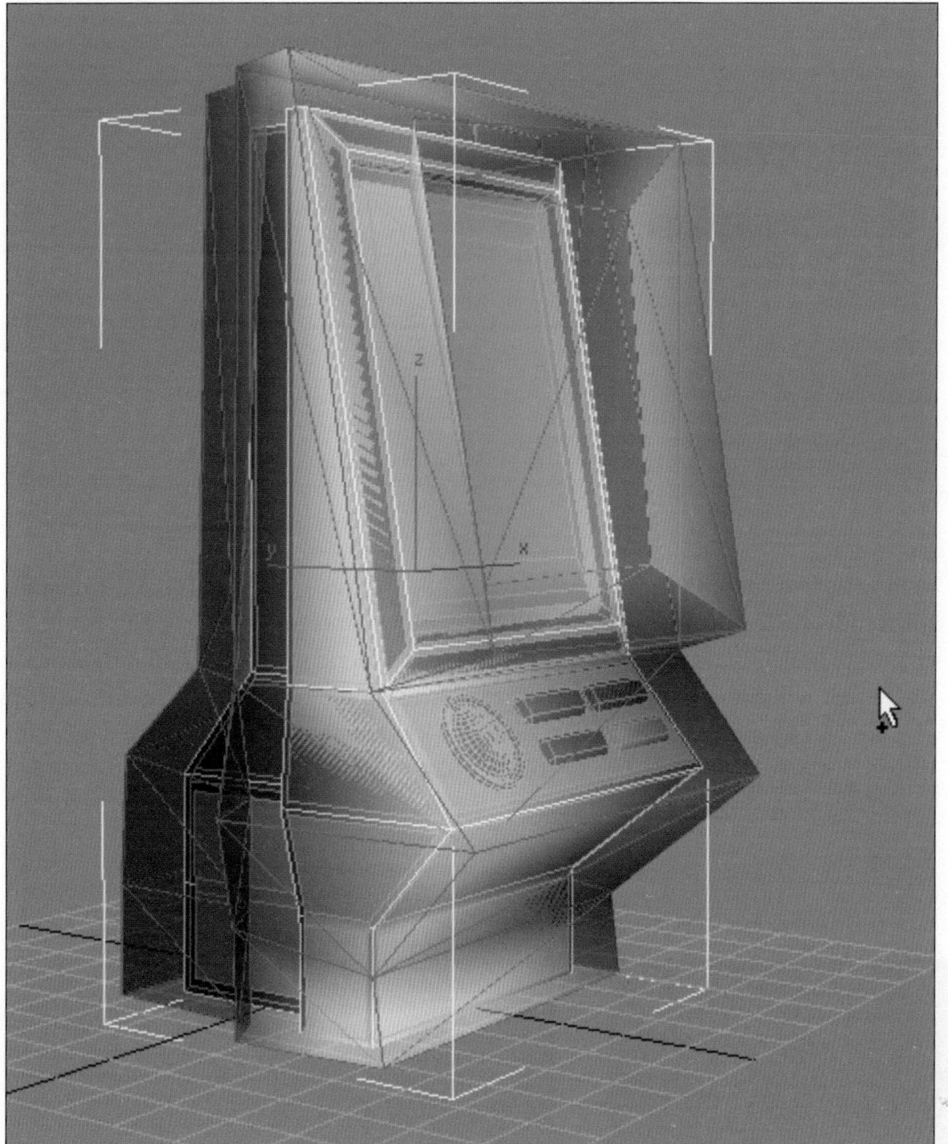


Figure 14.12

In general, as long as the cage completely surrounds the high-resolution detail, you should be able to get all of the data you need. The main drawback to this is that the areas near the back may begin to overlap, and the faces may inherit color and detail from the wrong surfaces. To change the shape of the cage, you can select the vertices and move them so that they contain any high-resolution mesh elements.

In the Render to Texture dialog, add the following two elements to the output: DiffuseMap and NormalsMap [Figure 14.13]. These will be used by the exported static mesh in the engine.

Figure 14.13

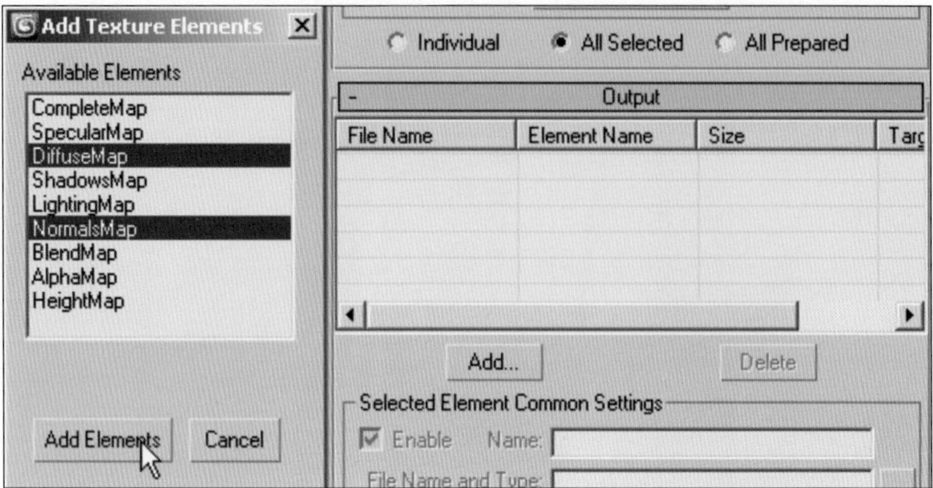


The output should produce two textures like Figures 14.14 and 14.15. By default, the Render to Texture dialog will set the two output sizes to 256 × 256. This is a good chance to look for missing areas. It's always best to spend some time making sure that the render will come out properly before increasing the resolution. The diffuse map [Figure 14.14] and the normal map [Figure 14.15] appear correctly, so we'll increase the resolution of those textures to 1024 × 1024.

Figure 14.14

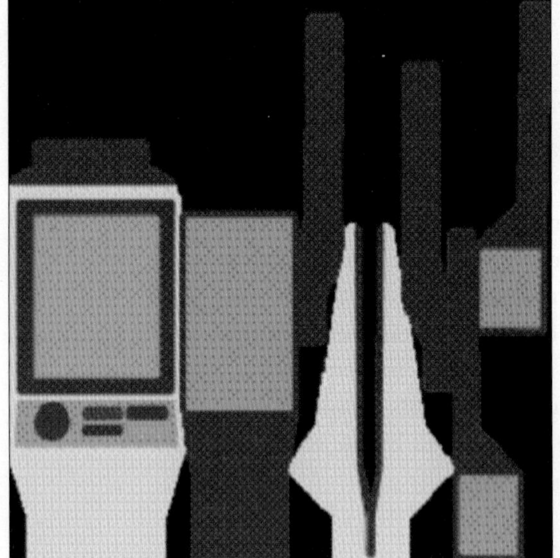

Figure 14.15

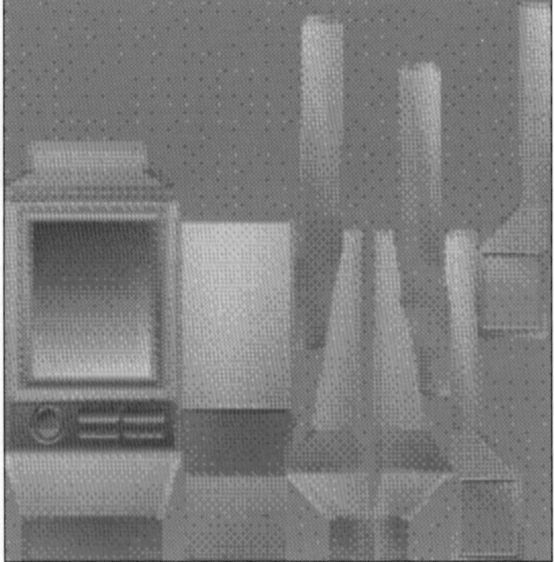

Figure 14.16

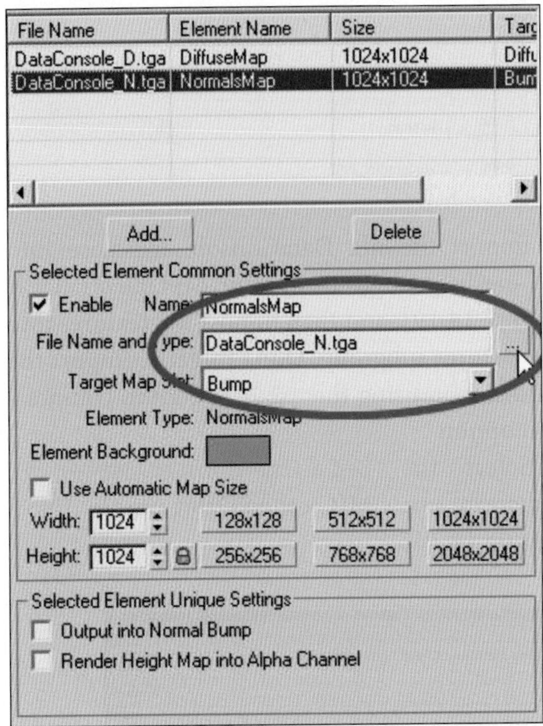


Figure 14.17

Figure 14.18

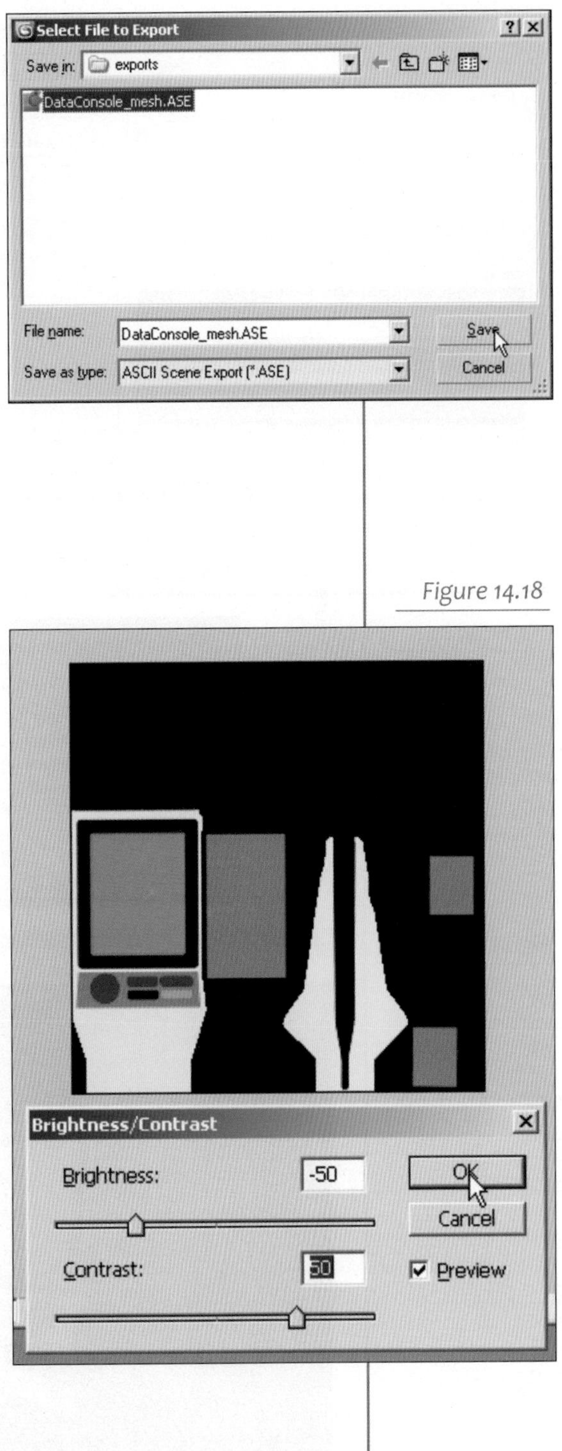


The new resolution should be sufficient for our purposes here. Set the File Name and Type to DataConsole_N.tga and DataConsole_D.tga [Figure 14.16] for the normal map and diffuse map, respectively. The names will make it easier to find the files when we need to import them into the engine.

Select the mesh and export it (using the Exported Selected option) to DataConsole_mesh.ASE [Figure 14.17]; this file will go into your exports folder together with the diffuse map and normal map textures.

Using GIMP, open the diffuse texture that we just created in 3D Studio Max. Select the menu item `Colors` → `Brightness-Contrast` and adjust the brightness and contrast sliders so that the diffuse image looks like Figure 14.18. Save the modified image to a file named DataConsole_S.tga. This image will be your specular texture.

Figure 14.19

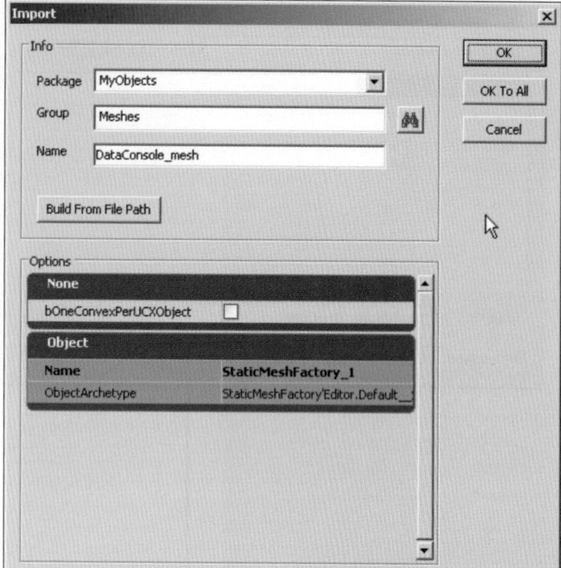


Figure 14.20

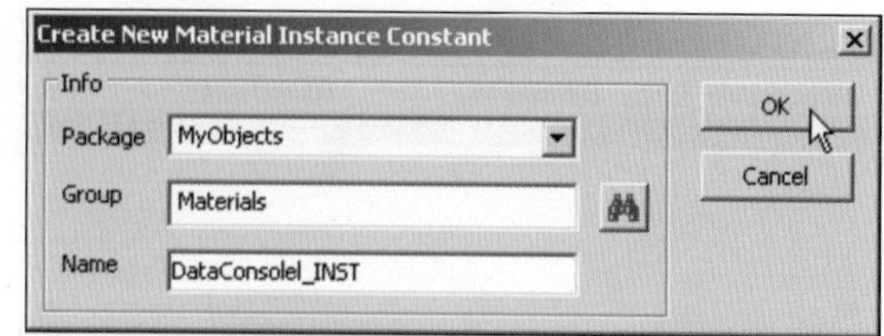


Import the file DataConsole_mesh.ase into the meshes subgroup in your MyObjects. UPK [Figure 14.19], and then import the textures into the textures subgroup. Don't forget to import the normal map using the `TC_NormalMap` compression option.

Select the `DefaultMaterial_Material` and create a new MIC called DataConsole_INST [Figure 14.20].

Figure 14.21

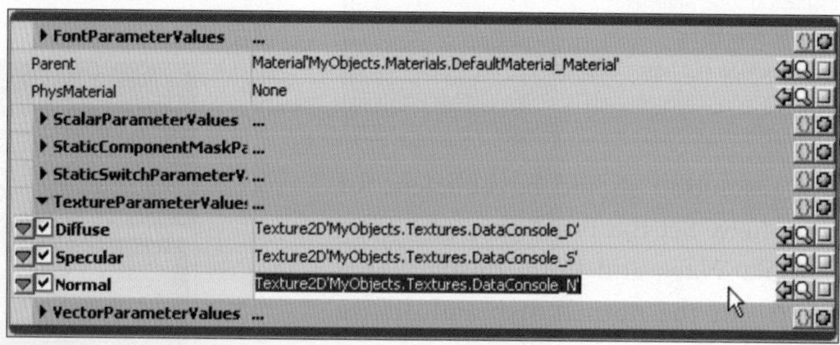


Figure 14.22

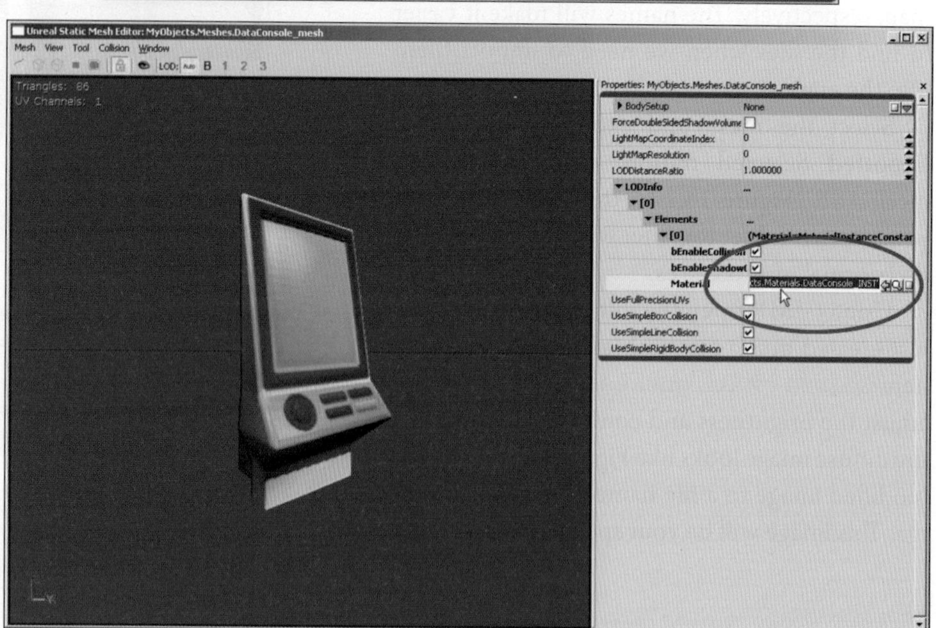

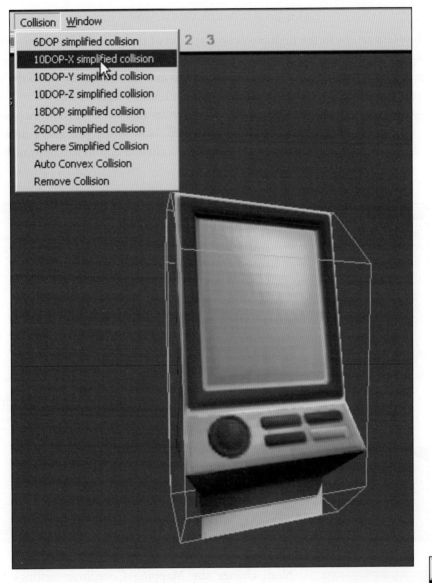

Figure 14.23

Figure 14.24

Figure 14.25

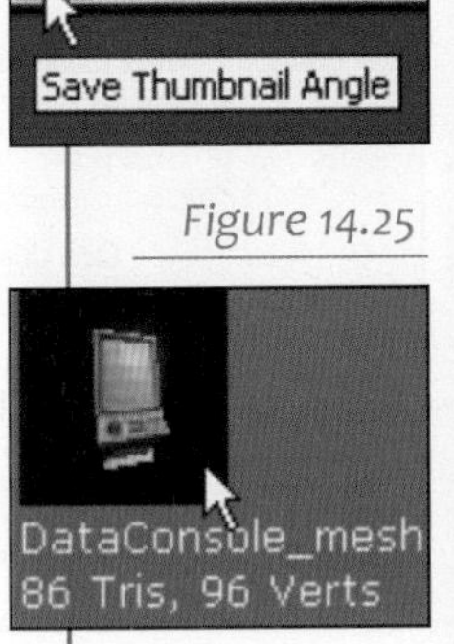


Add the imported textures to the material overrides in the TextureParameterValues [Figure 14.21].

Add the new MIC to the object's Material slot in the LOD0Info rollout menu [Figure 14.22].

Next create a simple collision box for the object [Figure 14.23].

Then create a new Thumbnail icon [Figure 14.24] to make the static mesh easier to identify in the Generic browser [Figure 14.25].

## Bake an Ambient Occlusion Texture

Now let's return to the high-resolution version of the console. This time, select the high-resolution mesh and open the Render to Texture dialog. To bake an ambient occlusion texture on this object, we'll need to use `mental ray`. So in the Render settings, select `mental.ray.photometric.light` [Figure 14.26].

Figure 14.26

To be able to render an ambient occlusion map, we need `mental ray` activated. Now when you add a new output texture, a new ambient occlusion option will be available [Figure 14.27].

Figure 14.27

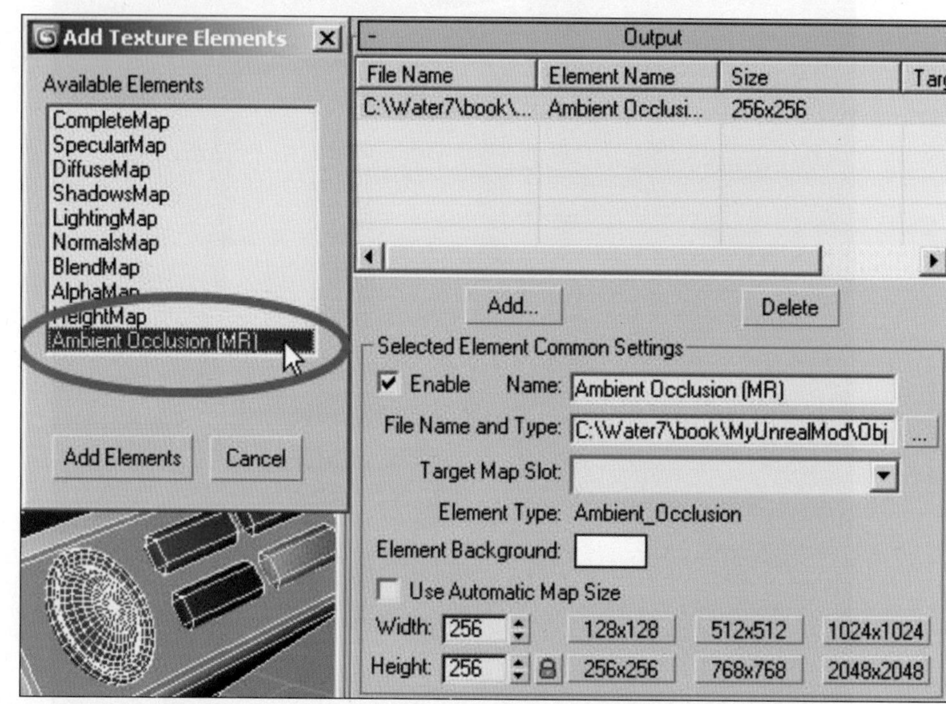


Figure 14.28

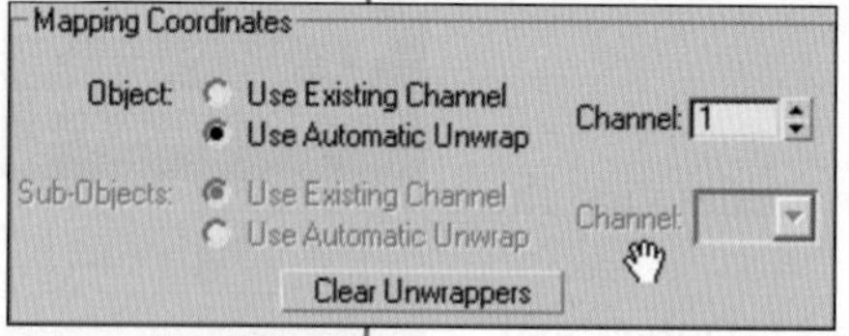


Next, change the Mapping Coordinate settings to `Use Automatic Unwrap` [Figure 14.28]. We never created UVs for our high-resolution mesh, so we'll let 3D Studio Max handle that for us.

After rendering the texture, create a new material—no material IDs this time—for the high-resolution object. Then assign the entire high-resolution object a single bitmap.

The first pass should produce something like this [Figure 14.29]—a bit chunky and not so great looking, but we didn't have to wait long to be sure that we're making some progress.

Figure 14.29

Figure 14.30

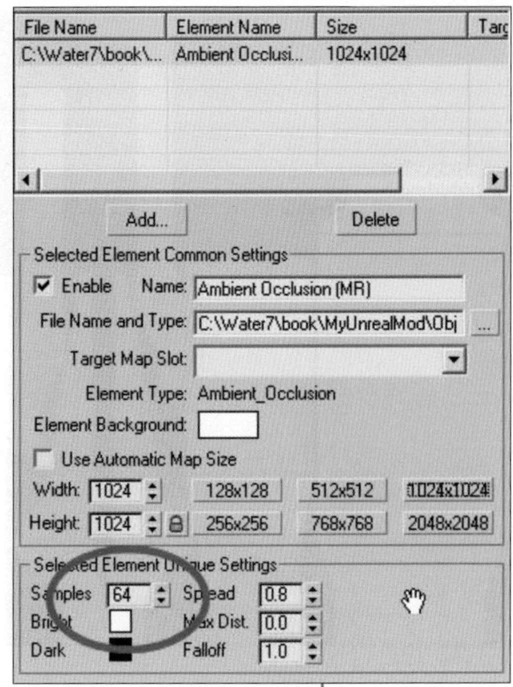


Increase the samples to 64, and increase the size of the texture map to 1024 × 1024 [Figure 14.30] or even 2048 × 2048 if you feel like waiting for a slightly longer render. This will improve the quality of the output. Finally, we have an ambient occlusion texture, but this is for the high-resolution object. The ambient occlusion texture was created for the high-resolution mesh because that mesh has interesting details that the lower-resolution mesh does not. Just as we transferred the diffuse color from the high-resolution mesh, we'll transfer the ambient occlusion to our low-resolution mesh. Only this time, we'll name the output of the Render to Texture tool DataConsole_AO.tga.

The result should look something like Figure 14.31. The areas around the panels have darkened, and the buttons now have shadows around them. You should remember to use the 3D Studio Max scanline renderer in the Render to Texture dialog when transferring textures. `Mental ray` is best used only for rendering the high-resolution object's ambient occlusion map.

Figure 14.31

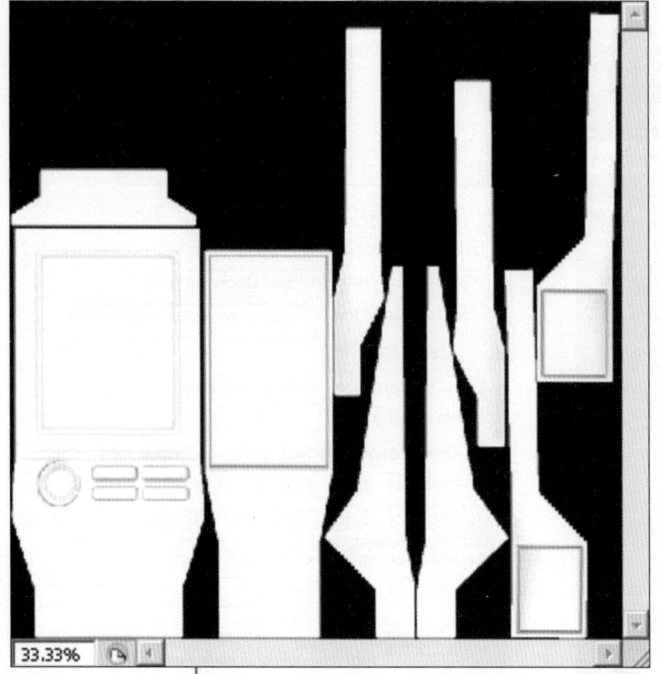


Select Open As Layers from the file menu and then select both the diffuse and ambient occlusion textures for the low-resolution object. Arrange the layers by dragging and dropping them so that the ambient occlusion is above the diffuse and then change the layers mode to "Multiply" [Figure 14.32]. This process is one of the most basic ways to add detail to a static mesh object. The object we created isn't the most fantastically detailed object ever; but as an example, it's simple and represents the steps required to make more interesting objects. To save the diffuse texture, right-click on the ambient occlusion layer and then select merge down.

Figure 14.32

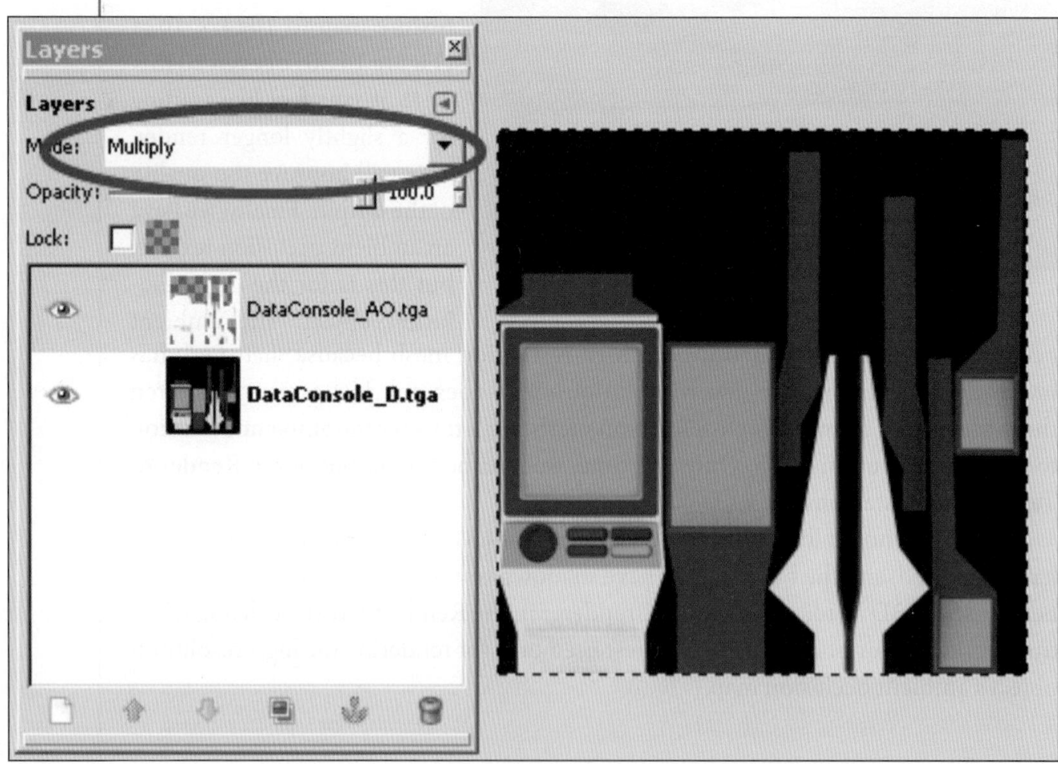

Using 3D Studio Max to generate textures can speed up your texturing process. You may have noticed that we hardly had to spend any time in GIMP or in any other texture editing tool.

As an alternative, we could have added the ambient occlusion into the texture as a node in the material editor. We wouldn't even have to use GIMP to combine our textures! You'll learn later in the materials editing chapters how this will work.

## On Your Own

Create a colorful specular map and see whether you can make a mother-of-pearl effect.

NVIDIA's Mental Mill is an amazing tool; take a look at it. It's similar to Unreal's Material editor. It will allow you to build materials in ways similar to how Unreal materials are built; then you can use these materials in 3D Studio Max!

# 15 Process and Methods

## *Staying Organized*

So far we've made several different assets; our projects up to this point have been pretty simple. To prepare for more complex tutorials and assets in Unreal, we're going to want to set up some basic practices.

This includes a few best practices when it comes to the Unreal Engine, as well as game development in general. Modeling, texturing, and animation are all specialized functions at a large game studio, where specialists fill each of these roles. An artist can find himself working as a technical artist, a hard-surface modeler, or a cinematics animator.

## What to Expect

So far, you've done some exploration of the 3D Studio Max and GIMP environments. You've imported some objects into Unreal and should be comfortable making packages for use in your game. You've created and applied materials to your objects. You've added collision to your objects and even interacted with them in Unreal.

Before diving into building complex objects in Unreal, we'll want to think about how to keep assets, textures, and our project under control. By the end of a completed game, you may be looking at hundreds of textures, materials, meshes, and animations. With so many assets lying all over the place, you'll want to keep them organized or you'll end up with a ton of wasted memory and data in your project that aren't in use.

I'll avoid getting too deep into the specifics of how you should work. After all, it's your game, your idea. I'll leave it up to you to dive deeper into both 3D Studio Max and GIMP to gain the specific skills for your project. This section is going to outline some do's and don't's when it comes to building objects and textures for the Unreal Engine. We'll also cover some basics when it comes to game engines in general.

## Unreal Package Organization

There's a lot you'll need to know to keep Unreal Engine's data organized. Unreal Engine arranges its data into separate assets called packages (UPKs). The UPKs that are grouped in your content folder contain meshes, textures, and asset-related data. Your package files need to be organized to allow Unreal Script to find, for instance, a weapon. Naming conventions become important at this point. You'll have to coordinate the Unreal script with the UPKs to ensure that an object can be instanced by Unreal Script.

PROJECT

### Moving Misplaced Resources

There's no direct way to move an object from package to package using drag-and-drop. The only method of moving an object around is to rename it. In this example, we have a material that's been created in the Meshes subgroup of PackageA.UPK [Figure 15.1].

Figure 15.1

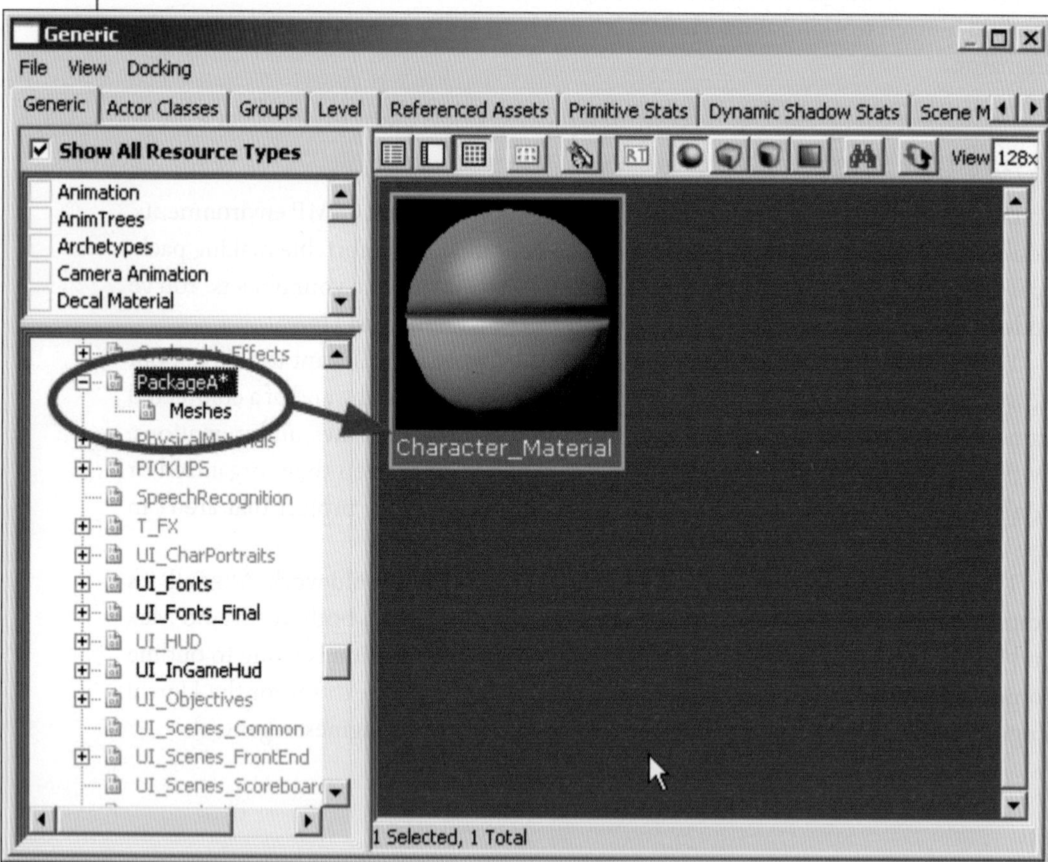

Figure 15.2

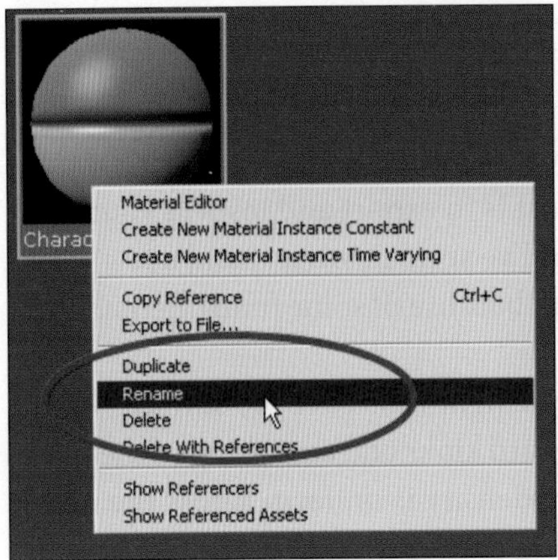


Figure 15.3

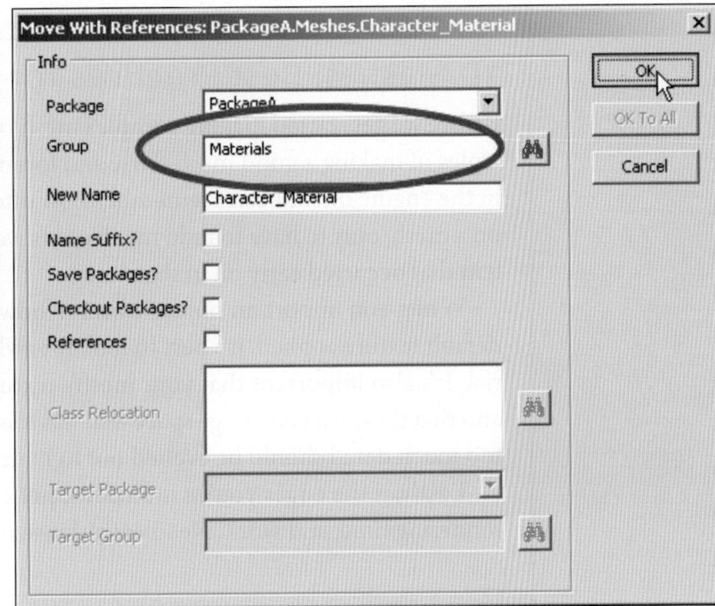


To change its subgroup, we're going to right-click on the object in the Generic browser and select Rename [Figure 15.2].

Notice that this window is called "Move With References:" [Figure 15.3]. In the Group text field, enter Materials and then hit OK. This is about all it takes to move objects around.

## Redirects

Redirects in Unreal work a bit like web page redirects. When a level loads, placed objects are instanced from the packages they live in. If the object has been moved to a new package, the redirect tells the level where to look for it. Redirects act as bookmarks that tell where an object has moved to.

Once the new address is found, the level can be saved with the updated information. Redirects exist as an invisible footprint where the object used to be. If an entire package were to be deleted along with its redirects, the level would not have any way to find out where the meshes it's looking for have moved to.

Before deleting old packages, it's best to update your levels so they can discover how an object has been renamed; otherwise, your level will need the objects replaced by hand. There are more efficient methods to update old levels, but those tools are beyond the scope of this book.

## 3D Meshes: Best Practices for Unreal Engine

Before we get started making complex mesh objects, I'd like to cover some basic principles of making a good mesh. First and foremost is to export and inspect your work in the engine often. I can't remember how often I've seen an artist spend a few weeks on a mesh, only to have to redo much of his work because of some fundamental problem that occurred early on in the work.

When you import an object, observe how the light rolls over the surface. With a default texture applied, it's best to look for awkward kinks and stretching of the material. It's also important that your mesh's texture density is uniform across the object and that there isn't any large space that has too low a texture density. Any area that has too much detail should be evened out to match the rest of the mesh's detail.

Lastly, if the edges you've modeled can't even be seen, then they're wasting data, rendering time, and work. Needlessly dense meshes are difficult to change.

## Mesh Density

The Unreal engine can handle quite a few polygons, but you shouldn't abuse this ability. Making a mesh so dense that it's difficult to model is problematic for many reasons. Model rigging and animation turn into a rather slow process when artists must deal with a needlessly dense mesh. I've managed to build and import characters with well over 80,000 triangles and I've met the bone limit with 255 joints. This turned into quite the heavy character; but once imported, the mesh was able to perform like any regular, if not overly detailed, character. Of course, these sorts of heavy, detailed characters are not intended for regular game play; this character was for a highly specialized demo focusing on photorealistic textures and facial animation software.

Judging the mesh density against how big something is on screen will help make decisions on how densely any model is built. Making a mesh too dense really has drawbacks only when there are a lot of such meshes on screen. However, when triangles are rendered to a region smaller than a pixel, you're simply wasting your time including them in the model, and you're wasting graphics card resources that can be better used elsewhere.

Add detail where it's needed, but not more than necessary. In most cases, a character in a video game will have more detail on his face than on his arms and legs. There are many resources on the Internet where you can get tips and suggestions on how best to model characters and objects for video games. It's a good idea to use those resources and gain the intuition that will tell you what sort of shapes should be modeled and what should be described in your texture maps.

## 2D Textures: Making Every Pixel Count

Texturing, above all else in a modern game model, is the most important part of any static mesh or character. When modeling, you should always keep in the back of your mind how much texture space the surface is going to use. Unreal Engine supports mirroring of UVs and lighting them correctly when the normals are flipped.

Mirroring UVs for a character is a great way to save texture space since humans, and indeed most bipeds, have vertical symmetry. Make use of this fact by mirroring the UVs on your character. Many objects can also have overlapping UVs to save space. In some cases, this can create some issues when lighting the object, but the solutions for those problems are beyond the scope of this book.

## Review

You should now have a good idea what it takes to build a 3D model. To learn more about adding details, you'll need to dive further into the inner workings of the Stack in 3D Studio Max. You should make the time to learn from the many resources on the Internet and in other books. The online community of 3D artists is growing, and it's easy to find a group of people to converse with and learn from.

In many cases, early attempts at 3D modeling push people away from texturing. The difficulty of painting makes many 3D artists shy away from learning how to use 2D editing software to achieve truly fantastic models. You're only hobbling yourself if you exclude painting skills from your skill set.

## On Your Own

It should be obvious that becoming a skilled modeler and texture artist is going to take quite some time. With a bit of talent and patience, creating an entire game is quite doable. Time and patience might be your best assets when it comes to tackling the art required for your mod.

# 16 Making Better Materials

*Connect the Dots . . .*

Basic materials are simple to build such as a single 2D-texture connected to a single output. To build a complex material, you start off with a basic material and add a few functions at a time. Large materials can have many dozens of nodes. You should attempt to make a material you can reuse for many different things. After spending hours of work on a single material, you'll want to make sure it's useful for more than one object.

Colors should be thought of as numbers. A texture is made of three channels: red, blue, and green. Each channel is made of 256 levels of grey, ranging from black to white. The material editor thinks of the range of grey from 0 to 1. If you multiply a color by the number 2, you can expect the resulting color to be twice as bright as the original.

The materials rendered to the scene will begin to bloom when their value exceeds 1. The range of color is not limited between 0 and 1. Some special effects even use negative colors to darken objects when rendered.

When building your materials, experiment and play with different combinations of nodes and textures. Just because the nodes represent math, there's no reason to be afraid of them. The nodes are doing the hard part; you just have to connect them together.

## What to Expect

The best practice when making a new material is to test what each node does on its own. Exploration is the most important part when it comes to learning how the Unreal Editor works. The parts of the editor by themselves are suited to simple tasks but hide a great deal of depth. The material editor is one of the more complex tools yet visually the most interesting.

Here's a periodic table of nodes that make up a material in Unreal Editor [Figure 16.1]. The vertical columns are groups of operations separated by what they do. The lower horizontal group is a set of nodes that have specific purposes only for

*Figure 16.1*

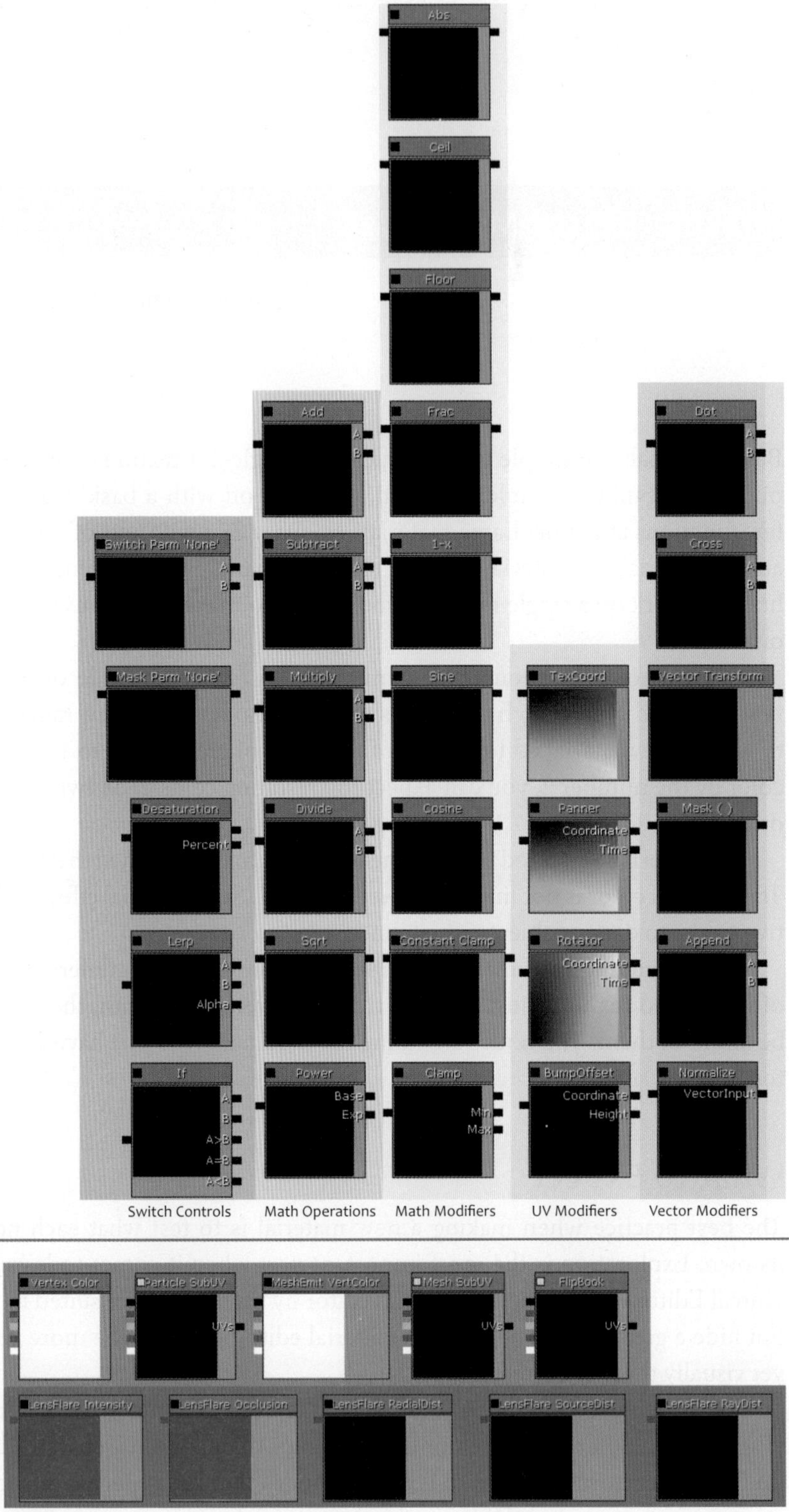

Abs
Ceil
Floor
Add
Frac
Dot
Switch Parm 'None'
Subtract
1-x
Cross
Mask Parm 'None'
Multiply
Sine
TexCoord
Vector Transform
Desaturation
Divide
Cosine
Panner
Mask ( )
Lerp
Sqrt
Constant Clamp
Rotator
Append
If
Power
Clamp
BumpOffset
Normalize

Switch Controls
Math Operations
Math Modifiers
UV Modifiers
Vector Modifiers

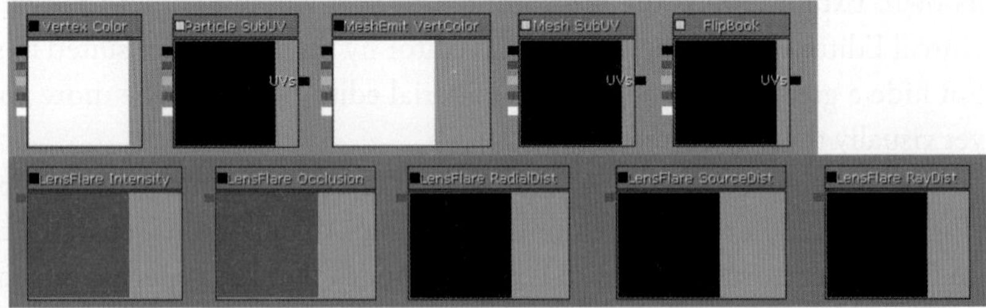

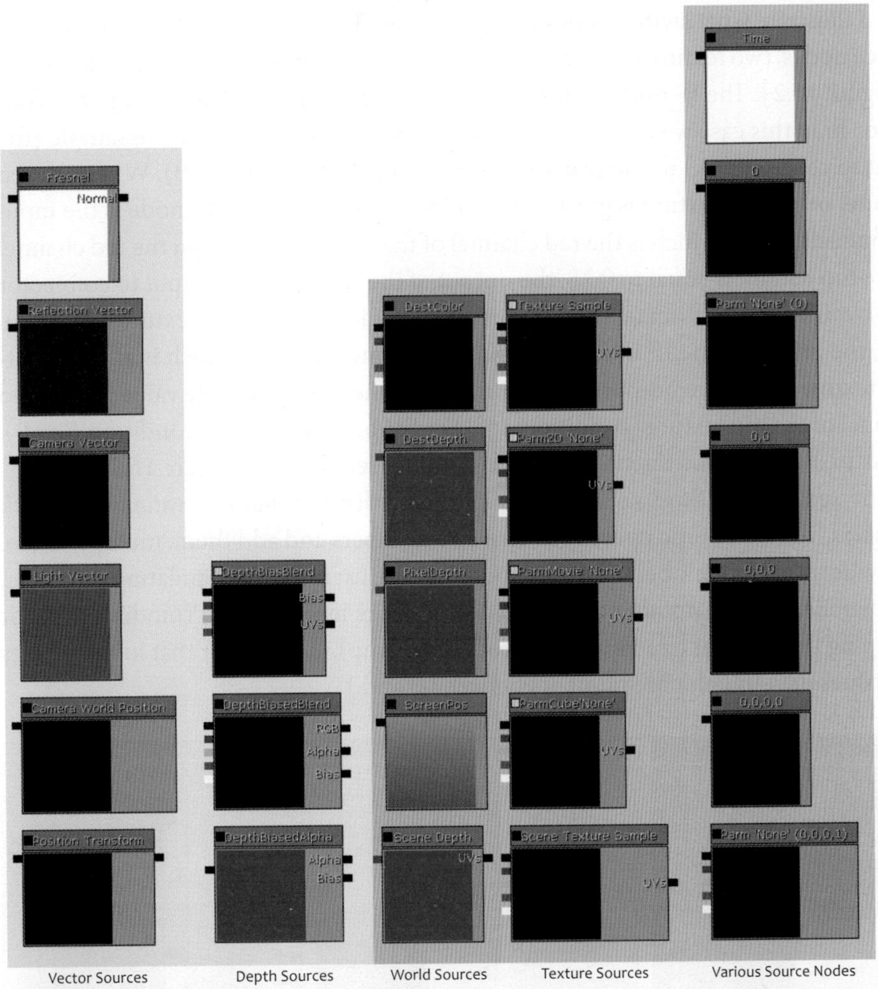

Fresnel
Normal
Reflection Vector
Camera Vector
Light Vector
Camera World Position
Position Transform
DepthBiasBlend
Bias
UVs
DepthBiasedBlend
RGB
Alpha
Bias
DepthBiasedAlpha
Alpha
Bias
DestColor
DestDepth
PixelDepth
ScreenPos
Scene Depth
UVs
Texture Sample
UVs
Param2D 'None'
UVs
ParamMovie 'None'
UVs
ParamCube'None'
UVs
Scene Texture Sample
UVs
Time
0
Param 'None' (0)
0,0
0,0,0
0,0,0,0
Param 'None' (0,0,0,1)
Vector Sources
Depth Sources
World Sources
Texture Sources
Various Source Nodes

Expression
FontParam 'None'
Font Sample

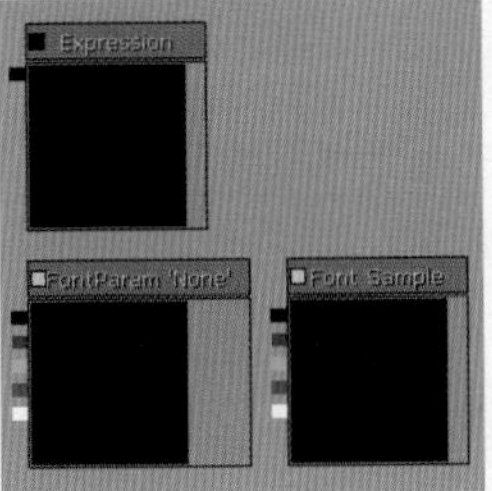

particles or lens flares, organized left to right, similarly to the rest of the chart. The columns are arranged from left to right with data modifiers on the left leading to various data sources on the right.

The first column of Figure 16.1 lists the *switch controls*. Switches allow you to add logic to your materials. These also allow you to use color data in a way more meaningful than just to add color. We'll see how these can be used with the following materials project.

To illustrate what switch nodes can do, let's work with an IF node. We have three source nodes, two texture nodes and a scalar node, going into the IF node [right image of Figure 16.2]. The IF node compares the input of connector A to the input of connector B. In this case we're comparing the red channel of the top texture sample (the input to connector A) to the scalar value 0.28 (input to connector B). When the red channel of the top texture is greater than 0.28, the output of the IF node is the input to connector A>B, which is the red channel of the top texture. When the red channel of the top texture is equal to 0.28, the output of the IF node is the input to connector A=B, which is the bottom texture. When the red channel of the top texture is less than 0.28, the output of the IF node is the input to connector A<B, which is also the bottom texture. Thus, the output of the IF node is either the gray-scale value for the red channel of the top texture (condition A>B) or the bottom texture (condition A<=B). A textured cube shows the output of the IF node [left image of Figure 16.2].

The second and third columns of Figure 16.1 list the *math operations and math modifiers*. The arithmetic operations take two numbers and add them, multiply them, or divide them. Other operations and modifiers are useful for manipulating a number, say, by reflecting the number about the center of the interval [0,1] (modifier 1-X) or clamping the number to an interval (modifier Clamp). Remember that in most cases the values of your color are numbers between 0 and 1.

Figure 16.2

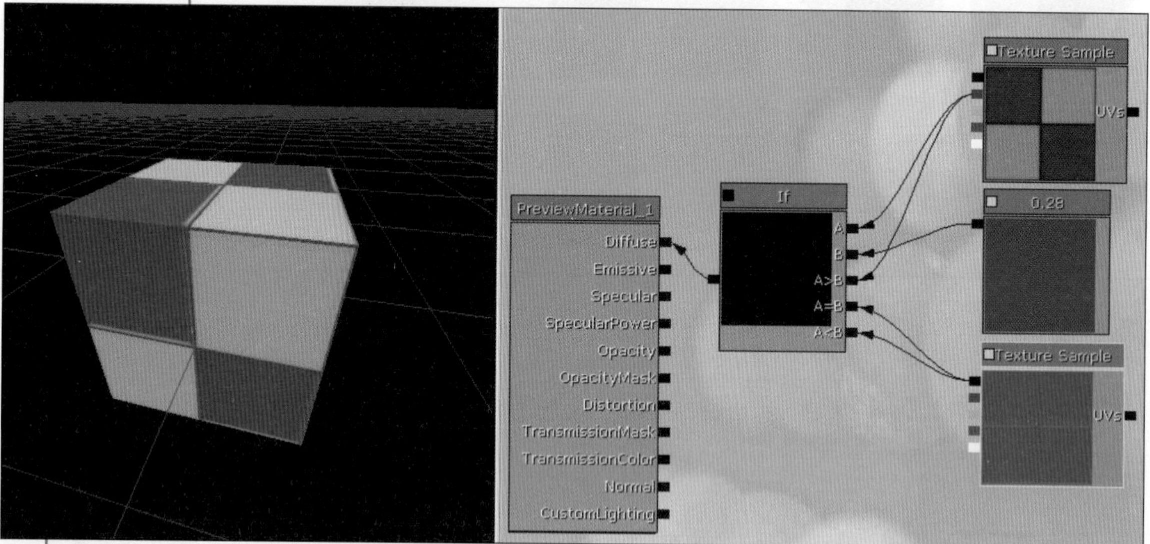

Figure 16.3

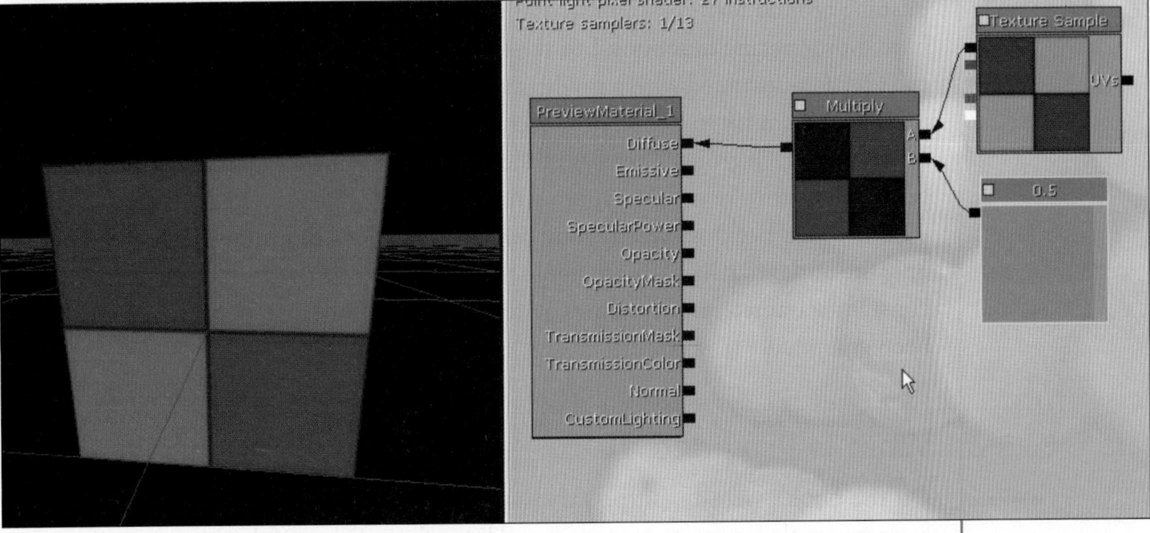


To half the brightness of any color, create a scalar node with a value of 0.5 and multiply it by another value. The result will be half the original value. In the following example, a scalar 0.5 is an input to the connector B of the Multiply node and the Texture Sample above it is an input to the connector A of the same Multiply node [right image of Figure 16.3]. The output of that node is the product of the inputs and is a color half as bright as the color of the original texture. A texture cube shows the result [left image of Figure 16.3]. The other math operations work in the same fashion.

The fourth column of Figure 16.1 lists modifiers for UVs. These allow you to manipulate texture coordinates for an image.

The fifth column of Figure 16.1 contains modifiers for vectors generally. Commonly encountered vectors that may be used as inputs to the vector modifiers are listed in the sixth column of Figure 16.1. That column also contains a node for transforming a position.

Some advanced blending effects require knowledge of depth values in the scene. The seventh column of Figure 16.1 contains nodes that may be used to achieve depth-influenced blending. Material colors may arise from world sources. Nodes to support such materials are listed in the eighth column of Figure 16.1.

Lastly, materials may be built from texture sources and number sources. The ninth and tenth columns of Figure 16.1 list nodes to support such materials. Simple single numbers and basic texture nodes are placed at the top. More complex data sources are placed at the bottom.

Rather than simply create a complex shader using a variety of the nodes, let's explore material nodes and possible uses. Nodes like panners and rotators are useful for pushing around textures, but the output is merely numeric data. Some of the nodes have more specific functions, but others are general purpose enough that their uses can't be demonstrated with a single material.

Rather than try to define how each node is used, we'll go through a selection of nodes from each group. The uses of the nodes within each group are similar; you can explore how they're used on your own.

Once you begin to create your own materials, it's important to remember that only the nodes that have Parameter in their name can be used with a material instance constant. Parameter nodes allow you to manipulate your material in real time after it's been compiled.

## What Is Provided

On the book's website (http://www.akpeters.com/unrealgamedev) are a bunch of extra materials for you to tear apart and learn from. Some of the common effects you see in many video games today have one or two cool tricks that are included in the materials on the disk. Effects like the rim-light that show up on a lot of characters are easy to recreate in the material editor.

More complex objects such as cube-reflections, heat distortions, smoke bombs, and so on are also supplied on the disk. So that you can see the variety of effects and materials in use in the scene, some basic particle effects are also supplied.

PROJECT

### The Universe of the Materials Editor

To get started, let's use our boxRoom.ut3 again and export a few basic shapes to use in the scene. I've created a basic cone, sphere, and cube. I'm also going to be using the default textures that were created for the previous material projects. These textures have colors that make them useful for more than just spotting an object that is missing a texture, as we'll see.

Create a new material and assign the material to our objects in the scene. This isn't the best practice when creating an asset for the game; but in this case we've got a small, isolated instance where we don't need to worry about the performance of the material we're building. It is important to see how the material reacts in a real-world situation, so we'll be using the boxRoom to see how our material reacts with lights and a few textures behind it.

Some of the material nodes also take into consideration various numbers based on where the materials are in the world. Some effects require an actor to be placed into the scene to supply the material with data, cube, and planar textures. The data and textures can be generated in real time and applied to the material.

It's also a good idea to have GIMP open while building new materials; you'll find a need for a specific shape or pattern when creating a complex effect. To decide how to

Figure 16.4

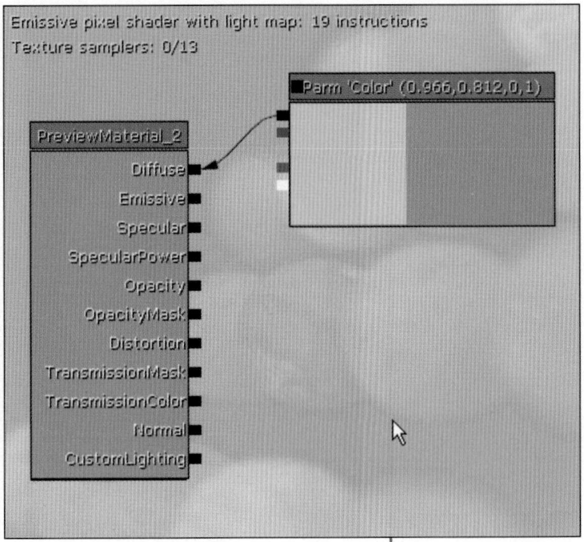

build a material, it's best to start off with some sort of goal in mind or a look you want to achieve. For this demo, I thought an interesting effect would be a teleport effect that would transform a regular material into a science fiction-like teleportation.

So what does the material look like? That question will define what sort of material we'll build to complete our effect. It will also keep us focused on using nodes that will lead to our goal of a flashy teleportation material effect. For simplicity, we'll go with a cascade of swirling, glowing dots that form over the character's mesh; as the glowing gets brighter, the texture underneath will begin to fade.

So let's get started.

Create a new material in the myMaterials.upk called `teleport_material`.

Figure 16.5

Let's start experimenting with some basic color. Add to the material graph a VectorColorParameter node that has a gold color. So far everything should be pretty simple and obvious. Compile the material and save the UPK.

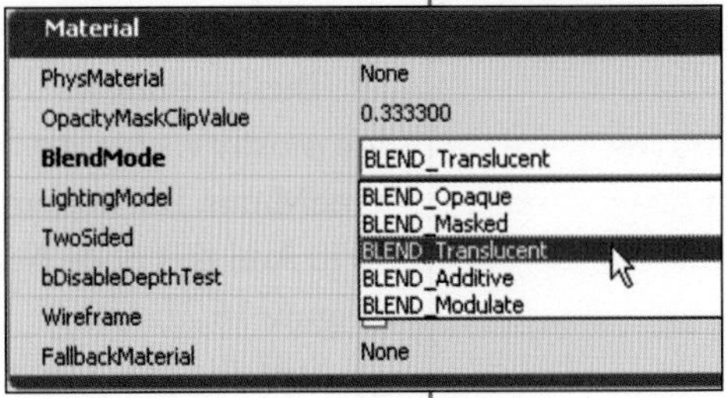

Next select the test object and assign the teleport material to it [Figure 16.4]. We should have a basic yellowish material. Open the material editor again, and let's change some of the basic parameters of the material. Select the various shading modes, and we'll switch to the `BLEND_Translucent` [Figure 16.5]. By default, most materials are single-sided; for translucent materials like this, we'll need to leave this as a single-sided material effect.

Now let's add in something more interesting. We'll want the object to look ghost-like, so to achieve this effect, we'll add to our scene a `Fresnel` node. One simple trick is to click on anything in the list of nodes on the right and then type the first few letters of the node you're looking for. This will jump the selection to the node you're typing the name of.

This is a node whose output is a number from 0 to 1 based on the angle between the surface's normal vector and the camera's view direction. To directly observe the effect of this node, connect it directly to the diffuse channel of the material [Figure 16.6]. Compile the material and take a look at the objects in the scene.

Figure 16.6

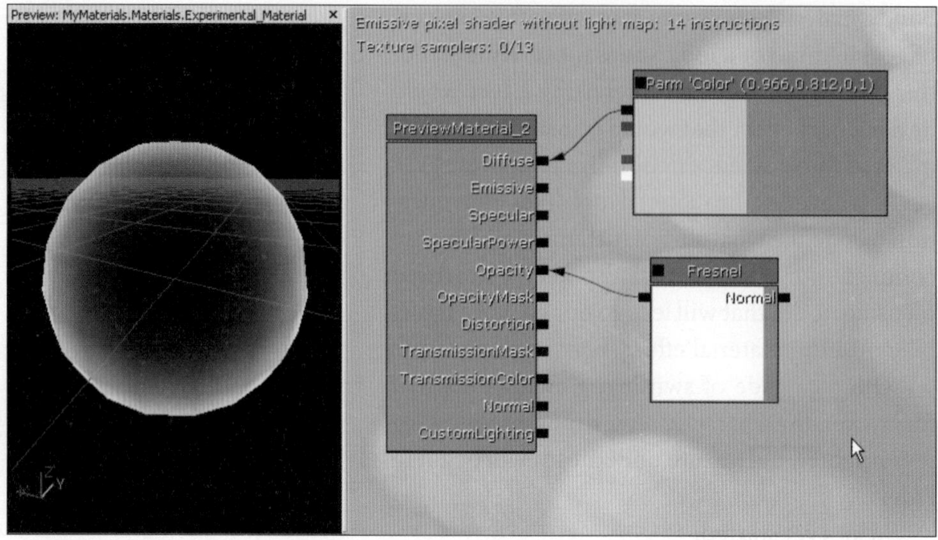


As you can see, the only areas that are solid gold are at the edges of the objects. The areas inside the object are dark. For the effect we're trying to achieve, we want the edges of the material to be invisible, so we'll use the Fresnel node to affect the opacity of the material.

The first thing we'll notice is that the face of the material is nearly invisible and the edges are mostly visible. To flip this effect, we'll use one of the math operations called 1-X or OneMinus. This node multiplies the data output from the Fresnel node by –1 and then adds 1 to it. Add this node between the Fresnel and the opacity tab and compile the material [Figure 16.7].

Still, the effect isn't as strong as I'd like. The opaque areas are too big for my taste, so I'd like to be able to adjust this in a MIC.

Figure 16.7

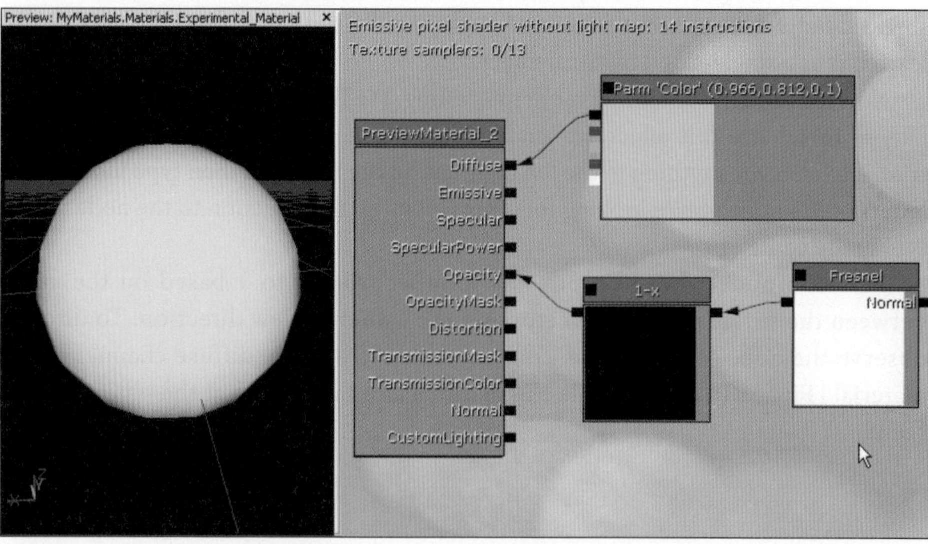

Figure 16.8

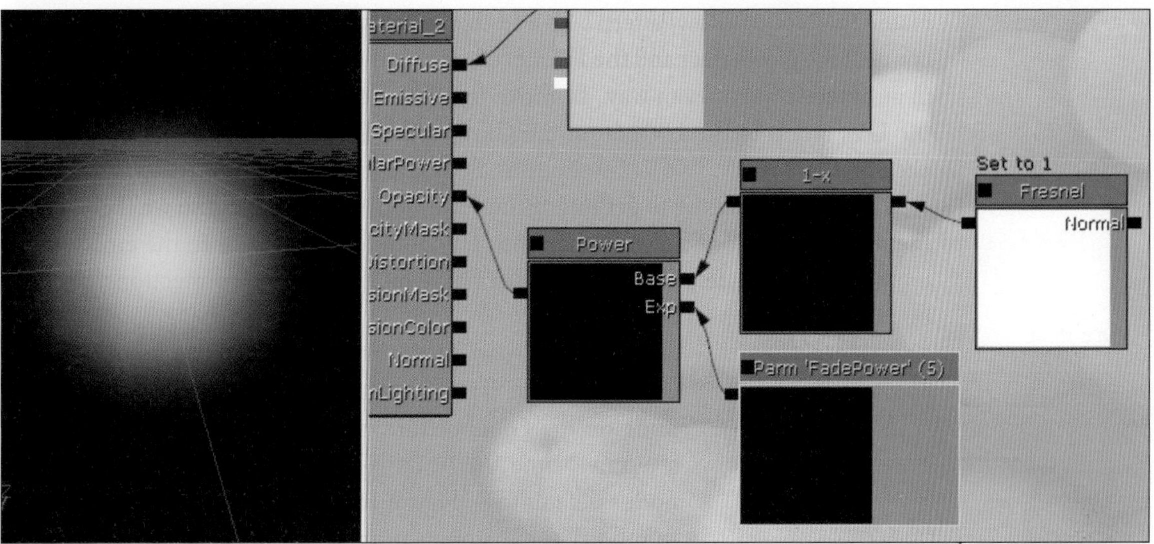


By adding a ScalarParm to a Math operation called Power, I can adjust the output value of the Fresnel node [Figure 16.8]. In the Fresnel node, I also set the output value to 1 to give me a better range of control on that node. The FadePower Scalar Parm allows me to easily adjust the range of the edge fade.

Figure 16.9

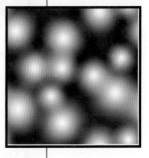

To continue, create a new material in GIMP. This is what we'll use to create the flow of dots that is going to swirl around on the mesh. Our new texture should look like this [Figure 16.9]. Using the gradient tool, add in a bunch of soft dots to the texture so there are a variety of levels of grey in the texture.

Next we'll import this texture and add it to our material using a `Texture2DSampleParameter` node. This will allow us to change the texture later if we want to make a material instance constant out of the material.

Figure 16.10

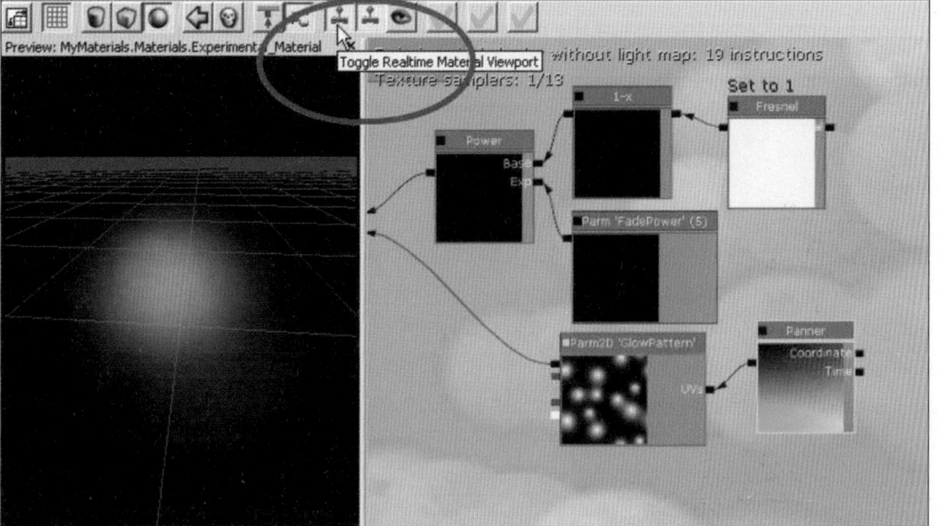

Name the Node "GlowPattern." To add this to the material, use a multiply node and connect the glow effect and the Fresnel effect together. This will modulate the opacity in an interesting, uneven way. To move the dots, connect a new Panner Node from the UVs group to the UV tab on the Glow node. To see the pan effect in real time, click on the `real-time view` buttons along the tool bar [Figure 16.10].

The effect is starting to get interesting! But nothing is glowing, so we'll go back to the material editor and also branch the glow node, connecting it to the emissive tab on the material node. All of the nodes can have many outgoing connections, but only one incoming connection.

Figure 16.11

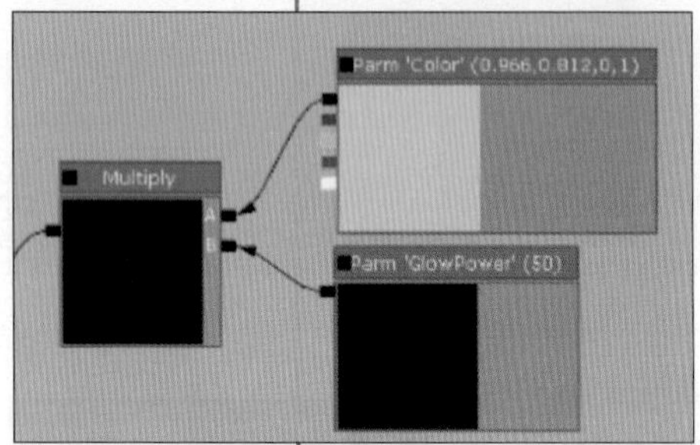


To make a part of the material glow, the value needs to exceed 1. So we'll use a Multiply node and a Scalar Parameter node on the Glow texture before connecting it to the emissive tab. Name the Scalar Glow "Intensity," and change the node's default to 3 [Figure 16.11]. This scalar should allow us to modify the materials property in real time when we make a new MIC based on this material. This is a number that can also be affected by Matinee, so you can change the effect's power for a cinematic, or it can be controlled by Unreal Script.

Our material is starting to look more interesting. But so far everything is pretty straightforward.

However, the main look of the material from the television show is that the glow scans across the object based on where the camera is looking at the material. This is not quite what we want for the material, so we'll modify the UVs on the texture again using some of the vector nodes to achieve our effect.

### A Short Diversion

To more easily observe the effect of the UV transformations, we'll directly connect the Panner node to the diffuse channel. This is where the experimentation and observation begins. Leave the rest of the nodes in the editor—you'll be hooking them back

Figure 16.12

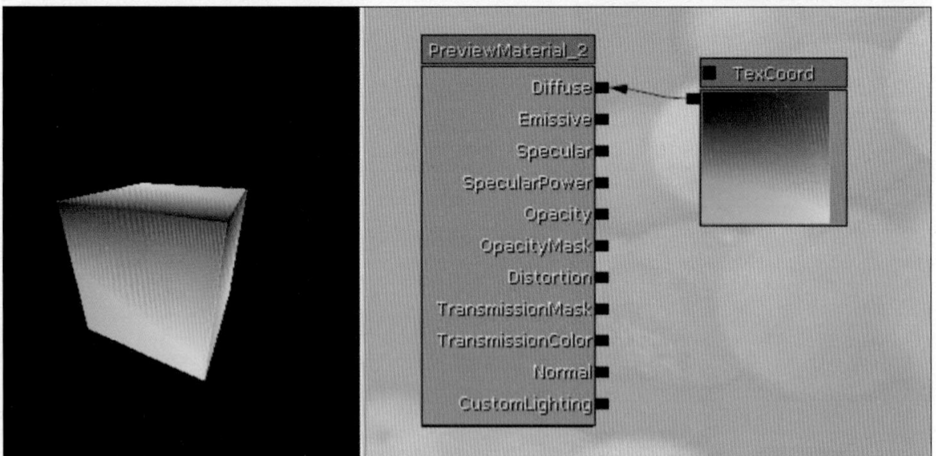

up later—but for now we're going to do a bit of direct observation. The editor can take control over several of the UV attributes. We're just experimenting, and this is the easiest way to observe the effect a node has on a material.

If we attach a regular TexCoord, or Texture Coordinate, node to the diffuse channel, we'll see a pretty strange orange and green color pattern [Figure 16.12]. But what are we looking at? To clarify, we can take a look at what a texture coordinate is in Max.

The U values range from 0 to 1 [Figure 16.13]. Of course, you can slide these values to negative and values greater than 1, but we don't need to worry about what that means just yet. If we want to see the V value of the TexCoord node, we can use the Vector Mask node and turn on only the G value.

Figure 16.13

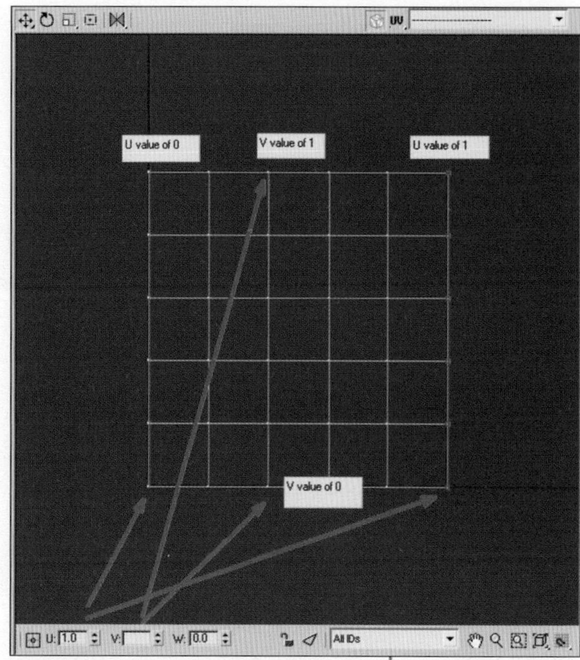

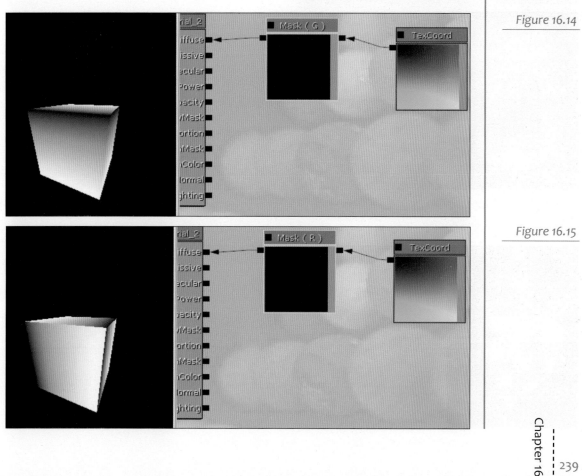

Figure 16.14

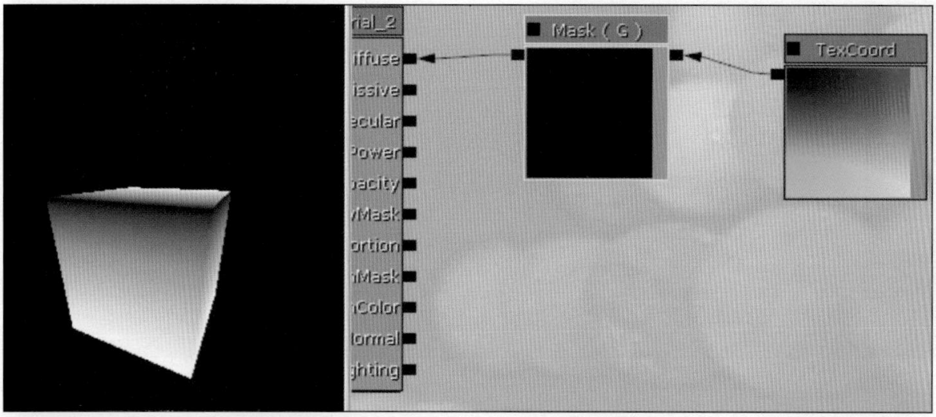

Figure 16.15

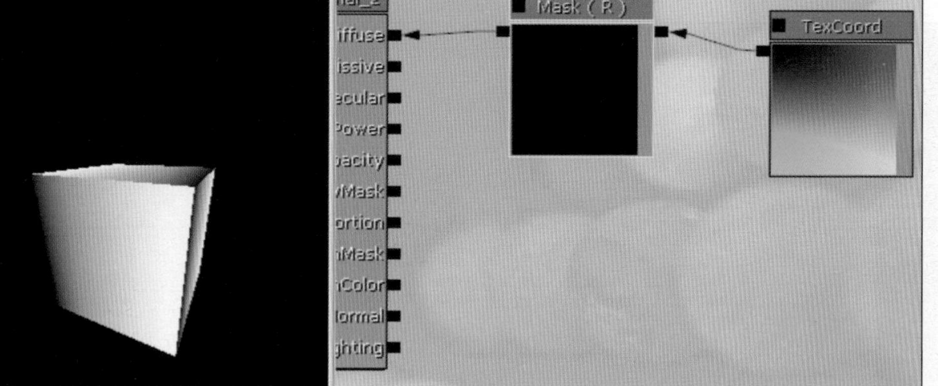

Figure 16.16

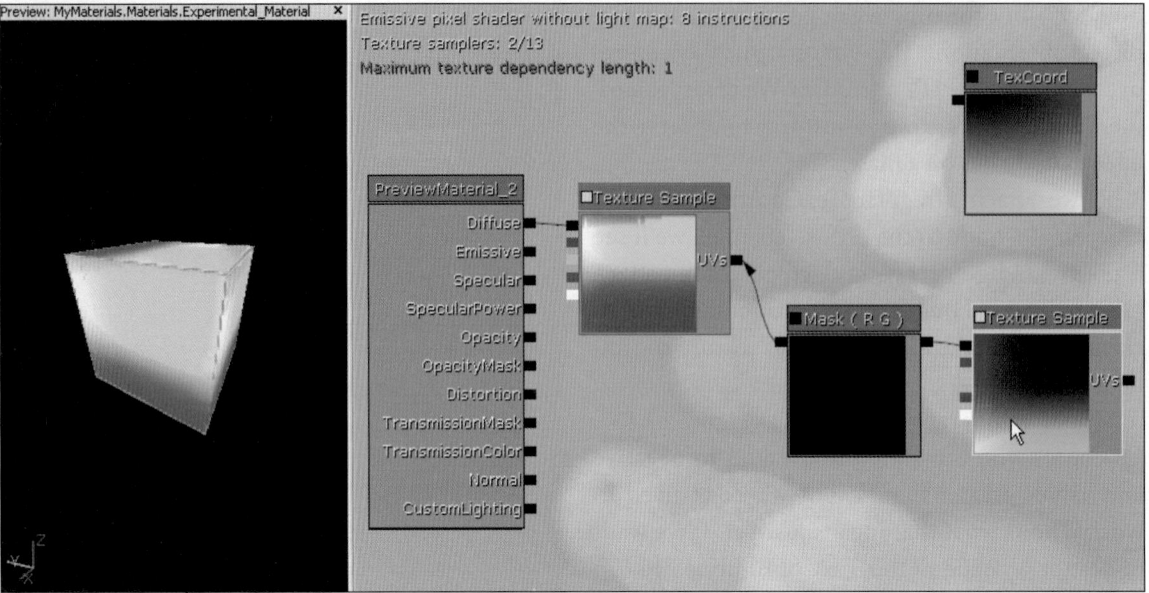


Figure 16.17

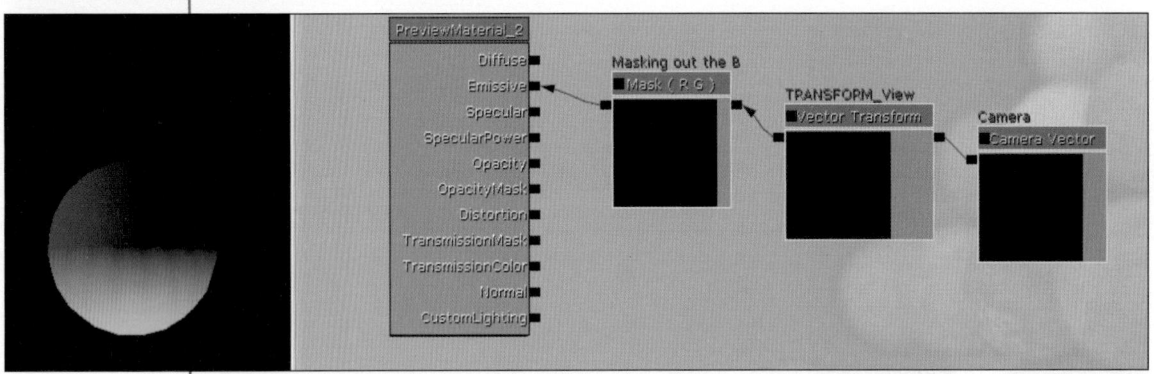


Figure 16.18

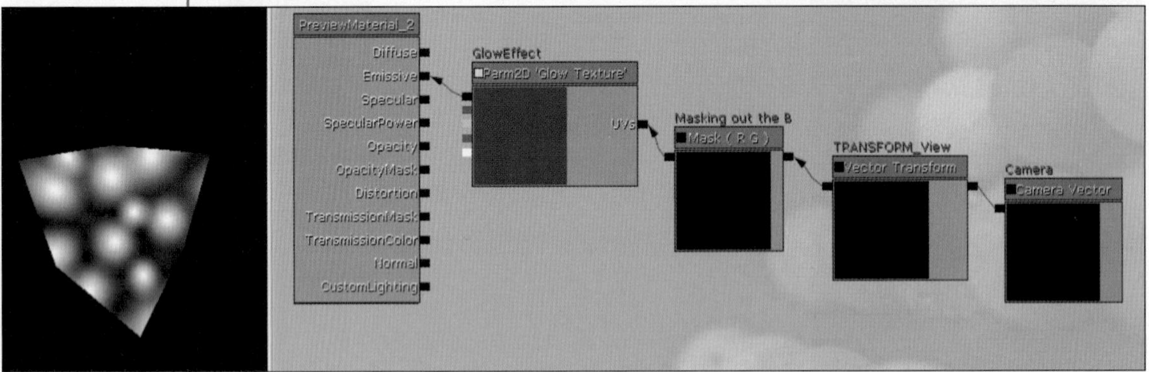

Figure 16.19

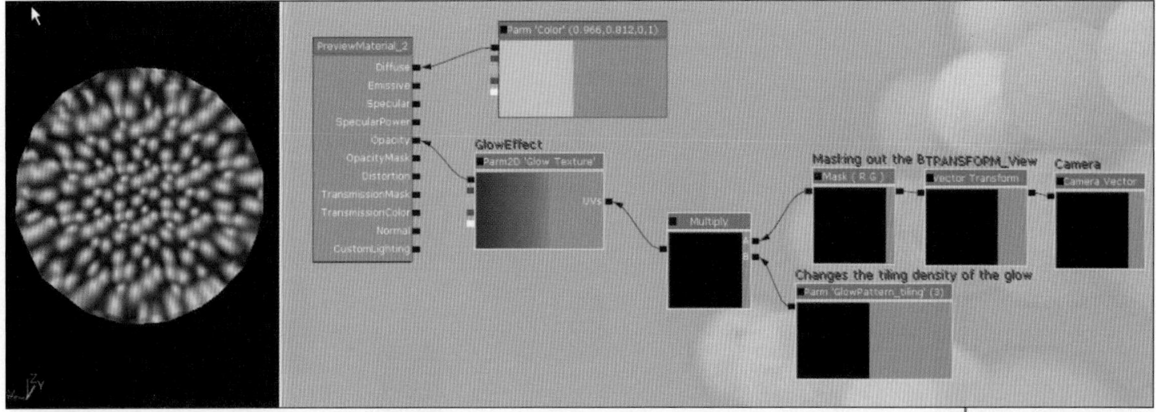


With only the Green channel we'll see a vertical gradient [Figure 16.14]; this is the equivalent of the V value in 3D Studio Max, a number starting at 0 and reaching 1.

Masking the red channel gives us a horizontal gradient from 0 to 1 [Figure 16.15]. What does this mean? Simply put, a UV map is a coordinate number from 0 to 1, and the texture coordinate when attached to a color channel is a color from 0 to 1. If the U is red and the V is green, then the two gradients overlaid on top of one another turn into the color values seen on the `TexCoord` node. In one of the GIMP textures we created, we did a similar thing. So what happens if we attach our specular texture to a material as its UVs?

Here's the comparison from the default UVs and the specular channels that were used for creating UVs [Figure 16.16]. Notice that the specular is giving us some strange distortion as well as flipping the material horizontally. We could try to fix this, but the main point is to observe how the texture behaves when different data is piped into the UV input.

### Back to the Task at Hand

Now, to experiment a bit, the effect we're going after is to clamp the texture to stick with the camera; so we'll start by attaching a `CameraVector` node to the diffuse channel [Figure 16.17]. However, this doesn't quite get us there. Next, to change how the UVs operate, we'll use a `VectorTransform` node to change the `Camera Vector` to the view.

This should look a bit familiar; we can use these as UVs for the glowing texture. Notice how the red starts off bright on the left of the object and gets darker to the right of the object. As well, notice how the green starts off bright on the bottom and fades toward the top [Figure 16.17]. This is not exactly the same as the regular TexCoord node, but it's similar. The next thing you'll notice is that the colors don't move with the object. They're locked to the camera!

Spin the different primitive shapes around and you'll notice that the material is pinned to the camera and not the object's UV coordinates [Figure 16.18]. To change the density of the pattern, we multiply the UVs by a scalar [Figure 16.19].

Figure 16.20

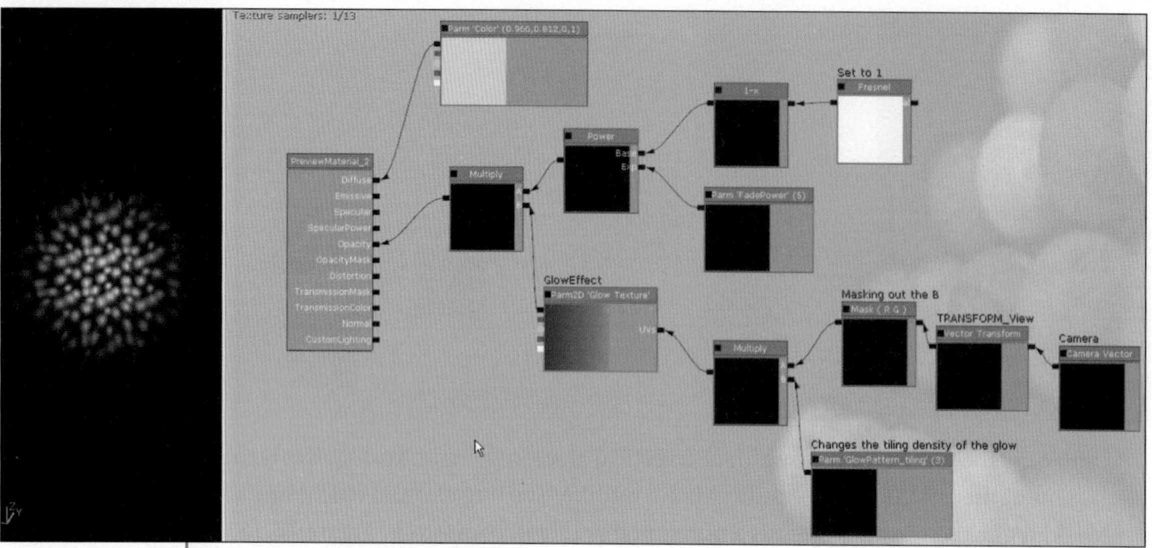


Before the GlowEffect texture node gets its UVs, a number is multiplied into the previous chain. We're also adding back in some of the previous effect so that we can see the results. Let's add back in the Fresnel from before with a simple Multiply node [Figure 16.20].

Our effect is already getting rather complex. But this is only the beginning.

Add in a panner and attach it to the Add node [Figure 16.21]. In effect, the panner is constantly adding a value to the UVs. Set the Panner's SpeedY property to 1.0; this will cause the pattern to scroll upwards. Add back in the GlowIntensity and crank it way up. When first adding different values together, like the Panner node, try the various basic math functions until you get the effect you're looking for. It's simply a matter of adding a node and connecting things until you get the result you're looking for.

Figure 16.21

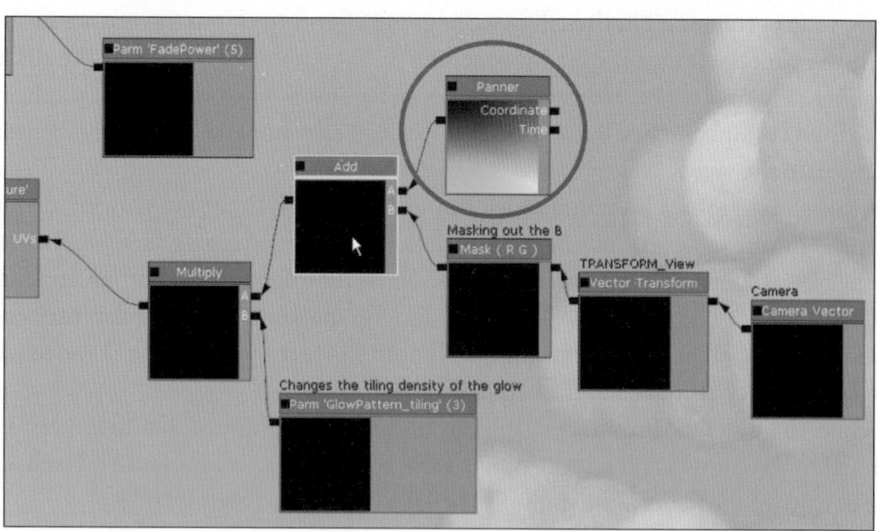

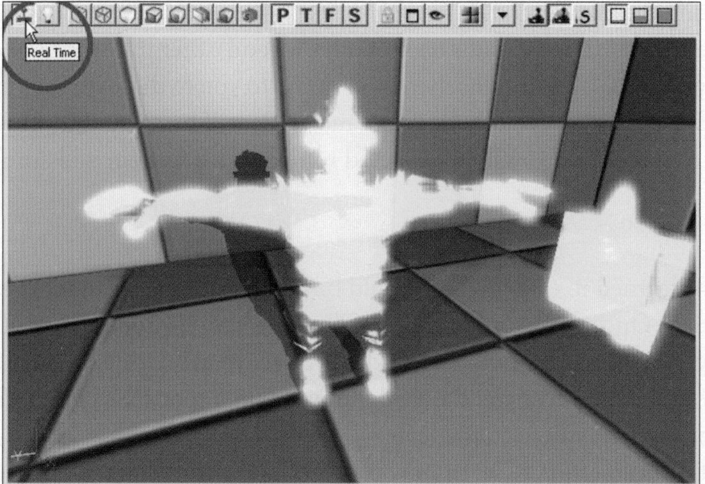


Figure 16.22

We can get an interesting glowing material effect for when our character teleports! Using the Add node, we could layer multiple effects to create more complex patterns on the surface of the character. Don't forget to turn on the `real-time view` button in the viewport in the level editor so you can watch your material move [Figure 16.22].

Copy and paste the network; then add the two groups back together [Figure 16.23]. Change some of the numbers before they are added together to get some variation out of the effect. The UVs are not affected on the entire object by one set of nodes having different UV data.

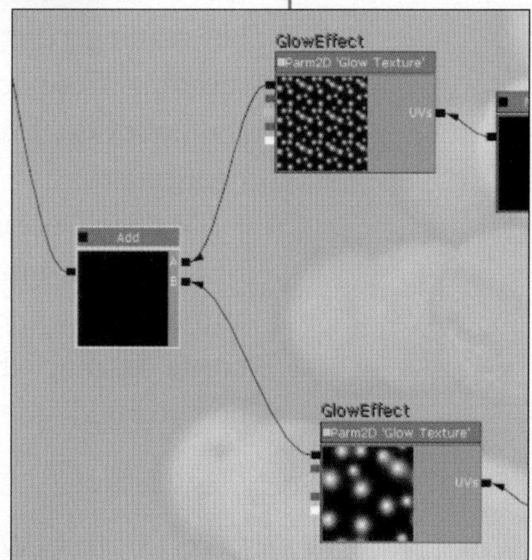


Figure 16.23

Figure 16.24

By adding the Captain's diffuse color back to the diffuse channel, we get a result like Figure 16.24. Mixing various uses of the UVs and other transforms allows you to layer many patterns over one another. Now it's up to you to discover the various math and transform nodes on your own. More materials will be created for the rest of the following chapters, but you'll be expected to deconstruct them and study them for yourself.

## Review

The lessons learned in this project should be applied to many other types of effects and materials. Once you've got a grasp of how the various nodes work, it should be easy to experiment and try out various ideas you may have. Using the small tricks and clusters of nodes, you like you'll be able to build up a tool set of methods to use in every other material you need to create.

All of this is an effort to learn how to experiment with the materials editor. The tool is far too deep to try to explain one node at a time. Doing so would be somewhat like reading a dictionary. Without context, none of the definitions would have much meaning. Connecting various nodes directly to diffuse channels helps you see what the nodes do. Everything in the materials editor is a color of some kind, even UV coordinates!

Math in Unreal's materials editor is actually an interesting and fun tool to play with. LERP (linear interpolation) and the IF nodes give you ways to manipulate objects and materials in unexpected ways. Complex materials, when used on particles, can create dazzling effects. As much as you can, you should learn to explore and discover how to build more interesting and complex materials.

## On Your Own

Unreal Tournament also has a wealth of interesting materials. Once you learn how to build your own complex materials, you'll also be able to deconstruct the Unreal Tournament materials to better understand how they work. As with any other art project, it's best to start off simple and add complexity as needed.

On the book's website (http://www.akpeters.com/unrealgamedev) are several other materials with some interesting effects applied to them. I'll leave it up to you to open the materials and discover how they work. Using the method of wiring parts directly to the output to see what's going on should help you understand the purpose of each set of nodes.

# 17 Props and Objects

*Building the World, One Mesh at a Time . . .*

A regular environment built in most Unreal Engine games is going to be built primarily out of static mesh objects. Once a static mesh is in a scene, the CPU doesn't need to think about updating the mesh—it's static. And if you use the same object several times, the scene remains quick and light, as each object is an instance of the original. That basically means there's very little performance hit for every clone of the original object.

Props and other points of interest are important to any game, and we've already made several simple mesh objects and given those meshes materials and collision. The next logical step is to move on to building entire levels. Using BSPs and refining what you already know, this is something you should be able to accomplish on your own.

## Static Meshes in an Environment

Static meshes can be used for streets, buildings, and even terrain. The complexity of the mesh doesn't necessarily have a direct effect on the scene's complexity. Mesh objects that either move or have moving parts need to be placed in a level as an interpolated object. These do get updated with every frame by the CPU, so they're not so cheap. Interpolated mesh objects have either a script or animation that makes them move. Either way, the mesh needs to be updated with each frame, even if the animation isn't playing. That's because the CPU has to be ready at any frame for the mesh to start to move, and the CPU doesn't necessarily know when that will be.

The textures can be dynamic and may be used to give a static mesh a dynamic feel. Materials in your scene can help make your world come alive with movement. Computer monitors, lights, and some simple movement can help add interest to any environment. Animated textures are simpler to create than you might have guessed, but we'll get to that later in the chapter.

Figure 17.1

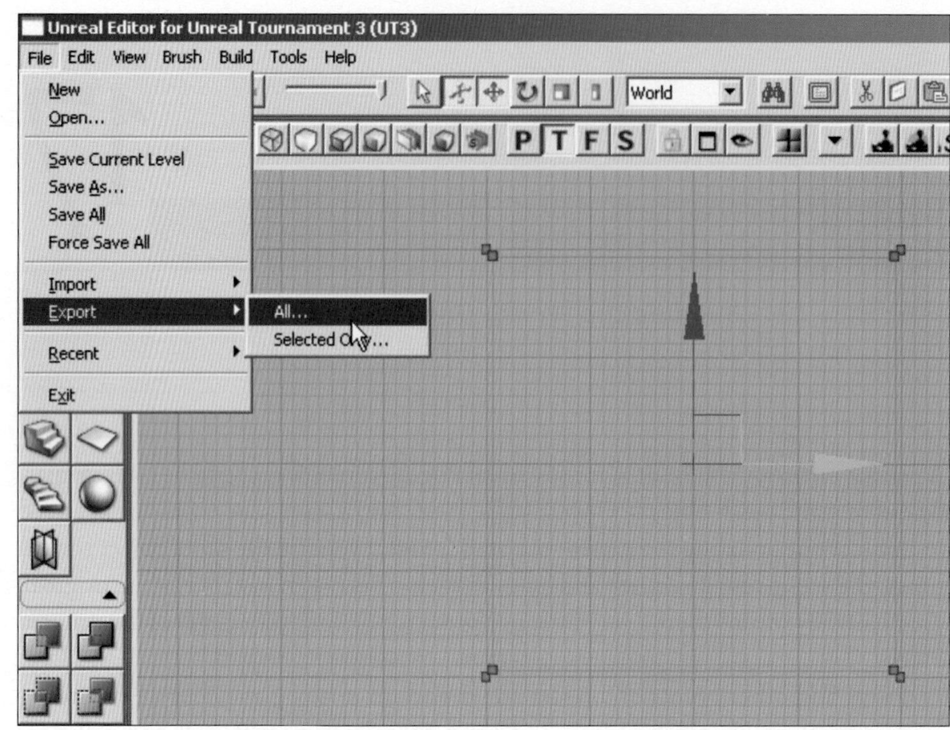


Figure 17.2

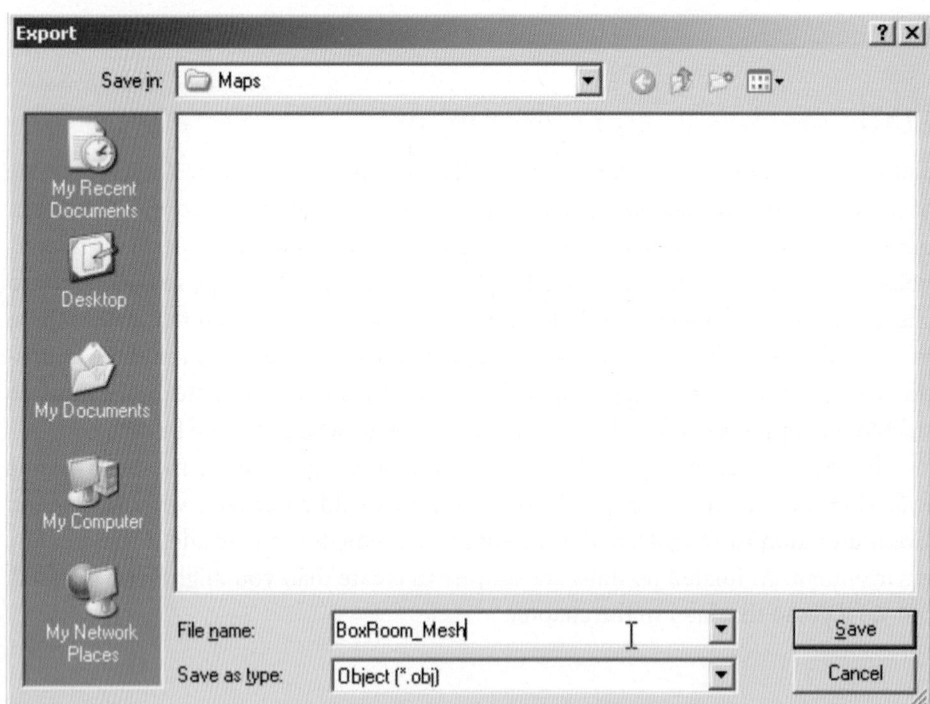

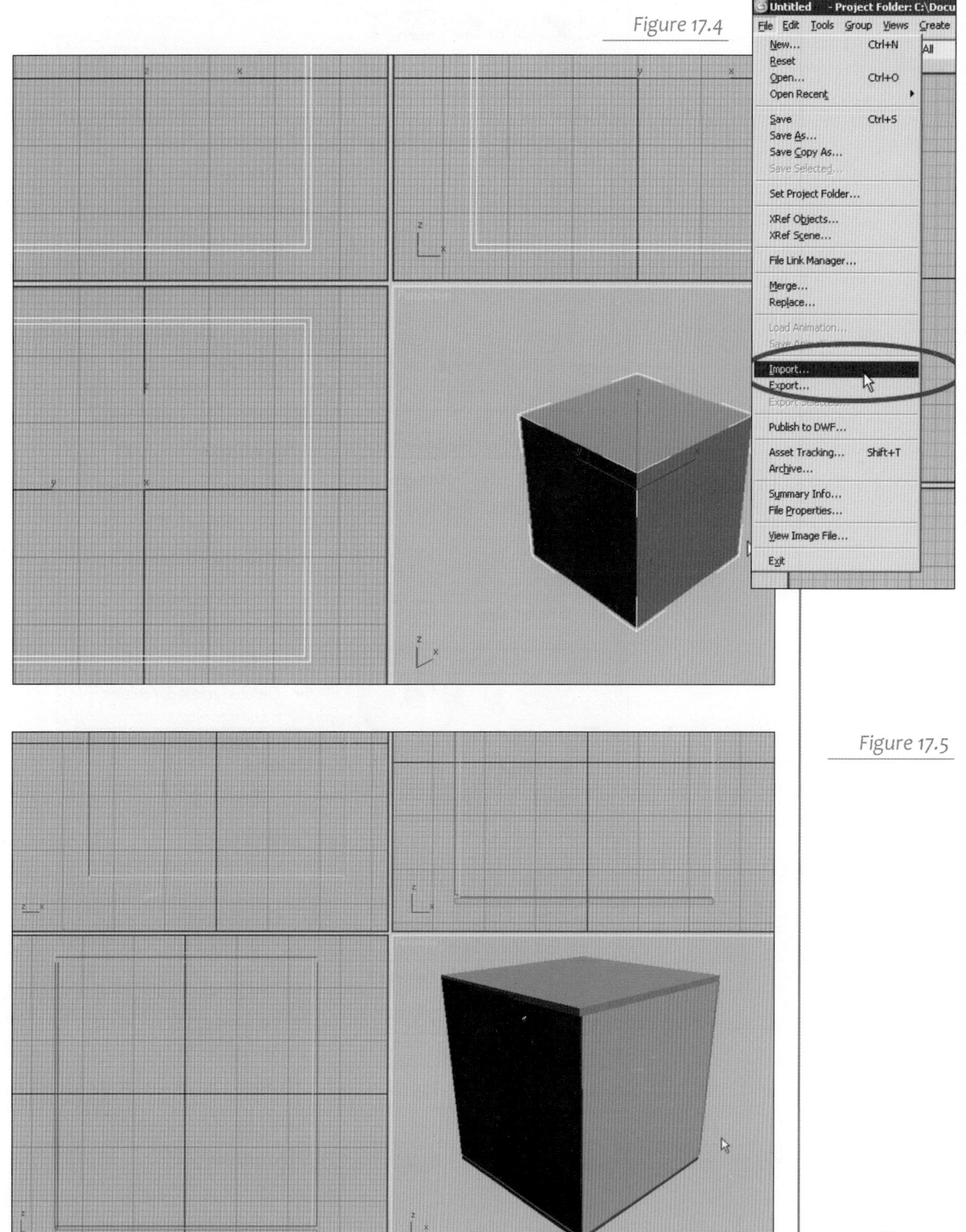


Figure 17.3

Figure 17.4

Figure 17.5

Figure 17.6

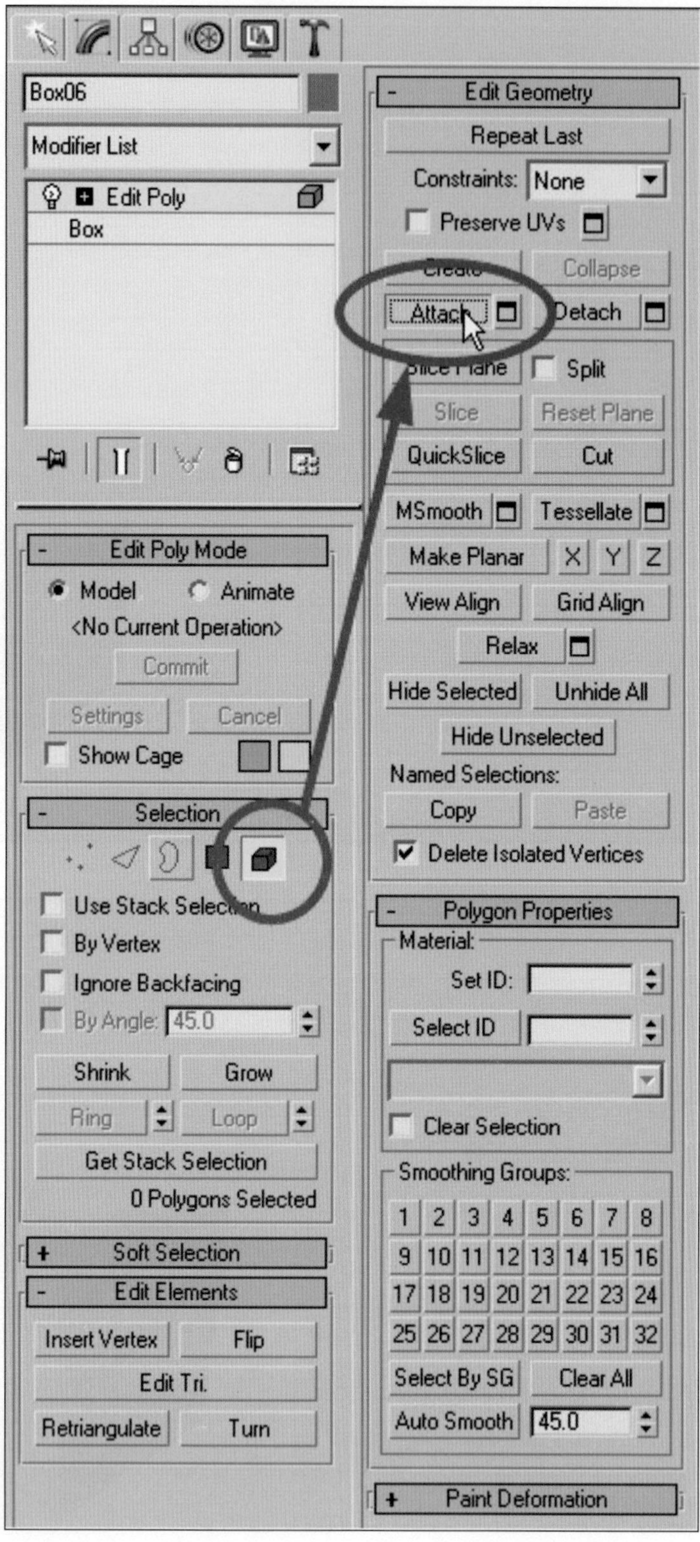
Box06
Modifier List
Edit Poly
Box
Edit Poly Mode
Model
Animate
<No Current Operation>
Commit
Settings
Cancel
Show Cage
Selection
Use Stack Selection
By Vertex
Ignore Backfacing
By Angle: 45.0
Shrink
Grow
Ring
Loop
Get Stack Selection
0 Polygons Selected
Soft Selection
Edit Elements
Insert Vertex
Flip
Edit Tri.
Retriangulate
Turn
Edit Geometry
Repeat Last
Constraints: None
Preserve UVs
Create
Collapse
Attach
Detach
Slice Plane
Split
Slice
Reset Plane
QuickSlice
Cut
MSmooth
Tessellate
Make Planar
X
Y
Z
View Align
Grid Align
Relax
Hide Selected
Unhide All
Hide Unselected
Named Selections:
Copy
Paste
Delete Isolated Vertices
Polygon Properties
Material:
Set ID:
Select ID
Clear Selection
Smoothing Groups:
1 2 3 4 5 6 7 8
9 10 11 12 13 14 15 16
17 18 19 20 21 22 23 24
25 26 27 28 29 30 31 32
Select By SG
Clear All
Auto Smooth
45.0
Paint Deformation

## Building a Section of a Level from Your BSPs

For the project, you will need to export a level from Unreal Editor and import it into 3D Studio Max.

We'll use the most simple BoxRoom.ut3 for this example [Figure 17.1]. Use File Export All . . . and save the BSPs as an OBJ [Figure 17.2].

This will give us a starting point in 3D Studio Max to work from.

Inside 3D Studio Max, import the file that was just exported out of Unreal [Figure 17.3]. Simply say okay to all of the default import settings for the OBJ.

You'll simply see your mesh inside 3D Studio Max, looking about how it looked inside Unreal [Figure 17.4]. Unfortunately, the object will need to have collision created and assigned, just as with any other static mesh object.

In this case, I've created a set of six smaller cubes to act as my collision mesh [Figure 17.5]. I used the `Box` primitive to create these. You can turn on various vertex snapping options to help shape these collision boxes.

To combine the collision objects into one object, select one of the new boxes and add on a new `Edit Poly Stack Modifier` [Figure 17.6]. As you click on the other boxes in the scene, be careful not to include the original mesh in this operation. It might be a good idea to hide the original mesh before clicking and adding the rest of the boxes [Figure 17.7].

Your boxes should all be combined into a single collision object. For ActorX to know this is your collision object, we need to name the mesh with a UCX_ prefix [Figure 17.8].

You can refer to Chapter 12 if you have forgotten any of the ActorX options.

This is the same box room that was exported from the BSP scene in Unreal Editor and imported to 3D Studio Max [Figure 17.9].

Figure 17.7

Figure 17.8

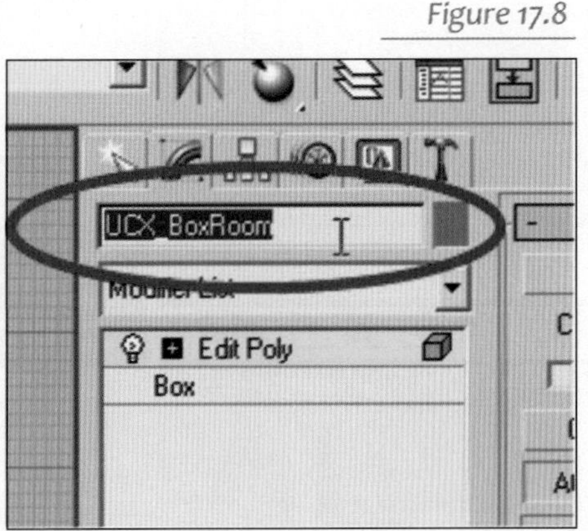

Figure 17.9

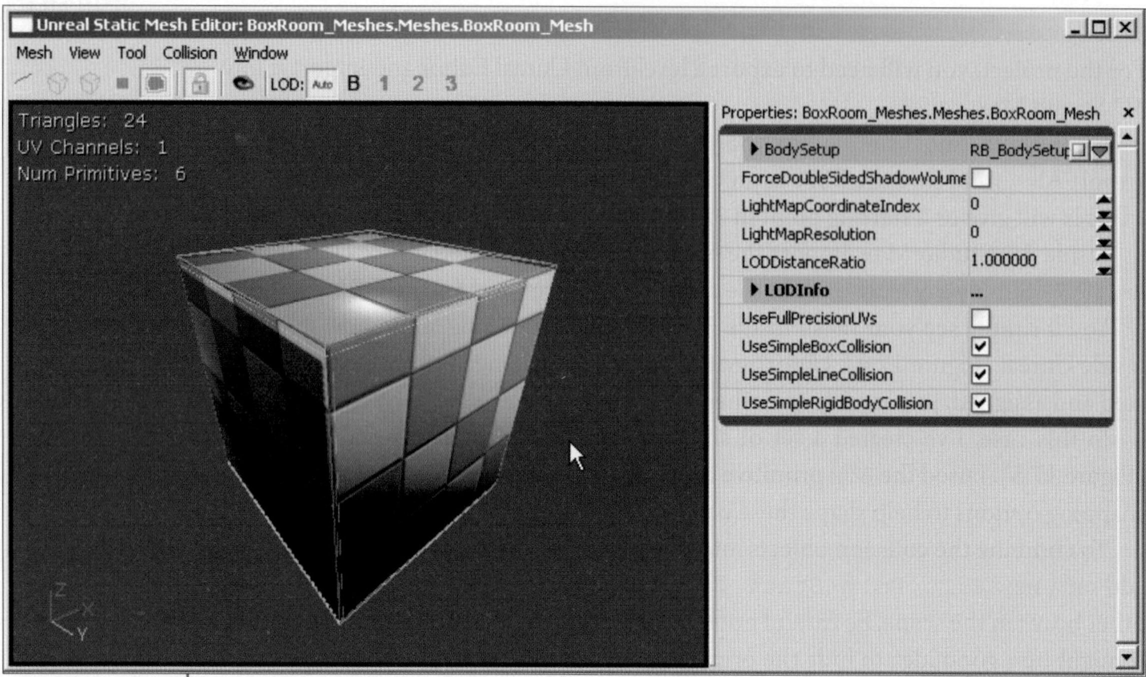


Figure 17.10

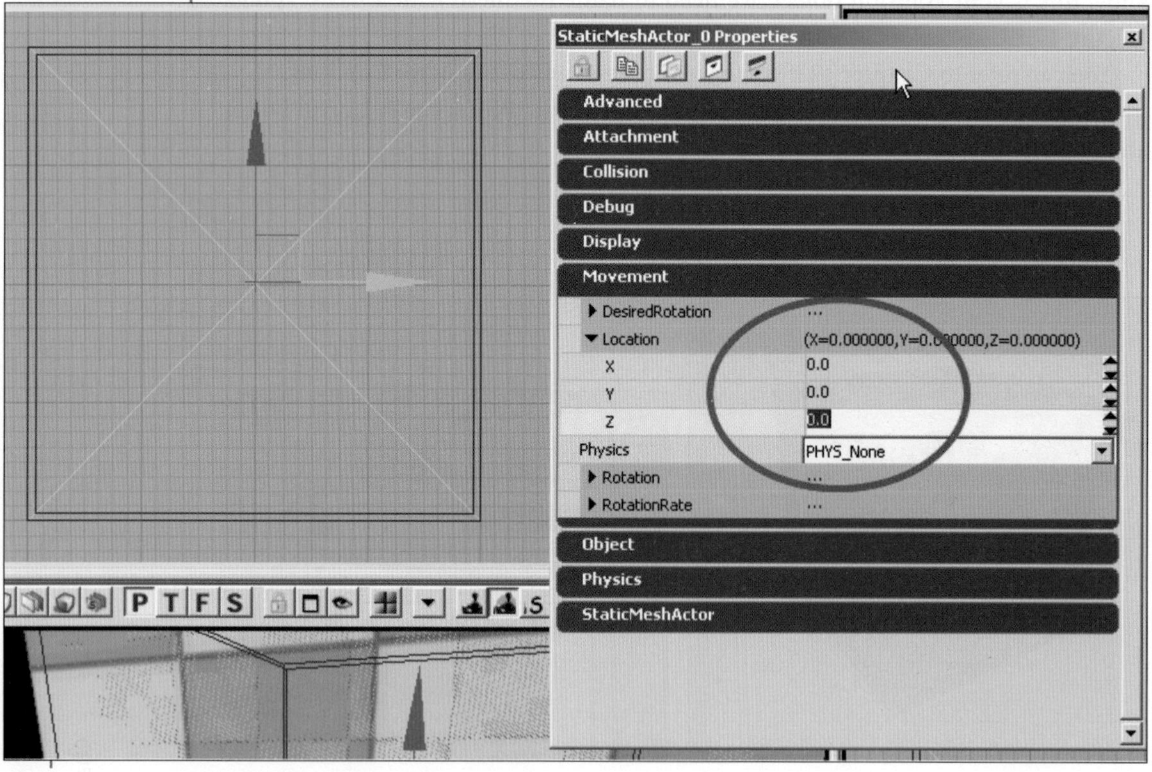

Figure 17.11

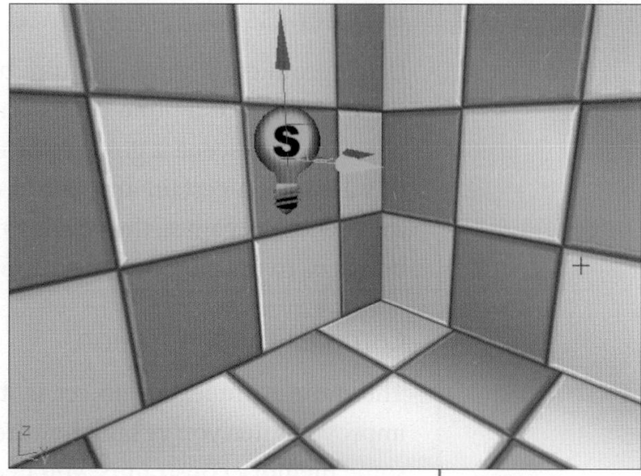

Place the Static Mesh into the scene and set the Location to 0,0,0 [Figure 17.10]. This should completely overlap with the original BSPs from the original scene. Using the show flags, you can hide static mesh objects so that you can select the BSPs in the world and delete them. Now you've got a static mesh version of your level [Figure 17.11].

So why are we doing this? Of course, we could simply build the entire level out of BSPs, and that would be great for iteration inside Unreal Editor. However, Unreal Editor doesn't have the same number of mesh editing tools that are available in 3D Studio Max. The amount of detail that can be accomplished in 3D Studio Max far surpasses the detail that can be created in Unreal Editor.

There's also a performance difference between BSPs and static meshes. Once a level gets highly detailed, BSPs are much slower to render when compared to the same level as a static mesh. The BSP rendering engine has long since been deprecated and is no longer in use.

### Interpolated Objects

These types of meshes require CPU calculation each frame, but they do move; however, they might move at any moment, so the game engine needs to check each frame whether there is anything updating an interpolated object.

## What to Expect

Keep these considerations in mind when building props for Unreal that include everything from bushes, rocks, and trees to computer consoles, spinning fans, and docking platforms. BSPs are typically used in a level only to roughly lay out the level. Unreal Engine 3 really has changed how game development and design is done.

The modern finished level no longer relies on BSPs. However, they're still quite useful. A BSP is a simple volume placed in the level. As soon as the shape is created, the engine can immediately light and evenly texture the new shape. That's convenient, until you need to make a specific detail or shape. The shaping tools provided in Unreal Engine can't compare to the tools provided for the same tasks in 3D Studio Max.

The big benefit of a BSP is that you can make big changes to an area and then play-test the new forms immediately. Compare this to building a level in 3D Studio Max, which requires exporting, importing, and then adjusting placement in your level before testing. This cycle reduces the speed at which you can iterate and play-test. Without a doubt, rapid iteration is important for good game play.

### Uniqueness vs. Performance

Large production games require balance among performance memory and quality. Building tons of unique props quickly leads to exceeding memory limits. If every object in your scene is going to be unique, you can't use too many of them. Of course, this assumes a certain amount of detail on each object; but for most photorealistically rendered games, the goal is to add as much detail as possible to each object. This brings us to the next consideration.

### Complexity vs. Iteration

The more complex an object is, the harder it is to iterate upon and to change or improve. When you've built hundreds or even thousands of objects and then finally hit some memory constraints, you need to make some sweeping changes. Usually these changes are broad texture changes, since it's nearly impossible to rebuild each object just to regain several kilobytes per object or just to regain a few megabytes for the overall level. In this case, overall quality is lost simply because the overall complexity was too high to easily make broad changes. This brings us to the last consideration.

### Scope vs. Reusability

When building a lot of different objects, you should always try to reuse each item as often as possible; but then you have to take into consideration how often you're going to see any given object. Usually you'll want to reuse an object a lot; but if you see it too often, you'll get bored looking at it. And if you want to cover a lot of space with unique items, you'll start to run into memory limitations. That brings us back to the first consideration, uniqueness vs. performance.

### So What Does That All Mean?

The tradeoffs are three-fold: forgoing uniqueness for performance, reducing complexity to retain flexibility, and reducing scope to reuse your work. There's a certain amount of work that is required for a given size level. Of course, the tradeoffs can be ignored if you have unlimited time and unlimited resources. The other possible extreme is to make a game entirely out of cubes.

To provide a constantly interesting game experience, you'll want to make sure that the player is always seeing or experiencing something interesting at regular intervals—that's uniqueness. This means lots of unique objects or events, which translates into how much work you'll need to do to entertain your player.

Then you'll want to have a deep experience as well, which usually means lots of space to wander through—that's your game's scope. Scope can also be thought of as how big you want the game to be. Achieving solid, unique game play in a small level will allow you to increase the complexity of the scene, as you'll be able to add more interesting objects and events to the level with less work. A large scene requires lots more work, but to make a large scene, you may have to trade off complexity.

## Level Modeling

With the modeling techniques we've built up so far, you should be able to manage building a simple environment. In the chapter folder provided on the disk is an example of an interior space built out of reusable sections: hallways and rooms, basically built like a set from a science fiction television show. You can see how these are arranged to make a complete level. The corresponding Unreal set is an example of how these parts can be used together to build a death-match level.

Provided are some parts so that you can make your own level out of simple building blocks. This is a much faster way to build in detail rather than try to use the BSP editor (which no one does nowadays anyway).

However, we won't dwell on the subject of level modeling too long. To remain focused on the more involved aspects of character modeling and implementation, we'll simply leave the level modeling for another book.

What we'll instead build upon are the skills required to realize a fully-rigged, animated character in Unreal Engine 3.

provided at http://www.akpeters.com/unrealgamedev. We want to learn the setup to give this object some interesting behavior once it is loaded in the engine. We'll start by building a skeleton for the object. What has been built already is a simple, pill-shaped object [Figure 18.1]. The upper half has two parts which form the object's lids. The lids will slide open or closed.

Figure 18.1

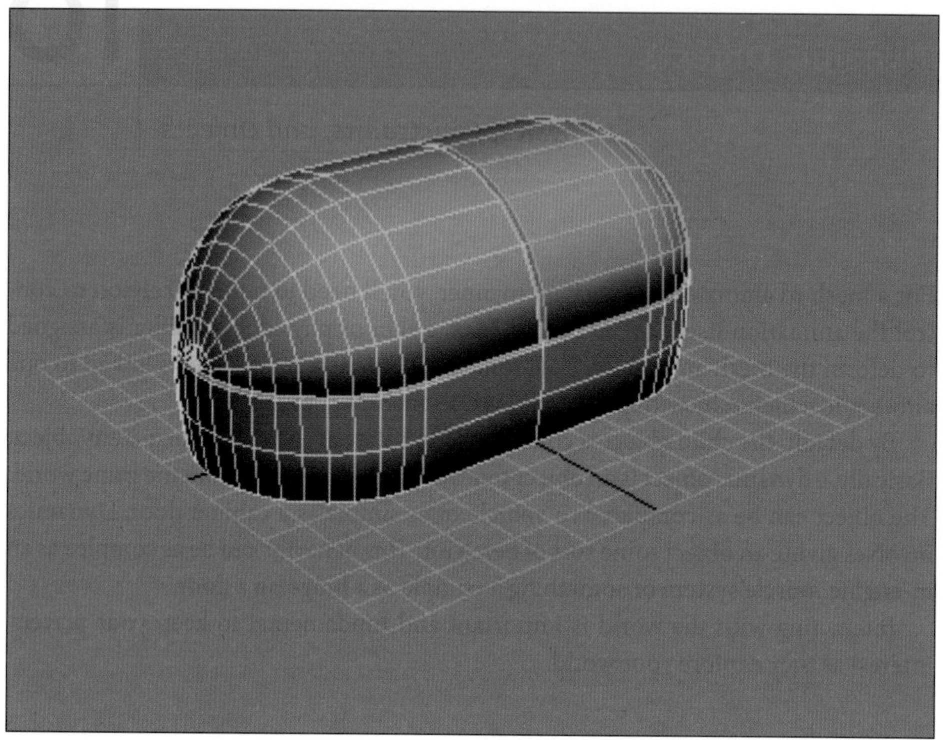

If our intent is simply to have an object that can be placed in a scene, we can stop here. However, we want to add some interactivity. The object is going to be a dynamic, pill-shaped item crate, so we're going to add some joints so it can be assigned a physics object once it's in the engine.

Figure 18.2

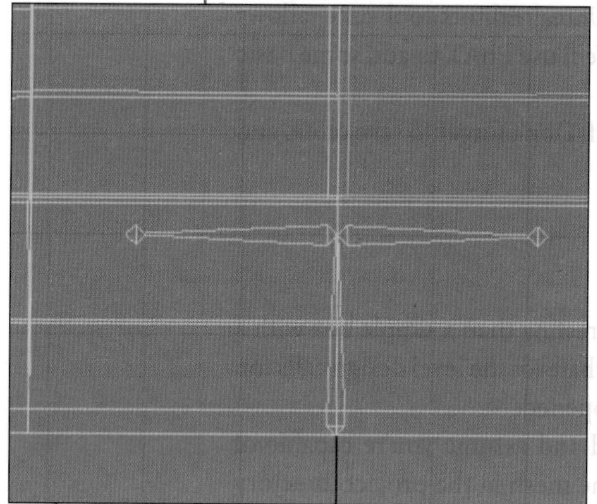

Each of the movable lids needs to have two joints assigned to it. A lid is connected to an end joint and has a joint in the middle of the crate to constrain it. The two pairs of joints, as well as the lower half of the crate, are connected to a root joint [Figure 18.2].

This is a pretty basic setup. Using the grid to snap the joints to this shape, the object can be built quickly. It's important to remember that the lids need to slide accurately for them to look like

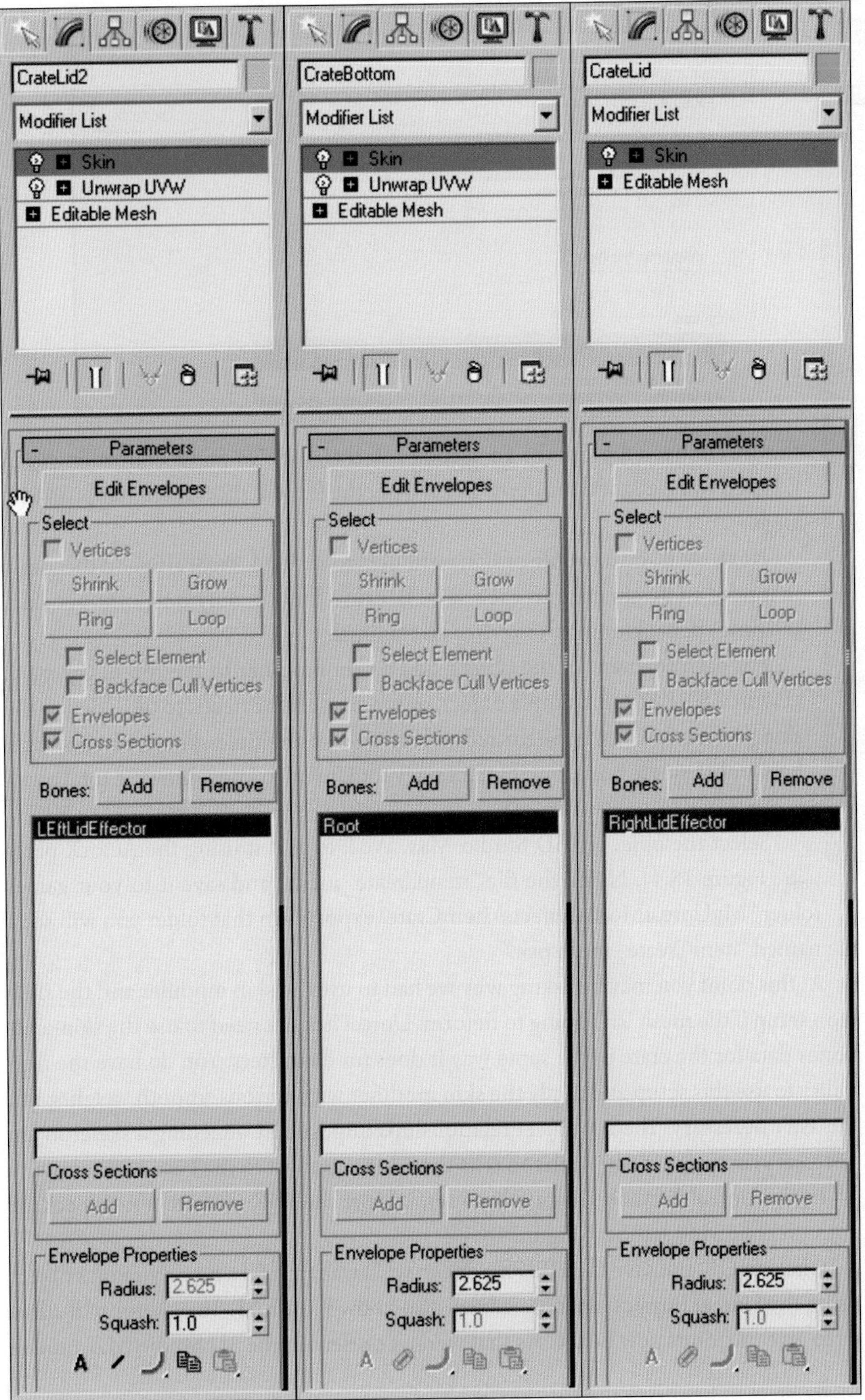
CrateLid2
Modifier List
Skin
Unwrap UVW
Editable Mesh
Parameters
Edit Envelopes
Select
Vertices
Shrink
Grow
Ring
Loop
Select Element
Backface Cull Vertices
Envelopes
Cross Sections
Bones:
Add
Remove
LEftLidEffector
Cross Sections
Add
Remove
Envelope Properties
Radius:
2.625
Squash:
1.0
CrateBottom
Modifier List
Skin
Unwrap UVW
Editable Mesh
Root
CrateLid
Modifier List
Skin
Editable Mesh
RightLidEffector

Figure 18.3

Figure 18.4

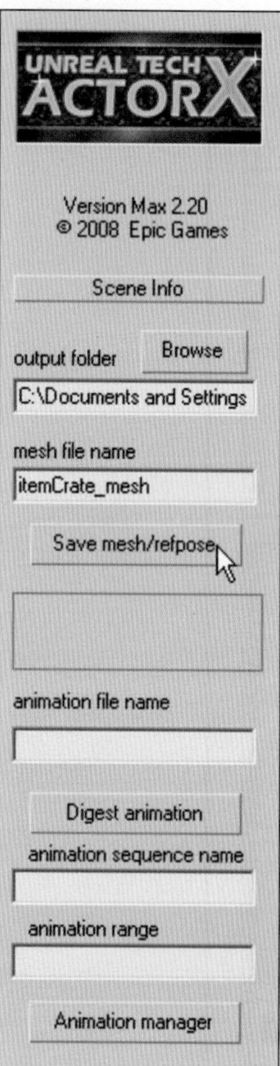


Figure 18.5

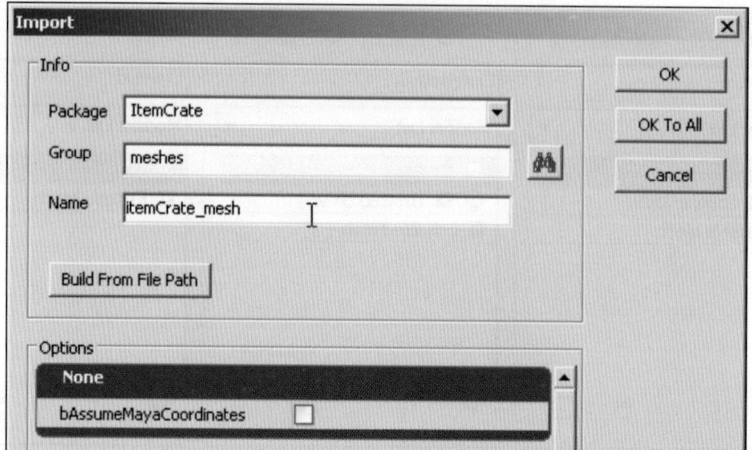


they're connected properly. To accomplish this, the two joints controlling each lid need to be aligned properly; otherwise, the lid will slide at an inappropriate angle.

Next, we'll add a couple of skin modifiers to each lid. We'll also add the joints that need to be attached to each skin. Because there is only one joint per skin, the time spent skinning the vertices is minimal.

For each segment of the object, add a skin modifier to the top of the stack [Figure 18.3]. For this simple object, only a single bone needs to be added to the skin parameters. It may seem redundant to have multiple skin modifiers, each have only a single bone, but it's necessary for Unreal to know how the total mesh is organized.

Select the object in 3D Studio Max. We'll export it using the ActorX plug-in [Figure 18.4]. Name the file "itemCreate_mesh" and save it to your games folder "MyUnrealMod\Objects\ItemCrate\exports." In that folder you will see a file named "itemCreate_mesh.psk."

At this point you may be asking why we had to use the skin modifier and the skeleton setup if the mesh isn't going to deform. Unreal doesn't need to use the skin-and-bones data for the crate in the same way it does for characters. You do have the flexibility to use this setup and apply the skin modifier with various smooth weights, but this isn't necessary. The subobject relationships imposed by attaching a skeleton are necessary; in this case, the skeleton tells the lids to connect to the base of the crate.

In the Unreal Editor's Generic browser, import the PSK file into a new package with the following settings [Figure 18.5].

Click on OK and save the UPK file. Next, we'll want to add a new dynamics object using the Unreal Physics attribute editor, also known as PhAT. This editor will allow us to give the joints new behaviors that weren't present in the 3D Studio Max model.

Of course, we could have assigned similar behaviors when using 3D Studio Max, but the attributes in 3D Studio Max's joint setup will not export to data that Unreal can use, so it would have been a wasted effort.

## Unreal Physics Asset Creation, PhAT

PhAT is a pretty interesting little tool. You will be able to modify and create different forms of physical constraints on objects. You'll be able to build ragdoll physics assets for your characters. Later, you'll be able to combine physics-driven objects with animated ones. Objects such as loose bits of armor or whip antennas on vehicles can be driven by physics, so they don't need to be animated.

### The PhAT UI map

Let's take a short tour of the UI

PhAT is divided into three sections: the main viewport, the toolbar, and the properties window [Figure 18.6].

Figure 18.6

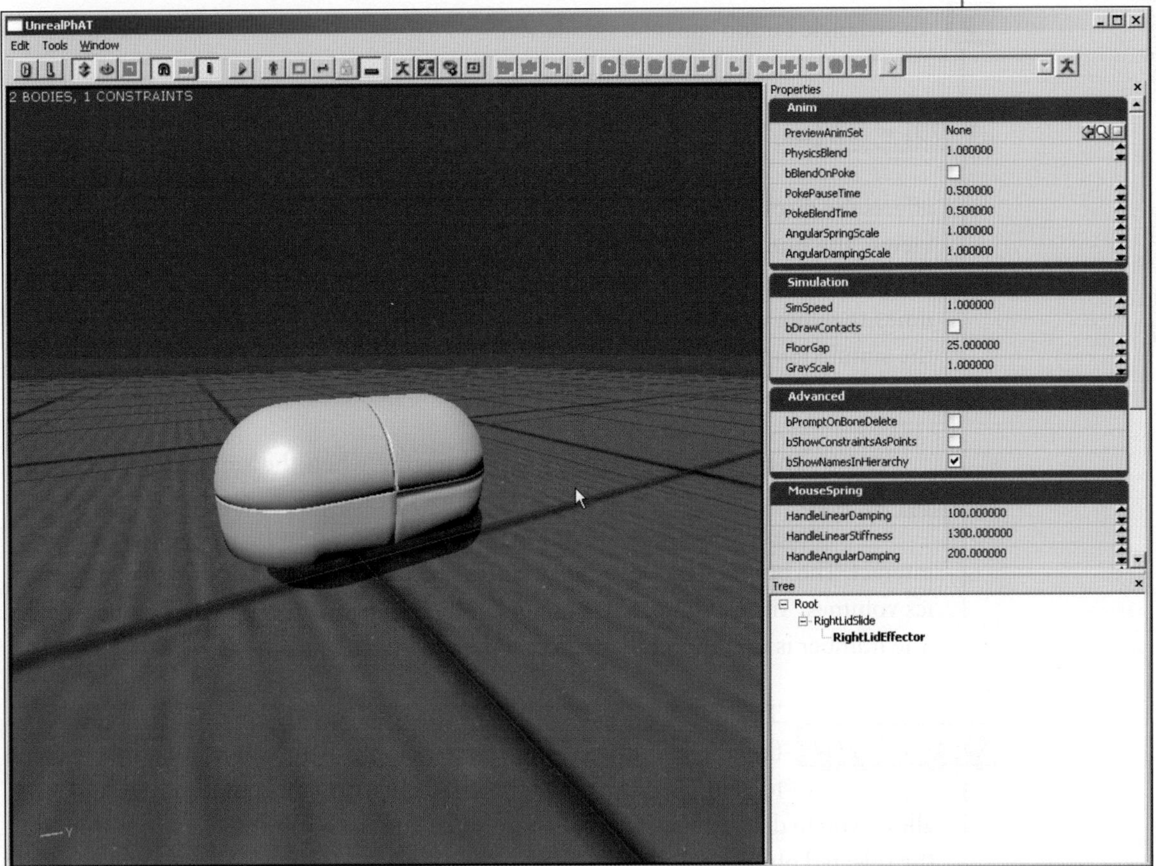

The toolbar contains several groups of buttons.

The first group has two buttons. The first button changes the editor from bone-editing mode to constraint-editing mode. The second button changes the transformation space when moving joints from world to local space.

The second group has three buttons. These are the translate, rotate, and scale buttons for changing the shape of a physics volume.

The third group has three buttons. The first button has a magnet icon. This button changes the movement behavior of the translate, rotate, and scale buttons, causing the objects to move in graded increments. When a volume or constraint is selected, the second button copies the properties of the currently selected joint to the properties of the next selected joint. The third button has an "I" icon. The button allows you to edit the joint or volumes properties.

When you press any of the buttons in the first three groups, several sets of parameters are exposed via a dialog for editing and adjustments.

The triangle button runs the simulation.

The next group of buttons changes the appearance of the various components in the editor. The first button is a toggle that displays the mesh in shaded view or wireframe view. The second button affects the display of physics volumes, cycling through shaded, wireframe, and hidden views. The button initially has a box icon, but the icon changes each time you press the button. The middle button changes how the constraints that hold the physics volumes together are displayed. The button with the lock icon shows which objects in the simulation are not affected by the dynamics in the scene. The last button in this group is a toggle that shows or hides the ground plane.

These buttons are used for debugging when the simulation is running. The first button displays the names of the joints that are in the skeletal mesh. The second button enables the tool to show when physics objects interact. The button with the eye icon shows which vertices are bound to which physics volumes. The last button displays a number at the center of each physics volume. The number is the amount of mass that the object contains.

This group of buttons is used to create and delete physics objects. The first three buttons allow you to add in a new sphere, pill, or box shape to your physics object. The button whose icon contains a box and red X allows you to delete a selected physics volume. The last button allows you to duplicate the selected physics volume.

This button is used to reset the center of action of a given constraint. If your default pivot is meant to be in the center of a given constraint, then you use this icon to set the center of the constraint. This isn't always the preferred behavior. A door's default position is usually not halfway open. With this tool, you'd set the center of action to the halfway point, and then you'd rotate the center of action to match the range of movement of the door. Resetting the center of action of a constraint might be a confusing topic. We'll get into how the operation is used in the next project.

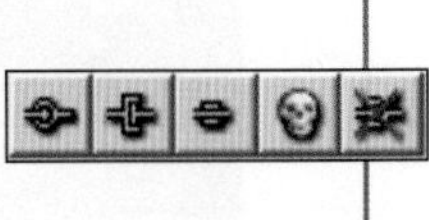

These buttons are active only when you select a constraint pivot. The first four buttons convert a constraint type to ball-and-socket, hinge, prismatic, or skeletal joints, respectively. The last button deletes the selected constraint.

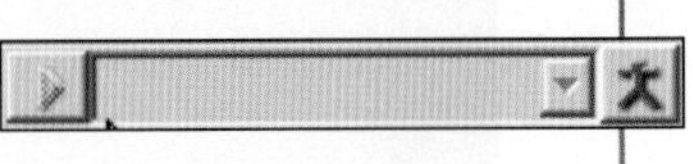

The final group of buttons is used to combine a skeletal animation into your physics simulation.

The properties window changes depending on which buttons you've got selected and which editing mode you are currently in. We're going to edit a lot of parameters. The parameter descriptions are provided as we encounter them in the next project.

PROJECT

## Physics Asset for the ItemCrate

To start, we'll right click on the ItemCrate skeletal mesh object in the Generic browser and then select "Create New Physics Asset" [Figure 18.7]. This launches a dialog that allows us to name and place our new object [Figure 18.8]. We'll want to be consistent with our naming the geometric object ItemCrate_mesh, so we'll call our physics object ItemCrate_Physics and save it with our group of meshes.

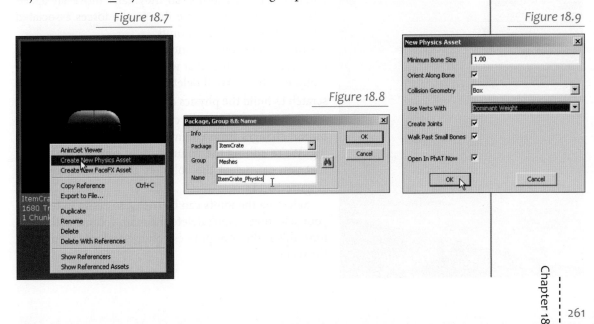

Figure 18.7

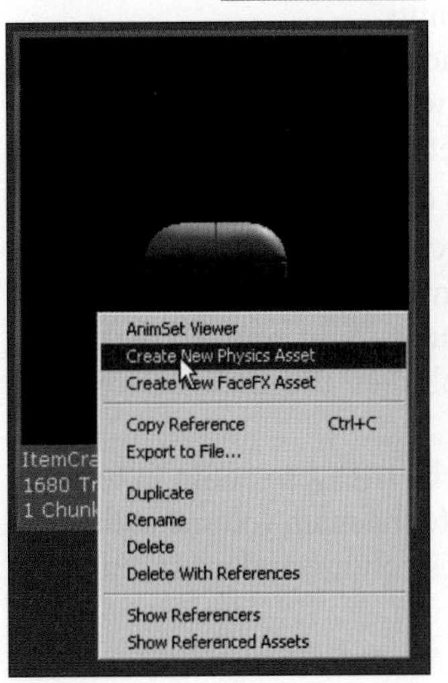


Figure 18.8

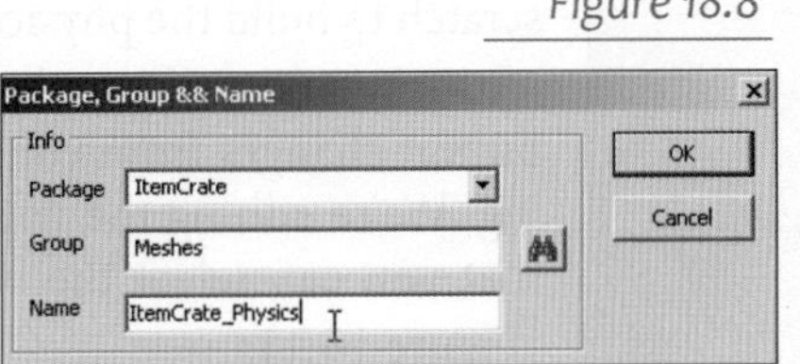


Figure 18.9

New Physics Asset
Minimum Bone Size 1.00
Orient Along Bone
Collision Geometry Box
Use Verts With Dominant Weight
Create Joints
Walk Past Small Bones
Open In PhAT Now
OK Cancel

Before the editor opens, we're prompted to enter a few settings to build our initial asset [Figure 18.9]. The asset will contain some primitive objects that we will modify. Select the settings, as shown in Figure 18.9, and click OK.

Once the physics editor is opened, our physics asset will have a couple of extra joints in the middle from the helper joints we created previously. Using the various view-mode buttons, change the viewport until it displays your mesh as a wireframe and the physics volumes as shaded boxes [Figure 18.10].

*Figure 18.10*

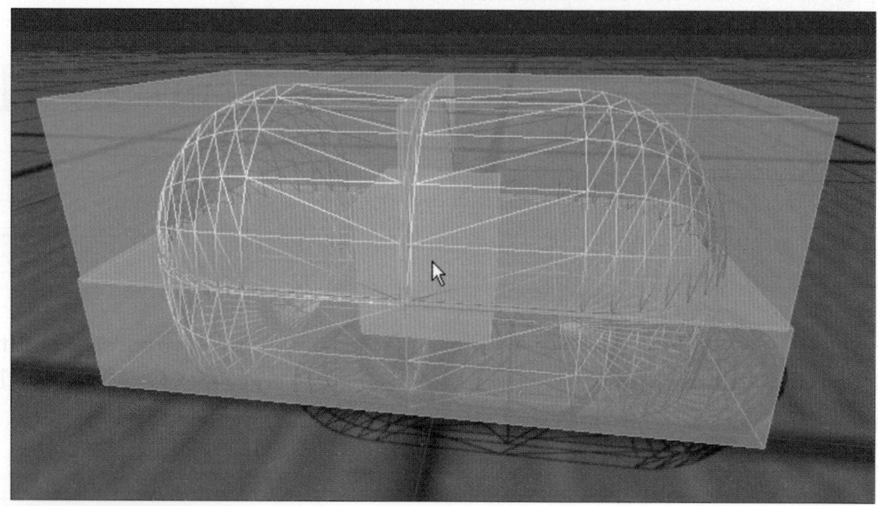

*Figure 18.11*

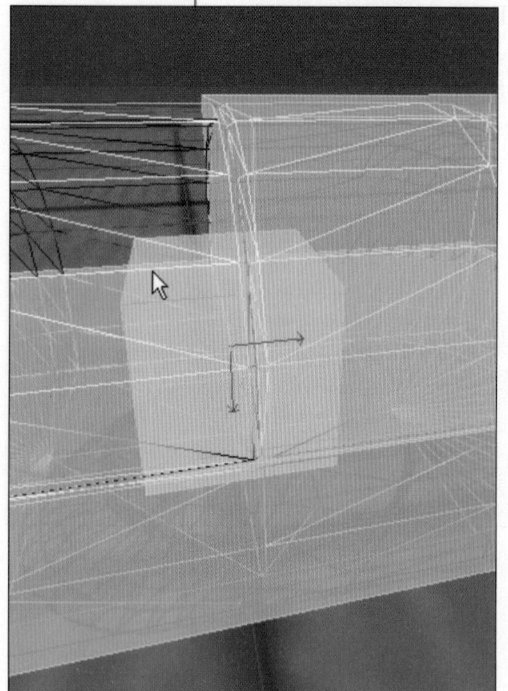

If we run the simulation using the button, the crate will try to break apart. The lids will push off the two smaller bones inside the crate. The lids are still constrained to be connected to each other, so they can't move far apart; rather, they simply wobble due to the forces associated with the bones and inner joints.

The default joint creation is usually inaccurate, and there are several rules that we need to obey when editing a physics object. We'll delete a few joints and start from scratch to build the physics objects for the lids.

Make sure you're in the correct editing mode. The button changes from volume editing to constraint editing. We're editing the volumes right now, so make sure that you can select the volumes and then delete them [Figure 18.11].

Selecting the joints can be tricky, so zoom in to make your selections. Don't delete the main volume at the bottom; this is the root physics volume and must remain in the scene.

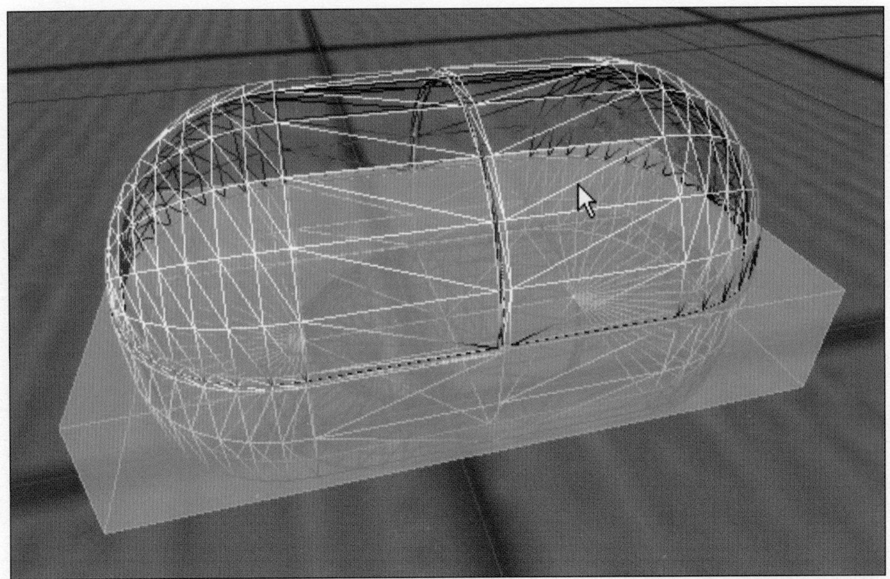

Figure 18.12

You should make the asset look like this so that we can build the proper objects as they're needed [Figure 18.12]. In volume-editing mode, click on the button to create a new bone [Figure 18.13]. Unreal PhAT requires at least one physics volume to edit, so the editor will not give you the option to delete the volume assigned to the root.

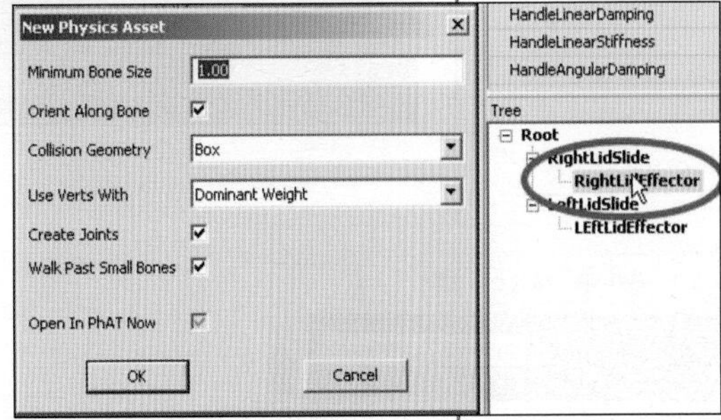


Figure 18.13

Double-click on RightLidEffector. A dialog will open. Click on OK. Repeat this for LeftLidEffector. Run the simulation to see the resulting motion of the

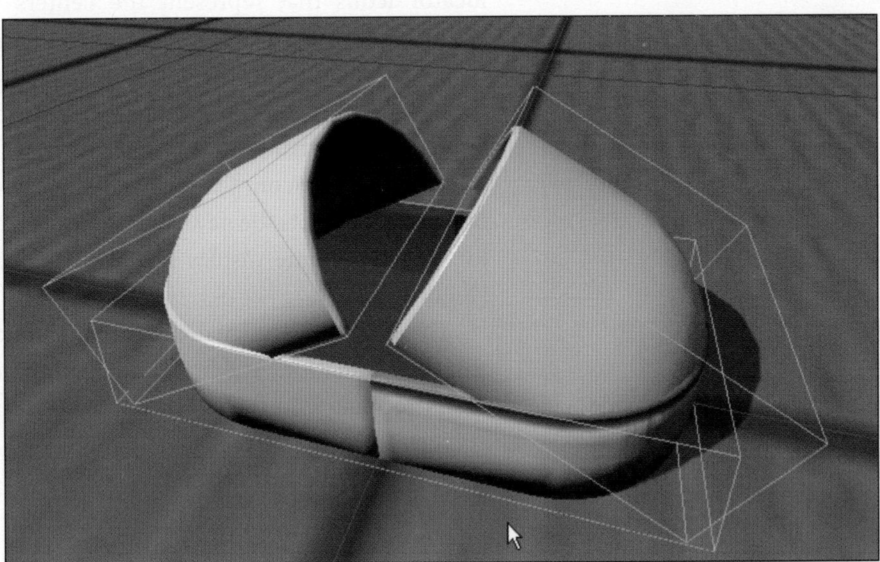

Figure 18.14

Figure 18.15

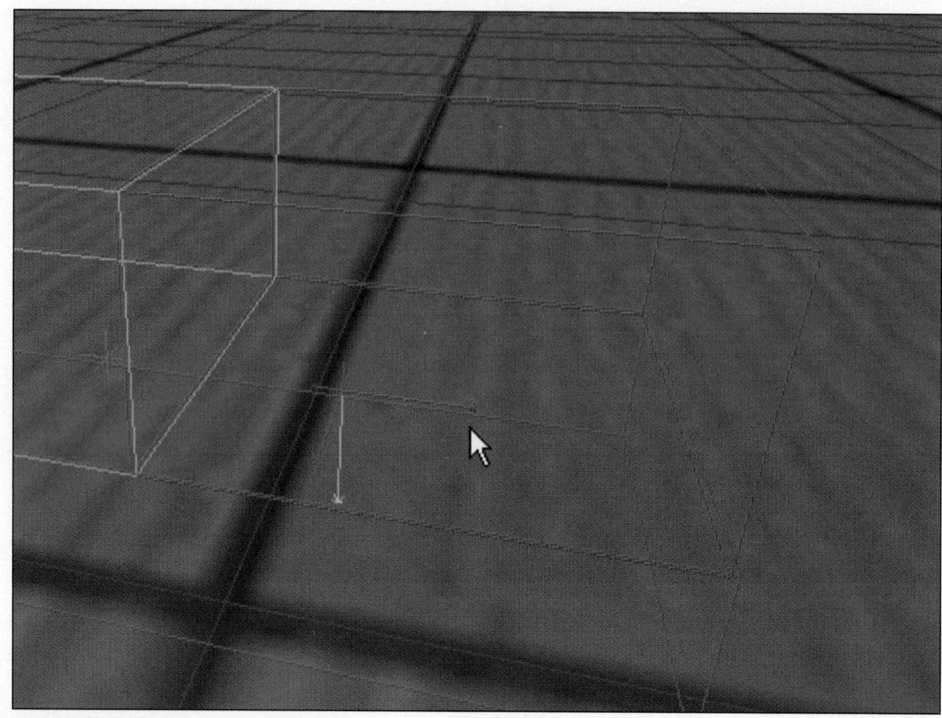

Figure 18.16

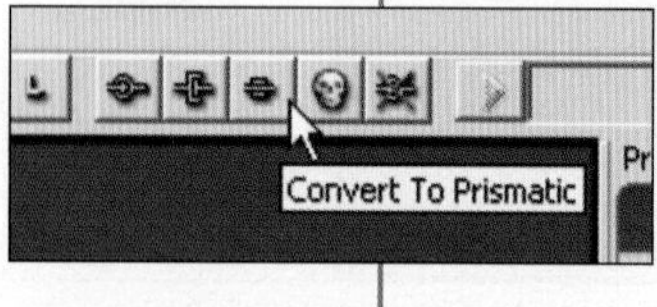


Figure 18.17

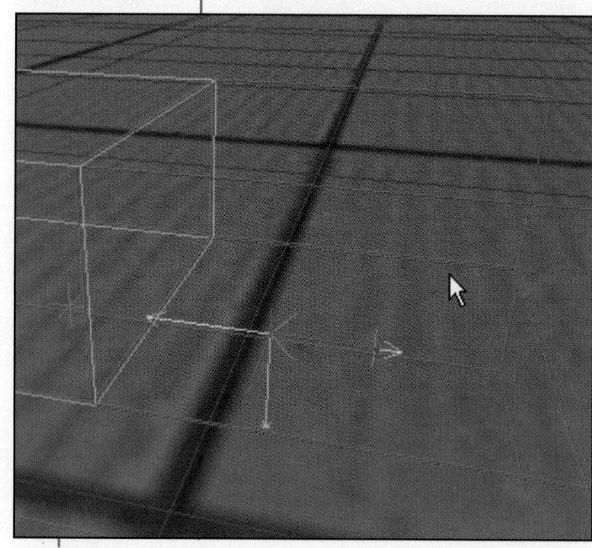

lids [Figure 18.14]. The lids drop into the bottom half of the crate, which is not interesting and, in fact, is not what we're looking for.

Switch into constraint-editing mode by pressing the button on the toolbar. The view is switched so that we can see magenta locator icons that represent the centers of action for the physics volumes [Figure 18.15].

Select one of the locators and then change the constraint type to prismatic by pressing the appropriate toolbar button [Figure 18.16].

The button's icon has changed slightly to one that represents the new constraint's behavior. The wireframe display has also changed [Figure 18.17].

To see how the prismatic constraint works, run the simulation. The lids slide open rather than dropping into the lower half of the crate [Figure 18.18].

However, the lids are sliding too far [Figure 18.19].

Figure 18.18

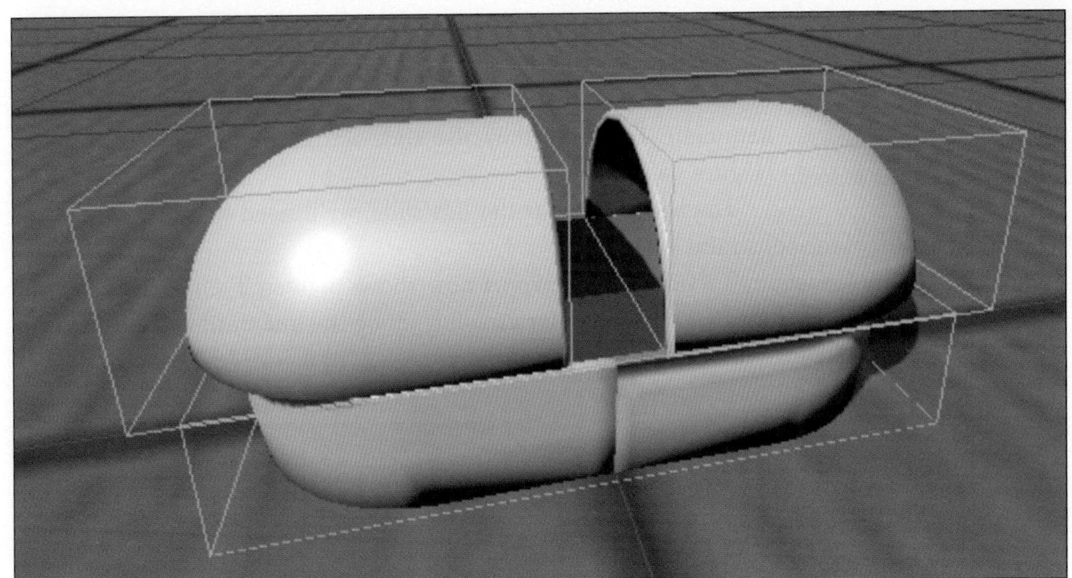

Figure 18.19

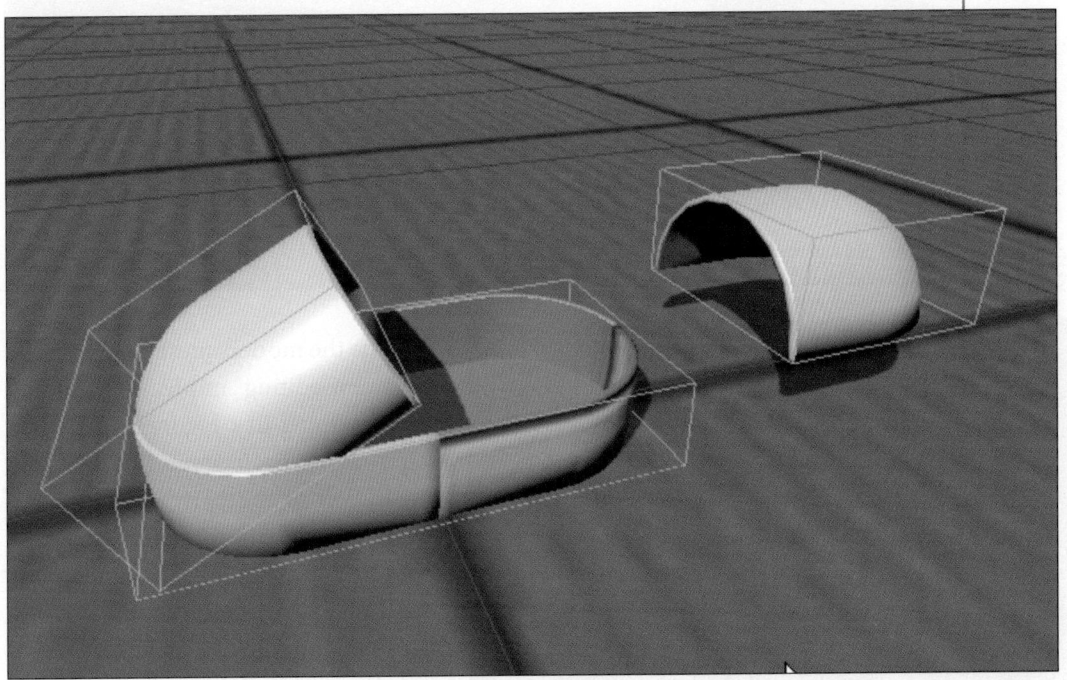

Figure 18.20

| Linear | |
|---|---|
| ▼ **LinearXSetup** | **(bLimited=1,L** |
| bLimited | 1 |
| **LimitSize** | 20.000000 |
| ▶ LinearYSetup | (bLimited=1,Limi |
| ▶ LinearZSetup | (bLimited=1,Limi |

We need to add some limitations to the motions of our physics parts. In the properties dialog for the constraint, set `bLimited` to 1 and `LimitSize` to 20. This keeps the lids from sliding off the base of the item crate. However, they also slide across the middle of the object [Figure 18.20].

To change how far the lids slide, we'll need to adjust where the center of the constraint is active.

The Constraint's icon in the viewport now shows a green T on each end of the constraint [Figure 18.21]. The center can slide along the line until it is at the inside end of the constraint action, shown as a red cross-hair in Figure 18.22.

Figure 18.21

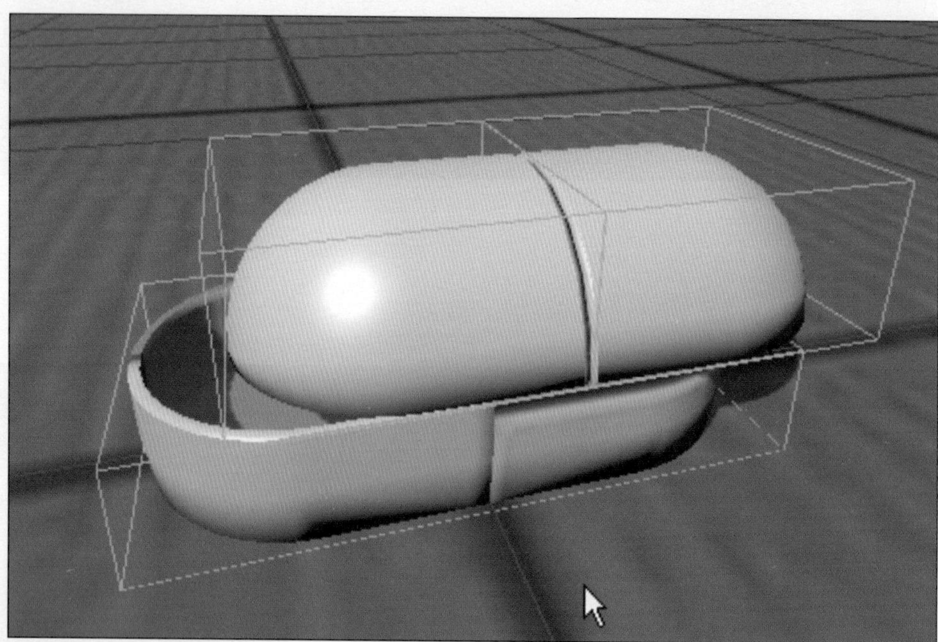

Figure 18.22

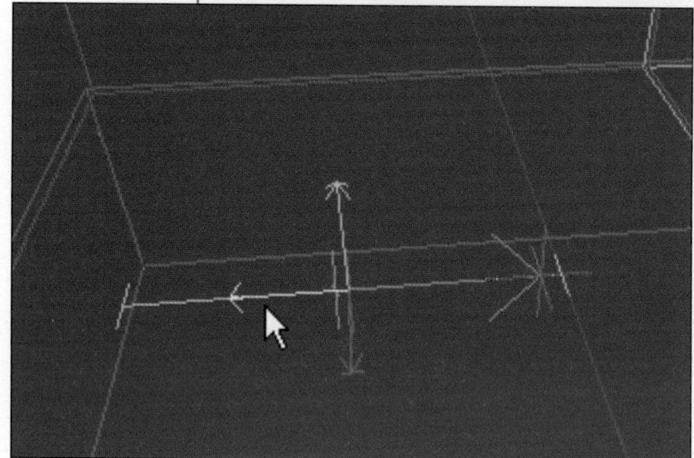

Hide the model's mesh. While in the constraint-editing mode, you should see something like Figure 18.23 when you're done. Each green line is a representation of the corresponding constraint's range of movement. A magenta cross-hair near the end of a green line represents the center of action. A cross-hair in the middle of a green line represents the center of the tool's handle.

Figure 18.23

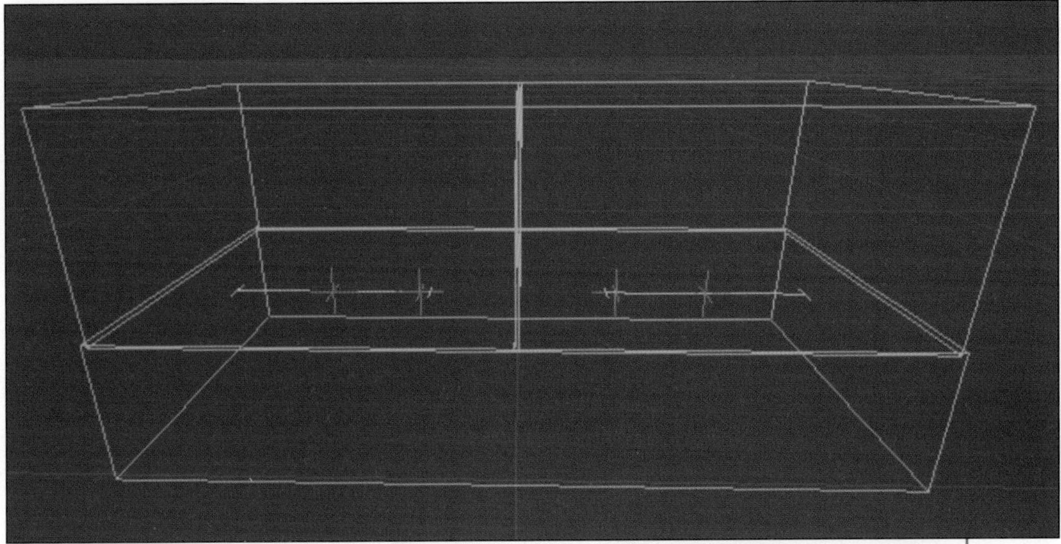

After some adjustment of the numbers you, should be able to constrain the object to behave something like this [Figure 18.24].

We have created a basic physics asset. Adding physics to the scene is a great way to obtain a lot of interesting things to play with. The physics volumes are also used for calculating how much of an object should cast shadows. Once the object is spawned into a scene by an `actorFactory`, the physics asset is connected to the object through the object's default properties.

Figure 18.24

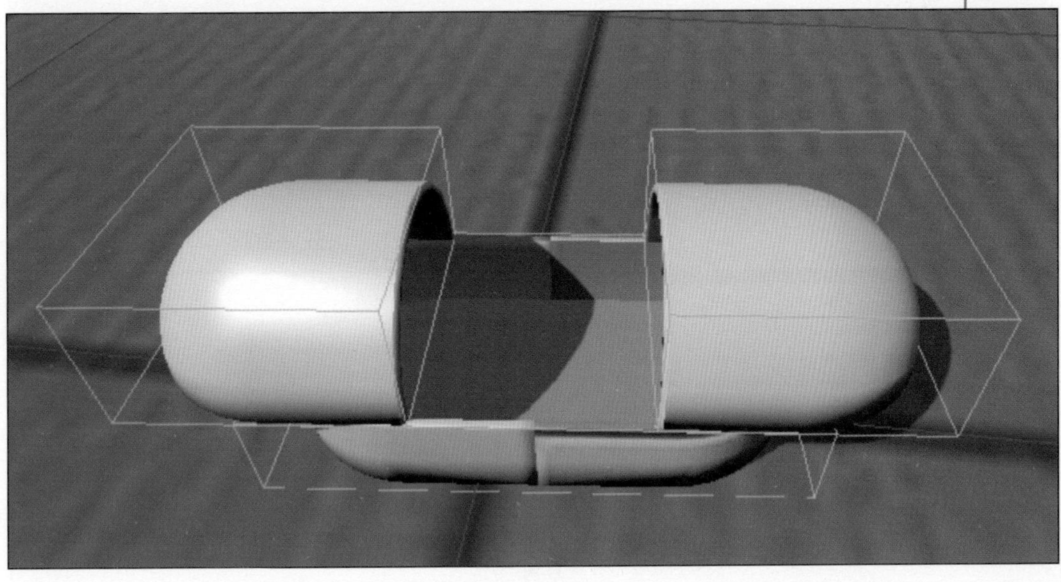

PROJECT

## Adding the Physics Object to a Level

Let's open up our boxRoom.ut3 for this project.

Let's start by adding a new PathNode to the scene [Figure 18.25]. For the sake of making something interesting, we'll position the PathNode above the static mesh object we created from the previous project.

Figure 18.25

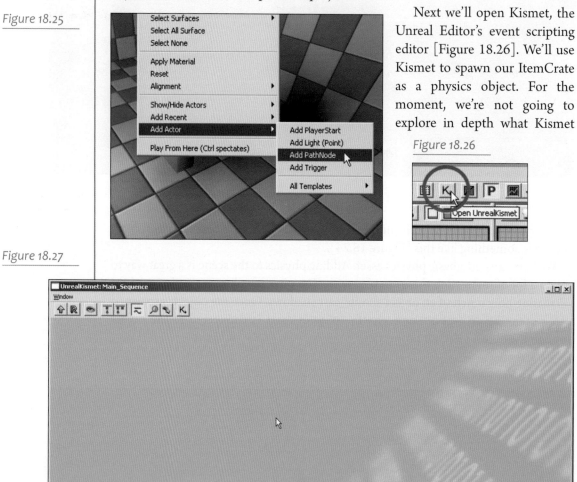

Next we'll open Kismet, the Unreal Editor's event scripting editor [Figure 18.26]. We'll use Kismet to spawn our ItemCrate as a physics object. For the moment, we're not going to explore in depth what Kismet

Figure 18.26

Figure 18.27

can do. We'll be building a very simple event for this task, so we'll just cover the specifics necessary to spawn a physics object into our scene.

The Kismet editor is shown in Figure 18.27. The middle area is the graph editor view where our Kismet sequences will be created. The properties window is displayed in the lower left of the editor. We'll focus on these two parts of the editor for now.

Right-click in the main panel's graph editor view and add a new event called "Level Loaded and Visible" [Figure 18.28].

Next, we'll add a new Action, called Actor Factory, in the Actor sub-menu [Figure 18.29].

We'll now connect the Level Loaded and Visible Event to the Spawn Actor tab of the Actor Factory node [Figure 18.30].

Select the apple icon in the level editor to create a path node. With the path node selected, add to the Kismet editor a `New Object Var Using PathNode_0` [Figure 18.31].

Kismet will use the object variable you just created. Such variables are used by Kismet in a manner similar to how UScript uses them. You create empty variables, name them, and then add data to them using various other nodes.

Figure 18.28

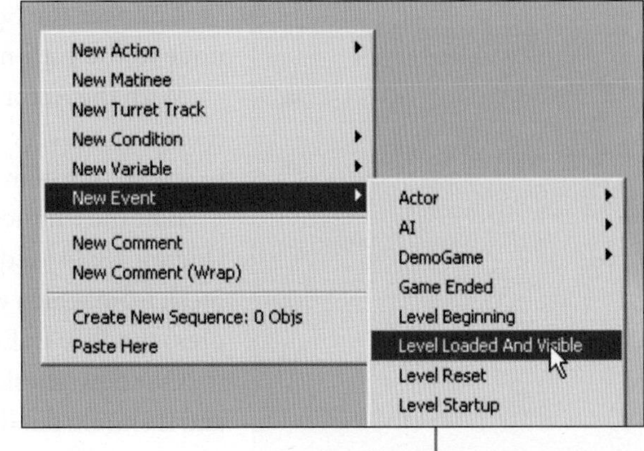


Figure 18.29

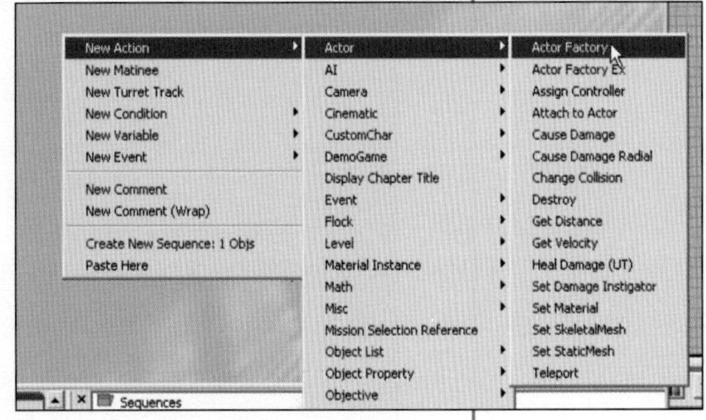


Figure 18.30

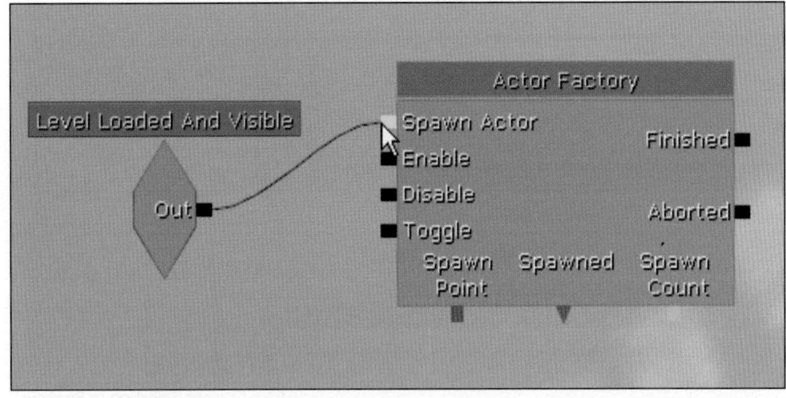


Figure 18.31

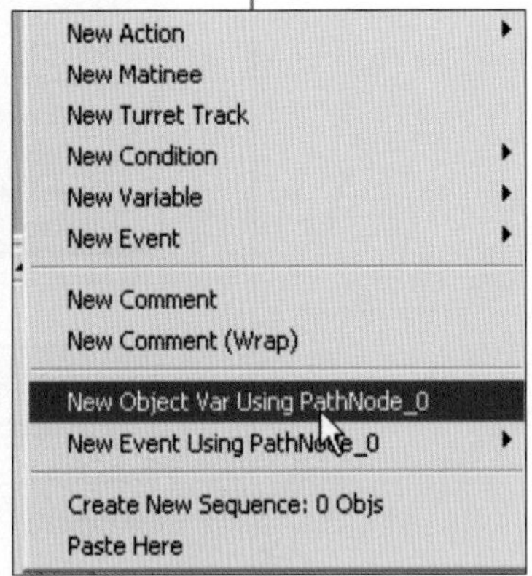

Figure 18.32

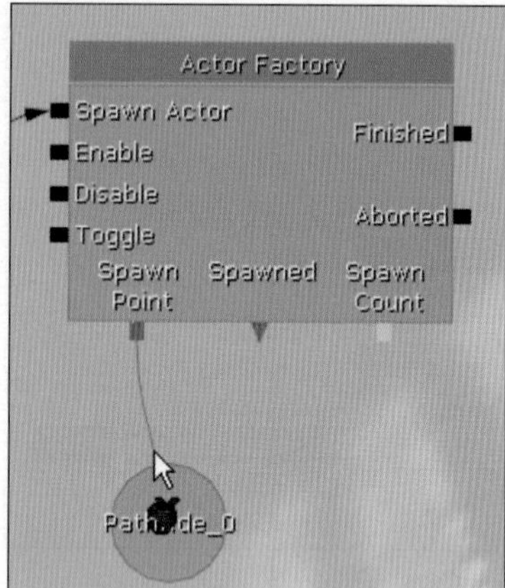


Connect the Spawn Point tab at the bottom of the Actor Factory node to the path-node variable we just added [Figure 18.32].

With the Actor Factory node selected, change the properties under `Factory` to `ActorFactoryPhysicsAsset` [Figure 18.33] in order to spawn our ItemCrate physics object.

Edit the PhysicsAsset property to use our ItemCrate's physics asset [Figure 18.34]. Edit the SkeletalMesh property to use the ItemCrate_ mesh from which we created the physics object. Save the level and then press the Play In Editor button.

Our new physics asset should spawn as soon as the level is created, and it should fall down over the box mesh [Figure 18.35].

Figure 18.33

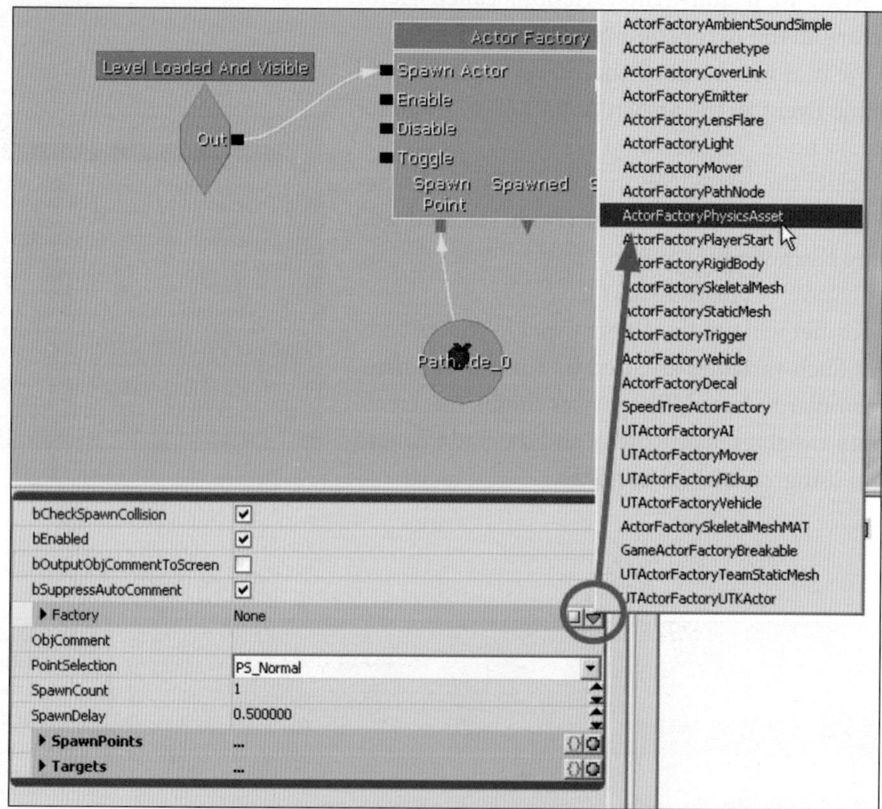


Figure 18.34

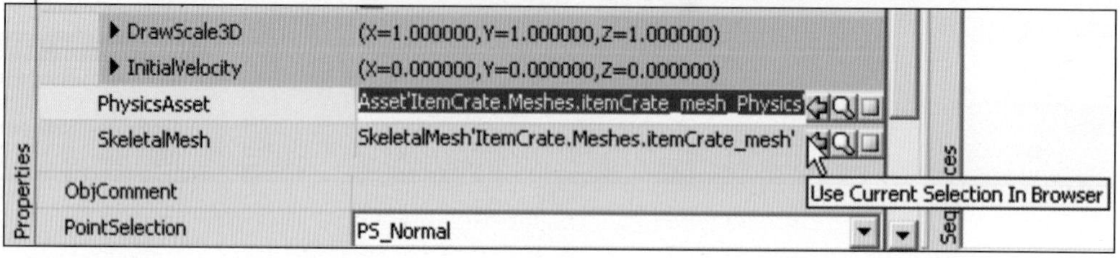

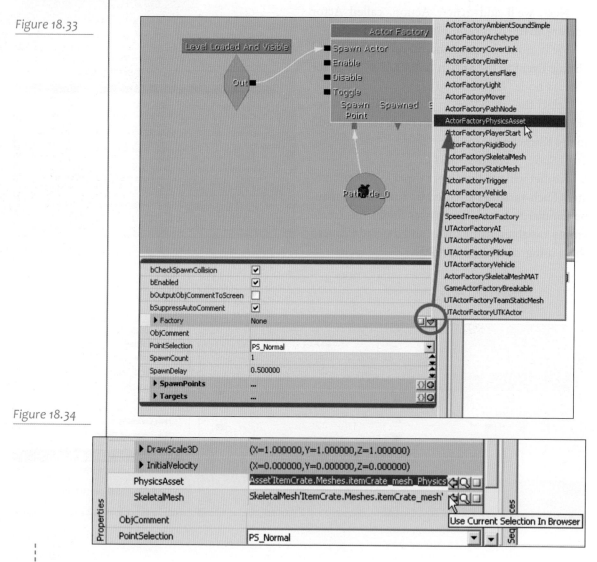

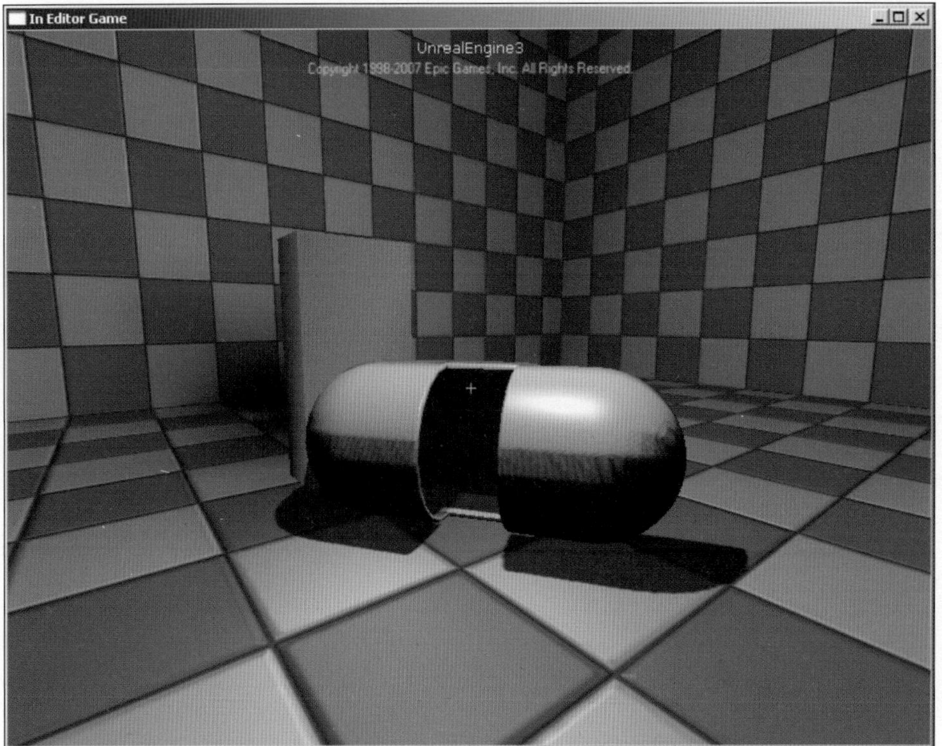


Figure 18.35

This is just the beginning of what we can do with physics and spawning objects in the scene. We'll be creating more detailed physics in later projects, making those projects more interesting than the one we just built.

Kismet is a pretty complex system. We'll be learning more about this later as we further explore animation and creating cinematics with characters; but for now, we'll stick to the basics of spawning objects into our scene.

## On Your Own

Building physics assets for most skeletal object is a necessity; it's something you'll need to do often. You should experiment with other constraint types to see how they work and how you can use them. Kismet is an amazingly powerful tool.

# 19

# Weapons

*Bullets, Missiles, and Laser Beams—pew, pew, pew!*

## Simple Animated Skeletal Mesh Objects

Weapons with moving parts have to be animated using joints. Joint translation and rotation are exported though the ActorX plug-in as a PSA file. Firing, reloading, idling, and other behaviors are then setup through the Animation Tree editor for the weapon. The weapon's state is driven by Unreal Script. Building animations requires a lot of steps; but you've gotten this far, so it's too late to turn back now!

The first thing we'll do is build a model for your new weapon. If the weapon has a few moving parts, then the parts will need to be rigged and animated.

PROJECT

### Modeling a Simple Ray Gun

We'll work through a few quick and simple techniques for building a simple, animated model. These techniques are also useful for modeling more complex items, which we will do later on. We'll go though some interesting steps that I've found rather useful when making quick props. The same techniques can be applied as well to character modeling and texturing.

The initial geometric model is shown in Figure 19.1.

I've assembled some primitive shapes, making sure the edges match by adjusting the edge counts on the primitive shapes. Using deformers from the modifier menu, I squashed the barrel into a tube shape [Figure 19.2].

In Figures 19.1 and 19.2, each part is shown in a different color so that you can see how the parts fit together.

When finished building the general parts, the extra faces hidden inside the mesh should be deleted. Extra edges that do not contribute to the profile are also deleted. Finally, the vertices are welded together after the parts were merged into a single object [Figure 19.3]. It's important that you save the primitive parts used to build the solid mesh. We'll be using these parts to build the high-resolution version of the mesh.

Figure 19.1

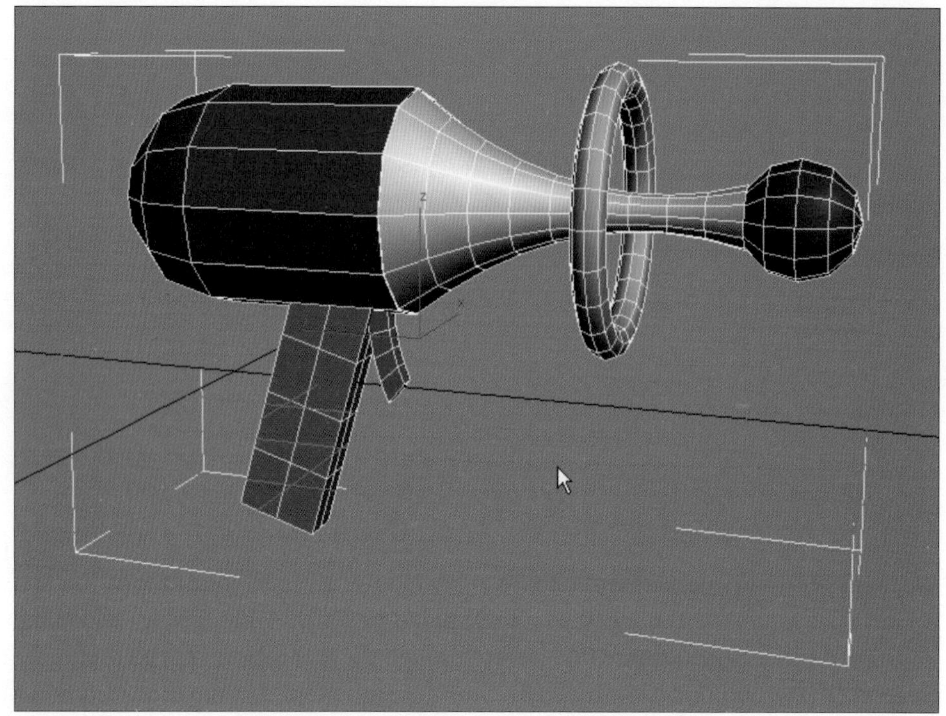

Figure 19.2

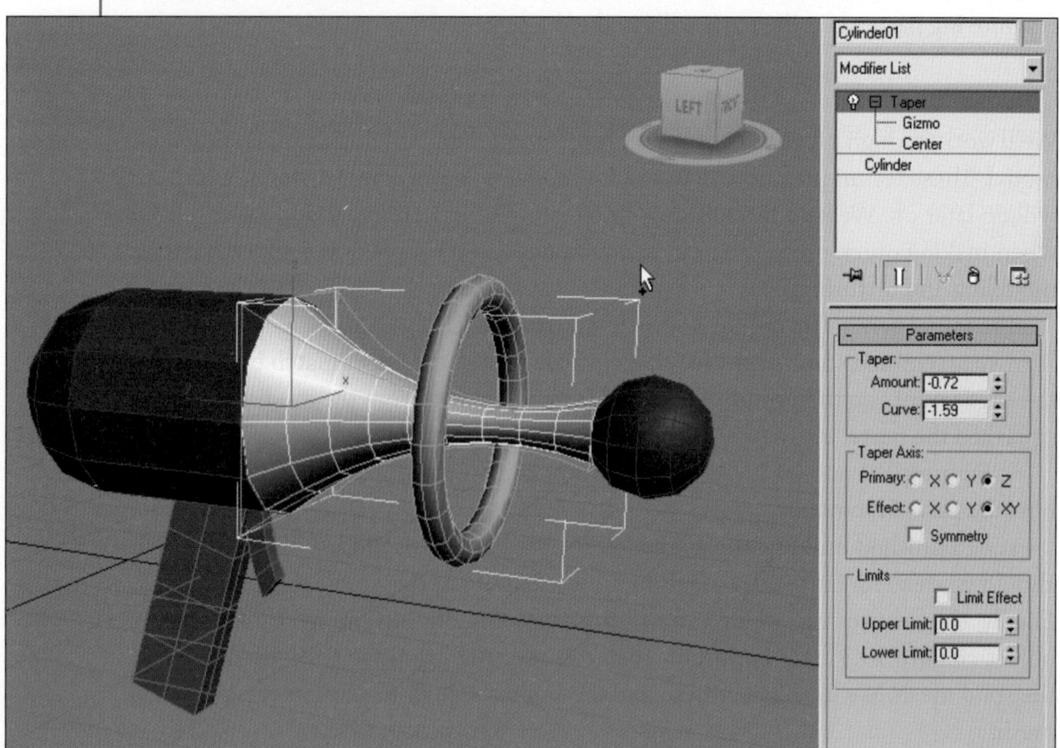

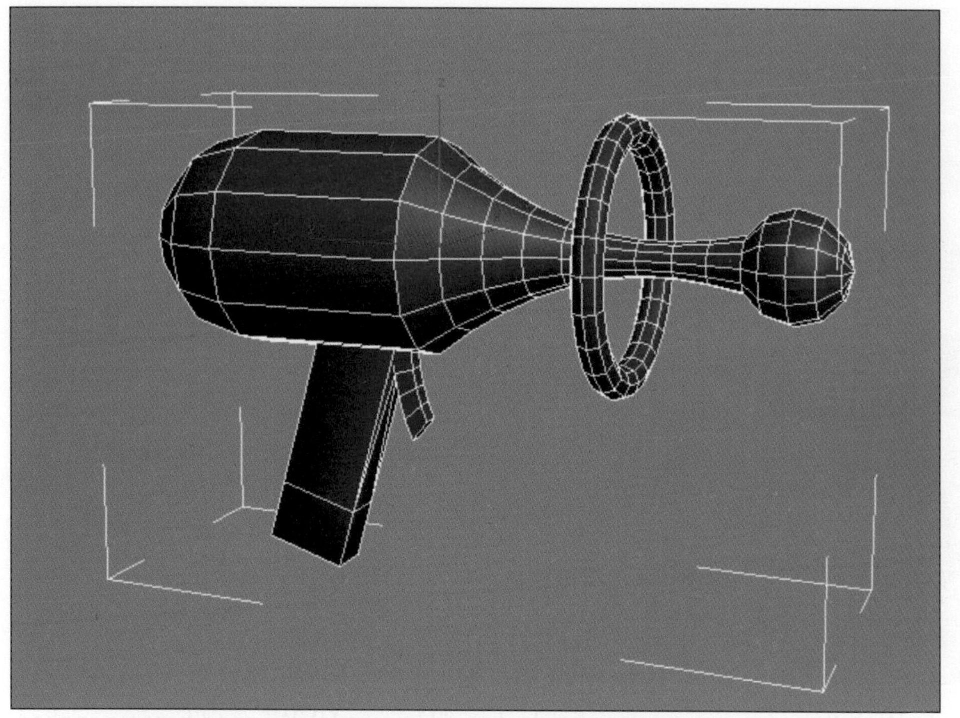

Figure 19.3

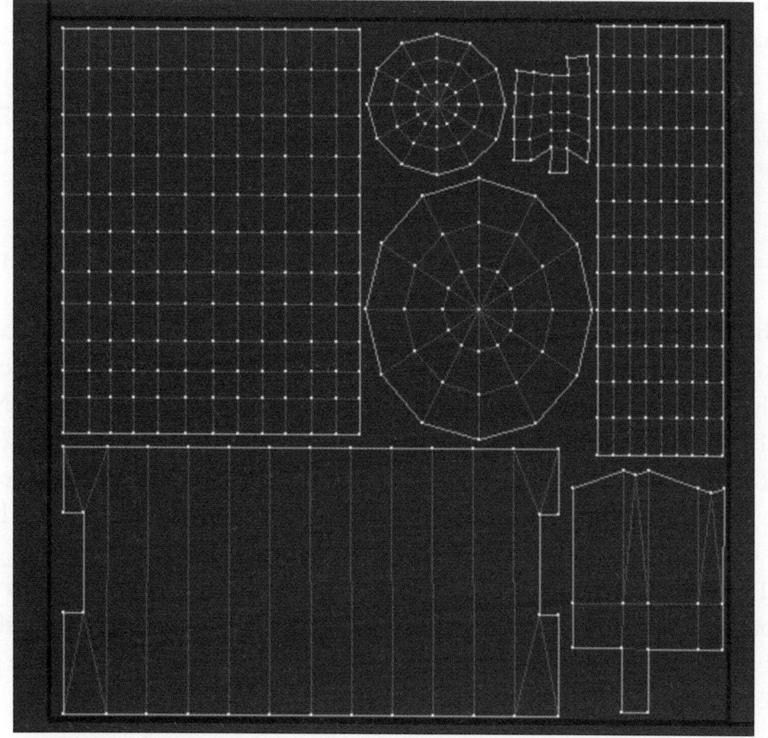

Figure 19.4

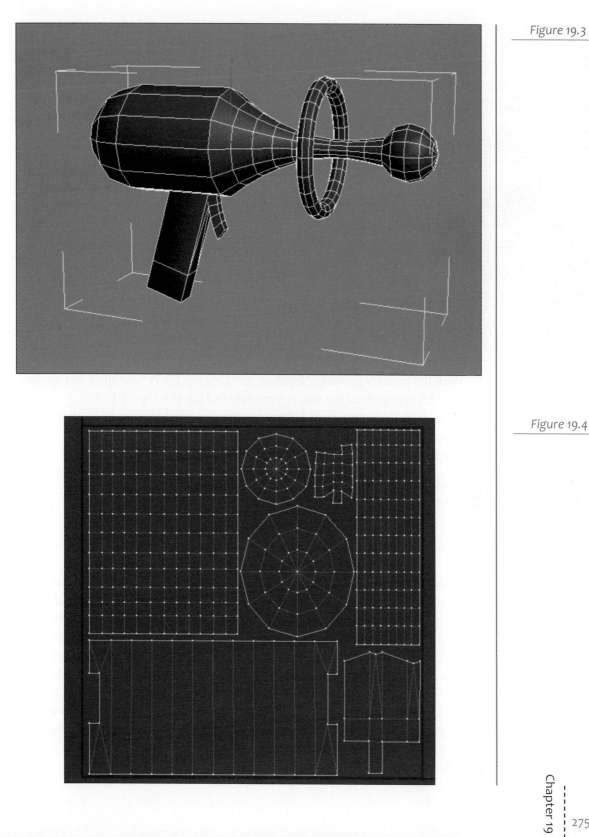

Figure 19.5

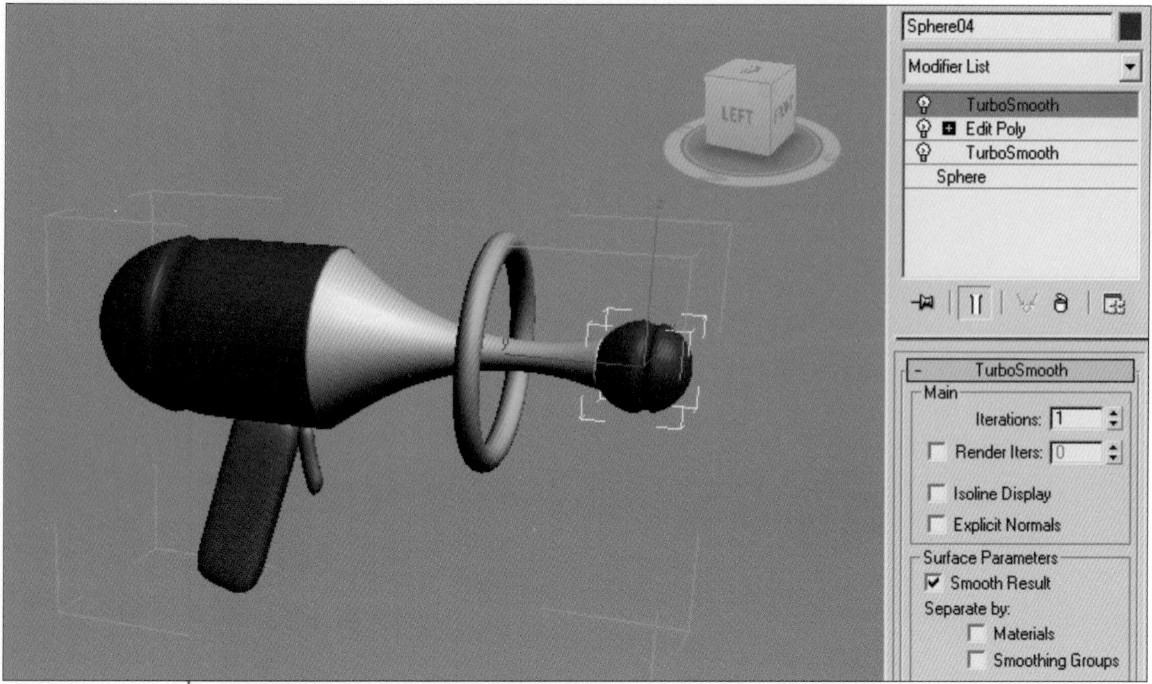


With the primary geometry finished, an "Unwrap UVW" modifier was applied, and the different parts of the model were flattened like this Figure 19.4.

Here are the primitive parts before they were merged [Figure 19.5]. A few edits were made to the geometry to add some simple detail. After the edits, I added a "Turbo Smooth" modifier to the objects to smooth them.

Figure 19.6

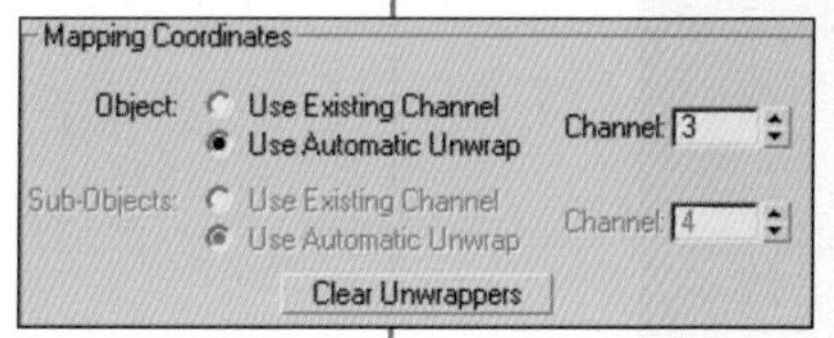


Once the high-resolution model is finished, it's a simple matter to bake the ambient occlusion into a texture to be used by the model. Automatically generated UVs are used to simplify the texture-baking process [Figure 19.6].

Bake the ambient occlusion map for the high-resolution model [Figure 19.7] and save the texture.

With the low-resolution mesh matched to the high-resolution mesh, bake the occlusion map from the high-resolution to the low-resolution texture channel. Similarly, bake the normal map to the low-resolution mesh [TaoPistol_N.tga of Figure 19.8]. Using GIMP, select portions of the model's textures and fill them with color in a separate layer. Multiply this layer by the occlusion map as a base color and save the result as the diffuse texture [TaoPistol_D.tga of Figure 19.8]. Make a brighter version of the diffuse texture and save it as the specular texture [TaoPistol_S.tga of Figure 19.8]. A new material for this weapon is an emissive texture, which is used to define parts of the textures that glow [TaoPistol_E.tga of Figure 19.8]. Brightly glowing parts of the pistol correspond to bright colors of the texture. Use black to prevent parts from glowing.

Figure 19.7

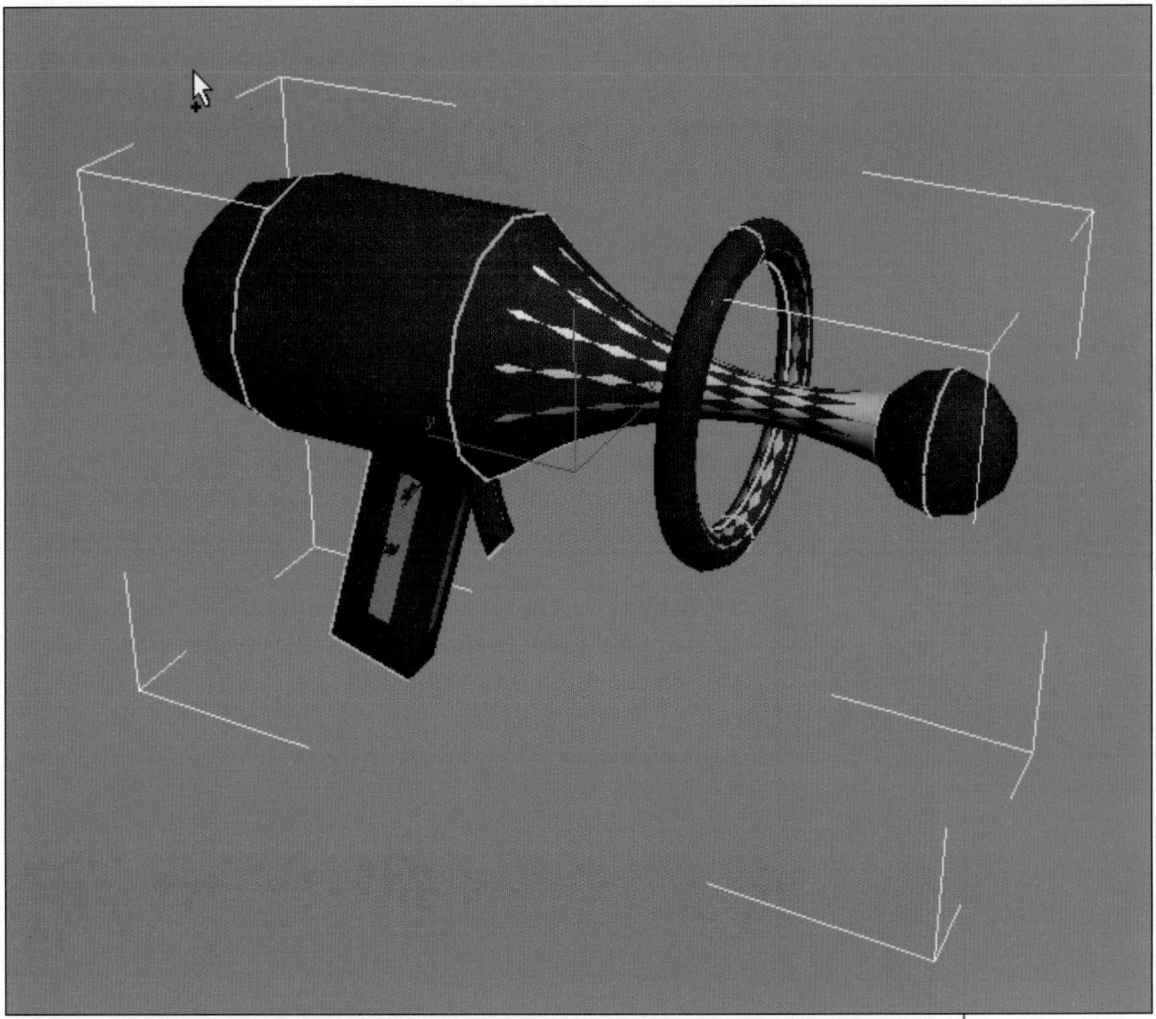

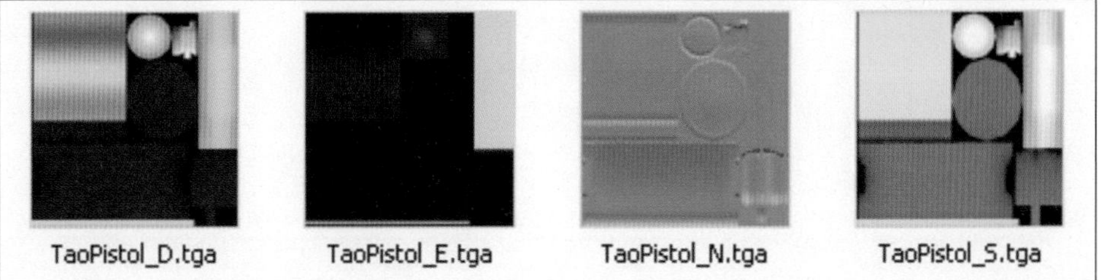


Figure 19.8

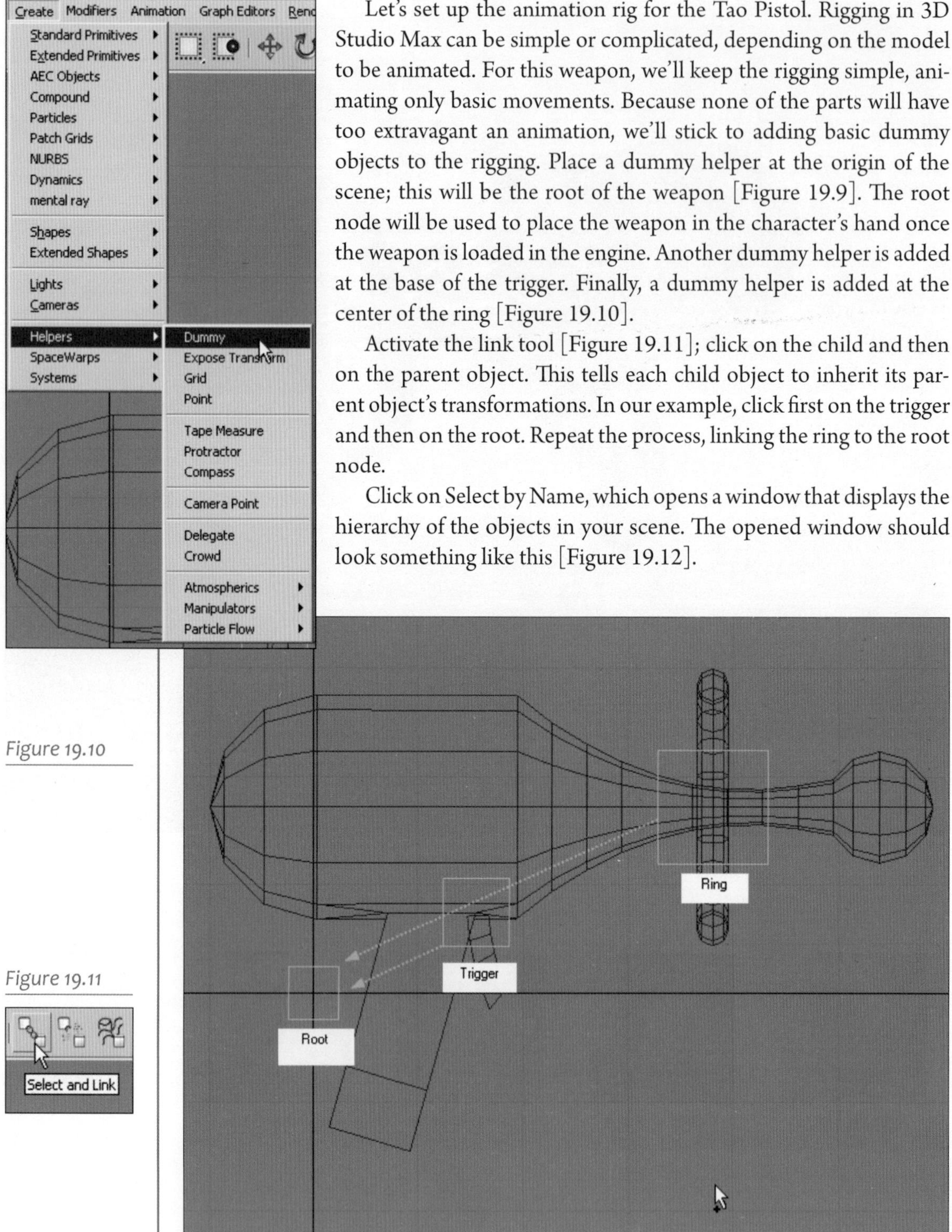


Figure 19.9

Figure 19.10

Figure 19.11

Let's set up the animation rig for the Tao Pistol. Rigging in 3D Studio Max can be simple or complicated, depending on the model to be animated. For this weapon, we'll keep the rigging simple, animating only basic movements. Because none of the parts will have too extravagant an animation, we'll stick to adding basic dummy objects to the rigging. Place a dummy helper at the origin of the scene; this will be the root of the weapon [Figure 19.9]. The root node will be used to place the weapon in the character's hand once the weapon is loaded in the engine. Another dummy helper is added at the base of the trigger. Finally, a dummy helper is added at the center of the ring [Figure 19.10].

Activate the link tool [Figure 19.11]; click on the child and then on the parent object. This tells each child object to inherit its parent object's transformations. In our example, click first on the trigger and then on the root. Repeat the process, linking the ring to the root node.

Click on Select by Name, which opens a window that displays the hierarchy of the objects in your scene. The opened window should look something like this [Figure 19.12].

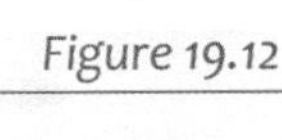

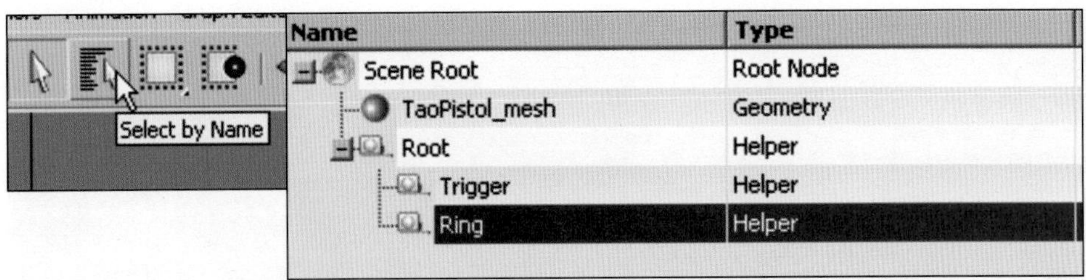


Figure 19.12

Figure 19.13

Figure 19.14

As in the dynamic-object project, add a single `Skin Modifier` to the mesh of the pistol. Attach the trigger to the trigger dummy, the ring end to the corresponding end of the joint chain, and the rest of the gun to the root dummy object. The selection-by-name tool is also useful to select the objects for the skin modifier [Figure 19.13].

This dialog allows us to turn the mesh into separate elements, each of which can be animated. Using ActorX, save the model and export the mesh as a PSK file named "TaoPistol_mesh."

If the ActorX tool warns you that the scene has no physique models, try checking the "all skin-type" check box in the ActorX settings roll-out [Figure 19.14]. Also check the boxes for persistent settings and persistent paths. This will make the tool remember where you like to save your PSK and PSA files.

Next, let's build the fire animation for the weapon. Select the Time Configuration button and set the length of the animation to 15 frames [Figure 19.15].

Before starting the animation, establish the animation loop by adding two key frames, one at the beginning and one at the end of the timeline.

The fire animation will play each time the Tao Pistol is fired. The animations on the two different parts are simple. First, animate the rotation of the trigger followed by the ring sliding in, and then off, the barrel [Figure 19.16]. At frame 0, export the skeletal mesh object using ActorX. Don't forget to save! Second, in a manner similar to the creation of the first animation, create a simple idle animation of the ring floating about.

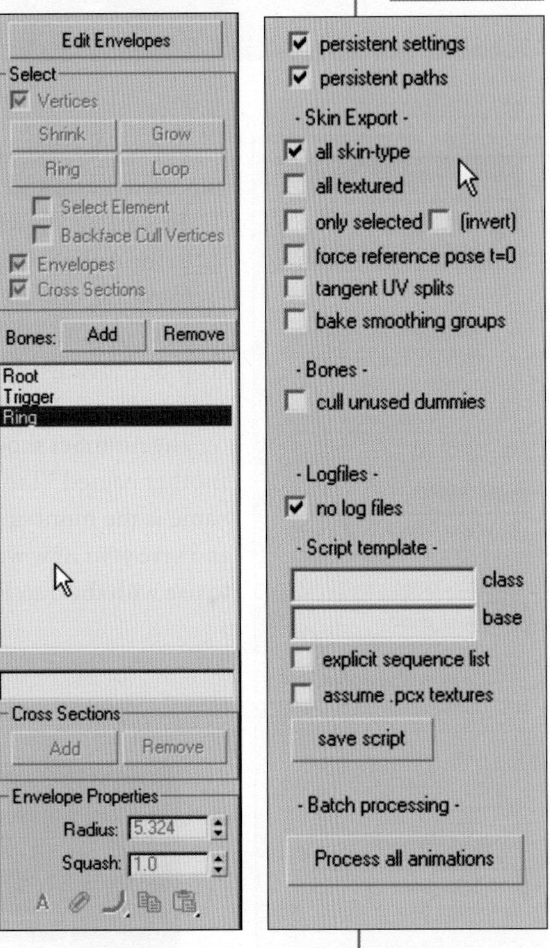


Figure 19.15

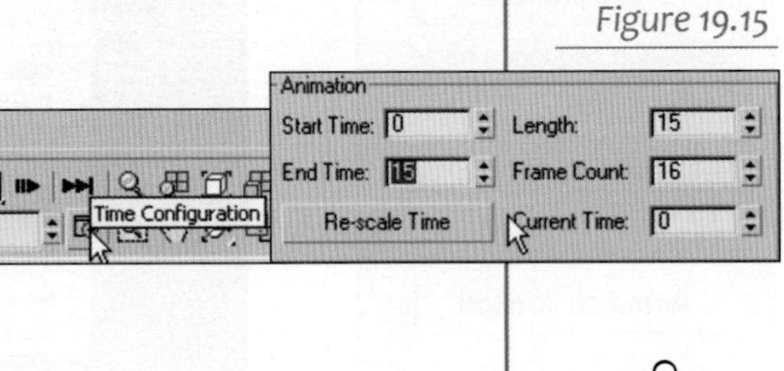

Figure 19.16

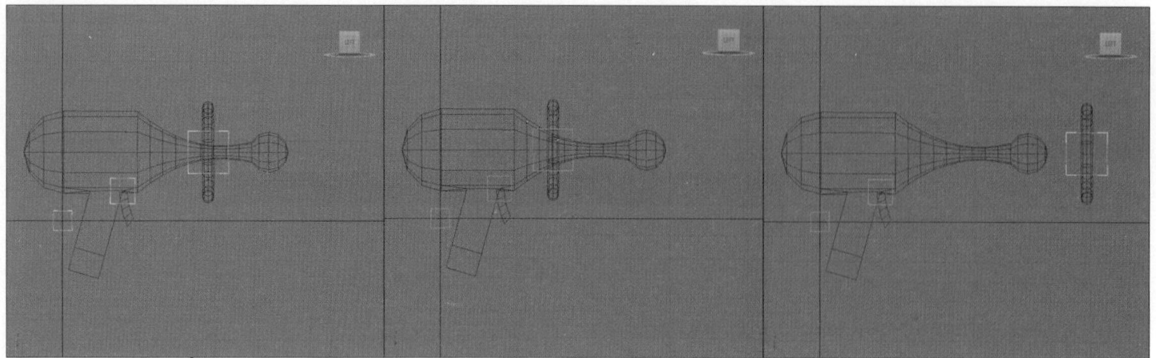

Figure 19.17

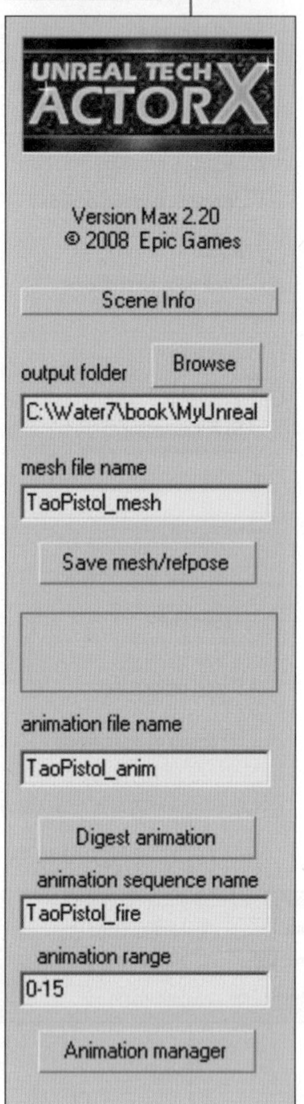


Import the skeletal mesh into the editor [Figure 19.17], right-click on the imported mesh, and then open the AnimSet Viewer [Figure 19.18].

This dialog allows you to import the new animations.

In the AnimSet viewer, select `File` → `New AnimSet` [Figure 19.19].

Name the new animation "TaoPistol_anims" and add it to a group named "Anims" [Figure 19.20]. Having a separate group for animations helps us to keep our various data files organized. Next, import the PSA file that was exported from 3D Studio Max [Figure 19.21].

The AnimSet should include a new item named "TaoPistol_fire[15]" and another named "TaoPistol_idle[15]." The number suffix on each animation name is the number of frames in the animation. Close the AnimSet viewer and save your new weapon package. A material is prepared and ready for you to use with the Tao Pistol. We have built a new type of weapon that is ready

Figure 19.18

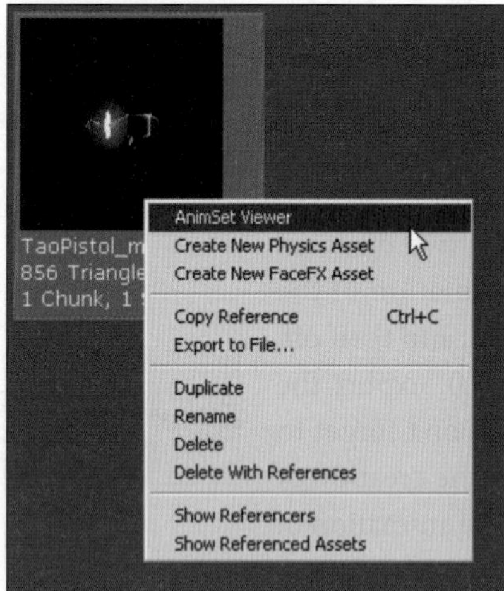


Figure 19.19

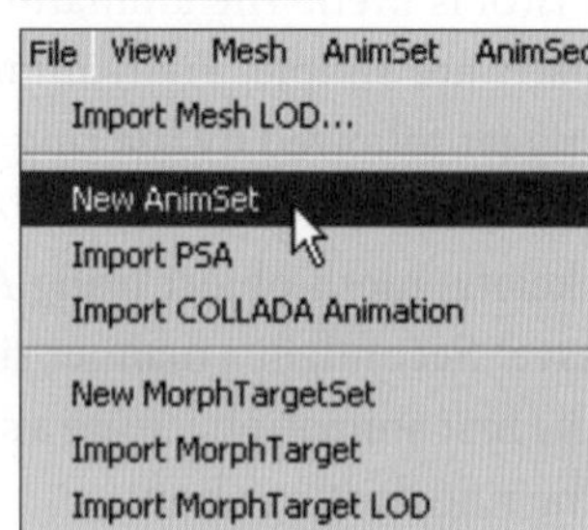

Figure 19.20

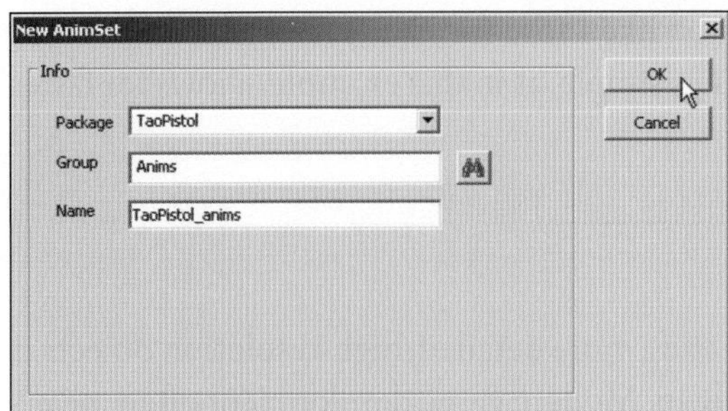


Figure 19.21

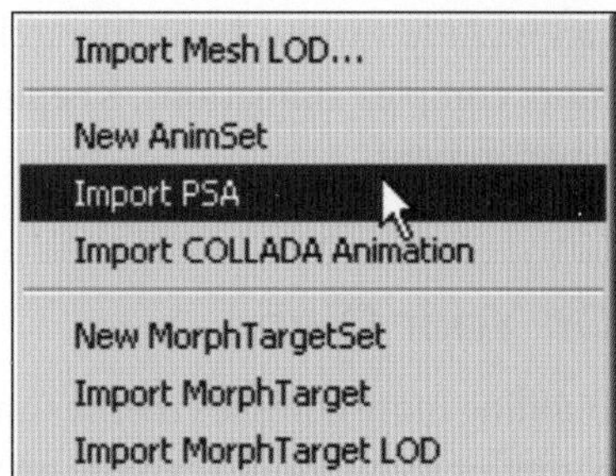


for Captain Hadron to blast space aliens with [Figure 19.22]! The UScript that drives this weapon will know about the AnimSet, including the animation names that will be played while the weapon is idle and when it's fired.

Figure 19.22

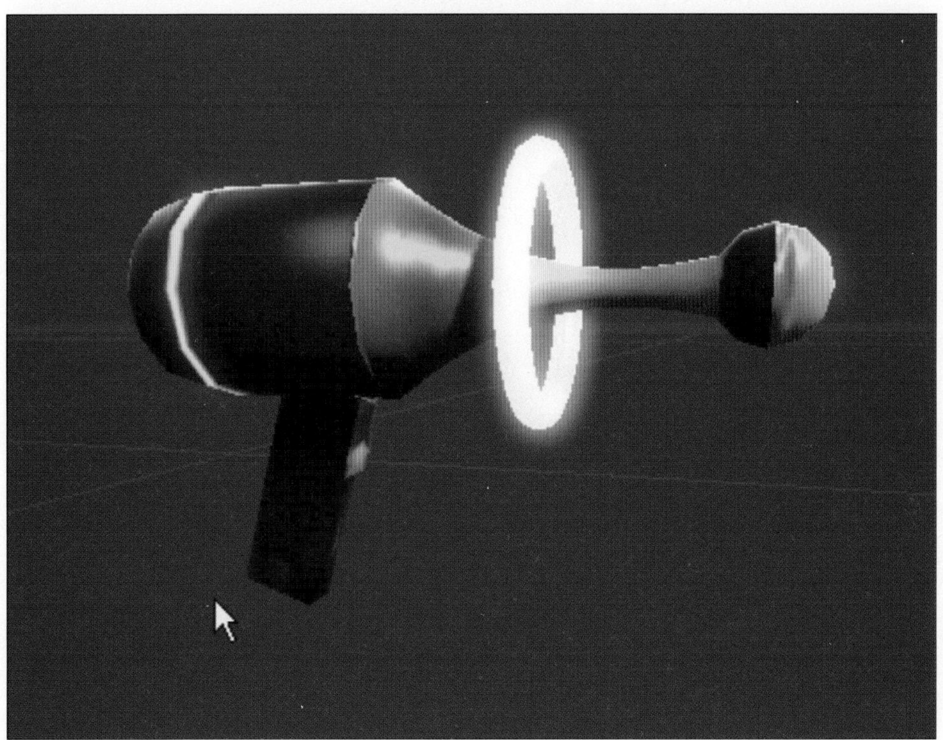

## Review

Creating a new weapon is somewhat like creating a new character. You'll need to animate a rig and then export the animations. The number of animations and the behavior of each can be as complex as those of a fully realized character, but for our demo we used only a few basic animations.

Of course, the Tao Pistol has only two moving parts—a trigger and a particle ring. Weapons found in Unreal Tournament are far more complex. Rigs for weapons can include various bone hierarchies, just like those for characters, which allow for more complex animations. Keeping things simple, as in this example, allows for faster development.

## On Your Own

Building more complex meshes and creating more detailed, high-resolution objects is something you should explore on your own. Modern game development often means rebuilding an object several times. High-resolution meshes don't always need to be built as a single part.

# 20 Cascade and Particle Systems

*Where There's Smoke, There's Fire*

Particle effects in the UnrealEngine3 are created using a tool called Cascade. Particles are basically sprites, which are flat, 2D images drawn in 3D space that originate from a point called an emitter. Once a sprite is emitted, it can be assigned various attributes such as velocity or initial speed at the time it's emitted; drag, which is the amount of speed the sprite loses as it travels; or even gravity and collision behaviors.

The amount of detail that a good particle system can add to a scene is remarkable, and the work needed to achieve such complexity is quite time consuming. We'll avoid in-depth discussions about the capabilities of Cascade, choosing instead to summarize only the basics of the tool. You will discover, though, how much fun the particle-editing system in Unreal Engine can be, and hopefully you'll take it upon yourself to explore the tool further.

## What to Expect

The following chapter covers the basics of Cascade. We'll make a simple texture, a very basic material with a special node designed for particle systems. Then we'll add the particle to the scene so we can see how it's going to look in our game mod.

### Cascade "Particle Man, Particle Man . . ."

PROJECT

We're going to create a new particle system in a package named "Effects" [Figure 20.1].

Make sure that the Factory is set to ParticleSystem. Another way to create a new object in the Generic browser is to use the file menu and select `New`. The options allow you to create anything that's also accessible through the right-click menu. Name the new particle system "TaoBlast" and then add it to the group named "Particles."

This will create our new particle system in the Generic browser [Figure 20.2]. A yellow border around the icon indicates that this object is a particle system. The icon initially contains the text "No Image," but this will change once we have something interesting to look at.

Figure 20.1

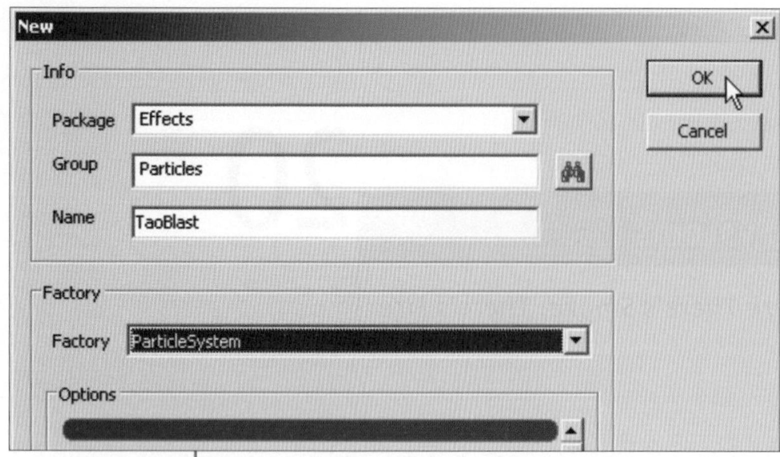


Figure 20.2

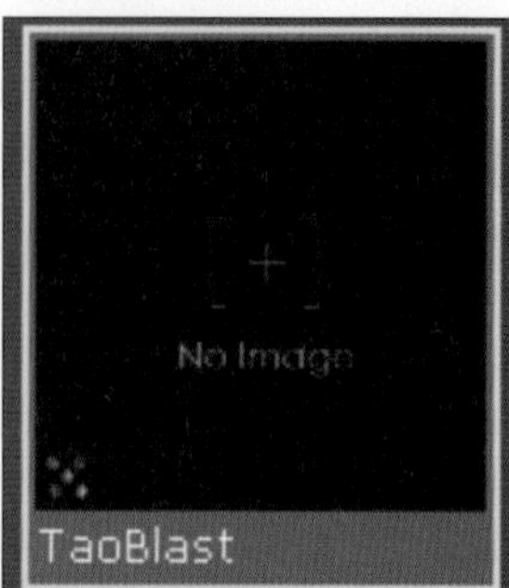


Figure 20.3

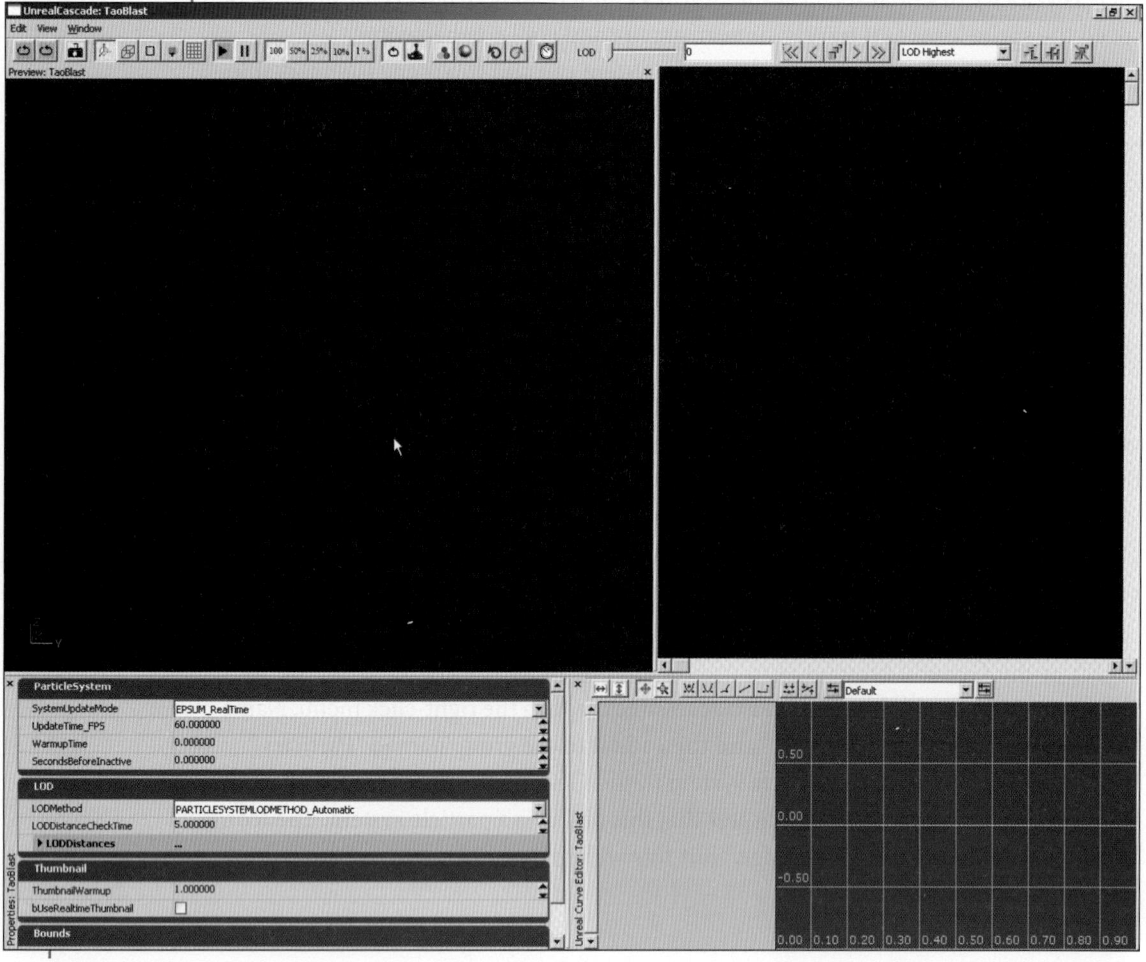

Figure 20.4

Figure 20.5

Here is the Cascade editor [Figure 20.3]. The empty panel on the left is the particle viewport. This is where your effect will be played repeatedly for you to observe your modifications. The blank panel on the right is the particle system node editor. This is where you'll be adding and selecting various parts of your particle system's behaviors. We'll learn more about adding behaviors later. The lower left window contains the selected component's properties. The lower right window is the curve editor for the selected behavior. The curve editor allows you to finely tune any behaviors that vary over time.

The toolbar at the top of the editor has several buttons of interest. To obtain a frame of reference that assists us in what we're doing, press the Toggle Grid button [Figure 20.4]. Next, we'll right click on the right pane of the editor. In the very small popup menu, select the New ParticleSpriteEmitter option [Figure 20.5].

Figure 20.6

Your new particle emitter is created with several default properties and modules [Figure 20.6]. First of all, your particle has an appearance, usually in the form of a camera-facing sprite. The Particle Emitter's name can be changed by right-clicking on the top-most node and selecting `Emitter` → `Rename Emitter`.

The top-most node is the main particle system. The three nodes below the particle are the modules that give our particle motion, color, and behavior. By adding and removing these modules, we can create complex and interesting particle behaviors; for example, we can quickly create smoke, fire, lightning, and many other basic effects in just a few modules.

Figure 20.7

To get a feel for how our particle is scaled and how it will look in something other than a black void with a blue grid, we'll place our particle system in the level BoxRoom.ut3. Highlight the TaoBlast icon in the Generic browser and use the right-click menu in the scene to add a new emitter: `Add Actor` → `Add Emitter: TaoBlast` [Figure 20.7].

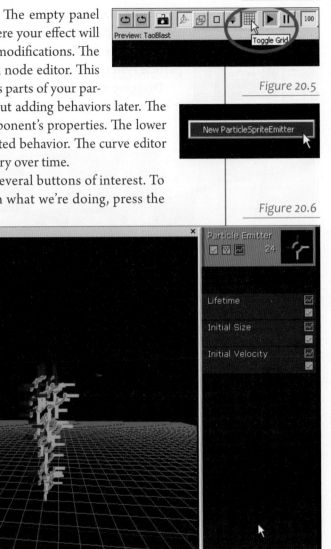

Figure 20.8

At first there is nothing in the level, so we'll need to turn on the `View In Real Time` button on the viewport options [Figure 20.8].

One of the fun things to do within the editor is to adjust the placement of a particle system in real time.

Dragging around the emitter allows us to see how the particle behaves when it's moved in the game [Figure 20.9].

Figure 20.9

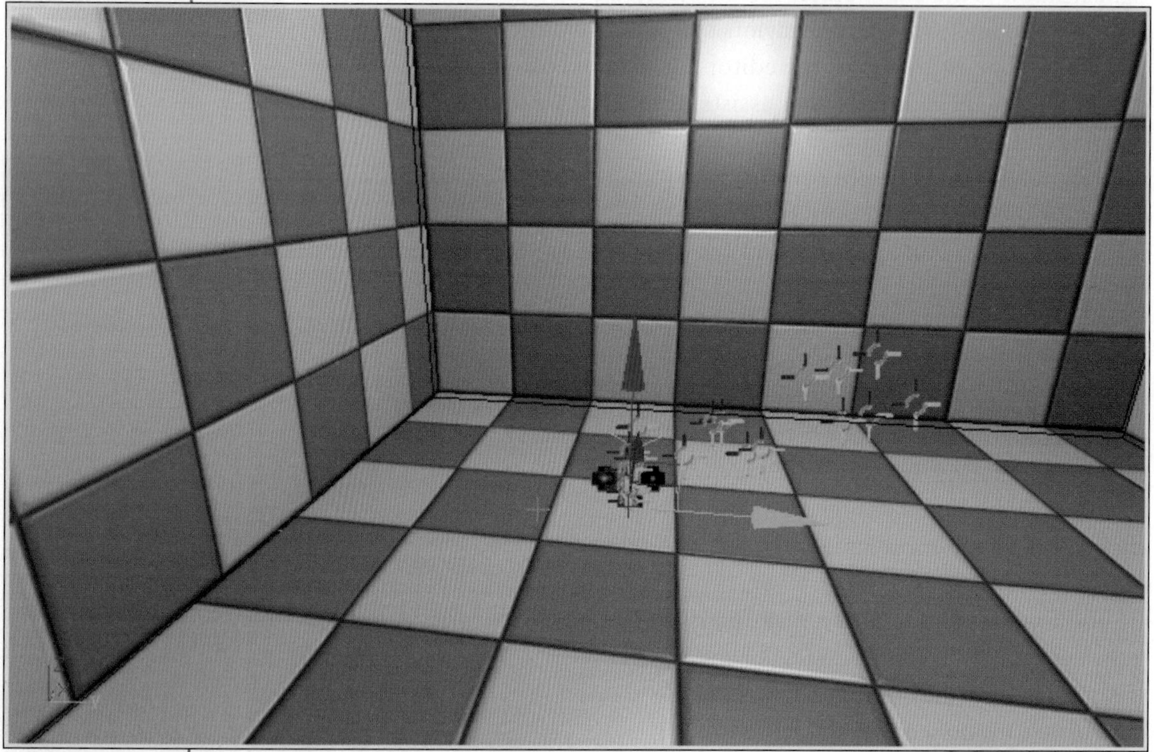

Figure 20.10

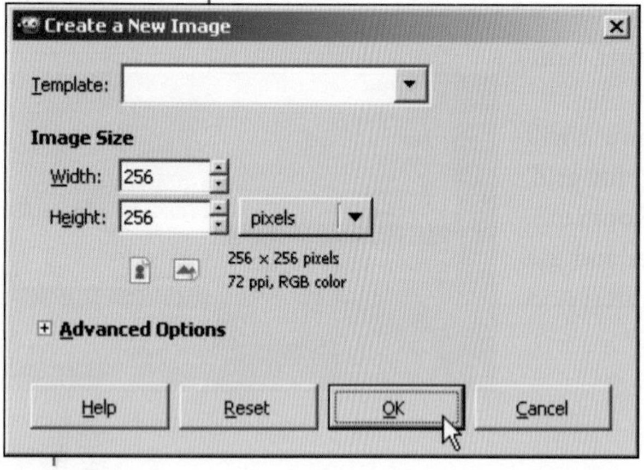

### Particle Texture, a Simple Sprite

Let's switch to using GIMP and create a texture for our particle. Right now we're looking at a strange circle with sticks coming out of it. Again, we'll stick to the basics to keep this chapter from becoming too big.

Create a new image; we're going to use a fairly small image, one that has 256 × 256 pixels [Figure 20.10]. We're planning on letting Unreal Engine tint the sprite with color, so we're going to create a white-on-black texture.

Figure 20.11

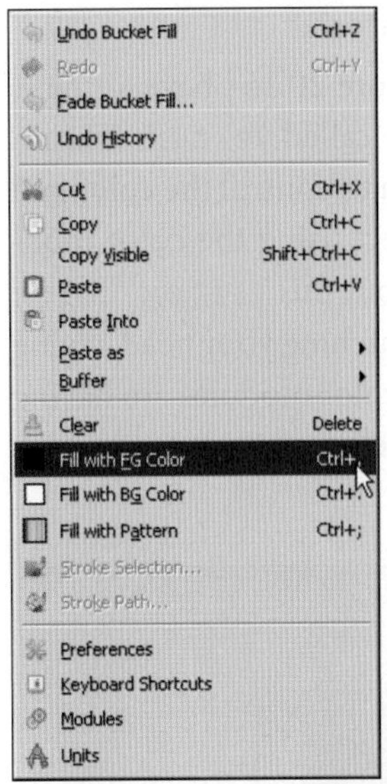


Figure 20.12

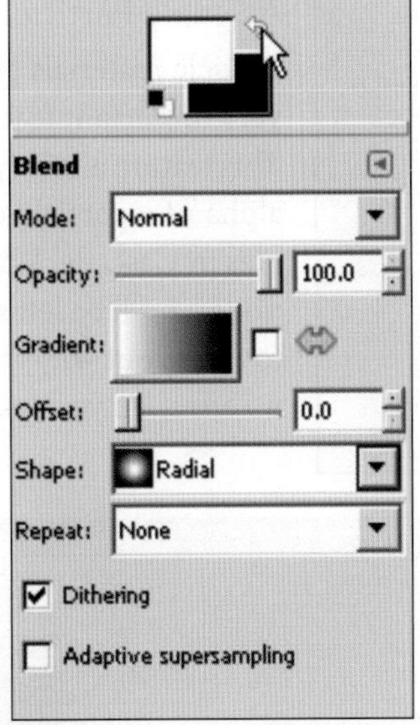


Figure 20.13

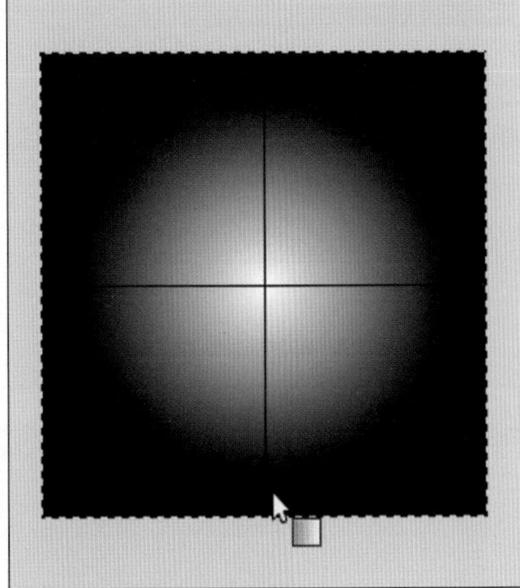

Fill the default canvas with Black [Figure 20.11].

Swap the foreground color with the background color and then change the shape of the gradient tool to Radial [Figure 20.12].

You might want to turn on snap-to-grid to ensure that your sprite is centered on the texture. Here the grid is showing—the actual texture does not have the two black lines crossing through it.

We're going to save this in the Effects folder and we're going to name it "Spark.tga" [Figure 20.14]. That's all we're going to do in GIMP for now.

Figure 20.14

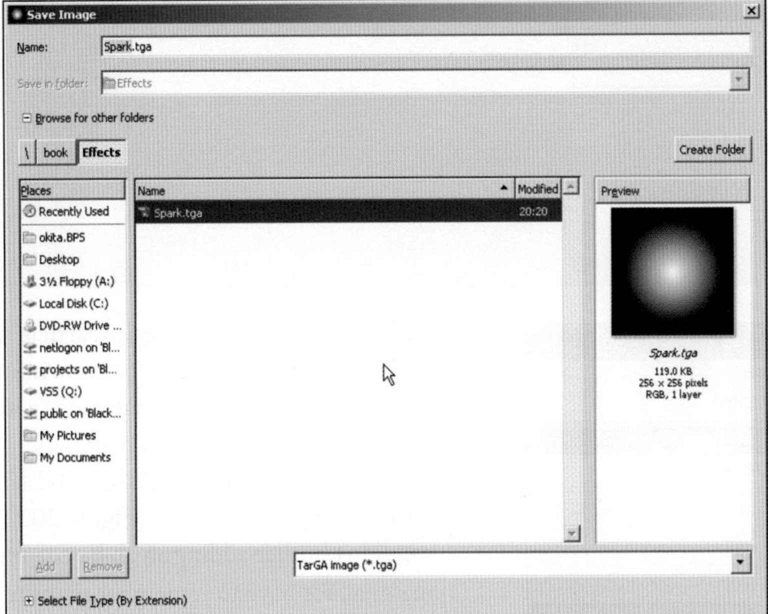

Figure 20.15

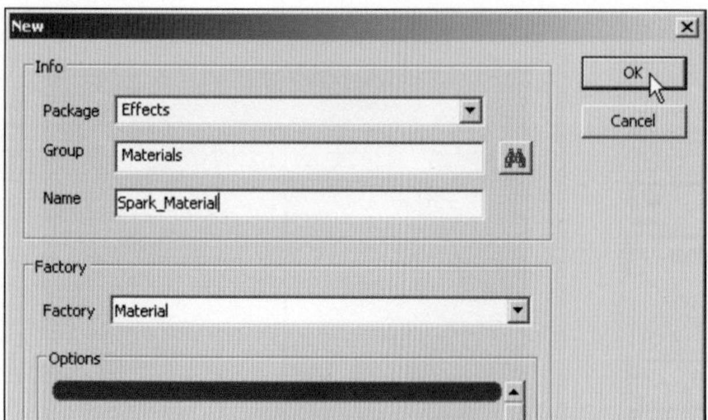


## A Simple Particle Material

Particle materials [Figure 20.15] have a single, very important feature called `vertex color`. This feature allows you to control the color and alpha of a particle effect using the color modules in Cascade. Without this `vertex color` node, you'll be left scratching your head, trying to figure out why the color modules are having no effect on your particle system.

Figure 20.16

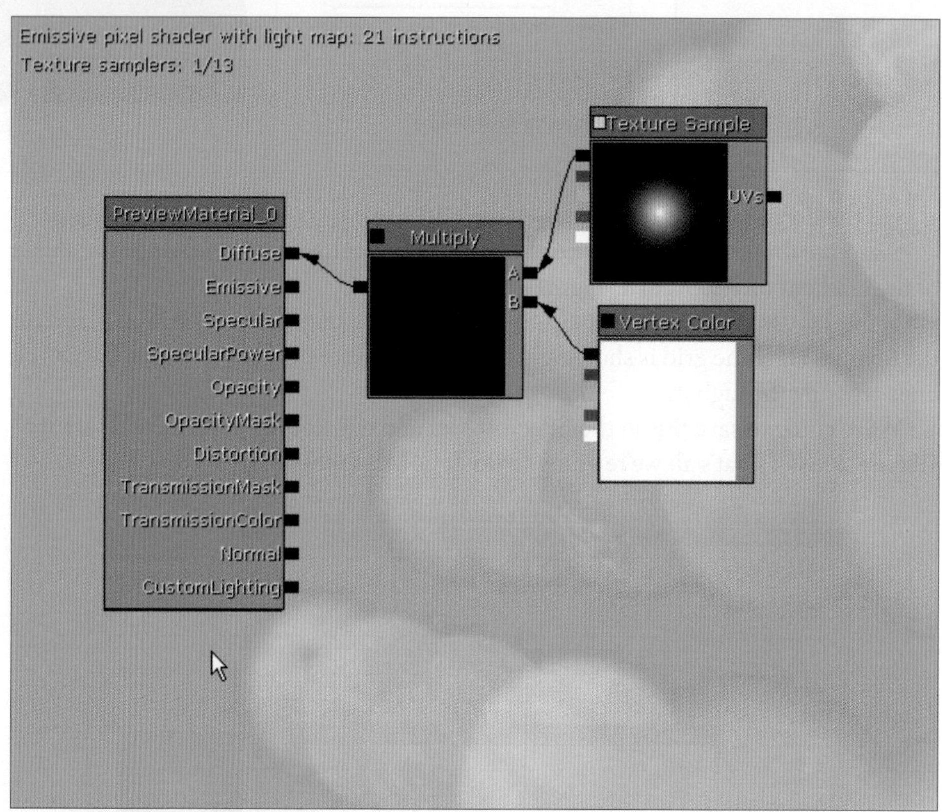


Figure 20.17

| Material | |
|---|---|
| PhysMaterial | None |
| OpacityMaskClipValue | 0.333300 |
| **BlendMode** | BLEND_Additive |
| LightingModel | MLM_Phong |
| TwoSided | ☐ |
| bDisableDepthTest | ☐ |
| Wireframe | ☐ |
| FallbackMaterial | None |

This is what your basic particle material looks like [Figure 20.16]. For more information on creating and editing materials, you should refer to the art chapters on materials.

The material node should have its BlendMode set to `Blend_Additive` [Figure 20.17]. Since we didn't bother adding an alpha channel to our material, we have to remember that the outside

Figure 20.18

| Usage | |
|---|---|
| bUsedAsLightFunction | ☐ |
| bUsedWithFogVolumes | ☐ |
| bUsedAsSpecialEngineMaterial | ☐ |
| bUsedWithSkeletalMesh | ☐ |
| **bUsedWithParticleSprites** | ☑ |
| bUsedWithBeamTrails | ☐ |
| bUsedWithParticleSubUV | ☐ |
| bUsedWithFoliage | ☐ |
| bUsedWithSpeedTree | ☐ |
| bUsedWithStaticLighting | ☑ |

Figure 20.19

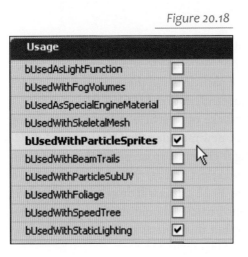

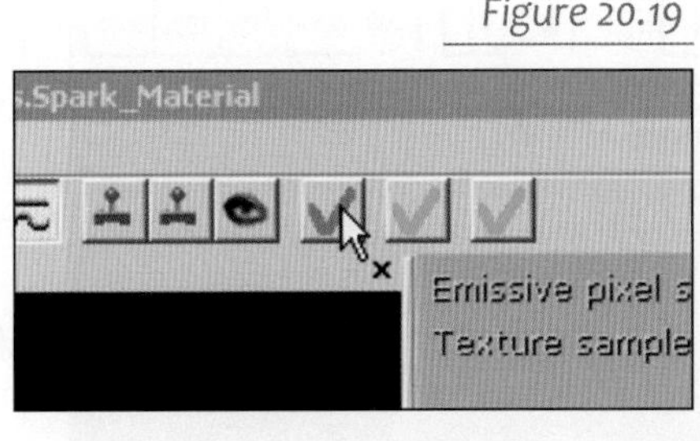


of the texture is black and the inside is white [the Texture Sample of Figure 20.16]. Additive materials will react only by adding color to the scene, dark colors and black colors are not added to the scene and will remain invisible.

The Usage dialog has a check box called `bUsedWithParticleSprites` [Figure 20.18]. This is usually automatically activated any time a material is assigned to a particle system, but it's a good idea to know where this check box is if a material seems to be incorrectly displayed later on.

The last steps are to rebuild the particle material and cache its shader data [Figure 20.19].

## Cascade: Adding Detail

In the Cascade tool, select the top-most particle node [Figure 20.20]. A couple of basic properties are listed for the particle system. We're going to replace the previous material with our new `Spark_Material` in the Material slot.

| EmitterName | Particle Emitter |
|---|---|
| ▼ RequiredModule | ParticleModuleRequired'Effects.Particles.TaoBlast:ParticleMod |
| Material | Material'Effects.Materials.Spark_Material' |
| ScreenAlignment | PSA_Square |
| ParticleBurstMethod | EPBM_Instant |
| InterpolationMethod | PSUVIM_None |
| bUseLocalSpace | ☐ |

Figure 20.20

Figure 20.21

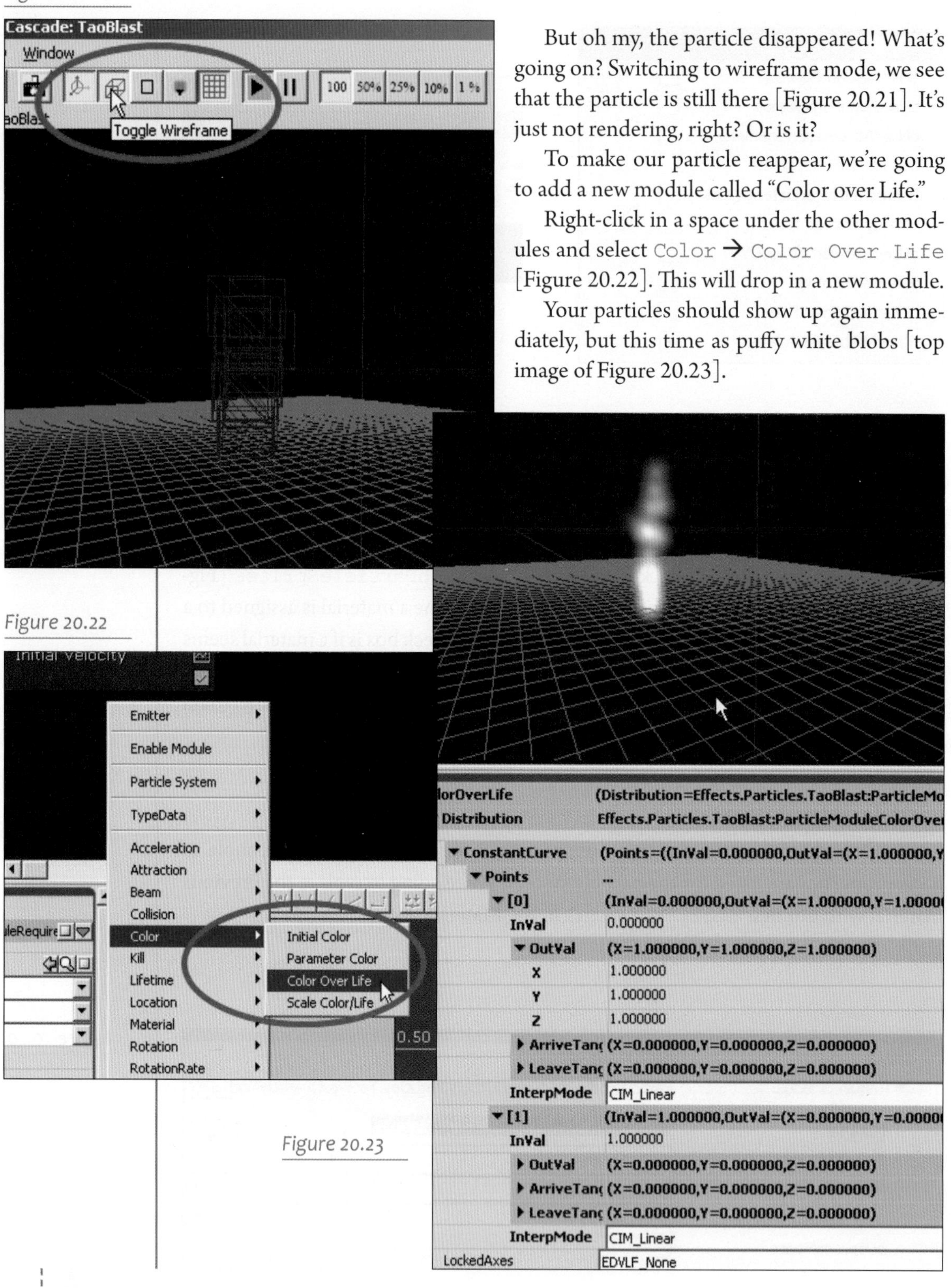


But oh my, the particle disappeared! What's going on? Switching to wireframe mode, we see that the particle is still there [Figure 20.21]. It's just not rendering, right? Or is it?

To make our particle reappear, we're going to add a new module called "Color over Life."

Right-click in a space under the other modules and select `Color` → `Color Over Life` [Figure 20.22]. This will drop in a new module.

Your particles should show up again immediately, but this time as puffy white blobs [top image of Figure 20.23].

Figure 20.22

Figure 20.23

Figure 20.24

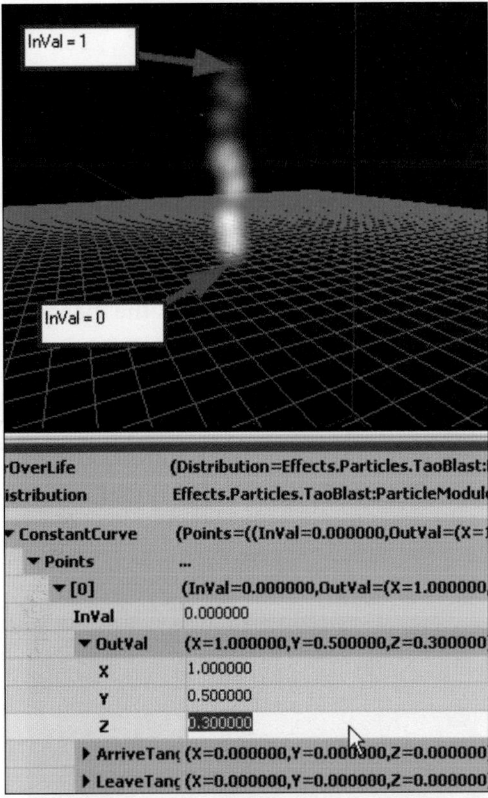


Figure 20.25

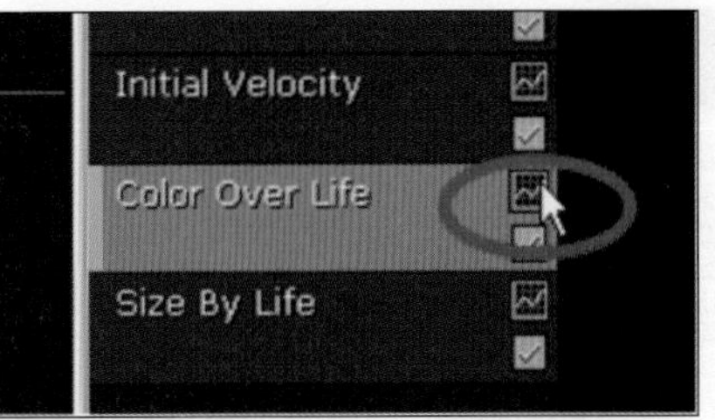


Figure 20.26

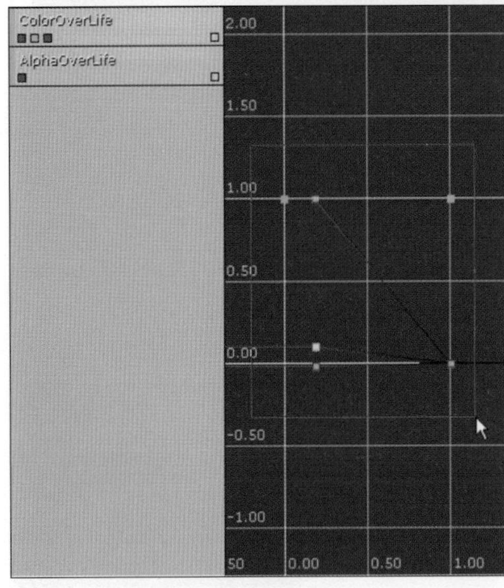


Expand the properties of the color-over-life module, and then expand the first OutVal roll-out menu [bottom image of Figure 20.23].

Make some modifications to the numbers in the OutVal fields [Figure 20.24]. The first thing you'll notice is that these numbers are not actually X, Y, and Z coordinates. They're mapped to red, green, and blue values, respectively, for our particle. The Points field refers to a graph. The InVal of 0 refers to the time of birth (creation) of the particle. The InVal on the second parameter is 1 [see Figure 20.23], which is the time that the particle's life ends. The OutVal of the first property is the starting RGB color for the sprite. The OutVal of the second parameter is the final RGB color for the sprite. In our example, the final color is 0,0,0 or black, which means our particle system fades as the particle's life reaches 1.

If you'd like to see what the point graph looks like, click on the graph icon on the module [Figure 20.25]. This will add the color-over-life's curves to the graph window on the lower right [Figure 20.26].

Using CTRL+ALT+LMB, you can box-select the various nodes in the graph editor (the box is shown in red) and change the curve's tension.

Figure 20.27

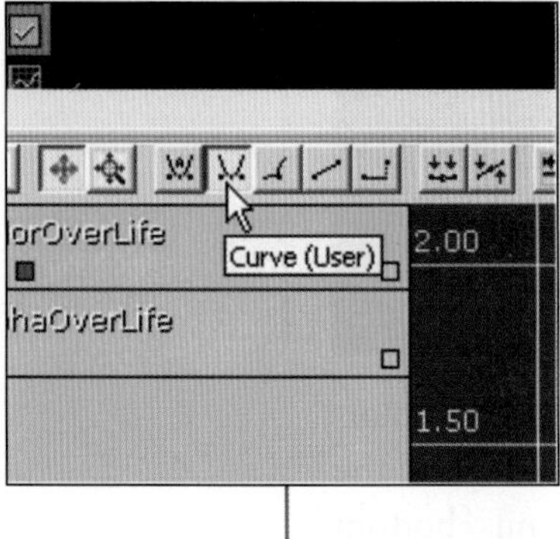


Setting the curve to User [Figure 20.27], the transition from a reddish color to black will be smooth [Figure 20.28].

Next, select the Initial Velocity module and set the properties to generate a particle system whose width is larger than what we had previously. We may choose the starting angles for the particles when they are emitted by the particle emitter [Figure 20.29].

The X- and Y-values are the angles at which the particles are emitted. The Z-value is the speed at which they are emitted. By fiddling with these parameters, you can change the behavior dramatically.

Our TaoBlast will be used as a muzzle flash for the TaoCannon. The cannon must emit a burst of particles rather than constantly stream the particles. We're going to change the EmitterLoops to 1 and set the constant SpawnRate to 0; then, in the BurstList field,

Figure 20.28

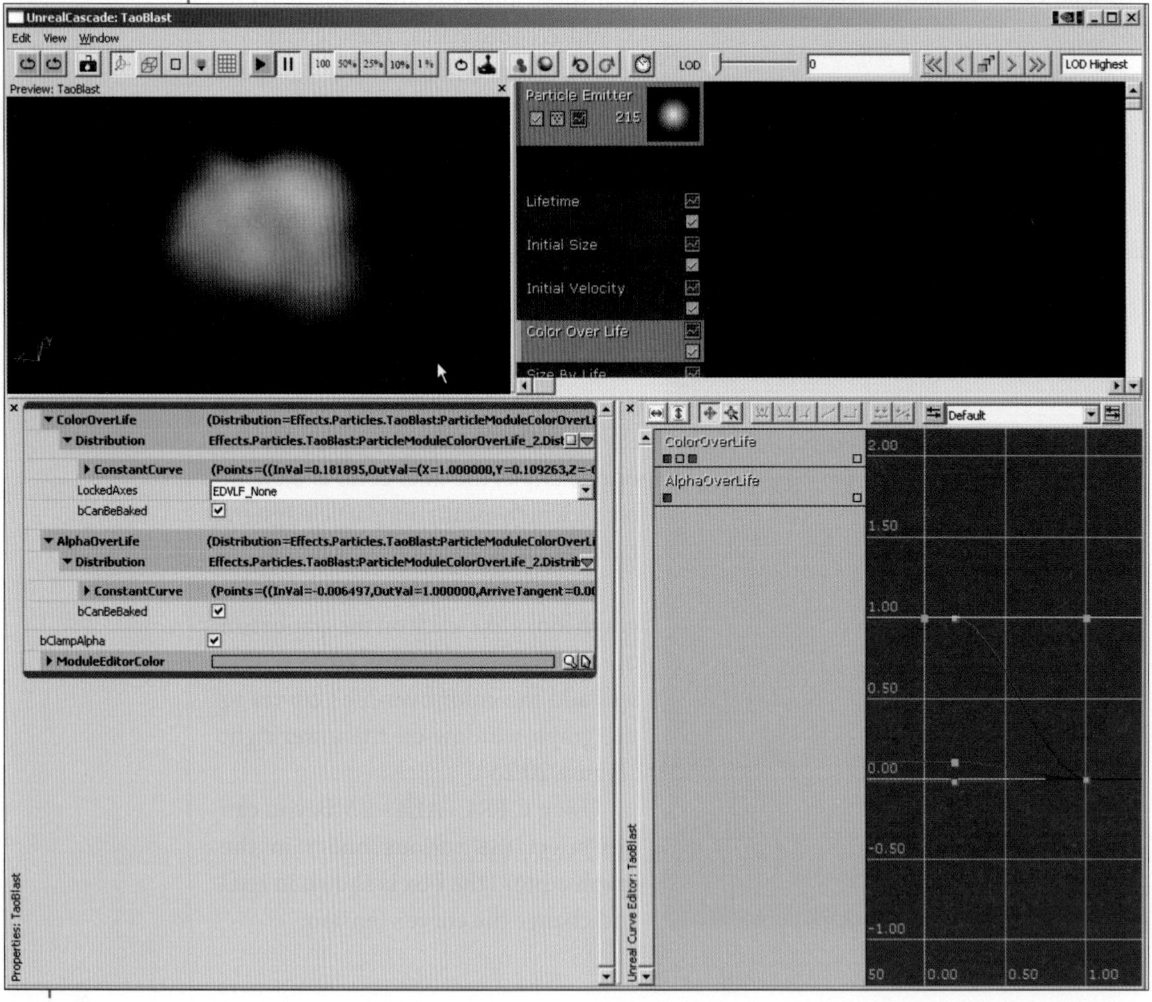

enter 200 in the Count number field [Figure 20.30]. Setting the EmitterLoops to 0 means that the emitter never dies and will constantly spawn new particles. The SpawnRate controls how many particles per second the emitter generates. Effectively, the BurstList is a controlled and timed event manager for the emitter. The Time field tells the burst at which point in the emitter's life it will release the number of particles specified by the Count number field.

Figure 20.29

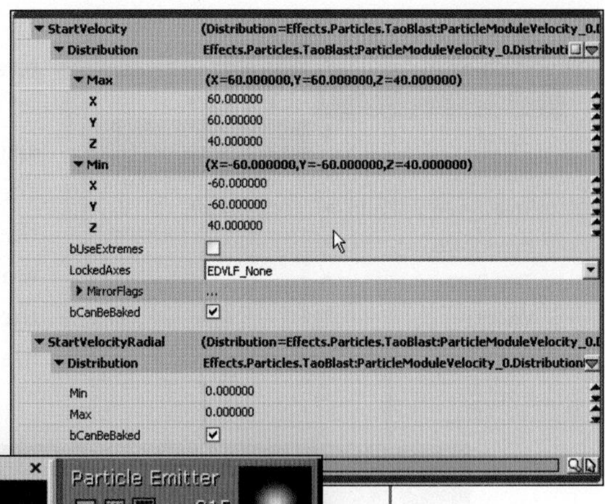

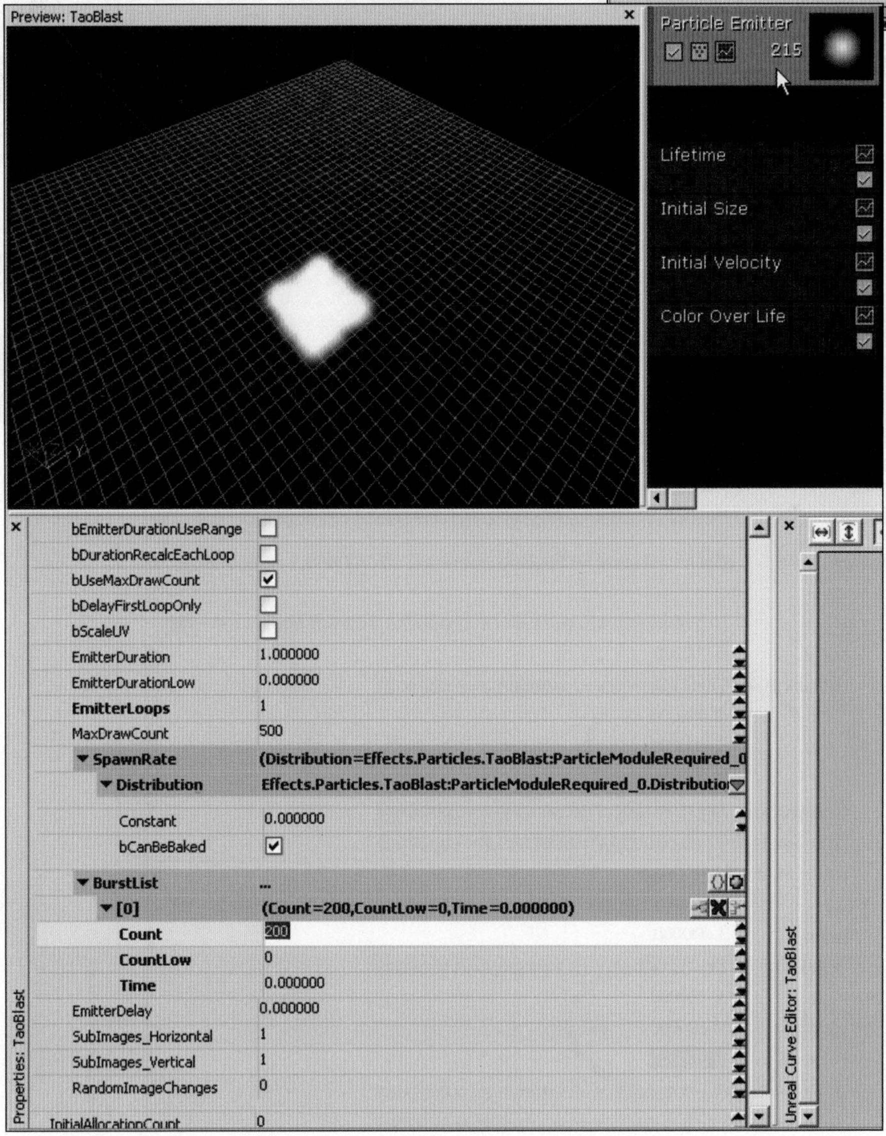

Figure 20.30

Figure 20.31

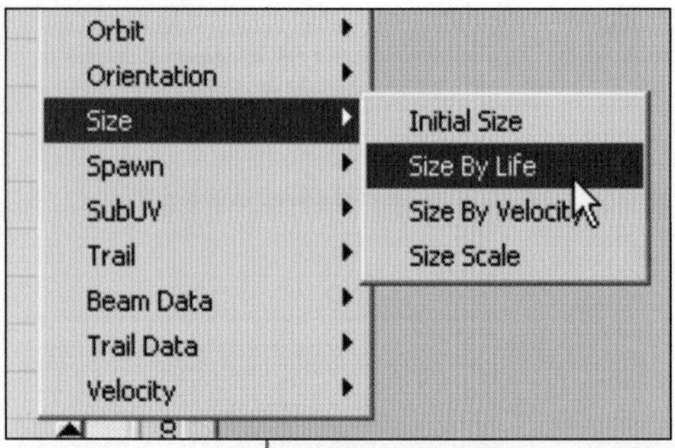


As a final touch to our burst of Tao Particles, we're going to add a Size By Life module [Figure 20.31].

The circled fields in Figure 20.32 show that the particle size starts at 2.0 and ends at 0.2, which means the particles shrink as they begin to die. It's important to remember that the second InVal must always be 1 for particles that have the word "Life" in the module. Remember: 0 is the time that the particle is created and 1 is the time that the particle's life ends.

Figure 20.32

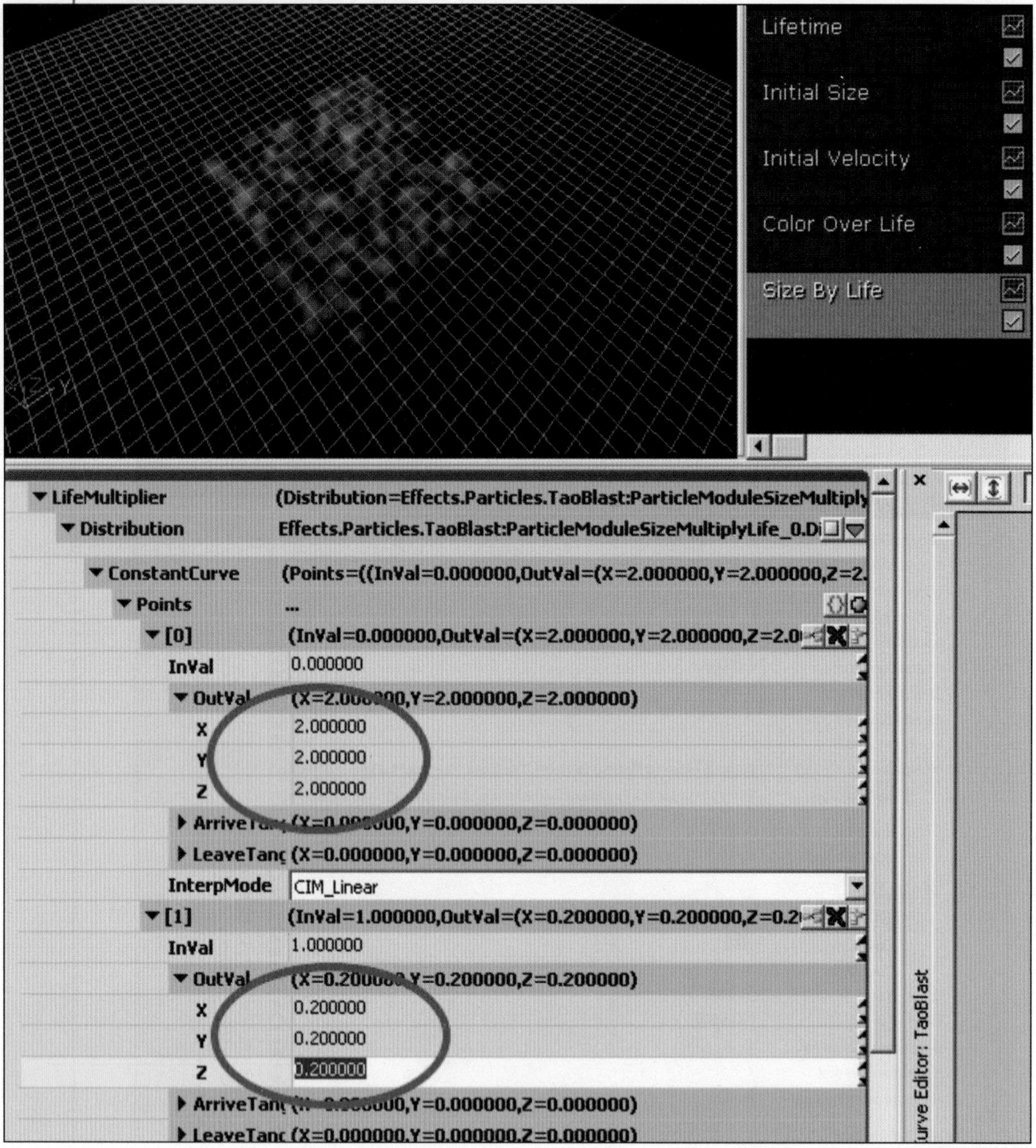

Figure 20.33

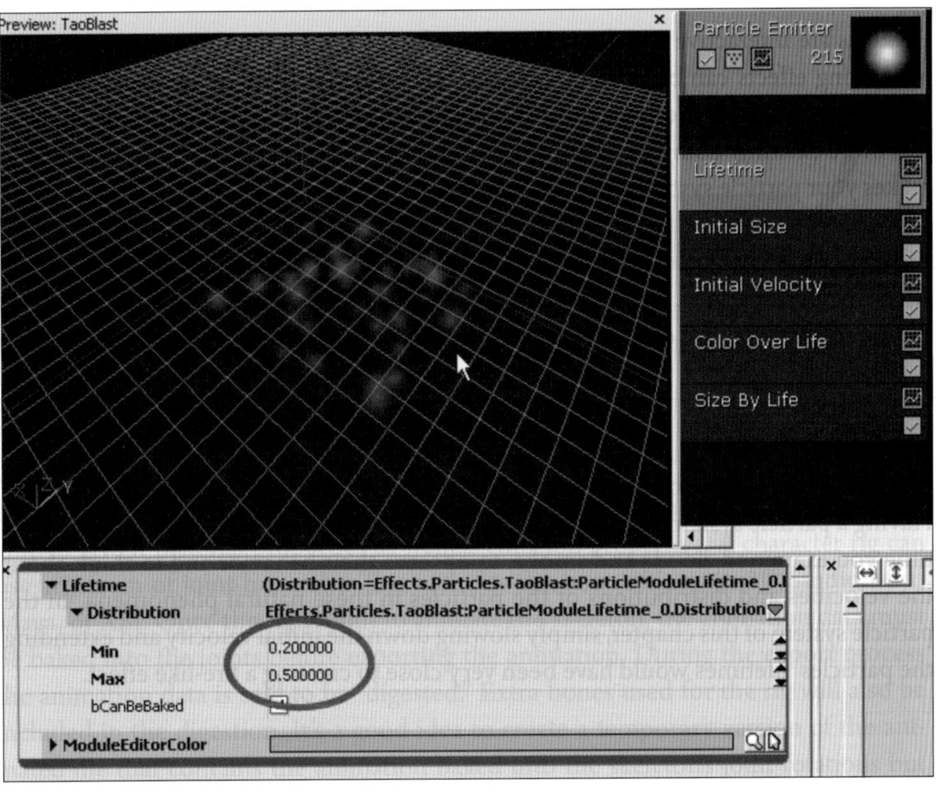


Figure 20.34

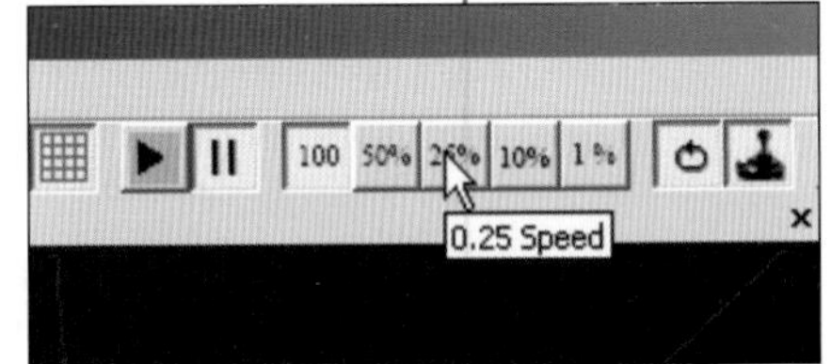


The Lifetime module allows us to change the life of the particle system [Figure 20.33]. Select the module and change the life of the TaoParticles to a range between 0.2 and 0.5. Notice that the particles still shrink and disappear smoothly.

To change the play-back speed of the particles, you can use the play-back speed buttons on Cascade's toolbar [Figure 20.34]. Once you've tuned your particle to look particularly cool, take a picture to update the particle's thumbnail in the Generic browser [Figure 20.35].

You should now have these three objects in your Effects.UPK [Figure 20.36].

Figure 20.35

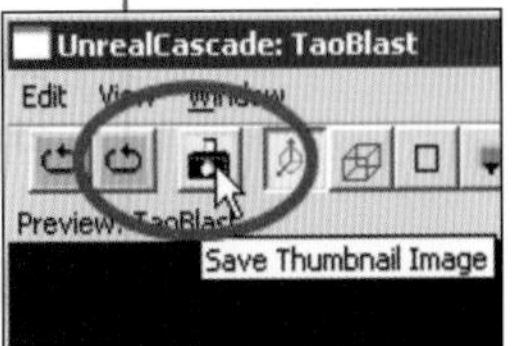


Figure 20.36

Figure 21.2

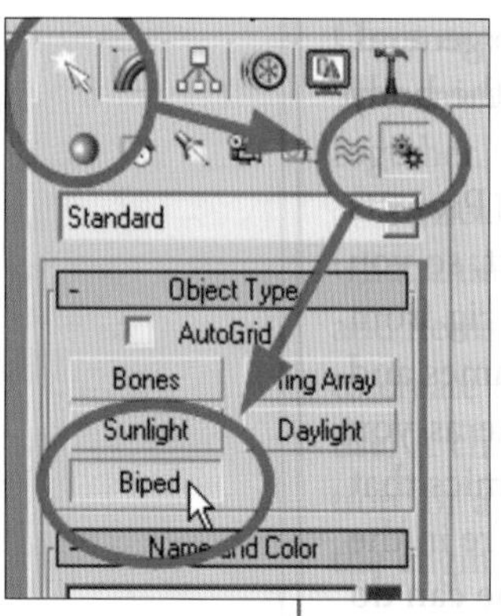


Figure 21.3

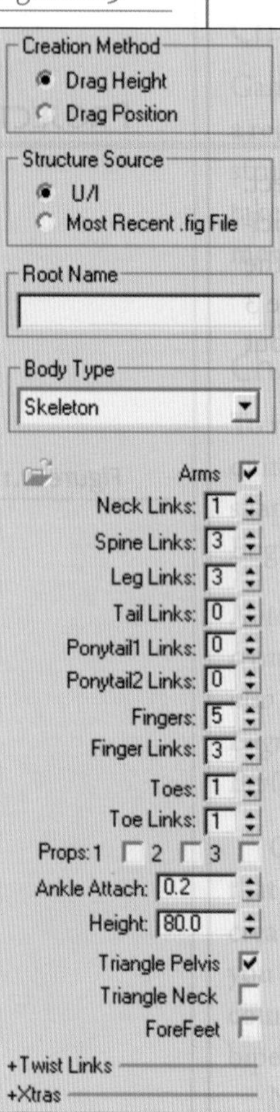


I've merged him in from a previous project. Next, we'll want to create a biped object.

*Note: Merging and importing into a fresh scene is a habit for my content pipeline; it is not necessary that you do the same. I prefer to have backup files of everything I do, thereby preserving older versions that I can go back to. In particular, the older versions allow me to try different ideas, and I don't have to worry about overwriting work that I want to keep.*

Select the Create tab [upper left red circle of Figure 21.2]. Select the Systems button [upper right red circle of Figure 21.2] and then select the Biped button [lower left red circle of Figure 21.2]. This will open the options dialog for our biped creation [Figure 21.3]. This is similar to bone creation when we rigged the item crate.

For our biped, we'll make a few changes to the default settings. Arms, yes, we'll want our biped to have arms. We'll need only one neck link, 3 spine links, 3 leg links, 5 fingers, 3 finger links, 1 toe, and 1 toe link. These joints will suffice for our Captain. He's wearing boots, so we don't need to worry about detailed toe rigging. And he's got a short torso, so we'll only need 3 spine links. For different characters, you'll want to adjust the number of joints and positions to match what you've built. However, I've found that having no more than 3 or 4 spine joints is sufficient for biped animation. A larger number of joints make adjusting the skin weights problematic, because the process can take quite a while to ensure smooth deformation as the character moves.

*Note: It's important to know that Unreal Engine can process no more than 255 joints. Any joints exceeding the limit will not import properly. Building a character with 255 joints is actually quite a chore. Adjusting and smoothing vertices for this many joints is quite a lot of work. For now, just keep things as simple as possible.*

To create a biped with the chosen settings, click near the origin of the scene and then drag vertically until our biped matches the height of the captain. You may also want to make sure that you're in Drag Height mode under the Creating Method roll-out menu.

Our biped should now be in place inside our Captain's mesh [Figure 21.4]. If you can imagine, the biped object is somewhat like our Captain's skeleton. One thing you might notice is that the biped is slightly offset from the center of the Captain's mesh. We'll adjust this so that the mesh and biped are centered on each other. This will make the skeleton a usable size. We'll be making a lot of adjustments to the biped structure, so don't worry yet about the proportions.

Figure 21.4

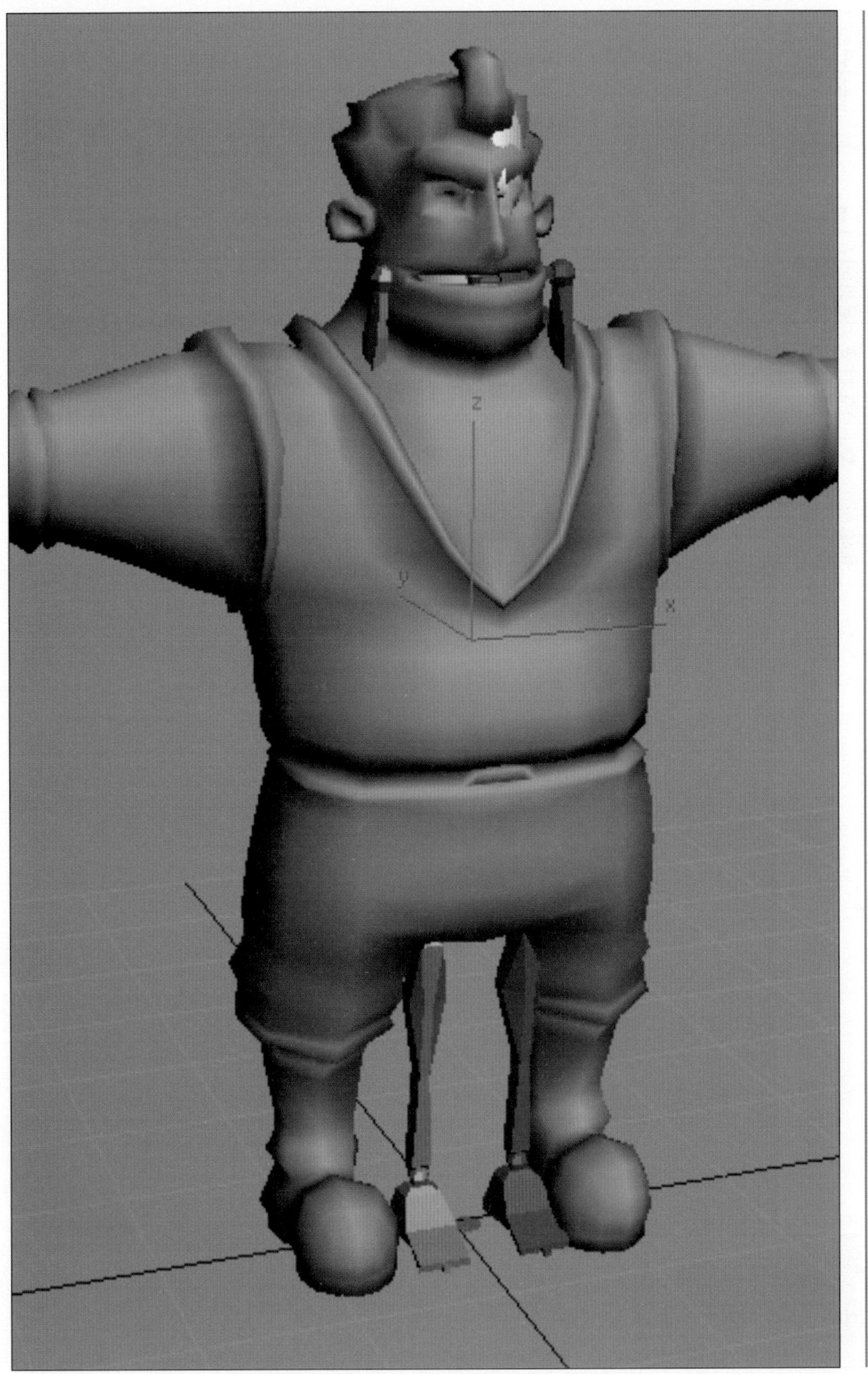

Figure 21.5

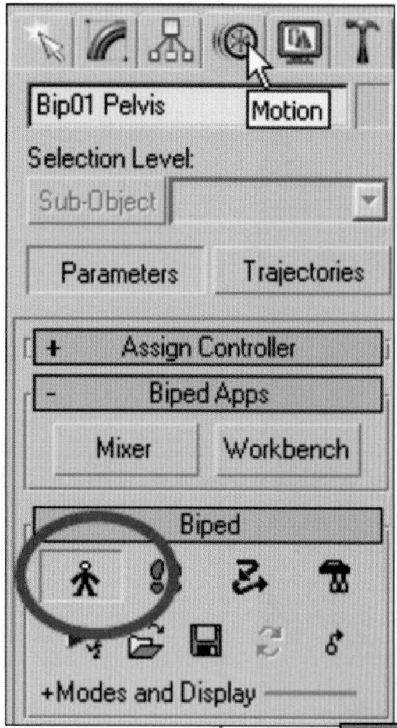


To adjust the biped, select the Motion tab and then click on the Figure Mode button [Figure 21.5]. It is important to edit the biped in Figure Mode; otherwise, editing the biped will tell Character Studio that you're animating him rather than changing his base proportions. While in Figure Mode, we can change the proportions of our biped to match our character. Select the small diamond shape in the middle of the pelvis [Figure 21.6], which is the character's center of gravity. You may select this to move the biped's entire structure at once.

Set the X and Y to 0 [Figure 21.7].

To adjust the Z, we'll switch to wireframe mode and drag the pivot of the biped to the character's center of gravity [Figure 21.8].

Matching the biped's pivot with the mesh's center of gravity is important to build the character correctly. The hips need to be matched on the Z-axis. When the mesh was built, the center of gravity was centered at the origin. It is important to remember where the character's root is to be located relative to the origin.

Figure 21.6

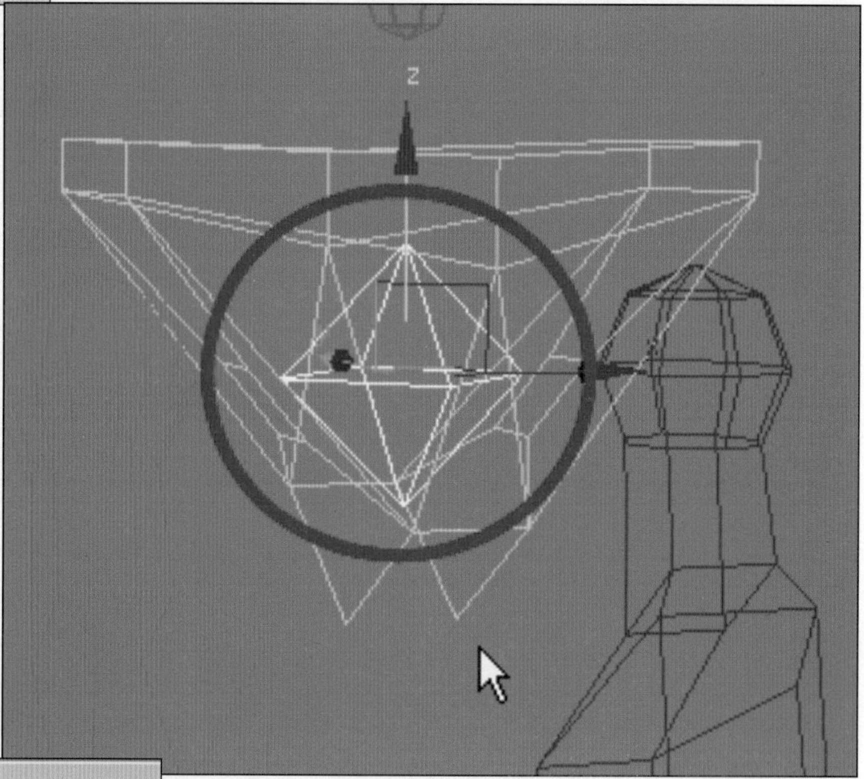

Figure 21.7

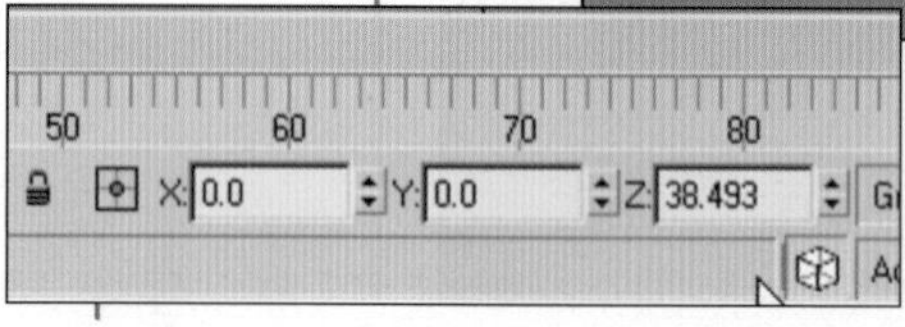

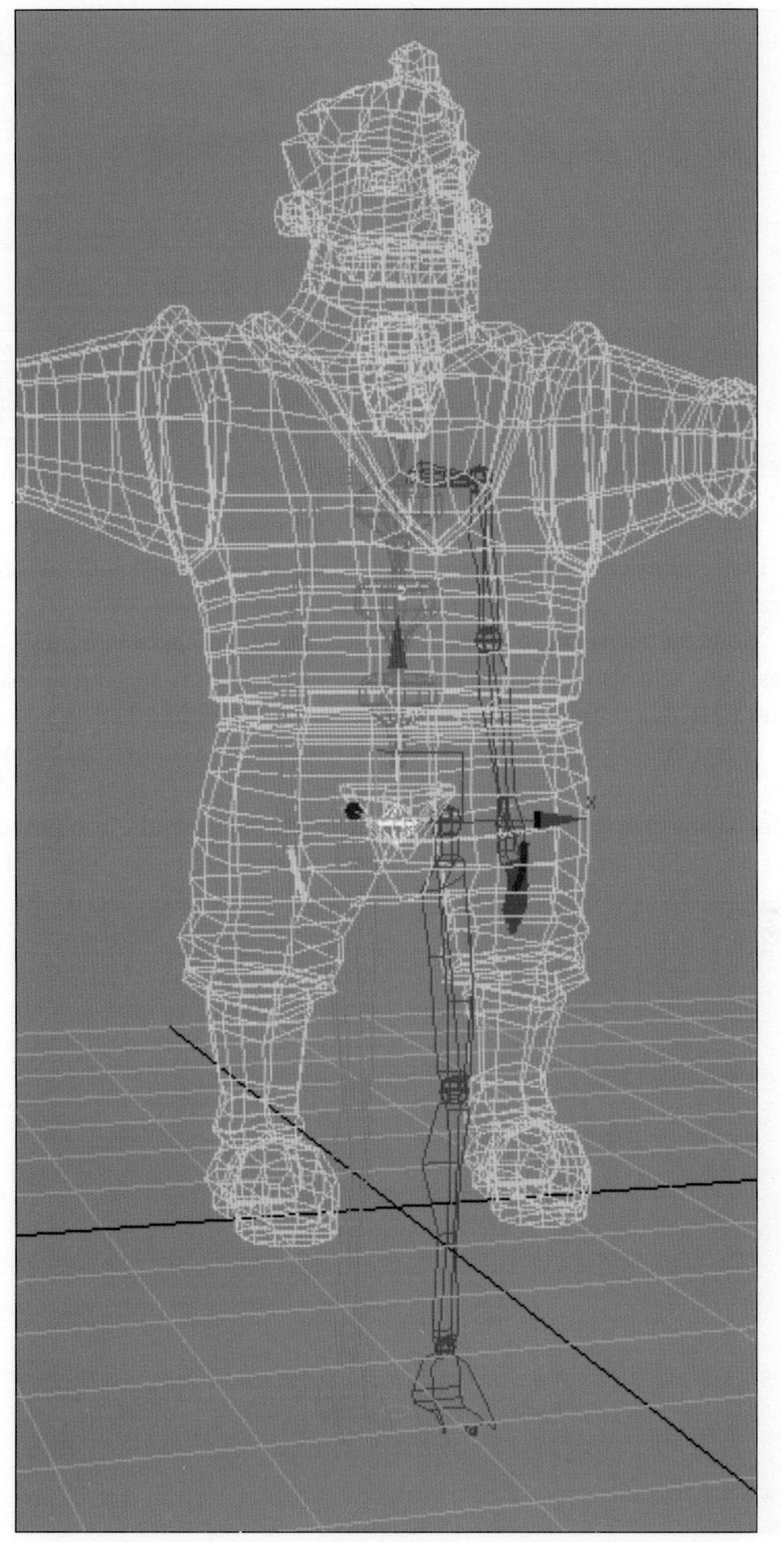

Figure 21.8

Figure 21.9

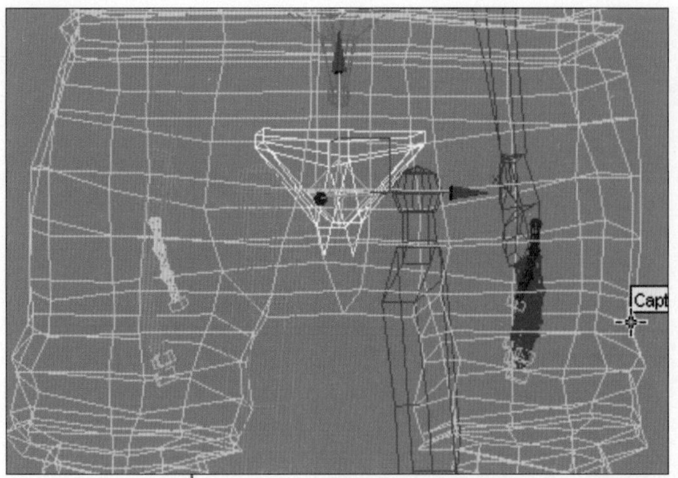


Figure 21.10

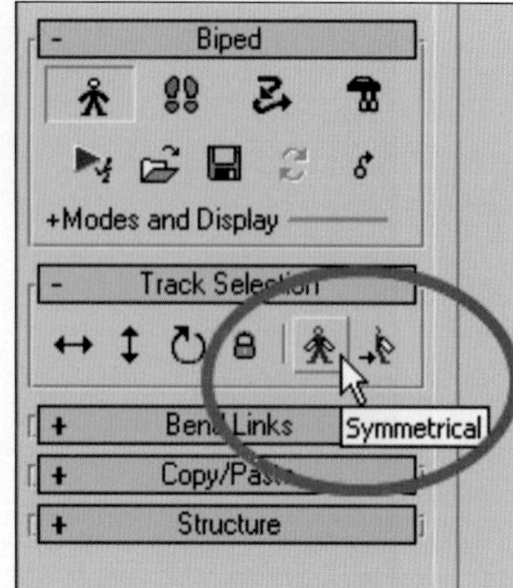


Figure 21.11

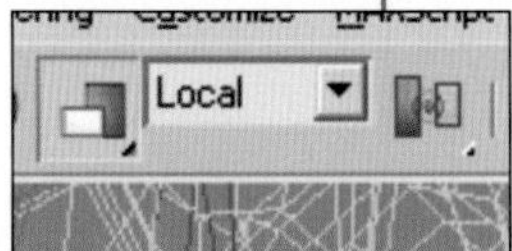


Select the pelvis object. This object is not to be confused with the center-of-gravity object, which is hiding inside of the pelvis [Figure 21.9].

Scale the pelvis out so the skeleton's legs match the character's mesh. In most cases you will also need to scale the rest of the limbs to match the character's mesh. Here's a simple tool that helps save time [Figure 21.10].

Select the left thigh bone of the biped. Click on the Symmetrical button of the dialog. You can now scale both thighs at the same time. Here are a couple more tools that will help you modify the biped. First, change to the non-proportional scale tool. Second, change the transform orientation to Local [Figure 21.11].

Figure 21.12

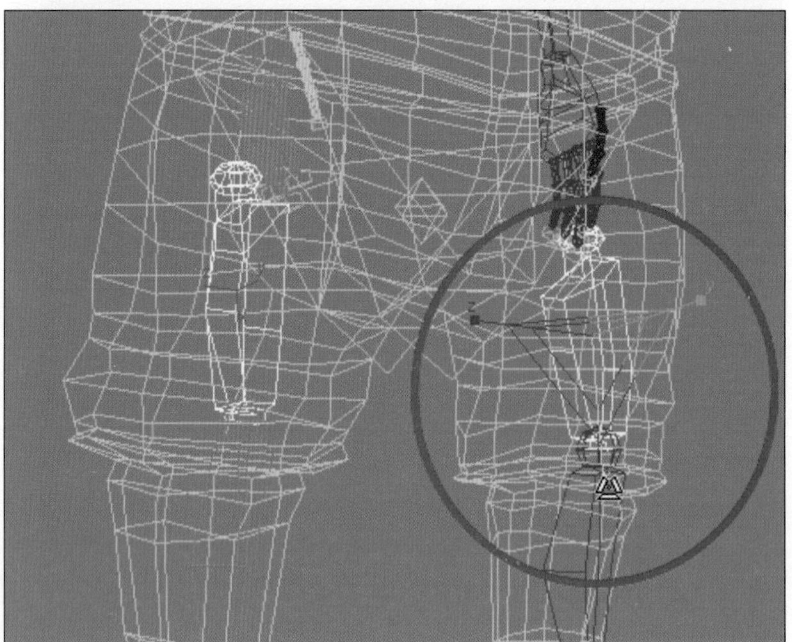

Now scaling the joints will be a bit simpler. 3D Studio Max will try to remember each tool's settings between local view screen and world space [Figure 21.12]. When you rotate joints into position and scale them to match your mesh, you'll want to make sure that they all move together. This mostly makes things easier when you're animating and pasting poses, which we'll discuss in a later project.

Don't forget to change the transformation space to Local for rotating joints.

By default, the rotation tool is set to View. If you rotate using this transformation space, both arms will rotate with each other [Figure 21.13], which is not so useful for positioning the model symmetrically.

Figure 21.13

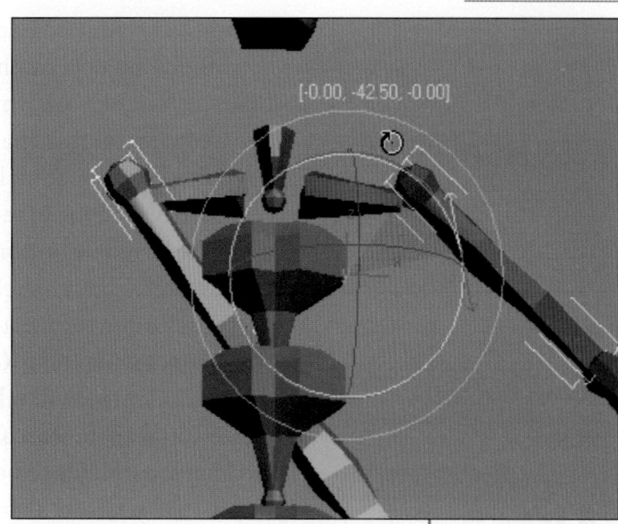


Figure 21.14

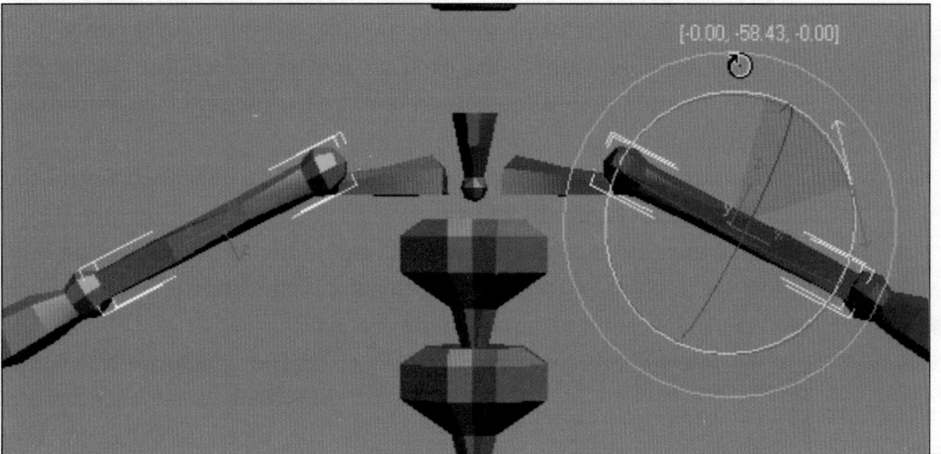


However, with the transformation space set to `local`, each arm will rotate properly in-place [Figure 21.14].

Use scale and rotate to adjust the rest of the skeletal joints, and then position them where they belong relative to the joints of the mesh. Once completed, you'll want to save your Character Studio biped object [Figure 21.15].

Figure 21.15

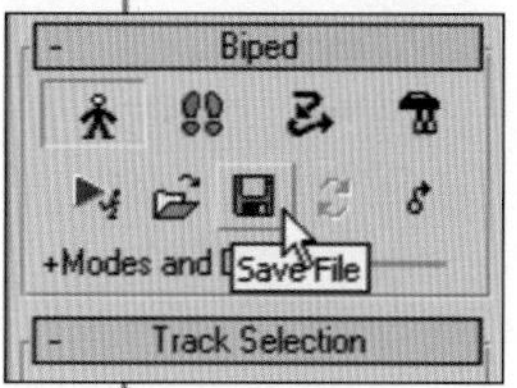


I've called my file "CaptainHadron_Tpose.fig" If you're having trouble positioning some of the joints in your biped, you can load my file into your biped to see how the joints should be placed. The Tpose.fig file is useful only for the character it was made for. It's important that you save a Tpose.fig file based on your character. The character rig is referred to as a biped or "bip." It is the base

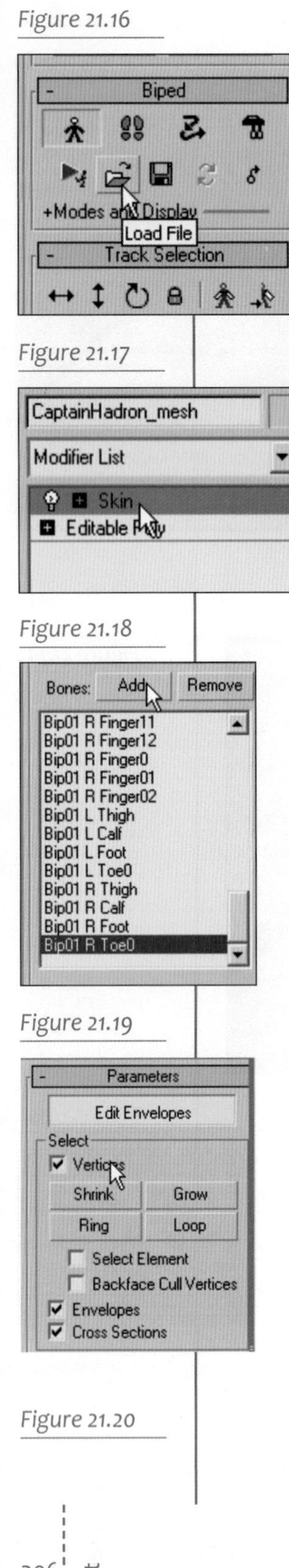


Figure 21.16

Figure 21.17

Figure 21.18

Figure 21.19

Figure 21.20

reference for your character's skeleton and contains joint positions and sizes. Biped objects can have different numbers of spine joints as well as different numbers of arms and legs for non-human characters. You can save a bip file for this character as CaptainHadron.bip. We'll be using the biped files for animation later on.

You may load the biped files using the Load File button, which is to the left of the Save File button [Figure 21.16].

Now we've built a skeleton to attach to our character's mesh. The FIG file is useful for several reasons. For whatever reason, if the scene loses some data, saving the FIG file will make things easier to recover. The animations in Unreal will rely on the biped's default pose and skeletal structure. If you want to start a new character mesh, you can create a new biped and load the FIG file to be used as your new mesh's skeletal structure. This means that you can share the previous characters' animations with the new character. As long as the skeletons line up, the animations will play properly in the engine without a hitch.

For this project, we'll use the skin modifier from the modifier list [Figure 21.17]. We're using the skin modifier for this project rather than physique, because Unreal doesn't have any way to import the muscle behavior that physique allows. Therefore, we'll omit any discussion about how physique works.

The skin modifier allows us to add those joints that will control the character mesh [Figure 21.18].

Click the Add button and select all the joints in the scene. The only object we don't need to include in this list is the "Bip01" object, which represents the center of gravity of the character.

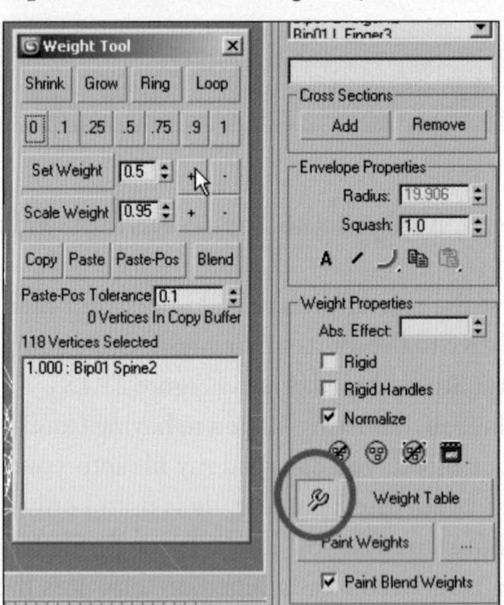


The automatic vertex weighting needs adjustment. The Biped tool has no way of knowing exactly how to deform your mesh, so you'll have to provide that information manually. To make these adjustments, activate the Edit Envelopes mode and turn on select the Vertices check-box to make your selections affect the models mesh [Figure 21.19].

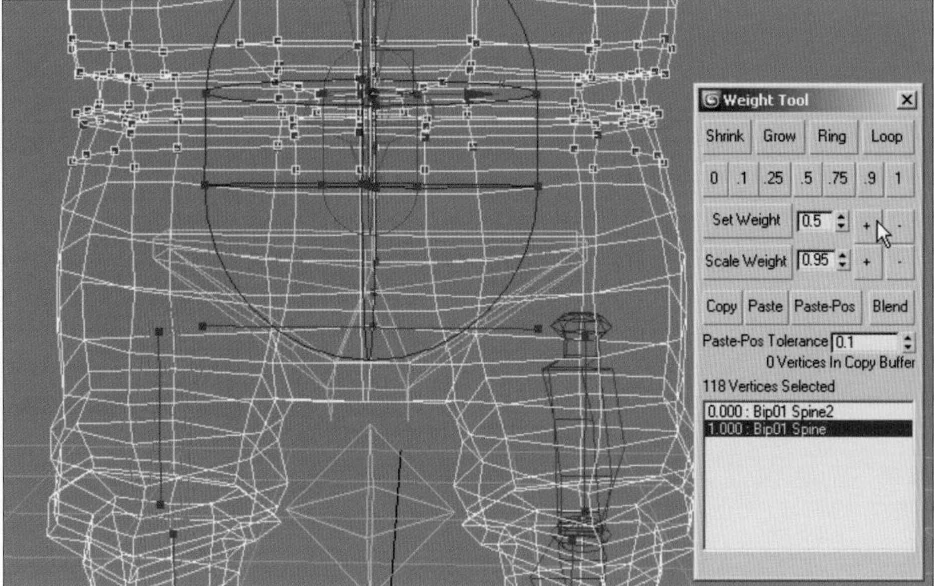


Figure 21.21

Next, select a group of vertices whose weights are to be modified. To modify the weights, open the Weight Tool located at the bottom of the modifier's options [Figure 21.20].

Modifying vertices can take quite some time. Selecting the vertices and then using the + button to set the weights is the best and most direct approach for assigning weights [Figure 21.21].

As you work, you'll want to test your skin weighting. Turn off the biped's Figure Mode before bending any of the joints.

At first, many of the vertices will be weighted like this [Figure 21.22], which is rough looking. The vertex weights will need a lot of adjustment to make the skinning look

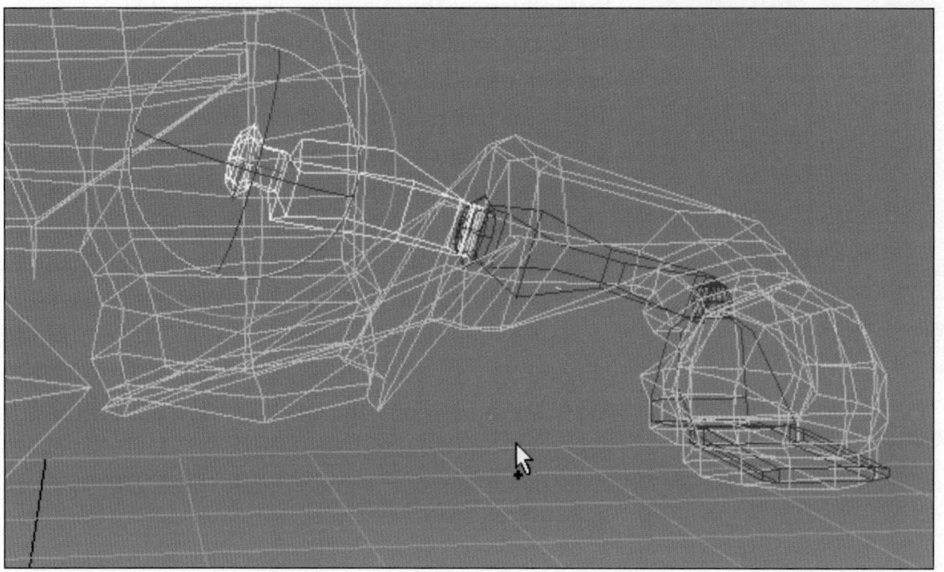

Figure 21.22

Figure 21.23

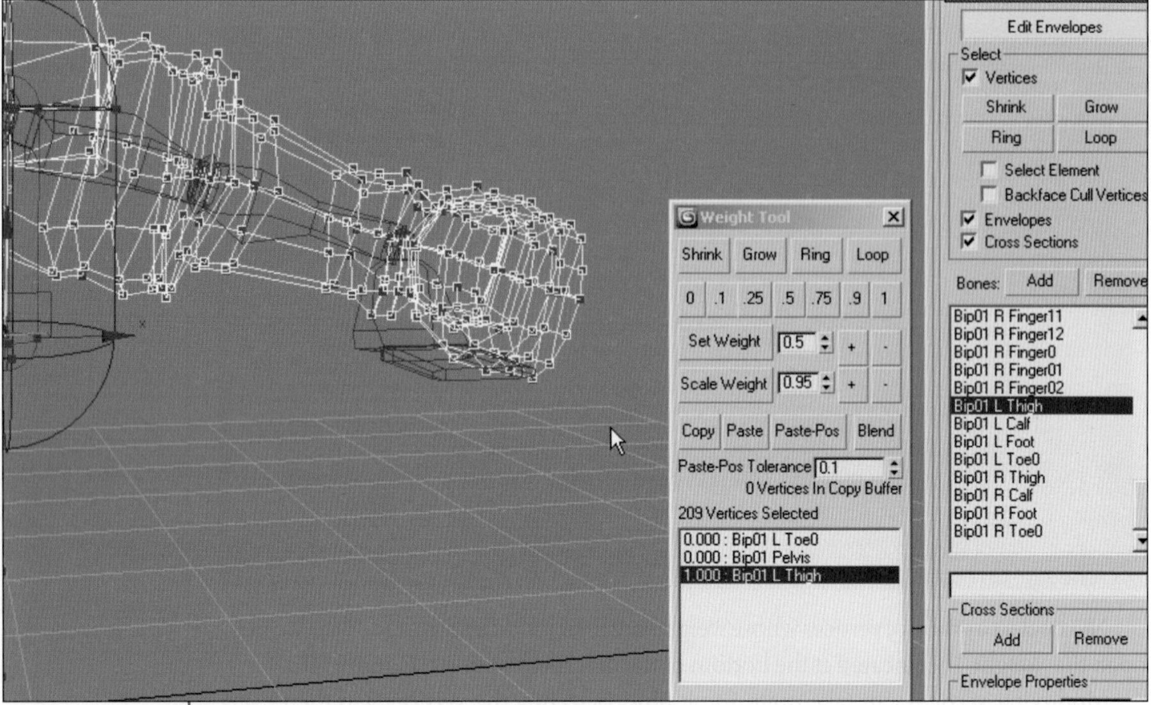


Figure 21.24

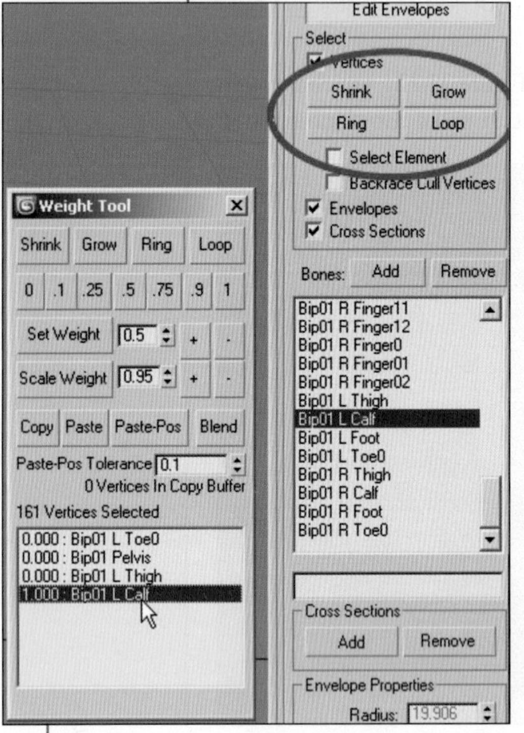


realistic. To correct this type of weighting problem, you'll want to select the vertices of the leg; then select the joint for which you need to assign weights to the vertices [Figure 21.23].

Use the Grow and Shrink buttons to change which vertices are selected, and then add weights to the joint that influences those vertices [Figure 21.24].

Next, shrink the selection again and weight the vertices that are influenced by the foot joint [Figure 21.25]. This is the first pass for weighting all of the vertices relative to the joints that influence them. Later, fine tuning is required to make the mesh deformations smooth.

Because of symmetry, we need only adjust the weights on one side of the character. We'll be able to mirror this information to the other side of the character.

Select Edit Envelopes and activate Mirror Mode [Figure 21.26]. We will use the Paste Blue to Green Verts button to copy the work we've done on the left side of the model to the right side.

Moving on, we should finely tune the model's deformations.

Figure 21.25

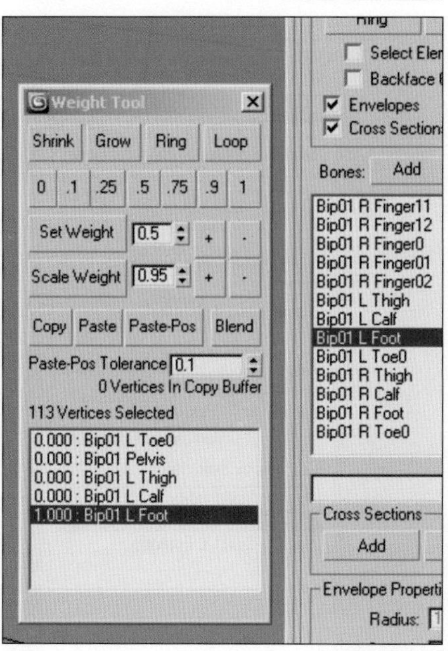


Figure 21.26

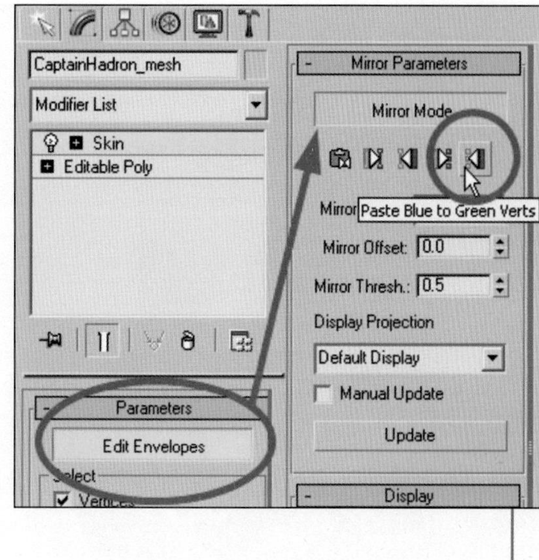


Figure 21.27

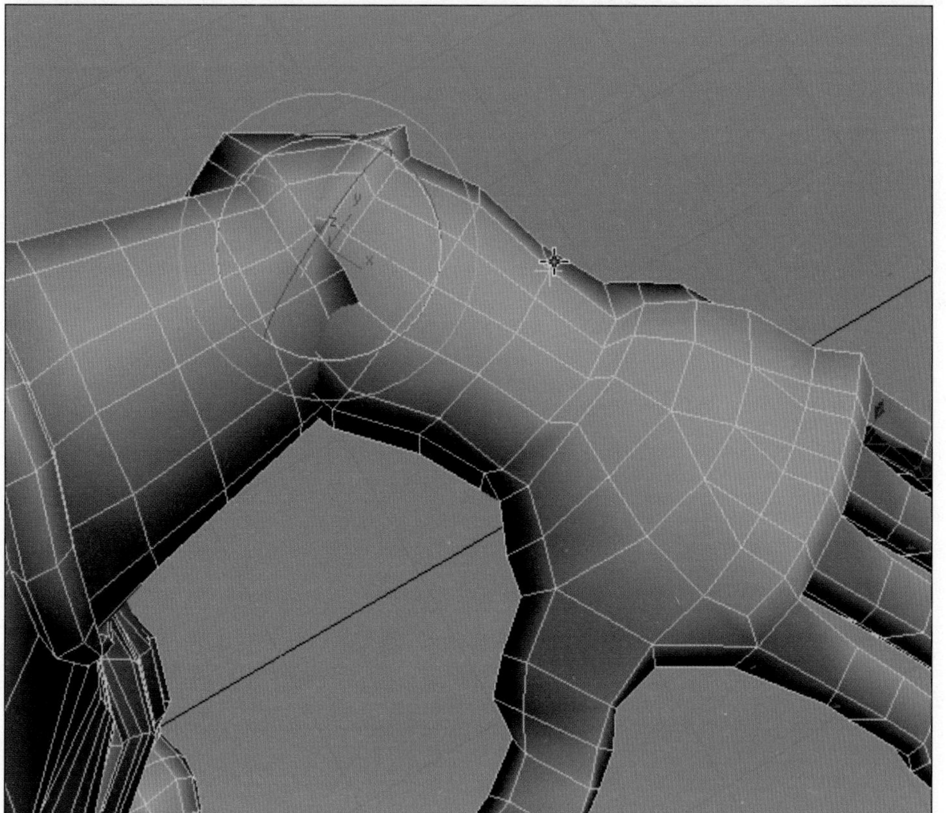

Figure 21.28

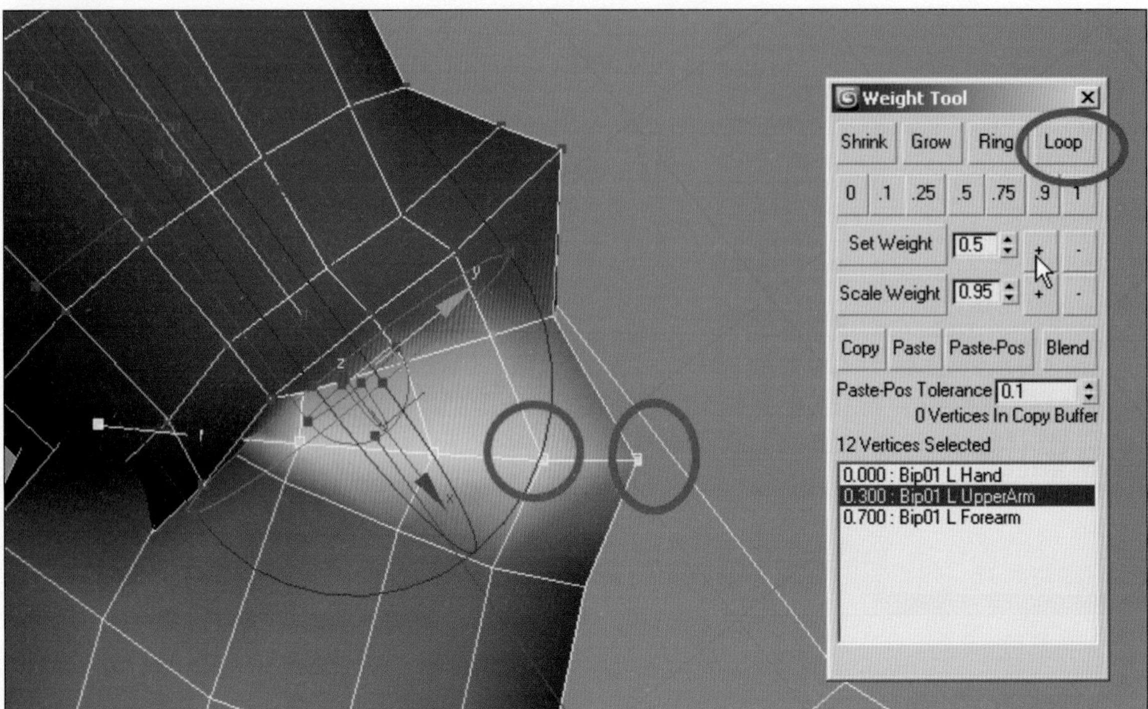


Figure 21.29

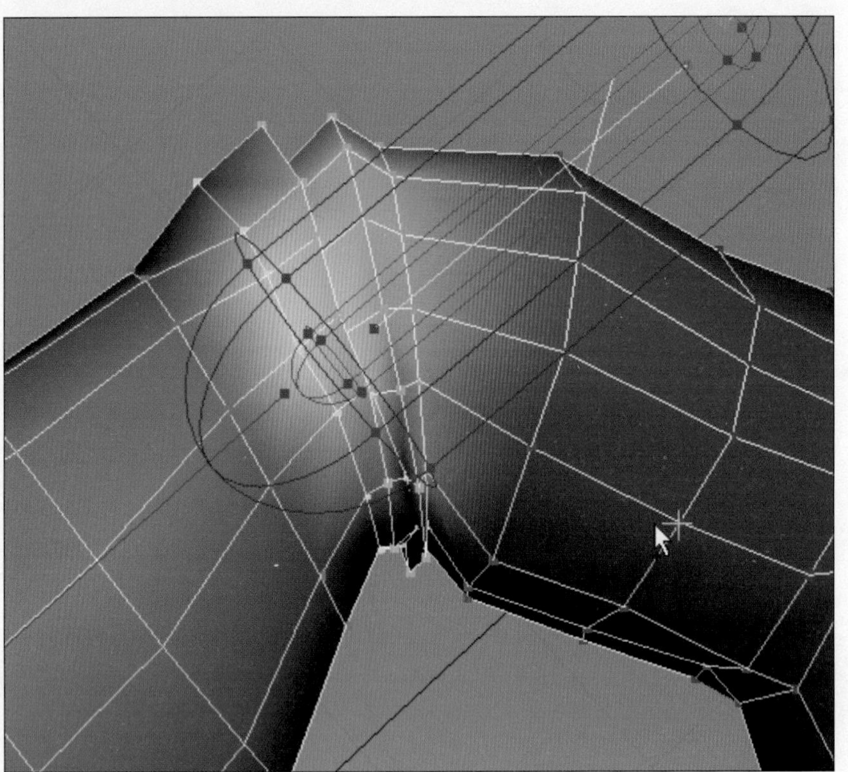

Figure 21.27 shows the elbow region on the left side of the character.

Select two vertices, say, the ones circled in Figure 21.28. Click on the Loop button on the Weight Tool dialog. Then use the + button to add weights to this loop of vertices until they are weighted approximately the same for both the UpperArm and the Forearm.

*Note: An edge loop (or "loop") is a series of edges that are connected and that create a loop around part of the mesh. In contrast, a ring is a series of edges that are not connected and that are nearly parallel to one another. Consequently, selecting an edge loop is different from selecting an edge ring. This is something you'll want to experiment with on your own to see how the behaviors differ.*

After spending a few minutes adjusting weights, we should come up with a deformation something like this [Figure 21.29]. Repeat the weighting process for each set of joints of the character. There are a few tools other than the Weight Tool that you can use for adjusting the weights on a character's mesh. 3D Studio Max's Weight Brush tool is similar to the tools found in other modeling packages, but may produce unreliable results. In the end, the Weight Tool is the only tool that gives me the most direct and accurate control over the weights for a character in 3D Studio Max.

You might have noticed that there are a lot of vertices with zero influence from a few joints assigned to them [Figure 21.30]. To eliminate these, scroll down the modifier's parameters and click on the Remove Zero Weights button [Figure 21.31].

This will clean up the Weight Tool's UI. Eliminating zero-valued weights is also important for the ActorX tool, because the tool cannot export a vertex that has been assigned more than four weights. Don't forget to save.

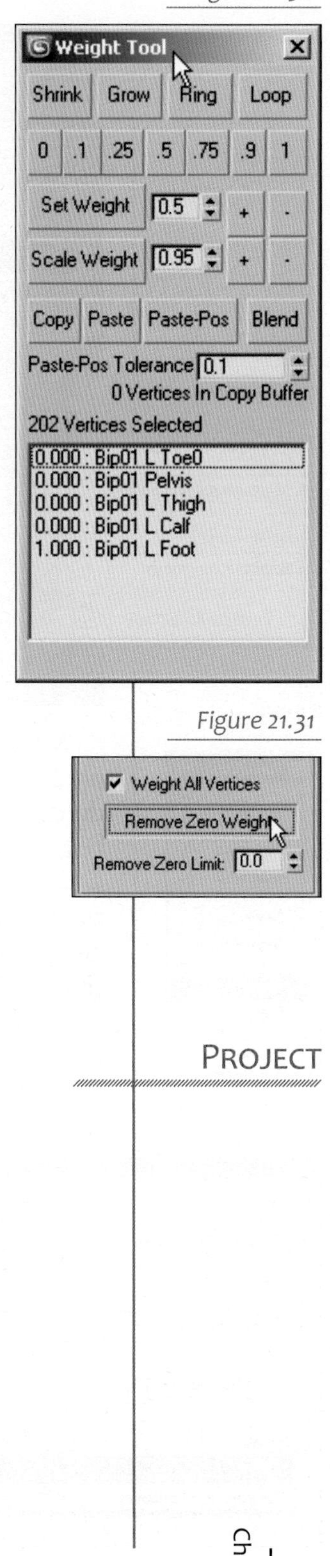


Figure 21.30

Figure 21.31



## Export and Setup in Unreal Engine

Now that we've got a completed character with a skeleton in 3D Studio Max, the next step is to get him into the Unreal Engine and set up his materials. In a previous project, we exported the skeletal mesh for an item crate using ActorX. Exporting a character is no different from exporting the item crate.

Before you export the character, make sure you've got his Tpose.bip file ready from the previous project. Load the FIG file. With the biped root node selected, click on the Figure Mode on the Motion tab. This will set the biped to the t-pose. Since it cannot be exported while in t-pose setting mode, now click the Figure Mode off. When the Figure Mode is off the figure will keep its pose and can be exported.

Figure 21.32

Figure 21.33

Figure 21.34

Make sure that the model is in his default T-pose before exporting him [Figure 21.32]; all of the animations created are based on deviations from this pose. Export the character mesh using ActorX. The process is the same as exporting a dynamic mesh [Figure 21.33].

Set your output folder to your work directory; this will be where your skeletal mesh and animations are saved. Set the mesh file name to "CaptainHadron_mesh" or to whatever you've named your character. Click on the `Save mesh/refpose` button, and your skeletal mesh file will be written to disk.

To import the mesh, open the Generic browser and select `File` → `Import` [Figure 21.34]. Navigate to your export directory, select the "CaptainHadron_mesh .psk," and select Open to see an import dialog [Figure 21.35].

Figure 21.35

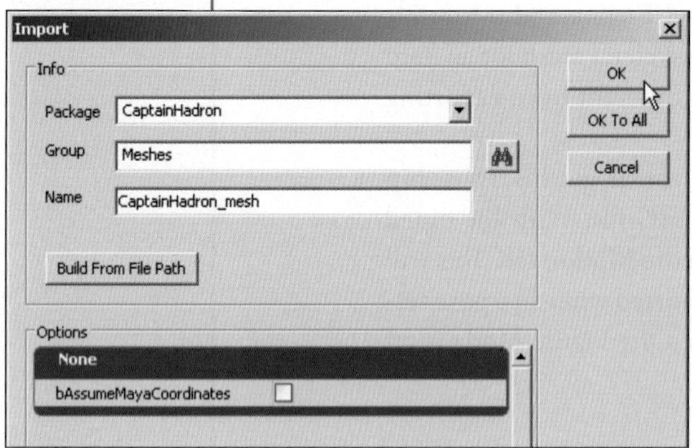


The dialog has some options for us to name the UPK file and to select the group to which the skeletal mesh is going to be saved. If you're going to use Maya for building characters, you'll need to click the `bAssumeMayaCoordinates`. Max uses a Z-up scene, whereas Maya uses Y-up. The only difference is that the character's orientation in one modeling package will be rotated relative to the orientation in the other modeling package.

Let's save the skeletal mesh into the "Meshes" group and name the UPK file "CaptainHadron." Click the OK button.

Before getting too far ahead, let's save the UPK file by right-clicking on the new CaptainHadron object in the browser. Save it to the custom-characters directory.

Next, we'll want to import the textures we created. The material assigned in 3D Studio Max will not be imported into our Unreal "CaptainHadron.upk." As in the previous projects, we'll need to rebuild a material after we import our textures.

With the CaptainHadron file selected, go to `File` → `Import` and select the CaptainHadron textures [Figure 21.36]. Remember that the normal map needs to be imported with the `TC_Normalmap` option [Figure 21.37], and the diffuse and specular maps need to be imported with the TC_Default compression options. Import the textures and put them into a Textures group in the "CaptainHadron.upk" file.

Figure 21.36

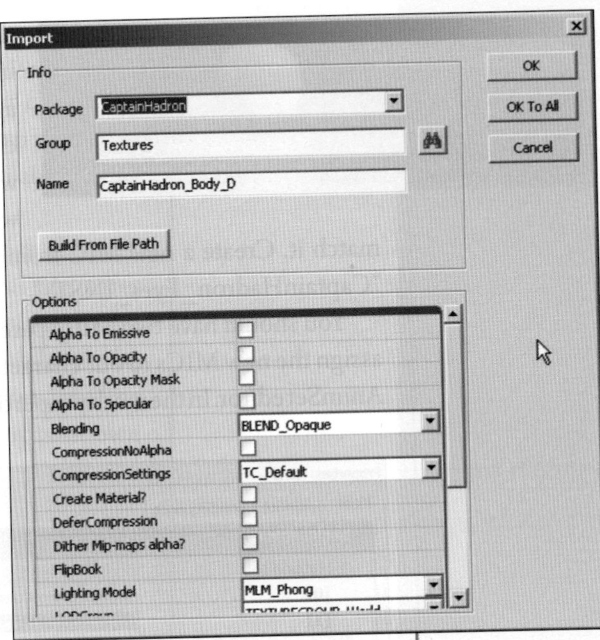


Figure 21.37

TC_Default
TC_Normalmap
TC_Displacementmap
TC_NormalmapAlpha
TC_Grayscale
TC_HighDynamicRange

From the previous materials project, open the "MyMaterials.upk" file. Select your Default_Material in the materials subcategory, right-click, and select Create New Material Instance Constant. Save this into "CaptainHadron.upk." Make a new group called "Materials" and then save the new MIC to it as "CaptainHadron_Body_INST."

Open the TextureParameterValues roll-out and assign your character's textures to the material instance [Figure 21.38]. The next time you open the file "CaptainHadron.upk,"

Figure 21.38

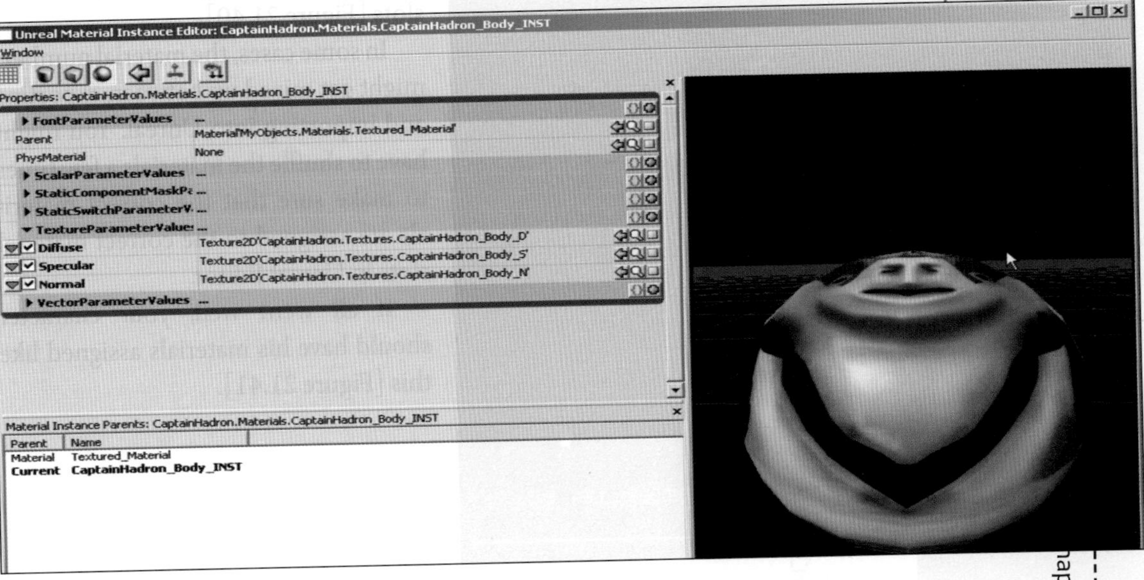

Figure 21.39

Figure 21.40

Figure 21.41

# 22 Character Animation

*Dance, Dance, Dance!*

## What to Expect

Character animation is another topic that alone can fill volumes of books. Human animation in 3D is a deep and complex subject. The human eye can detect subtle movements that turn into subconscious clues about a person's emotion and physical wellness. Turning these subconscious characteristics into key-framed animations is the skill of an animator. This skill can take years to master.

If you're already familiar with character animation, the following few projects may be a bit redundant; however, the information from these projects is still applicable to Unreal Engine's functions. The pipeline between your authoring tools and the engine is still relevant and the process is something that you'll need to learn.

### Create a Riggerobics Animation for Your Character

PROJECT

Riggerobics has two primary uses. The first use is to test your skinned mesh in 3D Studio Max so that you can fix any problems; for example, you might have accidentally selected a few foot vertices when adjusting weights for arm vertices. The second use is to import the skinned mesh into Unreal so that you can double check your work in the engine. If the skinned mesh was built properly, then the two mesh animations should look exactly the same. In some cases, the orientation of a joint can be shifted slightly; riggerobics will alert you to such deviations between two rigs.

After importing the "CaptainHadron_Bip.max" model, we'll save it as "CaptainHadron_Riggerobics.max." By creating a backup copy, we don't have to worry about overwriting our original model with an animated version of him. Separating the original mesh from the animations is important for a few reasons. First, for organizational reasons, it is easier to find a particular animation when the file is saved using a name that contains the animation name as a substring. Second, the separation allows you to share your work more easily with others. Once everyone has a copy of the original skinned mesh, each animator can work on different animations and not

Figure 22.1

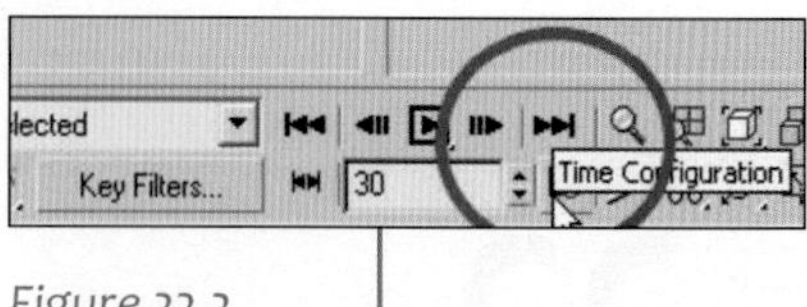


Figure 22.2

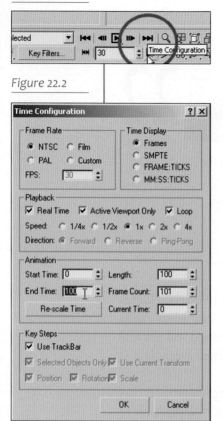

overwrite the original file. Third, it's important in case someone accidentally deletes or modifies something in the scene, making the file irreparable. In all cases, it's always better to have a clean, original file to work from, keeping the loss to a minimum.

Once we've loaded the scene, we're going to want to freeze the mesh. This allows us to select the Biped object underneath the mesh without having to deselect the character's mesh. We don't want to keep adding key frames to the mesh. Open the Time Configuration dialog by pressing the button shown circled in red in Figure 22.1.

The dialog itself is shown in Figure 22.2. By default, 3D Studio Max sets our timeline to 100 frames; see the highlighted End Time field of the dialog. Unreal Engine runs animations at 30 frames per second, so we'll leave the timeline at the default setting. You can increase this if you want a longer animation for the riggerobics test.

To start our animation, turn on the auto key button [Figure 22.3].

This feature allows us to move the joints around without having to click and tell 3D Studio Max to set a key for each adjustment.

Select upper joints and move them through various angles [Figure 22.4]. Using the slider button shown circled in red in Figure 22.5, increase the timeline by 10 frames before moving the joint to another angle.

Try to move every joint about its primary axis, and don't forget to twist or rotate the joints during this rigging test [Figure 22.6].

Figure 22.3

Figure 22.4

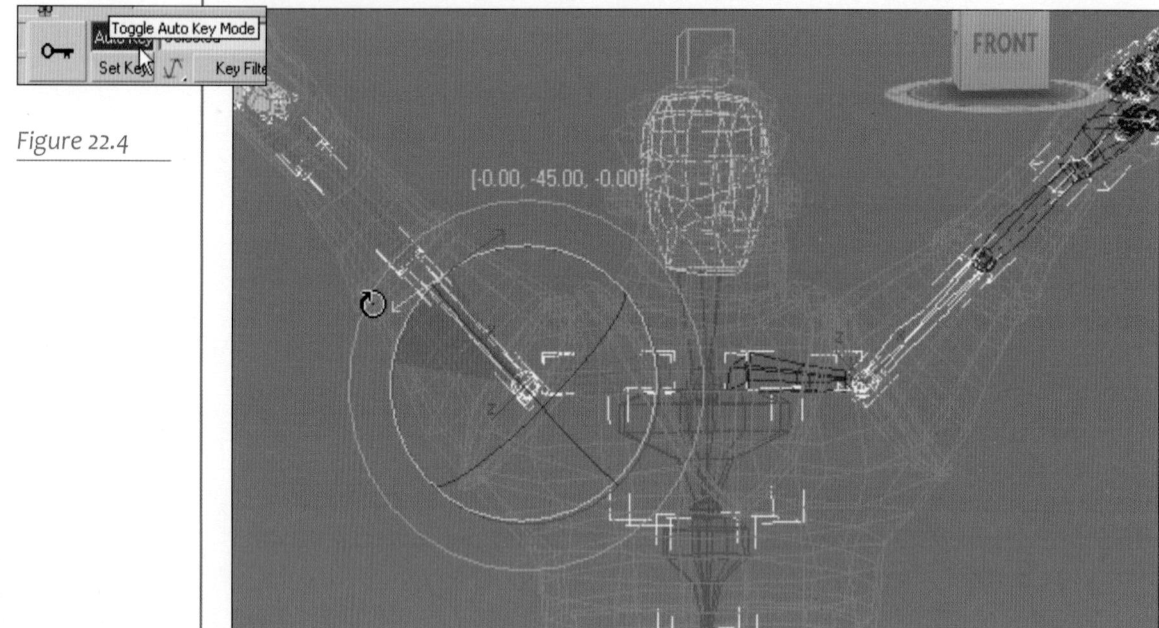

Figure 22.5

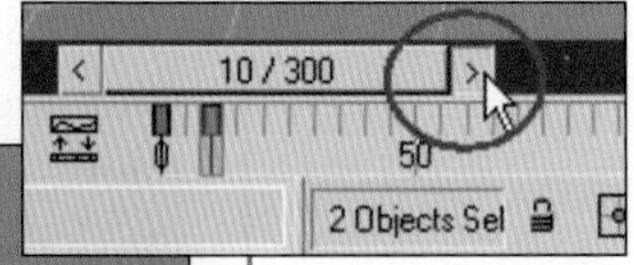


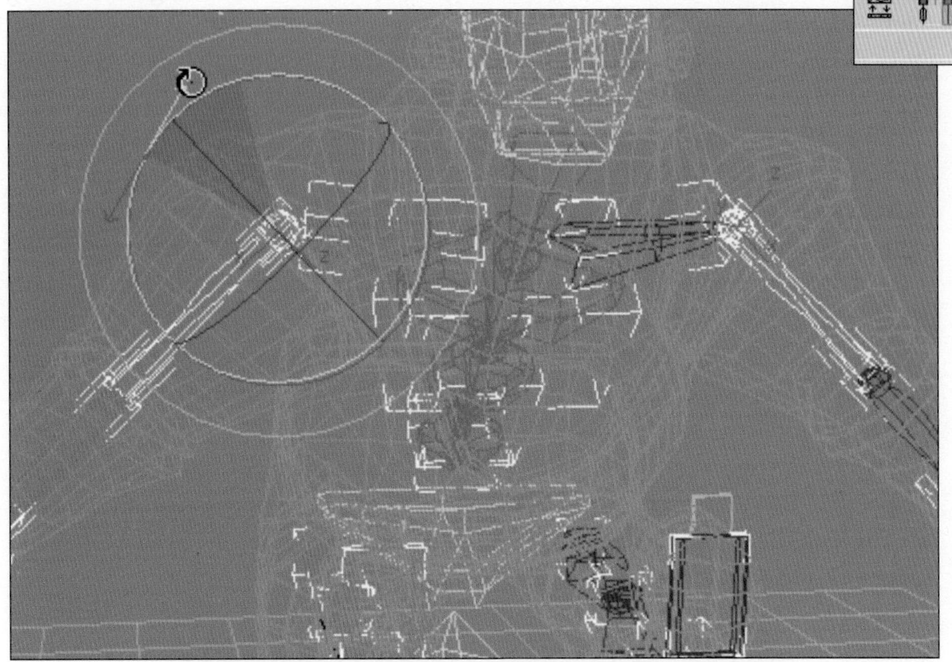

Figure 22.6

Figure 22.7

3D Studio Max should be setting keys as you move through the timeline; each of your operations consists of moving the time slider followed by rotating and twisting joints. There really isn't much of a method to riggerobics other than making sure you move the character using a wide range of rotations and positions. Many of the poses might look painful—but never fear, Captain Hadron can take it.

Now that you've added various rotations to the joints, it is a good time to fix some of the weighting issues that have come up. However, we've started a new scene for the riggerobics test [Figure 22.7]. Any changes we make will apply to the new scene, not to the default model we started with.

With the biped object selected, select the Motion tab and press the Save File button [Figure 22.8]. The dialog for saving the file is shown in Figure 22.9.

We're going to name the file "CaptainHadron_Riggerobics.bip." The file contains data only for biped animations and can be used by any other biped created with Character Studio.

Save your riggerobics file and close the dialog. Next, open the original "CaptainHadron_Bip.max" file. Select the biped object and then select the Motion tab. Click on the Load File icon under the Biped menu [Figure 22.10] and Open the "CaptainHadron_Riggerobics.bip" file [Figure 22.11].

Figure 22.8

Figure 22.9

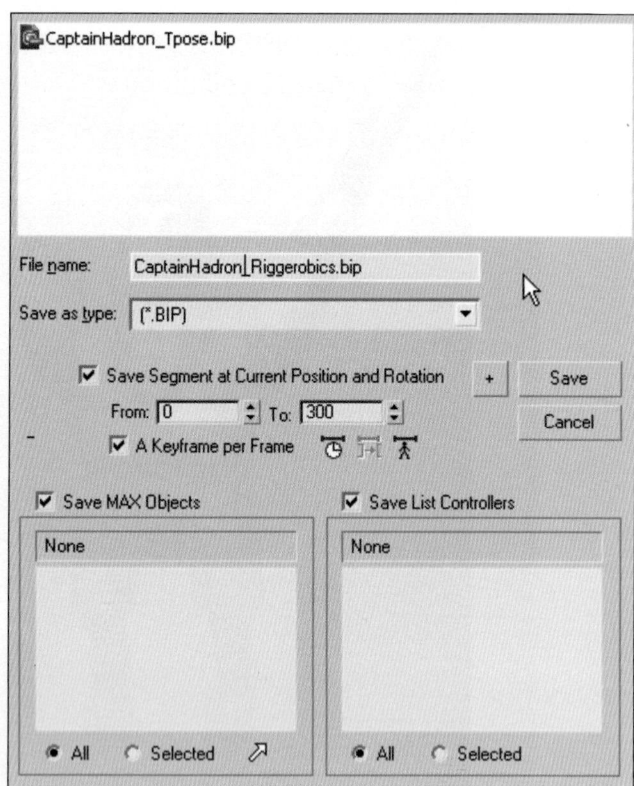

Figure 22.10

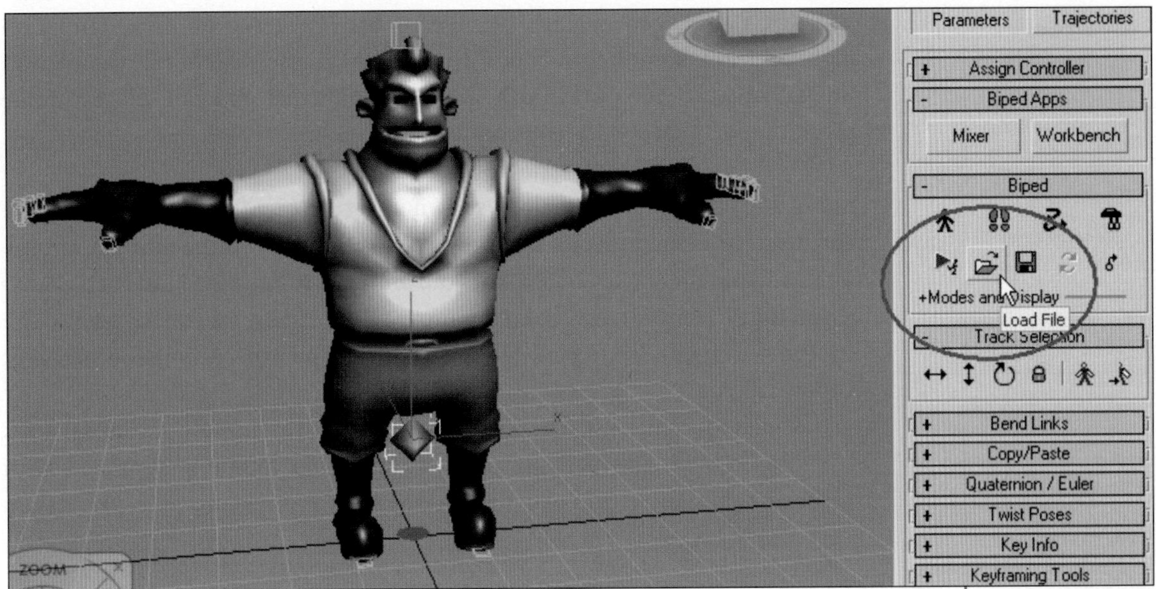


Figure 22.11

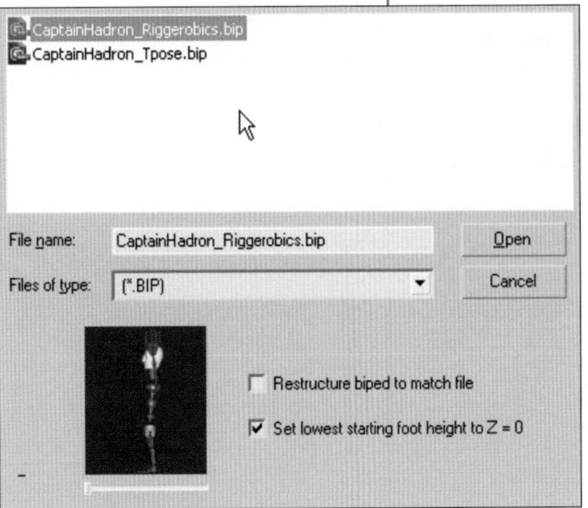


Fix your skin mesh weights, now that the mesh has some animations assigned to it. To restore the default pose, load the "Tpose.bip" file we saved when we first created the biped model for Captain Hadron. Click the Figure mode twice, once to activate it and once to turn it off. Loading the "Tpose.bip" file will delete the key frames in the scene and allow us to re-export our changes to the skin weights to Unreal Engine. Saving all of your various animations as BIP files allows you to create a reusable library of animations for any character that uses a biped skeleton. Biped animations are easy to reuse on different skeletons.



## Exporting Animation to Unreal

Load up ActorX rather than exporting a dynamic mesh as we did before. We'll be exporting animations using the ActorX plug-in, which creates a PSA file rather than a PSK file.

In the roll-out menu, select a name for the animation file [Figure 22.12]. In this example, I've named the animation "testAnims," which is the name for the group of animations, not for the individual animation sequence we're exporting. The name is also used for the file on disk that we'll import into Unreal's animation editor. We'll

Figure 22.12

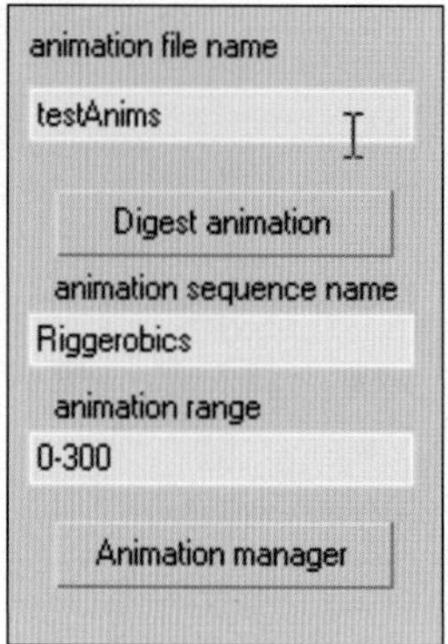


name the particular sequence of movements "Riggerobics." The animation range is set to match the timeline "0–300," which also matches the animation frames that we created previously. Keep in mind that you can select a frame range to export that is different from the full timeline.

Click on the Digest animation button [Figure 22.13].

A dialog box, similar to the one shown in Figure 22.14, will pop up once the animation has been digested. Basically, the dialog tells you the number of time frames and number of key frames for your animation. For each joint that is moving and for each time frame that it has moved, a key frame will be baked into the skeleton's animation sequence. Click on OK to open the Animation manager window [Figure 22.15].

The animation manager has gone through a few revisions in recent versions of 3D Studio Max. The manager allows you to build your animation files with the specific animations you plan on working with. For instance, you may have a

Figure 22.13

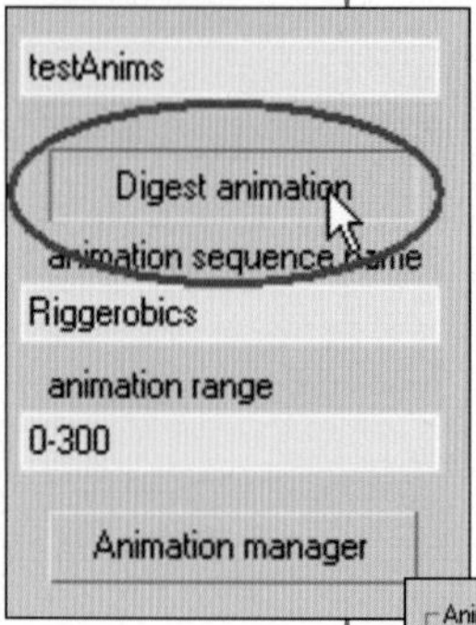

Figure 22.14

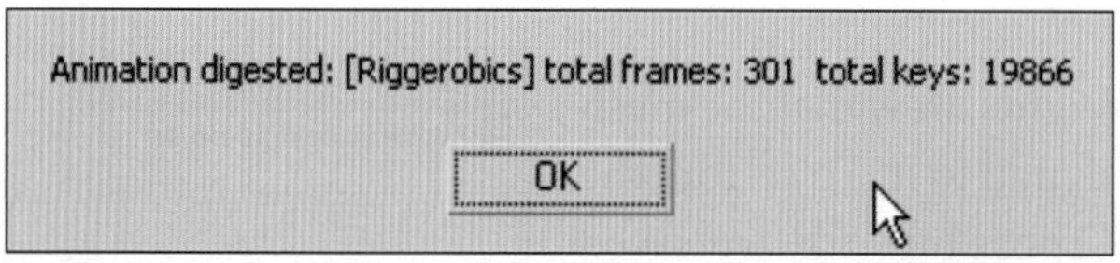

Figure 22.15

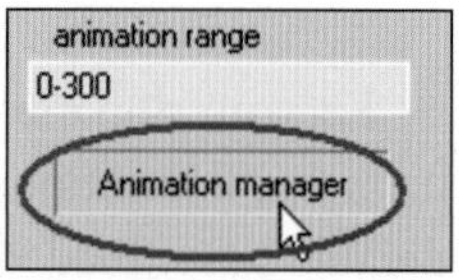

Figure 22.16

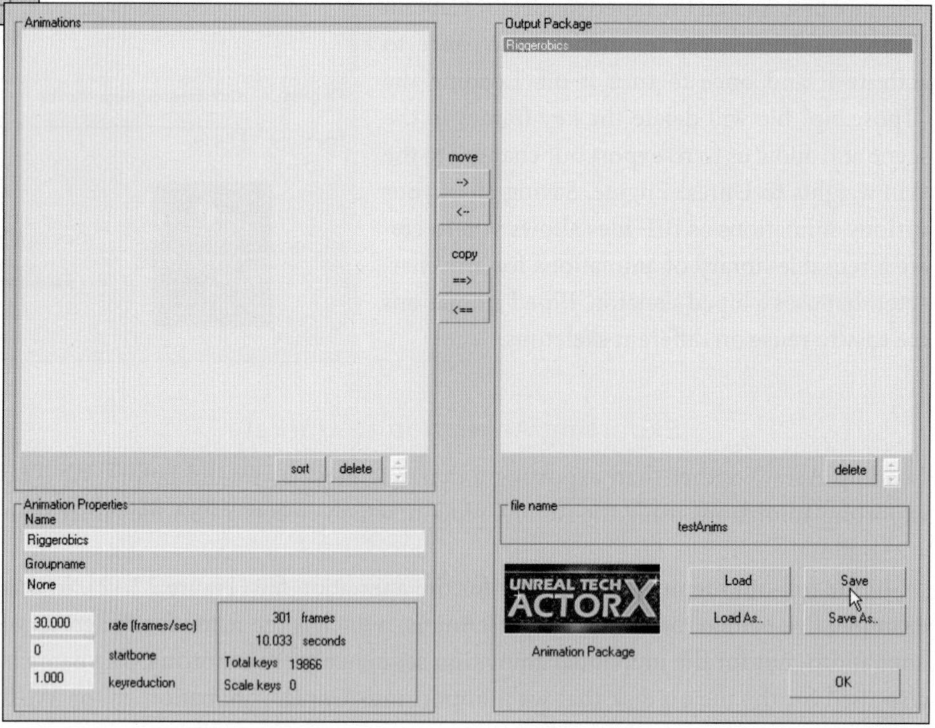

set of animations for running and walking; a set of animations for your cinematics; and a set for special actions such as power-ups, deaths, or idling. Each set of animations may be saved to its own file.

The animation manager dialog allows you to group, organize, and build separate collections for each set of animations [Figure 22.16]. In our example, we have only one file to work with, namely, the "CaptainHadron_anims" file, and one animation to add to the file, namely, "Riggerobics." When the dialog first opens, your riggerobics data appears on the left. The Animations pane is empty, which indicates that the file initially contains no animation data. If there were data, the contents would appear on the right. To copy or move the 3D Studio Max file data from the left pane to the right pane, click on the buttons located in the middle of the two panes. When you're finished organizing your animations, click the Save button on the lower right of the dialog. For now, we'll not assign a group name, because we're going to create only a few animations that do not need organizing into subcategories.

Figure 22.17

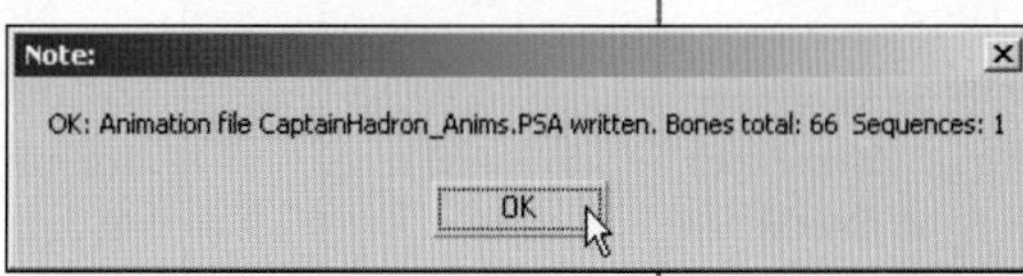


For future reference, groups are handy for organizing the animations into categories such as cinematic sequences, idling, running, deaths, and so on. The grouping is mostly useful when you've got to organize many different animations. A character can have several idle animations that can be played randomly so that the player doesn't see the same idle animation looped repeatedly. The AnimTree editor allows us to build such animations, which is something we'll get to in a later project.

A pop-up dialog confirms that the CaptainHadron_Anims.PSA file has been saved [Figure 22.17]. Click on OK. To close the ActorX window, click on the OK button on the lower right of the main dialog [Figure 22.16].

For now, we don't have to go too deeply into why we need to separate the various animations; however, keep in mind that each animation package has to be loaded in its entirety. The engine cannot load in one animation from one file and one animation from another file. If you were to store several megabytes of cinematics with all of your running and idling animations in the same file, you would be forced to load your cinematic animations when all that you wanted were the running and idling animations that enable the character to move in the scene. If you've got several characters and long animations for your cinematics, this is a waste of memory. Once in the AnimSet editor in Unreal, we're going to have additional control over animation data organization, so don't fret just yet.

Figure 22.18

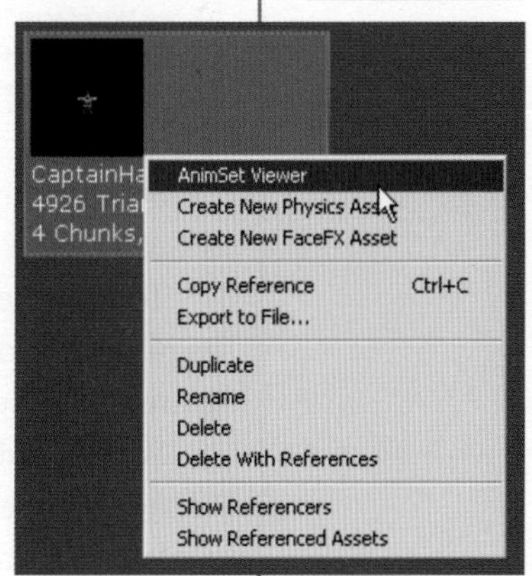


Returning to the Unreal Editor, open the "CaptainHadron.upk" file and then open the AnimSet Viewer [Figure 22.18]. Either double-click on your mesh, or right-click and select AnimSet Viewer. This is the same editor we used to assign materials to a mesh.

Figure 22.19

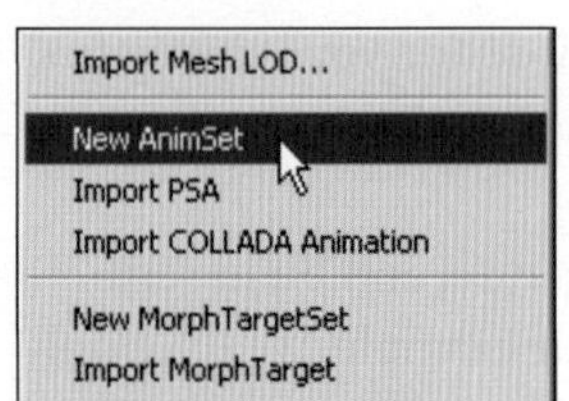


Figure 22.20

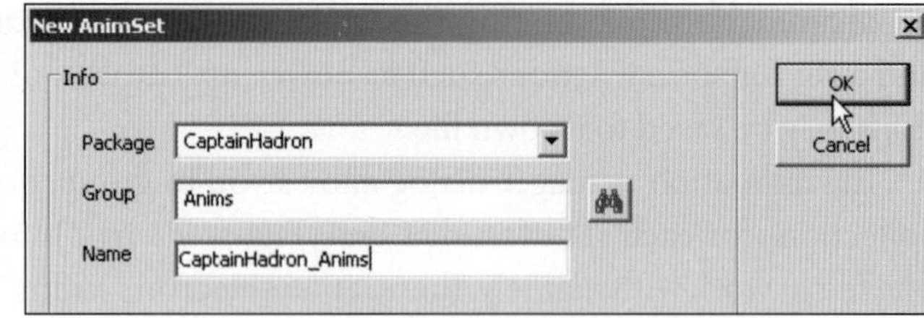


Figure 22.21

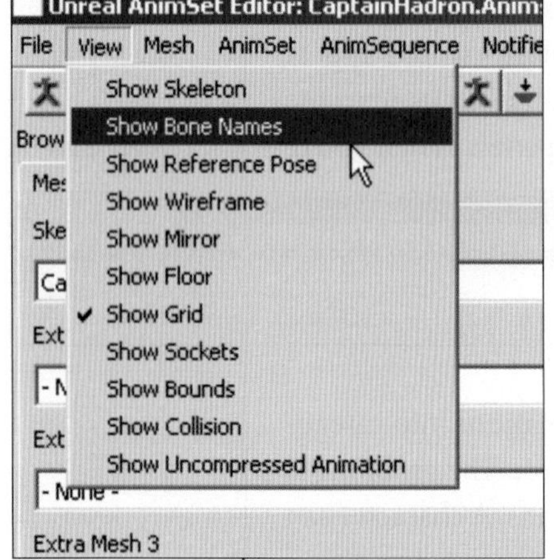


Create an empty AnimSet for your character by selecting `File` → `NewAnimSet`[Figure 22.19]. Name the new AnimSet "CaptainHadron_Anims" and store it into the group named "Anims" [Figure 22.20]. The AnimSet is initially empty.

Now we can import the "testAnims.psa" file into our empty AnimSet. These animations can't be played on another character unless the bone names match between the two characters. To show the bone names, select `View` → `Show Bone Names` [Figure 22.21].

To import new animations, select `File` → `Import PSA` [Figure 22.22].

Figure 22.22

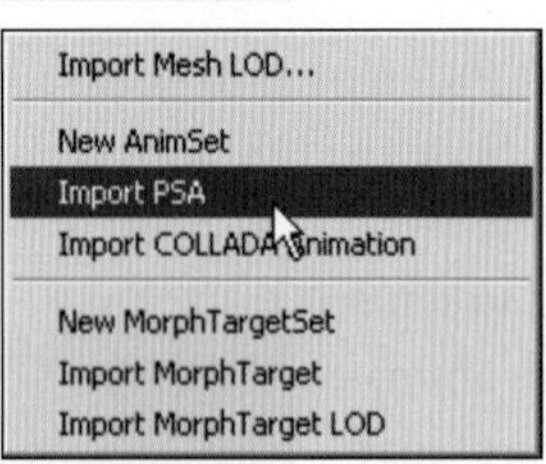


Figure 22.23

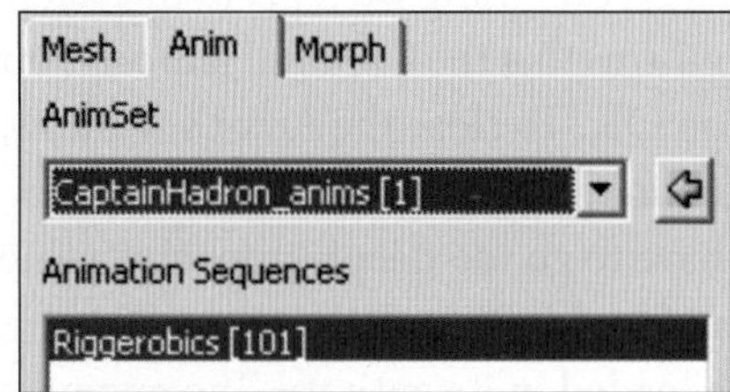


Select your previously exported file that was named "CaptainHadron_Anims .PSA" [Figure 22.23].

To play the animation, use the controls at the bottom of the viewport. If all went as planned, your animation should look the same in the AnimSet editor as it did in Unreal [Figure 22.24].

You should be able to scrub through your animation using the slider at the bottom of the AnimSet viewport.

It's important to remember that the animation data and the skeletal mesh are separated. In the editor, any characters whose skeletons have similarly named joints can share the animation data. This means that the animation data lives apart from the character it animates, because the animation can drive any number of skeletons. Skeletal animation is stored as a set of joints, each joint having an associated number of rotations for a specified timeline. Once the character is

Figure 22.24

spawned or created, the default parameters in the character's UC file (UScript file) need to connect the skeletal mesh and the AnimSet together. We'll go through an example of this in a later project.

PROJECT

## Animations and Movement

Okay, so riggerobics was a pretty simple animation to set up in Unreal, but it isn't useful for much more than bug testing. For our game, we'll want a few animations so that we can run around in our environment. Let's begin with a basic animation list. We'll want to animate these for basic movement in Unreal:

- Idle
- Run Forward
- Side-step Left
- Side-step Right
- Run Backward

The basic animations are required for any character in the Unreal engine. In addition to these, you'll want to animate a falling animation and a death animation. For the purpose of Unreal animation, there isn't much of a need for a jump animation.

The jumps happen so fast that a wind-up-and-launch animation takes too long to play. The usual "anticipation" in classical animation practices turns into "waiting" in a video game environment. Most video games are fast-paced, requiring twitch movements and split-second reactions. We'll avoid anticipation in the animation, since it's a traditional animation practice rather than a video game practice.

For a full game mod, you'll need to expand the basic animation list to contain all of the possible movements in your game, including animations for each weapon or item that your character is going to carry.

PROJECT

## A Quick Run Animation

Character animation is a topic that is too broad to cover in only a single chapter. There are a few tricks that can help you animate a run for the first time. Of course, you're encouraged to seek out more detailed animation tutorials, but the discussion here should give you a good starting point. If you're already familiar with animating in 3D Studio Max, then this project might be a bit rudimentary; however, there are a few hints that you might not know when creating an animation that will be used by the Unreal Editor.

Figure 22.25

Figure 22.26

Figure 22.27

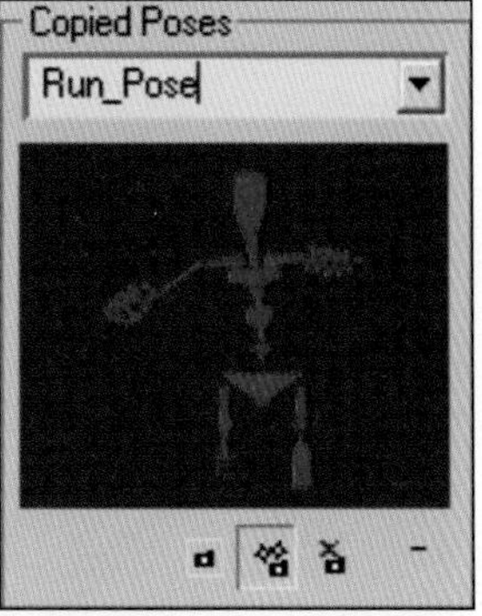


Figure 22.28

Figure 22.29

Start with a basic pose. Select the various bones on the character and rotate them into a position something like this [Figure 22.25], which illustrates an intermediate run with one foot forward and one foot backward.

Open the Copy/Paste section of the biped motion parameters and create a new collection of poses [Figure 22.26].

Select the Pose button and name the collection "CaptainHadron_Poses [Figure 22.27]. This collection will be a resource for your other animations. To loop an animation, the character should be in the exact same pose when he starts and ends the animation. When you're done with the pose, click on the "Copy Pose" button to launch the dialog of Figure 22.28.

Name the pose "Run_Pose" for future reference. An icon will be generated automatically to help you remember what the pose looks like. There are a few options for how the icon is generated, but you can experiment with this on your own.

When you're finished, click on the Save Collection icon [Figure 22.29]. The collection will be your library of poses. I saved mine with the Captain Hadron 3D Studio Max file in my character's project directory.

Figure 22.30

Figure 22.31

Toggle Auto Key Mode
Set Key
Key Fi

Figure 22.32

Figure 22.33

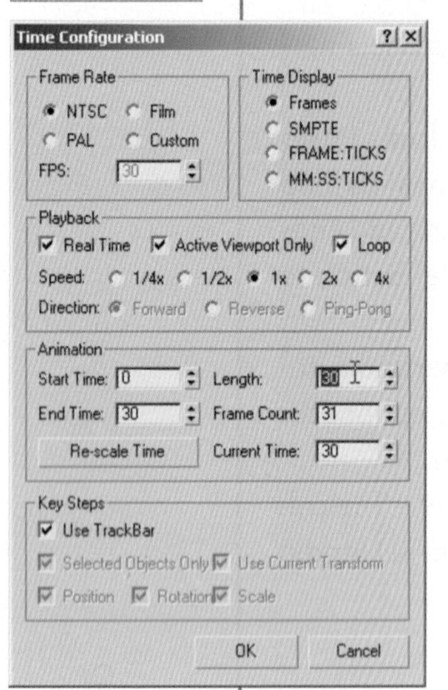


Switch to the side view so that you can see how far he's going to be moving with his pose [Figure 22.30]. We'll do a short, three-step run cycle that will start and end with the right foot forward. Figure 22.30 shows each step as a red arrow. The middle arrow is the portion of the animation where his left foot will be forward. The length of the character's stride is the distance between footsteps, which is approximately the distance from the back toe to the front toe.

Before proceeding, activate the auto key button [Figure 22.31].

At this point it is a good idea, although not necessary, to set the timeline to 30 frames.

Open the time configuration window [Figure 22.32] and set the length of the timeline to 30 frames [Figure 22.33].

On the first frame, paste the pose on the selected character. You can do so using the Paste Pose button of the Copy/Paste dialog; this button is the second from the left (under the Posture button). This ensures that the first time frame is key-framed properly.

Set a key frame for the biped diamond at the origin. Slide the time slider forward to 30 frames and then set another key frame corresponding to the character's motion over the distance marked

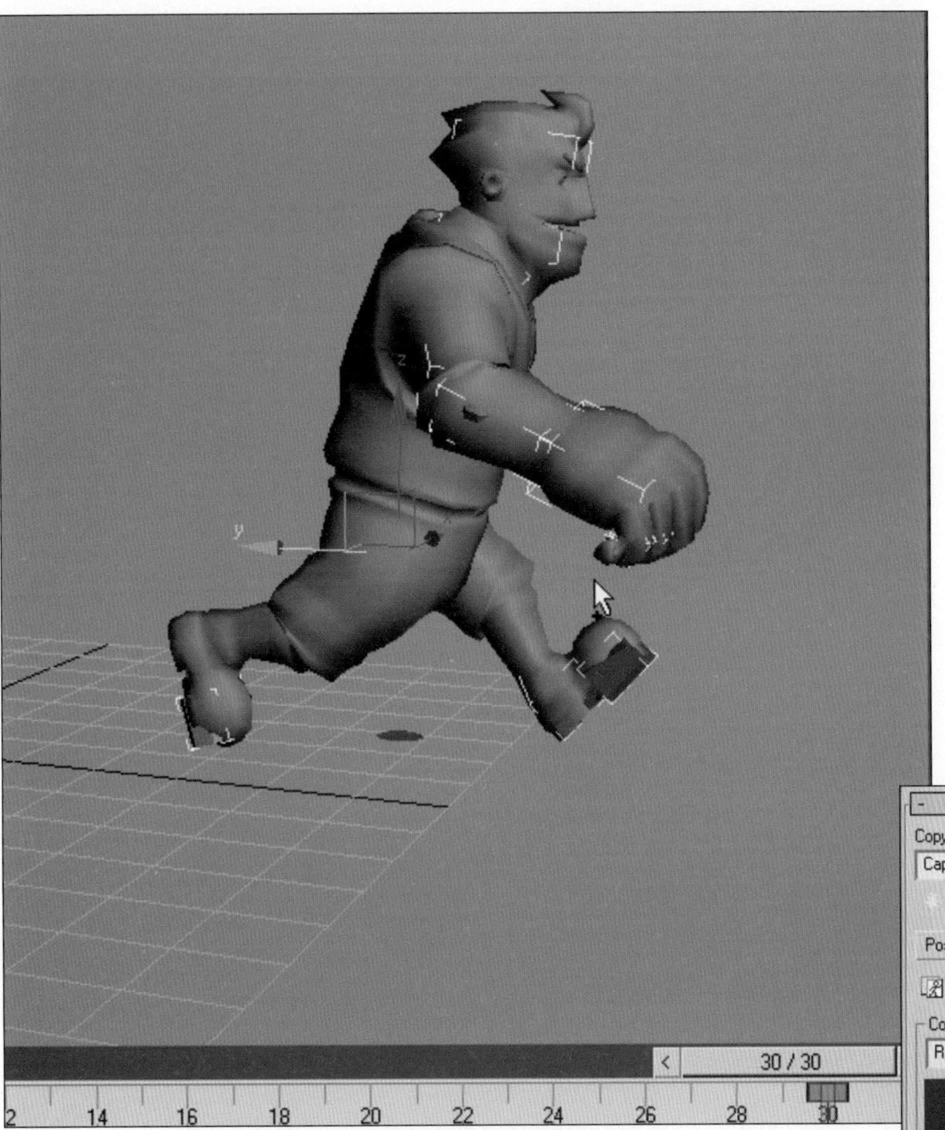


Figure 22.34

Figure 22.35

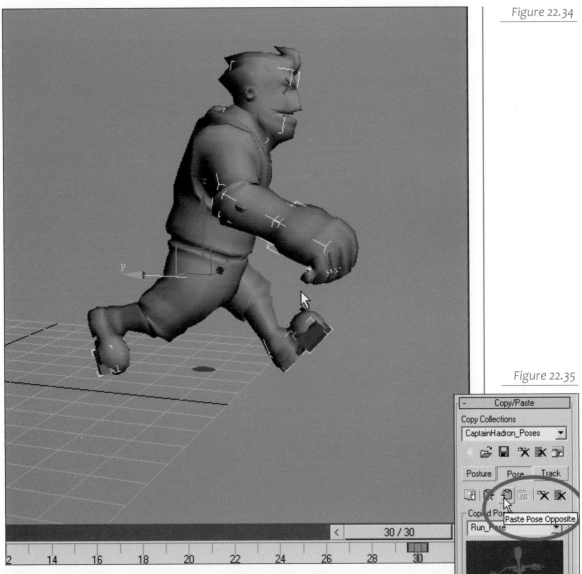

out previously [Figure 22.34]. As you scrub through the timeline, the character should now slide forward. Move the time slider back to the fifteenth frame; this is the midpoint of your character's animation. On the fifteenth frame, your character will need his left foot forward. You may accomplish this by selecting the Paste Pose Opposite button [Figure 22.35].

This operation pastes a mirrored image of the first pose at the halfway point of the animation [Figure 22.36].

It's important to remember the distance that the character is moving; this distance will be used later when building the character's animation tree. In our

Figure 22.36

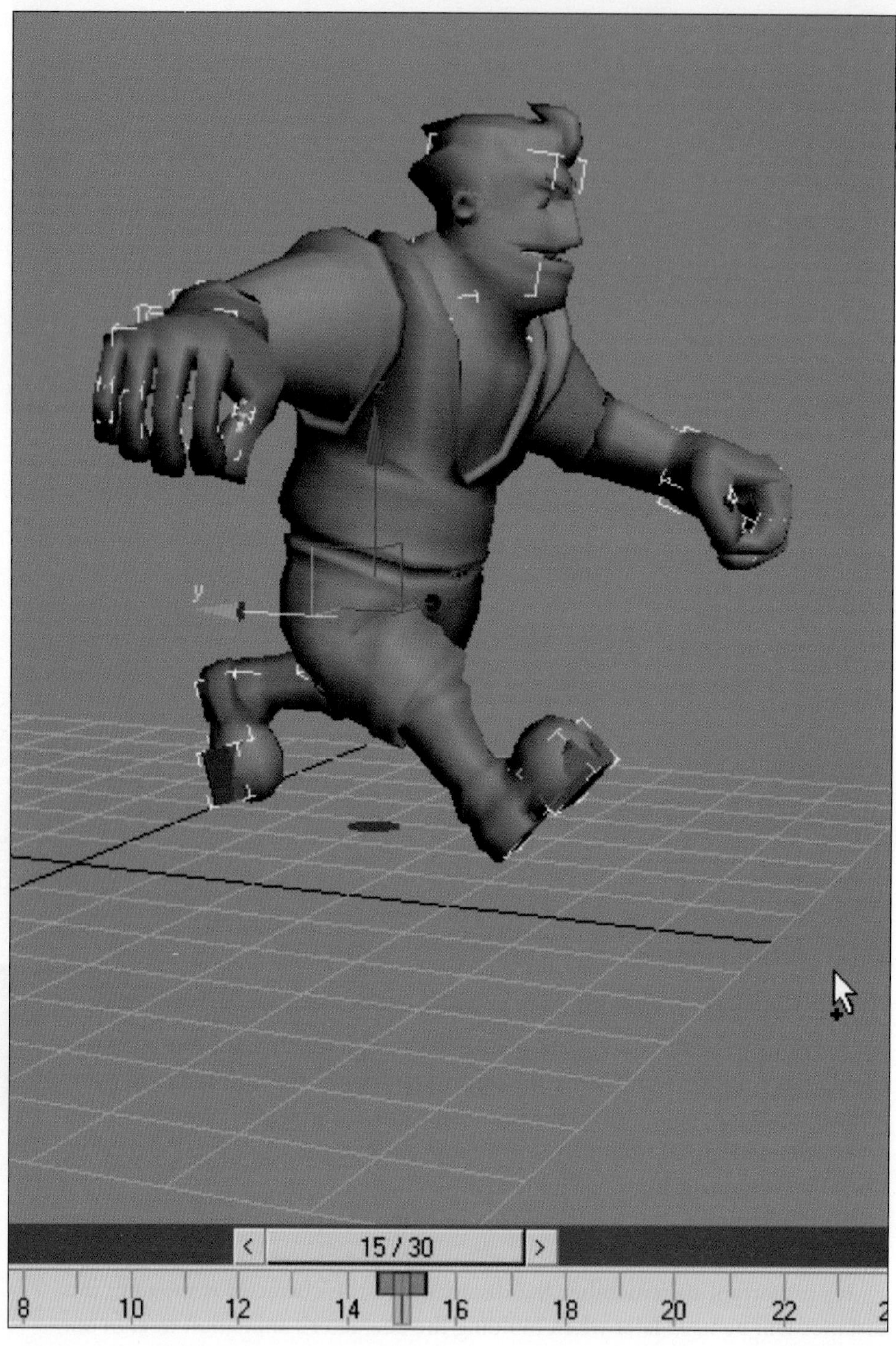

Figure 22.37

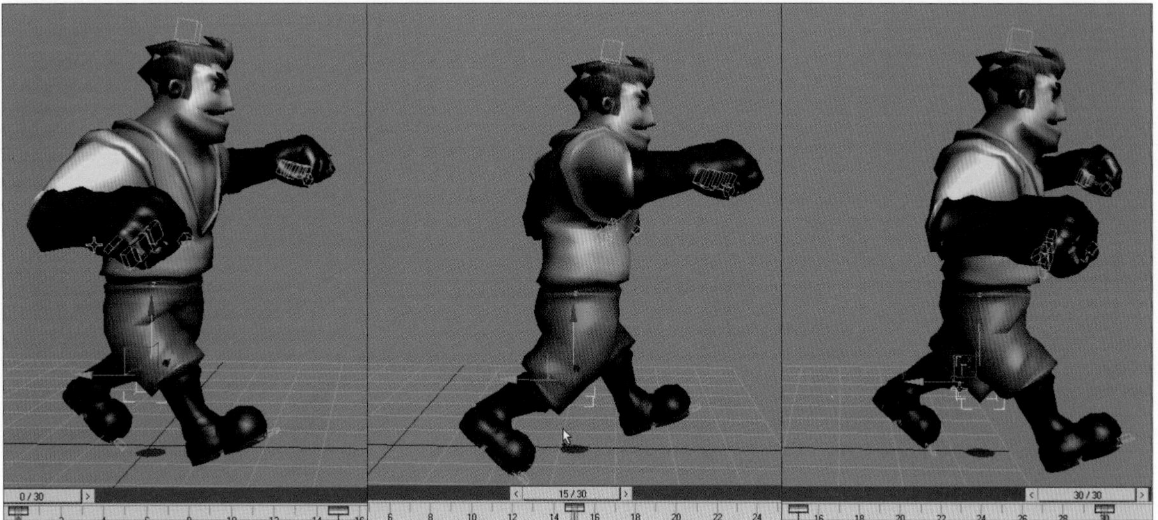


example, I set the last frame to -65 units away from the origin. At the midpoint, open the Copy/Paste roll-out dialog and select the Paste Pose Opposite button. Paste the regular pose at frames 0 and 30.

If you scrub through your timeline, you'll now have a rudimentary run cycle [Figure 22.37]. It's a bit stiff and lacks flare, but with a bit of tweaking, you'll have a useable run cycle. A good run cycle takes quite some time to build and includes bounce, follow-through, and other subtle features. A similar technique should be used to build an idle animation. In particular, the poses for the first and last frames should be the same.

An important point is that the first frame and the last frame must match. A second point is that the character needs to travel away from the origin. Many older-generation games require run cycles to keep the character in place at the origin. Unreal Engine, though, can use the traversed distance to calculate the speed at which an animation should be played. We'll learn how to use the traversed distance once we start building our AnimTrees.

Figure 22.38

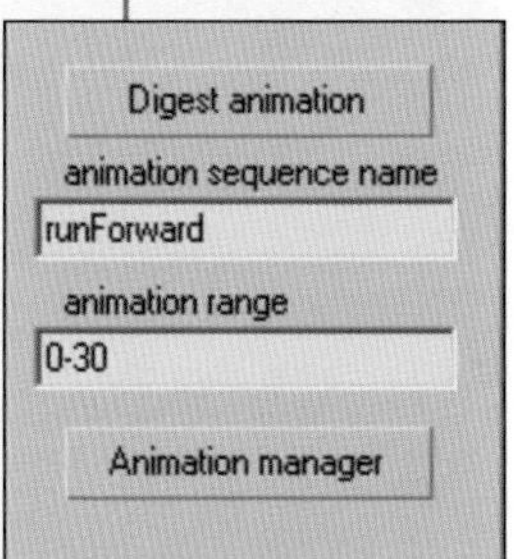


Figure 22.39

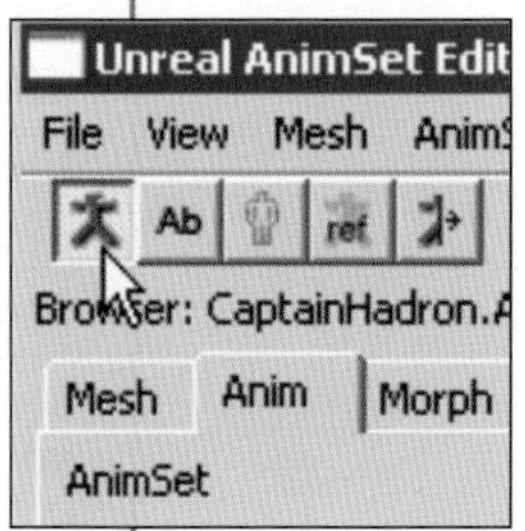


Open ActorX and name the animation sequence "runForward" [Figure 22.38]. Digest the animation in the scene, and then open the Animation Manager and press the `Load As` button. Open the animation file where you saved your riggerobics animation. Using the copy button, add the "runForward" animation. Save the PSA file in your exports directory so that we can get to it from the editor.

Open the Unreal Editor, if you didn't have it open already. Open the riggerobics animation set and import the PSA file we just saved from 3D Studio Max.

Turn on the show-skeleton button [Figure 22.39] and scrub to the end of the animation [Figure 22.40].

Figure 22.40

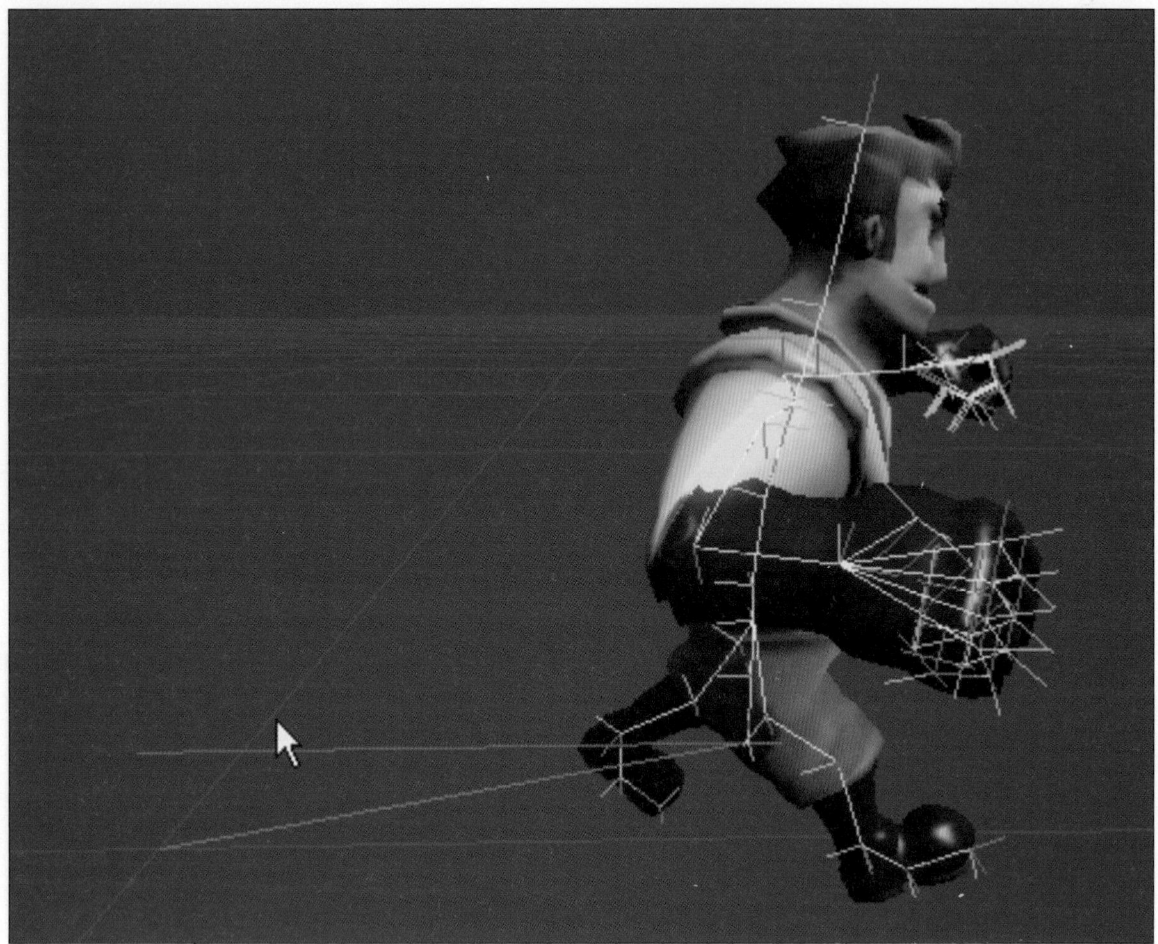

You should notice a couple of interesting, little lines originating from the Bip01 node in the animated scene. This is how Unreal detects the distance that the character has moved. The red line indicates the total distance the character has moved. The purple line points from the origin to the node that Unreal is using to calculate the distance. This distance is critical for use in the AnimTree editor; we'll get to that in the next chapter. For now, take for granted that Unreal can find this data in your animation.

3D Studio Max decides that the positive Y-axis is the direction that the front of your character faces [Figure22.41]. The lower left of the figure has a green line labeled Y, which indicates that the positive Y-axis is indeed the direction that the character faces. Unreal prefers that you use the positive X-axis for the forward-facing direction of your character. Rather than have to model and animate in 3D Studio Max with the character rotated to the left by 90 degrees (to face in the positive X-axis direction), we can rotate the character after he's been imported into the Unreal Editor.

LOD [0] Bones:66 Polys:4886 (Display Factor:2.62)
Verts:3077 (Rigid:2255 Soft:822)
Chunks:2 Sections:2
Pos: 0.0 pct, Time: 0.0000s, Len: 1.0333s

Figure 22.41

Figure 22.42

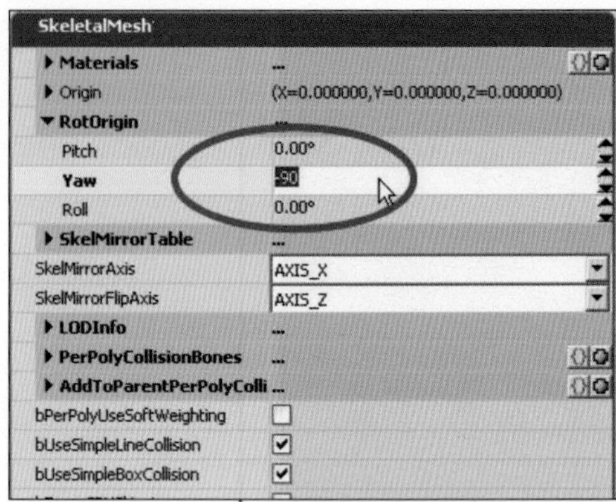


In the AnimSet Editor, you'll find ways to offset the origin of an imported SkeletalMesh object. Here we can set the character's yaw angle, which is the rotation angle about the up-axis, to –90 degrees [Figure 22.42] in order to turn him to face the positive X-axis [Figure 22.43].

In the event that the character was imported either floating or under the ground, you can use the Origin parameters (above the RotOrigin dialog field) to fix the character's placement. This is similar to how Maya might export models using a Y-up coordinate system.

Figure 22.43

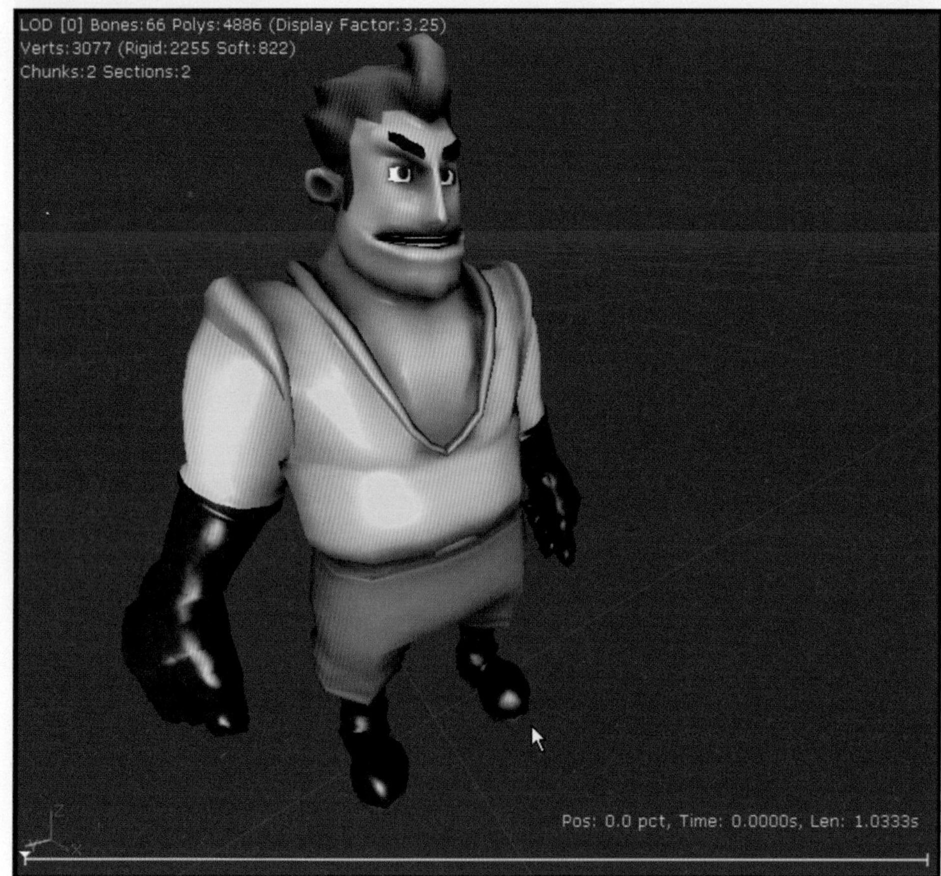


PROJECT

## Adding a Socket

For a pistol to find its way into the hands of our hero, we need to add what's called a "socket" for the weapon. By itself, a socket can't do a whole lot. UScript needs to know the name of the socket in order to connect a weapon to it.

Figure 22.44

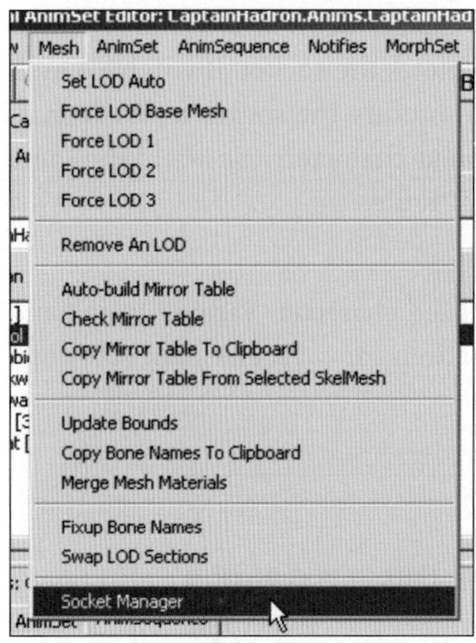


Figure 22.45

Figure 22.46

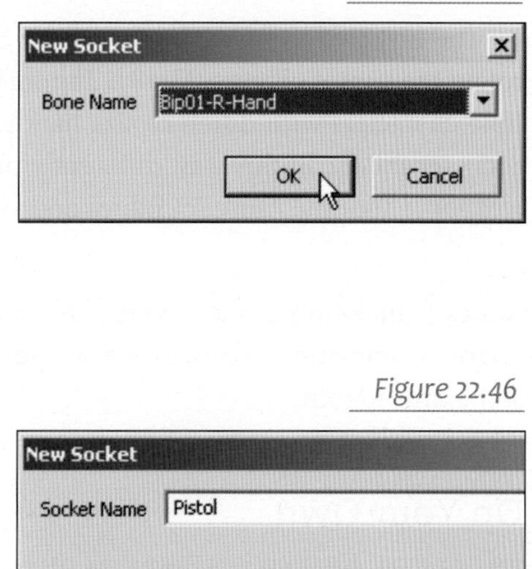


To add a socket to our hero, open `Mesh` → `Socket Manager` in the AnimSet editor [Figure 22.44]. A dialog prompts you to select a parent bone for the socket [Figure 22.45].

Select the `Bip01-R-Hand` and click on OK.

Name the new socket "Pistol" [Figure 22.46]. This name will be used by UScript to spawn the character's weapon.

A new 3D diamond icon will appear at the base of the right hand [Figure 22.47]. Using the arrows in the view, reposition the new socket to the middle of the palm.

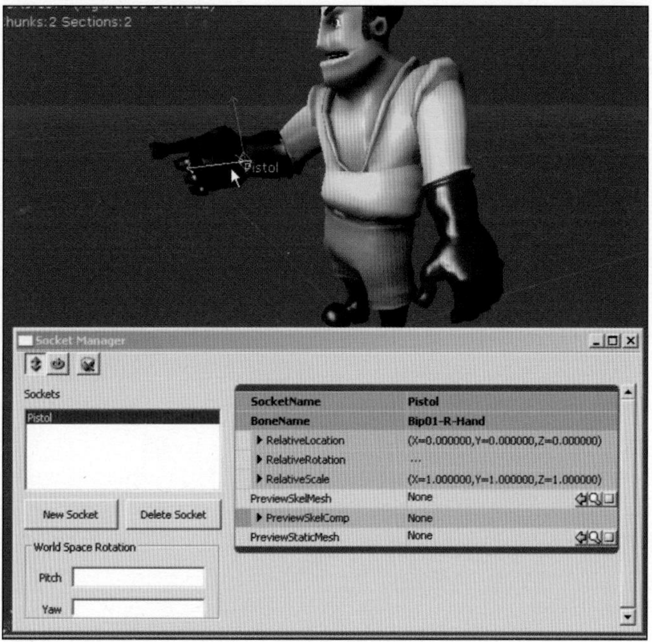


Figure 22.47

Figure 22.48

The first two icons at the top of the Socket Manager allow you to translate and rotate the socket [Figure 22.48]. The third icon deletes the socket. If you have multiple characters with different size hands, you can modify the socket for each character separately. In this way, differently proportioned characters can wield the same weapon. Close the AnimSet Editor and save the UPK file.

## Review

A lot of animation is required to build a fully realized character. Various armed and unarmed animation cycles, as well as special animations for cut scenes, can take quite some time to tune.

## On Your Own

The project directories contain another character, Officer Anyon. She's also rigged using Character Studio. You should be able to import the "riggerobics.bip" animation onto her skeleton. Try this, but just remember that you don't want to enable the "restructure skeleton to match imported bip" option, which would stretch her proportions to match the captain's skeleton. The skeletons are pretty different, so the stretching would create a rather odd looking officer.

Adding ragdoll physics is a fun way to see our character animate in the engine. It's also a great way to test the character's skin mesh modifier, in addition to the testing you can do with the riggerobics animation. Setting up a ragdoll is similar to our Item Crate project, except that we'll be using only the skeletal joint constraint type rather than the prismatic joint constraint type.

# 23 The AnimTree editor

## Telling Your Character How to Behave

The AnimTree's function is to blend many animations into a final result. The AnimTree applies logic to how various animations are to be blended together and when they should play. Adding this logic is done using the AnimTree editor. For instance, you can change which animations are played based on the weapon the character is carrying or which direction it is moving. Building up an AnimTree in this way makes complex animations easy to build and understand.

Blending animations together is usually a complex process. The AnimTree editor greatly simplifies this process through its simple to use and clearly defined functions. Unreal Engine has a few tricks built into the AnimTree editor that support tuning the animations after they've been authored. For example, one utility allows you to change the frame rate at which an animation is played. The rate can be linked to the speed of the character as it moves along a path.

## What to Expect

For a book this size, it would be difficult to replicate completely the number of behaviors and characteristics found in an *Unreal Tournament* or *Gears of War* character. We'll focus on building some basic animation behaviors for a character, creating what is required to control a character based on regular WASD key controls and to allow a character to carry a weapon.

The AnimTree used for the Unreal Tournament 3 characters was built specifically for weapons and animations used exclusively in Unreal Tournament 3. You'll want to focus on creating a new AnimTree for your particular project's needs. This is where custom UScripts may come into play. Once you've designed your own weapon, a few things must be set up before you can use the new script objects. You'll need a place for the weapon to attach to your character, and you'll need to change the animations to reflect which weapon the character is carrying.

To build the behaviors, AnimTree is used to blend animations. Like the material editor, you'll be connecting various data-containing nodes to other nodes that change how the data flows. The function that an AnimTree node performs depends on conditions such as movement, speed, and other in-game features, as the character interacts with the world.

Figure 23.1

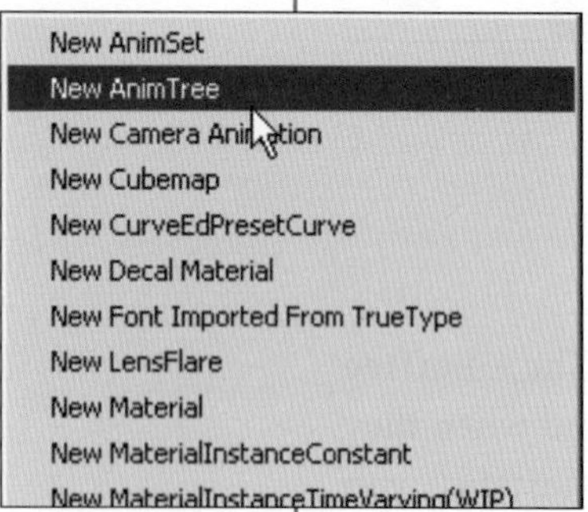


Figure 23.2

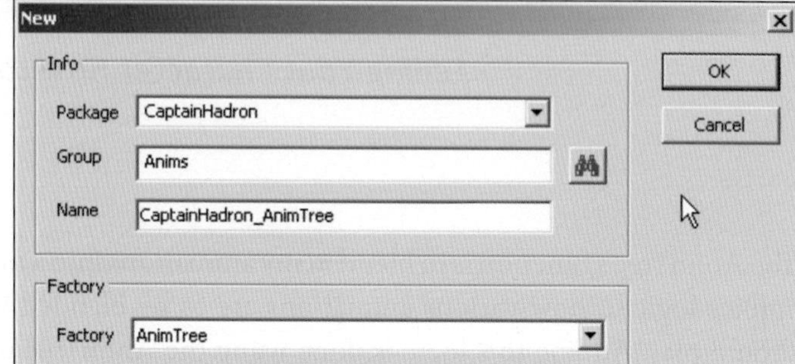


Figure 23.3

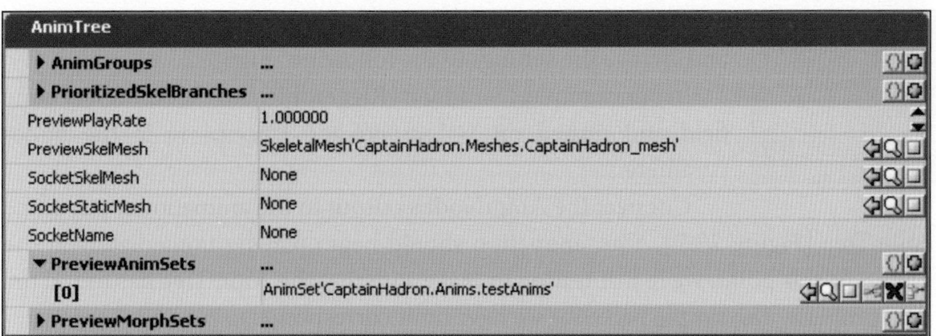


Figure 23.4

PROJECT

## AnimTree, Adding Behavior to the Animation

To assign a set of behaviors to a moving character, we'll use the AnimTree editor in the Unreal Editor. The AnimTree editor is a powerful animation blending and behavior editing tool. We'll also add in a couple of `AnimSlots` for use in Matinee. `AnimSlots` allow us to blend multiple animations together in order to build interesting behaviors for cinematic events.

In the Generic browser, right-click and select `New AnimTree` [Figure 23.1].

Name the AnimTree "CaptainHadron_AnimTree" and add this to the group of characters named "Anims" [Figure 23.2].

Select the `AnimTree` node in the middle of the graph editor [Figure 23.3]. Here you'll assign the mesh that you'll be using for previewing your behaviors, and you'll set the animations that you'll be working with.

Enter the name of your character mesh to the `PreviewSkelMesh` field of the editor; then add a new `PreviewAnimSet` and enter the name of your test animations [Figure 23.4]. Right-click in the node editor and select the `AnimSequence Player` option [Figure 23.5]. This creates a node that contains the name of an animation to play.

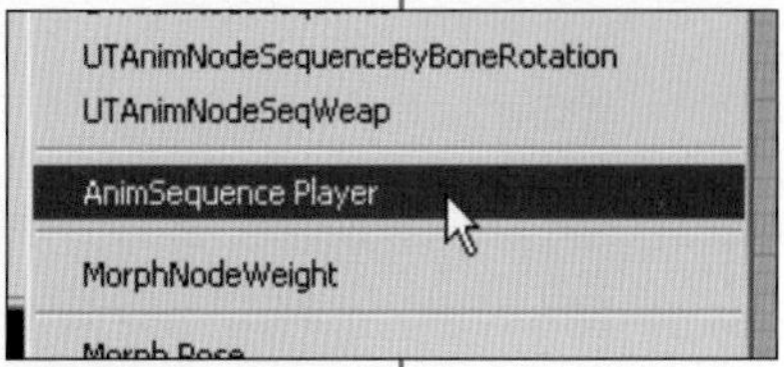

Figure 23.5

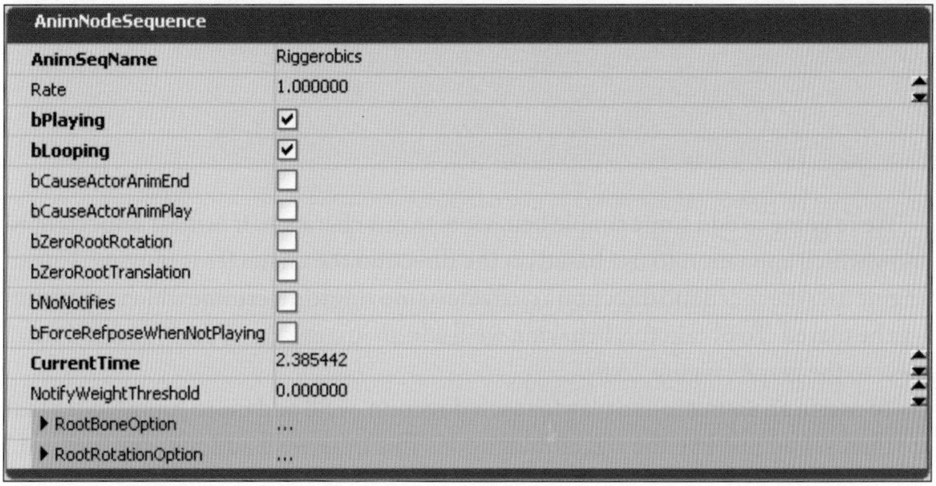

UTAnimNodeSequenceByBoneRotation
UTAnimNodeSeqWeap
AnimSequence Player
MorphNodeWeight

Figure 23.6

| AnimNodeSequence | |
|---|---|
| AnimSeqName | Riggerobics |
| Rate | 1.000000 |
| bPlaying | ☑ |
| bLooping | ☑ |
| bCauseActorAnimEnd | ☐ |
| bCauseActorAnimPlay | ☐ |
| bZeroRootRotation | ☐ |
| bZeroRootTranslation | ☐ |
| bNoNotifies | ☐ |
| bForceRefposeWhenNotPlaying | ☐ |
| CurrentTime | 2.385442 |
| NotifyWeightThreshold | 0.000000 |
| RootBoneOption | ... |
| RootRotationOption | ... |

Figure 23.7

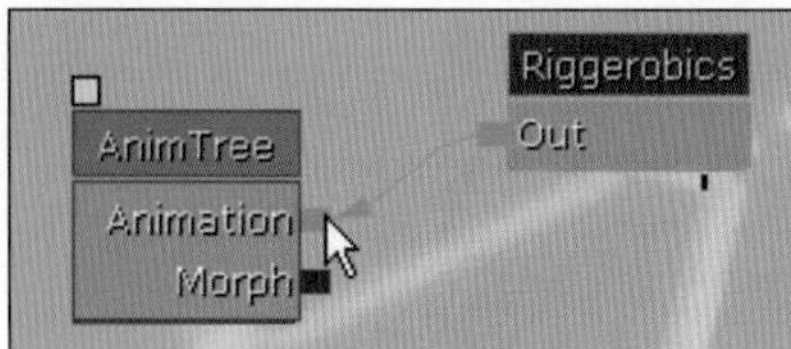


Once the node is in the graph editor, expand the parameters and change the settings to the following [Figure 23.6].

In our example, I've added "Riggerobics" to the AnimSeqName field and turned on `bPlaying` and `bLooping` in the nodes parameters.

Connect the AnimNode's output to the animation input of the AnimTree [Figure 23.7]. Your animation should begin playing immediately in the editor. At this point, we're just testing to make sure that the AnimTree has found the data properly. The simple behavior we have built corresponds to playing the riggerobics animation when the character is spawned—nothing too exciting yet.

Figure 23.8

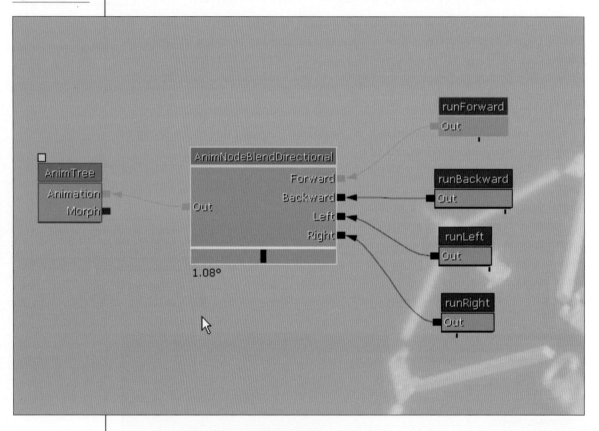

We're going to add some simple behaviors to our character. It is most important to know which animation to use based on the direction the character is moving. Unreal Engine uses the speed and direction a character is moving to determine which animation is to be played. To obtain this behavior, we'll add an `AnimNodeBlendDirectional` node to the graph [Figure 23.8].

To assign an animation to play for each direction, we'll add more AnimNodes that are then set up just like the riggerobics node. This time we'll add the "runForward,"

Figure 23.9

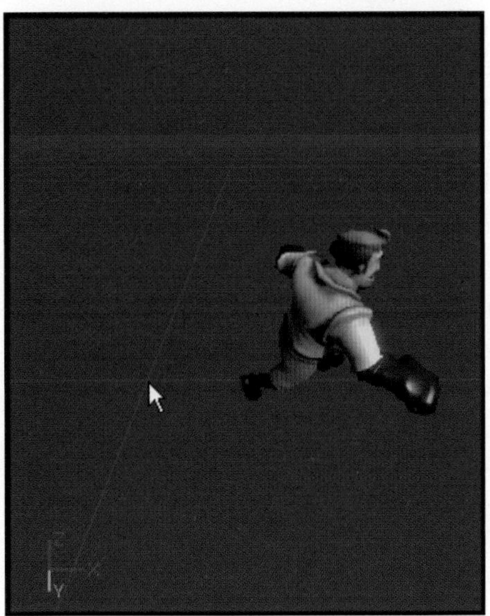

Figure 23.10

"runBackward," "runLeft," and "runRight" animations to the graph. To test how these animations blend together, use the slider at the bottom of the `AnimNodeBlendDirectional` node in the graph. Sliding the black bar changes the angle of the direction in which the player runs when playing the game. At the same time, the character is moving, just as we saw in the AnimSet editor and in 3D Studio Max [Figure 23.9].

This is a part of the plan—the character has a reference for how fast his animation is physically moving him. We want the engine to move him though, not the animation.

We could cancel out completely all of the character's origin transformations. If we did so, the character would lose the vertical bounce in his step and the vertical displacement from the scene's origin. You can see that the pelvis is now stuck to the scene origin at 0,0,0. However, we do have a couple of options. We don't want the character just translating in the X-direction or Y-direction when moving around. Instead, we're going to attach an AI controller or the Player's controller to move the character in those directions. The "RootBoneOption" roll-out near the bottom of the AnimNodeSequence options allows us to pick which axis to neutralize [Figure 23.10]. Set the RootBoneOptions to the following [Figure 23.11].

Figure 23.11

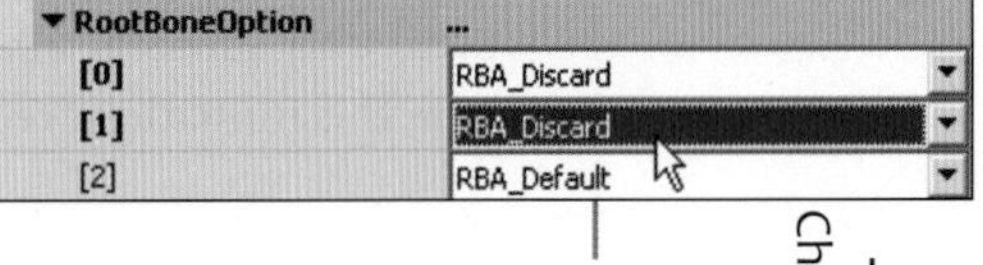

Figure 23.12

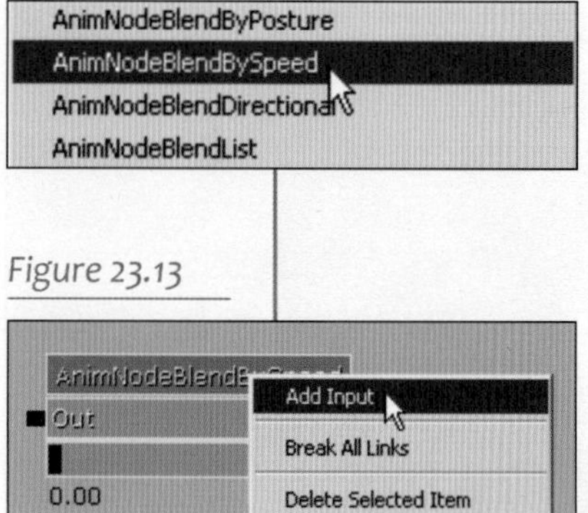


Figure 23.13

Changing the first two options to `RBA_Discard` will throw out the root-bone animation in the X and Y coordinates. Leaving the last slot at `RBA_Default` will preserve the character's bounce up and down. The bounce is merely a translation in the direction of the Z-axis. By now it should be clear that the three channels related to the RootBoneOptions correspond to the X-, Y-, and Z-axes.

Depending on which direction the character is moving, he'll play the designated animation. But what happens when he's not moving at all? We do not want to animation to translate the character when he should be stationary. To obtain this behavior, we'll add a node called `AnimNodeBlendBySpeed` [Figure 23.12].

To make this AnimNode blend together two animations, add a new input by right-clicking on the node and selecting Add Input [Figure 23.13]. The node now has two inputs.

When the character isn't moving, he'll want to play an idle animation. Attach the idle animation output to the first input of the `AnimNodeBlendBySpeed` node (the input is named Child1). Connect the `AnimNodeBlendByDirection` output to the second input (the input is named Child2). When the character begins to move, an animation is played based on the direction of motion. As you scrub the slider on the node, the character should now play the two different animations. However, Captain Hadron has short legs, so he doesn't run as fast as a regular Unreal Tournament character. We'll need to adjust the speed at which he'll start to play the "runForward" animation.

Figure 23.14

| AnimNodeBlendBySpeed | |
|---|---|
| BlendUpTime | 0.100000 |
| BlendDownTime | 0.100000 |
| BlendDownPerc | 0.200000 |
| ▼ Constraints | ... |
| [0] | 0.000000 |
| [1] | 65.000000 |
| [2] | 350.000000 |
| [3] | 900.000000 |
| bUseAcceleration | ☐ |

Adjust the node's first constraint to 65 [Figure 23.14]; this is the number with which he was moving in 3D Studio Max. Remove the unnecessary inputs. The distance traveled isn't negative as we had when moving the character in 3D Studio Max; Unreal only looks at absolute numbers for calculating the distance traveled. Here's where the animation tree becomes really interesting [Figure 23.15].

Figure 23.15

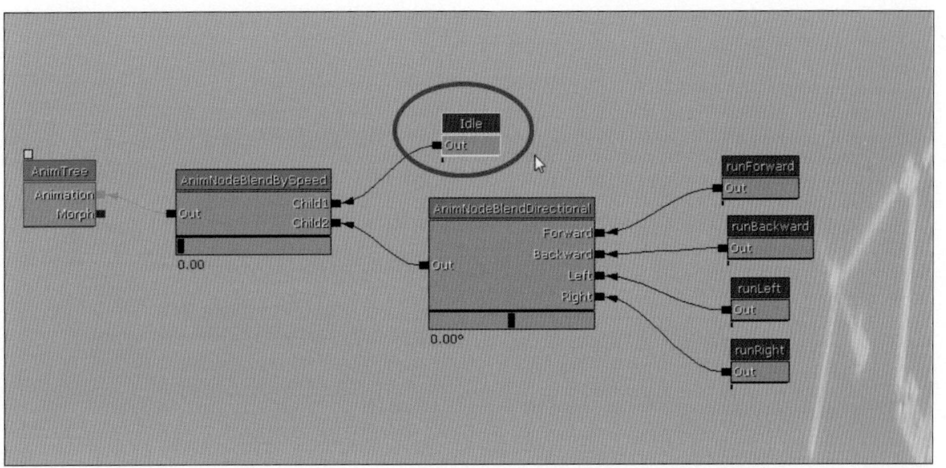


Add in a new `AnimSequencePlayer` with the idle animation set to play, and then choose the `RBA_Discard` settings for the X and Y translations. Connect the `AnimNodeBlendDirectional` output to the Child2 input of the `AnimNodeBlendBySpeed`. When the character's speed approaches or exceeds 65 units per 30 frames, the animations will blend to the `AnimNodeBlend-Directional` node, and then the `AnimNodeBlendDirectional` node will select an animation based on the direction.

Next, add in an `AnimNodeScaleRateBySpeed` [Figure 23.16]. This is a very interesting node. Once Unreal knows the distance the character is moving, it can recalculate the rate at which the animation should play based on how far the character is moving. Using the frame rate of the animation and the distance traveled, the engine can calculate which frame it should be at based on the speed of the character. Connect the node between the runForward and the `AnimNodeBlendDirectional` node. Do the same for the other three directional animations. The editor will also allow you to set the base speed of the node; add this into the Node's parameters [Figure 23.17].

Change the node's parameter to 65; again, we're using the number from 3D Studio Max's animation. Close the AnimTree editor and save your UPK file.

Your characters AnimTree should look something like Figure 23.18. You've made a pretty interesting behavior for your character's animation.

Figure 23.16

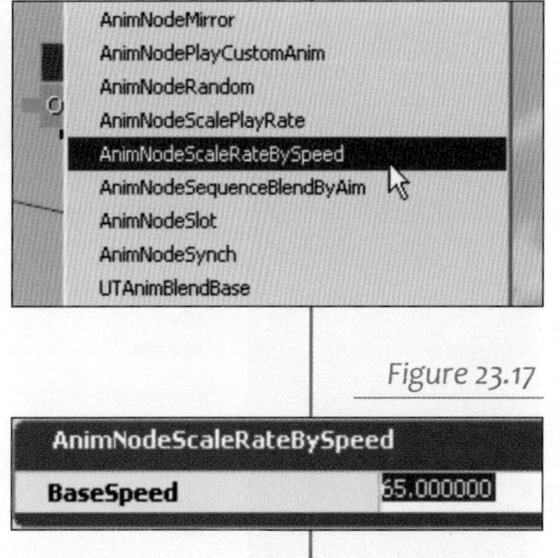


Figure 23.17

Figure 23.18

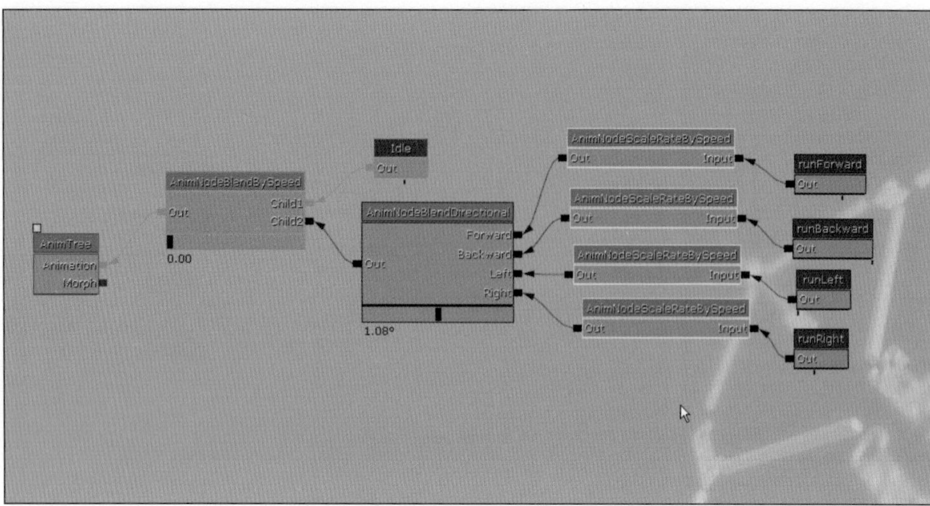


## Project

### Let the Engine Do the Animation

Open the BoxRoom.ut3 level again. We're going to add a character to run around in the level. Rather than animate the character running, we're going to let the engine decide which animation to play.

Select the character's skeletal mesh in the Generic browser. Add the character to the scene as a `SkeletalMeshMAT` object [Figure 23.19], which allows us to use his animations in Matinee. Open the Actor Properties dialog.

In the SkeletalMeshComponent property roll-out, expand the AnimSets roll-out and add the character's AnimSet, which contains the idle animation and various run animations [Figure 23.20]. This will tell the skeletal mesh in the scene which

Figure 23.19

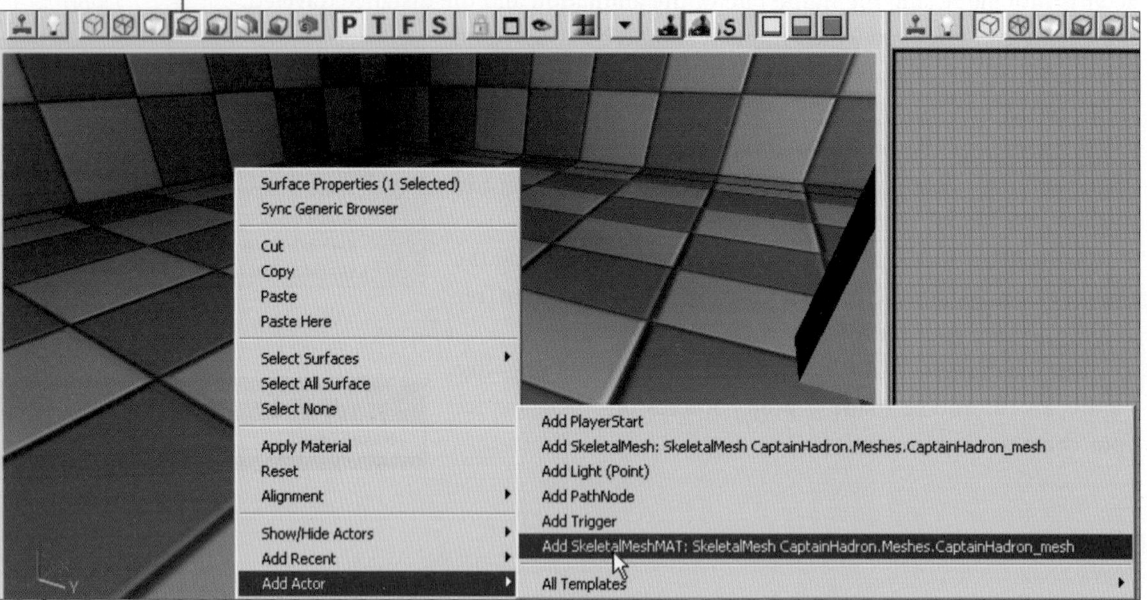

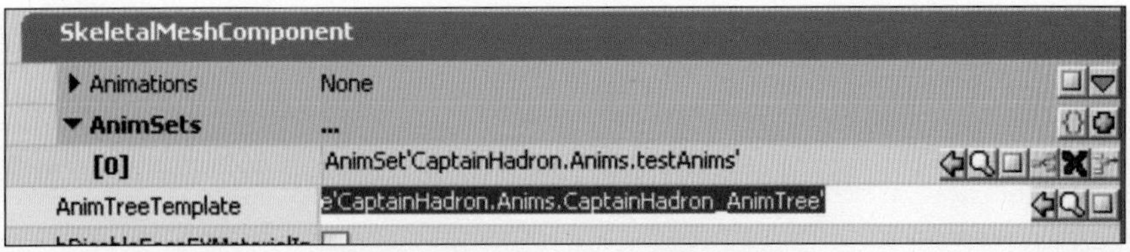

Figure 23.20

pool of animations it should draw from when animated. Now add in the Captain's AnimTree to the AnimTreeTemplate slot. This will tell the Actor in the scene which behaviors to use. Given a behavior, the Actor will know which animation to play. To tell the engine that the SkeletalMeshActor is going to be animated, you also need to change the Movement Property roll-out [Figure 23.21].

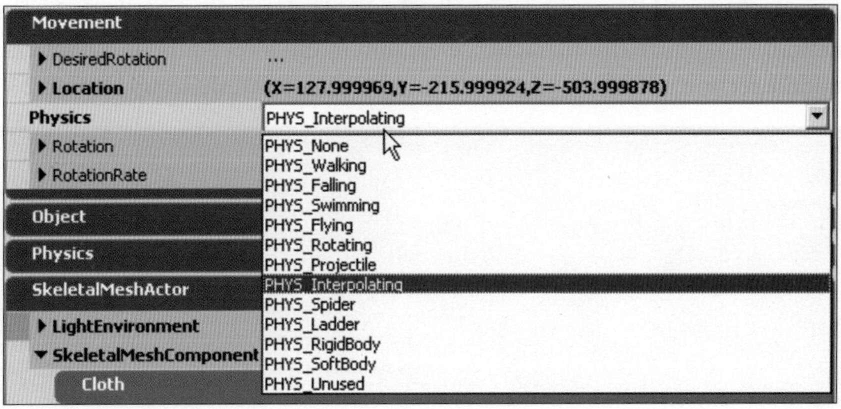

Figure 23.21

Select `PHYS_Interpolating`, which will send data about the character's movements to the AnimTree. Now your character is prepared for animation in Matinee. To add in an Unreal Matinee node, open Kismet and add a new Matinee object to the Kismet editor [Figure 23.22].

This is the Matinee node [Figure 23.23], which handles moving an interpolated mesh or triggering various particle and audio events. This node can also control the player's camera and play animated cut-scenes involving several characters and vehicles. For this project, we'll use the Matinee node to make the character walk around.

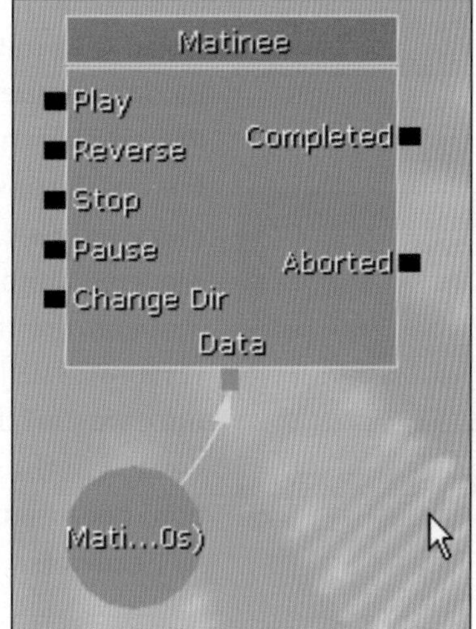


Figure 23.23

Figure 23.22

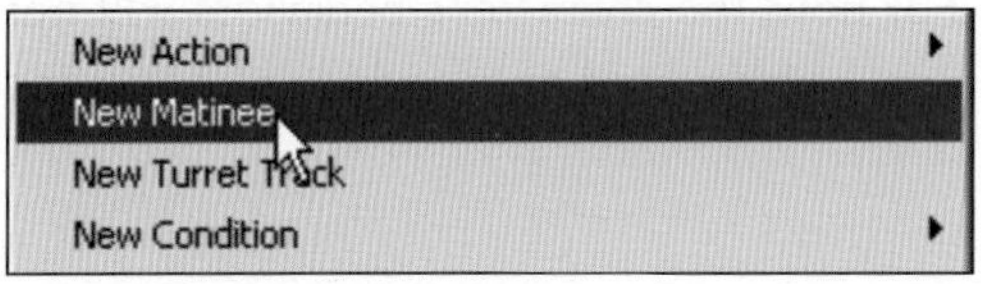

Figure 23.24

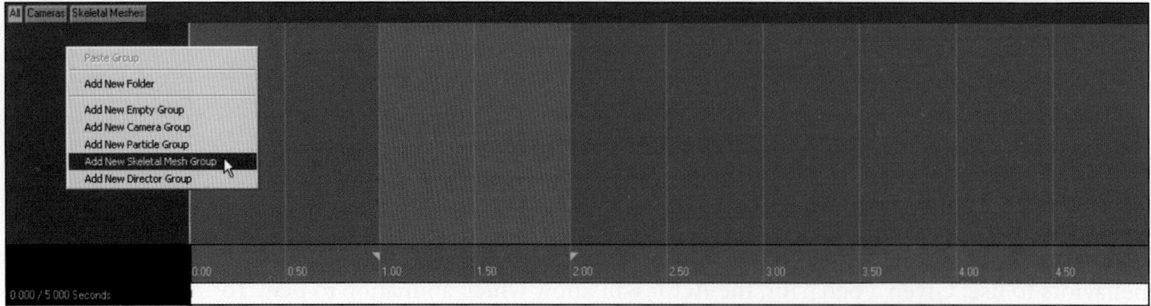


Matinee's main interface is split into three sections [Figure 23.24]. On the top is a graph editor, which is similar to the 3D Studio Max editor that allows you to edit animations. The middle section manages the track objects that you've selected for animation. To animate the character, select him in the level editor and right-click in the middle section to add the character as a NewSkeletalMeshGroup [Figure 23.25].

Figure 23.25

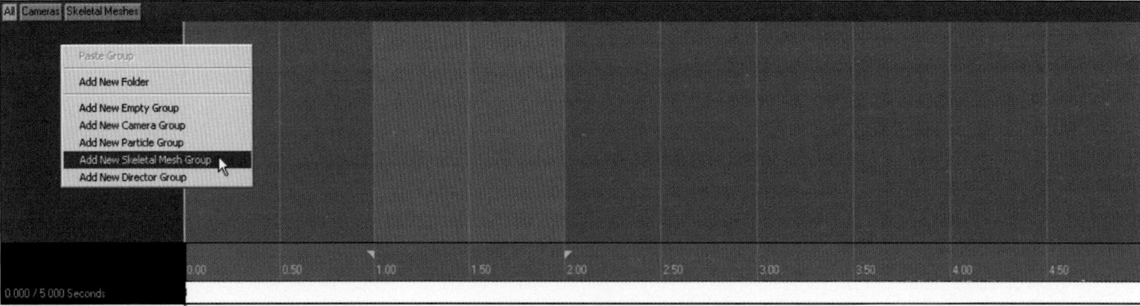


Figure 23.26

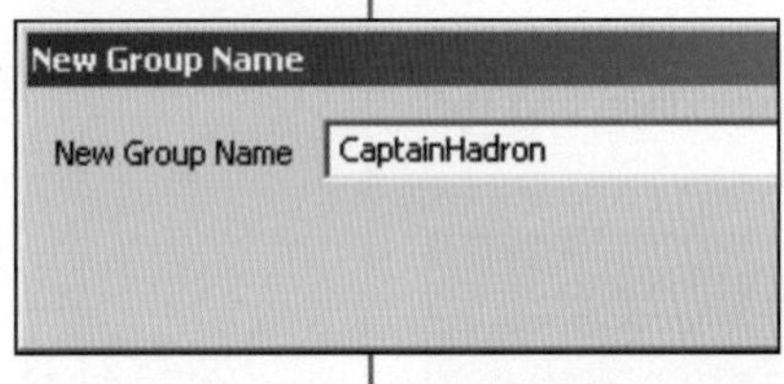


Figure 23.27

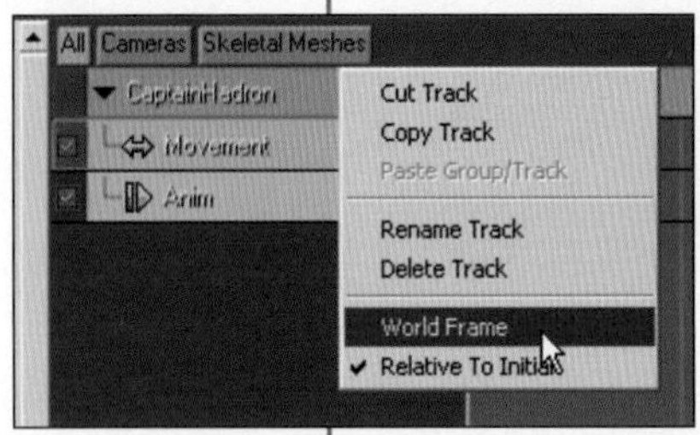


Once prompted, add the character as "CaptainHadron" and click on OK [Figure 23.26].

We'll be moving our character with the Movement track. To keep him from starting in strange places, right-click on the Movement Tracks and select World Frame [Figure 23.27]. The Relative to Initial option is used when playing a game. If the animation requires a character to stop and simply deliver a line of dialog, you'll want to play that wherever the character is at the time. For our purposes, we want our character to start in the same place every time we play this animation, so we'll use the world-frame movement mode.

Grab the time slider in the editor and drag it to 5 seconds [Figure 23.28]. This is enough time to see our animation playing once we start the level and to scrub through the animations you've created in the scene. For now, the character's behaviors will not play, because the scene is being edited only and is not executing its behaviors.

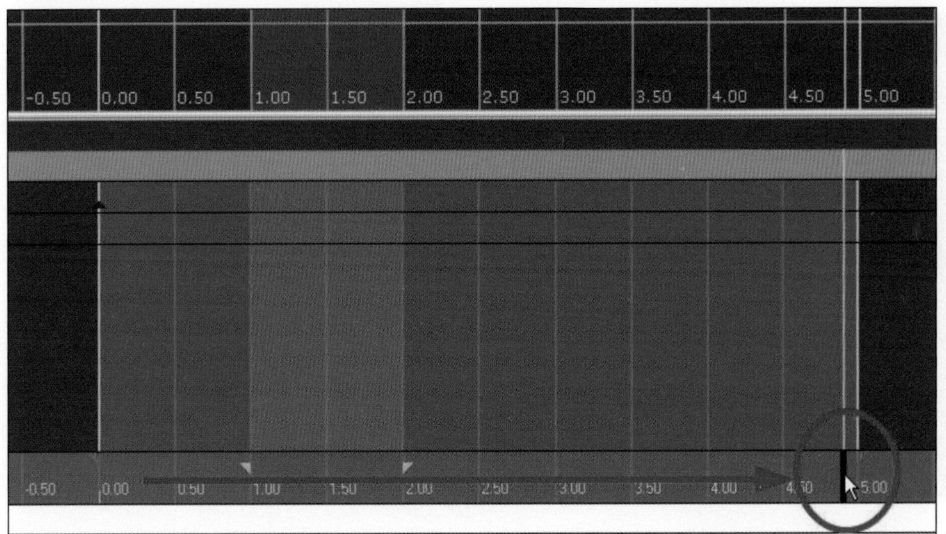


Figure 23.28

Moving the Captain forward, we can test our AnimTree [Figure 23.29]. Go back to the Matinee track and press [enter] with the movement track highlighted. This action adds a key frame to the timeline in Matinee [Figure 23.30].

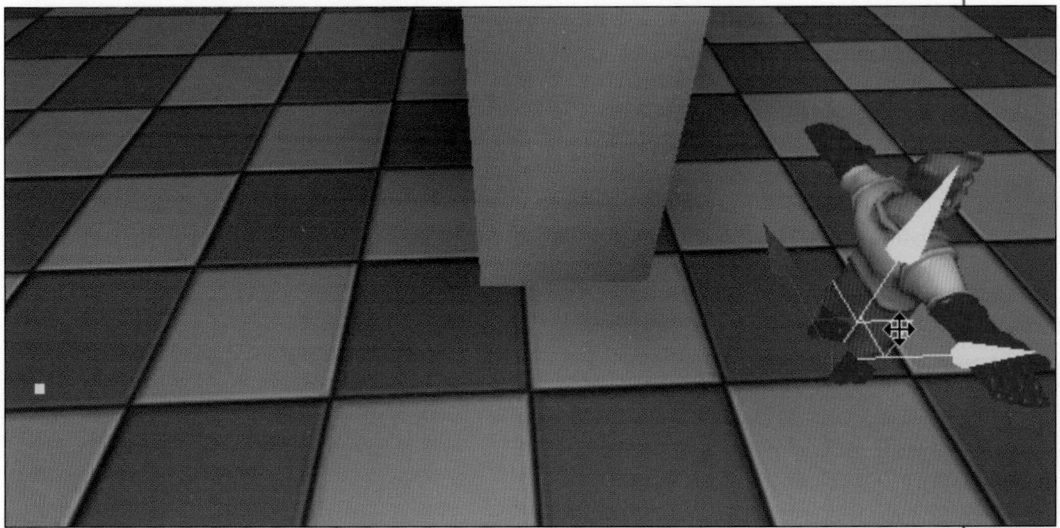

Figure 23.29

The key frames can be moved around in this editor, just like we moved key frames in 3D Studio Max. By right-clicking on the key-frame marker, you can adjust the properties numerically.

The editor's display window should update, showing a dotted line that indicates the character's movement [Figure 23.31]. Close Matinee and return to the Kismet

Figure 23.30

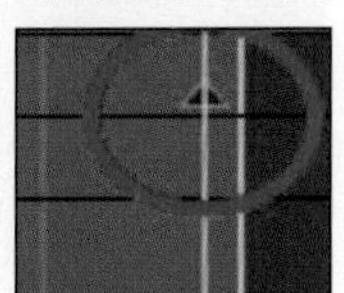

Figure 23.31

editor for the level. It's important to notice the spacing of the dots on the line. The closer together the dots are, the slower the animation will be. Similarly, the farther apart the dots are, the faster the animation will be.

Connect the output of the Level Loaded and Visible node to the Play input tab on the Matinee node [Figure 23.32]. This will cause the Matinee sequence to play when the level is started.

When the character moves, the animation starts off slowly. As the characters moves faster, the animation plays faster, thanks to the AnimNodeScaleRateBySpeed node in the AnimTree. When the character stops moving, the idle animation is activated, thanks to the AnimNodeBlendBySpeed node in the AnimTree. This character is ready for action!

Figure 23.32

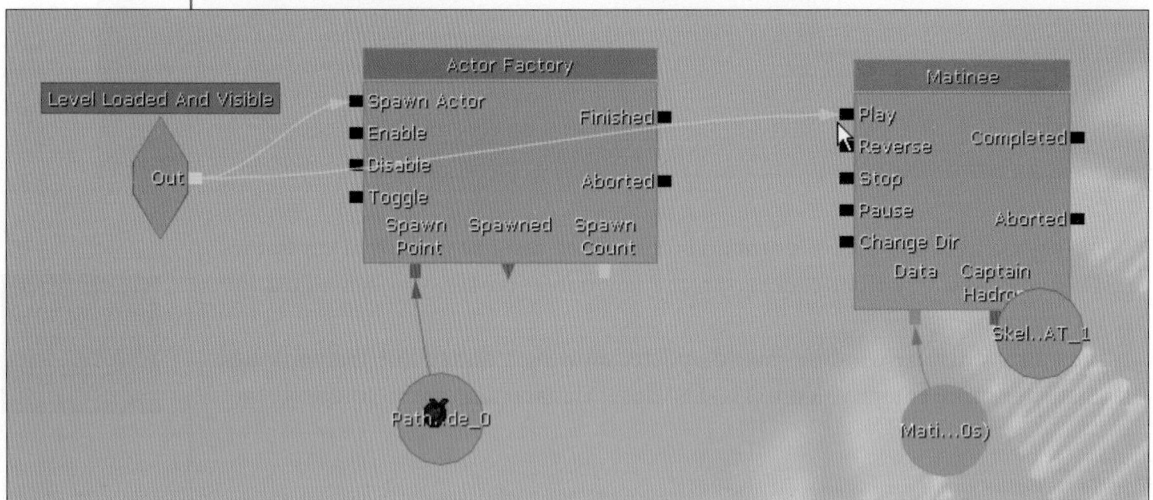

Once the animations in the AnimSet and the behaviors in the AnimTree are connected to the character's default properties via UScript, the behaviors are controllable as you would expect for a regular character. The WASD keys will work the same on this character as with any other character. This is just the tip of the iceberg when it comes to what the AnimTree can do. If you were to open the AnimTree of the Unreal Tournament characters, you'd see many blending nodes between weapons, vehicles, and various physics conditions.

You'll need to create a new set of animations for your weapon. Based on the unarmed animations, make the changes required to add a weapon. Once the animation set is complete, use UScript to create a new node to switch the set of animations from unarmed to armed. It's up to you to include as many animations as you have time to build.

## On Your Own

You'll need a lot of animations to complete your game. The AnimTree editor has many nodes with which you can experiment to discover new behaviors. Once you start adding weapon types and inventory items, you'll need to create new animations to support them. These can be added through the inventory of Unreal scripts, and you'll want to add your own weapons to the `AnimNodeBlendByWeapon` object.

A good place to start is to add in another `BlendBySpeed` child input for a slow walk cycle, a sneak cycle, or even a faster sprint cycle. As long as the stride starts with the same foot forward, the blend among all of the various animations will be seamless.

# Part III: Programming

*Breaking the Code: Programming the Unreal Way*

# 24 Why Learn Unreal?

## Learning How to Talk to Unreal

Welcome to the fascinating realm of video game programming. Game programmers are central to the game production pipeline and carry various responsibilities in ensuring the success of a game development project. Programmers can perform tasks in various areas like core engine development, gameplay, tools, audio/sound or game testing. The game engine is the central focal point of any game and drives the various aspects of the game's functionality and design. In this chapter we will introduce simple concepts with respect to the Unreal game engine.

Unreal Engine 3 is a complete game development framework for next-generation consoles and DirectX9-equipped PCs, providing the vast array of core technologies, content creation tools, and support infrastructure required by top game developers. Unreal Engine 3 is an excellent way to enter the game programming arena as it provides a simple scripting language called Unreal Script; for simplicity, we will call it UScript from now on.

UScript is easy to program with and can achieve a majority of features required for creating a video game from scratch. You are reading this book because you want to understand how games are made, and programming is what connects all the pieces in your game. With a powerful scripting language like UScript, you can reach your goals efficiently and with ease.

## What Is an Engine?

A game engine is a piece of software or code written by programmers to facilitate the game production pipeline. It can serve various needs specific to a particular game or in general to all games. A renderer is one component that is common to all game engines and is responsible for drawing the scene on your display. Some of the other common elements include camera systems, user interface, animation, physics and artificial intelligence.

## Introduction to Game Objects

Even though the term *game objects* may seem daunting, it is in fact very simple to understand. Objects are, simply put, everything that you interact with inside the video game. Consider a simple game like chess: the objects here are the checkered board and the different movable pieces.

Likewise, in video games, everything that displays interaction or behavior is called a game object. Every object has a set of unique properties that distinguishes itself from the rest. Again, going back to our chess example, a pawn has a certain look and a set of legal moves that make it different from a knight, which in turn has its own look and set of moves.

In programming terms, this set of properties is known as a *class*. When a programmer says, "I am creating a new class called pawn and writing code for that," what he means is that he is writing some code that will uniquely represent the pawn; and when objects are created using this particular code and placed in the game, they will behave like pawns.

### Objects in Unreal

When you play any Unreal game, you will come across all kinds of objects. It is important to note that, as a player, you are one of the objects in the game. You interact with other objects such as bots (computer generated enemies), other human players, weapons, doors and vehicles, to name a few. These are all objects that have been assembled and packaged together to provide an entertaining and engaging experience for the player. It is also important to note that for any object that you interact with in the game, there is written code that sits in a class buried somewhere in the entire game code.

As a game programmer, you will be learning how to manage all this code, add some new classes, modify some existing ones, and learn the process of creating a game that stems out of your unique ideas.

## Object Oriented Programming in Unreal

*Object oriented programming* simply means that the code written for the entire game is nicely packaged into simple modules and is not one giant piece of code. These modules can either be simple classes, as described earlier, or a collection of those classes. A simple analogy of object oriented code compares it to a human body. The human body is a complex entity made of different organs that work together as a whole. If one piece of the body stops functioning—say, the arm—it does not mean the entire body will come to a stop. Every part has its role to play, and the parts are nicely organized such that the entire body works as one unit.

Object oriented programming works exactly in that manner. Different objects are combined together to create unique experiences for the player; but if one of these objects fails to perform its task or exhibit the intended behavior, the game does not come crashing down. UScript is a purely object oriented language, and we will learn what that means in detail in the following chapters.

A basic principle of object oriented programming is that two classes shouldn't be doing the same thing. Let's consider this example: say you have a class called "automobiles." We can easily say that it is the parent class for cars, trucks, vans, and buses. So we can write all the code for automobiles inside of the "automobiles" class, for example, code that describes how a vehicle drives and what its speed is. These are properties that are exhibited by all automobiles.

Now we get into the "cars" class, which is a child of "automobiles" class. We add only code that will make the object represent a car and save all the common code that it inherits because it is also an automobile. In object oriented terminology, this property is called *inheritance.*

Let's consider these two weapons in Unreal Tournament 3: the Instagib Rifle and the Sniper Rifle. They do very similar things—consume ammo, fire an instant shot, do damage to a target, etc. They share so many similarities that much of their basic functionality and behavior can be achieved with the same lines of code.

Instead of duplicating this code between the two classes that represent the weapons, the common code is factored into a parent class, UTWeapon, which handles most of the basic operations of a weapon. They then extend that class, meaning a child class will exhibit all the behaviors of its parent class and add or tweak only properties that make it different.

This approach has many advantages. It makes it much easier to maintain the basic functions for all three classes, since they share code.

## The Tick

The Unreal Engine divides time into *ticks.* A tick is not a specific length or value and is dependent on the machine the player is using to play the game, which allows the Unreal engine to scale this value according to the power of the machine and the current load. A powerful machine will have a small value for the tick and vice versa. It is important to note that UScript provides a simple way to interact with the massive Unreal Engine codebase.

When you play a game that was created using the Unreal Engine, you cannot assume that all the functionality was written in UScript. What is certain is that some of the functionality is written in it, while a lot of the functionality is executed directly by the engine itself.

For example, say you picked up a weapon while playing Unreal Tournament 3 and opened fire. The engine automatically plays the animation and effects for the weapon fire and projectiles. But when the weapon's ammo hits a target, UScript takes control in the following manner:

- The weapon object is notified that it has hit a target.
- The weapon informs target: "I have hit you and you will now receive damage." The important thing to note here is that the target could have been friendly and may not take any damage due to the hit; however, the weapon does not care about this fact. This is known as *data encapsulation,* a powerful feature in object oriented programming.
- After being fired, the weapon could do any number of things, such as play the recoil animation, render a strike effect, play a sound that reflects the hit, and so on.
- The ammo that was used for the fire is removed from the player's inventory, and the bullets that were used as projectiles are removed from the game so they are no longer displayed.

The above sequence is executed by a program that was written for the weapon object using UScript. The important fact to note is that it will take the same amount of time to execute this sequence regardless of the machine that the user is playing the game on; however, the number of ticks taken to execute the sequence will vary depending on the power of the player's computer.

## The Virtual Machine

A *virtual machine* is a software implementation of a machine or a computer. The programming language Java implements a virtual machine that it runs on. This makes it operation system independent; similarly, UScript implements its own virtual machine and does all the processing in software.

Using a virtual machine may seem at first to be inefficient; however, the important thing to note is that all the performance intensive tasks are implemented in C++ or native code, and only gameplay-specific tasks are performed using UScript. In reality, UScript has a counterpart implemented in C++ that is hidden from the programmers. This arrangement hides all the complexity of the game engine and provides an easy way to achieve gameplay features necessary for the game.

To better illustrate this advantage, consider a scenario in which you throw a grenade at the enemy; its explosion results in the enemy's death. The three objects—you, the grenade, and the enemy—are all UScript objects: the processes of throwing the grenade, having it explode, and updating the death of the enemy are all handled by UScript. The rendering of the objects, skeleton transformations, and their collision and location update are performed by the native C++ code.

# 25 Introduction to Unreal Script

*Making Sense of It All*

## What to Expect

In this chapter we will learn the programming language that will be used to create our game using the Unreal Engine. This language is called UScript. The chapter goes into details to explain to the novice programmer the essence of programming involved in making a video game.

No programming background is necessary, as everything is explained from scratch. UScript was designed by Epic Games as a way to engineer Unreal Engine modifications without recompiling the engine's core, which is designed in C++. UScript syntax was designed based on Java and JavaScript, allowing many web developers, and even people who have done almost no code at all, easy access to coding some powerful game features.

### Set-up

UScript requires very few things; just a text editor, and a way to compile. UScript files are saved as .uc files, and you can set up simple shortcuts to compile and run the code that you will write. Compiling and running your own code is covered in detail in the next chapter.

You will want to have at least a general text editor running at this point since we are going to dive right into every part of the .uc file, from class definitions to default properties, explaining everything along the way.

### Classes

A class is a set of written code. Classes in Unreal are based on a hierarchy, ending with Object at the top, and Actor as the common favorite as the next link in the hierarchy, and so on until all classes are included. All classes in Unreal are then connected back to the Actor and Object classes.

UScript is a pure object oriented language, which means that any class that you can use in the game is an extension of the Object class. Every class that you create starts with a *class definition*, and the code for that looks like this:

```
class myEditor extends Editor;
```

The class definition states simply that the class `myEditor` extends the parent class `Editor`; a parent class is something that is above your current class. A *class declarative* is simply the word *class* followed by the class name, and then the word *extends*, followed by the name of the class you are extending. As with many programming languages, a semicolon terminates a program statement and informs the compiler that the logic for this line has ended.

## Variables

Variables store data in some form, from text to numbers. Variables are useful either in transferring data from one code segment to another or in calculating and storing new information in a code segment. Variables appear like this:

```
var [variable type] [variable name];
var int iHealth;
```

The types of variables in UScript are Integer, Floating Point, Boolean Value, Byte, String, Name, Enumeration, Actor Reference, Class Reference, Struct, and Conditionals.

### Integer

Integer variables store whole numbers; they cannot be decimals. For example, 250 is a valid integer, but 250.1 is not valid. Integer variables also allow operations applied to them, such as adding and subtracting to the number to increase or decrease it:

```
Var int iHealth;
iHealth++;
```

The first line of code declares an integer variable named `iHealth`. The second line of code increments the variable's value by 1, which is equivalent to the statement: `iHealth = iHealth + 1`. Notice how the *i* is lower case and *H* is upper case in the name `iHealth`; this is a good way of representing variables where the first letter shows what type of variable it is, in this case integer, and then what it represents—in this case, health value. Having a good variable naming convention goes a long way toward writing clean code.

```
iHealth--;
```

This line of code will subtract 1 from your number, which is equivalent to the statement: `iHealth = iHealth - 1.`

### Floating Point

Float values are much like integers in that they store numerical values, but these values can store both decimals and whole numbers. However, float values cannot interact with integers; you would have to convert all integers to floats if you wanted to obtain an answer other than an integer. When using expressions that involve both integers and floats, you need to remember that you will always get an integer back, but it will not be the number you wanted. If you need a more precise health variable, you could use it the following way:

```
var float fHealth;
```

Note that `fHealth--; and fHealth++;` will not work with float values. You will need to use:

```
Float = Float + 1;
```

### Boolean Value

Bools have been around for a shorter amount of time than other variable types. They are built around two words, *true* and *false.*

```
var bool bHealth;
```

The line of code declares a Boolean variable `bHealth` that stores whether an object in question is alive (`bHealth` is *true*) or dead (`bHealth` is *false*). Booleans are nothing but special byte values that store either 0 (false) or 1 (true).

```
var byte bByte;  if ( bByte == 1 ) {   Do Something... }
```

The previous code block is equivalent to the next code block.

```
var bool bBool;  if ( bBool ) {   Do Something... }
```

### String

A string is an ordered sequence of numbers and letters (alphanumerical characters) that is delimited by quotes. Here is an example of some things you could do with strings:

```
var string sString1;
var string sString2;
var string[25] sString3;
sString1 = "Uscript Tutorial";
sString2 = "Beginners Guide";
sString3 = sString1 $ sString2;
// concatenates sString1 and sString2 and stores the result in sString3
sString3 = Left(sString1, 1);
// finds the left most character of sString1
sString3 = Right(sString1, 1);
//finds the right most character of sString1
sString3 = Len(sString1);
//finds the number of characters in sString1
sString3 = Caps(sString1);
//converts the string to all upper case
```

The first two lines of code are simple declarations for strings sString1 and sString2. The declaration for sString3 has brackets containing the number 25, which means that the number of characters in the string must be less than or equal to 25. The two slashes // tell the scripting system that a *code comment* follows the slashes. These comments allow you to provide explanations about the code you wrote. Also, remember that when strings are given a value, the value must be in quotes.

### Name

Name variables are hardly used, but they still serve a purpose. Strings and Names both store alphanumerical values, and it can be easy to confuse names with strings, but remember that names are not strings. A string can be modified dynamically, but a name is simply a label for an object.

```
var name nName;
Name = 'Uscript';
```

Notice how names use single quotes instead of double quotes; names are a special type of strings and are used to identify various objects in your game. You can use the name to search for a particular object using your UScript code.

### Enumeration

An enumeration is a type that is defined by the script writer and consists of a set of identifiers chosen by the writer. Enumerations are often referred to as enum values. An example of an enumeration is as follows:

```
enum eName{    Mark,    Pat,    Jeff }; // define the enumeration and
        the values it can contain
var eName MyeName;  //declare a variable of that enum type
MyeName = Mark; // assign a value to the variable, note that if
        the value assigned is not either Mark, Pat or Jeff the code
        will not compile
```

Enumerations are helpful when you want to group certain properties together; for example, you could have an enum defined as `eHairColor;` you could predefine its values beforehand to contain only black, blonde, and brunette.

### Actor Reference

Actor references are different from other variable types as they refer to an actual object found inside the game you are coding for. These could be any Actor, including your main game character, weapons, vehicles, and enemies. Actor references are useful in creating various behaviors involving your main game character and other Non-Playing Characters (NPCs).

```
var Pawn Enemy; // declare the actor reference variable
Enemy = mainPlayer.Enemy; //assign the value to the actor
        reference variable
```

As you can see, the Pawn (special type of an Actor) is now in the class being declared as variable Enemy. Later in the code, it is assigned as the mainPlayer's current enemy. As you play the game, your current enemy could change to the one you are currently fighting against. So a variable that keeps track of your current enemy would be useful. Actor references are more common in modifications of games or in game cheats. Actor references can also be done in this way:

```
var Pawn Enemy, Target;
```

In this case, you would be referencing the Actor twice, under different names. As you can see, we use commas to separate and a semicolon at the end to save space; but you can achieve the same goal with

```
var Pawn Enemy; var Pawn Target;
```

Also, note that you can declare Actor references while keeping the original name of the actor.

### Class Reference

Class references are much like Actor references in that they reference something found within the game. Class references, unlike Actor references, don't reference an object in the game; rather, they reference a class. Here is an example of a class reference:

```
var class Reference;  // declare the class reference variable
Reference = Class'Pawn'; // define the class reference variable
```

As shown above, a class reference variable is declared, but we do not know what type of class it will be referencing at that time. Later in the game, we define it to refer to the pawn class. This is useful in situations in which the game does not know what class it might need to refer at compile time and that will become clear only at run time. If this sounds confusing, there is no reason to worry; we will be going over Actor and class reference examples in the next few chapters.

### Struct

Structs, also known as structures, are a way of defining a new variable made up of other variables. A struct is very similar to a class, except that it contains only variables. A class, on the other hand, can also contain functions. An example of a struct is as follows:

```
struct sPerson {var string sName; var integer iHealth;};
//define a struct
var sPerson Me, You;
// declare two variables that use the struct
Me.sName = "Mark";    Me.iHealth = 100;
//assign the values for the struct variables
Me = You;
//declare Me equal to You
```

In the above example, we used two variables and grouped them into a struct. A struct can have many more variables, if needed. The main reason to use a struct is to group together variables that make sense. A good example would be a struct that groups together all player properties such as speed, health, ammo, armor, and so on.

### Conditionals

Conditionals are useful when performing branching logic. Branching operations are common in game logic to test and perform various game-choice paths as listed in the game design. The conditionals are a combination of if/then/else statements along with a meaningful operator. The list of operators that can be used are:

- = = (Equal to)
- && (Logical And)

- || (Logical Or)
- != (Not equal to)
- < (Less than)
- <= (Less than or equal to)
- > (Greater than)
- >= (Greater than or equal to)
- ~= (Approximately equal to)

The code below gives examples of using conditional statements with appropriate operators.

```
var bool bMe; var int iAge;
if ( bMe ) {    // Code if bMe is True }
else if ( !bMe) {    // Code if bMe is False }
if ( iAge  > 10 ) {    // Code if Age is Greater than 10 }
if(bMe && iAge>10) { //Code if both bMe is true and iAge is
       greater than 10)
```

In the examples, we are checking for various conditions and appropriately taking the corresponding action.

## Flow Control

Flow control operations are essential in implementing gameplay elements that require traversing an array of game objects and picking the right one. Looping statements help us achieve this; there are different ways to code this logic. These are For Loops, Do Loops , While Loops, and Switch Statements.

### For Loops

For Loops are conditions in which a set of code is executed continuously until something is done to stop it, which can be anything you decide. Here is an example of a For Loop:

```
var int i; //Declare the variable i
for ( i=0; i < 2; i++) {    // Code here as long as i is less than 2 }
```

In the above code, we are looping our code starting *i* at value 0 until *i* is less than 2. This means that our loop will run two times.

### Do Loops

Do Loops are very similar to For Loops in that they compute a certain code until a condition is met. In Do Loops, you don't set an initial value for the variable, and you don't increase the value of the variable unless you add something into the loop. Here is an example of a Do Loop:

```
var int i;
do { i++;  //add more code that you require } until ( i == 2 );
```

It's very similar to For Loops, as you can see; but in this case, the loop terminates when the value of *i* is 2, and the variable *i* is incremented inside the loop.

### While Loops

While Loops are like Do loops, but the termination condition is tested at the beginning of the loop, whereas Do loops test the termination condition at the end of the loop. Here is an example of a While Loop:

```
var int i;
while ( i < 2 ) {   // Code Here   i++; }
```

### Switch Statements

Switch statements are, in short, over-complicated *if* statements that serve a purpose greater than your average *if*. Switch statements are used to go through certain sections of code, depending on the value of a variable. Switch statements are followed by case statements for all possible switch values, as shown in the code below:

```
var int i;
switch ( i ) {   case 0:  // Code  break;   case 1:  // Code  break;
default:  //Code break; }
```

The default case is executed when there is no corresponding case available for the current value of variable *i*. Switches are useful in selecting among the various states for the game objects. For example, an enemy in the game could be in various states such as wander, attack, sleep, defend, etc. Switch statements can help code the logic for switching among the enemy's various states, depending on the variable *i*.

### Functions

Functions are blocks of code that sensibly belong together. For example, you could have a function called `attackTheNearestEnemy`. In this function, you would first want to find what your current location is and what are the enemies near you. Then you would sort the enemy list, using the distance between you and enemy as the sorting parameter. These operations will require you to write a few lines of code and sometimes even call on some other functions. Here is another simple function example:

```
function Msg (string Message)
{
if ( Me != None )    {     Me.ClientMessage(Message);    }
}
```

You will notice how the function `Msg` is set up to make client messages, where the variable "Me" is an Actor that represents the current player. Notice that this function uses built-in features for the Actor class variable `Me`. However, functions could be completely independent and still perform a specific task. Here is an example of a function that calculates the factorial of a number. Notice how this function returns a value by using the return statement. Also interesting to note is that this function is recursive, which means that the function calls itself and runs the risk of going into an infinite loop. In the example, however, the recursion terminates for two reasons. First, the recursive call is applied to a number one less than the caller's input (the Number value decreases with each call). Second, the function has a nonrecursive case when the Number is nonpositive.

```
function int Factorial( int Number )
{
   if( Number <= 0 )
      return 1;
   else
      return Number * Factorial( Number - 1 );
}
```

### States

States are code written within a class that gets executed when the object that represents that class is in that state. Every object in Unreal can be in only one state at a given point of time. For example, an enemy could be in any of these states: dying, wandering, attacking, following, etc. UScript allows you to program complex behavior by the use of states and, specifically, state machine logic. Here is a simple code that shows how states are used in code:

```
state() openDoor
{
   function touchDoor( actor Other)
   {
       bDoor = true;
   }
}
// Trigger turns the light off.
state() closeDoor
{
   function touchDoor( actor Other)
  {
       bDoor= false;
   }
}
```

Here we can see two states for the door object; both of them call the `touchDoor` function and set the Boolean value for `bDoor` to true or false depending on the state the door is in. Another important feature of writing state code is the ability to use latent functions. A latent function contains code that does not get executed immediately and waits for some time to elapse. Here is code that explains this function:

```
state() openDoor
{
Begin:
   function touchDoor( actor Other)
   {
       Log( "The door is now touched by the Actor!" );
       Sleep(2.0);
       bDoor = true;
       Log( "The Door is now Open!" );
       goto 'Begin';
   }
   GotoState('closeDoor');
}
```

Here you will notice that the function `touchDoor` inputs text to the game's log file and calls the latent function `Sleep`, which waits two seconds before setting the Boolean variable `bDoor` to true. Also important to note is how labels can be used in the state code to compartmentalize various aspects of the code. In the above example, the label Begin is used to track the starting point of the state. You can have labels in the state code and use goto statements to jump to those labels. Lastly, you can also go from one state to another using the `GotoState` function.

## Default Properties

The *defaultproperties* code block is the conclusion to your classes; it is also used to define your variables' default values, which can be overwritten throughout your class in functions. Default Properties appear as so:

```
defaultproperties {
        variable1=value1
        variable2=value2
        bMovable = false
}
```

There is no need to use semicolons in default properties, but you can if you want. You can specify the default values for your class-specific variables in here. You can also override the values specified by your parent classes in the hierarchy. As shown in the code above, we have two class-specific variables, `variable1` and `variable2`, and we set their values. We also have one derived variable, `bMovable`, that is defined in the Actor class; we are overriding its value in our class by setting it to *false*. This means that the class we are creating cannot move initially in the game.

## Review

This chapter should give you a good understanding of the basics of the UScript language. You can also get more information from the Unreal Developers Network (UDN) website at http://udn.epicgames.com/Three/UScriptReference.html.

As with any programming language, the familiarity will grow only when you start writing code and trying out its various features. In the following chapters, we will be building the foundation for UScript and game programming in general. We are confident that you will be able to independently program any feature in your game once you have finished reading this book.

# 26 Mutators

*Make Unreal Yours*

## What to Expect

In this chapter, we will learn the concept of what a mutator is in the Unreal Engine. Mutators are simple changes that can be made to the playability of the Unreal game without requiring major changes to the engine or script code. A mutator is a simple script that can be enabled or disabled during play time to add additional gameplay elements.

Mutators can be as simple as slowing the speed of a player depending on the gun he carries or as more complex as having all enemies converge to attack the player when he is weak and running away from him when he is strong.

Unreal Tournament 3 has a very flexible system that renders it an ideal platform to make changes and customize gameplay. You can achieve various levels of customization by creating a simple mutator, a custom game mode, or a total conversion mod. In this chapter we will focus on the Mutator, a short snippet of UScript code that can be run as a set of new rules in any game type, either on a server or in single player via Instant Action.

Mutators make only small changes to the game—and *should* make only small changes. However, you can create a variety of Mutators and mix and match them achieve unique behavior and engaging gameplay.

## Getting Started

First, you need to know a bit about how Unreal Tournament 3 is set up. Unreal Tournament 3 stores everything in *packages*—that includes resources like 3D models, textures, maps, sounds, and, in our case, UScript code. Packages are collections of game resources and generally have the extension .upk.

A code package tends to have the extension .u, but this does not necessarily mean that it contains only code. Code packages can also contain things such as sounds and textures that the code depends on. Placing all these things in one package keeps things organized and easy to manage.

Since UScript is an object oriented scripting language, whenever we want to make changes or additions, instead of writing a lot of new code or changing old code, we can instead override or *extend* existing code to suit our needs.

In fact, you should never modify the stock Unreal Tournament 3 script files as this will prevent you from playing online. The UScript files are available to download by following this link: http://udn.epicgames.com/Files/UT3/Mods/UT3ScriptSource_1.5.rar.

Copy the files from the above link, and save them to your default Src directory.

### Windows XP

```
C:\Documents and Settings\My Documents\My Games\Unreal Tournament
3\UTGame\Src
```

### Windows Vista

```
C:\Users\*YOUR USERNAME*\Documents\My Games\Unreal Tournament 3\
UTGame\Src
```

You may need to create this directory if it does not exist. Don't forget to supplant the placeholder YOUR USERNAME with your own Windows user name. You will now create a folder to house your script code, to separate it from the existing UT code. Add a folder in Src called "FirstMutator" [Figure 26.1] and a second folder under that called "Classes" [Figure 26.2].

Figure 26.1

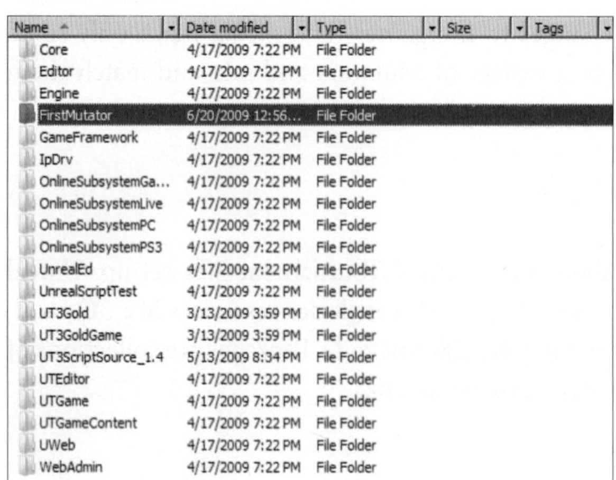

Name
Date modified
Type
Size
Tags
Core 4/17/2009 7:22 PM File Folder
Editor 4/17/2009 7:22 PM File Folder
Engine 4/17/2009 7:22 PM File Folder
FirstMutator 6/20/2009 12:56... File Folder
GameFramework 4/17/2009 7:22 PM File Folder
IpDrv 4/17/2009 7:22 PM File Folder
OnlineSubsystemGa... 4/17/2009 7:22 PM File Folder
OnlineSubsystemLive 4/17/2009 7:22 PM File Folder
OnlineSubsystemPC 4/17/2009 7:22 PM File Folder
OnlineSubsystemPS3 4/17/2009 7:22 PM File Folder
UnrealEd 4/17/2009 7:22 PM File Folder
UnrealScriptTest 4/17/2009 7:22 PM File Folder
UT3Gold 3/13/2009 3:59 PM File Folder
UT3GoldGame 3/13/2009 3:59 PM File Folder
UT3ScriptSource_1.4 5/13/2009 8:34 PM File Folder
UTEditor 4/17/2009 7:22 PM File Folder
UTGame 4/17/2009 7:22 PM File Folder
UTGameContent 4/17/2009 7:22 PM File Folder
UWeb 4/17/2009 7:22 PM File Folder
WebAdmin 4/17/2009 7:22 PM File Folder

Figure 26.2

Core
Editor
Engine
FirstMutator
Classes
GameFramework
IpDrv
OnlineSubsystemGameSpy
OnlineSubsystemLive
OnlineSubsystemPC
OnlineSubsystemPS3
UnrealEd
UnrealScriptTest
UT3Gold

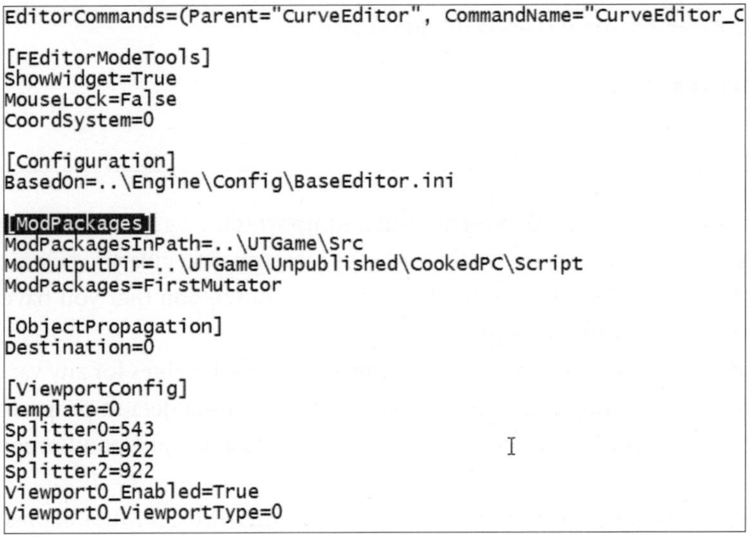

```
EditorCommands=(Parent="CurveEditor", CommandName="CurveEditor_C

[FEditorModeTools]
ShowWidget=True
MouseLock=False
CoordSystem=0

[Configuration]
BasedOn=..\Engine\Config\BaseEditor.ini

[ModPackages]
ModPackagesInPath=..\UTGame\Src
ModOutputDir=..\UTGame\Unpublished\CookedPC\Script
ModPackages=FirstMutator

[ObjectPropagation]
Destination=0

[ViewportConfig]
Template=0
Splitter0=543
Splitter1=922
Splitter2=922
Viewport0_Enabled=True
Viewport0_ViewportType=0
```

*Figure 26.3*

The Classes folder is where we will be keeping all our UScript that we're about to write—and we're just about ready to get started, but before we do we need to make sure that the game knows where to find our new code, so we need to find UTEditor.ini in our Unreal Tournament 3 directory. Use the system search to find it—this is a very useful tool for finding files in Unreal Tournament 3. Once in the file, find the section marked `[ModPackages]` [Figure 26.3].

Right at the end of this section, add `ModPackages=FirstMutator`. This tells the UScript compiler where to find your code. If you look in the start menu, you'll notice that you have shortcuts to both the editor and the game. Look at their properties, and you"ll notice something similar: both shortcuts point to the same program.

The editor is accessed by adding the editor command switch to the end of the target entry. We can access the UScript compiler the same way: copy the shortcut for UnrealEd and replace the editor command switch with make—the command used to tell the game to build the script. Name the shortcut something useful, and put it somewhere handy, perhaps as a shortcut on the desktop or in the same directory as the script. You are now done with set-up.

## Writing the Mutator

We need to create our first script file. Create a new text file using any text editor, and call it FirstMutator.uc. The .uc file extension is how the compiler recognizes a UScript text file. This means you can keep code snippets and old code in your working directory by changing the file extension, and the compiler will ignore them. You could use .OLD and .SNIP to keep things organized, but the choice is yours.

Open this text file; it's time to write our first lines of code.

```
class FirstMutator extends UTMutator;

DefaultProperties
{
}
```

Okay, this code doesn't do much—but it's important. `Class FirstMutator` is the new UScript class you are writing. Always remember to give your class the same name as your text file—otherwise, the compiler will tell you that you have a class/filename mismatch and refuse to compile.

The default properties are where you store the default values for any variable you might create for the mutator. It is not necessary to include default properties if you don't intend to include any default values (a rarity), but it's just good programming practice.

Now we need to tell our mutator to do something. The UTMutator class that we are extending contains a lot of useful functions that allow us to change the way the game plays. You should be able to find the file containing the UTMutator class and open it if you downloaded the source during set-up.

If you've programmed before, read through the UTMutator class and become familiar with it. If you haven't programmed before, then you're probably going to find the class a bit too difficult to understand right now, so don't worry about it.

In this mutator, we're going to change the gameplay! As the game progresses, the player's head will grow in size. As the head grows, the player's speed will decrease until the head reaches a scale of 5 or until the player is moving less than 100 units a second.

The first thing we are going to do is write a function to grow the player's head.

```
simulated function GrowHead() //What to do every time the timer ticks
{
        local UTPawn P;
        //Variable of the "UTPawn" class

        foreach DynamicActors(class'UTPawn', P)
        //iterate through non-static actors of the class 'UTPawn'
        {

        if(P!=none) //is there a player to modify?
        {
                P.SetHeadScale(P.HeadScale+0.4); //add 0.4 to the
                player's head scale
                P.GroundSpeed-=30; //subtract 30 from the player's
                ground speed
```

```
            if((P.HeadScale>=5)||(P.GroundSpeed<100))
            {
                  P.SetHeadScale(1);
                  P.GroundSpeed=440;
            }
      }
   }
}
```

Now we need to call this function every two seconds. We will do this in `PostBeginPlay()`.

```
simulated function PostBeginPlay() //function to be called after
game starts
{
      SetTimer(2, true, 'GrowHead');
      //This will call the function GrowHead every 2 seconds

      super.PostBeginPlay();
      //We don't want to override PostBeginPlay(),
      //this way everything that Unreal
      //does is preserved and we only add
      //to the default functionality
}
```

This mutator still feels like it is missing something. You can now run the mutator after compiling it as described in the next section. To make this mutator balanced, we will do some additional checks to see if the player's health is less than 50 and then set the head size and speed to default values. To do this, we will be adding a function calling that from within the `GrowHead` function.

The new function will be called `RestoreDefaults`.

```
simulated function RestoreDefaults(UTPawn P)
{
    P.SetHeadScale(1);
    P.GroundSpeed=440;
}
```

Now we need to update `GrowHead` to use this function and add the health check.

```
simulated function GrowHead() //What to do every time the timer
ticks
{
    local UTPawn P; //Variable of the "UTPawn" class
//iterate through non-static actors of the class 'UTPawn'
    foreach DynamicActors(class'UTPawn', P)
    {
        if(P!=none)//Is there a player to modify?
        {
            P.SetHeadScale(P.HeadScale+0.4); //add 0.4 to the
            player's head scale
            P.GroundSpeed-=30; //subtract 30 from the player's
            ground speed

            if((P.HeadScale>=5)||(P.GroundSpeed<100)||(P.
            Health<50))//Property checks
            {
               RestoreDefaults(P);
            }
        }
    }
}
```

The reason for having a separate `RestoreDefaults` function is to keep the code modular and easy to read. If other functions want set the default values, they can easily do so by calling the `RestoreDefaults` function. Here is the code for the entire mutator:

```
class FirstMutator extends UTMutator;

simulated function PostBeginPlay() //function to be called after
game starts
{
    SetTimer(2, true, 'GrowHead');
    super.PostBeginPlay(); //We don't want to override PostBeginPlay()
}

simulated function GrowHead() //What to do every time the timer ticks
{
    local UTPawn P; //Variable of the "UTPawn" class
//iterate through non-static actors of the class 'UTPawn'
    foreach DynamicActors(class'UTPawn', P)
    {
```

```
        if(P!=none)//Is there a player to modify?
        {
              P.SetHeadScale(P.HeadScale+0.4); //add 0.4 to the
              player's head scale
              P.GroundSpeed-=30; //subtract 30 from the player's
              ground speed

              if((P.HeadScale>=5)||(P.GroundSpeed<100)||(P.
              Health<50))//Property checks
              {
                 RestoreDefaults(P);
              }
        }
    }
}

simulated function RestoreDefaults(UTPawnP)
{
    P.SetHeadScale(1);
    P.GroundSpeed=440;
}

defaultproperties
{
}
```

## Compiling the Code

Compiling the code you write is very easy. You will need to create a shortcut of your UT3.exe and place it at a good location (preferably on the desktop). You will then right-click on the shortcut and open its properties [Figure 26.4]. At the end of the line, we will add the Make switch.

This will now compile any new code added to the game and then be available when you run it. Once you run UT3.exe via the shortcut, the code should compile without any errors or warnings. If you do get errors or warnings, you might want to step back and take a look at what they're telling you. Chances are you've made a small mistake, and it's easily rectified.

Figure 26.4

When you compile the code, the script compiler will automatically generate a package file with your compiled code in it and a configuration ini file if necessary. You'll find your package file in your Unreal Tournament 3 directory, which by default is

- Windows XP—`C:\Documents and Settings\My Documents\My Games\Unreal Tournament 3\UTGame\Unpublished\CookedPC\Script\FirstMutator.u`
- Windows Vista and Windows 7—`C:\Users\*Your User Name*\Documents\My Games\Unreal Tournament 3\UTGame\Unpublished\CookedPC\Script\FirstMutator.u`

## Final Touches

One last little thing remains to be done before this mutator is really ready. You can already theoretically jump into the game by selecting FirstMutator from the menu and playing with it. But the mutator doesn't have a name or a description that's of any use, and you'll have to run the game with another command switch (the -useunpublished switch) in order for it to show up.

This is where that configuration ini file comes in. Use Windows search to find the configuration file (hint: look for FirstMutator). Open it, and find the section `[FirstMutator UIDataProvider_Mutator]`. Under that you should add (or alter if it is already there)

```
ClassName=FirstMutator.FirstMutator
FriendlyName=First Mutator
Description=My First Mutator!
```

This section of the ini file controls how your mutator will show up in the mutator menu.

Figure 26.5

We can run the game by creating a new shortcut in the same way we accessed the UScript compiler—by adding the command switch Useunpublished—but this is no good if we want to give our mutators to someone. In order to do that, we need to move all our files from the unpublished directory; just copy them all over (remembering to keep the same directory structure!) into the published directory, and you're done [Figure 26.5].

Figure 26.6

Double-click the shortcut to run Unreal Tournament. On the main menu, select Instant Action [Figure 26.6].

You should now see a new menu [Figure 26.7].

Select the Map option at the top of the screen, select Arsenal in the list on the right, and then select the Next button at the bottom of the screen. You should see another menu [Figure 26.8].

Select the Mutators button at the bottom of the screen. You will see yet another menu [Figure 26.9].

Figure 26.7

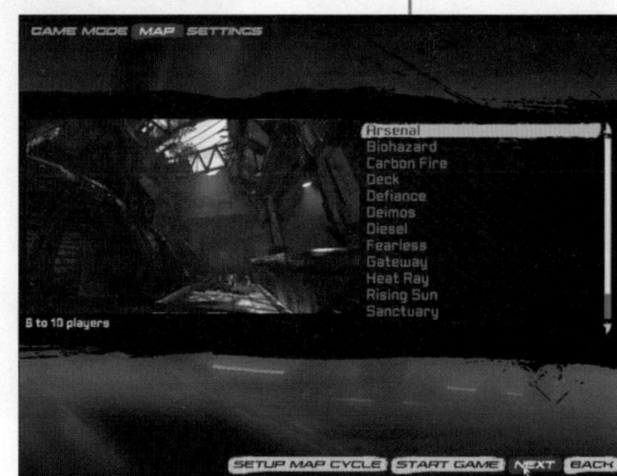


Figure 26.8

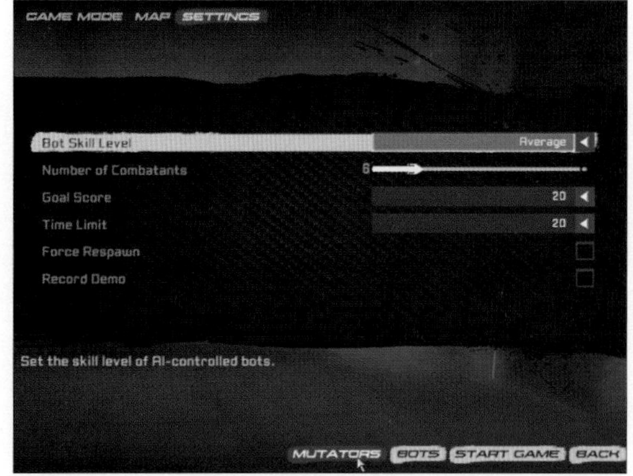


Figure 26.9

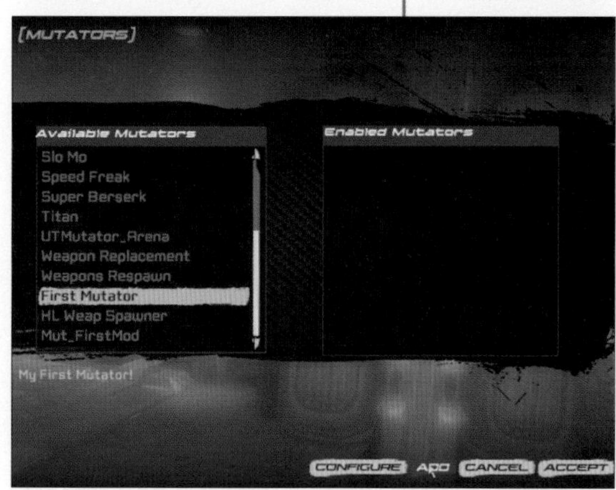

Figure 26.10

Select First Mutator in the list on the left of the screen and then select the `Add` button at the bottom of the screen. This enables your first mutator. Figure 26.10 shows a character using the first mutator.

# Mods

# 27

*Making Your Mod Real*

## What to Expect

In this chapter we learn how to author an Unreal mod and look at the various steps involved in that process. A mod is a complete modification of the Unreal game. The chapter will cover elements of data management and project setup.

### Getting Started

When working on a mod, it is very easy to lose files. The easiest way to avoid this problem is by setting up our mod directories to be as simple and efficient as possible while still adhering to the UT3 standards. In UT3 all modding is done in the "My Games" folder. Let's start by setting up our source folder. At this point, you should already have the UT3 UScript set up. If you don't, go back to Chapter 2 and set it up. This source is to be used as a reference and should be kept separate from your mod source code [Figure 27.1].

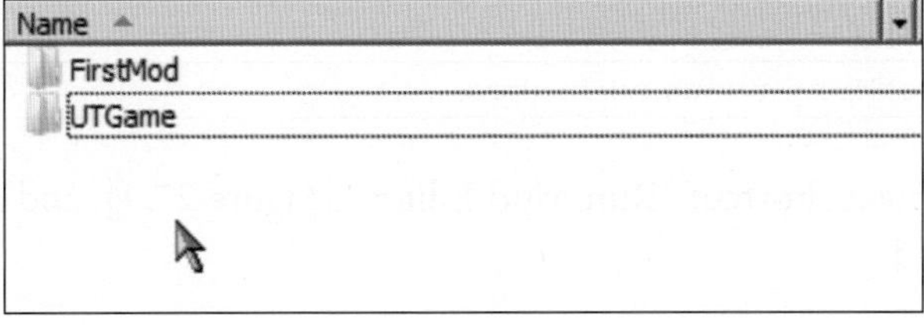


*Figure 27.1*

In your Unreal Tournament 3 directory within your "My Games" directory and create a new folder. Let's name it "FirstMod." This is our mod's main folder. Within that folder, create another folder named "Src."

```
\Unreal Tournament 3\FirstMod\Src\
```

Now create another folder and name it "FMod." Within this new FMod folder, create a folder named "Classes." This is the folder where we will do all of our coding. The final path will be

```
\My Games\Unreal Tournament 3\FirstMod\Src\FMod\Classes\
```

Figure 27.2

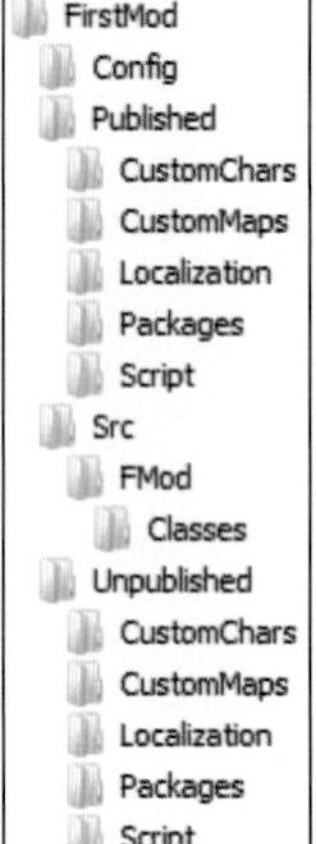


Now let's set up the folders for all the other assets our mod will use. Within your main mod folder, create three new folders. Name them "Config," "Unpublished," and "Published." Within Unpublished and Published, create folders named "CustomChars," "CustomMaps," "Localization," "Script," and "Packages." The directory tree should look like Figure 27.2.

Figure 27.3

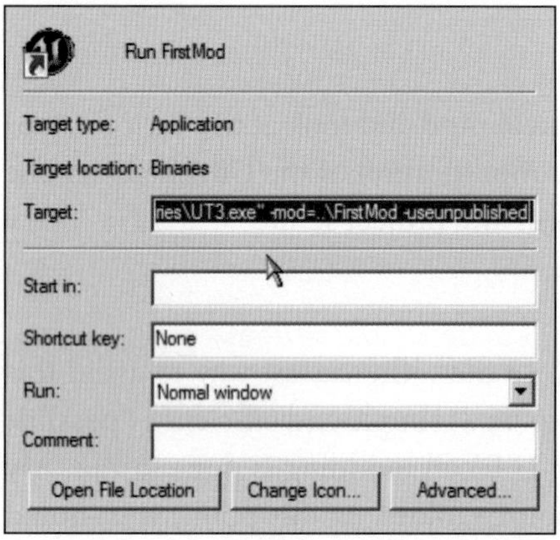

Figure 27.4

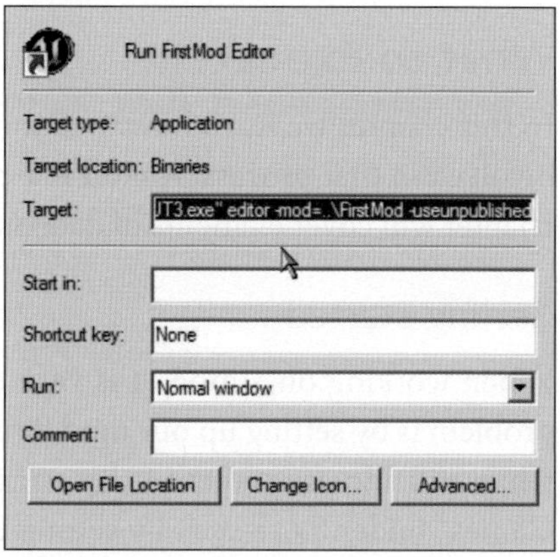

Now we are going to make three shortcuts. These shortcuts will be in our main mod folder, FirstMod. Create a shortcut to your UT3 executable and name the shortcut "Run FirstMod" [Figure 27.3]. In the shortcut properties, add this after the executable location in the Target field:

```
-mod=..\FirstMod -useunpublished
```

Name the next shortcut "Run Mod Editor" [Figure 27.4], and at the end of the Target field add:

```
editor -mod=..\FirstMod -useunpublished
```

Name the last shortcut "Rebuild FirstMod" [Figure 27.5], and at the end of the Target field add:

```
make -mod=..\FirstMod -useunpublished
```

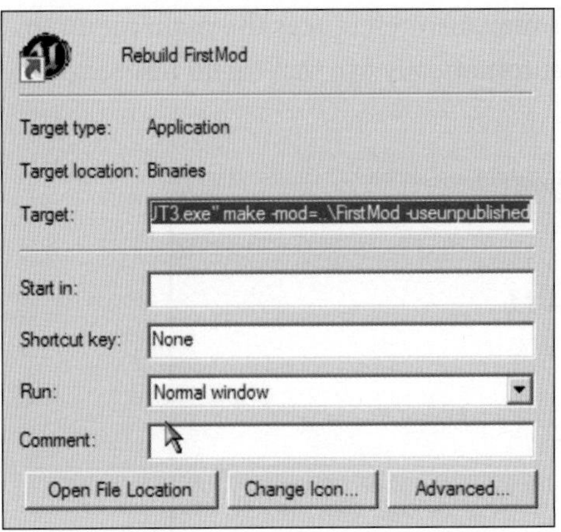


Figure 27.5

Now, when you need to rebuild your code, you just have to click "Rebuild FirstMod"; when you need to run the level editor, you just click "Run FirstMod Editor"; and when you want to play the game, you just click "Run FirstMod" [Figure 27.6].

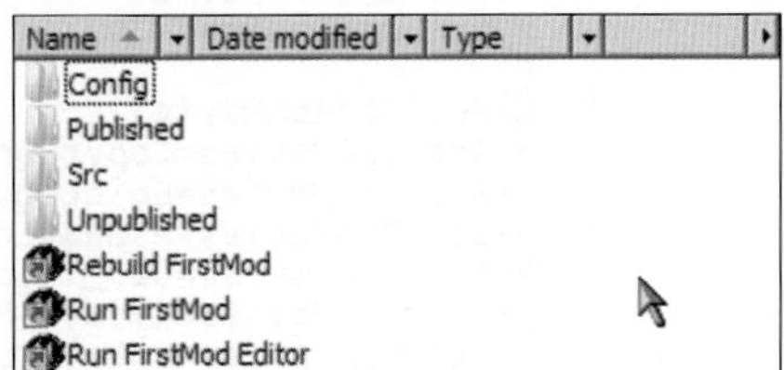


Figure 27.6

## Creating a Basic Game Framework

In the Config folder you will have to create two ini files called DefaultEditor.ini and DefaultEngine.ini. These files will help set some basic settings that your mod will need. It also lists the paths for content specific to your mod, such as code packages, maps, and other art resources.

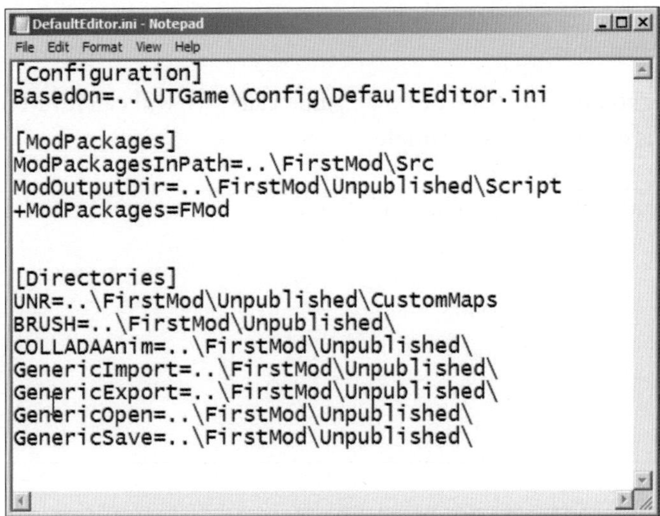


```
[Configuration]
BasedOn=..\UTGame\Config\DefaultEditor.ini

[ModPackages]
ModPackagesInPath=..\FirstMod\Src
ModOutputDir=..\FirstMod\Unpublished\Script
+ModPackages=FMod


[Directories]
UNR=..\FirstMod\Unpublished\CustomMaps
BRUSH=..\FirstMod\Unpublished\
COLLADAAnim=..\FirstMod\Unpublished\
GenericImport=..\FirstMod\Unpublished\
GenericExport=..\FirstMod\Unpublished\
GenericOpen=..\FirstMod\Unpublished\
GenericSave=..\FirstMod\Unpublished\
```

Figure 27.7

The important thing to remember is to reference the UScript packages that you will be creating in the DefaultEngine.ini under the `[ModPackages]` as shown below [Figure 27.7]. In the DefaultEngine.ini, you can remove all the splash screens and set the map to load when the game starts. This map also references the main menu that you created in the Design lessons and will automatically use that menu instead of the default Unreal menu [Figure 27.8].

Figure 27.8

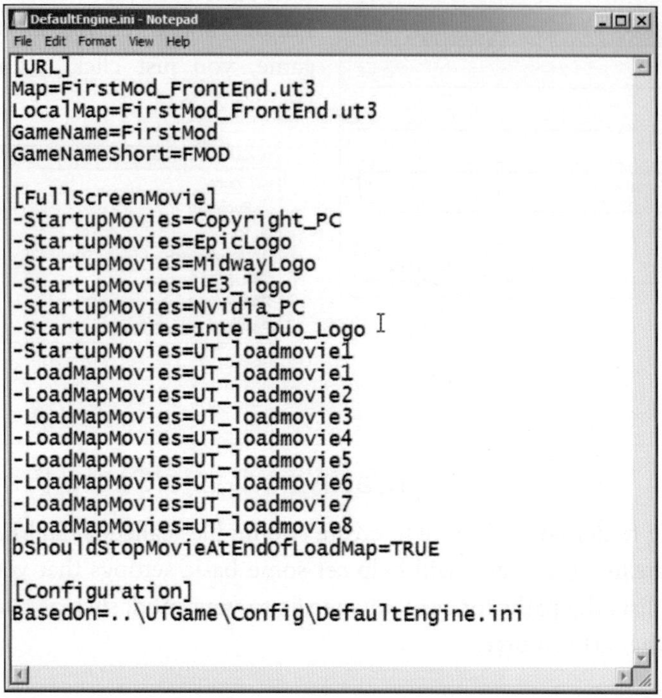

```
DefaultEngine.ini - Notepad
File Edit Format View Help
[URL]
Map=FirstMod_FrontEnd.ut3
LocalMap=FirstMod_FrontEnd.ut3
GameName=FirstMod
GameNameShort=FMOD

[FullScreenMovie]
-StartupMovies=Copyright_PC
-StartupMovies=EpicLogo
-StartupMovies=MidwayLogo
-StartupMovies=UE3_logo
-StartupMovies=Nvidia_PC
-StartupMovies=Intel_Duo_Logo
-StartupMovies=UT_loadmovie1
-LoadMapMovies=UT_loadmovie1
-LoadMapMovies=UT_loadmovie2
-LoadMapMovies=UT_loadmovie3
-LoadMapMovies=UT_loadmovie4
-LoadMapMovies=UT_loadmovie5
-LoadMapMovies=UT_loadmovie6
-LoadMapMovies=UT_loadmovie7
-LoadMapMovies=UT_loadmovie8
bShouldStopMovieAtEndOfLoadMap=TRUE

[Configuration]
BasedOn=..\UTGame\Config\DefaultEngine.ini
```

## Adding a Main Menu

The first thing to do is to create our own game class; we will call it FMGame.uc. The code for this is going to be very simple.

```
class FMGame extends UTTeamGame
simulated function PostBeginPlay()
{
   Super.PostBeginPlay();
}
defaultproperties
{
}
```

In the above code, you are extending from a UTTeamGame game type and calling the simulated function `PostBeginPlay`; the simulated label makes it available for all clients in case of a networked game. In your class, you are not doing anything yet. All you are doing is the playing the default team game by using `Super.PostBeginPlay`.

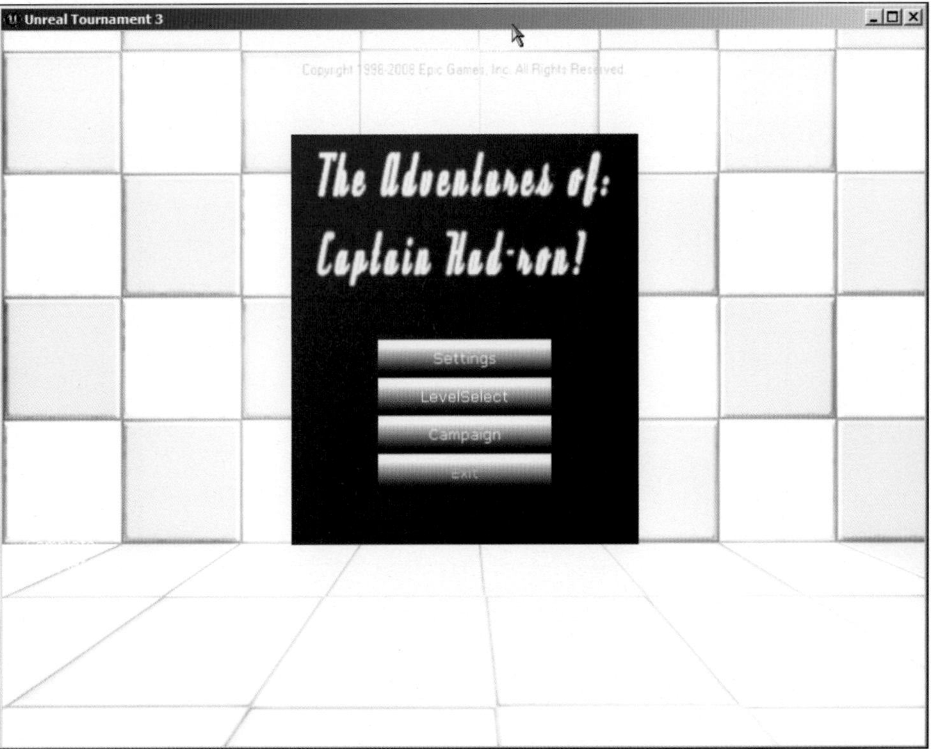


Figure 27.9

In the design lessons, you learned how to create a simple UI Scene (UIscenes.upk) and attach that to a map in the editor. Now is the time to use that map (FirstMod_FrontEnd.ut3) and bring it in as the starting menu. If you look at the above DefaultEngine.ini image, you will notice that the first few lines have references to the FirstMod_FrontEnd.ut3 map. These are needed to load this map as the starting menu.

To keep things simple, we have four menu options. If you now compile and run the game, you should see the main menu with its options being displayed instead of the Unreal menu. Run the game now and it should look like Figure 27.9.

# 28 Weapons and Characters

Now that we've created some of the basics required for starting your mod, we're going to need to fill our new game with something to set it apart from other versions. Adding new weapons and characters is the perfect way to give your mod a life of its own.

## What to Expect

This chapter will go into detail about the programming required in UScript to bring in custom weapons and characters. Most mods obtain their new look and feel by modifying the GUI and the levels created using the level editor. The real playability of the game comes, though, when weapons and characters interact with each other to provide various behaviors that make the players' experiences unique. In this chapter we discuss strategies for creating that unique experience.

### Creating a Custom Character

We will create a custom character and set its properties using UScript. We will also assign the right art and animation packages for our character. If you have completed all the art lessons in the book, you will realize that the default player mesh we will use is the same Captain Hadron mesh you used in the art lessons.

In Unreal, a pawn is a dynamic game object with intelligence and behavior. A pawn will need to be communicating with a controller class that handles the behavior. We will therefore need to create code for these two classes.

```
class FMPawn extends UTPawn placeable;
DefaultProperties
{
	ControllerClass=class'FMod.FMPlayerController'
	DefaultMesh=SkeletalMesh'CaptainHadron.Mesh .CaptainHadron_mesh'
	SoundGroupClass=class'UTPawnSoundGroup_Liandri'

	GroundSpeed=200
	AirSpeed=200
	DodgeSpeed=200

    Begin Object Name=WPawnSkeletalMeshComponent
	SkeletalMesh=SkeletalMesh'CaptainHadron.Mesh.CaptainHadron_mesh'
	PhysicsAsset=PhysicsAsset'CH_AnimHuman.Mesh.SK_CH_BaseMale
	_Physics'
	AnimTreeTemplate=AnimTree'CaptainHadron.Anims.CaptainHadron_AnimTree'
	AnimSets[0]=AnimSet'CaptainHadron.Anims.CaptainHadron_Anims'
	AnimSets[1]=AnimSet'CaptainHadron.Anims.CaptainHadron_Anims'
	Translation=(X=0.0,Y=0.0,Z=0.0)
	Scale3D=(X=1.0,Y=1.0,Z=1.0)
    End Object

    DefaultTeamMaterials[0]=MaterialInterface'CaptainHadron.Mat.Face
    _Mat'
    DefaultTeamHeadMaterials[0]=MaterialInterface'CaptainHadron.Mat
    .CaptainHadron_Mat'
}
```

In the above code, you will see that there is a keyword called `placeable` at the end of the class definition for the `FMPawn`. This is needed for objects that can be placed in the maps via the editor. You will also notice that all the art assets that you created in the art lessons are now being brought in and referenced via code for Captain Hadron. As mentioned earlier we will need to create the controller for `FMPawn`. The code for this is given here.

```
class FMPlayerController extends UTPlayerController;
simulated function PostBeginPlay()
{
    super.PostBeginPlay();
    SetBehindView(true);
}

/** Loads the player's custom character from their profile. */
function LoadCharacterFromProfile(UTProfileSettings Profile)
{
       // no code is needed, however this function needs to be
       overridden
}
defaultproperties
{
    bBehindView=true
}
```

You will also notice that we changed the camera to third person using the controller setting `bBehindView` to true. This is helpful as we can now see the entire mesh and set of animations for the captain.

We also need to modify the default properties of FMGame.uc to reference the pawn and the controller as the defaults.

```
defaultproperties
{
       PlayerControllerClass=class'FMod.FMPlayerController'
       DefaultPawnClass=class'FMod.FMPawn'
}
```

Compile and run the game now. You will see your main menu appear. Now select Campaign. If you had designed the main menu correctly in the design section, you will notice that it opens up the terrain map that you had created in the terrain chapter. You will also notice that the main character for the game is the captain [Figure 28.1].

Figure 28.1

## Creating a Custom Weapon

We can now easily bring in the Ray Gun that we created in the art chapters and attach it to the captain. The first thing we need to do is to clear the default weapon inventory and add just the Ray Gun to it so that it is the only weapon available in the game. We will change our FMGame.uc to achieve this.

```
simulated function PostBeginPlay()
{
        local UTGame Game;
        Super.PostBeginPlay();
        Game = UTGame(WorldInfo.Game);
        if (Game != None)
        {
                Game.DefaultInventory.Length = 0;
                Game.DefaultInventory[0] = class'FMod.FMWeap_TaoPistol';
        }
}
```

You will see that the inventory now has only one item and that it references the Ray Gun (Tao Pistol). So now we will need to create a class for the Ray Gun. We will extend this class from the Shock Rifle and change the default properties to reference the appropriate mesh and animation resources.

```
class FMWeap_TaoPistol extends UTWeap_ShockRifle;
defaultproperties
{
	Begin Object class=AnimNodeSequence Name=MeshSequenceA
	End Object
	// Weapon SkeletalMesh
	Begin Object Name=FirstPersonMesh
		SkeletalMesh=SkeletalMesh'FMWeaps.mesh.TaoPistol_mesh'
		AnimSets(0)=AnimSet'FMWeaps.anims.TaoPistol_Anims'
		Animations=MeshSequenceA
		FOV=60.0
	End Object
	AmmoCount=99
	LockerAmmoCount=99
	MaxAmmoCount=99
	ShotCost(0)=0
	ShotCost(1)=0
	AttachmentClass=class'FMod.FMAttachment_TaoPistol'

	Begin Object Name=PickupMesh
		SkeletalMesh=SkeletalMesh'FMWeaps.mesh.TaoPistol_mesh'
		Scale=0.48
	End Object

	InstantHitMomentum(0)=+00000.0
	InstantHitMomentum(1)=-00000.0
	WeaponFireTypes(0)=EWFT_InstantHit
	WeaponFireTypes(1)=EWFT_InstantHit
	InstantHitDamage(0)=45
	InstantHitDamage(1)=45
	InstantHitDamageTypes(0)=class'UTDmgType_ShockPrimary'
	InstantHitDamageTypes(1)=class'UTDmgType_ShockPrimary'
	WeaponFireAnim(0)=TaoPistol_fire
	WeaponFireAnim(1)=TaoPistol_fire
	WeaponPutDownAnim=TaoPistol_PutDown
	WeaponEquipAnim=TaoPistol_equip
	WeaponIdleAnims(0)=TaoPistol_fire
	PlayerViewOffset=(X=46,Y=15.0,Z=-28.0)
	MuzzleFlashSocket=MuzzleFlashSocket
	MuzzleFlashPSCTemplate=Effects.Particles.TaoBlast
	MuzzleFlashAltPSCTemplate=Effects.Particles.TaoBlast

	name="Default__TaoPistol"
	ItemName="Ray Gun"
	PickupMessage="Ray Gun"
}
```

Every weapon also has an attachment class that puts the weapon in the player's hands, so we will need to write the code for that. The attachment is referenced by the code above; see the line of code: (AttachmentClass=class'FMod.FMAttachment_TaoPistol').

```
class FMAttachment_TaoPistol extends UTAttachment_ShockRifle;

defaultproperties
{
	// Weapon SkeletalMesh
	Begin Object name=SkeletalMeshComponent0
		SkeletalMesh=SkeletalMesh'FMWeaps.Mesh.TaoPistol_Mesh'
		Scale=0.48
	End Object
	MuzzleFlashPSCTemplate=Effects.Particles.TaoBlast
	MuzzleFlashAltPSCTemplate=Effects.Particles.TaoBlast
	WeaponClass=class'FMod.FMWeap_TaoPistol'
}
```

*Figure 28.2*

You will also notice that we have now added the Muzzle flash particles effect that we created in the Design lectures. Compile and run the game now, and you will see the Ray Gun in the hands of the captain with your own Muzzle flash appearing on fire [Figure 28.2].

# 29

## AI

*I Command You: LIVE!*

### What to Expect

In this chapter we get deeper into UScript programming and provide for advanced gameplay behaviors inside the mod. This chapter covers various ways of making the non-playable characters behave the way you would like them to. You can give them abilities that make the game interesting and engaging. We will create an enemy character and have the character change between the states of roaming and jumping.

#### Creating a Non-Playing Character (NPC)

As in our previous chapter, we will need to create a class for the NPC and a controller that manages its behavior. To keep things simple, we will extend the NPC from FMPawn class. Unreal also has a NPC-based controller class, called UTBot, that has tons of AI and state logic that you can incorporate into your own NPC class as necessary. We will extend the controller for the NPC from the UTBot class.

```
class FMBotPawn extends FMPawn placeable;

DefaultProperties
{
	ControllerClass=class'FMod.FMBot'
	DefaultMesh=SkeletalMesh'TM_Char.Mesh.TM_Mesh'
	GroundSpeed=440
	AirSpeed=440
	DodgeSpeed=500
```

```
        Begin Object Name=WPawnSkeletalMeshComponent
                SkeletalMesh=SkeletalMesh'TM_Char.Mesh.TM_Mesh'
                PhysicsAsset=
                        PhysicsAsset'CH_AnimHuman.Mesh.SK_CH_BaseMale
                        _Physics'
                AnimTreeTemplate=
                        AnimTree'CH_AnimHuman_Tree.AT_CH_Human'
                AnimSets[0]=
                        AnimSet'CH_AnimHuman.Anims.K_AnimHuman_BaseMale'
                AnimSets[1]=
                        AnimSet'CH_AnimHuman.Anims.K_AnimHuman_BaseMale'
                Translation=(X=0.0,Y=0.0,Z=0.0)
                Scale3D=(X=1.0,Y=1.0,Z=1.0)
        End Object
}

class FMBot extends UTBot;
var int numJumps;
function SetAttractionState()
{
        if ( Enemy != None )
             GotoState('Dancing');
        else
             GotoState('Roaming');
}
state RangedAttack
{
Begin:
     GotoState('Roaming');
}
state Dancing

{
Begin:
     numJumps = 4;
     while(numJumps != 0)
     {
          Sleep(1);
          Pawn.DoJump(true);
          numJumps--;
     }
```

```
    goto('DoneDancing');
DoneDancing:
    GotoState('Roaming');
    numJumps = 4;
}
state Roaming
{
    ignores EnemyNotVisible;

Begin:
       MoveToward(Enemy,FaceActor(1),GetDesiredOffset(),
              ShouldStrafeTo(MoveTarget));
       Sleep(4);
       GotoState('Dancing');

}
defaultproperties
{
}
```

In the above class, you will see that the NPC shifts from roaming to jumping every four seconds. We also override the state RangedAttack so that the enemy doesn't fire. We also need to change the default properties of FMGame.uc to add the NPC as the default bot.

```
defaultproperties
{
       PlayerControllerClass=class'FMod.FMPlayerController'
       DefaultPawnClass=class'FMod.FMPawn
       BotClass=class'FMBot'
}
```

Figure 29.1

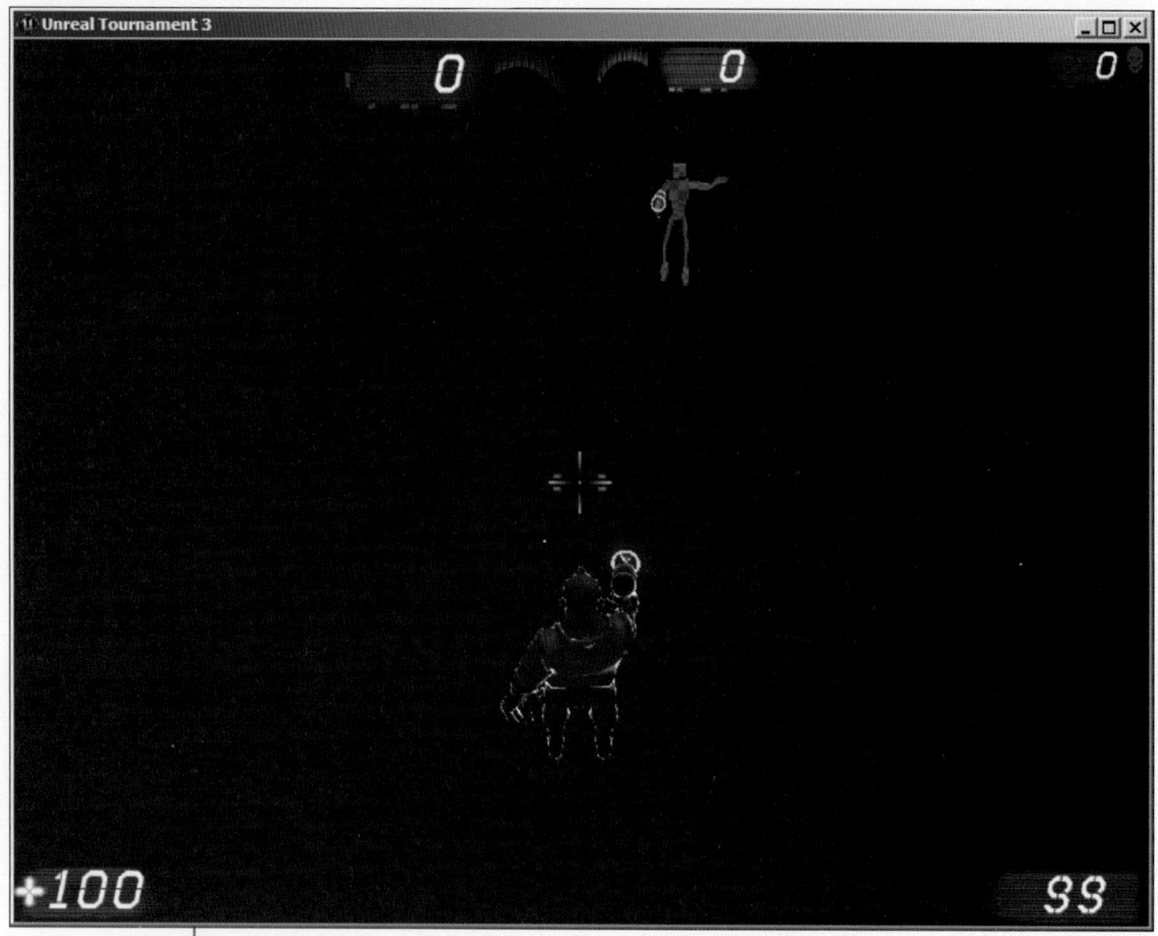


Compile and run the code now, and you should be able to see a box-like enemy character running and jumping in the level [Figure 29.1].

# 30 Finishing Touches

*Bringing It All Together*

## The Story So Far . . .

The last chapter puts all the above instruction together. You should have a working mod with fully-evolved characters, weapons, and a heads-up-display (HUD) all working cohesively and seamlessly to create a rewarding player experience. We will continue with the effort so far and try to display some meaningful information using the HUD. One of the things that is good to know, especially when you are in the debug phase, is what state the NPC is in. We will write simple code to display that on the screen, and we will also display the health value of the NPC. We also include step-by-step instructions on how to author a mod using the recently released Unreal Development Kit (UDK) by Epic Games.

## Creating a Custom HUD

The way to customize the HUD is to extend from the UTHUD class and add desired functionality. The two main functions that you can override are `DrawLivingHud` and `DrawGameHud`. In our case, we will override the `DrawLivingHud` to display the necessary information as this needs to be drawn while the player is alive. We will create a new class called FMHUD and write the code for it.

```
class FMHUD extends UTHUD;

function DrawLivingHud()
{
        DrawCustomHudInfo();
}
function DrawTextRA(coerce string Text, float X, float Y, optional
bool CR)
{
       Canvas.CurX = X;
       Canvas.CurY = Y;
```

```
        Canvas.DrawText(Text,CR);
}
function DrawCustomHudInfo()
{
      local FMPawn P;
      local int PCount;
      PCount = 0;

      foreach WorldInfo.AllPawns(class'FMPawn', P)
         {
            if(P.Controller != none)
            {
                  if(P.Controller.IsA('AIController'))
                  {
                        DrawTextRA("Enemy Health: "$P.Health,100,100+(PCo
                        unt*50),true);
                        DrawTextRA("Enemy State: "$P.Controller.GetStateName
                        (),100,60+(PCount*50),true);
                        PCount++;
                  }
                  else if(P.Controller.IsA('PlayerController'))
                  {
                         DrawTextRA("Player Health: "$P.Health,100,10,true);
                  }
            }
      }
}
defaultproperties
{
}
```

We also need to change the FMGame.uc and add the reference to this new HUD.

```
defaultproperties
{
        HUDType=class'FMod.FMHUD'
        PlayerControllerClass=class'FMod.FMPlayerController'
        DefaultPawnClass=class'FMod.FMPawn'
        BotClass=class'FMBot'
}
```

Compile and run the game, and you will notice that the health and state information for the NPC is displayed; as the NPC takes damage, the HUD automatically updates that information [Figure 30.1].

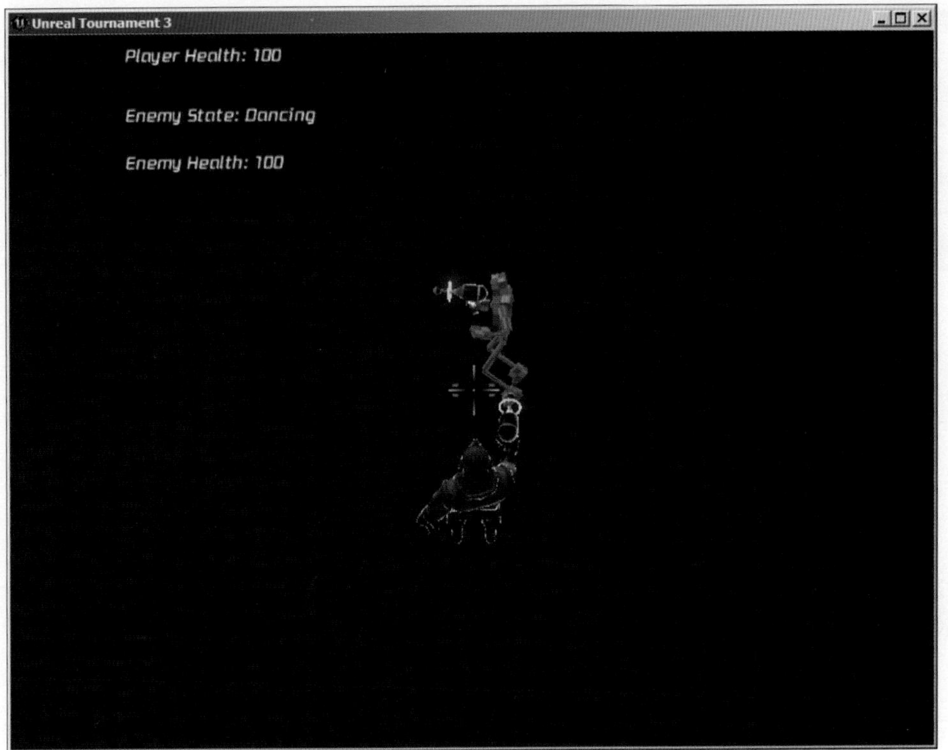


Figure 30.1

## UDK

Epic recently announced that they will release the Unreal Development Kit (UDK) for anyone interested in creating games using the Unreal Engine 3. However, we were almost done with the book when this news came out. To take advantage of the UDK and to help readers who would rather use UDK than UT3, we have added the following tutorials that explain the setup and development steps needed to get mutators and mods working with the UDK.

## Mutators in UDK

1. Install the UDK. We refer to the directory where UDK is installed as the root UDK directory.
2. In the root UDK directory, there should be a folder named "Development." In that folder, there is a subfolder named "src." In the src folder, create a new folder named "FirstMutator." This should start to sound familiar. The process is fairly similar to making mutators for UT3.
3. In your shinny new FirstMutator directory, create a folder named "Classes." Copy the FirstMutator.uc file into this folder (see Chapter 26 for how to create this file).

Figure 30.2

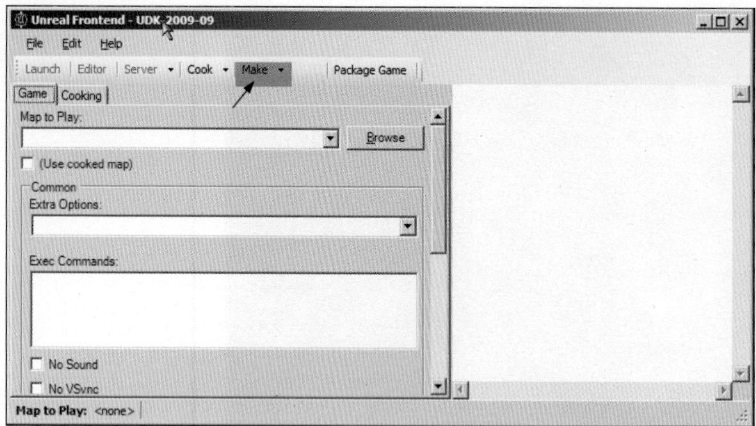


4. Compile the code by launching the UDK frontend. This can either be done by using the shortcut in the start menu, or by running UnrealFrontend.exe in the folder [Root UDK directory]\binaries. There should be a button named Make [Figure 30.2]. Click it to compile the code. The right window shows if the code has compiled correctly; if the code does not, the window will display any errors or warnings.

5. Go to the Config folder, open UTEditor.ini. and search for `[ModPackages]`. Make the follwoing changes to that section:

```
[ModPackages]
ModPackagesInPath=..\..\Development\Src
ModOutputDir=..\..\UTGame\Script
ModPackages=FirstMutator
```

6. Now open UTGame.ini, which will contain a block of options for other mutators. We need to add the following lines along with those written for the other mutators:

```
[FirstMutator UTUIDataProvider_Mutator]
ClassName=FirstMutator.FirstMutator
```

7. Go to the folder [Root UDK directory]\UTGame\LOC\INT\. There should be a file named "utgame.int." Open this with Notepad, and again look for a block with information about mutators (which will be identified by a big block of comments). In that section, add the following code:

```
[FirstMutator UIDataProvider_Mutator]
FriendlyName=First Mutator
Description=My First Mutator!
```

These lines let the game know where to find the mutator and it lets the UI know that to display in the menu.

8. Now open the frontend, and hit Make again to compile the mutator code without any errors or warnings. Once done that is done, click Launch, select the FirstMutator, and play the game. The heads for the bots increases and their pace becomes slower over time.

## Mods in UDK

1. Copy the "FMod" folder to [Root UDK directory]\Development\Src\ (see Chapter 27 for how to create code for the Mod). Some code changes will need to be done in the .uc files in order to get them to work with the UDK. Open the file FMPawn.uc and add the following lines of code:

```
simulated function class<UTFamilyInfo> GetFamilyInfo()
{
    return class'FMod.FMFamilyInfo_CaptainHadron';
}
```

Open FMBotPawn.uc and add the following lines of code:

```
simulated function class<UTFamilyInfo> GetFamilyInfo()
{
    return class'FMod.FMFamilyInfo_EnemyChar';
}
```

Create a new .uc file called "FMFamilyInfo_CaptainHadron.uc" and add the following lines of code:

```
class FMFamilyInfo_CaptainHadron extends UTFamilyInfo_Human
      abstract;

defaultproperties
{
    FamilyID="FMTC"

        CharacterMeshName="CaptainHadron.Mesh.CaptainHadron_mesh"
        CharacterMesh=SkeletalMesh'CaptainHadron.mesh.CaptainHadron_mesh'
}
```

Create another .uc file called "FMFamilyInfo_EnemyChar.uc" and add the following lines of code:

```
class FMFamilyInfo_EnemyChar extends UTFamilyInfo_Human
        abstract;

defaultproperties
{
    FamilyID="FMTC"

       CharacterMeshName="TM_Char.mesh.TM_Mesh"
       CharacterMesh=SkeletalMesh'TM_Char.mesh.TM_Mesh'
}
```

The above steps represent the new way of bringing the mesh properties for pawns into UDK. The UDK doesn't support the defaultMesh property and can bring in the mesh by creating familyInfo classes for the various objects in the game.

2. The folder [Root UDK directory]\UTGame\Content has folders for all your content (maps, characters, etc.). The maps for the Mod will go in the Maps folder, and so on. Create a folder under Maps called "FMod," and copy the .ut3 files into it. You do this in order to organize your Maps folder better and to better locate where your Mod's maps are. Similarly, create a FMod folder in the folders Characters, Effects, and UI, and copy the corresponding .upk files into those folders.
3. Now we need to change the properties in some .ini files. In [Root UDK directory]\UTGame\Config, locate files with names like "DefaultEngine.ini" and "DefaultEditor.ini." For every line that is added or changed in the .ini files for UT3 mods the equivalent line needs to be added or changed in the default .ini files for the UDK. DefaultEngine.ini will need the follwoing changes:

```
[URL]
MapExt=ut3
Map=FirstMod_FrontEnd.ut3
LocalMap=FirstMod_FrontEnd.ut3
TransitionMap=EnvyEntry.ut3
EXEName=UTGame.exe
DebugEXEName=DEBUG-UTGame.exe
GameName=FirstMod
GameNameShort=FMOD
```

and

```
[UnrealEd.EditorEngine]
EditPackagesOutPath=..\..\UTGame\Script
FRScriptOutputPath=..\..\UTGame\ScriptFinalRelease
+EditPackages=OnlineSubsystemLive
+EditPackages=OnlineSubsystemPC
+EditPackages=UTGame
+EditPackages=UTEditor
+EditPackages=UTGameContent
+ModEditPackages=FMod
;ModEditPackages=MyMod
AutoSaveDir=..\..\UTGame\Autosaves
InEditorGameURLOptions=?quickstart=1?numplay=1
```

DefaultEditor.ini will need these changes:

```
[ModPackages]
ModPackagesInPath=..\..\Development\Src
ModOutputDir=..\UTGame\Script
+ModPackages=FMod
```

Figure 30.3

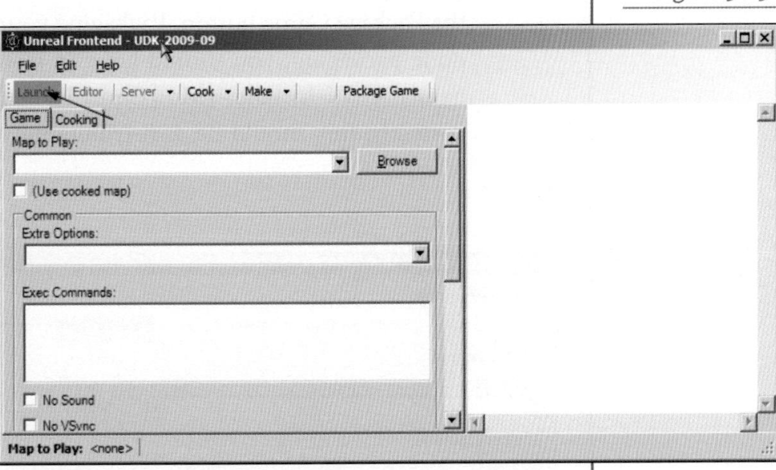


4. You will also need to open all of your maps in the UDK version of the editor and rebuild the lighting. Major changes were made to the lighting engine between the release of UT3 and the release of the UDK. Depending on the complexity of the lighting in the map, it could take awhile for the lighting to build. You can build the game by clicking Make in the frontend. It might give you a few warnings, which you can ignore. Click Launch [Figure 30.3] and you will be able to play your mod.
5. The next step is to cook your maps. This is done by launching the front end, clicking on the Cooking tab, entering the file names of all of the maps that

Figure 30.4

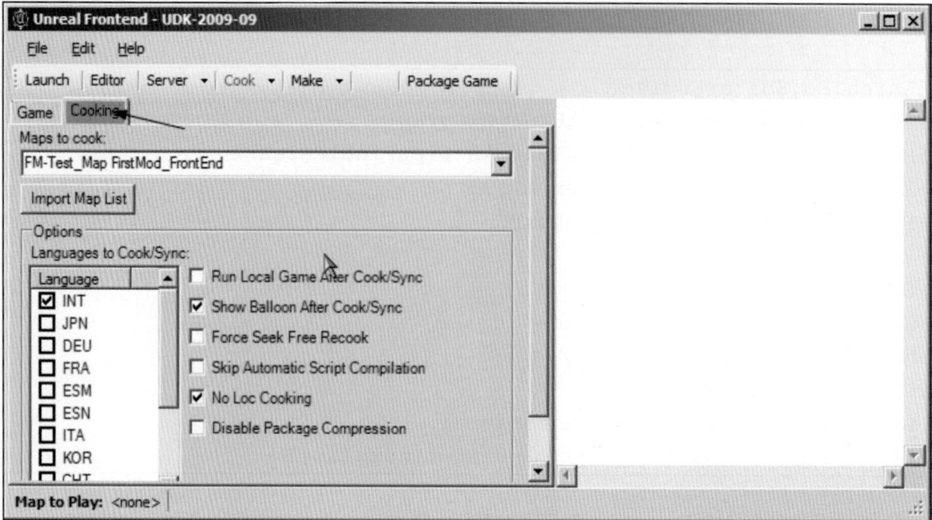


you want to cook (it will autofill the names as you type them), and then clicking the Cook button at the top [Figure 30.4]. If you do not cook your maps, they will not be packaged with your Mod.

6. Once your maps are cooked, it is time to package the Mod. In the frontend, click on the Game tab [Figure 30.5]. It should bring up a window asking for the long name, and short name, for your mod. Enter the names and then click the Package Game button. Packaging your mod may take a while. Once it is done packaging, you should have an installer in your UDK root directory named UDK-Installer-[Mod Short Name].exe. If you have done everything correctly, this should be a distributable version of your mod that you can release.

Figure 30.5

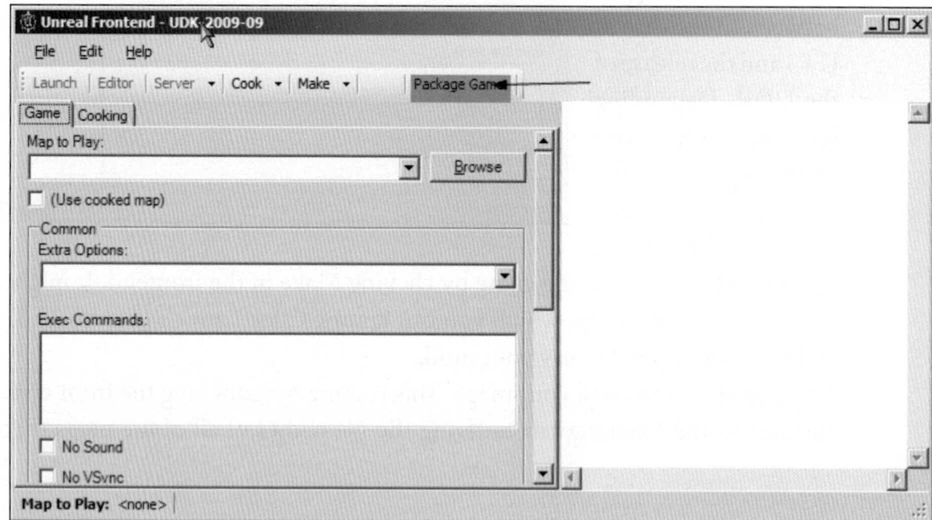

## Wotgreal Setup

Wotgreal is a neat editor for Unreal script that highlights syntax and helps browse the source files and their classes with ease. Below are the steps needed to get it working with UT3.

1. Download the latest version (development build) of WOTgreal from http://www.wotgreal.com/.
2. Install WOTgreal, and paste the content of the development build in to the WOTgreal installation directory.
3. Launch WOTgreal. A few broken menus will come up. Just keep clicking Next until you get to the one that asks if you want to associate .uc files with WOTgreal. Select Yes.
4. When WOTgreal opens, go to Options -> Preferences [Figure 30.6].
5. Under Game Information, set the game type to "UT3," and then change "Source Root Dir(s)" to point to your source directory. If you have a directory with your code and a separate directory with the Unreal code, you can use both of these by separating them with a semicolon: for example, "C:\Users\ashish\Documents\My Games\Unreal Tournament 3\UTGame\Src; C:\UDK\UDK-2009-09\Development\Src".

We recommend that you use Wotgreal only as an editor and use the shortcuts for compiling and running your mod or the frontend if using the UDK.

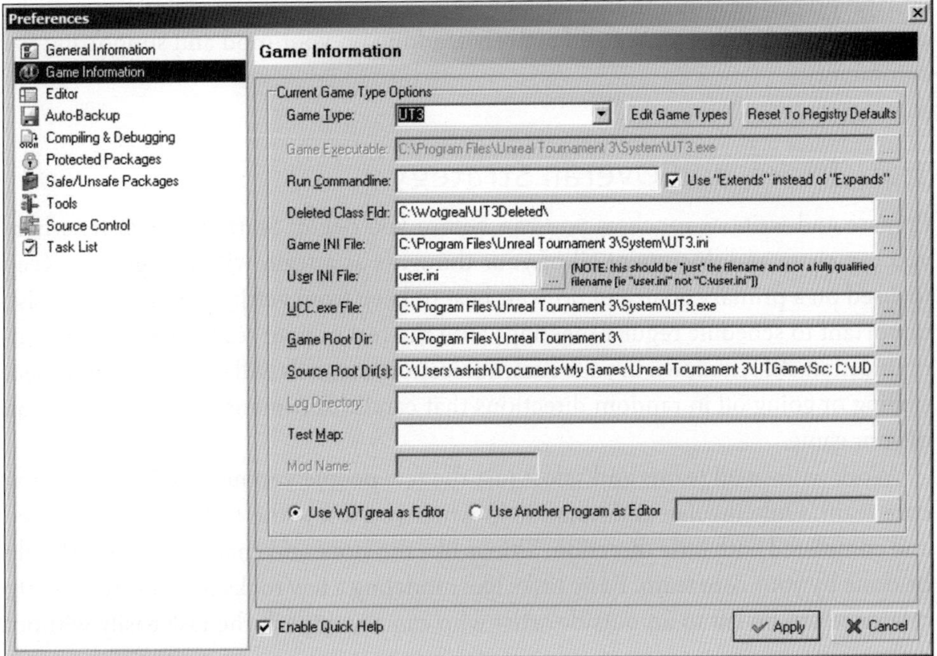


Figure 30.6

## Final Polish and Debug

With what you've got now you're well on your way to creating a complete third-person shooter. Your skill with unreal script will only grow as you dive deeper into the code. Learn from online resources and from the script files provided with Unreal Tournament's source updates available from Epic Games. These scripts can shed light on how to accomplish everything from the most basic to the most complex tasks.

If you get lost looking for how a function works, use WOTgreal to search for how the function was used by other scripts. Learn how the function is used and repurpose it for what you want to accomplish. Move in very basic steps, first thing is first. If you want to create a new object that animates when the player is near it, start by learning how to spawn a new object. Next learn how to trigger animations. Then learn how to check for distances between the object and the player. Finally glue the accrued knowledge into a single script that accomplishes all of these features.

Once you're nearing the completion of your mod, you'll want to package up the contents and prepare it for public release—but only to a select few. Build a small community of beta testers who will volunteer to help you polish the best mod you and your team can produce. Once things reach an acceptable level of completion, release your mod to the world, and sit back and watch your fan list grow.

The added number of players will also create an increase in potential feedback. Rather than ignore or deny the importance of user feedback, use it to prepare an update. Preparing and announcing new releases and updates is a great way to let your fan base feel that you're still actively working on your mod and supporting the community.

## Tips, Tricks, and Overall Strategy

Prepare and write as much as you can before you begin. Starting a website where you can share and document all of your thoughts as a team will help greatly. Keep focused on a primary goal, and do your best to keep from getting distracted. It's also important to schedule regular meetings with the rest of your team to maintain communication. A breakdown in your communication channels will result in your project stalling or going off in random directions that can be detrimental to the production of your game.

Work with small teams and select just the few people you need to build a strong core team. Only involve additional help when you know the tasks can be assigned and completed with little direction. Things like the story and character design should be done by your core team. Basic tasks like modeling a few rocks or trees from photo reference can be left to an outside artist who can accomplish the task easily without daily input.

One of the duties as a member of the core team is to help maintain focus. If you feel that there may be too many features or assets, it's always a good idea to reconsider the goal of the project. You should ask what is necessary and what can be cut out of the scope of the project in order to finish your project. Features and assets can always be released with project updates and add-ons.

## Closing words

We've covered quite a lot of topics: particles, textures, materials, cut-scenes, and animation trees. I think we've covered a lot of ground in a short amount of time. Unreal Engine affords you quite a lot of control from the get go, but that also means there's quite a lot to learn. Your adventure has just started with what you've learned in this book, and it's up to you to dive deeper into each topic.

The tutorials have been purposefully simplified for your benefit. Creating a more complex object from the beginning would have added additional steps, which would have lead into issues that distract from the task at hand. Creating and developing more detailed objects found in Unreal Tournament and other games that use the Unreal Engine takes time, patience, and skill. The skill required to create detailed Unreal Tournament props and objects comes from practice and learning skills beyond the scope of this book.

From here on out you should be seeking additional tutorials and lessons to add to your 2D and 3D skill set. As your texture and model work improves, you'll be able to apply the new meshes and materials to the lessons learned here and create higher and higher quality scenes and levels. In addition, as you learn new coding techniques, your characters behaviors and actions will also improve. Before too long, you'll be the creating triple-A games of your dreams!

When you begin planning your own project, remember to keep things simple. Collect and manage all of your thoughts in a central location where everyone can contribute and make changes and updates. Once you're started, keep everyone informed as to what you're doing and don't let yourself relax too much or the project might stall.